Royal Air Force &
Australian Flying Corps

Squadron Losses

1st April – 30th June 1918

W.R. Chorley

AVIATION
BOOKS
LIMITED

First published in the United Kingdom in 2018 by Mention the War Ltd. Leeds LS28 5HA, England.

Cover design: Topics – The Creative Partnership www.topicdesign.co.uk

Front cover image: RAF war grave headstone (Gosnold family).
Rear cover image: Andrew Chorley.

A CIP catalogue reference for this book is available from the British Library

ISBN 978-1-911255-26-0

If I rise on the wings of the dawn,

If I settle on the far side of the sea,

Even there your hand will guide me,

Your right hand will hold me fast.

(Psalm 139)

DH9 C1211 VI of 218 Squadron RAF, which made a forced landing on 29th June 1918 at Breskens, Holland, after suffering engine failure. The crew, Lts. W. Purvis and LH Locke, were interned (White family via Steve Smith).

By the same author:

In Brave Company - 158 Squadron Operations
To See The Dawn Breaking - 76 Squadron Operations
Royal Air Force Bomber Command Losses of the Second World War
[presented in eight volumes]

Contents

Introduction   6

Squadron losses 1st April 1918 - 30th June 1918   8

Acknowledgements   286

Sources   287

Glossary of Terms   289

Appendix A - Squadron losses table 1st April 1918 - 30th June 1918   290

Appendix B - Squadron losses by aircraft type 1st April 1918 - 30th June 1918   294

Appendix C - Squadron locations 1st April 1918 - 30th June 1918   300

Roll of Honour   307

Aircraft Types Used by the RAF and AFC 1st April – 30th June 1918   325

Introduction

When war broke out in Europe in August 1914, the Royal Naval Air Service and the Royal Flying Corps between them could muster only a handful of squadrons and, in truth, it was far from clear what rôle was expected of them. However, with the British Expeditionary Force in France and the German army advancing through Belgium and threatening to March on Paris any input that the two air arms might provide would be more than welcome. At this point it is worth explaining that the Royal Flying Corps had only existed for two years and the few squadrons that were active in the late summer of 1914, were equipped with a myriad of types, many of them quite unsuited for operational duties. Nevertheless, a start had to be made and it was the good citizens of Amiens that became aware of British aerial activity with the arrival on the 13th of August, of two squadrons* equipped in part to carry out reconnaissance operations on behalf of the army. Before the year was out they had been joined by four more squadrons, by which time that mind-numbing feature of the *Great War,* namely the trench system that ran from that small fragment of Belgium denied to the enemy down to the border with Switzerland was in place.

For the Allies the next three years brought a series of disappointments with each attempt to break the enemy front ending with little to show for the terrible loss of life inflicted by the Germans ensconced in their well constructed defences; Ypres, Loos, the Somme and Cambrai in particular are now remembered as battles that wiped out generations of young aspiring lives as dutifully they obeyed the order to make that perilous advance across 'No Mans Land'.

In the air advances in aerial technology had seen an eruption of squadrons and aircraft types more suited in carrying the aerial war to the enemy, though still remained a degree of vulnerability in their structure with their open cockpits affording little in the way of protection for the crews muffled well against the elements. Throughout the three-and-a-half years of war the twin air arms had provided sterling support for the ground forces, particularly in the areas of reconnaissance and photography.

Thus, this begs the question that if the two existing forces were performing well, why introduce a third force? In part the question is answered by events at home where public disquiet in the wake of German air raids, the first of which occurred way back in January 1915, carried out by airships, had more than the rumble of alarm, a situation heightened in the early spring of 1917, when Gotha bombers appeared in the skies over Eastern England going about their business with little or no interference from the dozen or so home defence squadrons.

The hierarchy in the Admiralty and the War Office viewed with alarm the idea of a third force [Trenchard recalled in the autumn of 1917, from overseeing air operations on the Western Front was vehemently opposed to the setting up of a separate air arm] which as winter drew nigh was occupying the minds of the War Cabinet.

It is beyond the remit of this book to become bogged down by the minutiae of inter-departmental squabbles succinctly described by Richard Overy in his commendable treatise *The Birth of the RAF 1918;* here it is suffice to say that 'The Air Force [Constitution] Act', the precursor to the formal establishment of the Royal Air Force, received royal ascent in late November 1917, after which the prime minister David Lloyd George set about making appointments that would carry the Act to its fruition.

Thus, with the birth of the third air arm, my first volume will now report in some detail the losses inflicted on its squadrons, and those of the Australian Flying Corps, up to then of June 1918. Although operational losses were frequent, many occurred on the airfields or over territory held by the Allies. Practice flying also brought its fair share of losses while the condition of the airfields played no small part in adding to the toll of casualties. Reliability of engines and airframes were still in relative infancy with numerous summaries reflecting these shortcomings. A forced landing owing to engine failure usually ended with little more than a few anxious moments for the pilot but in cases of structural failure the consequence were in most cases fatal.

It is highly unlikely that every loss of an aircraft has been covered for a myriad of reasons; lack of or loss of records being a major factor and though I am reasonably confident that the majority of Western Front casualties are reported, losses from other theatres of war are less easy to establish. Additions and amendments will appear in the second volume which will cover the period from the 1st of July 1918 through to the armistice on the 11th of November 1918.

Another feature that will readily be apparent are the number of Dominion and Commonwealth airmen involved and more than a scattering of Americans, either flying as members of the Royal Air Force or attached from their own air arms.

Through the medium of papers such as the *London* and *Edinburgh Gazettes* I have been able to report many of the citations accompanying awards made to those who feature in the summaries, while the odd snippet or two has been extracted from *Flight* which reported the air war and the burgeoning development of air power in some depth.

Finally, the purpose of this book and the next, which will carry the reporting of losses through to the armistice, is to illustrate the scale of casualties and to salute the fortitude of a long since departed generation of airmen who set in place the cornerstone of the Royal Air Force now celebrating its centenary.

* No 2 Squadron and No 3 Squadron latterly based at Farnborough and Netheravon respectively.

Corrections, additions and observations please email to:-
wr.chorley@gmail.com

Squadron losses 1st April 1918 - 30th June 1918

Monday 1 April 1918

An historic day in our country's military history; the Royal Naval Air Service*and the Royal Flying Corps merged to form an independent Royal Air Force. The merger came at a time of great uncertainty as to how long the war was going to last. Apart from the first few months of the conflict when it seemed an all conquering German army would march into Paris, both sides had settled into the interminable misery of trench warfare and though both armies had made gains here and there the well recorded battles up to the beginning of 1918 had done little to bring any hint of victory for either side while the cost in lives to those who were called upon to go 'over the top' in battles that in the eyes of the commanders would change the direction of the war in their favour were now measured in their hundreds of thousands. Even the latest spring offensive by the German army, now referred to by historians as the *Kaiserschlacht,* had started with much promise but like all the offensive operations of the past it had ended without that decisive break-through necessary to deliver victory to the Kaiser.

Nevertheless, for Field Marshal Douglas Haig commanding the British Expeditionary Force on the Western Front the implications, both militarily and politically, of the past three weeks were justifiably alarming. Although the enemy offensive had been halted, much ground had been lost and there was little prospect of a quick counter-attack. As if this were not enough, Haig's relations with the French were under considerable strain, added to which was a near complete breakdown in trust between himself and the prime minister David Lloyd George. The only light to lift his gloom was the knowledge that the build up of American forces were proceeding apace which would counter the effects of events in Russia where fighting had virtually ceased in December 1917 [the Treaty of Brest Litovsk was signed on the 3rd of March, eighteen days before the start of the *Kaiserschlacht*, thereby allowing the German army to redeploy valuable and much needed divisions from the Eastern Front to the Western Front.

This was the far from promising background that witnessed the birth of the third arm of our fighting services. For those already serving in what had been two separate air arms life would carry on much as before; bombing, reconnaissance, patrolling et al would be the norm until the armistice with much hard fighting yet to be done for the German Air Force was a particularly skilful opponent, their scout pilots, frequently operating in strong formations, posing a constant threat to our two-seater bomber and reconnaissance squadrons.

Of note during the day, enemy aircraft raided the airfield at Haute Visée where No 101 Squadron was based resulting in the death of Second Lieutenant Ronald Stonehouse, an observer on the squadron. His titled parents, Sir Edmund and Lady Stonehouse, commemorated their son's death by donating a parcel of land for the building of a hostel for nurses employed at Clayton Hospital in Wakefield. Air Mechanic Leslie George William Carter was also killed during the attack and three of the squadron's FE.2bs are described on Andrew Peverell's exceptional website as being 'riddled with shrapnel'; A5624, A5643 and A5786. However, despite significant damage, Andrew's careful investigation of the numerous AIR 1 Class files, I am able to report that 'A5624' eventually ended up in the hands of No 102 Squadron until written off on 16 September 1918; 'A5643' went to No 58 Squadron on 5 July 1918, thence to No 83 Squadron on the 28th of September 1918, and, finally, No 102 Squadron [which Andrew explains was at the time a demobilisation squadron responsible for receiving aircraft from squadrons returning to the United Kingdom, and then ferrying home and handing them over to an Aircraft Depot for crating or disposal] on 20 January 1919, after which there is no further trace. Similarly, 'A5786' went to No 58 Squadron on 8 June 1918, but was eventually struck to No 2 Advanced Salvage Depot and no further trace after 14 October 1918. Trevor Henshaw's close study of air activity in the *Great War* reports that a Private McCoy won a Distinguished Conduct Medal for his actions for although being badly wounded in the pre-dawn raid he insisted on helping others whose wounds he considered were worse than his own. Quoting from the 'Official History', Trevor indicates a third, as yet unidentified, person died.

Also of importance for the 1st April was the arrival at St Omer of the DH.9s of No 98 Squadron. Commanded by Major H O'Malley their arrival arrived carved a special niche in the history of the newly formed Royal Air

Force by being the first squadron to arrive in France as a Royal Air Force formation. Remaining on the Western Front for the remainder of the war its existence can be described as "Nomadic" for between arriving and the armistice '98' moved eight times and, prior to returning to Shotwick on 21 March 1919, it 'upped sticks' two more times.

* At the time of the merger the Royal Naval Air Service boasted sixteen squadrons, all engaged on operations on the Western Front and equipped with types synonymous with their Royal Flying Corps counterparts. In order to avoid confusion the Royal Naval Air Squadrons were prefixed with two digits, thus No 1 Squadron Royal Naval Air Service became No 201 Squadron of the Royal Air Force. Observant readers will note the absence of No 212 Squadron**which did not form until the 20th of August 1918, hence the final re-numbering finished with the DH.4 equipped No 217 Squadron. America had finally declared war on Germany in April 1917, and by June of that year fourteen thousand troops of the American Expeditionary Force had arrived in France under the command of Major General John J 'Black Jack' Pershing. Meanwhile, in Russia the February 1917 revolution had witnessed the abdication and subsequent imprisonment of Tsar Nicholas II cousin to George V.

** Formed at Hondschoote [the village being a commune in the Nord *département* of France] on the 8th of June 1917, as a training unit of No 1 Wing, No 12 Squadron Royal Naval Air Service disbanded on the day of the merger between the Royal Naval Air Service and the Royal Flying Corps. Interestingly, *The Camel File* shows 'B3760' as being issued to No 12 Squadron Royal Naval Air Service on the 26th of March 1918, and written off as No 212 Squadron on the 5th of April 1918. The wreck was surveyed at No 4 Advanced Salvage Dump on the 28th of April and deleted on the 15th of May 1918.

| 1 Squadron | Lt D M Bisset | Safe | Unemployed list 5 February 1919: Lt |
| SE.5a B4881 | | | |

T/o Ste Marie Cappel for an offensive patrol and to include low-level bombing. In the course of the operation 'B4881' was badly shot about and the ammunition drum from the top mounted Lewis gun fell into the cockpit jamming the rudder controls. As a consequence of this Lieutenant Bisset was unable to control the landing and crashed, damaging his aircraft beyond worthwhile repair. Formerly of the Gordon Highlanders, as a second lieutenant he was seconded for duty with the Royal Flying Corps with effect from the last day of August 1916 [*gazetted* 26 September 1916, issue 29764]. Following his departure from the Royal Air Force, it appears he joined the Territorial Army Reserve of Officers and effective from the 29th of January 1929, was attached to the 5th/7th Battalion Gordon Highlanders [issue 33460 of 25 January 1929], until resigning his commission on the 23rd of December 1933, retaining the rank of lieutenant [issue 34007 published on 22 December 1933].

| 1 Squadron | 2Lt P J Clayson | Safe | See 8 May 1918 - 1 Squadron |
| SE.5a C9624 | | | |

T/o Ste Marie Cappel similarly tasked and on return, and while preparing to land, the engine failed. Unable to avoid a bank which lay in his path Second Lieutenant Clayson crashed, damaging 'C9624' beyond repair; it had been on squadron charge since 5 March 1918. Commissioned to the General List of the Royal Flying Corps, he was confirmed in his rank on 28 September 1917 [*gazetted* 16 October 1917, supplement 30342]. A scout pilot of merit, Percy Jack Clayson was *gazetted* with the Military Cross 22 June 1918 [supplement 30761]; *'For conspicuous gallantry and devotion to duty. When on low-flying offensive patrol, he engaged an enemy scout and shot it down, with the result that it crashed to earth. He has brought down several hostile machines, one of which he forced to land in our lines, and has engaged massed enemy troops and transports from very low altitudes with machine-gun fire inflicting heavy casualties. He has displayed the most marked determination, courage and skill.'* Promoted acting captain, he was awarded the Distinguished Flying Cross on 3 August 1918 [supplement 30827]; *'A patrol leader of great skill, and a skilful marksman, whose personal fighting successes have proved of much value to his squadron. Captain Clayson's patrol frequently encountered enemy formations in superior numbers, but invariably succeeded in inflicting serious losses.'* Postwar, he was granted a short service commission with effect from 24 October 1919, in the rank of flying officer [*gazetted* 24 October 1919, issue 31616]. During the Second World War he rejoined the service and was commissioned to the Administrative and Special Duties Branch on 20 December 1941 [*gazetted* 3 March 1942, issue 35476] and continued to serve until relinquishing his commission, ranked flight lieutenant, under the provisions of the Navy, Army and Air Force Reserves Act, 1954. I believe his birthplace may have been Rhodesia.

| 3 Squadron AusFC | Lt J L Smith | Safe |
| RE.8 B2253 | Lt J L Withers | Safe |

T/o Abeele tasked for reconnaissance on the Franco/Belgian border and in particular the four km between Comines and Warneton, the latter being southwest of Comines [Nord]. All went well initially until when flying at five thousand feet the engine failed and the crew were obliged to forced land, circa 1025, at map reference 2831b88.

| 3 Squadron AusFC | Lt T L Baillieu | Safe |
| RE.8 B6491 | Lt F J Mart | Safe |

T/o Abeele*for a *Flash**reconnaissance but force-landed near the aerodrome after 'choking' the engine. Salvaged, but struck off charge on the 5th; thirteen hours and forty minutes total flying recorded. Thus, on this day with the coming into existence of the Royal Air Force and with it the inclusion of the Royal Australian Flying Corps in the summaries, the Corps had lost their first aircraft on the Western Front.

* Abeele was one of a clutch of airfields in the Ypres Sector and was located some sixteen km west-southwest of Ypres close to the French border. It is now the site of one of the many Commonwealth War Graves Commission cemeteries in the Sector, named appropriately 'Abeele Aerodrome Military Cemetery'. It contains one hundred and four burials from the *Great War* all from various British army units.

** A *Flash* reconnaissance was a method whereby an observer, either from a ground position, or in the air would report the position of enemy artillery pieces from the flash given off when the gun was fired.

| 4 Squadron | 2Lt T O Henderson | Safe | See 14 September 1918 - 4 Squadron |
| RE.8 B7721 | 2Lt G H Olney | Safe | Unemployed list 1 April 1919: Lt |

T/o Chocques*tasked for artillery observation but stalled and crashed into an orchard adjoining the airfield. Taken on charge on 16 March 1918, 'B7721' flew for a mere eight hours and fifty minutes. Tom Ormand Henderson was confirmed in his rank on 17 February 1918 [*gazetted* 22 March 1918, supplement 30589].

* Sited four km northwest of Béthune in the Pas-de-Calais 'Chocques' is the site of a Commonwealth War Graves Commission cemetery. It is a large cemetery with one thousand seven hundred and two identified burials.

| 8 Squadron | Lt D McLean | Injured |
| FK.8 C3684 | Lt E J Brabrook | Injured Etaples Military Cemetery |

T/o 0620 Vert Galand for an artillery patrol; force-landed west of Hernicourt in the Pas-de-Calais[map reference reported as V25b]. Formerly of the London Regiment [London Irish Rifles], Edward John Brabrook died from his wounds on 20 April 1918, in one of the many hospitals in the Etaples area. His father, Edward Frederick Brabrook was a Bachelor of Laws. Postwar, his parents submitted for inscription on Edward's headstone; *'Ever In Our Thoughts Mother, Eth & Mae.'*

| 8 Squadron | Lt A J Allen | Safe |
| FK.8 C8507 | Lt D R Sharman MC | Safe |

T/o Vert Galand similarly tasked and on return, and landing, ran onto rough ground which led to the under- carriage giving way; struck off charge on the last day of the month. While in the service of the Royal West Surrey Regiment and still only a temporary second lieutenant, Donald Risborough Sharman won the Military Cross [*gazetted* 10 January 1917, issue 29898]; *'For conspicuous gallantry in action. He displayed great courage and determination in holding an isolated trench under very heavy fire and was indefatigable in collect- ing and sending down wounded men.'* It appears that Donald Sharman remained in the postwar air force as his name appears in various editions of *The London Gazette,* for example, issue 33446 of 11 December 1928, reports his transfer as a flying officer from Class A of the Reserve to Class C, with effect from 28 October 1928. Then, on the 22nd of April 1937, he was granted a commission in Class C as a flight Lieutenant from the rank of captain, thus suggesting he had spent time with army [*gazetted* 8 June 1937, issue 34405]. During the Second World War he served with the Administrative and Special Duties Branch until relinquishing his commission under the provisions of the Navy, Army and Air Force Reserves Act of 1954.

| 10 Squadron | 2Lt C R Strudwick* | Safe |
| FK.8 C3644 | Lt R S Mackenzie | Safe |

T/o Abeele briefed for a counter attack patrol. On return Second Lieutenant Strudwick misjudged his approach and flew into a hedge. Delivered to the Aeroplane Acceptance Park at Newcastle on 7 February 1918, 'C3644' was accepted by the squadron on the 20th of February and at the time of what proved to be its final flight had logged fifty-four hours.

* A 'Second Lieutenant C R Strudwick' appears in my summary for the loss of No 35 Squadron FK.8 C3535 on 22 May 1918, raising the possibility that two officers with the initials and surname 'C R Strudwick' were serving at the time, though I cannot be certain. Access to service records should provide an answer; however, what is known a 'C R Strudwick' was appointed to a permanent commission on 1 August 1919, serving until 4th November 1945, when as a wing commander he relinquished his commission on the grounds of ill-health.

| 12 Squadron | 2Lt A J Coleman | Injured |
| RE.8 B4029 | | |

T/o Soncamp authorised for flying practice and having climbed to nine hundred feet lost control and nosedived to the ground. Accepted by the squadron on 23 March 1918, 'B4029' was deemed beyond worthwhile repair and was struck off charge on the 12th; its total flying hours being recorded as fourteen hours and twenty-five minutes.

| 20 Squadron | Major J A Dennistoun [Canada] | Safe | See 11 April 1918 - 20 Squadron |
| Bristol F.2b A7240 | Lt H G Crowe | Safe | |

T/o 1725 Ste Marie Cappel for a reserve patrol during which the Bristol was crippled by anti-aircraft fire resulting in a forced landing near Wulvergem [West-Vlaanderen] in the Ypres Salient. Formerly of the Canadian Infantry, Manitoba Regiment, Major Dennistoun was seconded to the Royal Flying Corps in the rank of temporary captain and was promoted temporary major with effect from 10 July 1917, as promulgated in *The London Gazette* dated 9th October 1917, supplement 30327. His secondment ceased on the 9th of June 1919 as reported in supplement 31505 of the paper published on 14 August 1919. His observer, Henry George Crowe formerly of the 6th Battalion Royal Irish Regiment was seconded for duty with the Royal Flying Corps on the 5th of September 1917, and was attached to No 20 Squadron on 28 November 1917. Soon after the incident, here reported, Henry was successful in his application for pilot training and a year later, having been awarded his Flying Badge he was attached to No 106 Squadron [RE.8]. Meanwhile, he had been *gazetted* [26 July 1918, supplement 30813] with the Military Cross; *'For conspicuous gallantry and devotion to duty when taking part in many low-flying bomb raids and reconnaissances as an observer. On every occasion he brought back very accurate and valuable information. On three occasions his machine was shot down by enemy fire, but he continued his work, and his great fearlessness and fine spirit have been an invaluable example to others. He has taken part in several air combats and been responsible for the destruction of many hostile machines.'* On the 17th of November 1921, [now ranked flying officer] he was granted a permanent commission [*gazetted* in issue 32576 of 13th January 1922]. His service now followed a path similar for all permanent officers and, perhaps, not surprisingly he specialised in photography filling the post of Photographic Officer in Iraq Command between February 1925 and October 1926. Flight Commander duties with No 14 Squadron [DH.9A] based in Transjordan occupied him for the next two years and then it was back to the United Kingdom and Staff College at Andover. On 13 February 1933, following a refresher flying course with the Central Flying School, he arrived at Biggin Hill to take command of No 23 Squadron [Hart and Demon]. Then, with the advent of the crisis in Abyssinia '23' was detached to the Middle East and while *en route* the intended reforming of No 74 Squadron from a flight of No 23 Squadron took place and Squadron Leader Henry George Crowe became its Commanding Officer, handing over to Squadron Leader D S Brookes in May 1936. This was his last flying tour and for the remainder of his service he was appointed to various staff duties, culminating as Air Officer Commanding No 223 [Composite] Group at Peshawar. Born in Ireland on the 11th of July 1897, Air Commodore Henry George Crowe retired on 28th December 1945, his death being announced on the 26th of April 1983, at Thornton-le-Dale in North Yorkshire. In addition to his Military Cross Air Commodore Crowe had received a number of civilian honours.

| 20 Squadron | Lt R B T Hedges | Injured |
| Bristol F.2b C4615 | Lt A G Horlock | Injured |

T/o Ste Marie Cappel similarly tasked and was brought down in circumstances similar to those reported in the previous summary, the Bristol descending shortly before 1000 in an area known as Pypegaale [West-Vlaanderen] and about midway between Ypres and Diksmuide. It is reported that a fire broke out soon after touching down. Commissioned to the General List of the Royal Flying Corps, Lieutenant Hedges was confirmed in his rank of second lieutenant on 6 September 1917]gazetted 25 September 1917, supplement 30311]. As a lieutenant he was appointed to a permanent commission on the 1st of August 1919, but this was subsequently cancelled on the 4th of November 1919 [issue 31628 of the paper published on that date]. Lieutenant Horlock's service began with the Territorial Forces attached to the East Kent Regiment. Postwar, he was granted a temporary commission in the rank of second lieutenant as an Observer Officer with his seniority backdated to the 1st of April 1918 [gazetted 14th March 1919, issue 31230]. It appears, however, that he returned to Territorial duties attached to the 4th Battalion The Buffs until relinquishing his commission, having reached the age limit, on 19 July 1933, retaining lieutenant rank [gazetted 18 July 1933, issue 33961].

| 23 Squadron | Lt N R Joyce [Australia] | + | Arras Flying Services Memorial* |
| SPAD S.13 B6858 | | | |

T/o 1250 Bertangles for an offensive patrol and was observed to fall away, apparently out of control, at map reference 66EC9c. Norman Roy Joyce came from Neutral Bay, Sydney. During the month the squadron flew their final SPAD S.13 sorties and began re-equipping with Sopwith 5F.1 Dolphin, the third squadron to do so.

* The Arras Flying Service Memorial is located in the Pas-de-Calais at Faubourg-d'Amiens Cemetery and commemorates the name of nine hundred and eighty-nine airmen of the Royal Naval Air Service, Royal Flying Corps and Royal Air Force who have no known grave. For further information, please consult the Commonwealth War Graves Commission website.

| 24 Squadron | Lt W Selwyn | Safe | See 25 April 1918 - 24 Squadron |
| SE.5 A8900 | | | |

T/o Conteville for a low-level offensive patrol during which a connecting rod fractured which in turn led to total failure of the crankcase. Crash-landed near Boves [Somme], eight km southeast of Amiens and though sent for repair was struck off charge on the 12th of April 1918. This early production SE.5 [it was the third aircraft off the line from a batch of fifty built by the Royal Aircraft Factory, Farnborough] by 6 May 1917 had been assigned to No 56 Squadron at Vert Galand in whose hands nine hostile machines were claimed [some being shared with other SE.5s]. On 15 October 1917, it was taken on charge by No 60 Squadron and following further maintenance arrived with No 24 Squadron on the 24th of March 1918. Three days later, while being flown by Captain George Edward Henry McElroy,*it shot down an Albatros D near the by now ruined hamlet of Chipilly in the département de la Somme.

* This officer features in a number of summaries, the first of which appears on 7 April 1918.

| 24 Squadron | Lt E P Crossen | Safe | See 4 April 1918 - 24 Squadron |
| SE.5a B1 | | | |

T/o Conteville similarly ordered but collided with a telegraph pole and damaged beyond repair. This was the first production SE.5a and as such was issued to No 56 Squadron as 'K' on the 10th of August 1917, surviving at least three serious accidents. Later to No 84 Squadron but while being flown by Second Lieutenant Edmund Otto Krohn*of Funchal on the Spanish Island of Madeira landed on frozen snow at Izel-lès-Hameau on 27th December 1917, sustaining some damage that necessitated removal to a repair facility. 'B1' arrived with No 24 Squadron on 23 March 1918, and in total logged forty-seven hours and twenty minutes flying.

* Killed in action on the 1st of March 1918, he now rests in Chauny Communal Cemetery British extension, age nineteen.

| 27 Squadron | 2Lt F Carr | Safe | |
| DH.4 B2102 | 2Lt J H Holland | Safe | See 16 June 1918 - 27 Squadron |

T/o 0850 Ruisseauville to attack targets at Péronne in the Somme *département*. Subjected to anti-aircraft fire, shrapnel from one burst caused serious damage to the DH's wings. Force-landed 1110 [presumably at base] where it was deemed beyond repair.

32 Squadron	Captain D M Faure	Safe	Unemployed list 6 September 1919: Captain
SE.5a C6413			

T/o 0900 Beauvois tasked for escort duties during which he was obliged to force-land with the oil tank shot through near Esclainville [possibly Esclainvillers in the Somme some fifteen km northwest of Montdidier] close to the lines, from where it was dismantled by infantry and taken to No 2 Aero- plane Salvage Depot; here it was struck off charge on 22 April 1918. Douglas Munro Faure was initially seconded to the Royal Flying Corps on 23 April 1916 for Observer Officer duties [*gazetted* 10th May 1916, supplement 29575]. He returned to active service on 23 August 1939, when he was commissioned to the Administrative and Special Duties Branch [*gazetted* 8 September 1939, supplement 34674] and continued to serve until his commission was relinquished on 9 July 1954, under the provisions of the Navy, Army and Air Force Reserves Act of 1954. At the time he was ranked wing commander.

32 Squadron	2Lt H F Proctor	Injured	
SE.5a D265			

T/o 0910 Beauvois for an offensive patrol during which he drove down an Albatros out of control, only for himself to be shot down soon after, sustaining serious wounds. No longer fit for flying duties, Second Lieutenant Proctor transferred to the Administrative Branch until his health deteriorated to the point where he was unable to continue in air force service. He relinquished his commission on 30 July 1919.

35 Squadron	2Lt B L Norton	Safe	Unemployed list 14 June 1919: Lt
FK.8 B3380	Lt R W Briggs	Safe	

T/o 0730 Abbeville having being briefed for a fighting patrol and while flying over the Somme and in the general vicinity of Villers-Bretonneux, where German infantry were active, came under sustained accurate rifle fire which hit the engine and radiator, necessitating a forced landing; burnt.

35 Squadron	2Lt W E Josephs	Safe	
FK.8 B5834	2Lt G W Owen	Safe	

T/o Abbeville similarly tasked and sustained serious damage in the same area as that outlined in the previous summary. Salvaged, 'B5834', which had been issued to the squadron's C Flight on 5 December 1917, was struck as not worth repairing on the 14th with a total of seventy-seven hours and thirty minutes flying recorded.

35 Squadron	2Lt A McGregor	Safe	See 1 July 1918 -35 Squadron
FK.8 C3642	2Lt M Balston	Safe	See 3 April 1918 - 35 Squadron

T/o Abbeville similarly charged and force-landed with a longeron shot through, the circumstances being similar to those previously reported. Postwar, and decorated with the Distinguished Flying Cross, Second Lieutenant McGregor was appointed to a permanent commission.

35 Squadron	Captain L G Paling	Safe	Unemployed list 30 October 1919: Captain MC
FK.8 C8502	Captain J R Fasson	Safe	Unemployed list 2 February 1919: Captain

T/o Abbeville for a offensive patrol in the course of which the crew flew into a hailstorm of such severity that they were forced down with a smashed propeller into a wood north of Belloy [*sic*]. Held by the squadron since the 29th of March 1918, 'C8502' was struck off charge on 14 April 1918, with just eight hours and twenty minutes flying recorded.

41 Squadron	Lt S A Puffer [Canada]	Safe
SE.5a B177		

T/o Fienvillers and headed for Alquines where on landing 'B177' turned over as it touched down, a strong blustery wind being a contributory factor. Lieutenant Puffer of the Canadian Expeditionary Force was attached to the Royal Flying Corps for flying duties on 11 December 1917 [*gazetted* 25 January 1918, supplement 30497].

Of the Alberta Regiment, his attachment ceased a year and a day later, as published in supplement 31141 of the paper issued on 21 January 1919.

54 Squadron   2Lt J L Horne   Injured
F.1 Camel B9259
T/o Conteville for an offensive patrol only to collide with the airfield's wind direction indicator and crash out of control.

54 Squadron   2Lt N F Spurr   Safe
F.1 Camel B9281
T/o 1500 Conteville similarly tasked and so badly shot about by anti aircraft fire that it was deemed not worth the expense to repair. Commissioned to the General List Second Lieutenant Norman Franklin Spurr was confirmed in his appointment on 3 December 1917 [*gazetted* 28 December 1917, supplement 30452]. Returning to the service in the Second World War, Norman Spurr was commissioned with effect from 17 March 1941, in the Administrative and Special Duties Branch. He resigned his commission on 15 February 1945, when holding the rank of flight lieutenant [temporary] [*gazetted* 8 May 1945, supplement 37067].

54 Squadron   2Lt C J Mason   Safe   See 3 April 1918 - 54 Squadron
SE.5a C1585
T/o Conteville similarly tasked and on return to the airfield, and landing safely, ran into an unmarked hole and tipped onto its nose; damaged beyond repair.

54 Squadron   Captain G C Cuthbertson MC   Injured St Sever Cemetery, Rouen
F.1 Camel D6529
T/o 1500 Conteville similarly ordered during which the Camel was hit by anti-aircraft. Badly wounded by shrapnel George Chapman Cuthbertson managed to regain the lines where he force-landed. Taken to one of the many hospitals in Rouen, Captain Cuthbertson succumbed to his wounds a week later. Details of his commission as a temporary second lieutenant with effect from 10 February 1915 appeared under the heading 'Alexandria, Princess of Wales's Own [Yorkshire Regiment]' and its sub-heading '12th Battalion [Teesside Pioneers]' [*gazetted* in issue 29117 published on 30 March 1915]. The citation for his Military Cross appeared on page 4825 of the supplement to *The London Gazette* of 22 April 1918; *'For conspicuous gallantry and devotion to duty. During a period of two months he has destroyed two enemy machines, one of which was a triplane, and sent down one other completely out of control. He has also carried out at very low altitudes several valuable reconnaissances at a long distance behind the enemy lines, and has set an example of the greatest pluck and determination to all ranks.'* Consulting *The Camel File,* an entry against 'B5432', delivered to No 54 Squadron on 20 January 1918, names George Cuthbertson as destroying in the mid-morning of February 3rd, an Albatros DV over Honnecourt,*his victim being described as painted yellow with a green tailplane. Twenty-four hours earlier he had downed an Albatros over Bellenglise [Aisne], followed on the the 1st of March with a Fokker DrI which went down out of control near Esnes [Nord]. On both occasions he was flying Camel B6293. This had been a heavy day for the squadron; four aircraft written off and a flight commander slowly dying.

* Probably Honnecourt-sur-Escaut in the *département du Nord*.

56 Squadron   Lt F Beaumont   pow
SE.5a C5433
T/o 1125 Valheureux for an offensive patrol and was last seen at around 1245 over the Somme near Fricourt* fighting a Fokker DrI. 'C5433' arrived in France on the 11th of March 1918, and was accepted by the squadron on the 29th. Confirmation of his capture appeared in *Flight* May 16, 1918. Postwar, Frank Beaumont was appointed to a permanent commission, his career for the better part of his service being concerned with Staff Duties, his final post being Air Attaché in Belgrade. Born on the 10th of May 1896, his senior education was spent on the Continent, first at Lille and later at Leipzig and his knowledge of European culture was to stand him in good stead both in the latter stages of his Royal Air Force service and in retirement for on leaving the air force on the 18th of January 1949, he took up the post of Director of the British Information Service, Bipartite Control Office in Frankfurt. In retirement he settled in Bavaria where he died at the relatively early age of seventy-two on

27 December 1968. The Imperial War Museum hold a number of photographs concerning, or associated with Frank Beaumont, one depicting a Bristol F.2b H1403 *Lady Cherry* on the ground at Cranwell when flown by him as an instructor. This would be circa August 1923 to October 1925, prior to his attachment for flight commander duties with No 24 Squadron.

* Fricourt was the scene of intense fighting on the opening day of the *Battle of the Somme* [July 1st, 1916].

| 56 Squadron | 2Lt B McPherson | pow |
| SE.5a C6351 | | |

T/o 1125 Valheureux similarly tasked and was last seen over the Somme at 1255 caught up in a stiff fight with Triplanes, believed to be from *Jasta 1*, over Guillemont.*Fitted with an Hispano-Suiza 'C6351' was the first of a batch of one hundred and fifty SE.5a fighters built by Wolseley Motors of Birmingham and was delivered to No 1 Aeroplane Acceptance Park Coventry by 15 November 1917. By various stages 'C6351' reached '56' at Baizieux on the 12th of March 1918, and moved with the squadron to Valheureux on the 25th. Notification of Second Lieutenant McPherson's capture appeared in the same issue of *Flight* as that for his squadron colleague summarised above, but with the additional detail that he had sustained wounds.

* Similar to Fricourt, Guillemont was one of the many villages along the Somme front that was fought over during the offensive that lasted between July and November 1916. At Guillemont the fighting was particularly hard between the 3rd and 6th of September when the German 2nd Army successfully defended their positions agains thrusts from divisions of General Sir Henry Rawlinson's 4th Army.

| 57 Squadron | 2Lt E Whitfield | + | Arras Flying Services Memorial |
| DH.4 A7401 | Lt W C F N Hart | + | Arras Flying Services Memorial |

T/o 0730 Le Quesnoy with orders to raid Bapaume which had been taken by German infantry on 24 March 1918 during the early stages of the *Kaiserschlacht*. Last sighted engaged in combat with fighters. Edgar Whitfield had been commissioned to the General List of the Royal Flying Corps on 7 June 1917 [issue 30170 of *The London Gazette* published on 6 July 1917]; his observer William Cecil Frederick Nicol Hart received his commission on 3 January 1915 [*gazetted* 5 January 1915, issue 29030] following cadetship with his school's Officer Training Corps and had come to the Royal Flying Corps from the 11th Battalion King's Own [Royal Lancaster Regiment].

| 57 Squadron | 2Lt D P Trollip [South Africa] | + | Arras Flying Services Memorial |
| DH.4 A7872 | Lt J D Moses [Canada] | + | Arras Flying Services Memorial |

T/o 0820 Le Quesnoy similarly instructed and was last seen by other crews in the formation near their objective. From Mount Prospect in the Eastern Cape, Douglas Price Trollip was commissioned as a temporary second lieutenant on the General List, Royal Flying Corps on 21 June 1917 [*gazetted* 6 July 1917, issue 30170]. His observer, James David Moses, formerly of the Regimental Depot [Manitoba] had come to the Royal Flying Corps from the Canadian infantry.

Note. A fifth No 57 Squadron death is reported for the 1st, namely Corporal Edward Charles Lovelock of Ball, Pewsey in Wiltshire, who is buried in St Pol British Cemetery, St Pol-sur-Ternoise. Corporal Loverlock, who was twenty-one years of age, was flying as an observer in DH.4 A7406 [see my summary for 20 May 1918] which made a safe return.

| 58 Squadron | Lt G L Castle | Safe | See 1 July 1918 - 58 Squadron |
| FE.2d A6398 | Lt F C Dixon | Safe | |

T/o 2005 Auchel having been briefed for bombing operations over the *département du Nord* at Douai and reported to have made a forced landing near Arras. Lieutenant Castle had been seconded from the Royal Artillery to the Royal Flying Corps on the last day of July 1916, as promulgated in supplement 29720 of *The London Gazette* published on 23 August 1916. He returned to Royal Artillery establishment on 9 January 1920 [*gazetted* 10th March 1920, supplement 31818] and served until resigning his commission on the 18th of August 1923. Frank Charles Dixon was commissioned to the Administrative and Special Duties Branch on 8 May 1940 [*gazetted* 28th May 1940, issue 34859] and remained in service until leaving the air force under the provisions of the Navy, Army and Air Force Reserves Act of 1954.

59 Squadron   2Lt J Stanley   Safe
RE.8 C5038

T/o Lealvilliers for a practice flight but while in the process of banking the RE's engine failed and 'C5038' side-slipped to the ground. Second Lieutenant Stanley clambered from the wreckage, shaken, but unharmed. Issued to the squadron on the 1st of February 1918,*'C5038' had been well used for when written off it had flown for a total of one hundred and forty-two hours and fifteen minutes.

* It has been pointed out by Andrew Pentland that it is highly probable that 'C5038' was received prior to the 1st as some information pertaining to issues made in December 1917 and January 1918 have been lost.

65 Squadron   2Lt F H Whiteley   Safe
F.1 Camel C8290

T/o Conteville tasked for an offensive patrol during which the guns jammed. Damaged beyond repair after landing at Bertangles and running into a ditch. Its service had lasted for less than a month; built by Rushton, Proctor & Company of Lincoln, 'C8290' was ready for shipment by the 4th of March, arriving in France on the 14th and issued to No 65 Squadron on the 26th. As reported in my appreciation for James Kennedy on April 2nd, it scored at least one aerial victory before its demise. I strongly suspect Second Lieutenant Whiteley to be Frank Hardenbrook Whiteley who during the Second World War received a commission in the Equipment Branch and served until relinquishing his commission as a squadron leader under the provisions of the Navy, Army and Air Force Reserves Act 1954.

65 Squadron   Lt P R Cann   Injured St Sever Cemetery, Rouen
F.1 Camel D1811 *Posholi*

T/o 0630 Conteville similarly ordered during which Truro College educated Percy Reginald Cann was attacked, and shot down, by *Leutnant* Eugen Siempelkamp*of *Jasta 4* at around 0800 German time, just to the southeast of Fouilloy in the Somme, sixteen km east of Amiens. Lieutenant Cann survived the encounter and was taken to one of the military hospitals near Rouen where he died from his wounds on the 4th of April 1918.

* *Posholi* was a presentation aircraft from the Paramount Chief and the Basuto Nation and replaced F.1 Camel B3859 which had been struck off charge on the 16th of February 1918, while attached to the Anti-Gotha Patrol Flight. For Eugen Siempelkamp, this was his first aerial combat success; in late July 1918 he took over command of *Jasta 64* but was badly wounded during the course of his fifth and final victory on the 14th of September 1918. Initially, Eugen flew Fokker DrIs but on taking over *Jasta 64* he appears to have switched to the Pfalz IIIa.

65 Squadron   2Lt J R Greasley   +   Arras Flying Services Memorial
F.1 Camel D6474

T/o 1050 Conteville and failed to return. John Richard Greasley was commissioned to the General List of the Royal Flying Corps on 27 September 1917 [*gazetted* 2 October 1917, issue 30320].

73 Squadron   2Lt A W Gallie   Safe
F.1 Camel C1578

T/o Beauvois for ground strafing of enemy positions near Fresnoy [probably Le Fresnoy] on the north-northeast side of Lille. Ran out of fuel and force-landed. On squadron charge since 22 March 1918, 'C1578' was re-covered to a repair facility but was struck off charge on 14 April 1918.

80 Squadron   2Lt O C Bridgeman   Safe   Unemployed list 11 April 1919: Lt MC
F.1 Camel B9247

T/o Belleville Farm for an offensive patrol but 'choked' the engine, lost control and crashed into a tree. Orlando Clive Bridgeman was commissioned from a cadetship to the General List of the Royal Flying Corps on the 17th of March 1917 [*gazetted* 10 April 1917, issue 30012]. There is one further *gazette* entry for an 'Orlando Clive Bridgeman' [4 March 1932, issue 33805] notifying his death and showing his rank as 'Captain' and advising persons having any claim to his estate to contact Bailey, Shaw and Gillett of 5 Berners Street, London W1, Solicitors for the said executor, Reginald Francis Orlando Bridgeman MVO CMG.

80 Squadron	2Lt J J Meredith	Unknown	Unemployed list 8 August 1919: F/O

F.1 Camel C1681

T/o 1515 Belleville Farm similarly tasked and believed to have been lost over the Somme near Moreuil. The note in *The Camel File* indicating Second Lieutenant Meredith perished is incorrect; two entries in *Flight* and the subsequent *Gazette* entry published on 5 September 1919, issue 31539, establishes his survival. Returning to *Flight,* in their issue of May 9,1918, he is officially reported as 'missing' while on 8 August 1918, the magazine repeats the official list issued by the German authorities for British aircraft claimed over the Western Front for April 1918 and under the heading for '20 Sopwith' appears the name of Second Lieutenant Meredith with the rider 'fate unknown'. It is possible, therefore, that he made his way back through the lines or evaded capture by reaching Holland, which throughout the *Great War* was a neutral country. Of interest is the ranking of J J Meredith as 'Flying Officer' on the Unemployed List for it was only with effect from the 1st of August 1919, that the now familiar officer titles of pilot officer, flying officer et al was officially promulgated.

82 Squadron	2Lt A R Wardle	Safe	Unemployed list 26 April 1919: Lt
FK.8 B3304	2Lt R T North	Safe	Unemployed list 28 May 1919: Lt

T/o Agenvillers for a dusk reconnaissance and on return crash-landed having misjudged the position of the flares. Struck for repairs, 'B3304' was removed from charge on 20 April 1918. Since delivery to the Aeroplane Acceptance Park at Lympne on 7 November 1917, it had flown for a total of forty-two hours and forty minutes, most of this total being logged since its arrival with the squadron on 15 March 1918. On the 17th of November 1920, Alfred Randles Wardle returned to the air force having been granted a short service commission spending the better part of the next five years on Fleet Air Arm duties serving for two spells on the aircraft carrier HMS *Pegasus* before being appointed to a permanent commission on 20 May 1925. Following a year [1931] attending Staff College he went out to India where he served as a flight commander with No 5 Squadron [Wapiti] before taking command of No 11 Squadron [Hart] at Risalpur. This was his final flying appointment and was followed by staff duties until going out to Ceylon in February 1947, as Air Officer Commanding, Air Head-quarters Ceylon. His final post was Air Officer Commanding No 66[Scottish] Group. Retiring in air commodore rank on 2 December 1952, his death was announced on the last day of July 1989.

84 Squadron	Lt S H Winkley	+	Arras Flying Services Memorial

SE.5a B174

T/o 1630 Conteville for a strafing mission and failed to return having been last sighted over the Somme near Démuin. Stanley Hugh Winkley was commissioned to the General List of the Royal Flying Corps on 10 May 1917, as *gazetted* in issue 30100 published on 29 May 1917. Twenty-five years of age, Stanley was an 'Old Tamensian' [Lord William's School, Thame, Oxfordshire]. Prior to enlistment he had worked as an engineer; his father is recorded as being a 'Master Butcher'.

203 Squadron	Lt O P Adam [Canada]	+	Maroc British Cemetery, Grenay

F.1 Camel B3798

T/o Treizennes for an offensive patrol and forced down north of Loos*in the Pas-de-Calais where it was destroyed by shell fire. 'B3798' arrived on the Western Front in the late summer of 1917 and was allocated to No 3 Squadron Royal Naval Air Service on the 5th of September of that year, since when it had been involved in numerous patrols, participating in many aerial combats either destroying or sharing in the destruction of a trio of hostile machines. Orval Patrick Adam hailed from Westport, Ontario.

* Loos [or to give its full name Loos-en-Gohelle] is for ever etched in the history of the *Great War* for it was here between the 25th of September and the 8th of October 1915, that the fiercest battle of the year was fought. It was notable for a number of 'firsts'; it witnessed the first use of poison gas by the British and the first large scale involvement of what is oft referred to as 'Kitchener's New Army'. The outcome fell well below the expectations of the Allies; the release of chlorine gas was of mixed blessing for a change in the wind direction resulted in much of its insidious cloud drifting back over the British lines as the infantry prepared to advance. This, tragically, caused many casualties, adding to those inflicted by the German machine gunners. In the aftermath of the battle recriminations at the highest level of Command led, eventually, to the removal of Field Marshal Sir John French as Commander-in-Chief of the British Expeditionary Force and the advancement of General Sir Douglas

Haig who commanded the First Army during the battle. Some historians are of the opinion that it was Haig's closeness to the King that in part led to this prestigious appointment.

209 Squadron   Captain F E Banbury DSC   +   Hazebrouck Communal Cemetery
F.1 Camel B7247   [Canada]

T/o Clairmarais ordered for a reserve patrol and as reported on the University of Toronto Service Roll suffered a heart attack when in the air and crashed. Fred Everest Banbury, born 27 October 1893 in Wolseley, Saskatchewan, features on a number of websites and is credited with eleven combat victories spanning the period from the last day of May 1917 to 26th March 1918, the first two being secured flying Sopwith Pups and the remainder on Camels. It seems he learnt to fly in the United States of America after leaving his home town in March 1916, and traveling to Newport News in Virginia where he enrolled with the Curtiss School of Flying. On completing his training he crossed to England and was commissioned to the Royal Naval Air Service on 28 June 1916, though, as yet, I have not been able to trace his name on *The London Gazette* website. Neither have I been able to find the entry for his award of a Distinguished Service Cross, but *Flight* in its issue of May 2, 1918, repeats the list of awards *gazetted* on 26th April 1918, thus confirming its authenticity. Further information regarding this officer is held by The National Archives in ADM 273/10/1.

Losses for the first day of the newly established Royal Air Force came to forty-two aircraft missing in action, written off as a result of battle damage, or in practice flying. The official communiqué released from General Headquarters, as repeated in *Flight* in their issue of April 11, 1918, under the banner 'Aircraft Work At The Front' states eleven of our aircraft were reported missing, while on the credit side ten enemy aircraft were destroyed and six others were driven down out of control. The communiqué also emphasises the good work carried out by the reconnaissance squadrons which enabled *'... much work to be done with the artillery, and many hostile batteries were engaged by our guns with observation from the air.'* Meanwhile, other squadrons were carrying out low-level attacks on enemy troops with a mixture of bombs and strafing runs during which thousands of rounds were fired. As night fell, raids were carried out on rail communications at Cambrai, where many tons of bombs were dropped, and on lines south and southeast of Douai, all aircraft returning safely.

Tuesday 2 April 1918
Trevor Henshaw in his excellent treatise concerning air fighting in the *Great War* by the British, Commonwealth and United States Air Services heralds his analysis of the day with the headline 'General Foch's*Dictum on the use of Air Power'. Instructions for the use of air power by the Allied air services on the Western Front had been received by the newly formed Royal Air Force headquarters during the day and it was abundantly clear on reading the general's dictum that better co-operation between the air arms of the British and the French would be necessary in future in order to ensure the most effective way of defeating the common enemy both in the air and on the ground, the latter being the priority as the following extract states; *'At the present time the first duty of fighting aeroplanes is to assist troops on the ground by incessant attacks.'* The instructions continued; *'Air Fighting is not be sought except so far as necessary for the fulfilment of duty.'* This last statement, I suggest, was in many cases only loosely adhered too. And, as Trevor comments; *'Interestingly, there was no mention of protecting corps machines.'* The general did emphasise the importance of co-ordinated bombing attacks on railways and key communications.

* By the end of 1916, both Foch and Joffre had fallen out of favour, and were assigned to posts which might best be described as 'paper' only. On page 244 of his book defending the reputation of Field Marshal Sir Douglas Haig, John Terraine writes [of Joffre]; *'... the Briand Ministry removed Joffre from direct control of the French Armies, appointing him 'technical advisor' to the Government, with an office in Paris and undefined duties.'* And on the same page he notes Foch's reduction of influence to that of *'advisor'.* To soften the hurt that must have been felt by Joffre, the French President, Poincaré, bestowed upon General Joffre the title 'Marshal of France' which, as Terraine writes, led the British Ambassador, Lord Bertie to communicate to Haig that Joffre was *'... being put on the shelf for Ornamental China and not for use.'* As history now reveals, Foch's relegation was not terminal and in May 1917, following the dismissal of the elegant and dashing General George Nivelle whose reputation had soared so brightly only to die like a snuffed out candle, Foch was appointed to the post of Chief of Staff under the new Commander-in-Chief, Pétain.

| 10 Squadron | Lt E D Jones | + | Lijssenthoek Military Cemetery |
| FK.8 C3522 | 2Lt W Smith | + | Lijssenthoek Military Cemetery |

T/o Abeele for observation duties over the enemy trenches near Ypres and circa 1320, while flying at a low height fire from the ground struck the cockpit of the FK.8, wounding Evan Davies Jones. From information posted on the 25th County of London Cyclist Battalion website [which I acknowledge], the pilot is thought to have slumped over the controls and moments later crashed just inside the allied lines. Those who witnessed the impact immediately ran to the scene to render aid but both airmen were so grievously hurt that they died within minutes of being freed from the wreckage. Evan Jones, a graduate of Trinity College, Cambridge, where he gained a Master of Arts degree, had been attached from No 4 Squadron; Wansey Smith had served formerly as a private solder with the 2nd Battalion London Regiment and later, still with the regiment, with the 25th County of London Cyclist Battalion, seeing considerable action on the Western Front. Recommended for a commission he returned to England and was attached to an Officers' Training Corps at Rhyle, after which it seems he was attached to the 11th East Lancashire Regiment. It is hinted that he had some prewar aviation experience and this, I suggest, prompted his request to join the Royal Flying Corps. Although the crash location is not given, it is likely to have occurred near Lijssenthoek in West-Vlaanderen, some twelve km west of Ypres.

| 11 Squadron | 2Lt A R Knowles [Bahamas]* | + | Péronne Road Cemetery, Maricourt |
| Bristol F.2b C4862 | Lt E A Matthews | + | Péronne Road Cemetery, Maricourt |

T/o 1700 Remaisnil for an offensive patrol and was last seen diving from fourteen thousand feet in the direction of an enemy aircraft. Believed to have fallen over the Somme, possibly in the general area of Maricourt. Arthur Ralph Knowles hailed from Eleuthera in the Bahamas; his observer/air gunner, Ernest Alan Matthews, was formerly of the Somerset Light Infantry.

* The Casualty Card raised in respect of Second Lieutenant Arthur Ralph Knowles can be viewed online via the Royal Air Force Museum Story Vault.

| 22 Squadron | Lt F Williams | + | Arras Flying Services Memorial |
| Bristol F.2b A7286 | 2Lt R Critchley | + | Arras Flying Services Memorial |

T/o 1515 Vert Galand for an offensive patrol and when last sighted was going down streaming flames near Vauvilliers. According to the Aerodrome website [which I acknowledge], 'A7286' accounted for a Albatros DV near Lomme on the 11th of March 1918, the victorious pilot being Second Lieutenant Stanley Wallage*. A photograph taken by Second Lieutenant David McLellan at Vert Galand on the 1st of April 1918, showing seventeen of the squadron's pilots and observers, one of whom was Roland Critchley, can be seen on the Imperial War Museum website [which I have pleasure in acknowledging] catalogue number Q 11993. All have gathered in front of one of the squadron's Bristols, which bears the letter 'D' the majority being in their flying clothing and all appear confident and cheerful.

* Undoubtedly Stanley Harry Wallage of the General List and Royal Air Force *gazetted* with the Military Cross on 13 September 1918, supplement 30901, the citation reading; *'For conspicuous gallantry and devotion to duty during recent operations. He personally destroyed seven enemy machines. He showed a fine spirit of dash and tenacity, and his skill and success as a fighting pilot was a fine example to others in his squadron.'* Andrew Pentland advises that Stanley's Medal Card is held at The National Archives as is his Army record of service, the relevant class numbers and files being WO 372/20/195117 and WO 339/104406.

Note. During the night of 4-5 April 1943, when Bomber Command raided the Baltic Sea port of Kiel, Squadron Leader Stanley Norman Tuttell Wallage of No 57 Squadron failed to return. His entry on the Commonwealth War Graves Commission website identifies his father as 'Flight Lieutenant S H S Wallage MC'. Unfortunately, despite an extensive search of *The London Gazette* I have not been able to trace any Royal Air Force officer with the initials and surname 'S H S Wallage', but I am of the opinion there is a connection linking him to the Second Lieutenant Stanley Wallage mentioned in my summary.

| 24 Squadron | Captain A K Cowper MC | Safe | Retirement 13 February 1920: |
| SE.5a C5311 | [Australia] | | |

T/o Conteville for an offensive patrol in the course of which a connecting rod broke and a forced landing was made near Vast [sic]. First issued on 20 November 1917, to No 60 Squadron but struck for repairs following a landing accident on 10 January 1918 [Second Lieutenant A Carter], 'C5311' arrived at Conteville as recently as 29 March. Andrew King Cowper was commissioned to the General List of the Royal Flying Corps and confirmed in his rank [temporary second lieutenant] on the 12th of August 1917 [*gazetted* 1 September 1917, supplement 30265]. The award of the Military Cross was promulgated on 22 April 1918, supplement 30643, his rank being shown as temporary second lieutenant; *'For conspicuous gallantry and devotion to duty. Whilst leading a patrol of six machines he observed four hostile triplanes, one of which he attacked, succeeding in causing it to break up in the air. The remaining three enemy machines were destroyed by the rest of the patrol. On the return journey he encountered an enemy scout, and shepherding it by the most skilful piloting west of the lines, forced it to land undamaged on one of our aerodromes. On a later occasion, during three separate combats, he and his patrol brought down one machine completely out of control, and two others with their observers wounded, and later in the same day three other machines completely out of control. Previously to this he has assisted in destroying six other enemy scouts, displaying at all times the greatest courage and determination.'* Andrew King Cowper's biography on *Wikipedia* is extensive and indicates he was subsequently awarded First and Second Bars to his Military Cross, these being *gazetted* in the same supplement published on 22 June 1918. On returning to Australia he worked on his parents sheep farm though later, and after marrying, his main business centred on his wife's florist store, specialising in gladioli. During the Second World War he joined the Royal Australian Air Force, serving in the Administrative and Special Duties Branch, rising to squadron leader rank before being discharged on the 2nd of March 1945. Born on the 16th of November 1898, at Bingara, New South Wales, he died in his 81st year on 25th June 1980, at Randwick, New South Wales.

32 Squadron	2Lt W B Green	Safe
SE.5a B8345		

T/o Beauvois for an offensive patrol and damaged beyond worthwhile repair after crash-landing on rough ground, near the airfield, having running out of petrol.

40 Squadron	2Lt N D Willis	Safe	See 1 June 1918 - 40 Squadron
SE.5a B4863			

T/o Bruary for an offensive patrol and on return, and landing, ran against a ridge and nosed over. Salvaged, but struck off charge on 7 April 1918. Issued to No 56 Squadron on 5 September 1917, 'B4863' was much favoured by Captain James Thomas Byford McCudden [see my summary for 9 July 1918] who between the 19th of September and the 21st of October 1917, drove down five hostile machines. Then, ten days later, and with Lieutenant Richard Aveline Maybery*in the cockpit, a combat southwest of Roulers resulted in a scout being driven down but in turn Richard Maybery was obliged to force-land at Bailleul, home of No 1 Squadron, with the petrol tank shot through. Repairs were put in hand and in gloomy weather on November 2nd, Lieutenant H Slingsby, who had been tasked to recover 'B4863', set off on the forty-two km flight southwest for Estrée Blanche but by the time he arrived darkness had fallen and in trying to land he crashed against a house. Repaired, the SE.5a was taken over by No 40 Squadron at Bruary on 23 February 1918. Concerning No 40 Squadron, comments, observations and the like, I respectively acknowledge David Gunby whose account of the squadron's rich history is written in *Sweeping the Skies*, now regarded as one of the finest squadron histories of all times.

*Killed in action on Wednesday, 19 December 1917, and buried in Flesquieres Hill British Cemetery.

43 Squadron	2Lt A K Lomax	pow	Unemployed list 10 September 1919: F/O
F.1 Camel C8293			

T/o 1220 Avesnes-le-Comte for an offensive patrol; failed to return. Commissioned to the General List of the Royal Flying Corps, Second Lieutenant Lomax was confirmed in his rank on 26 October 1917, as promulgated in supplement 30385 of the paper published on 17 November 1917. 'C8293' had been on squadron charge for just nine days.

48 Squadron	2Lt K W D Pope	Injured
Bristol F.2b B1269	2Lt W J Buttle	Injured

T/o 1705 Conteville heading for operations over Villers-Bretonneux during which the crew were shot about and wounded; force-landed at map reference 62DO25a19. Salvaged, it seems 'B1269' was considered ready to resume service and on 1 July 1918, it was taken in hand at Planques by No 62 Squadron. However, an air test revealed unsatisfactory flying characteristics and it was immediately struck for further inspection. This resulted in the airframe being deemed not worth repairing and on 29 July 1918, with a total of eighty hours and fifteen minutes flying appended, it was removed for charge.

| 48 Squadron | 2Lt C E Glover | Safe |
| Bristol F.2b C4701 | Cpl W Beales | Safe |

T/o Conteville similarly charged and badly damaged in combat in the vicinity of Villers-Bretonneux. Returned to base, but struck off charge on the 12th as not worth repairing.

| 48 Squadron | 2Lt C D B Stiles | Injured | Unemployed list 21 February 1919: Hon. Lt |
| Bristol F.2b C4707 | 2Lt F F Walker | Injured | St Sever Cemetery, Rouen |

T/o 1705 Conteville similarly charged and force-landed in the same vicinity as that summarised above. Neither Bristol had survived for long; 'C4707' having been received on 15 March followed the next day by 'C4701'. Second Lieutenant Stiles was confirmed in his rank on 8 October 1917 [*gazetted* 27 October 1917, supplement 30354]. His wounds were serious and effectively ended his service as a pilot. However, he remained in the air force and transferred, with effect from 8 August 1918, to the Administrative Branch, this being promulgated in issue 30918 of 24 September 1918. Sadly, his observer, Frank Frederick Walker succumbed to his wounds on 14 April 1918.

| 52 Squadron | 2Lt E D Jones | + | Lijssenthoek Military Cemetery |
| RE.8 A3868 | 2Lt R F Newton | + | Arras Flying Services Memorial |

T/o 1200 Abbeville for a bombing raid and lost thirty minutes later over Belgium. Evan Davies Jones is recorded in the cemetery records as attached to No 2 Squadron but seconded to No 10 Squadron. Prior to his military service he had graduated with a Master of Arts degree from Trinity College, Cambridge. His observer, Robert Francis Newton has no known grave; his presumed death is annotated '3 April 1918'.

| 54 Squadron | 2Lt R C Crowden | Safe | See 4 April 1918 - 54 Squadron |
| F.1 Camel B5223 | | | |

T/o Conteville for an offensive patrol and wrecked here in a landing accident. Strong winds were said to have been a contributory factor leading to the loss of the Camel.

| 54 Squadron | 2Lt R T Cuffe | Safe | See 21 July 1918 - 54 Squadron |
| F.1 Camel C8295 | | | |

T/o Conteville similarly tasked and as with the Camel reported above came to grief on landing, 'C8295' running into a hole; salvaged, the airframe was struck off charge on 14 April 1918. Richard Thomas Cuffe from Swinford in Co Mayo was one of well over one hundred cadets commissioned as temporary second lieutenants to the General List of the Royal Flying Corps on 13 September 1917, their names being published in supplement 30327 of the paper issued on 9 October 1917. 'C8295' had arrived with the squadron five days previously.

| 54 Squadron | 2Lt R N MacLean | Injured |
| F.1 Camel D6505 | | |

T/o 1805 Conteville similarly ordered and was over the Somme and when last sighted south of Moreuil, seemingly under control. Commissioned to the General List of the Royal Flying Corps, Second Lieutenant MacLean was confirmed in his rank on 16 November 1917 [*gazetted* 4 December 1917, supplement 30416]. Received in France from the Aeroplane Acceptance Park at Norwich, 'D6505' was issued to the squadron on the 26th of March 1918. Second Lieutenant MacLean was later treated for wounds received in combat.

| 56 Squadron | Lt J G Moore | Safe |
| SE.5a C9531 | | |

T/o Valheureux for practice flying and on return to the airfield was badly damaged while in the process of landing. Taken to No 2 Advanced Salvage Dump it is likely that 'C9531' languished until struck off charge on 7 May 1918.

59 Squadron   RE.8 A3676   Split longeron discovered, thought to have been caused by either a heavy landing or weather related. Deemed uneconomical to repair and struck off charge on 12 April 1918. First issued to No 12 Squadron on 5 August 1917, 'A3676' overturned on landing from an operational patrol [strong winds being a factor] on 25 November 1917 [Lieutenants Mann and Godfrey uninjured]. Repaired and ferried to Courcelles-le-Comte for No 59 Squadron on 19 February 1918, and thence to Lealvilliers on 22 March 1918.

60 Squadron   2Lt E W Christie [Canada]   +   Arras Flying Services Memorial
SE.5a B8236
T/o 1730 Fienvillers for an early evening offensive patrol and believed to have been shot down at 1816 by Jochann [or Johann] Puetz of *Jasta 66.*

60 Squadron   2Lt R K Whitney   Safe   See 18 July 1918 - 60 Squadron
SE.5a C1069
T/o Fienvillers similarly tasked and returned to the airfield with his aircraft so badly shot about that it was struck to No 2 Advanced Salvage Dump, where it was declared not worth repairing; struck off charge on the 7th.

60 Squadron   2Lt F W Clarke   Safe   See 12 April 1918 - 60 Squadron
SE.5a C5332
T/o Fienvillers simllarly instructed only for the engine to 'cut'; crashed, and effectively damaged beyond repair in the forced landing at map reference 57DH5B72. 'C5332' was one of one hundred and fifty SE.5a airframes [C5301-C5450] built by Vickers Limited of Crayford, Kent, arriving with the squadron on 22 December 1917. When written off it had accounted for six hostile machines [some being shared], five of the six at the hands of Captain F O Soden [subsequently granted a permanent commission], his final success in 'C5332' coming during the late morning of the 5th of February 1918, when he drove down an Albatros near Becelaere [West-Vlaan-deren] after which his guns jammed. Diving to near ground level he hedge-hopped towards home but while still over Belgium he sighted another Albatros and drove it into a tree near Ten-Brielen.

60 Squadron   Lt K P Campbell [Canada]   Safe   See 30 May 1918 - 60 Squadron
SE.5a C5388
T/o Fienvillers similarly ordered and returned to base circa 1845 so badly shot up that it was struck off charge ten days later. Formerly of the Saskatchewan Regiment and seconded for duty with the Royal Flying Corps on 12 December 1917 [*gazetted* 13 February 1918, supplement 30524], Keith Preston Campbell died on 28th November 1918, and was laid to rest in Ruislip [St Martin] Churchyard extension. At the time he was not attached to a squadron.

65 Squadron   2Lt H Dean   pow
F.1 Camel C8230
T/o 1055 Conteville for an offensive patrol and was last seen over the Somme east of the line Moreuil on the south end and Démuin to the north-northeast, a distance of about seven km. 'C8230' was issued to the squad-ron on the 20th of March 1918. Listed as 'missing' on the Roll of Honour prepared by the Air Ministry and repeated in *Flight* May 16, 1918, his status as a prisoner of war [wounded] appeared in the magazine's issue of October 24, 1918. He was repatriated on 18 December 1918.

65 Squadron   2Lt L L F Towne   pow   Unemployed list 11 July 1919: Lt
F.1 Camel C8294
T/o 1100 Conteville similarly tasked and went down in the same area as that reported for Second Lieutenant Dean. Commissioned to the General List of the Royal Flying Corps, Second Lieutenant Towne was confirmed in his rank on 27 October 1917 [*gazetted* 16 November 1917, supplement 30390]. The diligence of the Air Ministry in widely distributing their Rolls of Honour tables is reflected by three entries in *Flight* concerning Lieutenant

Towne; 'missing', 'previously reported missing but now believed prisoner of war' and finally 'repatriated', issues for May 9, July 4 and 19 December 1918. 'C8294' had been on the squadron's establishment for eight days.

65 Squadron	2Lt F A W Nunn	+	Arras Flying Services Memorial

F.1 Camel D1780

T/o 0650 Conteville also ordered for operations and seen to crash in enemy lines near Fresnoy in the Pas-de-Calais. Frederick Arthur William Nunn had served previously with the 1st Battalion London Regiment [Royal Fusiliers]. His attachment to the Royal Flying Corps, effective from the last day of December 1917, was *gazetted* in a supplement to *The London Gazette* issue 30497 published on 25 January 1918.

65 Squadron	Lt J G Kennedy	Safe	See 4 April 1918 - 65 Squadron

F.1 Camel D1830

T/o Conteville similarly instructed but swung badly and collided with a tree; crashed and damaged beyond repair. James Gilbert Kennedy was just eighteen years of age and his brief time with No 65 Squadron life had been full of drama. On the 27th of March he was caught out in fog while flying in 'B2412' and his attempt to force-land in a field that had been put to the plough near Poperinge ended with the Camel standing on its nose, James sustaining minor injuries. Three days later he was back in the air and flying in 'C8290' [see my summary for the 1st of April] and when in the vicinity of Lamotte [probably Lamotee Warfusée in the Somme] crashed an Albatros. Forty-eight hours later this brave young pilot from Finnarts on the Ayrshire coast of Scotland was dead.

73 Squadron	2Lt G L Graham	Safe

F.1 Camel B2311

T/o Fouquerolles authorised for a practice flight and damaged beyond repair after making a forced landing in a cornfield, thereby ending a most eventful eleven months of service. From the Air Acceptance Park at Lincoln, the Camel was in the hands of No 45 Squadron on 10 August 1917, serving until the 27th of October when Second Lieutenant J E Child force-landed at Poperinge on the western side of Ypres. Repaired, 'B2311' was taken on by No 70 Squadron on 26 November but was struck from squadron strength following a landing accident on 13 January, Second Lieutenant J Todd walking away unhurt [as did Second Lieutenant Child]. On 27 March, No 80 Squadron took over 'B2311' but by the end of the month it was again in the hands of the repair shop following a burst tyre on take-off, probably at Belleville Farm - Second Lieutenant J R Orr escaping injury. Thus, on the 11th of June this well travelled scout arrived at Fouquerolles where it was accepted by No 73 Squadron.

81 Squadron*	Lt J G Moore	+	Lincoln [Newport] Cemetery

F.1 Camel D6470

T/o Scampton for a training flight during which nineteen year old Jack Greville Moore lost control and spun to the ground. Educated at St Bees School in West Cumbria his name, along with other 'Old St Bechians' who fell in the *Great War*, is commemorated in the school's chapel. It is noted, however, that St Bees, which was founded by the then Archbishop of Canterbury Edmund Grundal in 1583, formerly closed in July 2015.

* Formed at Gosport on the 7th of January 1917, and equipped from the outset with Camels the remit for the squadron was training, though throughout its existence it carried 'squadron' status without the nomenclature 'training' being added. Eight days after forming the squadron moved to Scampton where it disbanded on the 4th of July 1918.

82 Squadron	2Lt C C Summers	Safe	
FK.8 B3381	Lt J H M Yeomans*	Safe	Unemployed list 14 February 1919: Lt

While taxing at Agenvilliers for take off the FK.8 ran into a deep rut. The time of the incident is given at 1400 [Army Form W 3347] with substantial damage to the undercarriage, propellor, left-hand lower plane and the fuselage severely strained. Up to this point 'B3381' had flown for a total of twenty hours and forty minutes.

* Possibly former Acting Captain J H M Yeomans MC of the North Staffordshire Regiment who relinquished his acting rank when ceasing to command a Company, effective 20 September 1917 [*gazetted* 30 October 1917,

supplement 30357]. However, the entry for Lieutenant J H M Yeomans for 14 February 1919, when with a host of others he was transferred to the Unemployed list, makes no mention of a Military Cross.

| 82 Squadron | Captain G I Paterson [Canada] + | Hangard Communal Cemetery extension* |
| FK.8 C8524 | Lt J Findlay | Injured |

T/o Agenvilliers for a tactical sortie over the lines and was probably brought down in the general vicinity of Hangard*[iSomme] some five km south of Villers-Bretonneux. George Irving Paterson was formerly of the 152nd [Weyburn-Estevan] Battalion of the Canadian Infantry which arrived in the United Kingdom during October 1916.

* The village of Hangard was on the junction of the Commonwealth and French armies where following the German offensive of the 21st of March 1918, was now heavily engaged in denying the enemy their intention of severing contact between the two armies. Forty-eight hours after Captain Paterson of Regina in the province of Saskatchewan lost his life, Hangard and its environs was the scene of bitter fighting which lasted until the 25th of April but it was not until the 8th of August 1918, that the village was eventually cleared of the enemy by the 1st and 2nd Canadian Mounted Rifles.

| 84 Squadron | Lt G O Johnson | Safe |
| SE.5a B699 | | |

T/o Conteville ordered for operations and force-landed at Longeau [sic] with a seized engine. Loaded onto a trailer further damage occurred which resulted in the aircraft being struck off charge on 12 April 1918. Following brief service with No 68 Squadron 'B699' arrived with '84' on 5 March 1918, and in less than a month accounted for three hostile machines, two being shared, all with Lieutenant Johnson at the controls. As a second lieutenant he was confirmed in his rank on 27 September 1917 [*gazetted* 19 October 1917, supplement 30347].

| 210 Squadron | Flight Sub-Lieut* A L Jones | Safe |
| F.1 Camel B3808 N | | |

T/o Treizennes for an offensive patrol and on return to the airfield crashed while landing. Struck off charge six days later.

* The recording of ranks applicable to the new service had yet to catch up with No 210 Squadron when reporting the crash, hence the entry in Air-Britain's *The Camel File* reflects his Royal Naval Air Service rank of Flight Sub-Lieutenant.

Note. In marked contrast to the 1st when the weather was fair, heavy banks of cloud hampered reconnaissance over the trenches, though low-level attacks continued to good effect. Enemy air activity between Albert and Moreuil was particularly prevalent with a number of aerial combats resulting. During the evening heavy and continuous rain prevented concentrated night raiding until conditions improved after 0300 hours, thus enabling a handful of attacks on enemy billets in the rear areas of the front. This inclement weather was to persist for the next week.

Wednesday 3 April 1918
During the day General Ferdinand Foch's assumed overall command of all Allied forces fighting on the Western Front, thus implementing the decision reached at the Doullens Conference on March 26th. Air activity from all participants was much reduced owing to the weather.

| 4 Squadron | 2Lt J E Sharp | Injured Unemployed list 3 April 1919: Lt |
| RE.8 B3436 | Lt E V Gilliat | Injured |

T/o Chocques for an artillery observation patrol during which a forced landing became necessary. Delivered to the Aeroplane Acceptance Park at Lympne by 20 August 1917, 'B3436' arrived on the squadron on 23 September, since when it had accumulated a very useful two hundred and four hours of flying. Under the banner 'Special Reserve of Officers' 'Infantry' with effect from the 1st of July 1917, Second Lieutenant Gilliat of the West Yorkshire Regiment was promoted lieutenant [*gazetted* 12 November 1917, supplement 30376]. He was seconded to the Royal Flying Corps on 3 February 1918, promulgated in supplement 30549 of 28 February 1918; postwar he appears to have rejoined his Regiment.

17 Squadron	2Lt St J Salmon-Backhouse	+	Sofia War Cemetery
FK.8	Lt G Still	+	Sofia War Cemetery

T/o Mikra Bay and failed to return. Both officers were formerly of the Cameron Highlanders and in the case of StJohn Salmon-Backhouse service with the Royal Fusilier and the 10th Battalion East Lancashire Regiment.

21 Squadron	Lt Walters	Safe
RE.8 D4813	Lt Wood	Injured

T/o La Lovie but stalled and crashed back to the ground and caught fire. Lieutenant Wood's injuries are described as 'slight'. Sent to France by sea, 'D4813' was accepted by the squadron on the day the Royal Air Force was formed; its total flying was a mere fifty minutes.

23 Squadron	2Lt E G S Mortimer [Canada]	+	Gezaincourt Communal Cemetery extension
SPAD S.13 B6881			

T/o Bertangles for practice flying; eyewitnesses report seeing the Spad flying at around eight hundred feet and then go into a spin from which if failed to recover. Ernest George Smith Mortimer hailed from Ottawa; his father, Major George Mortimer served with the Canadian Expeditionary Force.

27 Squadron	2Lt E J Smith	Safe
DH.4 A7640	Airman J Faulkner	Safe

T/o Ruisseauville for a test flight and on return overshot and crashed, damaging the DH beyond repair.

35 Squadron	Lt R M C MacFarlane	Injured
FK.8 C3682	2Lt A E Lancashire	Injured

T/o 0900 Abbeville for a contact patrol over the Somme during which the crew force-landed near Villers-Bretonneux where the FK.8 was destroyed by fire. Joining the squadron on 25 March 1918, 'C3682' had logged twenty-eight hours and fifteen minutes flying.

35 Squadron	2Lt Phillips	Safe	
FK.8 C8457	2Lt M Balston	Safe	Unemployed list 4 July 1919: Lt[RFA]

T/o 1400 Abbeville similarly tasked, heading for the Amiens area. Intercepted and badly shot about by enemy aircraft. For Second Lieutenant Balston, this was his second 'incident' in forty-eight hours [see my summary for the 1st of April for details]. Since its arrival on 23 March 1918, 'C8457' had completed overall fifty hours and fifty minutes flying..

48 Squadron	Captain C R Steele	Safe
Bristol F.2b B1349	2Lt E H Stanes	Safe

T/o Conteville to transit to the squadron's new airfield at Bertangles some thirty-four km to the south-southeast but ran into a hole and was damaged beyond repair. Charles Ronald Steele began his military service as a Royal Military College Sandhurst cadet and was commissioned to the Green Howards on 21 January 1916. His career as a junior second lieutenant serving with the infantry was brief for by 22 May 1916, he had qualified as a pilot and was attached to No 15 Squadron. His appointment as a flight commander with No 48 Squadron came in February 1918. The award of the Distinguished Flying Cross, *gazetted* 1 November 1918 supplement 30989, was reported as he convalesced in the United Kingdom having been severely wounded during an enemy night bombing raid on Bertangles on 24 August 1918, the citation reading; *'A bold and skilful leader who inspires confidence in those who serve with him. On August 13th, while leading an offensive patrol of five machines, he observed six enemy scouts; attacking these he shot down one out of control, his observer driving down a second. In this engagement he became separated from his patrol; seeing this, eight scouts dived to attack him, one of these his observer shot down out of control. Eventually he rejoined his patrol and led them back to the aerodrome. In all he has destroyed three enemy machines and driven down four others out of control.'* Postwar he was appointed to a permanent commission and for the better part of his pre-Second World War service he was engaged in Staff Duties, broken by fifteen months between January 1936 and May 1937 when he occupied 'the chair' with No 18 Squadron [Hart/Hind]. Throughout the Second World War and beyond he held senior posts with various commands, culminating as Air Officer Commander-in-Chief Coastal Command. Born at Netheridge in South Yorkshire on 9 November 1897, Air Marshal Sir Charles Steele died on the 14th of February

1973 at Trumpington in Cambridgeshire. In addition to British honours, his service was also recognised by the governments of Belgium, France and Greece. His observer was formerly of the 3rd Battalion, Manchester Regiment and owing to ill-health he had to relinquish his commission with effect from 14 October 1919. At the time he was ranked lieutenant and had been awarded the Military Cross.

| 52 Squadron | Lt E D Jones | + | Arras Flying Services Memorial |
| RE.8 A3868 | 2Lt R F Newton | + | Arras Flying Services Memorial |

T/o Abbeville for an operational mission during which the RE became the seventy-fifth victim of Manfred von Richthofen [the table listing his combat successes indicates this action as taking place on the 2nd of April] known throughout Germany as *Der Rote Kampfflieger* and commonly referred to by historians, writers and the like as 'The Red Baron'. The location for their demise is thought to have been Hill 104 north of Moreuil, a commune in the *département de la Somme*. Ernest David Jones had completed his education at Brecon Grammar School [then known as Brecon County School] whose website includes a detailed commemoration for the school's thirty-seven 'old boys' who lost their lives in the *Great War*. Ernest's entry is supported by a photograph of him taken after he was awarded his Flying Badge.

| 52 Squadron | 2Lt C M Swain | + | Picquigny British Cemetery |
| RE.8 B5063 | 2Lt S W Swaine | + | Picquigny British Cemetery |

T/o Abbeville for an operational patrol; lost control and spun in from four hundred feet near Bapaume in the Pas-de-Calais. Delivered to the Aeroplane Acceptance Park at Coventry on, or by, 24 September 1917, 'B5063' flew a total of one hundred and sixty eight hours since acceptance by the squadron on 2 October 1917. Bearing in mind the harsh conditions in which these comparatively frail aircraft operated, this was remarkable testimony to the ground crews who kept them serviceable and ready for operations. Bristolian, Clifford Maxwell Swain, was nineteen years of age; his observer, Sydney William Swaine, formerly of the Royal Field Artillery, was twenty. It is noted that their resting place is in the Somme some thirteen km northwest of Amiens and a considerable distance from Bapaume away to the northeast.

| 54 Squadron | 2Lt C J Mason | Safe | See 4 April 1918 - 54 Squadron |
| F.1 Camel C1560 | | | |

T/o Conteville for an offensive patrol and on return, and landing, the axle snapped resulting in damage that was deemed not worth repairing. Flown to France on 4 February 1918, and intended for the squadron, 'C1560' force-landed [owing to engine failure] near Villers-Carbonnel in the Somme some forty to fifty km east of Amiens, seriously injuring Lieutenant W H Kelly. Repaired, it eventually arrived on 24 March; on the last day of the month Second Lieutenant Mason drove down an Albatros southeast of Proyart a village in the Somme noted for its spectacular War Memorial. Sited in the public gardens this impressive memorial depicts a French soldier standing on a raised plinth beneath a stone arch on the face of which are the names of the village men who lost their lives in the *Great War*. It is further noted that on the 29th of August 1914, the village was overrun by the Germans in fighting that left the surrounding fields strewn with dead. However, during the critical *Battle of the Marne* in September 1914, Proyart was liberated and remained as such until the German offensive of March 1918, when once again the village fell to the enemy.

| 81 Squadron | Lt S Hughenin [USAS] | + | Brookwood Military Cemetery |
| F.1 Camel D6472 | | | |

T/o Scampton for a training flight [possibly for formation flying practice] during which a change in course was signalled and it was while carrying out this instruction that Stanley Hughenin's restraining belt became undone throwing him from the cockpit. Indications are that this awful tragedy took place at around three hundred feet. His name was published in the Wichita *Daily Eagle* of Tuesday, 23 April 1918, indicating his death was owing to an unspecified accident. On smashing into the ground the pilotless Camel killed two personnel of the United States Army Service, namely Private Nathan

Krantmann*and Corporal B J Siefert; both were on the strength of No 150 Aero Squadron but had been attached to No 60 Training [ex-Reserve] Squadron based at Scampton.

* Possibly Private Nathan 'Krantman' of Philadelphia in the State of Pennsylvania.

86 Squadron	Lt J B Jewell	+	Ruislip [St Martin] Churchyard extension
F.1 Camel C1684			

T/o Northolt and reported as spinning into the ground. John Belmont Jewell had been confirmed in the rank of Second Lieutenant with effect from 21 February 1918 [*gazetted* in supplement 30594 of the paper issued on the 22nd of March 1918]. From all accounts it appears he deliberately put the Camel into a spin but owing to a previous injury he was unable to centralise the rudder.

101 Squadron	Captain E D Hall	Safe
FE.2b A5559	Lt W S Aulton	Safe

T/o Haute Visée for a bombing raid during which the petrol tank was shot through by machine-gun fire, causing the crew to force-land near the airfield at Bertangles. Taken to No 2 Advanced Salvage Dump all trace of 'A5559' ceases on 30 June 1918. It is believed the 'adventures' on the 3rd of April was the last time this FE.2b took to the air. Lieutenant William Stanley Aulton was seconded to the Royal Flying Corps from the Army Service Corps on 13 January 1918, promulgated 5 February 1918, supplement 30509. On 17 April 1919, he was attached to the Administrative Branch [issue 31315 of the paper published on 29 April 1919], but by the autumn of 1921, William appears to have returned to army service. This service began early in the *Great War* when as a private soldier he was appointed as a second lieutenant from the Inns of Court Officers Training Corps to the West Riding Division Train of the Army Service Corps on the last day of August 1915 [*gazetted* 14 September 1915, issue 29295]. In the Second World War he returned to Royal Air Force service, obtaining a commission as a pilot officer in the Training Branch on 1 February 1941 [issue 35139 of 18 April 1941] and served until resigning his commission on the last day of February 1947, still in the rank of pilot officer.

Thursday 4 April 1918
This day signalled the end of the *Kaiserschlacht* though intense activity by the German armies continued unabated. Officially referred to as the *Battle of the Avre* which in turn became part of the *Battle of Villers-Bretonneux,* a total of fifteen German divisions went into action to the east of Amiens with the main infantry thrust aimed at securing the high ground surrounding Villers-Bretonneux from where Amiens could be exposed to artillery pounding. Throughout the day both sides fought hard and though close to exhaustion counterattacks from British and Australian units prevented the enemy from achieving their principal objectives.

2 Squadron AusFC	Lt L J Primrose AusFC	Safe	See 28 May 1918 - 2 Squadron AusFC
SE.5a D214			

T/o Fouquerolles for an offensive patrol during which the oil tank was shot through, thereby necessitating a forced landing near Amiens. Salvaged, but struck off charge on the 14th with seventy-two hours and forty-five minutes of flying recorded.

24 Squadron	2Lt E P Crossen	Safe	Unemployed list 12 March 1919: Lt
SE.5a B559			

T/o Conteville for ground target duties during which a forced landing was made near St Ouen. It will be recalled that Lieutenant Crossen had been involved in a mishap on the day the Royal Air Force came into being [see my summary for SE.5a B1].

24 Squadron	2Lt P J N Nolan	Safe	See 7 April 1918 - 24 Squadron
SE.5a B640			

T/o Conteville similarly tasked and damaged beyond repair while forced landing near the aerodrome. This particular SE.5a had an unfortunate past. Delivered to No 41 Squadron at Lealvilliers on the 7th of November 1917, it was involved in a fatal crash on the 22nd of the month when during take off it collided with SE.5a B33 resulting in the death of its pilot Second Lieutenant Reginald Maurice Whitehead who now rests in Doullens Communal Cemetery extension No 1, as does Second Lieutenant Edward Stanley Weiss who was at the controls of 'B640' and who sustained fatal injuries. Following repair it was taken on No 24 Squadron's establishment on 26 March 1918.

28 Squadron	Lt A F White	Injured
F.1 Camel B2454		

T/o Grossa but swung out of control and turned over; Lieutenant White's injuries were not thought to be too serious.

38 Squadron*	2Lt L Roebuck	+	Huddersfield [Almondbury] Cemetery
FE.2b A5508			

T/o Leadenham and while banking stalled; nose dived to the ground. Leonard Roebuck was confirmed in his rank on the 3rd of January 1918 [*gazetted* 8 February 1918, supplement 30517]. According to Andrew Pentland's examination of surviving *Great War* air records, 'A5508' was at Renfrew on or by 14 April 1917, and by 25th June had been issued to No 28 Squadron at Gosport where the squadron was still working up prior to deployment to the Western Front; on this day it was involved in a minor flying accident when it came down on a hedge near the aerodrome following engine failure, its crew, Lieutenant W F Findlay and his observer Second Lieutenant T Noad, alighting unharmed. The Court of Inquiry's findings was that failure of the engine occurred while switching from the service tank to the main tank. Repaired, its next entry pertains to the fatal accident, here summarised.

* Formed on the 1st of April 1916, at Thetford No 38 Squadron was re-designated No 25[Reserve] Squadron on 22nd of May, but re-formed at Castle Bromwich on 14 July 1916 under Captain A T Harris [the future Air Officer Commanding-in-Chief Bomber Command] who was to lead '38' until mid-September 1916, by which time Squadron headquarters was at Melton Mowbray. Its rôle while based in the United Kingdom was defence of the industrial Midlands from Zeppelin raids, detached flights being maintained at Buckminster, Leadenham and Stamford. With its background of night flying experience and with the threat from the Zeppelin raids abating, the squadron moved to France at the end of May, still equipped with FE.2b, for night bombing operations at which time Major C C Wigram was its commanding officer.

48 Squadron	2Lt F C Ransley	Safe	See 24 April 1918 - 48 Squadron
Bristol F.2b C4628	2Lt C W Davies	Safe	See 24 April 1918 - 48 Squadron

T/o Bertangles for an operational sortie over the Somme towards Villers-Bretonneux [a mere twenty or so km southeast of Bertangles] where fierce ground fighting was taking place. On return to base, the Bristol turned over while landing. Second Lieutenant Ransley was confirmed in his rank on 29 September 1917, and on the 15th of May 1918, was promoted temporary captain [it is noted he had qualified on both land and sea aeroplanes], the relevant *Gazette* entries being supplement 30344 of of 19 October 1917, and issue 30714 of 31st May 1918.

54 Squadron	2Lt R C Crowden	Safe	See 28 May 1918 - 54 Squadron
F.1 Camel B2483			

T/o Conteville for an air test and on return landed heavily, breaking the undercarriage.

54 Squadron	2Lt C J Mason	Safe	See 21 April 1918 - 54 Squadron
F.1 Camel B6386			

T/o Conteville having received instructions for a practice reconnaissance and damaged beyond repair following its return to the airfield where it came to grief on landing. This was Cecil John Mason's third mishap over the last four days; he was also involved in a crash on the 25th of March 1918.

56 Squadron	Captain W S Fielding Johnson	Safe
SE.5a C5394		

T/o Valheureux and on arrival at Bertangles, Captain Fielding Johnson misread the signals laid out on the airfield and touching down the SE.5a turned over; damaged beyond repair and was struck on the 7th.

65 Squadron	Lt J G Kennedy	+	Arras Flying Services Memorial
F.1 Camel D6552			

T/o Conteville and in the mid-afternoon when over Bois de Vaire dived on an enemy two-seater reconnaissance aircraft and sent it down in flames; this action had been spotted by some enemy scouts who immediately attacked the Camel and, unable to escape, James Gilbert Kennedy, reported on the 2nd, himself fell in a blazing mass.

66 Squadron	2Lt H B Homan [South Africa]	+	Montecchio Precalcino Communal Cemetery
F.1 Camel D5226			

T/o Treviso but when in the early stages of the climb the Camel's engine failed and with insufficient height in hand Henry Biorn Holman was unable to correct the spin before crashing just off the airfield. His entry in the cemetery register indicates that his family had connections with Scotland.

Friday 5 April 1918

Renewed attempts by the German divisions to the force the issue around Villers-Bretonneux failed and by the end of the day those of the enemy that had managed to occupy the eastern parts of the town were driven out. At this point, with the battlefield situation stabilised in favour of the Allies, von Ludendorff, principal architect of the *Kaiserschlacht* called off the offensive. Although Operation *Michael* had failed to drive a wedge between the Commonwealth forces to the north and their French allies to the south, nevertheless between the 21st of March and the 5th of April 1918, a vast bulge measuring sixty-four km at its central point had been punched into Fifth Army's lines and the territory taken would not be given up easily. The outcome of this retreat was the relieving of General Sir Hubert de la Pour Gough commanding Fifth Army, his place being taken by General Sir Henry Rawlinson who arrived at Gough's field headquarters in the early hours of 28th March, bringing with him his own staff officers, though some of Gough's staff remained to ease the transition of command. This was a sad end to Sir Hubert Gough's extensive career and in the years since students of the *Great War* believe he was the scapegoat for the failings of others. Reading the numerous accounts of his departure one is left with the impression that politics and jealousy played no little part in his sacking, a very sad reflection on the devious ways of those in high command. As a sop to lessen the disappointment that Sir Hubert Gough must have felt, Haig hosted a farewell lunch on the 5th of April but I doubt if Sir Hubert had much of an appetite for the fare placed before him. Of the Fifth Army, now commanded by Rawlinson, a new title was bestowed; the Fourth Army.

Born in London on the 12th of August 1870, Hubert de la Pour Gough outlived all his contemporaries, his death at the age of ninety-two being announced on 18 March 1963; he is buried in Camberley, Surrey.

In the aftermath of the German spring offensive much hard fighting remained and it would not be until August that the wheels of war would turn in favour of the Allies.

2 Squadron AusFC	Lt R W Sexton	Safe	See 8 June 1918 - 4 Squadron AusFC
SE.5a B185			

T/o Bertangles with the intention of flying to La Bellevue but engine failure intervened and 'B185' was damaged beyond worthwhile repair after forced landing at Doullens, twenty-two km north-northeast from the point of its departure.

2 Squadron AusFC	Lt J S Truscott	Safe	
SE.5a C1060			

T/o Bertangles with the same destination in mind and is known to have overflown Puchevillers roughly fifteen km north-northeast from Bertangles before forced landing owing to engine failure before reaching Marieux seven km further along on the same heading. All three locations fall within the Somme *département*.

55 Squadron	2Lt P H O'Lieff	pow	Unemployed list 28 May 1919: 2Lt
DH.4 A7553	2Lt S R Wells	pow	Unemployed list 8 March 1919: 2Lt

T/o Tantonville and failed to return from a raid on Luxembourg. Second Lieutenant O'Lieff was made a temporary second lieutenant for service with the Royal Flying Corps on New Year's Day 1918; formerly he had been a sergeant attached to the School of Technical Training. His observer had his rank confirmed on the day he was reported missing.

| 100 Squadron | 2Lt L E Collins | + | Fere-Champenoise French National Cemetery |
| FE.2b A844 | 2Lt N Ford [Australia] | + | Fere-Champenoise French National Cemetery |

T/o Villeseneux for a practice flight and crashed soon after, possibly in the general vicinity of the training area at Mailly-le-Camp in the Aube *département* and roughly twenty-seven km south-southeast of the airfield for both officers were buried here in the military cemetery until they were exhumed in 1932 and taken to their present resting place. Leslie Ernest Collins from Sidcup in Kent was nineteen years of age, his observer/air gunner, Norman Ford from Carters Tower in Queensland was twenty-seven. First issued to No 11 Squadron on 1 June 1917, 'A844' went next to No 18 Squadron, eventually arriving at Ochey and No 100 Squadron on 11 October. At the time of its demise it had logged one hundred and thirty-nine hours and five minutes of flying.

Saturday 6 April 1918

During the day No 65 Squadron departed Conteville in the Somme and flew the thirty-five km southeast to Bertangles, an airfield close to the battle lines and north of Amiens.

| 2 Squadron AusFC | SE.5a C5349 | During transit by road from Bertangles to La Bellevue sustained |

damage of an undisclosed nature. Taken to No 2 Advanced Salvage Dump and struck off here on the 9th.

| 2 Squadron AusFC | Lt L Benjamin | Injured |
| SE.5a D204 | | |

T/o Fouquerolles for an offensive patrol but owing to magneto trouble force-landed near Villers-Bocage. Salvaged and taken to No 2 Advanced Salvage Dump it, too, was struck as beyond economical repair before the end of April 1918. Lieutenant Benjamin's injuries were not serious.

| 3 Squadron | 2Lt D G Gold | pow | Unemployed list 5 May 1919: Lt |
| F.1 Camel C1577 | | | |

T/o 1445 Valheureux briefed to carry out low-level bombing on enemy positions facing Divisions of the Third Army*and failed to return. Arriving in France on 18 February 1918, 'C1577' was issued to the squadron on the 23rd of March. Second Lieutenant Gold's status as a prisoner of war appeared in the Air Ministry list, as repeated in *Flight* May 16, 1918.

* Commanded by General Sir Julian Byng whose command of the Third Army spanned the period 9 June 1917 to 22 March 1919. During this period his Divisions were engaged in the *Third Battle of Ypres*, the August 1918 *Battle of Amiens* and what is referred to as the 'Hundred Day' offensive.

| 3 Squadron | 2Lt J H Pascoe | Injured |
| F.1 Camel D6501 | | |

T/o Valheureux authorised to carry out practice flying during which Second Lieutenant Pascoe flew into telegraph wires near the aerodrome and crashed; his injuries are reported as 'slight'. 'D6501' was received by the squadron on the 30th of March 1918.

| 4 Squadron AusFC | Lt E R Sly | Safe | See 15 April 1918 - 4 Squadron AusFC |
| F.1 Camel B2498 | | | |

T/o Bruay with others to practice formation flying; on return clipped the brim of a ridge and turned over. By coincidence, its days with No 65 Squadron ended in similar circumstances when on 20 November 1917, Second Lieutenant Douglas Michael Sage landed short of Bailleul and running into a bank flipped onto its back. From Kroonstad in the Orange Free State of South Africa, eighteen year old Douglas Sage was killed when his Camel B2410 was shot down over Roulers [West-Vlaanderen] in the early afternoon of 18th of December 1917. He is buried in Belgium at Harlebeke New British Cemetery.

| 8 Squadron | 2Lt G de Gaye | Safe | Unemployed list 7 March 1919: Lt |
| FK.8 B4080 | 2Lt C P Henzell | Safe | Commission relinquished 1 April 1918: Lt [RFA] |

T/o Auxi-le-Château*tasked for photographic reconnaissance but turned back with the engine misfiring and on landing ran onto rough ground which caused an oleo cylinder to burst. Salvaged with a view to repair, 'B4080' was struck off charge on the last day of the month. Following the outbreak of the Second World War, Charles

Peregrine Henzell came forward to serve his King and country and was appointed in the rank of lieutenant to the General List on 14 January 1940; subsequently, he was transferred to the Intelligence Corps and on 16 May 1944, still ranked lieutenant, he resigned his commission, the relevant entries being supplements 34848 and 36523 published on 14 May 1940 and 23 May 1944.

* No 8 Squadron moved into Auxi-le-Château during the day from Vert Galand; thus, the operation here reported may have been mounted from Vert Galand.

13 Squadron	Lt S T Payne	+	Arras Flying Services Memorial
RE.8 C4570	2Lt R Hilton	+	Arras Flying Services Memorial

T/o Savy for an operational sortie from which it failed to return. Sydney Thomas Payne who formerly held at commission with the Royal West Surrey Regiment was transferred to the General List of the Royal Flying Corps with effect from the 7th of August 1916, as *gazetted* in issue 2996 of the paper published on the 9th of March 1917. His observer/air gunner transferred to air duties from the 5th Battalion Manchester Regiment; he was nineteen years of age.

23 Squadron	2Lt E R Varley	Injured	
SPAD S.13 B6878	Sgt J Meakin	Injured	Namps-au-Val British Cemetery
	Mechanic G Shenton	Injured	

T/o Bertangles for an offensive patrol during which Second Lieutenant Varley landed just to the south of the Amiens to Roye road where he picked up two wounded airmen [as recorded in the crew matrix] but while trying to take off the Spad [French built] was hit by a shell and completely wrecked. John Meakin died the following day, whether from his wounds caused prior to the attempted rescue or as a result of the shell hitting 'B6878' is debatable. Namps-au-Val [Somme] is about sixteen km southwest of Amiens. Early in the Second World War, Eric Ralph Varley was appointed to a commission in the Administrative and Special Duties Branch with effect from 28 August 1940 [*gazetted* 27 September 1940, issue 34954], serving until relinquishing his commission under the provisions of the Navy, Army and Air Force Reserves Act, 1954. His Military Cross [*gazetted* 22 June 1918, supplement 30761] was made for; *'Conspicuous gallantry and devotion to duty. Observing two enemy two-seater machines, he, by skilful piloting, obtained a position under the tail of one and opened fire at close range, with the result that the hostile plane fell out of control and crashed. On two later occasions he attacked and destroyed two other hostile machines, the pilot of one being taken prisoner. He has also shown great dash in attacking enemy balloons and hostile troops on the march, and has displayed marked gallantry throughout.'*

29 Squadron	Lt A G Wingate-Gray	Safe	Unemployment list 1 March 1919: Lt
Nieuport 27 B3601			

T/o La Lovie having received instructions to carry out a special mission and was last seen over Hollebeke [West-Vlaanderen] a village in 1918, but now part of the city of Ypres. Alexander George Wingate-Gray was commissioned to the Administrative and Special Duties Branch on 12 February 1940, promulgated in issue 34805 of the paper published on 5 March 1940, resigning his commission in squadron leader rank on 9 March 1944.

40 Squadron	Lt H Carnegie [Canada]	Safe
SE.5a B589		

T/o Bruay for an offensive patrol and report to have crashed at around 1035 north of Pont-à-Vendin in the Pas-de-Calais. Four days following this incident, Lieutenant Carnegie was tasked to carry out a low-level bombing attack during the course of which he was wounded by ground fire. Despite being in considerable pain he maintained control of his aircraft [SE.5a B191] and landed 1020 at Choques in the Béthune sector and taken to No 1 Casualty Clearing Station from where, I suspect, he was transferred to a permanent hospital, either in France or in the United Kingdom. Lieutenant Carnegie's service began with the 4th Canadian Reserve Battalion but who, as a temporary lieutenant, was seconded for duty with the Royal Flying Corps with effect from 6 July 1917, as *gazetted* in supplement 30221 of the paper published on 8 August 1917.

40 Squadron	Captain G H Lewis	Safe
SE.5a C5438		

T/o Bruay similarly tasked and crashed when his engine 'cut' at low level. Gwilym Lewis's account of his 'misfortune' is succinctly recorded by David Gunby on page 53 of *Sweeping the Skies*. Gwilym was indeed fortunate to emerge from the wreckage with only minor cuts and bruises for in his own words he somersaulted four or five times finishing up inverted with the tail section lying alongside the engine and his machine gun *'prattling merrily.'*

43 Squadron   Lt F 'D' Hudson   pow Niederzwehren Cemetery, Kassel
F.1 Camel B2431
T/o 1510 Avesnes-le-Comte for a special mission, during which the Camel was intercepted by *Lieutnant* H Weiss of *Jasta 11*. In the combat that followed Frederic 'Derek' Hudson was shot down and critically wounded crashing in the corridor between Cerisy to the north and Marcelcave to the south-southwest, a distance of around nine km, both being in Somme. Lieutenant Hudson died from his wounds on the 27th of April 1918.

43 Squadron   2Lt H S Lewis [Canada] + Roisel Communal Cemetery extension
F.1 Camel C8247   A mention in a despatch *Croix de Guerre* [France]
T/o 1400 Avesnes-le-Comte with similar orders and is though to have driven down a Fokker DrI before being last sighted, flying under control, north of Abancourt [Oise]. Possibly shot down by *Leutnant* Hans Kirschstein*of *Jasta 6* to the northeast of Lamotte-Warfusée [Somme] some twenty-six km to the east of Amiens at around 1525 [German time]. The son of the late Doctor Frederick Willows Lewis of Orahgeville, Ontario, Henry Stewart Lewis arrived in the United Kingdom in 1914 as a gunner attached to the Royal Canadian Artillery for service on the Western Front; he was commissioned during 1917.

* According to his *Wikipedia* profile, which I readily acknowledge, Hans Kirschstein was born in Koblenz on the 5th of August 1896. His early military service was as a combat engineer but in February 1916, following illness, he transferred to the air service, initially training to be a bomber pilot. In February 1918, came a change in direction when he transferred to fighters and was assigned to *Jagdstaffel 6*. His prowess as a fighter pilot was immediate and at the time of his death on the 16th of July 1918, he had been credited with twenty-seven combat victories and had been awarded the *Pour le Merite* [previously, he had gained at Iron Cross]. Ironically, his death at the age of twenty-one did not come in combat but in a flying accident when he was passenger in an aircraft captained by a newcomer to *Jasta 6 Leutnant* Johannes Markgraf.

43 Squadron   2Lt T R V Hill   pow Unemployed list 8 March 1919: Lt
F.1 Camel C8248
T/o 1645 Avesnes-le-Comte also tasked for a special mission and believed to have been driven down by *Leutnant* Weiss of *Jasta 1*. 'C8248' arrived with the squadron by way of the Aeroplane Acceptance Parks at Lincoln and Lympne with a brief interlude on establishment at Cranwell.

43 Squadron   Lt E Mather   + St Souplet British Cemetery
F.1 Camel C8281
T/o 1510 Avesnes-le-Comte for a special mission; possibly down in the vicinity of Saint-Souplet in the *département du Nord*. Edward Mather was nineteen years of age.

43 Squadron   2Lt M F Peiler   pow Unemployed list 24 March 1919: Lt
F.1 Camel D6452
T/o 1510 Avesnes-le-Comte similarly tasked and, possibly, fell victim to *Leutnant* Eric Just of *Jasta 11*. Second Lieutenant Peiler's name appears on the Air Ministry list, repeated in *Flight* May 16,1918, as being confirmed as a prisoner of war [this list also includes the name of his colleague Second Lieutenant Hill [see 'C8248']], his status being recorded as 'Missing'. During the afternoon of 24th of March 1918, Second Lieutenant Peiler claimed to have 'crashed' a Scout. By coincidence, a month earlier to the day, and while in the process of taking off from La Gorgue the engine in his Camel B2432 'choked' and the young Peiler was soon walking back to airfield from the ploughed field in which he had involuntary arrived. Repaired, it later went to No 54 Squadron and following a forced landing near Abbeville on 17 April was rebuilt as 'F5913'. Damaged for a third time [No 210 Squadron on 7 July 1918] it was passed to No 213 Squadron at Bergues - see my summary for the 9th of November 1918.

46 Squadron   Captain S P Smith   +   Arras Flying Services Memorial
F.1 Camel D6491 RG
T/o Filescamp Farm and in the mid-afternoon, and when over the Somme, had the awful misfortune to come under attack from Manfred von Richthofen who sent the Camel crashing to the northeast of Villers-Bretonneux and towards the eastern edge of the Bois de Hamel. Sydney Philip Smith had claimed a part share in the destruction of a two-seater Albatros when over Belgium on the 29th of March 1918.

48 Squadron   2Lt B G A Bell   +   Arras Flying Services Memorial
Bristol F.2b C4864   2Lt G G Bartlett   +   Arras Flying Services Memorial
T/o Bertangles for an offensive mission over the Somme to Lamotte-Warfusée and when last seen the Bristol was over Villers-Bretonneux, six km to the west of its intended destination.

60 Squadron   2Lt E A Sullock   Safe   Unemployed list 11 April 1919: Lt
SE.5a B103
T/o Fienvillers for an offensive patrol and damaged beyond worthwhile repair following a heavy landing. 'B103' had been on squadron strength since 20 January 1918.

70 Squadron   2Lt D V Gillespie   +   Villers-Bretonneux Military Cemetery
F.1 Camel C8252   A mention in a Despatch
T/o 1505 Fienvillers tasked to carry out an offensive patrol and is believed to have crashed at Cerisy-La Motte in the Somme. 'C8252' arrived with the squadron just over a week ago on the 28th of March.

79 Squadron   2Lt H G Dugan   pow   Unemployed list 8 March 1919: Lt
5F.1 Dolphin C3939
T/o Beauvais for an operational sortie from which it failed to return. Confirmation that he was a prisoner of war appeared in *Flight* May 16, 1918, when the magazine reproduced the list of casualties prepared by the Air Ministry. On August 15, 1918, *Flight* reported the list of names released by the German authorities pertaining to claims against Royal Air Force machines shot down during the month of April 1918. The list includes the ranks and names of Second Lieutenants Bell and Bartlett of No 48 Squadron, both being listed as 'fate unknown' but correctly showing they crashed in a Bristol F.2b. Second Lieutenant Dugan's name appears as 'Hugh Dugan' 'fate unknown' and placing him under the banner of '15 S.E.5 Single-Seaters'. It is known he arrived back in the United Kingdom on or by 30 December 1918. On the same page *Flight* carries a report of a leaflet raid over Vienna by Italian aircraft, the date not being specified, pointing out the futility of the Austrians to back the forces of Germany, referred to as 'Prussians'.

80 Squadron   2Lt E L Smithers   pow   Unemployed list 12 July 1919: Lt
F.1 Camel B2479
T/o 1615 La Bellevue for an offensive patrol and reported as being shot down over the Somme near Lamotte-Warfusée. 'B2479' had been on squadron strength since 14 March 1918. *Flight* of May 16, 1918, repeating the Air Ministry list of casualties confirms the prisoner of war status for Second Lieutenant Smithers.

201 Squadron   2Lt M H Findley*DSC   Safe
F.1 Camel B6419
T/o Fienvillers for an offensive patrol clashing in a strenuous encounter with an estimated eight Fokker DrIs from *Jasta 35 going* down over the Somme at around 1800 [German time] southeast of Morcourt and some thirty-two km east of Amiens, and falling just inside our lines between the first and second line of trenches. On returning to his squadron Second Lieutenant Findley stated that he fought with his opponents until his flying controls were shot away [possibly by *Leutnant Dellinger* operating from Favreuil near Bapaume]. Postwar, Maxwell Hutcheson Findley was appointed to a permanent commission.

* As yet I have not be able to trace this officer's award, all entries for 'Maxwell Hutcheson Findley' and with minor variations regarding his second Christian name and surname have drawn a blank.

| 205 Squadron | Lt G M Cartmel | + | Millencourt Communal Cemetery extension |
| DH.4 A7620 | Airman A J Lane | + | Millencourt Communal Cemetery extension |

T/o 1514 Bois de Roche for a raid on the aerodrome at La Motte; failed to return. George Musgrove Cartmel was nineteen years of age; Alexander James Lane was twenty. Both had served with No 5 Squadron Royal Naval Air Service where Alexander Lane was classified as a gun layer; his entry in the cemetery register shows him as a Private 1st Class of No 5 Squadron, which I suspect, alludes to his former naval service, though a private, I suggest, he would not have been.

| 208 Squadron | Lt W H Sneath | + | Arras Flying Services Memorial |
| F.1 Camel B7187 | | | |

T/o La Gorgue for an offensive patrol during which the Camels engaged with enemy scouts in the vicinity of the coal-mining area of the Pas-de-Calais near Lens. At around 1115 Wilfred Harry Sneath along with fellow Lieutenants G K Cooper and T F N Gerrard drove down a Fokker DrI; fifteen minutes later and Wilfred, too, was sent down out of control.

Sunday 7 April 1918

Although the main offensive, Operation *Michael,* had been terminated, the Germany army continued to press in Flanders with actions that are now referred to as the *Battle of Lys;* hopes of forcing the British Expeditionary Force out of the Ypres salient and back to the Channel ports was still uppermost in the minds of the German High Command. For the next three weeks a series of actions tested to the full the British Second Army holding the northern sector and what was regarded as a weakened First Army to the south. For the fledgling Royal Air Force this was a period of intense air activity all along the Western Front. On the 7th, over the Somme, enemy positions near Villers-Bretonneux continued to be attacked from the air as the ground fighting continued. It was also a day of some movement between squadrons; No 52 Squadron took its RE.8s from Boisdinghem to Abeele, while Major R S Maxwell, commanding No 54 Squadron oversaw the transfer*of their Camels from Conteville to Clairmarais; No 209 Squadron, also Camel equipped, departed Clairmarais for their new home at Bertangles, north of Amiens. The fourth squadron to move was No 101 Squadron [FE.2bs] from Haute Visée [severely attacked by the German air force on the 1st of April 1918] to Famechon.

* A move not without incident with two pilots, Second Lieutenants A A Sevastopulo [Unemployed List 8 February 1919] and Ian MacNair [see my summary for 12 April 1918] crashing on take off and a third, Lieutenant M L Campbell of the United States Air Service crashing on arrival [summarised below].

| 1 Squadron | Captain G B Moore MC | + | Arras Flying Services Memorial |
| SE.5a C1083 | [Canada] | | |

T/o 1250 Ste Marie Cappel for an offensive patrol and when over Hollebeke*at an altitude of two thousand feet was seen by his flight to burst into flames, an horrific sight for all who witnessed the tragedy. An experienced fighter pilot, Guy Borthwick Moore had shared in the destruction of one and personally destroyed a second hostile machine during two patrols on the 28th of March, the day after 'C1083' arrived with the squadron. From a cadetship he was commissioned as a temporary second lieutenant to the General List of the Royal Flying Corps on 26 April 1917, promulgated in supplement 30074 of the paper issued on 17 May 1917. Almost a year later to the day [13th May to be precise] he was *gazetted* with the Military Cross, supplement 30681: *'For conspicuous gallantry and devotion to duty. He led a patrol to attack hostile balloons. The patrol drove down three balloons in a collapsed condition, one of which he accounted for himself. He has also destroyed three enemy aeroplanes and driven down three others out of control. He has always shown splendid courage and resource.'* His death was the first from the squadron since the formation of the Royal Air Force.

* See my entry for No 29 Squadron on 6 April 1918, for an explanation regarding Hollebeke. Regarding the loss of this aircraft both the Casualty Ledger and card is dated the 7th of April, while the subsequent Casualty Report shows the 8th of April. However, as Andrew Pentland and Trevor Henshaw observe, rain curtailed extensive flying on the 8th.

| 4 Squadron AusFC | Lt J C Courtney AusFC | + | Arras Flying Services Memorial |
| Camel F.1 B5635 | [New Zealand] | | Villers-Bretonneux Memorial |

T/o 1100 Bruay for an offensive patrol and to include low level bombing and as described by Errol Martyn in his first volume dedicated to airmen with a connection to New Zealand was last seen fifteen minutes later, alight, after being hit by ground fire. The crash location is reported as Illies in the *département du Nord* some thirty-one km north of Arras. Errol reports that John Classon Courtney's body was recovered and buried at Marquillies which is south of Illies and separated by the N.41 highway. Born in Auckland, John arrived in the United Kingdom with his squadron which at the time had no aircraft and until the arrival of Camels used various types while preparing for operational duties on the Western Front. Meanwhile, he attended flying courses starting with attachment to the Central Flying School at Upavon [13 April 1917] ahead of rejoining No 4 Squadron Australian Flying Corps in November 1917, and transferring to France in mid-December.

| 8 Squadron | 2Lt Hooton | Safe | |
| FK.8 C3678 | Lt E I Wells | Safe | Unemployed list 14 April 1919L Lt MC |

T/o Auxi-le-Château for a contact patrol during which intense ground fire shot through the ailerons and holed the petrol tank; force-landed and damaged beyond repair. Accepted by the squadron on the 29th of March 1918, 'C3678' flew for a total of twenty-one hours and forty-five minutes. Starting his service as a private soldier with the London Regiment, Territorial Forces, Lieutenant Wells was appointed to the rank of second lieutenant in the Regular Forces on 21 November 1916, and was attached to the Rifle Brigade [*gazetted* 22 December 1916, issue 29875]. On 25 February 1918, he was transferred to the Royal Flying Corps, supplement 30589 of the paper issued on 19 March 1918.

| 9 Squadron | 2Lt J F V Rider | Injured | |
| RE.8 B5069 | 2Lt A S Hibbs | Injured | Unemployed List 8 May 1919: Lt |

T/o Proven for a counter attack patrol but owing to an error of judgement the task ended with the RE.8 stalling into the ground, whereupon it caught fire. On squadron squadron charge since 8 October 1917, 'B5069' had flown for a total of one hundred and eighty-nine hours and thirty minutes. As a second lieutenant, A S Hibbs was attached to the Nottinghamshire and Derbyshire Regiment with effect from 26 April 1917, promulgated in supplement 30349 of 23 October 1917. His transfer as an observer officer to the Royal Flying Corps came on the 9th of February 1918, supplement 30574 of the paper published on 12 March 1918.

| 10 Squadron | 2Lt S Jukes* | Safe | See 8 June 1918 - 10 Squadron |
| FK.8 B5824 | 2Lt W H Stanley | Safe | Unemployed list 11 April 1919: 2Lt |

T/o Abeele for a counter attack patrol during which the FK.8 was subjected to accurate anti-aircraft fire, sustaining damage to the rear tank. The crew force-landed, neither being hurt but were rather shaken by the entire experience. On squadron charge on 28 February 1918, 'B5824' had flown for seventy-eight hours and ten minutes.

* Possibly Lieutenant Sydney Jukes, age nineteen, of East Knoyle near Salisbury, Wiltshire, killed in a flying accident on 27 November 1918, while serving at one of the many Training Depot Stations. Buried in East Knoyle [St Mary] Churchyard extension his headstone is inscribed; *'The Lord Shall Be Thine Everlasting Light'*. His name appears on the Air Ministry Roll of Honour list for 11 December 1918, as repeated in *Flight* December 19th, 1918. Andrew Pentland adds; *'His military record shows Sidney, as does the casualty card. CWGC and the Gazette have Sydney.'*

| 11 Squadron | 2Lt R Fitton | Safe | Unemployed list 24 July 1919: Lt |
| Bristol F.2b B1143 | 2Lt R A West | Safe | |

T/o Fienvillers with orders to carry out a reconnaissance; on return, and landing, the tail skid became snagged against a ridge and, I suspect, overstressed the airframe as a result for 'B1143' was struck off charge on 22 April 1918. First issued to the squadron on 27 October 1917, the Bristol spent over three months undergoing repair and overhaul following a forced landing with magneto problems on 24 November 1917 [Captain G H Hooper and Lieutenant H G Kent] and it was only returned to the squadron on the 8th of March.

| 13 Squadron | Lt Buck | Safe | |
| RE.8 B7688 | | | |

T/o Fienvillers for a delivery flight to Izel-lès-Hameau, a distance of around thirty-six km and on a north-northeasterly track from the departure airfield. On arrival Lieutenant Buck misjudged his approach and crashed, writing off an RE.8 that had only thirty-five minutes flying time recorded having arrived in France by sea freight.

15 Squadron	2Lt A G Penny	Safe
RE.8 A3819	2Lt R Kearton	Safe

T/o Fienvillers having received orders to carry out a counter attack patrol during which engine failure overtook the crew who force-landed, without hurt, near Warloy*where it ran into a bank. To No 4 Squadron on 23 September 1917, 'A3819' was received by No 15 Squadron on the last day of March and when damaged beyond repair had accumulated one hundred and seventy hours and twenty-five minutes of flying. A *Gazette* entry for Second Lieutenant Kearton on 10 September 1918, issue 30892, records his rank as Honorary Lieutenant from 22 August 1918, ex-Observer Officer, after which he was transferred to the Technical Branch.

* Possibly Warloy Baillon which at various times in 1917, was used by Nos 3, 4, 7 and 22 Squadrons, its last user being No 3 Squadron which departed for Vert Galand on 25 March 1918.

20 Squadron	Lt P B Holgate	Safe
Bristol F.2b A7294		

T/o Boisdinghem authorised for a practice flight but unfortunately [and perhaps a little embarrassing] Lieutenant Holgate was of such short stature that he was unable to put his feet on the rudder bars and, as a consequence, with the speed increasing the Bristol began to swing and seconds later made rather violent contact with a tree. His commission was relinquished on the grounds of ill-health on 12 October 1918. Accepted by the squadron on 23 November 1917, 'A7294' had logged one hundred and nine flying hours.

21 Squadron	2Lt H A Walters [South Africa]	+	Mendingham Military Cemetery
RE.8 A3779	Captain H Eyden MC	+	Mendingham Military Cemetery

T/o La Lovie for an artillery spotting sortie in the Ypres sector; failed to return. Born in Nongoma in Zululand, Second Lieutenant Herbert Aidan Walters had married prior to leaving for the United Kingdom and operations over the Western Front. Herbert Eyden, whose military service had started as a cadet, was commissioned to the Royal Garrison Artillery on the 19th of November 1914 [*gazetted* 23 November 1914, supplement 28983]. His award of the Military Cross was *gazetted* on the 14th of January 1916, supplement 29438. Funds raised by the British Colony in Mexico have been 'married' to this aircraft; it flew for a total of one hundred and sixty-seven hours and fifty minutes.

24 Squadron	Lt P J N Nolan DFC*	+	Moreuil Communal Cemetery Allied extension
SE.5a B63			

T/o Conteville for an offensive patrol and lost, probably over the Somme, in circumstances not yet determined. Philip John Noel Nolan of Chelsea, London, was formerly of the Royal Field Artillery. He was just twenty years of age and had been involved in a forced landing three days previously [see my summaries for the 4th for details].

* The establishment of the Distinguished Flying Cross came on the 3rd of June 1918, and therefore for Lieutenant Nolan to be a recipient of this prestigious honour I can only think it was awarded retrospectively, and I have yet to find the citation or indication of the award being made.

24 Squadron	Captain G E H McElroy MC**	Injured See 19 June 1918 - 40 Squadron
SE.5A C1098		

T/o Conteville similarly tasked and return to the airfield flew into a tree while preparing to land. Captain George Edward Henry McElroy's injuries were only slight and a full description of his service is reported in subsequent summaries.

40 Squadron	2Lt I F Hind	Safe See 12 August 1918 - 40 Squadron
SE.5a C9534	[South Africa]	

T/o 0800 Bruay for an offensive patrol and on return to the aerodrome at 0950 crashed. Born at Naboomspruit in the Transvaal, Ivan Frank Hind escaped serious harm and continued to fly with the squadron until his death in action on the 12th of August 1918. Following a cadetship [he was one of sixty-four] he was commissioned as a temporary second lieutenant to the General List of the Royal Flying Corps on 10 May 1917 [*gazetted* 29 May 1917, issue 30200].

52 Squadron   RE.8 A3423   Reported as wrecked and abandoned; no further details apart from an entry stating 'A3423' had accomplished a total of two hundred and seventy-fours hours and thirty minutes flying.

52 Squadron   2Lt T Kileen   Safe
RE.8 B3423   2Lt J Napier   +   Arras Flying Services Memorial
T/o Abbeville tasked to carry out a reconnaissance over the Somme during which the RE.8 came under attack from enemy aircraft and driven down on the Allied side of the lines near Villers-Bretonneux. After vacating his cockpit, Second Lieutenant Kileen discovered his observer, James Napier, had been fatally shot through the head. As Second Lieutenant Napier is now recorded on the Arras Flying Services Memorial, I suggest the area where the forced landing was made was so close to the fighting that his body could not be recovered.

52 Squadron   2Lt R Duncanson   Safe   Unemployed list 11 March 1919: Lt
RE.8 B4034   2Lt C P Donegan   Safe
T/o Abbeville similarly tasked and force-landed near Bertangles aerodrome with a fractured rocker arm, the landing being made in conditions of rain and mist. Deemed beyond worthwhile repair.

54 Squadron   Lt M L Campbell USAS   Safe
F.1 Camel D6527
T/o Conteville for Clairmarais [see my lead-in for the day's activities] and on arrival, and in landing, flew into telegraph wires and crashed. Salvaged, 'D6527' was struck off charge on 20 April 1918. To No 54 Squadron fell the dubious distinction of losing ten of their aircraft since dawn on the 1st of April, ten to hostile action and two in non operational circumstances.

73 Squadron   Lt A V Gallie   Safe
F.1 Camel D6550
T/o Beauvois for an offensive patrol over the lines and shot down about one thousand three hundred and seventy metres west of Villers-Bretnonneux, and on the Allied side of the trenches.

73 Squadron   Lt R G H Adams   pow
F.1 Camel D6554
T/o 1050 Beauvois similarly tasked and was seen over Lamotte-Warfusée with hostile machines nearby. His status as being in the hands of the enemy was soon confirmed for his name appears in *Flight* May 16th, 1918, pertaining to the casualty lists released by the Air Ministry. His Camel had been issued to the squadron a mere twenty-four hours previously. Ronald George Hinings Adams was appointed as a second lieutenant [temporary] as early as 2 December 1914, thus indicating he had answered the call to arms at the outbreak of the *Great War*. Initially, he was earmarked for service as an infantry officer and as yet I am not able to report his attachment to the Royal Flying Corps. Soon after the resumption of hostilities in September 1939, he again volunteered his services and with effect from 18 November 1939, he was commissioned to the Administrative and Special Duties Branch. Appointed to the Most Excellent Order of the British Empire in the New Year Honours List for 1946, and now promoted to acting wing commander, he continued to be employed until one of the many culls of officers carried out under the provisions of the Navy, Army and Air Force Reserves Act, 1954.

79 Squadron   Lt J C Brooks   Safe   See 9 May 1918 - 79 Squadron
5F.1 Dolphin C3867
T/o Beauvais for an offensive patrol but turned for home early with a failing engine and with the airfield in sight force-landed in a ploughed field; damaged beyond repair.

81 Squadron   2Lt A L Simpson   Injured Toronto [Prospect] Cemetery
5F.1 Dolphin C8602

T/o Scampton for a training flight and crashed while attempting to land cross-wind. Critically injured, Arthur Lorrie Simpson died later in the day. There are no unit or next of kin information appended against his entry in the cemetery register where his rank is shown as 'Flight Lieutenant'.

| 84 Squadron | 2Lt E E Biccard | Safe | Unemployed list 20 April 1919: Lt |
| SE.5a C5346 | | | |

T/o Bertangles for practice flying and damaged beyond repair in a heavy landing.

| 92 Squadron | Captain N H England | + | Oving [St Andrew] Churchyard extension |
| Avro 504J B986 | 2Lt C Hackman | + | Winchcombe [Greet Road] Cemetery |

T/o Tangmere for a training exercise during which the Avro collided at three hundred feet over the airfield with a Sopwith Pup [see below]. From such a low altitude there was little hope for either pilot to effect an emergency landing.

| 92 Squadron | 2Lt V R Craigie [USA] | + | Oving [St Andrew] Churchyard extension |
| Sopwith Pup B5269 | | | |

T/o Tangmere for a training flight and lost in the manner previously described. Victor Raleigh Craigie came from Boston, Massachusetts, his father Captain Horace Walpole Craigie being described on the Military Forum website [which I acknowledge] as having served with the British Army. At the time the squadron was working up under the command of Major Arthur 'Mary' Coningham DSO MC for operational deployment to the Western Front. An Australian by birth but raised in New Zealand, Arthur Coningham was destined to become one of the key air force leaders during the Second World War with operational commands in the Western Desert and in Europe. Retiring at his own request in 1947, Air Marshal Sir Arthur Coningham was a passenger in the ill-fated Avro Tudor IV G-AHNP 'Star Tiger' which disappeared 29-30 January 1948, over the Atlantic *en route* to South America with a crew of six and twenty-five passengers.

| 205 Squadron | Lt L Jolly | Safe | |
| DH.4 N5961 | Gun Layer L James | Safe | |

T/o Bois de Roche and when landing the DH ran into a deep hole and was damaged beyond repair. Issued to No 5 Squadron Royal Naval Air Service on 28 February 1918, 'N5961' was still on charge at the time of the merger between the naval arm and the Royal Flying Corps to become the Independent Royal Air Force. Prior to this event, it 'scored' one combat victory when Flight Commander Charles Philip Oldfield Bartlett*and Gun Layer W Naylor shot down at Albatros over Busigny aerodrome on 13 March 1918.

* Captain Charles Philip Oldfield Bartlett in the course of his service was awarded a Distinguished Service Cross and First Bar. Remaining in the air force he retired in the rank of squadron leader on 26 August 1932. He went on to write two books; *Bomber Pilot, 1916-1918* followed by what some websites describe as a 'memoir' *In the Teeth of the Wind: The Story of a Naval Pilot on the Western Front, 1916-1918*. Used copies of the former are still available [Abe Books being one supplier] and, I suspect, a diligent internet search will find copies of his second. Furthermore, *Wikipedia* provides a potted biography of Charles Bartlett who, apparently, did not enjoy the best of health during his military service. It is also well worth mentioning that Gun Layer Naylor was an equally resourceful airman and his name will feature in many summaries pertaining to No 205 Squadron.

| 208 Squadron | Lt D C Hopewell | pow | Unemployed list 26 January 1919: Lt |
| F.1 Camel B6417 | | | |

T/o La Gorgue for an offensive patrol during which he became caught up in a general *mêlée* northeast of Loos and was forced down behind the enemy lines. Previously of the Royal Naval Air Service, Lieutenant Hopewell is named in the Air Ministry List of prisoners of war as repeated in *Flight* May 30, 1918. It is believed he may have been driven down by *Leutnant* Paul Billik of *Jasta 52* who finished the war credited with thirty-one victories and who, postwar, was killed in a civil flying accident on the 8th of March 1926. His entry on *Wikipedia* shows he was born in Haatsch [Silesia] on 27 March 1891, and like many of his era he was serving as an infantryman when war was declared in August 1914, and it was not until the beginning of 1917, that his application to join the air force came to fruition. Early in 1918, he was appointed to command the newly formed *Jasta 52* and it was as leader of this *Jagdstaffel* that he ran up an impressive list of victories before being shot down and made prisoner on 10 August 1918. His death in a landing accident while piloting a Junkers F.13 came at Staaken near Berlin. He was thirty-four years of age.

Monday 8 April 1918
The ground situation remained serious, though aerial activity appears to have been on a reduced scale. The Imperial War Museum, in their extensive photograph collection, has a picture of British walking wounded arriving during the day at No 43 Casualty Clearing Station at Frevent, some have hastily applied slings and one soldier is carrying a young colleague who appears to have suffered a lower limb injury to his left leg. Their footwear show signs of the all-clinging mud associated with many areas along the Western Front.

18 Squadron	Lt H R Gould MC	Safe	See 29 June 1918 - 18 Squadron
DH.4 A7770	Captain M S E Archibald MC	Safe	See 12 May 1918 - 18 Squadron
	A mention in a Despatch [Canada]		

T/o Treizennes for a dawn reconnaissance and on return, and landing, overstressed the airframe after turning sharply to avoid running into other aircraft. Brought to No 18 Squadron on 17 February 1918, 'A7770' accounted for a Pfalz on 10 March, its crew being Captain A G Waller and Sergeant M V Kilroy, the combat taking place in the early afternoon in the vicinity of Carvin-Fromelles*[Nord] some eight km northeast from Neuve-Chapelle [scene of a British offensive between 10 and 13 March 1915 in which the Royal Flying Corps worked well with the troops on the ground, gaining dominance in the air over the battlefield]. Herbert Ruska Gould, commissioned to the General List of the Royal Flying Corps on 5 July 1917 [gazetted 24 July 1917, issue 30203] and Max Stanfield Eaton Archibald, a Canadian from Truro in central Nova Scotia were each gazetted with a Military Cross in issue 30901 published on 13 September 1918, though neither lived long enough to savour the account. The citation for Herbert Gould reads; *'For conspicuous gallantry and devotion to duty. He has carried out 24 successful bombing raids, several of which he has led, and 26 low reconnaissance and bombing flights, as well as many low-flying, harassing and bombing patrols, during which many direct hits have been obtained and severe casualties inflicted. He has destroyed three enemy machines and has shown a very high spirit of zeal throughout.'* Equally impressive is the citation for Max Archibald; *'For conspicuous gallantry and devotion to duty. He has taken part in fourteen successful bombing raids, twenty-five successful low bombing and reconnaissance flights. On one occasion he was attacked by ten enemy scouts and drove down one completely out of control. He has engaged enemy troops from low altitude, and his excellent work, good spirits and total disregard of danger have been a fine example to all.'* Commissioned as a temporary second lieutenant to the Corps of Royal Engineers on 6 October 1915, issue 29316 of the *Gazette* published on 5 October 1915, he is reported as having been wounded on the 23rd of April 1916. The next day No 18 Squadron moved to Serny.

* Fromelles is for ever ingrained in the annals of Australian military history of the *Great War* for during one night in mid-July 1916, and with great reservations from senior commanders, XI Corps, the 61st Division and the 5th Australian Division, Australian Imperial Force, were ordered to make a frontal assault on near impregnable enemy positions. By dawn the Australians had suffered over five thousand five hundred casualties and in the opinion of those most closely involved it was all to no avail.

18 Squadron	2Lt G W F Darvill	Injured	See 4 September 1918 - 18 Squadron
DH.4 A8035	Sgt H Wilkes	Safe	

T/o Treizennes with the intention of carrying out an engine test but ran over loose earth that had filled a shell hole. This unevenness caused the DH to swerve and before the pilot could take remedial action 'A8035' collided with a plough and was damaged beyond repair. Its active service had lasted for less than a fortnight. For an appreciation of the service of George William Francis Darvill, please refer to my detailed summary of September 18th, published in the second volume.

85 Squadron*	Lt J R Stacey [Canada]	+	Heston [St Leonard] Churchyard
5F.1 Dolphin C3845			

T/o 1820 Hounslow and crashed almost immediately after stalling off a climbing turn. John Randolph Stacey from Caughnawaga in Laprairie County, Quebec, was formerly of the 1st Battalion Canadian Infantry. His headstone bears the inscription; *'God Be With You Till We Meet Again'*.

* No 85 Squadron had formed under the leadership of Major R A Archer at Upavon in Wiltshire on the 1st of August 1917, but nine days later moved to Norwich in East Anglia before arriving at Hounslow on the 27th of November 1917, where it continued to train ahead of being deployed to the Western Front in late May as a fighter squadron. Its main equipment then became the SE.5a. Research by Andrew Pentland confirms that Dolphins were on establishment during March 1918, most being allocated from the Aeroplane Acceptance Park at Kenley, examples being C4155, C4156, C4157, C4158, C4159, C4160, C4161, C4162, C4163, C4164, C4165, C4166, C4167, C4168 and C4173.

90 Squadron	2Lt B S Crecine	Injured
5F.1 Dolphin C4140		

T/o Shotwick but having climbed to around one hundred feet the engine 'cut'. This was followed by a dive and while attempting to recover Second Lieutenant Crecine stalled at twenty feet and crashed heavily. As the war progressed so his health deteriorated and he relinquished his commission on 22 December 1919.

211 Squadron	Lt N Haigh	Safe	
DH.4 B9498	Lt C L Bray	Safe	See 19 May 1918 - 211 Squadron

T/o Petite Synthe to practice, with other crews, flying in formation; on return overshot the landing area, crashed and was damaged beyond repair.

Tuesday 9 April 1918
During the day*the German Sixth Army attacked the southern part of the Allied lines between Armentières and Festubert and succeeded in pushing back a Portuguese Division towards Estaires, where intervention by British reserve divisions managed to halt the advance. Nevertheless, a sizeable bulge had been driven into First Army lines and the situation was causing much concern with Béthune, Hazebrouck and Bailleul all under threat. For the Royal Air Force at least seven squadrons were re-deployed; from Treizennes No 18 Squadron [DH.4s] went to Serny where they should have been joined by the Camels of No 208 Squadron. However, rain and fog at La Gorgue [one of a cluster of airfields in the Ypres Sector] prevented the squadron from taking off and with the imminent threat of the airfield being overrun [Estaires bordered the southwest corner of the airfield] Major Christopher Draper**took the decision [not lightly made] to gather sixteen Camels together in the centre of the airfield where they were put to the torch. Also on the move out of Treizennes were Nos 203 and 210 Squadron, both flying the seven km southwest to Lièttres, while from Choques in the Pas-de-Calais No 42 Squadron flew northwest for seventeen km to take up temp- orary residence at Treizennes before heading for Rély later in the month. Meanwhile, No 41 Squadron went from Alquines to Savy and No 74 Squadron from Téteghem, an airfield in the Dunkerque-Niewpoort sector, to nearby La Lovie [see below for airfields in Ypres sector].

* The official history marks this day as the opening of *The Battle of Lys* [9th to 29th April] during which time a number of important engagements were fought, each of which received there own distinctive titles. For the Germans, the 9th marked the opening of their third offensive referred to as Operation *Georgette* with aim of of denying the British Second Army the key road and rail links in Flanders which, if successful, would effectively isolate the Ypres Salient from the army's right flank with the French. Thus, the initial phase, 9th to 11th, is referred to as *The Battle of Estaires* and is commented upon above in my lead in to the day's activities from the air perspective.

** Squadron Commander Christopher Draper, to give him the rank conferred on him when to took command of No 8 Squadron Royal Naval Air Service, was one of the colourful characters associated with not only the early days of military aviation but between the wars and the 'grey' years that followed in the wake of the Second World War. Frequently reduced to a near penniless state but always an advocate on behalf of service veterans whom he considered received a raw deal from successive governments after both wars put to use his con- siderable flying expertise to draw attention to their cause by flying under bridges which he knew would attract the attention of the media. His memoirs were published by Aero Publishers in 1962 under the title *The Mad Major*. Born on the 15th of April 1892, Christopher Draper died on the 16th of January 1979, aged eighty-six.

1 Squadron	Lt G A Mercer [Canada]	pow
SE.5 A8933		

T/o Ste Marie Cappel for an offensive patrol in support of the Lys offensive and while south of Armentières*
came under sustained fire from the ground which forced the SE.5 down. Formerly of the Canadian Cyclist
Corps, news of Lieutenant Mercer's failure to return was reported in *Flight* May 2,1918, under the 'Missing' list;
his status as a prisoner of war appeared in the magazine's issue on May 16, 1918. News of his release [1st of
December 1918] and return to the United Kingdom was published by *Flight* on Boxing Day 1918. 'A8933' was
issued to the squadron on 28 March 1918, following repair to damage caused on 19 September 1917, when
Captain R L Chidlaw-Roberts of No 60 Squadron overturned while landing in a strong and gusting wind.

* For the soldiers who fought on the Western Front, and survived, associated Armentières with that well known,
and loved, melody *'Mademoiselle from Armentières'*.

4 Squadron	2Lt G H Langley	Safe
RE.8 B5074	2Lt C Sunderland	Safe

T/o Choques with the intention of flying to Treizennes in order to rejoin the rest of the squadron which had made
the transit twenty-four hours previously but lost control, crashed and damaged beyond repair.

4 Squadron AusFC	Lt J H Weingarth AusFC	Safe
F.1 Camel B7395		

T/o Bruay tasked for low-level bombing. Shot through and on return to the airfield hit a sharp ridge on landing.
Deemed not worth repairing the Camel was struck off charge on the 12th. Its active service had lasted for
eleven days. Jack Henry Weingarth survived the war and according to his entry in the cemetery register at
Leighterton [St Andrew's] Churchyard in Gloucestershire, he was still on the establishment of No 4 Squadron
Australian Flying Corps when he died on 4 February 1919. However, at the time his squadron was part of the
Occupation Force in the Rhineland and stationed at Bickendorf, where it disbanded on the last day of February
1919. But, at Leighterton there were two training squadrons, the 7th and the 8th of the Australian Flying Corps
and I strongly suspect Jack Weingarth was attached to one of these as a flying instructor.

18 Squadron	2Lt D W Gordon	Injured
DH.4 A7999	Corporal J Lewis	Safe

T/o Treizennes and on arrival at Serny crashed on landing; consumed by fire.

20 Squadron	Lt R H Harmer	Injured
Bristol F.2b B1221	Lt N Peters	Safe

T/o Boisdinghem tasked for low-level bombing but encountered very thick fog which caused the crew to become
uncertain of their position. While attempting to find a familiar landmark the Bristol flew into sand hills near
Wimereux in the Pas-de-Calais. I suspect the impact was quite severe for although Lieutenant Peters escaped
injury, nevertheless he was very badly shaken. At the time of his discharge, Lieutenant Harmer was no longer
employed on flying duties and was attached to the Administrative Branch and with his health being less than
robust his commission was relinquished with effect from 7 August 1919. 'B1221' had been delivered to the
squadron on 21 February 1918, since when it had flown for sixty-five hours and thirty minutes, including testing
and ferrying.

22 Squadron	2Lt C E Taylor	Safe
Bristol F.2b B1152		

T/o Vert Galand for local flying practice in the course of which the Bristol's engine failed. Second Lieutenant
Taylor managed to get back to the airfield but landed on soft ground which resulted in damage deemed not
worth repairing. Since arriving with the squadron on 3 December 1917, 'B1152' had flown for a total of eighty-six
hours and twenty-five minutes.

40 Squadron	Lt R E Bion	+	Arras Flying Services Memorial
SE.5a D3534			

T/o Bruay tasked to carry out a low level bombing mission against enemy troops now engaged in actions in the
Arras sector. Rupert Euston Bion's service began prewar with a cadetship in his Officer Training Corps from
which he graduated in October 1914 and was one of eleven ex-cadets appointed as temporary second lieu-

tenants to the Royal Field Artillery on the 10th [*gazetted* 13 October 1914, issue 28935]. His service with the Royal Artillery was relatively short for on the 25th of March 1915, he was accepted as a second lieutenant, on probation, with the 20th Hussars.

42 Squadron	Captain R A Archer MC	Safe
RE.8 A3658 *Junagadh No 1* 2Lt D G Smith		Safe See 10 April 1918 - 42 Squadron

T/o either from Chocques or Treizennes for an artillery observation patrol. Hit by machine-gun fire from the ground 'A3658', a presentation aircraft, was declared beyond worthwhile repair and was struck with a total of one hundred and ninety-eight hours and ten minutes flying. Captain Archer, late of the Royal Artillery, appears to have been attached to the Royal Flying Corps since [at least] 1 July 1917, as *gazetted* in supplement 30208 of 27 July 1917.

42 Squadron	Lt Bryers	Safe
RE.8 A4202	2Lt J Paisley	Injured

T/o Chocques with the likely intention of transiting to Treizennes but went out of control and crashed against a building, whereupon it caught fire. On squadron charge since 5 April 1917, 'A4202' had built up an impressive total of three hundred and fifty-two hours and forty-five minutes flying.

42 Squadron	Lt W Beart	Injured Unemployed list 11 July 1919: Lt
RE.8 A4212	Lt G W Gotch	Safe See 13 April 1918 - 42 Squadron

T/o either from Chocques or Treizennes for an artillery observation patrol; forced landing in front of La Fosse [*sic*], Lieutenant Beart having sustained a wound to his arm. It seems he attempted to take off but flew into a telegraph pole which effectively ended the active flying service of 'A4212'. Lieutenant Geoffrey William Gotch, formerly of the Royal Garrison Artillery, having completed his tour of duty as an observer died while serving in the United Kingdom on the 22nd of October 1918. He is buried in High Wycombe Cemetery. As an officer cadet he was commissioned to the Royal Garrison Artillery on 20 December 1916, promulgated on the 8th of January, 1917, supplement 29895. His attachment to the Royal Flying Corps probably took place on, or by, the 13th of December 1917, at which date he was promoted lieutenant [*gazetted* 22 March 1918, supplement 30589].

Note. At least two [and probably all three] of the RE.8s summarised here for No 42 Squadron came under the aegis of No 7 Brigade and in addition to the flying hours recorded for 'A3658', 'A4202' and 'A4212' chalked up significant totals of three hundred and fifty-two hours hours and forty-five minutes and three hundred and thirty-two hours and fifty minutes respectively, thereby illustrating the frequency of vital operations carried out by the Corps reconnaissance squadrons operating on the Western Front.

65 Squadron	2Lt G Duerden	Injured Picquigny British Cemetery
F.1 Camel C8265		

T/o Bertangle for a practice flight during which George Duerden, late of The Loyal North Lancashire Regiment, lost control and spun in. Alive when extracted from the wreckage, he died the following day in one of the casualty clearing stations at Picquigny [Somme], some fourteen km west-southwest from Bertangles. I very much suspect Second Lieutenant Duerden was a recent arrival with the squadron for his entry in the cemetery register is devoid of his unit detail. His was the squadron's first fatality since arriving at Bertangles on the 6th of April 1918.

70 Squadron	2Lt J W Gower	Safe
F.1 Camel D1802		

T/o Beauvois authorised for practice flying but lost control and crashed; salvaged, 'D1802] languished until the 8th of May 1918, when it was struck off charge at No 2 Advanced Salvage Dump.

205 Squadron	Lt H D Evans	Safe
DH.4 A8084	Sgt P L Richards	Safe

T/o Bois de Roche for bombing operations, landing at Breteuil and it was while taking off from here that engine failure occurred and moments later the crew were back on the ground, their DH damaged beyond repair.

208 Squadron   F.1 Camel   B3773, B3785, B3794, B3853, B3936, B6260:A, B7189, B7193, B7196, B7201, B7253, D3330, D3335, D3339, D3352 and N6342 all burnt on the ground at La Gorgue to prevent them from falling into enemy hands. Nearly all had seen operational service with many having destroyed, or driven down, hostile machines. 'N6342' had flown for a total of two hundred and sixteen hours [though not all with '208'] while in contrast 'D3352' had been with the squadron for just four days and had only one airborne hour to its credit.

Wednesday 10 April 1918
With the ground fighting around Estaires still fluid, the German Fourth Army attacked in strength the line north of Armentières. In places the situation was becoming critical, even though enemy advances were restricted on a limited front. Nevertheless, by the end of the day Messines had fallen. In the air the Western Front squadrons continued with their daily tasks of reconnaissance and roving offensive patrols, both activities guaranteed to provoke a response from the enemy scouts and ever alert ground forces.

During the day Major-General Sir Hugh Trenchard's, Chief of the Air Staff, letter of resignation was accepted by the War Cabinet, a fact conveyed to him by the Air Minister, Lord Rotheremere.

1 Squadron	Lt W D Patrick	pow	Unemployed list 11 February 1919: Lt
SE.5a B8371			

T/o 0940 Ste Marie Cappel for an offensive patrol in the direction of Armentières and was last sighted over the fighting at Messines. From Austin's Longbridge Plant near Birmingham, 'B8371' arrived with the squadron as recently as the 3rd of April. Lieutenant Patrick's name appears in the Air Ministry list for Royal Air Force officers reported 'Missing' and repeated in *Flight* May 16, 1918. Subsequently, his status as a prisoner of war was confirmed by the Air Ministry on 21 October 1918, as recorded by *Flight* October 24, 1918.

4 Squadron	2Lt C A Mason	Safe
RE.8 B3405	Mechanic Williams	Safe

T/o Chouques [possibly] and reported to have crashed on arrival at its new base. As the squadron moved to Treizennes on April 8th, the incident reported here may have occurred at Treizennes. Received on, or by, the 23rd of July 1917, at the Aeroplane Acceptance Park at Coventry, 'B3405' went through the usual processing and once in France was issued to the squadron on 14 August 1917, since when it had flown for most of its two hundred and seventy-four hours and thirty minutes.

4 Squadron	Lt W A S McKerrell	+	Chocques Military Cemetery
RE.8	Lt S Ramsden*	Injured	Longuenesse [St Omer] Souvenir Cemetery

T/o Treizennes for an operational task. William Archibald Struthers McKerrell was formerly of the 8th Battalion, Royal Scots. Samuel Ramsden was critically wounded and though taken to one of the many military hospitals in the St Omer area he died the following day.

• Andrew Pentland advises that according to records, Samuel Ramsden was wounded on the 11th and died on the 12th from his injuries [his date of death is supported by Commonwealth War Graves Commission records], thus suggesting two RE.8s [as yet unidentified by the airframe serials] were lost from the squadron on the days in question.

4 Squadron AusFC	Lt R King	Safe

F.1 Camel B2478 *Australia No 17, New South Wales No 16, The Upper Hunter Battleplane*
T/o Bruay tasked for bombing but got into the slipstream of another aircraft and 'choked' his engine; lost control and crashed. A presentation aircraft 'B2478' was issued to No 71 Squadron at Castle Bromwich by November 1917, the squadron becoming No 4 Squadron Australian Flying Corps on 19 January 1918. Prior to its crash, and while being flown by Lieutenant J W Wright during the mid-afternoon of March 26th, was hit by ground fire while making a strafing run northeast of Bapaume in the Pas-de-Calais. In considerable discomfort Lieutenant Wright made it back to base where he was treated for wounds to his back.

4 Squadron AusFC	Lt H K Love AusFC	pow
F.1 Camel B9302		

T/o 0800 Bruay for an offensive patrol and bombing of enemy positions. Driven down behind enemy lines by machine-gun fire and seen to turn over after crashing against a fence. Emerging from the Boulton and Paul works 'B9302' was delivered to the Aeroplane Acceptance Park at Norwich by 24 January 1918, and arrived with the squadron on 18 February 1918. Lieutenant Love's name appears in *Flight* May 23, 1918, in their repeat of an Air Ministry list of casualties.

8 Squadron	2Lt L G B Spence	Safe
FK.8 C8536	2Lt G E Davis	Safe

T/o Auxi-le-Château tasked to carry out a line patrol but while travelling at speed suddenly lost power and finished up, wrecked, in a ditch. With effect from 2 February 1920, Lieutenant Spence had to relinquish his commission owing to his health being effected by wounds received during the war.

18 Squadron	2Lt D B Richardson	Injured
DH.4 B9437*	Airman J Perigo	Injured

T/o Treizennes to transit to Serny where the main body of the squadron had arrived on the 9th but 'choked' the engine and crashed.

* B9437 was one of six DH.4s built at Yeovil, Somerset, by Westland Aircraft Works and intended for use by the Royal Naval Air Service with airframe serials N6382-N6387, but all were re-batched as B9434-B9439 ahead of delivery. All were fitted with RAF 3a engines.

23 Squadron	Lt G G MacPhee	pow	Commission relinquished on return to
SPAD S.13 B6860			Territorial Forces 29 April 1919: Lt

T/o Bertangles for an offensive patrol and was last seen over the Somme in the vicinity of Villers-Bretonneux. Late of the Highland Light Infantry, Territorial Forces, Lieutenant MacPhee was seconded for flying duties with the Royal Flying Corps on the last day of August 1917, as promulgated in supplement 30299 of 21 September 1917. His name, along with his squadron colleague summarised below, appeared in *Flight* May 30 1918, both being confirmed as prisoners of war. Lieutenant MacPhee was repatriated on the 1st of December 1918, with Second Lieutenant Hopgood following him home later in the month on the 18th.

23 Squadron	2Lt F J Hopgood	pow	Unemployed list 18 April 1919: Lt
SPAD S.13 B6864*			

T/o Bertangles similarly tasked, the duties for the two pilots to include bombing enemy positions.

* There is an interesting report in *Flight* August 15, 1918, in which the magazine repeats the official German list notifying claims for aircraft brought down over the Western Front in April 1918. A total of fourteen Spads were claimed and the names of Lieutenant MacPhee and Second Lieutenant Hopgood are mentioned and in the case of the latter his Spad is reported as 'S 1217' while MacPhee's aircraft could not be identified. The report continues; *'In the case of 2 Spads the numbers of the machines could not be ascertained; the occupants were dead. In the case of 2 Spads the numbers could not be ascertained; the occupants prisoners [one was an American NCO]. In the case of 7 Spads the numbers of the machines and the names and fate of the occupants could not be ascertained.'* Again, the expert knowledge of Andrew Pentland comes into play who points out that 'S 1217' would have been applied by the French manufacturers prior to transfer to the Royal Air Force and would have remained on the tailplane; however, Andrew states that 'S 1217' was applied to a Spad VII and that 'F4338' was the serial matched to 'B6864'. As to why the German authorities quoted 'S 1217' is not clear.

35 Squadron	2Lt J E Phillips	Safe	See 16 September 1918 - 35 Squadron
FK.8 C8528	2Lt H W White	Safe	

T/o Poulainville for an operational sortie; driven down over the Somme to force-land near Villers-Bretonneux.

35 Squadron	2Lt A Macgregor	Safe	
FK.8 D5011	2Lt J H Shooter MC	+	Longueau British Cemetery

T/o Poulainville similarly tasked and driven down by hostile aircraft to crash close to the French lines. Accepted by the squadron on 30 March 1918, over eleven days [and its previous times on test and delivery] 'D5011' had accumulated twenty-six hours and five minutes of flying. Of the Territorial Forces, cadet John Harold Shooter was commissioned to the York and Lancaster Regiment on 25 January 1917 [*gazetted* 8 February 1917, supplement 29934] and it was while serving with his regiment that he was honoured with the Military Cross [17th September 1917, supplement 30287]; *'For conspicuous gallantry and devotion to duty in carrying out a daylight patrol to clear up an obscure situation. Accompanied by a private, he showed most exceptional skill and daring in proceeding over unknown and difficult ground in order to ascertain the enemy's forward positions. They returned with valuable information, having attacked an enemy post and dispersed its garrison, one of whom was shot by the private. Their courage and intelligence proved of the greatest assistance in locating the enemy.'* His headstone at Longueau British Cemetery bears, at the request of his parents, the inscription; *'Having Unselfish Heart God Give The Rest'.*

| 40 Squadron | Captain C O Rusden | pow | Unemployed list 25 June 1919: Lt |
| SE.5a C5437 | | | |

T/o Bruay having been briefed to carry out low-level bombing on enemy troop positions and while doing so the 'C5437' lost engine power and, as a consequence, Captain Rusden was obliged to force-land near Gorre [*sic*] and though his aircraft was relatively undamaged, its proximity to enemy trenches meant it would be a hazardous operation to attempt its recovery. However, this was achieved and 'C5437' was recovered to No 1 Aircraft Salvage Depot on the 8th of May 1918, where on examination its condition was deemed beyond repair and the airframe was struck off charge the next day. Formerly of the Middlesex Regiment, Captain Rusden [then ranked lieutenant] was at the School of Instruction during 1917. Following his placement on the unemployed list, I believe he rejoined his Regiment.

| 42 Squadron | 2Lt N McC Anderson | Injured |
| RE.8 A4306 | Lt M J Pottie | Injured |

T/o Treizennes for a contact patrol in the course of which the RE.8 came under intense rifle and machine-gun fire, causing wounds to both members of crew. Lieutenant Pottie was formerly of the Seaforth Highlanders. On squadron charge 24 June 1917, 'A4306' went to Italy with the squadron and thence back to the Western Front.

| 42 Squadron | 2Lt R E Holthouse [Australia] | + | Arras Flying Services Memorial |
| RE.8 B5099 | 2Lt D G Smith | + | Arras Flying Services Memorial |

T/o Treizennes for operations associated with the latest German offensive; failed to return. Both officers had considerable military experience. Twenty-three year old Donald Graham Smith had enlisted in August 1914*and had served with the 4th Battalion, Middlesex Regiment seeing action in Italy, Egypt and Salonika while Arthur Reginald Holthouse, born in Riverton, South Australia on 28 May 1885, had enlisted on the 14th of June 1915, and having reached the United Kingdom transferred to the Royal Flying Corps on 16 March 1917. Information regarding Second Lieutenant Holthouse can be read on the RSL Virtual War Memorial website which I have much pleasure in acknowledging. It is also noted that Corporal Arthur Henry Winall attached to No 42 Squadron died this day; he is buried in Lillers Communal Cemetery which at the time was well within German artillery range as their forward troops in the Lys offensive were now at Robecq, a mere eight km east-northeast of Lillers.

* I strongly suspect that Donald Smith was one of thousands who responded to Field Marshal Lord Kitchener's call 'Your King and Country Need You' which by the end of September 1914, had recruited a staggering total of half a million men.

| 52 Squadron | 2Lt H L Taylor | Injured |
| RE.8 B6641 | 2Lt W I E Lane | Injured |

T/o Abbeville for an operational sortie during which the crew had the misfortune to encounter a force of nine Fokker Triplanes whose fire forced the crew to come down, under control, close to the enemy lines near Bois de Gentelles, both being wounded.

| 52 Squadron | 2Lt T Killeen | Safe | Unemployed list 16 December 1919: Lt |
| RE.8 C4595 | Lt W H Higham | Safe | |

T/o Abbeville similarly tasked and on return executed a heavy landing, causing the undercarriage to collapse.

| 54 Squadron | 2Lt T R Hostetter [USA] | Safe | See 27 September 1918 - 3 Squadron |
| F.1 Camel C6721 | | | |

T/o Clairmarais to conduct a weather test; crashed on landing.

| 65 Squadron | 2Lt G B J Stoddart | + | Picquigny British Cemetery |
| F.1 Camel C8286 | | | |

T/o Bertangles for a practice flight which ended with the Camel spinning into the ground. Eighteen year old George Benjamin Johnstone Stoddart was one of those extremely patriotic and determined young men who, as outlined in the note above, came forward eager to play there part in the conflict that lay ahead. George, who was just fifteen*years of age at the time, enlisted on the 1st of September and was accepted by the 2nd Dragoon Guards with whom he served as a cavalry machine gunner on the Western Front until January 1916. Unusually for an officer serving in the *Great War* a service number has been appended against his name; '89720' and this may have been his pre-commissioning number, details of which I have yet to trace. The distance from the airfield, by way of Ailly-sur-Somme, to where he is buried is fourteen km.

* Usually in the many cases identified of underage 'men' volunteering and being accepted by the armed services, came from poor or troubled backgrounds. Some were from large families where it was a constant struggle to bring food to the table and one less to feed helped to relieve the burden on hard-pressed mothers. But George Benjamin Johnstone Stoddart's parents would, in 1914, have been regarded as well born and educated; George's stepfather was a doctor and their address 'Harcourt House' in London's fashionable Cavendish Square was a very desirable residence. In recent times, a one-bedroom apartment in this very substantial residential block has a rentable value of over one thousand five hundred pounds per calendar month.

| 82 Squadron | 2Lt N C Simpson | Safe | |
| FK.8 C3526 | 2Lt W Spencer | Safe | |

T/o Agenvilliers tasked for a reconnaissance sortie during which engine failure occurred. Forced landing, the crew landed in a field but Second Lieutenant Simpson was unable to prevent his RE.8 from running onto a road where it was damaged beyond repair. Accepted by the squadron on 29 March 1918, it had logged a total of ten hours and five minutes flying.

| 99 Squadron | 2Lt Q W Bannister [Canada] | + | Toronto [Mount Pleasant] Cemetery |
| DH.9 C6189 | 2Lt E J Kidd | Injured | Addingham [St Peter] Churchyard |

T/o Old Sarum for a training flight and crashed near the airfield after Quinton Wolstenholme Bannister lost control while making a turn close to the ground. From Toronto, his body was later taken back to Canada for burial in his home city. Alive when removed from the wreckage, Ernest John Kidd, formerly of the 5th Battalion, West Yorkshire Regiment [Prince's Wales's Own], died later the same day. This was the squadron's last fatal crash ahead of leaving for St Omer on the 25th of April 1918, and subsequent operations on the Western Front.

| 111 Squadron | 2Lt T L Steele MC | + | Jerusalem Memorial Panel 57 |
| Nieuport 17 B3594 | [New Zealand] | | |

T/o Ramleh in the company of three other aircraft for an offensive patrol during which the quartet were attacked by an estimated force of nine enemy scouts, plus a two-seater aircraft. Thomas Lancaster Steele crashed behind enemy lines at Nablus on the northern West Bank roughly fifty km north of Jerusalem. Formerly with a machine-gun squadron attached to a New Zealand mounted brigade, Thomas held the rank of lance corporal when commissioned on 7 August 1917, as a temporary second lieutenant on transfer to the Royal Corps [*gazetted* on the 13th of November 1917, issue 30383]. The announcement of his award appeared long after he had been posted 'missing' for it was not until issue 30862, a supplement of the paper published on 23 August 1918, that the citation duly appeared; *'For conspicuous gallantry and devotion to duty. When instructed to attack a hostile concentration he encountered heavy machine gun and rifle fire, his petrol tank being pierced. Despite the risk of his tank catching fire he continued to his objective, where he obtained excellent results from bombs dropped from 400 feet. On a later occasion, though shot through his arm, he continued to his objective and obtained excellent results. His courage and determination were most praiseworthy.'*

| 142 Squadron | Lt G J Turner [Canada] | + | Ramleh War Cemetery |
| RE.8 | Lt P L Ward | Injured | |

T/o Julis and lost in circumstances presently unknown. George James Turner had been attached to the Royal Air Force from the Canadian Infantry, his regimental depot recorded as being at Manitoba.

Thursday 11 April 1918

During the day, No 98 Squadron having moved from St Omer to Clairmarais on the 3rd operated for the first time in its bombing rôle with the despatch of fifteen DH.9s to raid targets at Wervicq in the *département du Nord* and practically on the border with Belgium. In the event twelve crews returned claiming to have bombed their primary objectives, two were obliged to force-land and one crashed while taking off [see my summary]. Again, inclement weather hampered daylight operations but as the summaries show supreme efforts were being made to harass the enemy at every opportunity. On the ground the Allies were being severely pressed and reports of the ground fighting arriving at general headquarters were giving rise to increasing concern. For Sir Douglas Haig it was one of the most stressful periods of his entire Command; pleas to the French and Foch in particular were not meeting the response that he so desperately needed and it was against this background that he wrote an 'Order of the Day' which the historian John Terraine states has entered into the British Army's heritage. Written in his near indecipherable scrawl and disseminated to army and corps headquarters for distribution to all formations and ranks of British Forces in France the Order read; *'Three weeks ago today the Enemy began his terrific attack against us on a 50-mile front. His objects are to separate us from the French, to take the Channel ports and destroy the British Army. In spite of throwing already 106 divisions into the battle and enduring the most reckless sacrifice of human life, he has yet made little progress towards his goals. We owe this to the determined fighting and self-sacrifice of our troops. Words fail me to express the admiration which I feel for the splendid resistance offered by all ranks of our Army under the most trying circumstances. Many amongst you now are tired. To those I would say that victory will belong to the side that holds out the longest. The French Army is moving rapidly and in great force to our support. There is no other course open to us but to fight it out! Every position must be held to the last man: there must be no retirement. With our backs to the wall, and believing in the justice of our cause, each one of us fight on to the end. The safety of our homes and the freedom of mankind alike depend on the conduct of each one of us at this critical moment.' 'D Haig F. M.'*

| 1 Squadron | Lt E M Forsyth | Safe |
| SE.5a B597 | | |

T/o Ste Marie Cappel tasked to carry out low bombing of enemy positions. Returning from the mission, engine failure overtook the 'B597' which made a forced landing to the south of Flêtre [Nord] where a mere three km to the north is the Commonwealth War Graves Commission military cemetery of Bertenacre. First issued to No 84 Squadron on 14 October 1917, 'B597' was seriously damaged on 22 November 1917, when Second Lieutenant A F W Beaumont Proctor*force-landed in a field that had been to the plough near Belle-Église [Oise], north of Paris and on the northeastern fringes of what is now the *Parc Naturel Régional du Vexin Français*. Repairs were put in hand at No 2 Advanced Salvage Dump from where it was issued to No 1 Squadron 13 January 1918.

* South African, Andrew Frederick Weatherby Beauchamp Proctor born 4 September 1894, at Mossel Bay on the eastern seaboard of the Cape Province, was to distinguish himself during the *Great War* initially serving as a private soldier in the Duke of Edinburgh's Own Rifles and experiencing action in the German Southwest Africa campaign. On the successful conclusion of this campaign, Andrew Proctor was demobilised and returned to college in order to complete his degree in engineering. Then, in 1917, he rejoined the service, this time as an air mechanic accepted for pilot training, arriving in the United Kingdom in the early spring of that year. Successfully completing all his courses he was attached to No 84 Squadron and with '84' he arrived in France on 23 September 1917. During the next thirteen months Andrew Proctor excelled in his rôle as a fighter pilot, so much so that his commanding officer Major William Sholto Douglas [subsequently Marshal of the Royal Air Force Lord Douglas of Kirtleside] in his whose own words described Andrew as *'that little man who had the guts of a lion'* be honoured with the Victoria Cross. This was duly approved, though at the time Andrew was recovering in hospital from serious arm wounds received in combat on 8 October 1918. Postwar Andrew Frederick Wetherby Beauchamp Proctor was granted a permanent commission, after which he was given special permission to take a year's leave in South Africa. On return, and in June 1921, he was attached to the Central Flying School at Upavon and it was here on the 21st that he took off in Snipe E8220 to practice aerobatics. Tragically, while at

the top of a loop he lost control and spun into a Wiltshire meadow near Enford on the A345 and south of the air-field. First buried at Upavon, his body was exhumed and returned to his homeland by way of the SS *Balmoral Castle* arriving in Cape Town on 8 August 1921. Fittingly, he was afforded a State Funeral. For further details pertaining to this officer, please consult Chaz Bowyer's published work on the Air VCs.

| 2 Squadron | 2Lt J W D Farrell | Safe | Unemployed list 3 July 1919: Lt |
| FK.8 B243 | Lt F Ambler | Safe | |

T/o Hesdigneul*to carry out a practice contact patrol but when over the lines came under sustained rifle and machine-gun fire from our own forces. Such was the accuracy of their aim that the crew limped home with the FK.8 well and truly shot through. Deemed not worth repair 'B243' was struck with a grand total of three hundred and twenty-nine hours and fifty minutes flying. Second Lieutenant Farrell was granted the acting rank of captain on 30 November 1918, at which time he had been attached to the Administrative Branch [*gazetted* 7 January 1919, issue 31112]. Frederick Ambler was commissioned to the Administrative and Special Duties Branch on the 26th of September 1939, promulgated in issue 34700 of the paper issued on 3 October 1939, and continued in service until having to relinquish his commission under the provisions of the Navy, Army and Air Force Reserves Act of 1954. This may have been implemented on 11 May 1954, at which time he held the rank of squadron leader.

* The airfield at Hesdigneul was located southwest of Béthune [Pas-de-Calais] and during the *Great War* was 'home' to No 2 Squadron between 30 June 1915 and 30 June 1918. Briefly, it was occupied between the 19th and 26th of October 1918, by No 21 Squadron. According to the website Wartime Memories Project [which I acknowledge] it is now covered by housing and a sports ground.

| 3 Squadron AusFC | 2Lt A W Rees | Injured |
| RE.8 A3541 | Lt G A Paul | Injured |

T/o Poulainville for an operational sortie during which the crew were attacked, and wounded, by half-a-dozen Albatros scouts. 'A3541' arrived with the squadron on 26 March 1918, following reconstruction after being struck by No 5 Squadron.

| 4 Squadron | 2Lt C A Mason | Injured |
| RE.8 B5047 | Lt C R Pilcher | Injured Unemployed list 17 September 1919: F/O |

T/o 0545 Treizennes for operations in support of XV Corps [Lieutenant-General John Philip Du Cane]. Force-landed near La Gorgue [Nord] and close to the Franco-Belgian border southwest of Armentières. Abandoned, both officers having sustained wounds. On squadron establishment since 20 September 1917, 'B5047' had logged, overall, two hundred and eighteen hours in the air.

| 4 Squadron AusFC | Lt J P G Basclain | Injured |
| F.1 Camel B2387 | | |

T/o 1345 Bruay for a bombing patrol and damaged beyond economical repair after crashing five minutes later just off the airfield. Army Form W 3347 [kindly forwarded by Andrew Pentland] indicates the crash was caused by Lieutenant Basclain 'choking' the engine [130 hp Clerget]; a detailed analysis of the damage has been appended. For most of its seven months of active service, 'B2387' was in the hands of No 70 Squadron with whom it crashed on landing on 28 September 1917, and again on the 11th of November, the last involving the death of, or serious injury, to a soldier and injury to Second Lieutenant E B Booth*who earlier had force-landed at Sainte-Marie-Cappel in the *département du Nord* after encountering a severe storm. Its total flying time totalled seventeen hours and thirty minutes.

* Possibly Second Lieutenant Edwin Borgfeldt Booth who died on the 7th of April 1918, and is buried Toronto [Mount Pleasant] Cemetery. His unit is shown as '43 Training Squadron'; *Flight* in its issue for May 16th, 1918, in which the Air Ministry list of casualties are recorded shows Second Lieutenant E B Booth under the heading 'Accidentally killed'.

| 5 Squadron | 2Lt J F Good | Injured |
| RE.8 B5123 | Lt A W Mackay | Injured |

T/o Le Hameau tasked for photo reconnaissance. While so engaged, the crew came under attack from enemy aircraft and both were wounded. In considerable discomfort they managed to get their badly damaged aircraft back to base. Struck to No 1 Aeroplane Supply Depot 'B5123' was officially removed from charge on 23 April 1918; sixty-four hours and thirty-five minutes being appended on its records.

7 Squadron	Lt H Hughes	+	Mendingham Military Cemetery
RE.8 A3792	Lt W H King	+	Mendingham Military Cemetery

Malaya No 32 The A N Kenion

T/o Proven East for local flying practice though according to the accident card the RE.8 had been armed with bombs. It seems that Harold Hughes attempted a flat turn at a low altitude and sideslipped to the ground, whereupon the bombs exploded; the remarks column states *'Not to blame'*. He was twenty years of age; William Hugh King, like many observers at the time, had an army background having served with the 2nd/8th Essex Regiment and the 2nd/5th North Staffordshire Regiment.

7 Squadron	2Lt L M Gerson	pow	Unemployed list 21 November 1919: Lt
RE.8 B4033	2Lt H Inman	pow	

T/o 1650 Proven East for a *Flash* reconnaissance; failed to return. The names of both officers appear in *Flight* May 16, 1918, under the heading 'Missing', while confirmation that they were prisoners of war was published by the magazine on October 24, 1918. Second Lieutenant Inman was formerly of the Territorial Forces and attached to the Manchester Regiment.

7 Squadron	Captain A W F Glenny	Safe	Retirement circa 10.40: Air Commodore
RE.8 B6489	MC* DFC		MC* DFC *Croix de Guerre* [Belgium]
	2Lt J P Bosman	Safe	Unemployed list 19 August 1919: Lt

T/o Proven East for an operational sortie during which a forced landing was carried out between the lines in the Lys Plain near Nieppe [Nord] and close to the Franco-Belgian border. To prevent it from falling into enemy hands, 'B6489' was set alight by nearby infantry. Arthur Willoughby Falls Glenny began his military service as a Gentleman Cadet at the Royal Military Academy Sandhurst and on graduating was commissioned as a second lieutenant to the Royal Army Service Corps with effect from 13 January 1915 [*gazetted* 12 January 1915, issue 29038]. Captain Glenny remained commissioned to the Army Service Corps until his appointment to a permanent commission with the Royal Air Force on 1 August 1919. His photograph, reproduced on the Air of Authority website [which I am grateful to acknowledge] shows he trained initially as an observer, qualifying as such on, or by, the 2nd of February 1916, though by the 1st of July 1916 [the opening day of the *Battle of the Somme*] he gained The Royal Aero Club Certificate No 3205. Posted to the Western Front his name quickly came to the attention of his senior officers and he was *gazetted* with the Military Cross on 19 September 1917 [issue 13143 of the Edinburgh edition of the paper]; *'For conspicuous gallantry and devotion to duty when in co-operation with our artillery. By dint of great perseverance, skill and very gallant flying he has accomplished splendid work under very difficult circumstances. On one occasion, during a gale of wind, he successful ranged three of our heavy batteries on an enemy battery, which was completely obliterated. He has consistently set a very fine example to his squadron.'* A First Bar appeared in the supplement [13296] of *The Edinburgh Gazette* on 29 July 1919; *'For conspicuous gallantry and devotion to duty, both in reconnaissance and as an artillery observer. On one occasion, although shot down* [This refers to the loss of 'B6489'] *he brought in valuable information. On several occasions he conducted successful knock-out shoots with various batteries, obtained excellent photographs, and did much work of a very high standard.'* A richly deserved award of the Distinguished Flying Cross was published in *The London Gazette* on 3 December 1918, supplement 31046; *'This officer has rendered valuable and gallant service on many occasions when on photographic and other reconnaissances. On 16th May, when directing fire on a hostile battery, he was attacked by twelve hostile scouts; his observer's gun jammed, and he was driven down to 2,000 feet, but, handling his machine with great skill, he avoided serious damage; after the scouts had been driven off he returned and carried on the shoot with successful results. In this flight, which lasted four hours, he succeeded in taking fifteen photographs over corps' counter-battery areas.'* In the years following the cessation of hostilities, Arthur Glenny spent time in India where between the 1st of August 1922 and the early winter of 1923, he commanded No 28 Squadron [Bristol F.2b]. On his return to the United Kingdom he attended Staff College and from then on was mainly concerned with Staff Duty appointments, returning to India in the winter of 1938, where on Christmas Eve of that year he was appointed Officer Commanding No 1[Indian] Group at Peshawar. Born on 2 March 1897, Air Commodore Arthur Willoughby Falls Glenny died on 29th January 1947, two months short of his fiftieth birthday. In addition to the decorations reported in the summary, he received a mention in a despatch.

| 10 Squadron | Lt R Hood | Safe |
| FK.8 D5014 | Lt E L H Macleod | Safe |

T/o Abeele for a bombing mission. On return, and landing, an oleo cylinder burst and on coming to rest 'D5014' had sustained damage of such severity it was deemed not worth the cost of repair. Lieutenant Macleod's commission was relinquished on 22 July 1919, owing to his unfitness to serve as a consequence of wounds.

| 11 Squadron | 2Lt A E Magee | Safe |
| Bristol F.2b C4847 | 2Lt A H Craig | Safe |

T/o Fienvillers briefed to carry out a reconnaissance but turned back after Second Lieutenant Magee was taken ill. On landing crashed into the No 57 Squadron DH.4 summarised later, the impact being reported as between the two cockpits and with a force sufficient to break the DH into two pieces.

| 13 Squadron | Captain C K M Douglas | Safe | |
| RE.8 B5087 | Lt G Dania | Safe | Unemployed list 13 April 1919: Lt |

T/o 1720 Izel-lèz-Hameau for artillery observation duties during which the crew came under attack from enemy aircraft east of Arras. Issued to the squadron on 23 November 1917, 'B5087' was seriously damaged by fire on the 13th of December when an armourer accidentally discharged the aircraft's signal pistol while removing it from its stowage. Struck for repair, 'B5087' returned to the squadron on 5 March 1918. As a temporary second lieutenant Charles Kenneth Mackinnon Douglas of the Royal Scots was seconded to the Royal Flying Corps as an observer officer on 25 June 1916, promulgated in supplement 29659 of the paper published on 10 July 1916, and on which day he was placed on the General List. Like so many of his generation service began as an officer cadet and in his case commissioning as a temporary second lieutenant [gazetted on 29 December 1914, issue 29021], his seniority being from the 28th of December 1914. According to a website devoted to meteorologists, a profile written by M Field of Arundel in Sussex, Charles Douglas, born in Edinburgh on 29 May 1893, showed a keen interest in weather observations from the age of eleven. Educated at Edinburgh Academy and King's College, Cambridge, where he read mathematics, he carried his desire to learn more about the weather into his service life. The author of the profile [whom I gratefully acknowledge] remarks that while training to become a pilot Charles was seriously injured in a training accident and that during his active service he was wounded on five occasions. Such was his determination to excel in the field of meteorology that he wrote a number of papers on the subject which in turn gained the attention of Lieutenant-Colonel Gold, Officer Commanding the British Meteorological Service on the Western Front. This very learned, and lengthy, article opens with the words; 'Charles Kenneth Mackinnon Douglas was to many the greatest synoptic forecaster this century.' In retirement Charles Douglas lived in Devon where he died on the 19th of February 1992. He was honoured with the Most Excellent Order of the British Empire and the Air Force Cross. Lieutenant Dania was formerly of the Royal Field Artillery.

| 15 Squadron | 2Lt R G Hart MC | Injured |
| RE.8 B844 | 2Lt L F Handford MC | Injured |

T/o Vert Galand for an operational mission in the course of which the crew came under attack from hostile aircraft wounding both and causing major damage to the RE's flying controls, thereby necessitating a forced landing near Contay [Somme] some twenty-three km northeast of Amiens. Formerly of the Territorial Forces and attached to the London Regiment, Second Lieutenant Handford had been seconded to the Royal Flying Corps on 20 March 1918 [supplement 30679 of the Gazette published on 11 May 1918]. His release from active service was as a result of wounds, most likely the injury to one of his knees inflicted on the 11th of April, was effective from 21 December 1918.

| 16 Squadron | 2Lt L Leiper | Safe | |
| RE.8 B3415 | Lt C H Stilwell | Safe | Retirement 1 January 1945: W/C |

T/o Camblain l'Abbe with the intention of carrying out an artillery observation patrol but got no further than a nearby haystack as a consequence of the engine 'choking' on take off. Christopher Holt Stilwell was commissioned to the The East Surrey Regiment following graduation from the Royal Military Academy Sandhurst on the 17 April 1915 [*gazetted* 16 April 1915, issue 29133]. An entry in the paper issued on 27 April 1920, lists a table of army officers re-seconded for duty with the Royal Air Force for a further two years with effect from the 1st of August 1919, their ranks ranging from group captain to pilot officer and it is the last category that Christopher Stilwell's name is mentioned. It appears he was retained in the air force for promotion to flight lieutenant on 1 January 1924, was promulgated in supplement 32893 of New Year's Day 1924, while elevation to squadron leader came on 1 December 1932 [issue 33889 of 6 December 1932]. Wing Commander rank was signalled with others on 1 March 1940, with the rider that promotions were 'temporary' [issue 34810 of 12 March 1940]. It is noted that throughout this long period of service he was attached to the General Duties Branch.

| 16 Squadron | Captain T B Jones | + | Aubigny Communal Cemetery extension |
| RE.8 B6522 | Lt V King | + | Aubigny Communal Cemetery extension |

T/o Camblain l'Abbe tasked to carry out an artillery observation patrol in the course of which the RE.8 was attacked by a trio of hostile aircraft and driven down out of control at around 1715. Vernon King had been attached from the Royal Marines; he was thirty-one years of age.

| 18 Squadron | 2Lt L J Balderson | Safe | See 26 May 1918 - 18 Squadron |
| DH.4 A7991 | Lt G Bullen | Safe | |

T/o Serny to test the DH's RAF 3a engine during which it seized and in the forced landing that followed 'A7991' was damaged beyond repair. It had spent a mere twenty-four hours on squadron charge.

| 19 Squadron | 2Lt G H Rogers | Injured |
| 5F.1 Dolphin C3837 | | |

To Savy for an offensive patrol only to crash, out of control, near to the aerodrome.

| 20 Squadron | Major J A Dennistoun [Canada] | Injured | |
| Bristol F.2b B1275 | Lt J J Scaramanga | Injured | See 10 July 1918 - 22 Squadron |

T/o Ste Marie Cappel for an offensive patrol during which Major Dennistoun was wounded by machine-gun fire from the ground. A forced landing was successfully executed just across the Franco-Belgian border, coming down near the village of Neuve-Eglise in the Ypres Salient. James John Scaramanga*also required hospital treatment for his wounds. For details concerning Major Dennistoun, please refer to my summaries for the 1st of April 1918.

* According to his profile reported by *Wikipedia* James John Scaramanga was born on the 25th of July 1898, into a wealthy family of Greek origin. It would seem that James enlisted below the required age for military service and it is reported he was attached to No 20 Squadron as an observer officer by late December 1916, his initial flying being in the squadron's FE.2d. Following conversion to Bristol F.2b James scored his first aerial victory on 9 March 1918, when he sent down an Albatros DV over Comines in the *département du Nord*. Regarding the downing of 'B1275' it is indicated he was seriously wounded and on his recovery was posted to Serny where he was attached to No 22 Squadron on 6 June 1918. At the time of his death [details reported in my summary for the 10th of July 1918] he had been credited with twelve aerial victories. An interesting aside is the connection of the family name by way of James's first cousin George Ambrose Scaramanga to Ian Fleming, a tale of friendship fostered when both were at Eton College followed later by an acrimonious falling out, hence, it is suggested, by the villein in Fleming's 'The Man With the Golden Gun', being given the name 'Scaramanga'.

| 21 Squadron | Captain Jones | Safe |
| RE.8 C5042 | Lt Clarke | Safe |

T/o St Inglevert for a counter attack patrol over the Ypres Salient where it was brought down by a combination of anti-aircraft and machine-gun fire.

| 32 Squadron | Lt P E Wood | Safe |
| SE.5a B4896 | | |

T/o Beauvois for an offensive patrol but became lost and, subsequently, crashed near Rély airfield. Allocation of 'B4896' was intended for No 60 Squadron but while *en route* to Ste Marie Cappel on the 6th of January 1918,

Lieutenant George Barton Craig,*a No 60 Squadron pilot, crashed and following repairs 'B4896' was issued to No 32 Squadron on 8 March.

* From Waterhole in the Canadian province of Alberta, George Barton Craig was killed on the 21st of February 1918; he is buried in Belgium at Moorseele Military Cemetery.

| 35 Squadron | 2Lt E C Grimes | Safe | Unemployed list 28 September 1918: Lt |
| FK.8 C3629 | 2Lt N Bowden | Safe | See 25 April 1918 - 35 Squadron |

T/o Poulainville for an operational sortie during which it became necessary to force-land near Cachy [Somme], fourteen km southeast of Amiens having been hit by anti-aircraft fire.

| 40 Squadron | 2Lt D F Murmann | Safe | See 13 August 1918 - 40 Squadron |
| SE.5a B875 | | | |

T/o 1220 Bruay tasked for an offensive patrol and, in addition, to carry out bombing. Forty minutes after departing Bruay Second Lieutenant Murmann returned and crashed near the airfield. His rank had been confirmed on the 5th of December 1917, as published on New Year's Day 1918, in supplement 30318.

| 42 Squadron | 2Lt P Carrie | Safe | |
| RE.8 A3598 | 2Lt P E Turner | Safe | |

Punjab No 10 Kalabagh

T/o Treizennes intending to carry out an artillery observation patrol only to have the misfortune to fly into a telegraph pole and then crash, out of control, against a tree. Taken on establishment on 28 July 1917, 'A3598' was well travelled having been detached with the squadron to Italy*during which time it was involved in a minor flying accident on 8 December 1917. When written off it had flown for a total of one hundred and twenty-three hours and thirty minutes.

* The main body of the squadron departed Fienvillers on 17 November 1917, and over the next five months operated from Santa Pelagio [arriving here on 2 December], Istrana, Grossa, San Luqa and, finally, Poggia Renatico before returning to the Western Front and Fienvillers on 14 March 1918.

| 43 Squadron | Lt B H Bostick | Injured | |
| F.1 Camel D6518 | | | |

T/o Avesnes-le-Comte for a practice flight; crashed on the aerodrome and damaged beyond repair.

| 48 Squadron | 2Lt A C Campbell | Safe | |
| Bristol F.2b B1348 | Airman M Lynch | Safe | |

T/o Bertangles for an operational sortie but ran onto soft ground when the engine 'choked'. Damaged beyond repair.

| 53 Squadron | Lt R D Best | Injured | |
| RE.8 B4021 | Captain C G White MC | Safe | See 21 April 1918 - 53 Squadron |

T/o Abeele for a counter attack patrol; force-landed after machine-gun fire from the ground wounded Lieutenant Best. His observer, Cecil Godfrey White was formerly of the Royal Field Artillery and was attached, as a second lieutenant, to the 1st [City of London] Brigade with effect from 25 September 1914, as promulgated in the *Gazette* on 21 October 1914, supplement 28946. His award of the Military Cross preceded his attachment to the Royal Flying Corps and was *gazetted* on 25 August 1917, supplement 30251; *'For conspicuous gallantry and devotion to duty. Although in considerable pain from an unhealed wound, he continued to command his own and another battery for four days, keeping up a successful bombardment of enemy strong points and craters. Upon conclusion of the bombardment he was compelled to go sick. His conduct throughout has been magnificent.'*

| 53 Squadron | Lt J Craig | + | Meteren Military Cemetery |
| RE.8 B8890 | Lt K Hall | Injured | |

T/o Abeele similarly instructed; crashed in flames near Berthen, a commune in the *département du Nord* at the foot of Mont des Cats, and a couple of km to the north where James Craig is buried.

| 53 Squadron | Lt R S Barlow | Safe |
| RE.8 E18 | 2Lt F Pashley | Safe |

T/o Abeele similarly tasked and while carrying out the duty came under accurate machine-gun fire from ground troops which smashed the propeller; force-landed and wrecked after running into an old shell hole. The crew had been ordered to carry out their patrol between Holebeke and Wytchete. Accepted on the 1st of April, 'E18' had only managed four hours and twenty minutes of flying in total.

| 54 Squadron | Lt O J F Jones-Lloyd | Safe |
| F.1 Camel D1786 | | |

T/o Clairmarais for an offensive patrol but the controls jammed and he was unable to avoid the crash that resulted. 'D1786' had been on squadron charge for eleven days.

| 57 Squadron | 2Lt F A W Mann | Injured See 20 July 1918 - 57 Squadron |
| DH.4 A7901 | 2Lt J T White | Injured See 20 July 1918 - 57 Squadron |

T/o Le Quesnoy for a photo reconnaissance sortie on completion of which the crew landed at Fienvillers where the exposed plates were handed to the Photo Section. Still on the ground, and while preparing to return to Le Quesnoy, 'A7901' was struck amidships by the Bristol Fighter summarised earlier. Received on 7 January 1918, Sergeant E R Clayton accompanied by Second Lieutenant L L T Sloot and Captain A Roulstone and Lieutenant D F V Page [see 21 September 1918] shot down Albatros scouts on 19 January and 13 March respectively, while four days later Captain Roulstone, this time with Second Lieutenant W C Venmore in the rear cockpit, fought off a sextet of Albatros fighters. A third, and final combat victory was celebrated on the day the independent air force came into existence when Captain F McD C Turner*and Second Lieutenant A Leach [he was wounded during the fight] drove down a scout shortly before midday over the Somme near Irles.

* Please refer to my summary of 9 August 1918 and the loss of 57 Squadron DH.4 D8428 for notes pertaining to Captain Turner's service.

| 60 Squadron | Captain K Crawford | + | Arras Flying Services Memorial |
| SE.5a C5445 | | | |

T/o Fienvillers for an offensive patrol from which the SE.5a failed to return. Kevin Crawford's previous service had been with the Machine Gun Corps. He was the squadron's last casualty before moving the next day to Boffles some twenty km to the north-northwest thereby departing the Somme in favour of the Pas-de-Calais.

| 65 Squadron | Lt L J Rimmer | Injured |
| F.1 Camel D6486 | | |

T/o Bertangles for a practice flight over the trenches. On return, and while making ready to land, the undercarriage of his aircraft became caught up in a No 70 Squadron Camel C8289 [Lieutenant J Williamson who was on a practice flight from Fienvillers]. Lieutenant Rimmer's Camel was damaged beyond repair but 'C8289' was repaired and passed to No 73 Squadron who in turn wrote it off in a fatal crash on 17 June 1918 [see my summary for this day].

| 65 Squadron | 2Lt J L M White [Canada] | Safe |
| F.1 Camel D6548 | | |

T/o Bertangles similarly ordered and crashed at Boffles in the Pas-de-Calais. Second Lieutenant White had been seconded to the Royal Flying Corps from the Canadian Machine Gun Corps. With the loss of these two aircraft, the squadron, since the 1st, had now lost a dozen Camels, eight on operations and a quartet on non-operational flights. On 7 July 1919, Lieutenant White's secondment to the Royal Air Force ceased; it is noted that he had been awarded the Distinguished Flying Cross.

| 73 Squadron | 2Lt J G Hunter | Injured |
| F.1 Camel C8275 | | |

T/o Beauvois for practice flying which ended with the Camel crashing into a partially constructed Bessoneau* hangar. Eyewitnesses to the accident state that Second Lieutenant Hunter had made several attempts to land but went round again each time until his final approach when he touched down but bounced and crashed as described. Indications in *The Camel File* that he died from his injuries appear to have been groundless.

* Of wood and canvas construction the *Bessoneau* hangar was widely used by the French and British air forces throughout the *Great War* with examples surviving until the Second World War and beyond.

73 Squadron	2Lt A F Dawes	Safe
F.1 Camel C8292		

T/o Beauvois with the intent of carrying out an engine test but in those last seconds before lifting off the starboard tyre burst. Second Lieutenant Dawes made a valiant attempt to become airborne but as the Camel swung so one of the hangars loomed into view and in trying to clear this latest obstacle he stalled and crashed. As to whether or not it was the same hangar that his colleague Second Lieutenant Hunter struck [see the summary above] is not known.

Note. Some documentation reports this incident occurring on the 12th of April 1918.

73 Squadron	2Lt R G Lawson	pow
F.1 Camel D1827		

T/o 1725 Beauvois for an offensive patrol from which Second Lieutenant Lawson failed to return. His name, under the heading 'Missing', appeared in *Flight* May 16. 1918 but it was not until the magazine's issue of August 8th that his status was confirmed as that of a prisoner of war and in a wounded state.

74 Squadron	Lt B Roxburgh-Smith	Safe
SE.5a C1788		

T/o La Lovie and headed for the squadron's new home at Clairmarais where on landing it came to grief. Initially considered for repair the airframe was struck off charge on 23 April 1918.

79 Squadron	2Lt A C R Tate	Injured See 2 May 1918 - 79 Squadron
5F.1 Dolphin C3834		

T/o 1735 Beauvais with other squadron Dolphins briefed to carry out low-level bombing on enemy positions. Ran low on petrol and on landing at an advanced landing ground at Beaumetz touched down on soft ground and turned over, Second Lieutenant Tate sustaining facial injuries.

83 Squadron	Captain J N MacRae	+	Lapugnoy British Cemetery
FE.2b A5781	F/S A Westwood*	+	Lapugnoy British Cemetery

T/o Auchel for an engine test which ended with 'A5781' crashing into a telegraph pole and its wires. Completing his education at Malvern College, where he was a member of the Junior Division, Officers Training Corps, John Nigel MacRae was commissioned to the Nottinghamshire [Sherwood Rangers] Yeomanry as a second lieutenant on the 1st of June 1911 [*gazetted* 14 July 1911, issue 28513]. However, according to a profile published in the April 25, 1918, issue of *Flight,* John later joined a battalion of the Black Watch commanded at the time by his uncle Colonel John MacRae-Gilstrap [an entry in *The London Gazette* published on 16 February 1915, issue 29070, under the heading 'Infantry' shows Second Lieutenant MacRae as being appointed as a temporary second lieutenant with effect from 15 February 1915]. In October 1915, he transferred to the Royal Flying Corps gaining his Flying Badge on the 1st of February 1916, and proceeding in March to France where he served for the next eight months before being 'rested' as a flying instructor. His return to the Western Front was as recent as the 5th of March. From Auchel Captain MacRae's body, along with that of Arthur Westwood, was driven some six km east-northeast for burial at Lapugnoy.

* Flight Sergeant Arthur Westwood's entry on the Commonwealth War Graves Commission website shows his unit as No 24 Squadron, a scout formation equipped with SE.5a; his entry in *Airmen Died in the Great War* shows him as attached to No 83 Squadron as an observer.

98 Squadron	2Lt C G Tysoe	Safe	
DH.9 C6081	2Lt N C MacDonald	Safe	Unemployed list 13 April 1919: Lt

T/o Clairmarais in the company of fourteen fellow squadron crews all having received orders for the squadron's first operational task of the *Great War,* an attack on enemy positions at Wervicq-Sud in the *département du Nord* and practically on the border with Belgium some twenty km south of Ypres. As the DH.9s gathered speed the crew of 'C6081' lost control in the slipstream of the bomber ahead of them and crashed. Salvaged, with a view for possible repair, the airframe was struck of charge on 25 April 1918, thus becoming the squadron's first write off since arriving in France on the 1st of April from Old Sarum. Two days after the incident, here summarised, the squadron flew from Clairmarais near St Omer to Alquines some twenty plus km to the west-southwest. On the 26th of May 1919, Lieutenant Tysoe was obliged to relinquish his commission owing to ill-health contracted on active service.

100 Squadron   FE.2b A5746   On start up at Villeseneux in readiness for a practice flight the engine backfired causing the carburettor to burst into flames. Such was the intensity of the blaze that followed that 'A5746' soon became a burnt out wreck. Fortunately, Second Lieutenant S C Harker, who had been authorised to make the flight, escaped unharmed. Having survived the war he, like thousands of his fellow officers, was placed on the unemployment lists, in his case the 26th of September 1919. However, within a year Seymour Haley Harker who had first been commissioned to the General List of the Royal Flying Corps on 8 March 1917, promulgated on the 8th of March 1917, supplement 29975, was re-employed and granted a short service commission in the rank of flying officer with effect from 27 July 1920 [*gazetted* 10 August 1920, issue 32012]. It is none too clear as to how long he served but by the late '20s he was on the Reserve of Air Force Officers from where on the 30th of August 1938, he was granted a commission in his rank of flight lieutenant to the Administrative and Special Duties Branch [*gazetted* 9 November 1939, issue 34727] serving until resigning his commission on 28 April 1945, and permitted to retain his rank of acting squadron leader.

203 Squadron   Lt S Smith   +   Outtersteene Communal Cemetery extension,
F.1 Camel B7277   Bailleul
T/o Lièttres with others from the squadron for an offensive patrol during which the flight came under attack from half-a-dozen Albatros scouts, one of which 'flamed' the Camel near Neuve-Eglise which is just inside Belgium and in the Ypres Salient some twelve km south of the town. The Commonwealth War Graves Commission maintains a cemetery here, titled Nieuwkerke [Neuve-Eglise] Churchyard, containing one hundred and six burials from the two wars. It will be noted that Sidney Smith is buried in France thus suggesting the Camel crashed on the French side of the border.

210 Squadron   2Lt Lt E Swale   Safe   Unemployed list 5 February 1919: Lt DFC*
F.1 Camel B3817 A
T/o Lièttres having received instructions for low-level bombing but became hopelessly lost and wrecked while forced landing in a field near Hazebrouck [Nord]. On 2 November 1918, in supplement 30989, Edwin Swale was *gazetted* with the Distinguished Flying Cross; *'A successful and skilful pilot who has destroyed three enemy machines and one kite balloon* [flying 'D3392' on 5 June 1918], *and has, in addition, driven down four aeroplanes out of control. On the 15th of September he attacked one of five Fokker biplanes; this machine was driven down out of control, and, on attempting to land, crashed.'* On 3 December 1918, supplement 31046, a First Bar was *gazetted; 'A gallant and determined officer. On the 1st of October Captain Swale led his patrol* ['D3332'] *to attack eleven Fokker biplanes; in the engagement that ensued he drove down the leader, which crashed and caused a second machine to fall out of control. In addition to the foregoing, this officer has destroyed nine hostile 'planes and driven down five out of control.'* Soon after the outbreak of the Second World War, Edwin Swales, along with several hundred fellow 'veteran' officers, was commissioned on the 26th of September to the Administrative and Special Duties Branch, all as probationary pilot officers as *gazetted* 3 October 1939, issue 34700. he served until relinquishing his commission in the rank of wing commander on 24 August 1954, under the provisions of the Navy, Army and Air Force Reserves Act 1954. Service to his country was not yet over and in the coming years he was made a Member of the Most Excellent Order of the British Empire and in the Queen's Birthday Honours list for 1964, was appointed Companion of the Order of St Michael and St George. Born 28 June 1899, in Chesterfield, Edwin Swale died on the 19th of July 1978. His *Wikipedia* entry states he was the leading Camel ace in No 210 Squadron with seventeen confirmed victories, fourteen against the formidable Fokker DVII.

| 210 Squadron | Lt M T McKelvey | pow |
| F.1 Camel B5750 | | |

T/o Lièttres tasked for low-level bombing and was last sighted east of Armentières. Lieutenant McKelvey was confirmed as a prisoner of war in *Flight* magazine published on October 24, 1918, and in a wounded state, a status previously considered likely.

Thursday-Friday 11-12 April 1918 - Zeebrugge
Primarily, this was to be a Royal Navy operation with block-ships being scuttled in the harbour entrance to prevent vessels from leaving. Great secrecy surrounded the operation which to the chagrin of all concerned was thwarted by adverse weather which forced a postponement until later in the month [see my leader for 23 April]. However, three Handley Page equipped bomber squadrons took off from which three were lost.

207 Squadron	Captain J R Allan DSC	+	Arras Flying Services Memorial
HP 0/100 1462	[Canada]		
	Captain P Bewsher	Safe	
	2Lt M C Purvis	Safe	

T/o Coudekerque borrowed by No 215 Squadron and while *en route* to the target an engine caught fire and '1462' ditched at around midnight off the Belgian port of Oostende. As a Flight Sub-Lieutenant Captain John Roy Allan, along with Flight Lieutenant Lancelot Giberne Sieveking, was *gazetted* with the Distinguished Service Cross on 29 August 1917, supplement 30258; *'In recognition of their services in dropping bombs on enemy railway lines and ammunition dumps during the night of the 11th-12th July 1917.'* No 215 Squadron had formed as No 15 Squadron Royal Naval Air Service at Coudekerque as recently as the 10th of March 1918, personnel and equipment coming from Nos 7 and 14 Squadrons of the Royal Naval Air Service, receiving a handful of Handley Page O/100s of which two have been identified '1462' and '3128'. With the merger of the Royal Naval Air Service and the Royal Flying Corps on April 1st, its numberplate became '215' and as such the squadron returned on the 23rd of April to the United Kingdom to re-equip at Netheravon with Handley Page O/400 and it was not until 4 July 1918, that the squadron returned to the Western Front following a period of working up Andover.

214 Squadron	Captain E R Barker DSC	Interned	Unemployed list 9 July 19: Capt DSC
Handley Page O/100	Lt F H Hudson	Interned	Unemployed list 21 Jan 19: Lt
3119	2Lt D C Kinmond	Interned	Unemployed list 2 Feb 19: Lt

T/o 2350 Coudekerque similarly tasked and came down in neutral Holland. It is reported that '3119' was burnt. Edward Robert Barker was born in Liverpool on 21 April 1898, entering the Royal Navy in July 1916, direct from schooling at Shrewsbury. He died in Bramley, Surrey, age seventy-eight on 8 July 1976. His medals [a group of six, including the Distinguished Service Medal and two from the Second World War] were offered for sale by Harland Military Antiques. During the Second World War, Edward Barker served with the Royal Air Force and was demobilised in October 1945.

214 Squadron	Lt E L McIlraith	Safe
Handley Page O/0100	Lt W H Matthews	Safe
3129	Lt A R Clark	Safe

T/o 0005 Coudekerque similarly tasked and, subsequently, force-landed near Fort-Mardyck on the western fringes of Dunkerque. It is believed enemy action along with inclement weather conditions played a part in the loss of this bomber.

Friday 12 April 1918
With the Lys offensive continuing, this day saw the British First Army [General Sir Henry Horne] committed to defending the Hinges Ridge by the 3rd and 4th Divisions under the aegis of Brigadier-General H S Horne, these actions being part of the *Battle of Hazebrouck* which would continue for the next three days. As will be seen from the summaries that follow, aerial activity was intense leading Trevor Henshaw, author of *The Sky Their Battlefield,* to observe that in the improving weather attacks by fighters and bombers were pressed home with the greatest vigour while the more than hazardous tasks undertaken by crews flying the artillery observation and contact patrols were of the highest value: the Royal Air Force was not found wanting.

1 Squadron	Lt R B Donald	Safe	Commission relinquished 9 March 1919: Lt

1 Squadron
SE.5a C9610 — Lt R B Donald — Safe — Commission relinquished 9 March 1919: Lt

T/o 1155 Ste Marie Cappel for an offensive patrol, returning to base at 1318 so badly shot about that it was struck off charge later in the month.

3 Squadron   Lt A A MacD Arnot MC   +   Knightsbridge Cemetery, Mesnil-Martinsart
F.1 Camel B5580

T/o 1740 Valheureux for an offensive patrol and was last seen in the direction of woods near Aveluy*in the *département de la Somme* and is likely to have crashed between Aveluy and Mesnil-Martinsart. Arthur Alison MacDonald Arnot was commissioned from a cadetship to the General List of the Royal Flying Corps on the 5th of July 1917 [*gazetted* 24 July 1917, supplement 30203]. A year later, and just nineteen years of age, he was *gazetted* with the Military Cross [supplement 30761 of 22 June 1918]; *'For conspicuous gallantry and devotion to duty. When engaging hostile troops with bombs and machine-gun fire, he was attacked by a large number of enemy aircraft. He engaged the hostile machines in a most gallant manner, one of which he destroyed. On a previous occasion he shot down another enemy plane, which fell in flames. During the last four months he has carried out offensive patrols at very low altitude under adverse weather conditions with conspicuous skill and success'.* It is known that in March 1918, Second Lieutenant Arnot shot down two Albatros scouts while flying Camel B5448.

* Now the site of a Commonwealth War Graves Commission cemetery the first burials were made in June 1916, shortly before the opening of the Somme offensive on the 1st of July. At this time it was an area referred to by the army as 'Lancashire Dump'. Following the withdrawal by the Germans to the *Hindenburg Line* in February 1917, Aveluy Wood remained relatively 'peaceful' until the bitter fighting of April 1918, when German troops occupied part of the wood remaining in situ until eventually forced to retire in the August of that year, after which the cemetery was brought back into use.

3 Squadron AusFC   2Lt L Fryberg   Injured
RE.8 A4758   Lt O H Suess   Injured

T/o Poulainville for an artillery observation patrol only to fly into a haystack. At the time 'A4758' had flown for a total of two hundred and two hours and ten minutes, an excellent achievement and a tribute to the ground crews who maintained their charges.

3 Squadron AusFC   Lt G W Best AusFC   +   Vignacourt British Cemetery
RE.8 B3435   Lt O G Lewis AusFC   +   Vignacourt British Cemetery

T/o Poulainville for an artillery observation patrol which ended in tragedy when the RE stalled and dived into the ground, bursting into flames as it impacted. George William Best hailed from Hobart in Tasmania, this being reflected by the inscription on his headstone *'Born Hobart, Tasmania, Feb.1st, 1896 Love Is Not Enough'*. Owen Gower Lewis came from the State of Victoria; his headstone is inscribed *'Rest After Toil Port After Stormy Seas'*.

4 Squadron   2Lt P C Westhofen   +   Arras Flying Services Memorial
RE.8 D4692   [South Africa]
     Lt A W Miller   pow

T/o 1350 Treizennes for an operational sortie from which it failed to return. Nineteen years of age, Philip Charles Westhofen came from Cape Town.

4 Squadron AusFC   Lt N C Trescowthick   Safe
F.1 Camel B6393 F

T/o Bruay for an offensive patrol including low-level bombing on enemy positions. Within sight of the trenches engine failure occurred which resulted in the Camel coming down on the Allied side of the lines near Robecq in the Pas-de-Calais and about eleven km to the northwest of Béthune where it was set alight as the infantry retired in the face of strong enemy pressure. According to *The Camel File* Lieutenant Trescowthick only discovered this after he made his way back to his aircraft following a telephone call to his squadron explaining his predicament!

| 5 Squadron | Lt L Mogridge | + | Aubigny Communal Cemetery extension |
| RE.8 B7691 | Lt R H Boyd | + | Aubigny Communal Cemetery extension |

T/o Ascq for an artillery observation patrol and reported to have gone into a nosedive at five hundred feet, crashing near Haute-Avesnes in the Pas-de-Calais roughly twelve km northwest of Arras. Originally from Exeter, Lewis Mogridge had previously served with the 8th Battalion, The King's [Liverpool Regiment].

| 7 Squadron | Lt D W Millar | Safe |
| RE.8 B3423 | | |

T/o Proven East authorised for local circuits and landings practice during which 'B3423' crashed near the airfield. Its flying hours are recorded as two hundred.

| 10 Squadron | Captain A M Maclean | + | Arras Flying Services Memorial |
| FK.8 B271 | Lt F B Wright | + | Arras Flying Services Memorial |

T/o 1530 Abeele for a counter attack patrol and lost in circumstances not yet resolved. Alexander Murchison Maclean was late of the Scottish Horse; his observer Francis Beattie Wright was formerly of the Royal Field Artillery. Later in the day and with dusk descending No 10 Squadron moved to Droglandt.

| 10 Squadron | Lt R O Williams | Safe | See 22 June 1918 - 10 Squadron |
| FK.8 B324 | | | |

T/o Abeele for the transit flight to Droglandt arriving here after dark and without the aid of flares crashed heavily while attempting to land. Delivered to the Aeroplane Acceptance Park at Newcastle on, or by, 30 July 1917, 'B324' had logged one hundred and twenty-eight hours and ten minutes of flying.

| 10 Squadron | Lt L H Short | Safe | See 30 May 1918 - 10 Squadron |
| RE.8 B3326 | | | |

T/o Abeele for a counter attack patrol and lost in circumstances similar to those reported for Captain Maclean.

| 10 Squadron | Lt A A Webster | Safe |
| RE.8 B3328 | 2Lt J P Mackenzie | Safe |

T/o Abeele and lost in circumstances as reported for Lieutenant Williams. Earlier in the day, Lieutenant Short [see 'B3326'] accompanied by Second Lieutenant E L H McLeod took off from Abeele at 1545 tasked for a counter offensive patrol during which ground fire wounded the observer. It is also noted that on the 17th of February 1918, 'B3328' had been slightly damaged while carrying out night flying practice from Abeele, its pilot on that occasion being Lieutenant F W Burdick [see my summary for 16 June 1918, and No 4 Squadron].

| 10 Squadron | Lt C T Aulph | Safe | See 17 April 1918 - 10 Squadron |
| RE.8 B3373 | Lt F W Rushton | Safe | Unemployed list 20 May 1919: Lt MC |

T/o Abeele and lost in the manner as reported for Lieutenant Williams, and others. Lieutenant Rushton was commissioned to the Essex Regiment from unattached lists on 1 November 1917 [gazetted 1 November 1917, supplement 30361].

| 10 Squadron | Captain A R Churchman | Safe | |
| RE.8 B5791 | Lt G A E Norgarb* | Safe | Unemployed list 27 March 1919: Lt |

T/o Abeele with the intention of recovering RE.8 C3548 [summarised below] which had force-landed with its pilot wounded fairly close to the lines. Arriving over the area, Captain Churchman, I suspect, was faced with a pretty tricky situation and his best approach to land was by sideslipping. Unfortunately, he lost control and though neither himself or Lieutenant Norgarb were hurt, both aircraft had to be left to their fate as they were well within range of enemy fire. Born on 2 January 1896, Allan Robert Churchman's service began as a sailor with the Royal Navy but it seems he left the navy in preference for the army and was subsequently commissioned to the Royal North Devon Hussars though his *Gazette* entry merely describes him as a cadet granted the temporary rank of second lieutenant on 19 December 1916 with the Territorial Forces attached to the Yeomanry [29888 of 2 January 1917]. However, at some point during the year his allegiance switched to the Royal Flying Corps where he quickly came to fore and the supplement [13300] to *The Edinburgh Gazette* of 7 August 1918, published the citation for his award of the Distinguished Flying Cross; *'Within the past month this officer has been successful in rendering vary valuable service in directing our artillery fire on enemy positions. Owing to his skill and judgement on many occasions concentration of our fire was brought on enemy batteries with such precision that great damage was effected.'* Postwar, Allan Churchman was appointed to a permanent commission after which his service followed a pattern similar to the majority of officers holding a permanent commission with spells of flying duties intermixed with staff appointments [between 14 September 1935 and 14 May 1937, he commanded No 45 Squadron, the myriad of tasks demanded of the squadron during his tenure being described between pages 112 and 116 of Wing Commander 'Jeff' Jefford's excellent history of the squadron]. Promoted air commodore on the 1st of June 1943, his final appointment was Air Officer Commanding Northern Ireland from which post he retired on 2 November 1946. Post-retirement he became General Inspector with the Ministry of Health and Local Government in Northern Ireland until stepping down in 1961. Meanwhile, in the New Year Honours List for 1959, he had been made a Companion of the Order of the Bath. Allan Robert Churchman died on the 13th of January 1970.

* Although not digitised the a file concerning Gustav Adolph Eugen Norgarb is held at The National Archives under WO 339/115111.

10 Squadron	Lt E C Harrison	Injured	
RE.8 C3548	2lt J C Anderson	Safe	See 17 April 1918 - 10 Squadron

T/o 0650 Abeele for a counter attack patrol during which Lieutenant Harrison was wounded. A controlled forced landing was accomplished and, as has been summarised above, a salvage attempt was made but without success. All in all what with operations and transiting to a new airfield the 12th had been a disaster with seven of their aircraft written off.

18 Squadron	2Lt G N Wilton	Injured Unemployed list 12 May 1919: Lt	
DH.4 A7800	Lt W Miller	Safe	

T/o Serny for an operational sortie during which the DH was so badly shot about by an enemy aircraft that it was struck off charge before the end of the month. Accepted by No 18 Squadron on 5 January 1918, it had been fired on or tangled with the enemy on two occasions; on 17 February during a raid on Ascq when crewed by Second Lieutenant F Jones and Lieutenant A C Morris it was attacked and though an escape was made, Arthur Cuhelyn Morris, formerly of the 19th Battalion Royal Welsh Fusiliers, was mortally wounded. The son of the Reverend Morris of Wrexham, Denbeigh, he was laid to rest in Aire Communal Cemetery. its next 'brush' with the enemy came on 27 March when Second Lieutenant D A Stewart with Captain L I Collins as his observer accounted for a Fokker DrI *'Dreidecker'* near Albert. Second Lieutenant Stewart, it is noted, had gained a Military Cross.

20 Squadron	Lt A L Pemberton	pow	Unemployed list 9 April 1918: Lt
Bristol F.2b B1257	Corporal F Archer	pow	

T/o 1510 Ste Marie Cappel for an offensive patrol and bombing; last sighted near Neuf-Bequin [Nord] and close to the Franco-Belgian border. Reported as wounded, Lieutenant Pemberton's name appeared in the Air Ministry list of casualties, and repeated in *Flight* in their issue of May 16, 1918, under the heading 'Missing'. Andrew Pentland has a note on his Royal Flying Corps history website that Corporal Archer is thought to have been interned in Switzerland. However, Andrew's subsequent trawling through the files of the Red Cross [references R51583 and R51619] has unearthed much fascinating detail. It seems that Corporal Archer was captured at Moerville [sic] and, initially, taken to Fürstenfeldbruck [a town in Bavaria some thirty-two km west of München] suffering from nervous shock, and thence to Lechfeld from where on 31 August 1918, he was interned in Switzerland. The files indicate a total of four hundred and one prisoners of war were so transported from Lechfeld on that date.

20 Squadron	Lt D G Cooke	Safe
Bristol F.2b C4605	Lt H G Crowe	Safe

T/o 1514 Ste Marie Cappel for a special patrol and was damaged beyond worthwhile repair after encountering severe enemy fire. For an appreciation of Henry George Crowe's service, please refer to his entry on the 1st of April 1918.

21 Squadron   RE.8 A3747   Reported in AIR 1/1019 weekly return as shot down by hostile aircraft. However, information, regarding the identity of the crew is absent. It appears to have been a presentation aircraft bearing the title *Australia No 20 New South Wales No 18 The McCaughrey Battleplane*. AIR 1/14 listing presentation aircraft indicates it was a gift from Sir Samuel McCaughrey of North Yanko Yanko and John McCaughrey. Meanwhile, an email from Andrew Pentland states the official history for No 21 Squadron records all killed, wounded and missing officers but has no such information for the day in question. Andrew continues; *'A comparison of weekly returns shows the only machine unaccounted for is B5021, listed as 'wrecked and burnt 14.4.18' so this could be the Meredith machine'*. [see my summary for the 13th and Edward Mercer Meredith]. I am, however, leaving the entry as shown as Commonwealth War Graves Commission report, Second Lieutenant Meredith's death as occurring on the 13th, this being backed by Chris Hobson's entry in *Airmen Died in the Great War*.

21 Squadron	Lt H A Marshall [Canada]	Safe
RE.8 C4578	Lt M C L Whiting	Safe

T/o 0545 La Lovie for a counter attack patrol over the Ypres Salient during which machine-gun fire from the ground forced the crew to make an emergency landing, fortunately on the Allied side of the lines.

27 Squadron	2Lt G E Ffrench	Safe	See 3 May 1918 - 27 Squadron
DH.4 B2099	2Lt W Spencer	Safe	See 3 May 1927 - 27 Squadron

T/o Ruisseauville ordered for bombing during which the crew landed at Planques and it was after departing this airfield to return to base that it was damaged beyond repair following a forced landing. George Edward Ffrench, eighteen years of age, was born in Shinrone in Co Offaly, though at the time of his air force service his father, the Reverend Le B Edward Ffrench was residing in Kilconnel Rectory, Ballinasloe, Co Galway. George, having served with the Officer Training Corps at Trent College, Long Eaton, Derbyshire, was commissioned to the General List Royal Flying Corps on 6 December 1917 [*gazetted* 11 December 1917, issue 30425]. Owing to the common nature of his Christian and surname, William Spencer's details have not been traced.

29 Squadron	Captain C H R Lagesse	Safe
SE.5a D3926	[Canada]	

T/o Téteghem for what is reported 'practice flying' but as the SE.5a had only arrived with the squadron earlier in the day [possibly from No 1 Air Issues Section at Rély] it may be that Captain Lagesse was carrying out an acceptance test flight. Whatever the reason, he apparently tried to pull 'D3926' into the air before obtaining full flying speed and as a consequence of doing so he stalled. Moments later, a wingtip dug into the ground and the resultant damage was beyond economical repair. It was the squadron's first loss of an SE.5a having given up their Neiuports in favour of the type. Camille Henri Raoul Lagesse began his service as a cadet and was commissioned to the General List of the Royal Flying Corps in the rank of temporary second lieutenant on 26th September 1917 [*gazetted* 3 October 1917, supplement 30320]. Towards the end of the *Great War* he was *gazetted* with the Distinguished Flying Cross, followed on 11 February 1919, by a First Bar [*The Edinburgh Gazette* issue 13400 of that date]; *'A scout leader of marked ability and daring who, since 28th August, has destroyed thirteen enemy aeroplanes, displaying at all times brilliant leadership and courage. On 2nd October, when leading a patrol of four machines, he dived on eight Fokkers; four of these were destroyed, Captain Lagesse accounting for one.'* A Croix de Guerre was conferred on him by His Majesty King of the Belgians on the 15th of July 1919 [*gazetted* 15 July 1919, in the Eighth Supplement to the paper published on 11 July 1919]. I suspect he left the service soon after the *Great War* but returned in October 1940, when he was granted a commission within the General Duties Branch in the rank of pilot officer for the duration of hostilities, effective from the 7th [issue 34982 of the 29th of October]. Postwar, he continued to serve until relinquishing his commission under the provisions of the Navy, Army and Air Force Reserves Act of 1954.

38 Squadron	Lt W A Brown	Injured
FE.2b A5578		

T/o Melton Mowbray for an anti-Zeplellin patrol and reported to have crashed near the aerodrome at Coventry, seriously injuring Lieutenant Brown.

41 Squadron	2Lt M E Gadd	Safe	See 11 June 1918 - 41 Squadron
SE.5a B8271			

T/o Serny for operations to Bac-sur-Maur and on return landed on rough ground which caused the under-carriage to collapse. Issued on, or by, 5 December 1917, to the Aeroplane Acceptance Park Coventry, 'B8271' was issued to the squadron on the 18th of March. Postwar, Second Lieutenant Gadd transferred to the Administrative Branch, effect from 9 January 1919, promulgated 7 March 1919, issue 31217.

43 Squadron	Lt A C Dean [Canada]	pow
F.1 Camel D6428		

T/o 0935 Avesnes-le-Comte for an offensive patrol and is believed to have been shot down circa 1020 by scouts from *Jasta 47* near Frelinghein [Nord] and on the border with Belgium to the northeast of Armentières. Lieu-tenant Dean, formerly of the Central Ontario Regiment and who was seconded to the Royal Flying Corps with effect from 18 December 1917, was named in *Flight* May 2, 1918,*under the heading 'Missing'.

* Heading the page on which the Roll of Honour is reported, *Flight* published the results of The RFC Hospital Gramophone Fund appeal, in which a young lady from Hartlepool [identified only by her initials V B] sent a donation along with a poem which captures totally the patriotic feelings of the nation to our servicemen and in this case to those who took to the air:

> 'Up, high in the boundless sky,
> The airman flies on his lonely way,
> A thousand trials are his, unknown
> To those who on earth do stay.
> Yet never he falters, or shirks his task,
> His brave heart knows no craven fears,
> Though his hands be frozen to the wheel,
> And shells burst round him as he steers.

> 'Hourly his life the airman risks,
> And untold suffering oft he knows,
> And bears it all for England's sake,
> That conquered should be England's foes.
> All ye who stay upon the ground,
> Nor knows the perils of the air,
> Be grateful to our airmen who
> For us so many dangers dare.

43 Squadron	Lt L A Greenwood	Injured	St Hilaire Cemetery extension, Frevent
F.1 Camel D6514			

T/o Avesnes-le-Comte for a practice flight and on return to the airfield crashed, sustaining injuries from which he succumbed the next day. 'D6514' arrived in France and No 1 Aeroplane Supply Depot on the 2nd of April 1918, transferring the next day to No 2 Aeroplane Supply Depot before issue to the squadron on the 7th.

43 Squadron	Lt G H Kissel USAS*	+	Pont-du-Hem Military Cemetery, La Gorgue
F.1 Camel D6558			

T/o 0935 Avesnes-le-Comte for his first offensive patrol and is believed to have been shot down by scouts from *Jasta 47*. Gustav Hermann Kissel had been attached to the Royal Flying Corps from the Aviation Section, Signal Reserve Corps of the United States Army. It is likely his Camel fell near the hamlet of Pont-du-Hem [Nord] which lies roughly midway between Armentières to the northeast and Béthune to the southwest. At the time of his death the area in which I believe he fell was the scene of intense fighting and the hamlet eventually fell into enemy hands around the middle of the month and remained so occupied until mid-September. There can be little doubt that what remained of the hamlet was effectively destroyed at this time.

* The Library of Congress, which I am pleased to acknowledge, in their section for Veterans History Project, shows that Gustav Hermann Kissel graduated from Harvard in 1917, just as America was entering the war. Owing to a shortage of facilities in the United States, he was sent to the United Kingdom for flight training. During this time he kept a diary, his final extract, written on the 10th of April 1918, has been entered by the Library; *'Tonight a regiment marched by, each battalion playing its band and the men singing as they went up to the trenches. It was a most impressive thing to hear & and filled one's mind with the wonders of war.'* As his name suggests, the family roots lay in Germany. A website devoted to images of Gustave Hermann Kissel indicates his mother lived in Morristown in Morris County, New Jersey.

48 Squadron	2Lt R S Wimpenny	Safe	Unemployed list 13 November 1919: Lt
Bristol F.2b C816	Mechanic E North	Safe	

T/o 2 Air Issues Park for a transit flight to Bertanlges where on arrival the Bristol crashed. Including its pre-arrival in France on 2 April 1918, and its subsequent flying, 'C816' only achieved four hours and forty-five minutes of flight time.

| 53 Squadron | 2Lt F Green | Injured |
| RE.8 A4376 | Lt Adem | Injured |

T/o Abeele for a transit flight to Clairmarais*where on arrival as dusk was falling the crew crashed heavily, Lieutenant Adem's injuries being reported as serious.

* The main body of the squadron would make the thirty km move southwest from the Ypres Salient to Clairmarais near St Omer twenty-four hours later.

| 54 Squadron | Lt J R Sandford USAS | + | La Touraine Cemetery |
| F.1 Camel B5424 | | | |

T/o 0750 Clairmarais for an offensive patrol and when last sighted at 0820 was southeast of Armentières. At 0830, *Oberleutnant* Hans-Georg von der Marwitz*of *Jasta 30* claimed a Camel over Wambrechies which is a small town directly east of Armentières and on the northwest fringes of Lille. Joseph Ralph Sandford was born on the 16th of October 1895, at Skowhagen in Somerset County, Maine, arriving in the United Kingdom in August 1917, having been selected for flight training; it is believed he had been attached to No 54 Squadron for six weeks. Postwar, his remains were exhumed and returned to the United States for burial in the Sandford family plot. 'B5424' crashed on 12 December 1917, when one of Captain S J Schooley's feet became jammed against the rudder bar on take off; repaired, 'B5424' was reissued to the squadron on the 8th of March.

* Born on the 7th of August 1893 in the Silesian town of Ohlau Hans-Georg von der Marwitz came from a military background, his father being General of Cavalry and commander of Germany's Second Army. It is no surprise, then, that the young Hans-Georg began his service as a cavalryman in *Uhlan Regiment No 16* followed by a switch to the infantry, first with *Infanterie Regiment No 13* and thence to *Infanterie Regiment No 16* before the lure of flying took hold early in 1916. As a fighter pilot he is credited with fifteen victories, mainly when flying Pfalz DIII scouts. Surviving the war, and ranked *Oberleutnant,* Hans-George von der Marwitz died on the 12th of May 1925. I acknowledge the US Military Forum website for details concerning Joseph Ralph Sandford.

| 54 Squadron | Lt I MacNair | + | Arras Flying Services Memorial |
| F.1 Camel C1559 | | | |

T/o Clairmarais for an offensive patrol and when last seen was shooting up enemy troops west of Estaires in the *département du Nord.* First used by No 46 Squadron 'C1559' arrived with No 54 Squadron as recently as the 6th having needed repairs following combat on the 24th of March when Second Lieutenant R E Lindsay made it back to Filescamp Farm with a longeron shot through. With the loss of these two aircraft the squadron had, since the 1st, now lost eleven of their aircraft during operations, the first of any of the Royal Air Force squadrons serving on the Western Front to reach double digits. In addition, four had been written off under non-operational circumstances thus brining the overall total of aircraft written off to fifteen and with two of their pilots dead.

| 56 Squadron | Captain L W Jarvis | Safe |
| SE.5a C5430 V | | |

T/o Valheureux for an offensive patrol during which the SE.5a was hit by hostile fire resulting in engine failure. Force-landed near Querrieu*[Somme], eleven km northeast of Amiens. 'C5430' was much favoured by Louis William Jarvis who claimed an Albatros at around midday on 16 March 1918, and shared in driving down another Albatros during the early afternoon of the 17th; then, early in the evening of 11th April he sent down a Pfalz. Postwar, he was appointed to a permanent commission on 1 August 1919, retiring on or by the 24th of September 1943, when ranked group captain and recipient of a mention in a despatch.

* The little commune of Querrieu is steeped in military history going back in time to the capture of Amiens by the Spanish Netherlanders in March 1597, and the subsequent siege of the city by forces under the command of King Henry IV. On 29 August of that year, Henry was notified that a strong Spanish force was bearing down on

his camp which he had established north of Amiens and, gathering a small contingent of soldiers he sallied forth coming upon the leading Spanish scouts as they emerged from woods near Querrieu. Such was the vigour of the King's charge that the Spaniards were put to flight. During the Franco-Prussian war of 1870-1871, the fortress of Amiens was occupied in the November of 1870, and it was from here that the Commander of the Prussian Army launched an attack in the direction of Querrieu but his force was counter attacked by the French who were successful in repulsing the Prussians who retreated back to Amiens. By 1918, the commune was again in the spotlight; earlier, and prior to the Somme offensive of 1916, Sir Henry Rawlinson, commanding the British Fourth Army, established his headquarters in the castle at Querrieu and during that bitter year many famous visitors including King George V, accompanied by the Prince of Wales, called upon his headquarters. Two years on and the area was thick with British and Australian troops and on the last day of May 1918, General Monash commanding the Australian Corps set up his headquarters in a castle at Saint-Gratian, a stones throw away to the north of Querrieu. Not surprisingly, burials of servicemen took place here and Querrieu British Cemetery now contains one hundred and ninety-nine graves; one hundred and three from the United Kingdom, eighty-four from Australia and a dozen from Germany.

57 Squadron	2Lt R Willey	Safe	See 20 May 1918 - 57 Squadron
DH.4 A2153	2Lt H S G Palmer	Safe	See 20 May 1918 - 57 Squadron

T/o Le Quesnoy with orders to bomb enemy positions near Bapaume. On return, crashed and turned over. 'A2153' had been on squadron establishment since 17 August 1917.

59 Squadron	Lt C Curtis	Injured
RE.8 C2254	2Lt E G Thomas	Safe

T/o 1030 Lealvilliers*for a photo reconnaissance sortie; shot down by a hostile aircraft, Lieutenant Curtis being recovered in a wounded state.

* No 59 Squadron moved to Vert Galand on the 12th of April 1918.

60 Squadron	2Lt F W Clarke	Safe
SE.5a B668		

T/o Fienvillers*for an offensive patrol; engine failed and force-landed. A similar misfortune had overtaken Second Lieutenant Clarke of the 2nd of April while flying SE.5a C5332 [see my summary for the day].

* On this day No 60 Squadron left Fienvillers in the Somme for Boffles in the Pas-de-Calais some twenty km away to the north-northwest.

62 Squadron	2Lt C F Whistance	Safe	Unemployed list 11 June 1919: Lt
Bristol F.2b B1345	Sgt C Brammer	Safe	

T/o Planques for an offensive patrol and on return came to grief while landing. It appears 'B1345' had been allocated to No 62 Squadron on 30 March 1918. In total, it had flown for one hour and forty minutes.

65 Squadron	Captain T E Withington	Safe
F.1 Camel C8282		

T/o 1845 Bertangles for an offensive patrol and force-landed at Cachy [Somme] after a shell struck the fighter's centre section struck, this happening when he was in the vicinity of Hangard, which lies about five km to the south-southeast of Cachy. Owing to its proximity to enemy batteries, the Camel was abandoned to its fate. Thomas Ellames Withington was commissioned to the 3rd Battalion, Oxford & Buckinghamshire Light Infantry on the 1st of September 1914, promulgated that same day in issue 28886. By 1917, and now ranked captain, he had been seconded to the Royal Flying Corps; notification of his award of the Air Force Cross appeared in *The Edinburgh Gazette* of 5th June 1919, issue 13458. It seems he returned to army service with the Oxford & Buckinghamshire Light Infantry and though retiring in the rank of major on 6 July 1940, subsequent honours came his way; the Most Excellent Order of the British Empire was *gazetted* in the New Year Honours List for 1943, while the Polish honour *Order of Polonia Restituta* was *gazetted* in supplement 36283 of the paper published on 14th December 1943. Thomas Withington had a narrow escape from meeting his maker when in October 1917, and flying Camel B2407 'R' in the company of a fellow No 65 Squadron colleague, Captain C

Clark who was at the controls of 'B2401', the two machines came into collision over the English Channel. Both officers ditched off Eastbourne from where they were rescued, Thomas being picked up by the trawler *RX241*.

73 Squadron   Lt M F Korslund [USA]   +   Arras Flying Services Memorial
F.1 Camel D1850
T/o 1105 Beauvois for an offensive patrol and when last sighted over the Pas-de-Calais was west of Vieille-Chapelle where the *Battle of Lys* [and its associated actions] was still in full swing. It is possible that Milo Franklin Korslund was shot down by *Leutnant* Hans-Georg von der Marwitz of *Jasta 30* whose claim for a Camel was timed at 1125. Milo Korslund was the son of Mrs Anna Korslund of St Paul, Minnesota and the husband of Milo H Korsland of Coulee, Mountrail County in North Dakota. At the time of his death he was twenty-four years of age. In addition to his entry on the Commonwealth War Graves Commission website, he is also commemorated on the Canadian Virtual War Memorial which comes under the aegis of the Canadian Government, Veterans Affairs, Canada.

74 Squadron   Lt H G Clements [Canada]   Safe   See 20 May 1918 - 74 Squadron
SE.5a C1079
T/o Clairmarais for an offensive patrol; wrecked while landing. Lieutenant Clements, late of the Alberta Regiment, retired while in the United Kingdom. Issued when still in the United Kingdom, 'C1079' flew to France and St Omer when the squadron deployed on the 30th of March 1918, commanded by Major K L Caldwell.

74 Squadron   2Lt J I T Jones MM   Safe   See 18 June 1918 - 74 Squadron
SE.5a C1786
T/o Clairmarais similarly tasked and on return, and while preparing to land, its Viper engine 'cut' and in the ensuing forced landing near the aerodrome 'C1786' was damaged beyond worthwhile repair. Second Lieutenant Jones was *gazetted* with Military Medal on the 10th of August 1916 [supplement 29701] while serving as Air Mechanic First Class. Postwar he was appointed to a permanent commission. Similar to 'C1079', summarised above, 'C1786' was taken on charge while the squadron was still domicile in the United Kingdom.

80 Squadron   2Lt G L Murray [South Africa] +   Arras Flying Services Memorial
F.1 Camel B5154
T/o 1530 La Bellevue for an offensive patrol and shot down between Merville [Nord] and Radinghem in the Pas-de-Calais. Gordon Lautre Murray came from Somerset West where his father, the Reverend Andrew C Murray, had a living. Gordon was a gifted academic; a Rhodes Bursary Scholar he came to England to attend Oxford University. At the time of his death he was twenty-one years of age.

80 Squadron   2Lt A L Code   Injured
F.1 Camel C1683
T/o 1530 La Bellevue similarly tasked; failed to return. Subsequently, Second Lieutenant Code was reported by the Air Ministry to have been wounded [*Flight* June 6th, 1918], and it was owing to these wounds that his commission was relinquished on the 1st of February 1919.

80 Squadron   Lt W A Pell [Canada]   +   Arras Flying Services Memorial
F.1 Camel C1699
T/o 1530 La Bellevue similarly charged and was last seen near Le Paradis in the Pas-de-Calais. Now a well advertised camping holiday destination on the 27th of May 1940, it was the scene of an atrocity carried out by members of the 14th Company, SS Division *Totenkopf* commanded by *Haupsturmführer* Fritz Knöchlein when nearly a hundred men of the 2nd Battalion The Royal Norfolk Regiment were executed after briefly holding out in a farmhouse against the advance of *Waffen-SS*. Two of the battalion survived and postwar it was their evidence helped to convict Fritz Knöchlein who was executed in 1949.

82 Squadron   2Lt S Haigh   Safe
FK.8 C3680   2Lt W Spencer   Safe
T/o Agenvillers tasked for an offensive patrol; brought down and wrecked at Gentelles [Somme] some thirteen km southeast of Amiens.

84 Squadron   Lt C M McCann [Canada]   pow
SE.5a C1094

T/o 1645 Bertangles for an offensive patrol and was seen to go down, under control, and land on the German side of the lines northwest of Plessier *[sic]*. 'C1094' arrived with the squadron on the last day of March 1918. Lieutenant McCann was formerly of the Canadian Machine Gun Corps and was subsequently reported to be in enemy hands but in a wounded state [*Flight* May 23, 1918]. This same magazine later reported [Boxing Day 1918] that he was back in the United Kingdom. His secondment to the Royal Air Force ceased on 16 March 1918, as promulgated in supplement 31300 of the *Gazette* 15 April 1919.

85 Squadron   2Lt G W Bellin   Injured
5F.1 Dolphin C4144

T/o Hounslow and damaged beyond repair following a stall at thirty feet while in the process of turning on the down wind leg.

98 Squadron   2Lt H W Brown   Injured
DH.9 C6090   Lt D G J Odlam   Injured

T/o Clairmarais tasked for bombing and on return got into a flat spin and crashed, heavily, near the aerodrome. 'C6090' had been issued to the squadron at Old Sarum on 12 March 1918, and flew to France on the 1st of April. Salvaged, it was struck off charge on the 27th of April.

101 Squadron   2Lt J P Owen-Holdsworth MC   +   St Pierre Cemetery, Amiens
FE.2b A5728   2Lt H J Collins   Injured

T/o Famechon for an operational sortie; crashed as a result of being hit by anti-aircraft fire from French batteries. James Philip Owen-Holdsworth, nineteen years of age when killed, was *gazetted* with the Military Cross on 26 July 1918, in supplement 30813, the citation capturing his outstanding skill as a bomber pilot; *'For conspicuous gallantry and devotion to duty. In the last six months he has carried out fifty-two bombing raids on the enemy lines of communications, their aerodromes and their rest billets, often flying in very bad weather. Descending to low altitude he has attained several direct hits, both on their hangars and their billets. On several occasions he has returned with his machine riddled with bullets. He has set a fine example of courage and determination.'* Noting that his observer survived, I believe it feasible that, dying, he force-landed, though it was not unknown for an observer to carry out such an action after realising his pilot had been incapacitated.

205 Squadron   Lt R C Day   Safe   See 24 April 1918 - 205 Squadron
DH.4 A7486   Sgt S M MacKay   Safe   See 24 April 1918 - 205 Squadron

T/o Bois de Roche for an operational sortie; while returning to base came down at Dompierre *[sic]* and damaged beyond repair.

205 Squadron   Lt R Chalmers   Safe
DH.4 N6001   2Lt J E H Chadwick   Safe   Unemployed list 22 April 1919: 2Lt

T/o Bois de Roche for an operational mission which was aborted owing to engine problems. The crew turned back but crashed 1615, when landing. Delivered to No 5 Squadron Royal Naval Air Service on 24th July 1917, the DH saw extensive service and, it is noted, featured Gun Layer Naylor [see my summary for DH.4 N6000 on 17 April 1918] during an engagement in morning on 28th March when the DH came under attack from five Pfalz fighters, one of which Naylor shot shot. Then, a couple of Fokker DrIs appeared on the scene but as they jockeyed for position and with Naylor keeping a watchful eye their would be assailants collided and, locked in a final embrace, went down on fire. Meanwhile, earlier in the month on the 16th, and with the squadron's commander Stanley James Goble occupying the observer's cockpit, two Albatros scouts were sent down near Busigny Aerodrome. Flight Lieutenant S R Watkins was the pilot on this occasion, while Naylor's skipper was Charles Philip Oldfield Bartlett for whom I have supplied an asterisk note in the April 7th summary.

206 Squadron   Lt H Mitchell   Safe
DH.9 B7615   Mechanic C F Costen   Safe

T/o Boisdinghem for a bombing sortie and wrecked on the southeast side of the airfield as a result of turning over. It is not clear if the crew were outbound or inbound at the time.

| 206 Squadron | Lt R Robinson | + | Longuenesse [St Omer] Souvenir Cemetery |
| DH.9 B7617 | Sgt G Woodgate | Safe | |

T/o Boisdinghem similarly tasked and crashed. On impact a fire broke out and before nineteen year old Ralph Robinson could get clear of the cockpit the bombs which 'B7617' was carrying exploded.

| 206 Squadron | Lt E H P Bailey | Safe | See 10 June 1918 - 206 Squadron |
| DH.9 B7619 | 2Lt C E Anketell MM | Safe | See 11 May 1918 - 206 Squadron |

T/o Boisdinghem similarly tasked and damaged beyond repair in a landing accident. For notes regarding Charles Edward Anketell, please refer to my summary for the 11th of May.

This had been a quite remarkable day with fifty-three aircraft crashed or damaged to such an extent it was unlikely they ever flew again.

Saturday 13 April 1918

A day of intense German pressure and though Allied resistance was stiff and resolute, by nightfall Second Army divisions had fallen back in front of Bailleul [west of Armentières] conceding the town to the enemy. It was at this point in the Lys offensive that General Sir Henry Plummer, no doubt with great reluctance and having discussed the worsening situation at general headquarters, decided that a withdrawal towards Ypres was necessary. In the aerial activity for the day, losses were much reduced.

Major-General Sir Frederick Sykes appointed Chief of the Air Staff vice Major-General Sir Hugh Trenchard. It is widely reported that to say Sir Frederick Sykes and Sir Hugh Trenchard did not see eye-to-eye would be an understatement for Sykes could not stand the sight of his predecessor. The acrimony that existed between the two men, and the numerous disagreements between Chiefs of Air Staffs and their political masters et al are succinctly explained by the historian and author Richard Overy in his book *The Birth of the RAF 1918*.

| 10 Squadron | Lt A W Bennett | Safe | |
| FK.8 B5772 | 2Lt G A Cameron | Safe | |

T/o Droglandt ordered to carry out a counter attack patrol. On return, crashed in the process of landing. This was the squadron's first 'write off' since moving in from Abeele the previous evening. Allotted 15 September 1917, to the Aeroplane Acceptance Park at Lympne, 'B5772' was taken on the squadron's establishment on the 17th of October. When declared not worth the cost of repair it had logged a total of one hundred and thirty-eight hours and twenty minutes flying.

| 18 Squadron | 2Lt A C Atkey MC [Canada] | Safe | Unemployed list 3 May 1919: Lt MC* |
| DH.4 A7859 | Sgt H Hammond | Safe | |

T/o Serney having been briefed for bombing operations and damaged beyond repair following an emergency forced landing in a ploughed field near Isbergues in the Pas-de-Calais, owing to engine trouble. Twenty-four hours earlier, with Lieutenant H R Gould and observer Captain M S E Archibald as crew [both are summarised on 9 April and separately they would perish in action on 14 August and 12 May respectively], 'A7859' had been involved in a lively fight over the *département du Nord* during which the crew claimed a part share in the shooting down of two enemy scouts near Estaires. Three other DHs from the squadron took part; 'A7990' Lieutenant F J Morgan [see 16 May 1918] and Sergeant M V Kilroy, 'A7998' Second Lieutenant A C Atkey and Sergeant H Hammond and 'A8000' Captain A G Waller and Second Lieutenant J Waugh. Two of the DHs engaged in the fight would soon be lost [A7990 and A7998] while 'A8000' [see Tuesday 3 September 1918] would require a rebuild after being badly shot about in combat. Alfred Clayburn Atkey received a commission as a temporary second lieutenant on 19 October 1916, promulgated in supplement 29838 of the *Gazette* published on 25 November 1916. An award of the Military Cross appeared in the paper on 22 June 1918, supplement 30761; *'For conspicuous gallantry and devotion to duty. When engaged on reconnaissance and bombing work, he attacked four scouts, one of which he shot down in flames. Shortly afterwards he attacked four two-seater planes, one of which he brought down out of control. On two previous occasions his formation was attacked by superior numbers of the enemy, three of whom in all were shot down out of control. He has shown exceptional ability and initiative on all occasions.'* Alfred Atkey has an impressive biography on *Wikipedia* in which he is credited as being the fifth highest scoring Canadian during the *Great War* and the highest while flying two-seater machines such as the DH.4 and Bristol F.2b [he was posted to No 22 Squadron in late April 1918, serving in A

Flight] with an overall tally of thirty-eight hostile machines to his credit. The First Bar to his award was *gazetted* on 13 September 1918, by which time he was back in the United Kingdom. Born in Toronto on 16 August 1894, Captain Alfred Clayburn Atkey died there on 10th February 1971, though it seems he lived for many years in the United States.

| 20 Squadron | Lt H Wesley-Segui | Injured | Unemployment list 11 June 1919: Lt |
| Bristol F.2b C4616 | 2Lt W L Pinder | Injured | Unemployment list 12 February 1919: 2Lt |

T/o Ste Marie Capel*and reported to have crashed, heavily, while attempting to land at Clairmarais as dusk was falling, seriously injuring the crew. Henry Wesley-Segui was commissioned to the General List of the Royal Flying Corps, his appointment in the rank of temporary second lieutenant being confirmed on 12 February 1918, promulgated in supplement 30584 of the 15th of March 1918. A document pertaining to him exists in The National Archives under WO 339/119782.

* During the day No 20 Squadron left Ste Marie Cappel, their 'home' since the 15th of April 1917, and made for Boisdinghem which lies around twelve km to the west of St Omer and, I suspect, the crew were making a pre-cautionary landing at Clairmarais a mere five km northeast of St Omer. Andrew Pentland adds; *'The casualty book and Casualty cards are dated 12.4.18, although the casualty report is dated the 13th.'*

| 21 Squadron | 2Lt E M Meredith | + | Haringhe [Bandaghem] Military Cemetery |
| RE.8 B5021 *Montreal No 1* | 2Lt A E Heyes | Injured | Haringhe [Bandaghem] Military Cemetery |

T/o La Lovie or St Inglevert for it was on this day that No 23 Squadron moved from the former to the latter. It is likely that the RE.8 came down in the vicinity of Haringhe [West-Vlaanderen], a village some eighteen km north-west from Ypres. Austin Edward Heyes died twenty-fours later from his injuries. Copies of his Medal Card can be obtained from The National Archives [WO 372/9/165005]; it is noted that he enlisted as a private soldier.

| 22 Squadron | 2Lt O St C Harris | Safe |
| Bristol F.2b A7251 | Lt H F Moore [Canada] | Safe |

T/o Serny for an offensive patrol and damaged beyond repair when on return landed on rough ground at St Andre. On squadron charge since 24 September 1917, 'A7251' had accumulated a total of one hundred and eighty-four hours and fifty-six minutes of flying; it had been delivered to France crated. Lieutenant Moore of the Manitoba Regiment was seconded for duty with the Royal Flying Corps on 16 October 1917 [*gazetted* on the 13th of February 1918, supplement 30524].

| 42 Squadron | 2Lt H W Collier | Injured | Unemployed list 29 July 1919: Lt |
| RE.8 A3258 | 2Lt W E McLean | Injured | Unemployed list 2 July 1919: Lt MC |

T/o Treizennes for a combination of contact patrolling and bombing and reported to have crashed into trees while attempting to land in thick fog. Arriving with the squadron on the 18th of April 1917, 'A3258' is believed to have spent time in Italy before returning for duties on the Western Front. Well used by the squadron, it logged an impressive three hundred and seventy-one hours and twenty-five minutes of flying. William Elser McLean was awarded the Military Cross on 26 July 1918, as *gazetted* in supplement 30813 [his surname is incorrectly shown as 'MacLean']; *'For conspicuous gallantry and devotion to duty. During recent operations this officer carried out a contact patrol in a thick mist at a height of only 150 feet under heavy machine-gun and rifle fire, and flew daily during the misty weather at low altitudes, bringing back much useful information about the enemy, and harassing them with machine gun and bombs. It was greatly due to his magnificent work that headquarters were kept informed of the enemy's movements during the different phases of the battle. By his gallant and cheerful spirit at a time when the squadron was suffering heavy casualties he set a splendid example to others.'*

| 42 Squadron | 2Lt A W Welsh | Safe | Unemployed list 15 April 1918: Lt |
| RE.8 B6528 | Lt G W Gotch | Safe | |

T/o Treizennes for a sortie combining artillery observation and bombing. Caught out by fog and while attempting to land at Rombly*in the Pas-de-Calais crashed heavily; damaged beyond repair. It will be recalled that Lieu-tenant Geoffrey William Gotch, late of the Honourable Artillery Company and Royal Garrison Artillery had been involved in a serious crash on the 9th of April when acting as observer for Lieutenant W Beart [see my summary for details]. Geoffrey Gotch died on active service on 22 October 1918; he rests in High Wycombe Cemetery.

* *Wikipedia* indicates that Rombly, some eighteen km northwest of Béthune, is little more than a hamlet with a population averaging around forty-five between the years 1962 and 2006.

| 42 Squadron | Lt A D MacDonald | Safe |
| RE.8 C5073 | 2Lt J G Angus | Safe |

T/o Treizennes similarly tasked but crashed moments later owing to engine failure. Second Lieutenant Angus was seconded for duty with the Royal Air Force [as promulgated in *The London Gazette* of 22 February 1919, supplement 31197] from the 29th of April 1918 and as at 30 November 1918, to remain seconded; his battalion being the 5th Battalion of the Highland Light Infantry]. It would appear, however, that his service with the Royal Air Force was already in effect.

| 53 Squadron | 2Lt G L Dobell | Safe | See 8 May 1918 - 53 Squadron |
| RE.8 B791* |

T/o No 1 Air Issues for delivery to No 53 Squadron at Clairmarais on the northeastern side of St Omer but it would seem Second Lieutenant Dobell became uncertain of his position and sighting Boisdinghem [which is to the west of St Omer] decided to land and ask for directions. Unfortunately, in the last few seconds of flight 'B791' was caught by a sudden gust of wind and in the resulting crash was damaged beyond repair. Delivered to France by air, it had achieved a mere three hours of flying.

* Andrew Pentland adds that this *'unlucky machine'* had a most unfortunate genesis in that on its delivery flight in the United Kingdom it had crashed, but deemed repairable it was taken to the Southern Aircraft Repair Depot where the damage was repaired.

| 54 Squadron | Captain E Z Agar [Canada] | + | Merville Communal Cemetery extension |
| F.1 Camel D6461 |

T/o 1555 Clairmarais for an offensive patrol and when last sighted by his squadron colleagues he was over the *departement du Nord* near Neuf-Berquin and very close to the border with Belgium. Merville, where he now rests, had fallen to the Germans just three days previously having been held by the Allies in the wake of fierce fighting in early October 1914. Egan Zinkan Agar was formerly of the Canadian Infantry having enlisted in Regina.

| 66 Squadron | 2Lt R H Lefebvre [Canada] | + | Montecchio Precalcino Communal Cemetery |
| F.1 Camel B5410 | | | extension |

T/o San Pietro for a practice flight during which the Camel disintegrated in the air. Initially used on the Western Front by No 46 Squadron until it crashed near Cambrai [Lieutenant Richard Edmund Dusgate*] on 23 November 1917, 'B5410' underwent extensive repairs and then was 'exported' to Italy by rail on the 2nd of March 1918, and following a brief period storage at No 7 Aircraft Park handed to No 66 Squadron on the 29th.

* Twenty years of age, Richard Dusgate walked away from the crash near Cambrai, but on the 19th of December 1917, he died in captivity from wounds received in combat on the 30th of November while at the controls of Camel B2512, most likely in the vicinity of Cambrai. He is buried in Valenciennes [St Roch] Communal Cemetery.

| 84 Squadron | Lt W A 'Peter' Southey | Safe | Unemployed list 9 March 1919: Lt DFC* |
| SE.5a C1774 |

T/o Bertangles for an offensive patrol during which the propeller parted company with the rest of the SE.5a; however, within sight was the airfield at Bovelles Lieutenant Southey glided in for a forced landing but on touching down on a freshly ploughed strip 'C1774' turned onto its back. Removed to No 2 Advanced Salvage Dump 'C1774' was struck off charge on the 22nd of April 1918. Walter Alfred Southey was the squadron's second highest scoring 'Ace' behind Andrew Frederick Weatherby Beauchamp Proctor [see my summary and footnote for No 1 Squadron SE.5a B597 on 11 April 1918]. Walter opened his account during the afternoon of the 2nd of May when he drove down an Albatros near Abancourt [Oise] and closed it on the 30th of October when he claimed a Fokker DVII at around 0930 over the Forêt de Nouvion. During this six month period he was credited with thirteen hostile machines destroyed, plus two shared, and five observation balloons. Born on the 29th of April 1897 in Bermondsey, London, 'Peter' [as he was always known to his family and friends] Southey died on the 17th of April 1920, in the most tragic of circumstances as a consequence of falling from his motorcycle while on his way to work, sustaining a fractured skull. He was literally just days away from celebrating his twenty-third birthday; he is buried in Brockley and Ladywell Cemetery. To return to his military service, Walter Alfred Southey was commissioned in the rank of temporary second lieutenant to the Royal Flying Corps on 5th August 1916, *gazetted* in issue 29727 of the paper published on 29 August 1916. His award of the Distinguished Flying Cross and First Bar were published respectively on 2 November 1918 [supplement 30989] and 7 February 1919 [issue 31170]; the citations in order read; *'A gallant and skilful officer. On the 9th August, observing a large body of enemy troops and artillery on a road, he descended to 50 feet and bombed them, causing heavy casualties; he then engaged them with machine-gun fire, inflicting further loss and scattering them in all directions. He displays great courage in the air, having accounted for seven enemy aircraft.' 'An officer of ready resource whose skilful leadership is of the greatest value to his squadron. Since 23 August, Captain Southey has destroyed five enemy kite balloons and three machines, while he has also driven down two aircraft completely out of control.'*

101 Squadron	Lt G E P Elder	Injured Unemployed list 7 July 1919: Lt
FE.2b A5632	2lt S M Sproat	Injured Unemployed list 1 August 1919: Lt

T/o 0245 Famechon tasked for a raid on Erchies*but while *en route* came under anti-aircraft fire from French batteries and, having sustained serious damage, force-landed at Longpre.*

* I have been unsuccessful in tracing these locations, but 'Longpre' may be 'Longpré-les-Corps-Saints' in the Somme.

203 Squadron	2Lt J Denison	Injured Pernes British Cemetery
F.1 Camel D3347		

T/o 0615 Lièttres for a special patrol covering the six km corridor between Merville in the west to Estaires in the east during which eighteen year old John Denison*was mortally wounded in the head. Bravely, he attempted to fly the twenty odd km back to the airfield but crash-landed circa 0650 at map reference 36A.H5A where the remains of his Camel were burnt on site.

* I consider it a possibility that he was admitted to one of the two nearby Canadian Casualty Clearing Stations and it is a certainty that Second Lieutenant John Denison was one of the first to buried in what would become Pernes British Cemetery [designed by the architect Sir Edwin Lutyens] which came into use during April 1918. John's parents, who lived in Leeds, had the following poignant inscription carved into his headstone; *'John Beloved We Thank Our God Upon Every Remembrance Of You.'*

Sunday 14 April 1918
Throughout the day German forces continued to press hard, taking Neuve Eglise but following penetration of British positions near Bailleul were repulsed. Intense attacks near Merville, while east of Robecq the enemy sustained heavy losses in men and equipment. Also of note was the appointment of General Ferdinand Jean Marie Foch as Commander-in-Chief of Allied Armies in France.

1 Squadron	Lt J C Bateman	Safe Unemployed list 14 April 1919: Lt
SE.5a A8930		

T/o Ste Marie Cappel and on arrival at Clairmarais, and landing, sustained irreparable damage when it was struck by an RE.8 and a Bristol F.2b [neither identified]. An early production SE.5a 'A8930' was ferried from Farnborough to the Aeroplane Acceptance Park at Lympne on 13 June 1917, continuing to France the next day. Following storage, it was flown to Filescamp Farm, then home for No 60 Squadron under whose usage it served until 19th August when it was damaged. Repaired, it was issued to No 1 Squadron on 21 January 1918. On the 28th of February, 'A8930' was over the Ypres Salient when Second Lieutenant P J Clayson [featured in my summaries for the 1st and 20th of April] spotted an Albatros flying between Zonnebeke and Passchendaele where moments later it was driven down in an almost vertical dive under full power. This success added to a brace of Albatros scouts downed by Lieutenant S B Horn during its time with No 60 Squadron.

| 1 Squadron | Captain W L Harrison | Injured |
| SE.5a C6405 | | |

T/o Clairmarais and wrecked here while landing in the dark from a transit flight, possibly from Ste Marie Cappel which the squadron officially vacated twenty-four hours previously.

| 2 Squadron | 2Lt T Rawsthorne | Safe |
| RE.8 C3530 | Lt A H McLachlan | Injured |

T/o Hesdigneul for an artillery patrol to the Locon area of the Pas-de-Calais where it was hit by heavy machine-gun fire from the ground, wounding Lieutenant McLachlan. With effect from 12 August 1918, Second Lieutenant Rawsthorne was transferred to the Administrative Branch [*gazetted* 28 January 1919, issue 31147].

| 4 Squadron | Lt A E Doughty MM | + | Aire Communal Cemetery |
| RE.8 C4561 | 2Lt J A R Andrews | + | Aire Communal Cemetery |

T/o 1557 Chocques*for a contact patrol but within seconds of leaving the ground went out of control and spun in, bursting into flames on impact. John Alfred Raymond Andrews probably enlisted at the outbreak of the *Great War* serving initially as a rifleman with the 16th Battalion, London Regiment [Queen's Westminsters] but was subsequently commissioned on the 30th of May 1917, to the Lincolnshire Regiment and attached to the 6th Battalion [*gazetted* 18 October 1917, supplement 30339]. From his profile on the Stamford Boys website, which I have pleasure in acknowledging, it notes his father was a Solicitor's Law Clerk and that the young John Andrews was educated at Stamford School. His medals eventually reached his mother in 1921. The information that his pilot held the Military Medal indicates he, too, had been commissioned from the ranks. Earlier in the day the crew had had a narrow escape from injury for when taking off for an artillery patrol their RE.8 'B5893' was caught by a strong gust of wind and thrown onto its back, two shaken airmen scrambling out from beneath their badly damaged machine [see my summary for 10 August 1918, and No 6 Squadron]. Their respite, tragically, was short lived and it begs the question if their experience of such a narrow escape had a bearing on the awful events that were soon to follow.

* Air-Britain's records for squadron locations indicates No 4 Squadron was based at Treizennes having arrived here from Choques on the 8th of April 1918.

| 4 Squadron | Lt F H Creasy | Safe | Unemployed list 11 February 1919: Captain |
| RE.8 C5050 | 2Lt W Rowley-Redwood | Injured | |

T/o Chocques similarly tasked and on return, and landing, turned over. Struck off charge on 27 April 1918, with a total of one hundred and fifteen flying hours.

| 40 Squadron | Major R S Dallas DSO DSC* | Injured See 1 June 1918 - 40 Squadron |
| SE.5a B4879 | [Australia] | |

T/o 1030 Bruay accompanied by three of the squadron's most senior and experienced pilots to carry out a special reconnaissance. When over the station at Bailleul [Nord], Roderick Stanly Dallas spotted a lorry and immediately dived to attack. His decision was to have a serious outcome as troops in the vicinity opened fire on the SE.5a, wounding him and damaging his aircraft to the extent that on return it was deemed uneconomical to repair and it was struck off charge on the 20th of April 1918. For a detailed appraisal of this outstanding Commanding Officer, please refer to my summary of 1 June 1918.

Monday 15 April 1918
During the day another phase in *The Battles of the Lys* came to an end at Hazebrouck.

| 2 Squadron | 2Lt F H Baguley | Safe | Unemployed List 12 July 1919: Lt |
| FK.8 B218 | Lt R L Rice | Safe | |

T/o Hesdigneul tasked for an artillery observation sortie over the Pas-de-Calais and in the same area, Locon, as visited the day previous. While in the area 'B218' was hit by anti-aircraft fire and damaged beyond repair. Taken on charge on 19 June 1917, it had accumulated a very useful three hundred and forty-three hours and twenty minutes flying. Lieutenant Rice had been commissioned to the Royal Dublin Fusiliers and whose appointment as an observer officer was subsequently promulgated on 20 May 1918, in issue 30735 published on 7th June

1918. On 10 November 1919, now classed as a flying officer he resigned his commission on return to duty with his regiment [*gazetted* 20 January 1920, issue 31743].

| 2 Squadron | 2Lt G H Allison | Safe | See 19 April 1918 - 2 Squadron |
| FK.8 B248 | Lt F W Cundiff | Safe | |

Punjab 25 Kangra Gurdaspur

T/o Hesdigneul similarly tasked and written off in the manner described in the previous summary. On squadron charge 22 June 1917, this FK.8 racked up three hundred and fifty-eight hours and fifty-seven minutes flying. It is believed both officers served in the Second World War, Second Lieutenant Allison possibly in the General Duties Branch as an officer with these initials and a Service Number '06182' relevant to *Great War* service relinquished his commission on 11 May 1954, under the provisions of the Navy, Army and Air Force Reserves Act of 1954. Lieutenant Cundiff, of the Royal Field Artillery, Territorial Services, was seconded to the Royal Flying Corps on 1 November 1917 [*gazetted* 20 November 1917, supplement 30395]. Subsequent entries in the paper conclude on 2 July 1948, supplement 38340, when under the banner 'Regiment List - Royal Artillery' he relinquished his commission on 3 July 148, having exceeded the age limit, retaining the rank of major.

| 2 Squadron | 2Lt J H Jennings | Safe |
| FK.8 C3651 | 2Lt H Stanners | Injured |

T/o Hesdigneul similarly tasked and damaged beyond repair after being struck by heavy machine-gun fire which wounded Second Lieutenant Stanners. Accepted by the squadron on 10 March 1918, 'C3651' had flown for fifty-three hours and fifty-five minutes.

| 4 Squadron | 2Lt W Naylor | + | Arras Flying Services Memorial |
| RE.8 C4557 | Lt D Elliott | + | Arras Flying Services Memorial |

T/o Treizennes for an operational task over the front held by XV Corps [Lieutenant-General Sir Henry de Beauvoir De Lisle] from which it failed to return.

Note. Lieutenant-General Sir Henry de Beauvoir De Lisle had taken over command of XV Corps from Lieutenant-General John du Cane three day previously when his predecessor was appointed liaison officer between Field Marshal Sir Douglas Haig and the Allied Generalissimo Ferdinand Foch.

| 4 Squadron AusFC | Lt E R Sly | Safe |
| F.1 Camel B3903 | | |

T/o Bruay for an offensive patrol during which the Camel was badly shot about. Salvaged, the damage was deemed to be such that repairs would not be worth the expense. Since being issued to No 45 Squadron on the 26th of August 1917, 'B3903' had been involved in numerous actions and until a landing accident on the 21st of October 1917 [Second Lieutenant M B Frew] ended its time with '45' five hostile machines had fallen to its guns. Resuming active service, this time with No 4 Squadron AusFC, on 18 January 1918, four more enemy aircraft were sent down, one, in the afternoon of March 27th, being described by Lieutenant F J Scott as a white finned two-seater in enemy markings but looking remarkably like a Bristol F.2b. It was duly despatched northeast of Bray-sur-Somme. A summary concerning Lieutenant Sly is reported on the 6th of April.

| 22 Squadron | Lt G N Traunweiser [Canada] | + | Haverskerque British Cemetery |
| Bristol F.2b C4808* | Sgt S Belding | + | Haverskerque British Cemetery |

T/o Serny for an offensive patrol in the Lys sector and probably brought to earth in the general vicinity of the village of Haverskerque [Nord] which at the time was a mere five km behind the forward positions of British troops fighting hard to stem the continuing German pressure. Sadly, the demise of the crew was probably brought about by what is now referred to as 'friendly fire'. From Grand Forks in British Columbia, George Noble Traunsweiser is commemorated by a Special Memorial at Haverskerque, as is thirty-two year old Sydney Belding of Burnham Market in Norfolk.

* On 18 March 1918, 'C4808 was flown by William Frederick James Harvey, late of the Royal Dublin Fusiliers, who shot down an Albatros DV over Carvin. This was the second of the twenty-six victories attained by this officer who finished the war decorated with the Military Cross, Distinguished Flying Cross and First Bar.

| 48 Squadron | 2Lt A C G Brown | Safe | See 3 May 1918 - 48 Squadron |
| Bristol F.2b C4606 | 2Lt W Hart | Safe | |

T/o Bertangles for a low-level reconnaissance over the Somme and in the direction of Chaulnes where much fighting had been taking place. Hit by machine-gun fire and damaged to the extent that repairs were considered not worth the time and effort. Alexander Claud Garden Brown, who hailed from Whitwell on the Isle of Wight, was made a temporary second lieutenant on the General List of the Royal Flying Corps on 25 June 1917, as *gazetted* on 10 July 1917, supplement 30175. Interestingly, *Gazette* publications of 7 April 1911, and 31 December 1912, under the Admiralty headings report the appointment to the rank of Sub-Lieutenant in His Majesty's Fleet of Alexander Claud Garden Brown and his promotion on the last day of December 1912, to Lieutenant. His Royal Navy service is acknowledged on the Imperial War Museums website, which includes details of the death of his brother, Lieutenant Edward John Guy Brown of the Royal West Kent Regiment killed in action near Zillebeke on the 22nd of February 1915. Both were born in Swindrigemuir, Ayrshire, Alexander on the 19th of August 1890, and Edward on the 28th of August 1892. In conclusion, the British Aviation - Projects to Production website [which I acknowledge] in their table for 'Holders of RAeC Aviators Certificates 351 through 400' identifies Lieutenant Alexander Claud Garden Brown RN as gaining his certificate '398' on 21 January 1913, on a Bristol Biplane at Eastbourne. My search for additional details was rewarded by the following extract from *Flight* January 18, 1913, under the sub-heading 'Eastbourne Aerodrome'; '... *Mr. Fowler was out testing the Bristol. After making a solo he took up Yates for a short flight. Lieut. Brown then took up the pilot's seat, and after making several circuits Mr. Fowler sent him for his first solo which he completed in splendid style.'* The report goes on to say that Alexander made several more solo flights during the morning and so impressed his instructor that it was decided he '... *should go for his ticket.'* By the early afternoon he had successfully completed two tests '... *and he gives every promise of being a first-class pilot.'*

| 54 Squadron | Lt J R Moore | Safe |
| F.1 Camel C1573 *Malaya No 34 The Ashworth Hope No 2* | | |

T/o 0805 Clairmarais for an offensive patrol in the course of which enemy fire shot away the Camel's propeller, Lieutenant Moore forced landing amongst trenches in the area of the *Forêt*de Nieppe*. Parts of the aircraft were salvaged but the rest was put to the torch.

* During the summer of 1944, and with Bomber Command's support of the D-Day landings in full flow, numerous sorties targeted the *Forêt de Nieppe* where the enemy had numerous reserve deposits of stores.

| 54 Squadron | Lt R E Taylor | Safe |
| F.1 Camel D6500 | | |

T/o Clairmarais similarly tasked and wrecked in a landing accident on return to the airfield. Neither Camel had survived for long; 'C1573' arrived with the squadron on 20 March while 'D6500' arrived from No 1 Air Issues just three days previously. However, during its brief operational life, 'C1573' with Lieutenant Moore at the controls forced down a Rumpler on the 12th of April near Armentières.

| 206 Squadron | Lt A E Steele | Safe |
| DH.9 D5582 | Private F C Bevis | Safe |

T/o 1 Air Issues with the intention of delivering the bomber to the squadron base at Alquines*but landed on a strip of ploughed earth at Drionville and was damaged beyond repair.

* During the day No 206 Squadron vacated Boisdinghem in favour of Alquines some eight km to the west-southwest while Drionville where it came to grief is about fourteen km south-southeast of Alquines.

Tuesday 16 April 1918

In many ways a sad and humiliating day for the British Second Army [General Sir Herbert Plummer] for with the need to release reserve divisions to help counter German pressure along the Lys front, the line in the Ypres salient had to be shortened and this meant that the ruins of Passchendaele taken by the Canadians at considerable cost in the numbing horror of the *The Third Battle of Ypres* [31 July to 10 November 1917] were reoccupied by the Germans. Against this, and in the overall scale of things, the death of nineteen year old

Second Lieutenant Bouverie Walter St John Mildmay of No 70 Squadron might be regarded as yet another casualty in the ongoing grind to achieve victory, it is worth reporting for it occurred when he was flying F.1 Camel D1782 from Remaisnil to the squadron's new base at Fienvillers,*some twelve km away to the north. Ten minutes after departing Remaisnil, Bouverie Mildmay crashed with fatal consequences. His entry in the register for Gezaincourt Communal Cemetery extension is, however, of interest. The son of the Reverend Arundel Glaxtonbury St John Mildmay and Alys St John Mildmay of Old Wolverton Vicarage in Buckinghamshire the entry records "Count of the Holy Roman Empire" by inheritance, last of the line of the Hazelgrove Mildmays. Bouverie was confirmed in his rank with effect from 18 October 1917 [*gazetted* 15 November 1917, supplement 30382]. 'D1782' had been with the squadron since the last day of March 1918, and although struck off strength in April, Andrew Pentland reports; '*... the machine was later reconstructed and flown again on 17.7.18 with the new serial F6193. These reconstructed machines made a substantial contribution to the supply of aircraft to the Front.*' Turning to *The Camel File* 'F6193' eventually reached No 210 Squadron at Boussieres on 8 November 1918, and in the early afternoon of the day before the armistice came into effect Lieutenant K R Unger drove down a Fokker DVII. Postwar, 'F6193' was issued on 24 January 1919, to No 203 Squadron at Boisdinghem but had been reduced to produce by 9 February of that year.

* Both airfields were located in the Somme.

1 Squadron	Lt F R Knapp	pow	Unemployed list 29 September 1919: Lt
SE.5a B532			

T/o 1320 Clairmarais for an offensive patrol and was last sighted twenty minutes later over the *département du Nord* near the commune of Flêtre, some twenty-seven km east-southeast of the airfield. Lieutenant Knapp had been confirmed in his appointment [as a probationary Second Lieutenant] on 13 January 1918 [*gazetted* 25th March 1918, supplement 30594].

1 Squadron	Lt K C Mills	Safe	See 8 August 1918 - 1 Squadron
SE.5a D277			

T/o Conteville [No 49 Squadron] and on arrival at Clairmarais ran into a parked aircraft. Andrew Pentland has forwarded a copy of Army Form W 3347 the summary of which continues as follows: '*... causing the following damage:- Top starboard plane smashed, Starboard Ailerons smashed, Elevators smashed, Wing Struts smashed, Centre struts smashed, Centre section damaged, Centre section wires broken, compressions struts in fuselage smashed, Longeron, Tail plane & Rudder smashed. Engine damage unknown. Recommended to be struck off charge and remains to be returned. Pilot unhurt. Total flying time 5 hrs.15 mins.*' The parked aircraft was SE.5a C6416 belonging to No 1 Squadron, but there are no indications that it was damaged on this date [see my summary for 5 June 1918].

2 Squadron	2Lt J L Walton	Injured	
FK.8 D5026	Lt A E Cripps	Safe	Unemployed list 3 June 1919: Lt

T/o Hesdigneul for operations over the Pas-de-Calais and an area now very familiar to No 2 Squadron, namely Locon. Apparently, during the bombing run the pilot fainted and 'D5026' crashed near Béthune, some five km to the south-southwest injuring the pilot and leaving Lieutenant Cripps very badly shaken. Subsequently, Lieutenant Walton relinquished his commission, on account of ill-health caused by wounds, on the 14th of December 1918. Allotted to the Aeroplane Acceptance Park at Newcastle on 3 April 1918, 'D5026' arrived with the squadron from No 1 Air Issues on 13 April and when lost had flown for just two hours and forty minutes.

23 Squadron	Lt R A Way	Safe
SPAD 7 B6737		

T/o Bertangles and forced down after being hit near the lines by anti-aircraft fire, the Spad ending up about three hundred metres from the trenches. It is believed Lieutenant Way was first commissioned to the Wiltshire Regiment.

41 Squadron	SE.5a B60	Destroyed near the hangars while on the ground at Serny by a DH.4 from No 18 Squadron.

65 Squadron	Lt B Balfour	+	Arras Flying Services Memorial

F.1 Camel D1799 *Britons in Nicaragua No 1*

T/o Bertangles for an offensive patrol and shot down over the Somme to the southeast of Amiens. Bernard Balfour was formerly of the London Regiment, First Surrey Rifles. This presentation Camel was at No 4 Aero-plane Acceptance Park Lincoln by 15 March 1918, and ferried to France on the 1st of April. On the 7th it was flown to Bertangles for No 65 Squadron which had been in situ here for twenty-four hours and in the hands of Captain P J Gilmour it shot down a hostile aircraft early in the afternoon of the 11th, the location being reported as northeast of Moreuil Wood on the River Avre and scene of exceptionally fierce fighting on the 30th of March 1918, when a Canadian Cavalry Brigade attacked the 23rd Saxon Division, forcing the Germans to pull out of the woods.

80 Squadron	Captain A H Whistler	Safe	Singapore Memorial Column 409 1 March 1940
F.1 Camel B9293			Group Captain DSO DFC**

T/o La Bellevue for an air test during which Alfred Harold Whistler*indulged in what is described as 'contour chasing'. While doing so he began to feel faint so, climbing to a thousand feet, he set course for the airfield after which he could remember nothing. As to where he crashed is not reported but one assumes it was fairly close to La Bellevue and, it would seem, he was not badly hurt. Born on 30 December 1896, at Theddlethorpe, Lincoln-shire, the son of a clergyman, Alfred went to Oundle School near Peterborough, and thence to the Royal Military Academy Sandhurst from where he was commissioned as a second lieutenant to the Dorsetshire Regiment on the 16th of July 1916 [*gazetted* 18 July 1916, issue 29671]. However, the lure of the air beckoned and he was seconded to the Royal Flying Corps on 1 August 1917, as promulgated in supplement 30352 of 26th October 1917. His first operational attachment was to No 3 Squadron and it was probably while flying a Morane out of Lavieville on 29 January 1917, that he was wounded. Recovered and pronounced fit to resume operational flying, he joined No 80 Squadron and in August 1917, where he was made a flight commander but it was not until a year later that he was *gazetted* with the Distinguished Flying Cross on 3 August 1918, supplement 30827; *'A very courageous and enterprising patrol leader, who has rendered valuable services. He has done exceptionally good work in attacking ground targets, which he engages at very low altitudes. During the past month his patrol attacked eight enemy scouts who were flying above him. He attacked a triplane and brought it down in a crash, and while thus himself engaged another of his pilots destroyed a second enemy machine. The remainder of the enemy formation were then driven off.'* On 2 November 1918, supplement 30989 recorded the citation to his award of the Distinguished Service Order; *'During recent operations this officer has rendered exceptionally brilliant service in attacking enemy aircraft and troops on the ground. On August 9th he dropped four bombs on a hostile battery, engaged and threw into confusion a body of troops, and drove down a hostile balloon, returning to his aerodrome after a patrol of one and a half hours' duration with a most valuable report. He has in all destroyed ten aircraft and driven down five others out of control.'* Recognition of his fine fighting qualities were not yet at an end for in supplement 31170 of 8 February 1919, appeared the citation for an award of a First Bar to the Distinguished Flying Cross; *'This officer has twenty-two enemy machines and one balloon to his credit. He distinguished himself greatly on 29 September, when he destroyed two machines in one combat, and on 15 September, when, following two balloons to within twenty feet of the ground, he destroyed one and caused the observer of the second to jump out and crash. He has, in addition, done arduous and valuable service in bombing enemy objectives and obtaining information. Captain Whistler is a gallant officer of fine judgement and power of leadership'.* Retained in the postwar air force, he was appointed to a permanent commission on 1 August 1919. A spell as a flying instructor occupied him in the early '20s, *Flight* of November 9th, 1922, reporting his posting from No 2 Flying Training School [Inland Area] to RAF Cadet College [Flying Wing] [Cranwell], and it was not until 15 February 1926, still ranked flight lieutenant, that his association with Iraq commenced with a posting to Headquarters Iraq. On 1 July 1927, he was promoted squadron leader and on the 15th of the same month he assumed command on No 55 Squadron at Hinaidi, their venerable DH.9As continuing to provide sterling service and for their commanding officer a Second Bar to the Distinguished Flying Cross, supplement 33477 of 15 March 1929; *'In recognition of gallant and distinguished services rendered in connection with the operations against the Akhwan in the Southern Desert, Iraq, during the period November 1927-May 1928.'* Further promotions followed and by early 1940, he was in India with the rank of acting air commodore as Chief of Staff RAF India. Then, an awful tragedy struck when on the 1st of March 1940, he boarded the ill-fated Imperial Airways Handley Page HP.42 airliner G-AAGX *'Hannibal'*** to return to the United Kingdom which following departure disappeared over the Gulf of Oman. This gallant airman is now commemorated on the Singapore Memorial which stands in Kranji War Cemetery, a perpetual testament to the twenty-four thousand three hundred and seventeen servicemen who lost their lives on land and in the air [and while undergoing the most bestial conditions inflicted on prisoners by the Imperial Japanese Forces] and in Malaya, Indonesia and the whole of southern and eastern Asia and the surrounding seas and oceans.

* Although Christened 'Alfred Harold Whistler' many service documents and his entry on the Commonwealth War Graves Commission website refer to him as 'Harold Alfred Whistler'.

** The disappearance of *'Hannibal'* was reported in *Flight* March 7, 1940; *'The death of the four passengers and four crew of the Imperial Airways liner Hannibal must be presumed, as wreckage has been washed up on the Iranian coast at Ras al Kuh, about 25 miles east of Jask. There is no sign of any survivors, but the search by the Royal Air Force and the company is continuing. Hannibal was lost on her homeward trip between Jiwani [in Baluchistan] and Sharjah on March 1st, and carried as passengers Sir A T Pannirselvam, who was to join the Secretary of State's India Council in London. Other passengers were Group-Capt. Whistler, Capt. Bryn and Mr. H Hutchinson. Capt. Townsend was piloting Hannibal and had with him First Officer Walsh, Radio Officer Tidsbury and Flight Steward Steventon. It was a strange coincidence that Hannibal was a favourite of Capt. Dismore who died recently.'* The report continues with the comment that under normal circumstances *'Hannibal'* would have been replaced some years ago but for the fact that Imperial Airways had suffered from a shortage of aircraft, a situation not within their control, and since the outbreak of war much of the fleet had been impressed for war work and other diversions. In total, the loss of *'Hannibal'* was reported in *Flight* on six occasions, that for March 21, 1940, stating that the search had been called off and the earlier report of wreckage being found on the coast was subsequently proven to have come from *'an old boat.'*

Wednesday 17 April 1918
Intense German artillery bombardments followed by determined infantry assaults on the line between Forêt de Nieppe and Wytschaete which along with Merteren had to be given up. However, northwest of Diksmuide the Belgian army enjoyed some success taking around seven hundred enemy prisoner and capturing over forty machine-guns. During the day the British Second Army [General Sir Herbert Plummer] opened the *First Battle of Kemmel*. As may be gauged from the summaries, air activity was intense, particularly during the morning and early afternoon when breaks in the weather provided for good visibility. It will also be noticed that a number of training accidents occurred, thereby indicating the arrival of pilots new to the rigours of flying on the Western Front.

1 Squadron	2Lt F R Knapp	pow	Unemployed list 29 September 1919: Lt
SE.5a B532			

T/o 1320 Clairmarais heading in an easterly direction for an offensive patrol including low-level bombing in the direction of Messines and was last seen twenty minutes later and about twenty-five km from Clairmarais near Flêtre [Nord]. Delivered to No 56 Squadron on 2 October 1917, 'B532' was damaged on the 12th of November when Lieutenant B W Harmon crashed while landing on a *'new aerodrome'*. Repaired, 'B532' arrived with No 1 Squadron on 27 March and with Second Lieutenant Knapp at the controls 'flamed' a Pfalz DIII south of Armentières early in the evening of April 11th. On August 15, 1918, *Flight* reproduced the list, published in Germany, of British aircraft claimed by their forces during April 1918, in which Second Lieutenant Knapp is identified as being a prisoner of war having been brought down in a 'Sopwith'. I suspect the SE.5a was pretty badly smashed as the airframe serial could not be ascertained. Meanwhile, the Air Ministry had confirmed his prisoner of war status, this appearing in *Flight* on May 16.

2 Squadron	Lt D S Thompson	Safe	
FK.8 B5776	Lt A G Melanson [Canada]	Safe	See 9 May 1918 - 2 Squadron

T/o Hesdigneul tasked for artillery observation. Hit by machine-gun fire from the ground, possibly in the vicinity of Bellerive *[sic]* where the engine caught fire, after which the crew crash landed on Chocques aerodrome. Salvaged, but deemed not worth the cost of repair, 'B5776' was struck off charge on 25 April 1918, with two hundred and eighty-seven hours and ten minutes flying time to its credit; it had been on squadron charge since 27 September 1917, ex-2 Air Despatch and the Aeroplane Acceptance Park Lympne.

2 Squadron AusFC   Lt Davies   Safe
SE.5 A8906

T/o Fouquerolles for an offensive patrol and reported to have crash landed near Lens following a midair collision which broke one of the aircraft's ailerons. An early production SE.5 'A8906' was issued to No 68 Squadron at Baizieux on the 19th of December 1917, and was still in use when the squadron was retitled No 2 Squadron Australian Flying Corps on the 19th of January 1918.

4 Squadron   2Lt M L James   Injured
RE.8 B830   Lt O A Broomhall   Injured Ebblinghem Military Cemetery

T/o St Omer for an operational sortie; attacked by no less that seven enemy scouts and driven down to a controlled forced landing, both officers being wounded. Oscar Arthur Broomhall was almost certain to have been admitted to either the 2nd or the 15th Casualty Clearing Stations which arrived at Ebblinghem in April 1918; he succumbed to his wounds the next day. The cemetery where he now rests is roughly midway between St Omer and Hazebrouck. Oscar was commissioned from cadetship on 25 October 1916, to the Liverpool Regiment [*gazetted* 3 November 1916, supplement 29812] and was subsequently attached to the 5th Battalion The King's [Liverpool Regiment].

5 Squadron   2Lt A G Edwards   Injured
RE.8 C2274   Lt N Sworder   Injured La Targette British Cemetery, Neuville-St-Vaast

T/o 0750 Savy for an artillery spotting sortie on the Corps front and shot down circa 1025 by hostile scouts west of Farbus Wood, Norman Sworder dying the next day, probably while being treated at one of the casualty stations located in the Neuville-St-Vaast area of the Pas-de-Calais. A native of Maidenhead, Norman's former service had been with The Canadian Infantry [British Columbia Regiment]; his entry in the cemetery register indicates his brother, Malcolm Sworder, fell in action but of this I can find no details. Andrew Pentland, who has sent a copy of the report raised in respect of this loss, allows me to report that 'C2287' had achieved a total of twenty-nine hours and ten minutes of flying. The signature of No 5 Squadron's Commanding Officer seems to read 'C K Gardiner', Major.

7 Squadron   2Lt A S N Coombe   +   Arras Flying Services Memorial
RE.8 B5048   Lt S S Wright   +   Arras Flying Services Memorial

T/o Droglandt for an operational sortie and failed to return. Surviving records indicate that 'B5048' was first issued to No 34 Squadron, a Home Defence squadron, on 19 September 1917, but was flown to Bray Dunes circa 30 October where it was taken over by No 52 Squadron. Again, its tenure was brief and on 23 November it was issued to No 7 Squadron then at Proven East.

10 Squadron   Lt C T Aulph   Safe   Unemployed list 19 August 1919: Lt
FK.8 C3648   2Lt J C Anderson   Safe   See 16 June 1918 - 10 Squadron

T/o Droglandt for reconnaissance duties and on return, and landing, ran in to a pile of unyielding sandbags which damaged 'C3648' beyond any worthwhile repair. For both officers, this was their second 'incident' of the month [see my summaries for No 10 Squadron reported on 12 April].

12 Squadron   2Lt W J Crockett   Safe   See 19 September 1918 - 34 Squadron
RE.8 B814

T/o Soncamp authorised for practice flying but while taking off he 'choked' the engine, forced landing moments later in a field adjoining the airfield. Salvaged, 'B814' languished until struck off charge on 7 May 1918. Although I cannot be certain, I am of the opinion that the Lieutenant Wallace John Crockett buried in Italy in the extension to Montecchio Precalcino Communal Cemetery, killed while flying with No 34 Squadron [RE.8] on 19 September 1918, is one and the same person. His parents requested his headstone be inscribed *'Dulce Et Decorum Est Pro Patria Mori',* which is a line from a work by the Roman lyrical poet Horace; it translates as *'It is sweet and proper to die for the Fatherland'.* It is also noted that Wallace served in France as a private soldier with the Artist's Rifles between 1915 and 1917.

20 Squadron   Lt J H Corbert   Injured
Bristol F.2b C4748   2Lt R W Turner   Safe

T/o Boisdinghem tasked for reconnaissance during which engine failure overtook the crew who crashed while trying to force-land near Terdeghem, a commune in the *département du Nord*. Lieutenant Corbert clambered from the wreckage with cuts and bruises; his observer escaped unharmed.

| 28 Squadron | 2Lt W G Hargrave | + | Dueville Communal Cemetery extension |
| F.1 Camel B6342 | | | |

T/o 1020 Grossa for an offensive patrol and brought down following aerial combat at Colle della Madona. William George Hargrave was confirmed in his rank on the 5th of December 1917 [*gazetted* in supplement 30452 of the paper published on New Year's Day 1918]. His father served in the army, rising in rank to Company Sergeant Major.

| 54 Squadron | Lt C C Lloyd [South Africa] | + | Arras Flying Services Memorial |
| F.1 Camel D1837 | | | |

T/o 0600 Conteville for a first light offensive patrol and when last seen was over the *département du Nord* west of Bailleul. 'D1837' arrived with the squadron on the 2nd of April 1918. Colin Corden Lloyd hailed from Sea Point in the Cape Province of South Africa. Earlier in the month, on the 12th, he had walked away from a crash while landing at Clairmarais from an operational patrol. His Camel 'D1779' was repaired and issued to No 73 Squadron on 29 June 1918, but written off on the 14th of July [see my summary for details].

| 54 Squadron | 2Lt M H G Liddell | + | Arras Flying Services Memorial |
| F.1 Camel D1848 | | | |

T/o 1715 Conteville for an evening offensive patrol; failed to return. 'D1848' had been with the squadron for just five days. Matthew Henry Goldie Liddell was formerly of the 7th Battalion Cameronians [Scottish Infantry] and was seconded to the Royal Flying Corps on the 3rd of December 1917 [*gazetted* 2 January 1918, supplement 30454].

| 54 Squadron | 2Lt T S C Howe MC | Safe | |
| F.1 Camel D6523 | | | |

T/o Conteville for an offensive patrol; returned badly shot about and, subsequently, struck from charge. Despite this close call, Sydney Thomas Curzon Howe was tasked for a similar sortie at midday.

| 54 Squadron | 2Lt T S C Howe MC | + | Arras Flying Services Memorial |
| F.1 Camel D6583 | | | |

T/o 1215 Conteville for an offensive patrol and was last sighted fighting hard over Outtersteene [Nord], some five km southwest of Bailleul. Thomas Sydney Curzon Howe came to the air force following service with the Connaught Rangers. Information concerning the award of a Military Cross has to date eluded me.

| 65 Squadron | 2Lt M A Newnham | Safe | Unemployed list 18 March 1919: Lt DFC |
| F.1 Camel D6566 | | | |

T/o Bertangles authorised for practice air fighting against an unidentified Camel. In the excitement of the chase, Second Lieutenant Newnham lost control and spun into some trees near the aerodrome. Miraculously, he emerged from the remains of his aircraft with little more than bumps and bruises. 'D6566' had been received from No 2 Air Issues on 12 April 1918.

| 82 Squadron | 2Lt H F Flowers | Safe | See 14 October 1918 - 82 Squadron |
| FK.8 C8563 | | | |

T/o Agenvilliers authorised to practice take offs and landings and it was while landing from a circuit that Humphrey French Flowers had the misfortune to run into a plough. Such was the damage to the FK.8 that it was later struck off charge; of the offending plough, its fate is unknown.

| 84 Squadron | Sgt A Jex | Safe | See 22 April 1918 - 84 Squadron |
| SE.5a C5335 | | | |

T/o Bertangles authorised for practice flying but lost control and sideslipped to the ground; damaged beyond repair. Received by the squadron from No 2 Air Issues on 20 January 1918.

| 98 Squadron | Lt S B Walsh | Safe |
| DH.9 C6087 | Lt C T de Guise [Canada] | Safe |

T/o Alquines for a bombing raid during which hostile fire shot away the controls and the DH crashed in an attempted forced landing near Lynde [Nord], ten km to the west of Hazebrouck. 'C6087' was ferried from No 2 Aeroplane Acceptance Park at Hendon to Old Sarum on 6 March 1918, for issue to No 98 Squadron. It arrived in France with the squadron on the 1st of April, and now badly damaged it was struck off charge on the 25th. Of the Quebec Regiment, Lieutenant C T de Guise was seconded for duty with the Royal Flying Corps on 23rd October 1917, as published in supplement 31001 of the *Gazette* published over a year later on 9 November 1918. His secondment ceased on the last day of March 1919, promulgated in supplement 31333 of 9 May 1919.

| 205 Squadron | Lt W E MacPherson | Safe |
| DH.4 A8080 | | |

T/o 1545 Bois des Roche for a practice flight only to collide with a hangar, the DH being totally wrecked.

205 Squadron   DH.4 D8405   Damaged beyond repair when the DH summarised above came crashing down.

| 205 Squadron | Captain C R Lupton DSC | Safe | See 9 May 1918 - 205 Squadron |
| DH.4 N6000 | Airman A G Wood | Safe | See 9 May 1918 - 205 Squadron |

T/o 1237 Bois de Roche tasked for a raid on La Motte aerodrome during which the DH's rudder controls were badly damaged, thus necessitating a forced landing, this being attempted at Corbie, a small town in the Somme and about 15 km up river from Amiens. Unfortunately, in the final phase of landing the DH flew into telegraph wires and was wrecked. Flown by a number of highly skilled naval pilots, 'N6000' had been involved in many aerial combats, seven [at least] being recorded between 17 February and 7 April 1918 before it was damaged in a flying accident a mere five days before it was written off. First to score was Flight Lieutenant E Dickson and Gun Layer W Naylor who between them sent down a brace of Albatros scouts on the 17th and 18th while Captain Charles Philip Oldfield Bartlett accounted for an unidentified aircraft on 21 March followed on the 23rd by an Albatros; then, on April 1st a Pfalz was left smoking - all with Gun Layer Naylor, while on the 7th, this time with Airman A G Wood he claimed a couple of scouts, one of which he reported as a Pfalz. The flying accident alluded to also featured Captain Bartlett along with Airman F S Jackson, neither of whom were injured. Charles Roger Lupton was one of three officers awarded a Distinguished Service Cross in the supplement to *The London Gazette* on 18 December 1917 [issue 30437] and in order they are listed as Flight Sub-Lieutenant Charles Roger Lupton, Flight Sub-Lieutenant Euan Dickson and Observer Sub Lieutenant William Lawrence Hill; '*For conspicuous gallantry and devotion to duty in a bombing raid on Thourout Railway Station and Varsennaere Aerodrome on the 26th October 1917.These officers volunteered for the expedition in spite of extremely unfavourable weather conditions. They have all previously taken part in many bombing raids.*'

| 206 Squadron | Lt H Mitchell | Safe |
| DH.9 B7615 | Airman C F Costen | Safe |

T/o Alquines in the company others all having been briefed for a bombing raid. Reported to have force-landed about a km or so southeast of the airfield, turning over in the process.

| 206 Squadron | Lt R Robinson | + | Longuenesse [St Omer] Souvenir Cemetery |
| DH.9 B7617 | Sgt G Woodgate | Safe | |

T/o Alquines similarly instructed and, it is reported, crashed when landing and caught fire. I can only assume Sergeant Woodgate managed to get clear before a bomb that had not been released exploded. From Nottingham, Ralph Robinson was just nineteen years of age.

| 206 Squadron | 2Lt L M Whittington | Safe | See 23 April 1918 - 206 Squadron |
| DH.9 B7618 | Private S Jones | Safe | See 23 April 1918 - 206 Squadron |

T/o Alquines similarly tasked and on landing crashed heavily.

| 206 Squadron | Lt V C M Tiarks* | Safe |
| DH.9 B7599 | Private H W Williams | Safe |

T/o Boisdinghem and set course for Alquines where, on arrival, the DH crashed while landing. I much suspect 'B7599' had been in an unserviceable state when the squadron decamped to Alquines forty-eight hours previous.

* Identified as Victor Charles Morris Tiarks, born 24 May 1898, and a record may be obtained from The National Archives through AIR 76/507/2 which refers to a former reference in the original department as 'Book No. 235 Part 1.'

Thursday 18 April 1918
Heavy fighting in many areas along the Western Front, particularly around Givency-en-Gohelle in the Pas-de-Calais where the British Fourth Army [General Sir Henry Rawlinson] was forced to give ground.

| 1 Squadron | Lt R B Donald | Safe | Commission relinquished 9 March 1919: Lt |
| SE.5 A8929 | | | |

T/o Clairmarais for low level bombing sortie during which the SE.5 was hit by hostile fire, forced landing at Treizennes which was currently being used by No 42 Squadron. The damage was such that 'A8929' was struck as beyond economical repair. The writing off of this aircraft marked the tenth operational loss since the 1st of April. In addition three had come to grief in other circumstances.

| 2 Squadron | Captain N Deakin | Safe |
| FK.8 C3616 | Lt R L Rice | Safe |

T/o Hesdigneul for a contact patrol but was obliged to force-land, owing to engine failure, near Gonnehem in the Pas-de-Calais some eight km northwest from Béthune. Accepted by the squadron 28 February 1918, 'C3616' flew for a total of thirty-nine hours and five minutes. Lieutenant Rice was formerly of the Royal Dublin Fusiliers and with effect from 10 November 1919, he relinquished his Royal Air Force commission on return to army duties.

| 4 Squadron AusFC | Lt A Finnie AusFC | Safe | See 11 May 1918 - 4 Squadron AusFC |
| F.1 Camel D6580 | | | |

T/o Bruay for an offensive patrol which included a bombing task; on return to Bruay the wind was gusting with some strength and as a consequence Alexander Finnie crashed while attempting to land.

| 40 Squadron | 2Lt C W Usher | Safe |
| SE.5a B13 | | |

T/o 1405 Bruay with orders to carry out a balloon reconnaissance, which was accomplished. On return, and when about to land, the SE.5a was caught by a sudden gust of wind and crashed. Postwar, Cecil William Usher, who was known to his squadron colleagues as 'Pusher', was granted a short service commission on 8 February 1921 [*gazetted* 22 February 1921, issue 32235] and, subsequently relinquished his commission on completion of active and reserve service on 22 February 1937. But, as with many of his compatriots, realising war was becoming inevitable, Cecil rejoined the air force, this time with a commission in the Administrative and Special Duties Branch as from 16 May 1939 [*gazetted* 23 May 1939, issue 34628]. He served until 7 September 1954, when he was obliged to relinquish his commission under the provisions of the Navy, Army and Air Force Reserves Act 1954; at the time he held the rank of squadron leader.

Note. One of the plethora of scout pilots engaged this day was Lieutenant A B Ellwood flying Camel F.1 B7185 and tasked to carry out a special mission over the *département du Nord* between Merville and Estaires. On return to Lièttres the surface wind was gusting strongly and despite his best efforts Aubrey Beauclerk Ellwood lost control and crashed. Damage to his aircraft was slight and following repair it returned to service, subsequently rebuilt in the summer of 1918, and given the airframe serial 'F5966' as such it was issued on 9 July 1918, to No 213 Squadron at Bergues. However, it appears to have had many unresolved faults and, consequently, it was struck off charge on 24 July 1918, as not worth repairing. Picking up on Lieutenant Ellwood, postwar he was granted a permanent commission on the 1st of August 1919, and served with great distinction until retirement on 29 January 1952, his last appointment being Air Officer Commanding in Chief Transport Command. Knighted in the New Year Honours List of 1949, Air Marshal Sir Aubrey Ellwood died on the 20th of December 1992. A full analysis of service can be read on the RAF Commands website.

Thursday-Friday 18-19 April 1918

101 Squadron	Captain J A Middleton	Injured	
FE.2b A6408	Captain R E Smith	+	Longueau British Cemetery

T/o 2350 Famechon ordered for bombing operations and crashed near Dommartin [Somme], ten km or so to the south-southeast of Amiens. Ralph Eustace Smith was late of the Northumberland Hussars. Arriving with the squadron from No 2 Air Issues on 6 April 1918, 'A6408' had flown for a total of eleven hours and twenty minutes.

Friday 19 April 1918

Inclement weather along the Western Front with numerous reports of snowstorms.

2 Squadron	2Lt G H Allison	Safe	See 23 May 1918 - 2 Squadron
RE.8 D5010	2Lt C Sheil	Safe	

T/o Hesdigneul tasked for an artillery patrol but swung and before it could be recovered a wing came into contact with a lorry and ended up damaged beyond repair. Accepted by the squadron as recently as 14th April, 'D5010' had logged a total of six hours and twenty-five minutes flying. Second Lieutenant Allision had an alarming few minutes on the 15th when his aircraft was so badly shot up by anti-aircraft fire it had to be scrapped [see my summary for details]. Postwar he was granted a short service commission in the rank of flying officer on 19 December 1919, *gazetted* that day in issue 31685. His service in the 1920s has yet to be traced, but it is known he was transferred to Class C of the Reserve in the rank of flight lieutenant on 12th December 1926. I strongly suspect his Second World War service was with the Administrative and Special Duties Branch until he was obliged to relinquish his commission under the provisions of the Navy, Army and Air Force Reserves Act, 1954.

5 Squadron	2Lt H C Cooke	Safe	
RE.8 B6672	2Lt G B Pershouse	Safe	See 4 May 1921 - 12 Squadron

T/o Savy tasked for a night raid on Brebières and a reconnaissance of the area; reported that owing to snowstorms the crew force-landed at Veres [sic]. On charge from No 1 Air Issues on 27 March 1918, 'B6672' had logged fourteen hours and fifty minutes flying. Retained in the postwar air force, George Bradney Pershouse qualified as a pilot.

5 Squadron	2Lt R S Durno	Safe	Unemployed list 29 September 1919: Lt MC
RE.8 D4825	2Lt H L Page	Safe	Unemployed list 10 April 1919: 2Lt

T/o Savy similarly tasked. On return it was snowing, reducing visibility and as a consequence Second Lieutenant Durno misjudged his approach and finished up in a ploughed field next to the aerodrome, inverted. Taken on charge on 13 April 1918, 'D4825' was struck with just five flying hours to its credit. Robert Stewart Durno was *gazetted* with the Military Cross 22 June 1918, supplement 30761; *'For conspicuous gallantry and devotion to duty. When on photographic work he succeeded, despite the most constant and severe fire from the ground, in taking 16 photographs from a height of 1,300 feet. On the following day he took part in a low-flying attack on hostile troops, as a result of which, though his machine was riddle with bullets, he was forced to land, but succeeded in doing this behind our front lines. He has set a splendid example to his flight.'*

38 Squadron	Lt S A Leith	+	Coventry [London Road] Cemetery
RE.8 C2373			

T/o Radford having been collected by Lieutenant Sidney Angus Leith of No 38 Squadron based at Melton Mowbray and while in the process of turning spun to the ground.

53 Squadron	Lt A N Pitchford	Safe	Unemployed list 29 January 1919: Lt
RE.8 B7718	Airman J Harrison	Safe	

T/o Clairmarais for operations and damaged beyond repair while forced landing in a snowstorm. Commissioned to the General List of the Royal Flying Corp, Lieutenant Pitchford's appointment was approved on 5 December 1917 [*gazetted* New Year's Day 1918, supplement 30452], though a *Gazette* entry published on 13 February

1919, suggests he many have formerly served with the Lancashire Fusiliers and an entry in the paper published on 21 February 1921, I suggest, confirms this as against the Lancashire Fusiliers his commission is relinquished with effect from 29 January 1919 [see unemployed list above],retaining the rank of second lieutenant.

| 74 Squadron | Lt P F C Howe | Safe | See 25 April 1918 - 74 Squadron |
| SE.5a D274 | | | |

T/o Clairmarais for an offensive patrol and written on return to base when Lieutenant Howe crashed while attempting to land. Delivered to London Colney on 20 February 1918, 'D274' went with the squadron to Gold-hangar on 25 March and crossed to St. Omer five days later. Since then it had spent brief spells at Téteghem and La Lovie before arriving on the 11th at Clairmarais. In total, 'D274' flew for fifteen hours and fifteen minutes.

| 100 Squadron | 2Lt A R Kingsford | Safe | Unemployed list 18 July 1919: Lt |
| FE.2c B450 | Pte A Johnson | Injured | |

T/o 2230 Villeseneux tasked for a raid on enemy positions near Chaulnes but struck a flare standard with the bottom left-hand plane and was force-landed. While endeavouring to avoid other machines, nosed dived to the ground. Taken on charge from No 2 Air Issues on 25 January 1918, 'B450' had flown for a total of thirty-two hours and thirty-five minutes.

Saturday 20 April 1918

During the day the ground party of No 148 Squadron embarked for service in France. Activity in the air was considerable, both operational and with squadrons running training programmes. By 'close of play' at Capelle No 88 Squadron was settling in to its new home their Bristol F.2bs led by Major R T Leather having earlier crossed the Channel from Kenley to work up for operations which commenced on the 6th of May.

| 1 Squadron | Lt W A Smart | Safe | Unemployed list 11 January 1919: Lt |
| SE.5 A8908 | | | |

T/o Clairmarais for practice flying and wrecked in a landing accident. Taken in hand by the squadron on 29th January 1918, having seen prior service with Nos 60 and 84 Squadrons, 'A8908' accounted for at least two hostile aircraft and a kite balloon, all at the hands of Second Lieutenant P J Clayson - summaries for this officer are reported on 1 April and 8 May 1918.

| 2 Squadron | 2Lt W M Hirst | Safe | Unemployed list 11 September 1919: F/O |
| FK.8 B304 | | | |

T/o Hesdigneul tasked for night bombing but owing to engine failure was obliged to force-land near Houchin, a commune in the Pas-de-Calais some five km south of Béthune.

| 2 Squadron | 2Lt C Sheil | Safe | See 22 April 1918 - 2 Squadron |
| FK.8 B315 | | | |

T/o Hesdigneul tasked for an artillery observation patrol but had the misfortune to run into a ditch which damaged 'B315' beyond repair. From No 2 Air Issues to the squadron on 28 October 1917, it had logged a useful two hundred and seventy-two hours and forty-five minutes flying. No 2 Squadron was the first non-scout squadron to lose ten of their aircraft on operational duties since the 1st of the month.

| 2 Squadron AusFC | Lt G Cox | Safe | |
| SE.5a B150 | | | |

T/o Fouquerolles authorised for flying practice and wrecked when landing after an ammunition drum fell off the Lewis gun and jammed against the rudder bars.

| 3 Squadron | 2Lt D G Lewis* | pow | |
| F.1 Camel B7393 | | | |

T/o 1730 Valheureux for an offensive patrol and shot down by Manfred von Richthofen flying a Fokker DRI '425/17' of *Jasta 1* going down over Villers-Bretonneux a mere three minutes after Manfred had shot down David Greswolde Lewis's commanding officer and about six km away to the north-northeast. It was 'The Red Baron's' final combat victory.

* Possibly [as suggested by Andrew Pentland] the same 'Lieutenant H G Lewis' who is known to have hailed from Rhodesia and while with No 78 Squadron at Suttons Farm named his F.1 Camel B9309 *'Rhodesia'.*

3 Squadron   2Lt O H Nicholson   Safe   See 18 June 1918 - 3 Squadron
F.1 Camel C6711   [South Africa]
T/o Valheureux authorised for flying practice during which Second Lieutenant Owen Harrow Nicholson of Pepworth in the Natal collided with telegraph wires and crashed. Delivered to No 2 Aeroplane Acceptance Park Hendon on 27 December 1917, 'C6711' arrived with the squadron on 13 January 1918.

3 Squadron   Major R Raymond-Barker MC   +   Arras Flying Services Memorial
F.1 Camel D6439
T/o 1730 Valheureux leading his squadron on an offensive patrol over the Somme and at around 1840, now south of Bois de Hamel, came under attack from Manfred von Richthofen flying a Fokker DrI of *Jasta 1.* His aim was deadly and within seconds the Camel was a ball of fire as a result the fuel tank exploded. It was Manfred's 79th and penultimate victory. Richard 'Dick' Raymond-Barker was born in Forest Gate, London, on the 6th of May 1894, and was commissioned to the 12th Battalion of the Royal Northumberland Fusiliers on the 30th of November 1914 [*gazetted* 1 December 1914, issue 28993]. However, in mid-1915, he took a series of flying lessons at Hendon under the aegis of the Hall Flying School and on successful completion of his course [16th July] was granted Royal Aero Club Aviators' Certificate No 1460. Joining the Royal Flying Corps on the 6th of August 1915, 'Dick' Raymond-Barker saw active service with four squadrons before being appointed to succeed Major J A G de C Coucy as commander of No 3 Squadron on 17 September 1917, by which time he had been awarded the Military Cross [*gazetted* 17 September 1917, supplement 30287]; *'For conspicuous gallantry and devotion to duty when leading a fighting patrol. He attacked a large hostile formation, destroying two of them. He has also done excellent work in leading distant photographic reconnaissances, notably on two occasions when his skilful leadership enabled photographs to be taken of all the required hostile area in spite of repeated attacks from enemy aircraft. He has helped to destroy seven hostile machines, and has at all times displayed conspicuous skill and gallantry.'* He was succeeded by Major R St C McClintock.

4 Squadron   Captain F B Reece   Injured   Longuenesse [St Omer] Souvenir Cemetery
RE.8 D4693
T/o 1445 St Omer for a practice flight which ended at 1450 in a fatal nosedive to the ground, followed by fire. Alive when pulled from the burning wreckage, Frederick Bennett Reece, formerly of the Corps of Royal Engineers, died soon afterwards from his terrible burns.

4 Squadron AusFC   2Lt R G Smallwood   Safe   See 14 May 1918 - 4 Squadron AusFC
F.1 Camel B7385
T/o Bruay for an offensive patrol which was include low-level bombing but swung out of control and crashed. Taken on charge on 24 February 1918, when flown by Captain W B Tunbridge accounted for two enemy aircraft between the 10th and 22nd of March.

4 Squadron AusFC   Lt E Stanton   Injured
F.1 Camel B7412 Y
T/o Bruay authorised for practice flying; stalled while landing and damaged beyond repair. Taken on charge on the 15th of March 1918, 'B7412' flew for a total of forty-one hours and fifty-five minutes.

7 Squadron   RE.8 B3432   Wrecked on the ground at Droglandt after being struck by the FK.8 belonging to No 10 Squadron summarised below.

10 Squadron   Lt E J Riley   Safe
FK.8 B3330   Lt F W Rushton   Safe
T/o Droglandt to practice the art of reconnaissance and on return, and landing, ran into the RE.8 summarised above. Earlier in the month [11th] when the squadron was at Abeele, and with the crew comprising of Lieutenant

H W Holmes and Second Lieutenant I S Black, 'B3330' returned to base having been shot about and Second Lieutenant Black suffering from a knee wound.

16 Squadron	2Lt P C West	Safe	See 3 August 1918 - 16 Squadron
RE.8 C5031	Lt C V Todman	Safe	See 3 August 1918 - 16 Squadron

T/o Camblain l'Abbé tasked to carry out artillery observation; wrecked following a misjudged landing on return to base. An inquiry concluded this was owing to the inexperience of Second Lieutenant West.

18 Squadron	2Lt C W Snook	Safe	See 21 April 1918 - 18 Squadron
DH.4 A7818 G	2Lt B Tussaud	Safe	See 21 April 1918 - 18 Squadron

T/o Serny with others briefed for formation flying practice and in the aftermath of a misjudged approach and landing collided with a hut, 'A7818' initially being disposed to a repair park for inspection where it was struck off charge on 25 April 1918. Two decades later, and with another war with Germany becoming more of a certainty with each passing day, hundreds of officers who had served in the *Great War* came forward to serve their country in its hour of need and in the case of Courtenay Walter Snook he was commissioned to the Administrative and Special Duties Branch of the Royal Air Force in the rank of pilot officer on 19 September 1939 [*gazetted* 26 September 1939, issue 34694], his terms of engagement being for 'hostilities only' accept that in his case he continued in the postwar air force until relinquishing his commission under the provisions of the Navy, Army and Air Force Reserves Act 1954, his rank at the time being squadron leader.

18 Squadron	2Lt J Waugh	Safe	See 31 May 1918 - 18 Squadron
DH.4 A8045	Lt P W Anderson	Safe	

T/o Serney for bombing and when making an emergency landing near Renescure [Nord] ran into a ditch covered with camouflage; damaged beyond useful repair.

21 Squadron	Lt Lewis	Safe
RE.8 C5067		

T/o St Inglevert for practice flying and crashed near Calais after colliding with telegraph wires.

23 Squadron	Captain H V Puckridge	Safe	See 1 July 1918 - 23 Squadron
SPAD 13 B6875			

T/o Poulainville*for an engine test and crashed almost immediately owing to a faulty air pressure system. For Hugh Victor Puckridge service began as an officer cadet at the Royal Military Academy Sandhurst from where he graduated with effect from the 7th of April 1916, commissioned to The King's [Shropshire Light Infantry]. However, on 15 July 1916, he was seconded to the Royal Flying Corps, as promulgated in issue 29698 of the paper published on 8 August 1916. Additional information concerning this officer appears in my summary for 1st July 1918.

* No 23 Squadron was based at the time at Bertangles. Handed over in Paris as 'S4558' on 1 March 1918, the SPAD was delivered to No 23 Squadron on the 18th of that month, by which time it had received the airframe serial 'B6875'.

24 Squadron	2Lt J Palmer	Safe
SE.5a C9609		

T/o Conteville for an offensive patrol and wrecked while forced landing on the aerodrome, owing to engine failure. Intended for No 84 Squadron at Bertangles, I suspect the issue date of 8 April 1918 was a 'paper' issue for the 'C9609' arrived at Conteville and No 24 Squadron the next day.

25 Squadron	2Lt F F Keen	Injured	Unemployed list 10 June 1919: Lt
DH.4 A8058	2Lt W Rudman MC	Safe	See 21 April 1918 - 25 Squadron

T/o Ruisseauville tasked for a reconnaissance of road and rail lines of communication and wrecked in a forced landing, 'A8058' running into a shell hole near Acquin. Second Lieutenant Rudman had been attached from the Wiltshire Regiment. Twenty-four hours hence and he would be making *'neue Freunde'*.

35 Squadron	2Lt C M Sonnenberg	Safe	See 18 September 1918 - 35 Squadron
FK.8 C8543	[South Africa]		
	Lt A J Rose	Safe	

T/o Poulainville tasked for artillery observation. On return, and landing, ran into pickets supporting hangar ropes; damaged beyond repair. This was the squadron's tenth loss since the 1st, all being while engaged on operations and, thankfully, without any fatalities.

| 40 Squadron | Lt R G Landis USAS | Safe |
| SE.5a D3510 | | |

T/o 1235 Brauy for a line patrol and when over the Bois de Pachaut became embroiled in a combat with a couple of Albatros C-type two-seat biplanes. Coordinated fire from the two enemy aircraft damaged the SE.5a so badly that though Lieutenant Landis was able to land safely an hour after departing, 'D3510' was in such a sorry state that it was struck off charge a week later.

| 46 Squadron | 2Lt E R Watt | Safe |
| F.1 Camel C6722 | | |

T/o Filescamp for an offensive patrol. On return to base levelled off too high and stalled. Salvaged, but struck on 25 April 1918, as not worth repairing. 'C6722' had been on squadron strength since 23 March 1918.

| 49 Squadron | Lt B W Robinson | pow | |
| DH.9 D5578 | Sgt T Wills | + | Tyne Cot Cemetery |

T/o Petite Synthe for an operational sortie and when over the Belgian province of West-Vlaanderen came under sustained attack from six enemy scouts whose fire wounded the pilot and mortally injured his observer. It appears that despite his wounds Brian Wilfred Robinson was able to crash-land at a remote spot known locally as Keyem*which according to *Google Maps* lies north-northwest from Diksmuide and to the right of the N369. Both Lieutenant Robinson and twenty-nine year old Thomas Wills joined No 49 Squadron on 26 November 1917; his service number '11483' indicates he enlisted in the Royal Flying Corps at some time in 1915.

* Along with Keyem the location 'Lake Ghistelle' is mentioned but as far as I am aware no such lake exists in Belgium.

| 55 Squadron | 2Lt H E Townsend | Safe | See 21 May 1918 - 55 Squadron |
| DH.4 A7578 | Airman W C Taylor | Safe | |

T/o Tantonville for formation flying practice; stalled and crashed almost immediately.

| 56 Squadron | 2Lt A M Clermont | Safe | Unemployed list 29 September 1919: Lt |
| SE.5a B35 | | | |

T/o Valheureux for an offensive patrol but was forced to abort owing to an inability to keep up with the rest of the patrol. A technical examination concluded this was down to the age of the aircraft [sent to France, crated, via the port of Newhaven on 6 October 1917] which had been accepted by the squadron on *Guido Fawkes* day 1917, and since when had flown for a total of one hundred and twenty-six hours and twenty-five minutes.

| 56 Squadron | 2Lt H K Mulroy | Safe | See 18 June 1918 - 56 Squadron |
| SE.5a D237 | | | |

T/o Valheureux for practice flying which ended with a misjudged landing, damaging 'D237' beyond repair.

| 59 Squadron | 2Lt T A Royds | + | Toutencourt Communal Cemetery |
| RE.8 A3654 | | | |

T/o Vert Galand authorised for flying practice; force-landed and ran into a field kitchen, whereupon it burst into flames.

| 74 Squadron | Lt J R Piggott | Safe | Unemployed list 5 March 1919: Lt |
| SE.5a C1080 | | | |

T/o Clairmarais for an offensive patrol; damaged beyond repair when on return Lieutenant Piggott crashed while landing. 'C1080' arrived with the squadron when working up for the Western Front at London Colney. It flew for a total of twenty-three hours and twenty-five minutes.

79 Squadron	2Lt A S Colquhoun	Injured	St Pol British Cemetery, St Pol-sur-Ternoise
5F.1 Dolphin D5201			

T/o Beauvais authorised for practice flying; stalled at one hundred feet after losing flying speed; crashed.

81 Squadron	Lt C S Williams USAS	+
F.1 Camel C8209		

T/o Scampton for a training flight; broke apart in a spin.

83 Squadron	2Lt G W Higgs	Injured
FE.2b A5605	2Lt P A Bankes*	Injured

T/o Franqueville tasked for a raid on Armentières. Returning to base lost engine power and crashed while attempting an emergency landing.

* I am reasonably confident that this may be Percival Abbott Bankes, late of the Royal West Kent Regiment, who was awarded the Military Cross on 9 January 1918, supplement 30466; *'For conspicuous gallantry and devotion to duty during a hostile attack on our trenches. It was his steadiness and coolness during three hours' bombardment and during the actual attack that encouraged the men to put up such a stout resistance. He was the life and soul of the defence, and wherever the men appeared to waver he was there and encouraging them to hold out. When our men were driven out of the saps he at once attacked and recaptured all the saps except one. His quick grasp of the situation proved him to be a most valuable and gallant officer.'* Buried at Brockley Cemetery is a Lieutenant P A Banks MC of the Royal Air Force who died on the 22nd of February 1919. There are no next of kin or age information appended.

84 Squadron	Captain E H Tatton	+	Picquigny British Cemetery
SE.5a D270	A mention in a despatch		

T/o Bertangles and shot down at around 0715 over the Somme near Glisy, eight km east of Amiens, by anti-aircraft fire. Eric Hudson Tatton, formerly of the East Yorkshire Regiment, was appointed as a flight commander, and to be ranked temporary captain while so employed, on the 1st of August 1917 [*gazetted* 18 August 1917, supplement 30238]. From Edgware in Middlesex his father had entered Holy Orders.

205 Squadron	2Lt R C Day	Injured
DH.4 E4624	Sgt S M MacKay	Injured

T/o Bois de Roche briefed for a bombing raid which was subsequently aborted owing to inclement weather conditions. On return to the airfield, and landing, one of the bombs fell off and exploded, setting light to the DH which was completely wrecked. Both airmen had been involved in a serious crash on 12 April 1918, during which their aircraft was wrecked.

206 Squadron	Lt E J Stedman	Safe	Unemployed list 28 February 1919: Lt
DH.9 B7589	Airman C G Smith	Safe	

T/o Alquines along with other ordered for a raid; crashed on landing.

213 Squadron	Lt F L Cattle	Injured See 29 June 1918 - 213 Squadron
F.1 Camel B3782		

T/o Bergues and on return to the airfield flew into a ridge on landing; wrecked. On 13 July 1917, 'B3782' was issued ex-Dover storage to No 3 Squadron Royal Naval Air Service and in the coming months was frequently in action; however, on 20 November the Camel was returned to Dover and following storage was issued to the Seaplane Defence Squadron on 12 January 1918, this unit being titled No 13 Squadron Royal Naval Air Service three days later and in turn becoming No 213 Squadron on the 1st of April. Throughout its time with active units it saw extensive action, including an attack, with other Camels, on a U-boat which was forced to submerge east of the North Middelkerke Bouy on the 23rd of February. In the capable hands of various pilots it shared in the destruction of at least eight enemy aircraft, including seaplanes. Originally from the London borough of Hornsey, Frank Leonard Cattle was educated at Christ's Hospital School and at the Imperial College of Science and Technology South Kensington.

Sunday 21 April 1918

On this day the best known air 'Ace' of all time Manfred Albrecht Freiherr von Richthofen known the world over as '*The Red Baron*' died. My account of his passing, as published in *The Downsman*, February 2017, reads: '*The precise identity of the claimant for his death on the 21st of April 1918 over the départment of the Somme at Morlancourt Ridge near the village of Vaux-sur-Somme east of Amiens has occupied the minds of war historians for many years. What is not in dispute is that he sustained a mortal wound as he pursued at low level a No 209 Squadron Camel flown by Canadian born Lieutenant Wilfred May. The plight of Wilfred May, a relative novice, had been spotted by a fellow Canadian, Captain Roy Brown who dived steeply to attack the triplane, reporting later that he had to pull up steeply to avoid flying into the ground. By this time Manfred was extremely low and was over an area held by Australian infantry who immediately engaged the fast-flying Fokker DrI and it was at this point that Manfred was hit, the bullet entering below his right armpit and causing massive internal damage to his chest. With his life ebbing away he executed a forced-landing in a field close to where the Australians had seconds before poured round after round in his direction. Immediately, there was a rush to see if the pilot was alive and it seems Manfred was conscious when lifted from the cockpit. Some say his last word was "kaput" and so died 'The Red Baron' with eighty combat victories scored between the 17th of September 1916 and the 20th of April 1918, on which day he shot down two Sopwith Camels from No 3 Squadron, his final victim surviving to become a prisoner of war.*' When it was realised that the relatively undamaged aircraft was that of von Richthofen souvenir hunters as well as personnel charged with dismantling the Fokker reduced the airframe to components, few of which survive; however, as reported in the February 2017 issue of *Britain at War* [a Key publication which I have pleasure in acknowledging] a fuel tank stored in Australia's National Aviation Museum at Moorabbin Airport is believed to be one of the items removed from the Triplane. A photograph of this item along with photographs contemporary to the time are published on page 14 of the aforementioned magazine. And, as Trevor Henshaw writes in his analysis of Western Front losses, the news of Manfred's death spread to all corners of the Front, the men of his *Jagdgeschwader* were stunned to the quick, for it was recognised that not only had Germany suffered the loss of a great exponent of air fighting, but '*also a tactician and leader of exceeding skill.*'

1 Squadron	Lt E E Owen	Safe	See 12 June 1918 - 1 Squadron
SE.5a B570			

T/o Clairmarais for an air test. On return to the airfield the wind was gusting strongly making for a difficult landing which, in the event, ended with 'B570' on its back, turned over by a violent gust moments after touching down. Lieutenant Owen crawled from beneath unharmed but 'B570' with thirty-seven hours and thirty-eight minutes of flying behind it was struck off charge at No 1 Advanced Salvage Dump four days later. Arriving on the Western Front in the early autumn of 1917, and issued on 15 October to No 40 Squadron at Bruay it set out on a special patrol on 28 December with Second Lieutenant John Wilson Wallwork in command. Historian and author David Gunby takes up the story as he comments on pages 41 and 42 of his No 40 Squadron history of the problems encountered if the Foster mounting for the Lewis gun was incorrectly fitted; '*... it could slide back to hit the pilot on the head...and on 28 December it happened to Wallwork, who had just driven down an enemy aircraft out of control. The casualty report notes that the pilot was 'partially stunned by the Lewis gun falling on his head' and 'admitted to hospital with bruises to face and body and suffering from slight concussion.'* The near unconscious John Wallwork force-landed near Divion in the Pas-de-Calais, eight km southwest of Béthune. Commissioned to the General List of the Royal Flying Corps on 20 April 1917 [*gazetted* 6 June 1917, supplement 30117]. Recovered, and with his spirit undiminished, he went on to gain the Military Cross, promulgated in supplement 30813 of 26 July 1918; '*For conspicuous gallantry and devotion to duty. During recent operations he participated in many offensive and low-flying and bombing attacks, and carried them out with great courage and determination. From very low altitudes he bombed enemy troops and transport, inflicting heavy casualties. He caused, while on offensive patrol, more than one enemy machine to crash, and brought down others out of control. He set a magnificent example of courage and skill.*' John Wallwork was appointed to a permanent commission on 1 August 1919. In 1922, he took part in the Royal Air Force Pageant at Hendon, while earlier in the year at the Martlesham Heath dinner, *Flight* reports that in the short musical programme that followed the meal, he played '... *some lively tunes and popular choruses.*' Sadly, before the year was out he was dead, fatally injured after taking off from Gloster's factory at Brockworth on 18 December 1922, to deliver the Gloster Nightjar J6930 to Martlesham Heath, crashing owing to engine failure. Taken to Wooden Lodge Nursing Home in Gloucester, John Wilson Wallwork died later in the day.

1 Squadron	Lt H B Winton	+	Longuenesse [St Omer] Souvenir Cemetery
SE.5a D280			

T/o Clairmarais for an offensive patrol but while climbing away collided with an RE.8 and crashed on the airfield's perimeter, bursting into flames on impact. 'D280' had been on squadron charge for just four days. Harold Barkley Winton's entry in the cemetery register is extensive; educated at Sittingbourne and Shrewsbury School, Harold went up to Cambridge [Magdalene College] from where he enlisted in 1914 and served for three years as a private soldier with the 16th Battalion Middlesex Regiment in whose service he was wounded. In 1917, he was accepted by the Royal Flying Corps. It is further noted he was an Exhibitioner and Bachelor of Arts by proxy 1915. To this I am able to add that he was confirmed in the rank of temporary second lieutenant on 26 February 1918, as *gazetted* in supplement 30600 of the paper published on 27 March 1918.

12 Squadron	2Lt H R Caffyn	Safe
RE.8 B4051	2Lt W A Armit	Safe

T/o Soncamp having being briefed for an artillery observation duty. Flying at seven thousand five hundred feet over Boyelles in the Pas-de-Calais the RE attracted the attention of no less than eight enemy aircraft and, subsequently, was driven down to a forced landing near Simencourt, some seventeen km away to the north-northwest. Commissioned to the Royal Flying Corp, Second Lieutenant Caffyn's appointment was confirmed on 26 November 1917, as promulgated in supplement 30426 of the *Gazette* published on 11 December 1917.

15 Squadron	2Lt G A Penny	Injured
RE.8 C5046	2Lt H Atkinson	Injured

T/o 0800 Vert Galand for a photographic reconnaissance mission and five minutes later having climbed to one hundred feet stalled and spun to the ground. On impact the RE went up in flames. Second Lieutenant Penny was seriously injured, his observer less so, both, I believe, recovering in due course. Arriving with the squadron on 7 March 1918, 'C5046, flew for a total of sixty-three hours, though Army Form W 3347 [sent by Andrew Pentland] indicates engine running time as sixty-nine hours and twenty minutes.

18 Squadron	2Lt C W Snook	Safe	See 27 September 1918 - 18 Squadron
DH.4 A7700	2Lt B Tussaud	Safe	See 20 April 1918 - 18 Squadron

T/o Serny ordered for bombing duties and when landing in a cross-wind dropped onto its starboard wheel, ballooned back into the air and on its second arrival the undercarriage collapsed. An outline of the pilot's service is reported in the summary for the previous day.

20 Squadron	Lt C G Lankin	Safe	See 25 April 1918 - 20 Squadron
Bristol F.2b B1108	Lt J W McHattie	Safe	See 25 April 1918 - 20 Squadron

T/o Boisdinghem for an offensive patrol and on return wrecked owing to a poorly judged landing. James William McHattie was commissioned from the ranks to The York and Lancaster Regiment with effect from 21 December 1915 [*gazetted* 30 December 1915, supplement 29420].

24 Squadron	2Lt T T B Hellett	Injured
SE.5a B633		

T/o Conteville for an offensive patrol during*which Second Lieutenant dived steeply, pulled up, zoomed and as he arrived at about two thousand feet the engine 'cut'. Maintaining a semblance of control he force-landed in a ploughed field where the SE.5a promptly turned over. Relatively unscathed, Second Lieutenant Hellett was treated for facial cuts. 'B633' arrived with the squadron on the 24th of March 1918, following previous service with No 41 Squadron. Taken to No 2 Advanced Salvage Dump, it was struck off charge on 3 May 1918, with seventy-two hours and ten minutes flying recorded.

* Andrew Pentland has forwarded a copy of Army Form W 3347 where the location for the patrol is shown as being over the Fourth Army [General Sir Henry Rawlinson] front. Despite extensive damage, a recommendation was made that 'B633' be sent to No 2 Advanced Salvage Dump for repair, though no movement data appears after the 21st of April 1918.

| 24 Squadron | Lt E G McMurtrie | Safe | See 14 May 1918 - 24 Squadron |
| SE.5a B8411 | | | |

T/o Conteville for a practice flight and written off following engine failure and a misjudged forced landing near the airfield. On squadron charge since 16 March 1918, 'B8411' with Second Lieutenant R T Mark at the controls drove down a Pfalz near Ramicourt [Aisne] in the early evening of the next day; then at around the same time on the 23rd with Second Lieutenant P J Nolan in command a Rumpler was shared with two other SE.5s.

| 25 Squadron | 2Lt C J Fitzgibbon | pow | Unemployed list 11 April 1919: Lt |
| DH.4 A7563 O | 2Lt W Rudman MC | pow | See 20 April 1918 - 18 Squadron |

T/o Ruisseauville with orders to reconnoitre Valenciennes-Busigny, a distance of about forty-two km with Busigny almost directly south of Valenciennes. Reported down between the start point of the reconnaissance and Cambrai. Notification that both officers were in German hands appeared in *Flight* May 23 and July 25, 1918 respectively. 'A7563' was issued to No 57 Squadron on 7 August 1917 and over a period of just ten days shot down four enemy aircraft, all Albatros types and all claimed by Major E G Joy*and Lieutenant F Leathley*. Their first success came during the early evening of the 16th [the DH was over the Forêt d'Houthulst**] followed early next morning by three more during operations Kortrijk-Menin. This last engagement ended with the DH being force-landed with its engine shot through. Following repairs and storage it went to No 25 Squadron on 10th March 1918.

* Major E G Joy of Canadian Local Forces was appointed flight commander in the rank of major on 1 September 1917 [*gazetted* 28 September 1917, issue 30318], while Lieutenant Forde Leathley was one of a large number of officers selected for permanent commissions on 1 August 1919, in their rank, and *gazetted* that day, issue 31486. Concerning Forde's early service, which began before the outbreak of the *Great War,* he was commissioned as a second lieutenant to the Special Reserve of Army Officers [Infantry], his appointment being confirmed on 24 July 1914 [*gazetted* that day in issue 28852] with his battalion named at the 5th Battalion, The Prince of Wales's Leinster Regiment [Royal Canadians]. Following his attachment to the Royal Flying Corps he was awarded a Military Cross published on page 282 and 283 of the Supplement to *The London Gazette* January 10, 1918; *'For conspicuous gallantry and devotion to duty in making photographic reconnaissances and in fighting enemy aircraft. Since April he has taken part in numerous combats, during which seven hostile machines have been driven down and destroyed either by him of his Pilot, and although attacked in superior numbers of the enemy, his skill and offensive spirit have enabled him to carry out photographic reconnaissances.'* As noted earlier, Lieutenant Leathley was appointed to a permanent commission and it is known that he was sent out to Egypt in 1924 on posting to the Aircraft Depot on 21 June; however, the following January and with effect from the 27th, he was placed on the retired list. Then, in 1940, he returned to military service, not as one might have expected with the Royal Air Force but as a lieutenant attached to the King's Royal Rifle Corps and given the service number '152043'. There are eleven *Gazette* entries featuring this service number, but apart from his entry in issue 34992 published on 12 November 1940, the rest concern Squadron Leader John Charles Salvidant who retired at his own request on 28 March 1974. There are several interesting websites featuring Forde Leathley many of which show his birth as 17 February 1896 at Trillick in County Tyrone and his death at Cannes on the French Rivera on 25 August 1982.

** Houthulst Forest has its place in the history of the *Great War* for it was from near here on the 22nd of April 1915, that the poison gas released from enemy positions was used for the first time. There are a number of websites devoted to this first gas attack, one concerning the forest itself being of particular interest; written by Rob Ruggenberg and titled 'The Abomination of Houthulst' it has been translated into English by Ron Rowell.

| 25 Squadron | 2Lt J D Dingwall | + | Aire Communal Cemetery |
| DH.4 A8078 *Bombay No 1* | Lt C M Sinclair | Injured | |

T/o 1215 Ruisseauville for bombing operations during which the crew came under sustained attack from enemy scouts, reported as ten in total. At some stage John David Dingwall [commissioned to the General List of the Royal Flying Corps on 2 August 1917, issue 30249 published on 24 August 1917] was mortally wounded and died in the air. With consummate skill, and despite himself suffering painful wounds, Lieutenant Sinclair managed to effect a forced landing at Serny. It seems, thankfully, that he made a good recovery.

25 Squadron   DH.4   D8375   While parked on the airfield at Ruisseauville damaged beyond repair after being hit by the DH summarised below.

| 25 Squadron | 2Lt S Jones | Safe |
| DH.4 D9240 | Cpl H Edwards | Safe |

T/o Ruisseauville and on return from an operational flight crashed into D8375 [see above].

| 32 Squadron | 2Lt C J Howson* | Safe |
| SE.5a B164 | | |

T/o Beauvois for an offensive patrol and crashed at Choques when attempting an emergency landing owing to problems with the oil pressure. Earlier in the month, on the 7th, Second Lieutenant Howson sent down a Fokker DrI near Dumuin.

* On the 5th of July 1918, a Lieutenant Charles James Howson attached to No 95 Squadron at Shotwick was killed when struck accidentally by the propellor of Avro 504 D7068. He is buried in Liverpool [Anfield] Cemetery. Whether or not they are one and the same person, I am not able to say for certain.

| 53 Squadron | Lt E H N Stroud | + | Sanctuary Wood Cemetery |
| RE.8 C5037 | Captain C G White MC | + | Sanctuary Wood Cemetery |

T/o Clairmarais for an operational sortie over the Ypres Salient. Eric Hubert Noel Stroud was late of the Leicestershire Regiment; his observer, Cecil Godfrey White was formerly of the Royal Field Artillery and details of his service and the citation for his award may be read in my summary for his narrow escape on the 11th of April 1918, when he was acting as observer for Lieutenant R D Best.

| 54 Squadron | Lt R J Marion [Canadian] | + | Arras Flying Services Memorial |
| F.1 Camel B9315 | | | |

T/o 1140 Clairmarais for an offensive patrol and was last observed flying at three thousand feet over the Nord *département* near Estaires. Robert Jameson Marion, age nineteen and from Edmonton in Alberta, had abandoned his studies at the College of Dental Surgeons, Toronto, in order to play his part in the *Great War*, initially attached [November 1917] to the Canadian Dental Corps, an attachment that could have only lasted for a matter of weeks.

| 54 Squadron | Lt C J Mason | + | Arras Flying Services Memorial |
| F.1 Camel D6569 | | | |

T/o 1140 Clairmarais similarly charged and was last seen fighting hard with eight Fokker DrI scouts over Bailleul [Nord] and is thought to have fallen to the west of the town and between the two opposing lines of battle. Cecil John Mason had been involved in a landing accidents on the first, third and fourth days of the month when the squadron was operating from Conteville. The squadron's operational losses for the month now stood at twenty.

| 57 Squadron | 2Lt H Erskine | Safe | |
| DH.4 A7618 | Lt W A B Eastwood | Safe | Unemployed list 21 February 1919: Lt |

T/o Le Quesnoy for an operational sortie and almost immediately was obliged to force-land near the airfield owing to engine failure.

| 59 Squadron | Captain J S Green | Safe | |
| RE.8 C4566 | Lt J B V Clements | Safe | Unemployed list 17 November 1919: Lt DFC |

T/o Vert Galand for an air test and damaged beyond repair when the undercarriage snagged against an isolated tent on the airfield. 'C4566' arrived with the squadron, then at Lealvilliers, on 28 March 1918.

74 Squadron   Lt C E L Skedden [USA]   Safe   See 8 May 1918 - 74 Squadron
SE.5a D269
T/o Clairmarais for an offensive patrol; shot through and damaged beyond repair in a forced landing near Ste Marie Cappel airfield. Charles Edwin Lloyd Skedden from Minneapolis and formerly of the 173rd Battalion, Canadian Infantry, receives a number of mentions in the late Wing Commander Ira Jones book *'Tiger Squadron'* published in 1954, by W H Allen. Numerous copies remain available through a range of bookshops specialising in second-hand books, many of those currently advertised being reasonably priced.

74 Squadron   Lt S C H Begbie   Injured Lille Southern Cemetery
SE.5a D281
T/o 1720 Clairmarais similarly tasked and shot down, in flames, near Armentières. Twenty-one year old Sydney Claude Hamilton Begbie was pulled alive from the wreckage but succumbed to his terrible burns twenty-four hours later. His service life started when commissioned to the East Surrey Regiment and attached to the 3rd Battalion. Sydney was seconded to the Royal Flying Corps on 15 July 1916 [*gazetted* in supplement 29693 of 3rd August 1916].

80 Squadron   2Lt A L Code   Injured
F.1 Camel B4617
T/o 0850 La Bellevue for an offensive patrol and was forced down, with a wounded pilot, near Mercatel in the Pas-de-Calais some seven km south-southeast of Arras and a mere fifty metres or so inside the Allied lines.

82 Squadron   2Lt J Sangster   Safe   See 7 July 1918 - 82 Squadron
FK.8 C8483   Lt J S C Robinson   Safe
T/o Agenvilliers for an offensive patrol and on return overshot the landing area and ran on to rough ground; damaged beyond repair. Accepted by the squadron on 24 March 1918, 'C8433' accumulated fifty-two hours and fifty-five minutes of flying. Under the heading 'Territorial Forces', J S C Robinson of the Yorkshire Regiment was confirmed in his appointment as second lieutenant on 6 December 1916 [*gazetted* the same day, supplement 29850]. Postwar, he was appointed to a permanent commission but this was cancelled with effect from 21 October 1919, as promulgated in issue 31610 of that date. However, he was granted a short service commission, as an observer officer, on 28 November 1919, issue 31663.

84 Squadron   Lt C L Stubbs   Safe
SE.5a C5397
T/o Bertangles for an offensive patrol and damaged beyond repair here when the engine 'cut' as Lieutenant Stubbs attempted to land across the prevailing wind. 'C5397' arrived from No 2 Air Issues as recently as the 6th of April. Charles Lionel Stubbs was made a second lieutenant [temporary] from cadetship on 24 May 1917, and attached [with a host of others] to the General List of the Royal Flying Corps [*gazetted* 20 June 1917, supplement 30141]. Like so many of his generation the ominous situation facing our country in the late 1930s prompted him to return to the service and, subsequently, he was commissioned Pilot Officer on probation on the 21st of February 1939, in the Administrative and Special Duties Branch. Charles Stubbs served until relinquishing his commission on 17 August 1954, under the Provisions of the Navy, Army and Air Force Reserves Act 1954. Now of wing commander rank and appointed Commander of the British Empire he was permitted to retain his acting rank of air commodore.

89 Squadron   2Lt W E H Blyth   Injured Norwich Cemetery, Norfolk
Pup B5306   [South Africa]
T/o Harling Road for a training flight and on landing touched down at high speed. Moments later the undercarriage collapsed and 'B5306' turned over with considerable violence. Freed from the wreckage, nineteen year old Wilfred Ernest Hill Blyth was taken to hospital where he died the next day from his injuries; he was from Barkly West in South Africa's Cape Province famed for its diamond mining industries. His entry in the cemetery register incorrectly shows him as being attached to No 88 Squadron.

101 Squadron   2Lt A C Hine   Injured
FE.2b B453   2Lt H J Townson   +   Abbeville Communal Cemetery extension

T/o Famechon tasked for bombing but struck first one of the landing lights and then crashed against a telegraph pole. Herbert Johnston Townson had been attached from the 15th Battalion West Yorkshire Regiment [Prince of Wales's Own].

202 Squadron*   Lt G H Whitmill   +   Dunkirk Town Cemetery
DH.4 D1754
T/o Bergues for practice flying and crashed moments later, bursting into flames on impact. Although not traced via *The London Gazette,* nineteen year old George Harris Whitmill was appointed as a probationary flight officer in July 1917 [*Flight* August 9, 1917] as per Admiralty orders. The loss of this aircraft was the squadron's first since the establishment of the Royal Air Force on the 1st of April 1918.

* Renumbered from No 2 Squadron Royal Naval Air Service on the 1st of April, '202' at the time was equipped with both the DH.4 and DH.9. Unlike many of the Western Front squadrons which moved to various aerodromes twixt the merger of the air arms and the armistice, No 202 Squadron remained at Bergues throughout.

203 Squadron   2Lt D L Bawlf [Canada]   +   Aire Communal Cemetery
F.1 Camel B3795
T/o Lièttres for formation flying practice and while lingering at five hundred feet for the rest of the Camels to join him he lost control and sideslipped to the ground. From Winnipeg his headstone carries the inscription; *'His Life For His Friends Winnipeg, Canada.'*

204 Squadron   F.1 Camel B3856   Reported as crashed and completely wrecked; location and identity of the pilot is, at present, unknown. At the time the squadron was based at Téteghem in the *département du Nord*.

Monday 22 April 1918
A day of continued fierce fighting on the ground while the Royal Navy made their final preparations for the night attacks on Zeebrugge and Oostende.

1 Squadron   Lt R B Donald   Injured Commission relinquished 9 March 1919: Lt
SE.5a B4851
T/o Clairmarais having been briefed for an offensive patrol but while travelling at speed had to make an emergency swerve in order to avoid colliding with a squadron colleague. Moments later Lieutenant Donald cartwheeled out of control and 'B4851' was damaged beyond repair. Despatched to France in a crate it was the first aircraft in a batch of fifty SE.5as ordered from The Royal Aircraft Factory Farnborough, and initially went to No 56 Squadron [10 August 1917] being active over Ypres Salient until a crash on the 14th of September, necessitated salvage and repair. These completed it arrived with No 1 Squadron on 19th January.

2 Squadron   2Lt R Allan   +   Noeux-les-Mines Communal Cemetery extn
FK.8 D5005   2Lt C Sheil   +   Noeux-les-Mines Communal Cemetery extn
T/o Hesdigneul for an artillery observation patrol and was brought down circa 1830 near Le Brebis after being hit by anti-aircraft fire. Charles Sheil of Dublin was commissioned to the Royal Munster Fusiliers on the 1st of March 1917 [*gazetted* in supplement 30118 published on 7 June 1917]; he had escaped unharmed two days previously when his aircraft ran into a ditch during take off [see my summary for the 20th]. The deaths of this crew marked the first from the squadron since the 1st of April 1918.

2 Squadron AusFC   Lt E D Cummings   Safe   See 3 May 1918 - 2 Squadron AusFC
SE.5a D3924
T/o Fouquerolles for an offensive patrol but, subsequently, had to force-land on, or near, the airfield at Treizennes owing to a severe petrol leakage. The damage was such that 'D3924' was struck off charge as not worth repairing at No 2 Advanced Salvage Dump on the 4th of May 1918. It had been delivered to Fouquerolles from No 2 Air Issues as recently as 7 April.

4 Squadron   Lt F W McChesney   Safe
RE.8 C2276   2Lt J C Stack [USA]   Safe   See 30 April 1918 - 4 Squadron

91

T/o St Omer for an offensive patrol during which the RE attracted the hostile attention of a quintet of enemy aircraft. Despite their best endeavours they were unable to drive down the two-seater which returned to St Omer, shot about to a degree that repairs were deemed to be not worth the effort. On charge since 28 March 1918, it had logged forty-eight hours and five minutes of flying.

4 Squadron AusFC	Lt L A Storch AusFC	+	Lapugnoy Military Cemetery
F.1 Camel D6584			

T/o Bruay to conduct an air test and practice flying. It appears that a target had been spread out on the airfield and it was while diving towards this that Louis Albert Storch, twenty-three years of age and from Ambleside in South Australia realised he had seriously misjudged his speed and height. Attempting to recover, he pulled back with such violence that structural failure of the wings resulted and the Camel plunged into the ground. His body was taken five km northwards to his resting place; 'D6584' had flown into Bruay from No 1 Air Issues twenty-four hours previously.

7 Squadron	Lt D W M Miller	Safe	
RE.8 B6467 *Punjab 48 Beas*	2Lt R Lean	Safe	

T/o Droglandt having being briefed to carry out a *Flash* reconnaissance. On return to base, crashed and damaged beyond repair. Taken on squadron charge 24 September 1917, this presentation aircraft had logged a very useful two hundred and twenty-nine hours and twenty-five minutes flying, most of which would have been on operations.

8 Squadron	Lt F M F West	Safe	See 10 August 1918 - 8 Squadron
FK.8 C8445	2Lt J A G Haslam	Safe	See 10 August 1918 - 8 Squadron

T/o Auxi-le-Château for an anti-artillery patrol during which the FK was bracketed by anti-aircraft fire and to his concern Lieutenant West saw his ailerons being shot away. Maintaining control he force-landed, his aircraft now beyond repair. Accepted on 23 March 1918, it had flown for a total of forty-eight hours and fifty-five minutes. Formerly of the Royal Field Artillery, a non-digitised document for this officer is held at The National Archives under WO 339/56117. Additional notes pertaining to these officers are reported in my summary for the 10th of August.

12 Squadron	2Lt N Garland	Safe	
RE.8 B5894	2Lt G Terry	Safe	

T/o Soncamp with orders to conduct a photographic reconnaissance mission during the course of which the engine failed with the crew flying at seven hundred feet over Boisleux-au-Mont in the Pas-de-Calais. Now in a glide, 'B5894' continued in a northwesterly direction for about four km before coming down near Ficheux where it became entangled in barbed wire. Initially operated by No 15 Squadron [from 15 October 1917] it was shot about while on an artillery patrol on 20 November, the crew, Second Lieutenant G W Armstrong and his observer Second Lieutenant R Kearton, landing at Léchelle*aerodrome. Repaired, it arrived at the then squadron's base of Mons-en-Chaussée from No 2 Air Issues on 26 February 1918.

* Léchelle was used at various times by Nos 3 and 15 Squadrons. However, the German offensive of March 1918, witnessed the withdrawal of the Royal Flying Corps and the arrival of *Jagdgeschwader 1*. Then, in October 1918, it was the turn of the German Air Force to withdraw and the Royal Air Force reoccupied the aerodrome with Nos 3 and 15 Squadrons returning, and briefly it accommodated No 56 Squadron.

12 Squadron	2Lt C D Proudfoot [BWI]	+	Bac-du-Sud British Cemetery, Bailleulval
RE.8 C2255	2Lt R S Craig	+	Bac-du-Sud British Cemetery, Bailleulval

T/o No 2 Air Issues but having climbed to about one hundred and fifty feet and banking went into a steep dive from which it failed to recover. On impact the RE, which was being collected, burst into flames. Robert Stewart Craig was nineteen years of age, his pilot, Cyril Dallas Proudfoot of Kingstown in the British West Indies, had been commissioned to the South Nottinghamshire Hussars, a Yeomanry Territorial Forces unit from which he was seconded for duty with the Royal Flying Corps on 18 February 1918 [*gazetted* 26 March 1918, supplement 30596].

19 Squadron   2Lt J D Hardman   Injured
5F.1 Dolphin C4048
T/o Savy for an offensive patrol during which pressure was lost and Second Lieutenant Hardman [his injuries are described as 'slight'] was obliged to make an unscheduled landing near Hersin*sustaining damage which ended the flying life of 'C4048'. Accepted by the squadron on 28 March 1918, this Dolphin logged fourteen hours and thirty-one minutes flying.

* Possibly Hersin-Coupigny in the Pas-de-Calais, ten km west-northwest of the coal mining centre of Lens.

20 Squadron   Sgt Stansfield   Safe
Bristol F.2b C4802
T/o Boisdinghem for flying practice but made rather a hash of his landing and as a consequence the Bristol was damaged beyond repair. 'C4802' had flown sixty-nine hours and twenty minutes since its arrival with the squadron on 4 December 1917.

22 Squadron   2Lt F M Ward   +   Aire Communal Cemetery
Bristol F.2b C4810 *Gold Coast No 11*   Sgt A Burton   +   Aire Communal Cemetery
T/o Serny for an offensive patrol only to stall and crash with considerable force. At the Aeroplane Acceptance Park Bristol by the end of October 1917, 'C4810' arrived with the squadron on 19 January and by the time of its demise had flown, in total, for eighty-five hours and twenty-six minutes.

23 Squadron   2Lt L W Prescott   +   Arras Flying Services Memorial
SPAD S.13 B6857
T/o 1843 Bertangles for an offensive patrol and was last sighted flying on a northwesterly heading at five thousand feet over Corbie [Somme]. Lewis William Prescott, commissioned to the General List of the Royal Flying Corps, was confirmed in his rank on 5 January 1918, as published in *The London Gazette* 20 March 1918, supplement 30587.

Note. Trevor Henshaw author of *The Sky Their Battlefield* draws attention to the fact that No 23 Squadron which had commenced re-equipping in March 1918, with Sopwith Dolphin would soon be up to establishment, and the French manufactured Spads that had stood them in good stead since February 1917, would be withdrawn before the end of the month.

27 Squadron   2Lt E J Smith   Safe
DH.4 B2073   2Lt E C W Deacon   Injured Godewaersvelde British Cemetery
T/o Ruisseauville for a bombing operation during which the formation came under severe attack from at least seven Fokker DrIs, mortally wounding nineteen year old Ernest Cecil Watson Deacon. On landing he was rushed to a casualty clearing station at Godewaersvelde where he died soon after admittance. Ernest's father was the Reverend Ernest Deacon of Croxden Vicarage, Rocester in Staffordshire. 'B2073' had an eventful time while on No 27 Squadron charge; arriving at Serny on 23 November 1917 it was obliged to force-land at Bully-Grenoy in the Pas-de-Calais on the 30th, Second Lieutenant P Carr and his observer Second Lieutenant P W Plant, the latter formerly of the Notts and Derby Regiment [Sherwood Foresters], completing their journey to base the next day. Then, still at Serny, it was badly damaged on 15 December when Second Lieutenant G R Norman and Airman A Hughesden crashed on take off, the DH ending up on its back and its two occupants scrambling out with only minor cuts and bruises to show for their very fortunate escape.

29 Squadron   Lt R H Walker   Safe   See 8 May 1918 - 29 Squadron
SE.5a D3564
T/o Téteghem for a transit flight to St Omer where Lieutenant Walker landed in cross-wind conditions, lost control and crashed. 'D3564' had been on the squadron's establishment sine 11 April 1918.

29 Squadron   Lt A Bevan   Safe
SE.5A D5955

93

T/oTéteghem for a transit flight to St Omer where Lieutenant Bevan landed on uneven ground, damaging 'D5955' beyond repair; it had survived a mere four days of service with the squadron.

| 32 Squadron | 2Lt J W Trusler | Safe |
| SE.5a D273 | | |

T/o Beauvois authorised for flying practice and on return, and landing, ran into SE.5a C9612 which had landed earlier. 'C9612' was not too badly damaged but was wrecked in a take off accident on 29 June 1918 [see my summary for further details].

| 37 Squadron | 2Lt E G Mucklow | + | Stow Maries [SS Mary and Margaret] Chyd* |
| BE.12 C3240 | [Served as C L Milburn] | | |

T/o Stow Maries authorised for night flying; crashed. At the age of thirty-three, Edward Gerald Mucklow was above an age associated with frontline squadrons. Under his assumed name he flew as Second Lieutenant 'Cyril Lawson Milburn'. His death is reported in the May 16,1918 edition of *Flight* which adds; *'after over 14 months flying at the front.'* I can only assume this entry in the magazine, which appears under the banner 'Personals', was submitted by his mother, Ada Mucklow of Elton, Stone Park, Windemere.

* There are six service burials in this churchyard; five from the *Great War* and one from the Second World War, namely Group Captain Claude Alward Ridley DSO MC who at the age of forty-five most certainly saw service in the former conflict. Although I have shown 'BE.12 C3240', BE.2e B4535 is a possibility. Concerning Stow Maries, which is ten miles east of Chelmsford near Malden in Essex, it is one of only a handful of *Great War* air-fields where flying still exists[though for many years it reverted to farmland], principally in the shape of aircraft representative of that era. At the time the squadron was commanded by Major F W Honnett.

| 49 Squadron | Sgt S J Oliver | Injured |
| DH.9 C6138 | Sgt W Kelsall | Injured |

T/o Petite Synthe having received instructions for a bombing mission and was written off in most unusual circumstances for having climbed to ten thousand feet Sergeant Kelsall proceeded to test his Vickers machine-gun and while doing so he inadvertently shot away the propeller of the DH. Turning back, the propeller-less engine began to vibrate with such violence that eventually it fell from its frame. In the ensuring crash-landing both sergeants were injured, Oliver sustaining slight internal injuries while an embarrassed Kelsall was taken to hospital with a broken leg; according to the No 49 Squadron Association website he had been with the squadron since 26 November 1917.

| 84 Squadron | Sgt A Jex | Safe |
| SE.5a B637 | | |

T/o Bertangles for practice flying, an exercise that Sergeant Jex had indulged in five days previously and which ended with his SE.5a sideslipping to the ground and damaged beyond repair [see my summary], and while practising 'S' turns near the ground he lost control and crashed.

| 131 Squadron | Captain S T Saunderson | + | Shawbury [St Mary the Virgin] Churchyard |
| DH.6 C7215 | Captain N V Harrison | + | East Sheen Cemetery |

T/o Shawbury for a training flight and crashed near the airfield. Samuel Treherne Saunderson of Harristown in Co Kildare was late of the North Irish Horse. A record regarding his service is held by The National Archives under WO 339/23590, while the website The North Irish Horse in the Great War, which I have pleasure in acknowledging, has a comprehensive overview on his service with the army and later the flying services. Following flying instruction he served first with No 17 Squadron and with the squadron saw active service against Turkish forces both in the Sinai Desert and in Egypt's Western Desert. Between January 1916, and his attachment to No 131 Squadron which formed at Shawbury as a night bomber unit on the 1st of March 1918, he served with various units as a flying instructor.

| 201 Squadron | Captain G A Magor [Canada] | + | Arras Flying Services Memorial |
| F.1 Camel B6428 | | |

T/o 1028 Noeux for an offensive patrol and was last seen over the Somme near Hangard which is about twenty-one km southeast of Abbeville. This veteran Camel arrived with No 1 Squadron Royal Naval Air Service on the 9th of November 1917, and until becoming No 201 Squadron following the merger of the Naval and Army air arms had shot down, or shared in the destruction of, eleven hostile machines. As '201' it claimed one more, a Fokker DrI early in the afternoon of April 6th. 'B6428' was quite obviously the favoured aircraft of Captain Stanley Wallace Rosevear [see my summary for 25 April 1918] for he was at the controls for all twelve victorious combats.

| 201 Squadron | 2Lt W H Easty | + | Arras Flying Services Memorial |
| F.1 Camel N6377 | | | |

T/o 1020 Noeux for an offensive patrol and was last sighted flying near Captain Magor [see above]. First issued to No 3 Squadron Royal Naval Air Service on 16 June 1917, and named *'TIKI'*, 'N6377'. Subsequently, following maintenance in the Repair Shop at Dover, the Camel was issued to No 1 Squadron Royal Naval Air Service. Walter Harry Easty had crashed taking off for a practice flight five days previously, his Camel being repaired, but written off on 11 January 1919, in the hands of No 213 Squadron, which will be summarised in the third volume.

| 217 Squadron | Lt C F Parsons | pow |
| DH.4 A8063 | Aircraftman G S Gladwin | pow |

T/o Bergues for operations over the sea and it was while trying to bomb an enemy trawler that Lieutenant Parsons lost control and spun into the water; from here they were picked up by the crew of the vessel they were trying to sink.

Tuesday 23 April 1918

On this day the Royal Navy made an heroic attempt to deny the *Kreigsmarine* and particularly their U-boats using the Belgian port of Bruges-Zeebrugge by sinking three block-ships in the harbour entrance. In the event only two of the block-ships were scuttled and, unfortunately, not in the desired place and as a consequence of this the port was able to resume operations within a matter of days. Also, this day, the ground-attack capabilities of the Royal Air Force on the Western Front were bolstered by the arrival from Hounslow of No 87 Squadron and their Sopwith Dolphins. Commanded by Major J C Callaghan the squadron was initially lodged at St Omer, moving to Petite Synthe on the 27th of April.

Lord Rothermere, President of the Air Council, tendered his resignation, though this was not made public for several days. He had held the post since 26 November 1917 [see 26 April 1918 for his successor].

| 1 Squadron | Lt A H J Howe* | Injured |
| SE.5a C6384 | | |

T/o Clairmarais for a practice flight but almost immediately lost control and sideslipped into the nearby forest. 'C6384' had been on squadron strength for just nine days.

* Believed to be Alfred Herbert Jones How commissioned to the General List of the Royal Flying Corps on the 30th of August 1917 [*gazetted* 18 September 1917, supplement 30392] and transferred to the Unemployed List on the 16th of January 1919.

| 2 Squadron AusFC | Lt D'A K J Studdard | Safe |
| SE.5a C5382 | | |

T/o Fouquerolles and wrecked here in a heavy landing on completion of a practice flight. 'C5382' had been held by the squadron since 12 March 1918; its overall flying came to forty-four hours and forty minutes.

| 16 Squadron | 2Lt P H Sadler* | Safe | Unemployed list 30 August 1919: F/O |
| RE.8 B5892 | 2Lt G H B Richards* | Safe | |

T/o Camblain l'Abbé tasked for artillery patrol but while traveling at speed across the aerodrome collided with the RE.8 summarised below.

* Although I cannot be absolutely certain, I believe these officers to be Philip Herbert Sadler and George Henry Bruce Richards. If I am correct, then both served in the Second World War, and beyond, having received comm-

issions in the Administrative and Special Duties Branch, Sadler on 21 March 1941, and Richards on 4 July 1939. Both relinquished their commissions under the provisions of the Navy, Army and Air Force Reserves Act 1954, on 24 and 10 August 1954 respectively, both retaining their rank of flight lieutenant.

16 Squadron	Captain D J Nickle [Canada]	Injured	
RE.8 E17	Lt D L Reed	Injured	Unemployed list 7 March 1919: Lt

T/o Camblain l'Abbé similarly instructed and lost in the manner shown above. The two injured officers received slight burns, thereby indicating 'E17' went up in flames. Captain Nickle was appointed to the Royal Flying Corps in the rank of lieutenant from the Canadian Forestry Corps on the last day of August 1917 [*gazetted* 22 September 1917, supplement 30299]. He ceased to be employed with effect from 12 January 1919, as promulgated in supplement 31179 of the paper issued on 14 February 1919.

56 Squadron	Captain K W Junor MC	+	Arras Flying Services Memorial
SE.5a C1086	[Canada]		

T/o 1630 Valheureux for an offensive patrol and when last seen was in aerial combat over Bray-sur-Somme. Accepted by the squadron on the 25th of March 1918, 'C1086' was taken over by Kenneth William Junor who drove down a Fokker DrI on the 1st of April near Guillemont, followed on the 11th with an Albatros west of Aveluy, both actions taking place over the Somme, while on the 20th a he 'flamed' a Rumpler two-seater reconnaissance aircraft southwest of Puisieux in the Pas-de-Calais. From Toronto and formerly of the Canadian Machine Gun Corps, Kenneth Junor's Military Cross was posthumous, appearing in supplement 30681 of *The London Gazette* published on 10 May 1918; *'For conspicuous gallantry and devotion to duty in aerial fighting. He destroyed two enemy machines and drove down two others out of control, which crashed on landing. He always showed the greatest courage, skill and resource.'*

57 Squadron	2Lt W H Townsend [USA]	Injured	Huby-St Leu British Cemetery
DH.4 D8406	2Lt C C Souchotte	+	Huby-St Leu British Cemetery

T/o Le Quesnoy to bomb enemy positions near Bapaume [Pas-de-Calais] and when returning to base seen by other aircraft in the formation to suddenly dive away trailing flames from its engine. William Henry Townsend survived the crash but died later in the day; he hailed from Cambridge in Middlesex County, Massachusetts. A note in the cemetery register indicates he graduated from Dartmouth College in 1915. Charles Campbell Souchotte was appointed second lieutenant on probation from a cadetship on 13 November 1917 [*gazetted* 11 January 1918, issue 30473]. As far I can ascertain these were the sole squadron fatalities on the Western Front this day. Trevor Henshaw adds that Private A Mill and Mechanic J I Hardy raced to the scene of the crash, and without regard to their own safety managed to pull Second Lieutenant Townsend from the remains of the cockpit; subsequently, both were awarded the Albert Medal.

110 Squadron	Lt H V Brisbin [Canada]	Injured	Secondment ceased 24 April 1919: Lt
DH.9 C6071	Lt T Phillips	Injured	

T/o Sedgeford for a training flight only to stall and crash heavily, severely injuring Lieutenant Brisbin who had been seconded from the 1st Central Ontario Regiment.

123 Squadron	2Lt J R Wylie	+	Urmston Cemetery
DH.6 B2677			

T/o Duxford for a training flight. James Randolph Wylie was born in Belfast, though at the time of his death his parents had crossed the Irish Sea to reside in Manchester. Prior to his air force service, James was late of the Royal Dublin Fusiliers.

206 Squadron	2Lt L M Whittington	Injured	
DH.9 B7586	Private S Jones	Injured	

T/o Alquines with others for a bombing mission and when over Estaires [Nord] came under assault from half-a-dozen enemy scouts; force-landed near Busnes in the Pas-de-Calais having turned west. Both airmen are featured in my summaries for 17 April 1918.

| 210 Squadron | 2Lt A Baird | Safe |
| F.1 Camel B7221 | | |

T/o Lièttres tasked for an offensive patrol and escort duties. On return landed safely but while still running at speed a wheel sank into a rut causing the Camel to turn onto its back. A shaken, but otherwise unharmed, Second Lieutenant Baird emerged from his now wrecked machine.

Wednesday 24 April 1918

A notable day in the continuing Lys offensive with the start of a three day battle known as the *Second Battle of Villers-Bretonneux*. It was first occasion that German tanks entered the war in strength, fourteen of their twenty strong force of A7Vs being deployed and, thus, the first tank against tank encounter took place when three of the A7Vs came upon on a trio of British Mk IV tanks, two of which were 'female' armed only with machine-guns. Both 'female' tanks were shot about and had to withdraw, but the 'male' tank with its 6-pounder gun fired to good effect at the leading A7V which was quickly abandoned by its crew. At this point a number of British Whippet light tanks joined the battle and with the 'male' tank advanced until the 'male tank was disabled by enemy artillery fire and abandoned. Subsequently, both sides were able to recover their disabled assets. Meanwhile, two Australian and one British Brigade counter-attacked as night fell forcing the enemy back and partially surrounding Villers-Bretonneux. During the day, at Dover, No 218 Squadron formed as a light-bomber unit equipped with DH.9 and commanded by Major B S Wemp.

| 11 Squadron | 2Lt E W P Lamb | + | Doullens Communal Cemetery extension No 1 |
| Bristol F.2b C4673 | Sgt B J Maisey | + | Doullens Communal Cemetery extension No 1 |

T/o Remaisnil with orders to carry out a reconnaissance. Weather conditions were far from ideal and while flying at a low altitude the crew failed to see a belt of trees shrouded in fog; the resultant collision sent the Bristol down near Heuzecourt [Somme], some 27 km northeast of Abbeville. At the wishes of his parents, Edward Woollard Penistone Lamb's headstone is inscribed; *'A Good Son An Honourable Man A Workful Loss To His Home'*.

| 48 Squadron | 2Lt T G Jackson | Safe |
| Bristol F.2b A7114 | Lt A E Ansell | Safe |

T/o Bertangles for a contact patrol over Villers-Bretonneux where the crew came under sustained machine-gun fire from the ground, their Bristol absorbing so many hits that, subsequently, it was deemed not worth the cost of repair. First issued on 16 June 1917, to No 11 Squadron it was earmarked for issue to No 8 Squadron on the 29th of the month, but remained on No 11 Squadron's establishment. On 7 August, it force-landed near the Arras to Bucquoy road with the observer Second Lieutenant P Adams dangerously wounded having been shot through the spine and stomach [it would seem he recovered], while the Bristol was salvaged and sent for repair. On the 11th of October, it was taken on by No 22 Squadron only to be damaged five days later during flying practice, Second Lieutenant Charles Edgar Ferguson*escaping injury. Repaired for the second time, 'A7114' was issued to No 48 Squadron on 5 February 1918. Concerning Lieutenant Ansell, supplement 29256 of *The London Gazette* of 7 August 1915, under the heading 24th [County of London] Battalion, The London Regiment [The Queen's], shows a Private Arnold Edward Ansell from the 9th [County of London] Battalion, The London Regiment [Queen Victoria's Rifles] *gazetted* as a Second Lieutenant. Nine years later, issue 32974 of the paper under the heading 'Reserve of Air Force Officers' a Pilot Officer Arnold Edward Ansell was granted a commission in Class B, with effect from 16 September 1924. On 16 September 1933, and now ranked flying officer, he relinquished his commission on completion of service, but returned to duty on 29 August 1939, retaining his rank, and was transferred to the Administrative and Special Duties Branch. He served until 11 May 1954, when under the provisions of the Navy, Army and Air Force Reserves Act 1954, his commission was relinquished, retaining the rank of flight lieutenant. Although I cannot be certain that Private Ansell, Lieutenant Ansell and Flight Lieutenant Ansell are the same person, I suggest it is a very strong probability.

* Forty-eight hours after walking away from his flying accident, Second Lieutenant Charles Edgar Ferguson and his observer air gunner, Second Lieutenant Alexander Dick Lennox fell in action near Ingelmunster Station, their Bristol 'A7247' coming apart in the air following an attack from a Pfalz. Both rest in Sanctuary Wood Cemetery where Charles's headstone is inscribed; *'A Very Gallant Gentleman - Vivit Post Funera Virtus'*. Formerly of the

5th Battalion, Royal Scots Fusiliers, Alexander's parents requested that his headstone should carry the words; *'Faithful Until Death'*.

| 48 Squadron | 2Lt F C Ransley | Safe |
| Bristol F.2b C4886 | 2Lt C W Davies | Safe |

T/o Bertangles similarly tasked and subsequently written off through the circumstances described above. Both officers featured in my summary for 4 April 1918.

| 61 Squadron | 2Lt C A Brown | + | Edinburgh [Newington or Echo Bank] Cemetery |
| SE.5a C5339 | | | |

T/o Rochford and crashed out of control following a steep dive. The sole casualty during the period under analysis, No 61 Squadron was a Home Defence squadron and as far as can be ascertained after exchanging their Sopwith Pups in favour of SE.5a it saw no operational activity whatsoever.

| 65 Squadron | Lt H B D Harrington | pow | Unemployed list 24 October 1919: Lt |
| F.1 Camel D6436 | | | |

T/o 1120 Bertangles for an offensive patrol and when last seen was in the vicinity Villers-Bretonneux. *Flight* May 30th, 1918, lists Lieutenant Harrington as 'missing', indicating also that he was formerly on the Territorial Forces and commissioned to the London Regiment. The same magazine, July 4, 1918, states Lieutenant Harrington as believed held captive. 'D6436' arrived with the squadron on 2 April 1918.

| 82 Squadron | Lt L K W Barrett [USA] | + | Abbeville Communal Cemetery extension |
| FK.8 D5024 | 2Lt C A Procter | + | Abbeville Communal Cemetery extension |

T/o Agenvillers for an operational sortie but owing to poor visibility failed to see a line of trees into which the aircraft crashed and exploded. Leland Kelly Willson Barrett of Atlanta, Georgia had been involved in a taxying mishap at Agenvillers on the 12th of April, his observer on this occasion being identified as Second Lieutenant 'Potter' but I strongly suspect this was a misprint for 'Procter'.

| 84 Squadron | Captain A F W Beauchamp | Safe | See 28 May 1918 - 84 Squadron |
| SE.5a C1794 | Proctor [South Africa] | | |

T/o Bertangles for an offensive patrol and in the aftermath of running through intense ground fire force-landed on the Amiens to St Quentin road. For an extensive report for Captain Andrew Frederick Weatherby Beauchamp Proctor, please return to 11 April 1918, and my asterisked note for No 1 Squadron. SE.5a B597.

| 84 Squadron | Captain K A Lister Kaye | Safe |
| SE.5a C9623 | | |

T/o Bertangles similarly tasked and damaged beyond repair after being repeatedly hit by ground fire over Villers Bretonneux. On squadron charge since 13 March 1918, 'C9623' accounted for six hostile machines, all at the hands of Second Lieutenant W H Brown.

| 205 Squadron | Lt R C Day | Injured | |
| DH.4 E4624 | Sgt S M MacKay | Safe | See 9 June 1918 - 205 Squadron |

T/o Bois de Roche for a raid which was aborted owing to bad visibility. Crashed when landing, caught fire and after the crew had scrambled to safety one of the bombs exploded. Both airmen feature in a serious crash on the 1st of April 1918.

| 209 Squadron | Lt F C Stovin | + | Arras Flying Services Memorial |
| F.1 Camel B6311 | | | |

T/o 1645 Bertangles for a special mission from which nineteen year old Frederick Cecil Stovin failed to return.

Thursday 25 April 1918
Another busy day of air activity with much of the emphasis centred around Villers-Bretonneux where intense ground fighting by Australians, New Zealanders and British forces gradually forced the enemy out of the town. Heavy fighting was also reported from Kemmel Ridge where thirteen German divisions attacked, supported by a

vicious artillery bombardment and by dusk the Ridge was in enemy hands. Strengthening of the day/night bomber squadrons continued with the arrival at St Omer of No 99 Squadron which since August 1917, had been working up, initially at Yatesbury but latterly at Old Sarum with a variety of types before received DH.9s just weeks before their deployment to France. During this time the squadron had three commanding officers with their fourth, Major H MacD O'Malley now leading them for operations over the Western Front.

| 2 Squadron | 2Lt P F Balch | Safe |
| FK.8 B3377 | Lt J Thomson | Safe |

T/o Hesdigneul for an artillery patrol during which the engine began to vibrate so alarmingly that the crew made a forced landing on Mazingarbe airfield. Salvaged, the airframe was struck off charge on 28 April 1918, with a useful total of one hundred and nineteen hours and seven minutes flying recorded.

| 4 Squadron | Lt C B Hunt | + | Borre British Cemetery |
| RE.8 B5102 | 2Lt P H Whitwell | + | Borre British Cemetery |

T/o St Omer tasked for a contact patrol during which the crew were attacked by an enemy aircraft and sent down to crash at map reference 27W28B08. Charles Basil Hunt from Kenley in Surrey was nineteen years of age; his headstone is inscribed with the words; *'Peace Perfect Peace With Loved Ones Far Away'.* Patrick Henry Whitwell was formerly of the Yorkshire Regiment. No 4 Squadron was the first squadron operating on the Western Front to suffer the deaths of ten of its aircrew since the 1st of April while engaged on operations, while an eleventh death occurred during a training flight.

| 10 Squadron | Lt E J Riley | Safe |
| FK.8 C3582 | | |

T/o Droglandt for a practice flight but held the nose down for too long and, subsequently, the propeller struck the ground and was shattered, the airframe being damaged to the extent that with eighty three hours and fifteen minutes flying time recorded it was struck off charge.

| 10 Squadron | Lt H W Holmes | Injured |
| FK.8 C8553 | Lt H G Hooker | Safe. |

T/o Droglandt for a counter attack patrol during which the crew came under sustained machine gun fire from the ground. Force-landed but crashed into a shell hole at map reference 28N5a38, Lieutenant Holmes requiring treatment for wounds.

11 Squadron   Bristol F.2b B1252   Struck while parked on the aerodrome [Remaisnil] by a Camel belonging to No 70 Squadron.

| 20 Squadron | Lt C G Lankin | + | Longunesse [St Omer] Souvenir Cemetery |
| Bristol F.2b B1191 | Lt J W McHattie | + | Longunesse [St Omer] Souvenir Cemetery |

T/o Boisdinghem for an offensive patrol but while attempting to land at Ste Marie Cappel overshot, stalled and crashed; it will be recalled that both officers had had a similar experience four days previously [see my summary for details and information regarding the commissioning of James William McHattie]. James William McHattie rests beneath the inscription; *'A Silent Thought A Hidden Tear Keep His Memory Ever Dear.'*

| 24 Squadron | Lt W Selwyn | Safe | See 4 July 1918 - 74 Squadron |
| SE.5a C9518 | | | |

T/o Conteville and believed to have been damaged beyond repair following an attack on ground targets. According to *The SE.5a File* 'C9518' arrived on squadron charge on the 3rd of April 1918. Lieutenant Selwyn features in my summaries for the historic 1st of April 1918.

| 24 Squadron | 2Lt J Palmer | Safe |
| SE.5a D335 | | |

T/o Conteville briefed for a reconnaissance sortie and wrecked after striking a road during a thunderstorm. 'D335' had been with the squadron for just four days.

27 Squadron   DH.4 A7622   Struck by DH.4 B2145 [crew not identified] while parked at Ruisseauville. The damage to 'A7622' was terminal but 'B2145' continued in squadron service until the 9th of May 1918, when it was damaged beyond repair in a forced landing [see my summary for details].

| 35 Squadron | Captain G G Walker | Safe |
| FK.8 C8439 | 2Lt W W Jones | Safe |

T/o Poulainville for a special reconnaissance and, on return, wrecked in a crash by the edge of a wood close to the aerodrome.

| 35 Squadron | Lt A E G Williams | + | Villers-Bretonneux Military Cemetery |
| FK.8 C8552 | 2Lt N Bowden | + | Villers-Bretonneux Military Cemetery |

T/o Poulainville tasked for an artillery patrol over the Somme to Cachy in the course of which the crew came under ground fire, taking a direct hit from a shell. Norman Bowden twenty-one years of age and formerly of the 8th Battalion Sherwood Foresters [Notts and Derby Regiment] has on his gravestone the words; *To That Brightest Of All Meetings Brings Us Jesus Christ At Last'*. His pilot's entry in the cemetery register is devoid of any next of kin detail. In airframe serial order this was the squadron's twelfth operational loss but the first to result in fatalities.

| 43 Squadron | Lt A Eddleston | + | Avesnes-le-Comte Communal Cemetery extn |
| F.1 Camel D1819 | | | |

T/o Avesnes-le-Comte for a practice flight and while overhead the aerodrome suffered complete structural failure. Albert Eddleston was nineteen years of age and on the Commonwealth War Graves Commission website his Christian name is wrongly shown as 'Bert', the shortened version of 'Albert'.

48 Squadron	Captain T Colvill-Jones	pow	Berlin South-Western Cemetery
Bristol F.2b B1126	[Argentina]		
	Mechanic F Finney	pow	

T/o 1605 Bertangles for an offensive patrol in the direction of Villers Brettoneux some twenty km to the south-east of the airfield and was last seen at around 1700, flying at eight thousand feet, and diving towards a hostile machine near Wiencourt-l'Équipée [Somme] some two to three km east-southeast of his assigned area. Believed driven down by K Schattauer of *Jasta 16* at Marcelcave on the western side of Wiencourt-l'Équipée. Twenty year old Thomas Colvill-Jones of Buenos Aires died from his wounds on 24 May 1918; his elder brother, Captain Robert Colvill-Jones, an observer and holder of the Military Cross, lost his life with the end of the *Great War* in sight [see my summary for No 57 Squadron on 4 November].

| 48 Squadron | Captain H C Sootheran | Safe |
| Bristol F.2b B1346 | Lt P K Cockeram | Safe |

T/o Bertangles for a reconnaissance sortie over the Somme in the area of Villers-Bretonneux; crashed on landing.

| 49 Squadron | Lt F D Nevin | Safe |
| DH.9 C6182 | Sgt C Fathers* | Safe |

T/o Petite Synthe for bombing operations but stalled while climbing away; crashed. Salvaged, but deemed uneconomical to repair the airframe was struck off charge on 5 May 1918.

* No 49 Squadron Association website indicates the initial 'G' and notes Sergeant Fathers as being posted in on the 25th of April 1918, and posting out on the 4th of May 1918. His involvement in the crash here summarised has also been noted.

| 53 Squadron | Captain H M Gibbs | Injured |
| RE.8 B6615 | Lt A Lomax | Injured |

T/o Clairmarais ordered for a counter attack patrol to Kemmel, both members of crew being wounded during the operation.

54 Squadron	Lt O J F Jones-Lloyd	Injured

F.1 Camel B9283

T/o Clairmarais for an offensive patrol and on return crashed while attempting to land. Salvaged, it is believed for 'B9283' its flying days were over. Delivered to France, crated, by way of Newhaven it went to Warloy Baillon and No 3 Squadron on 17 February 1918, and was damaged during low-level bombing on the 6th of March, Second Lieutenant A P Freer escaping injury. Repaired, it arrived with No 54 Squadron seven days prior to the incident here reported.

56 Squadron	2Lt F C Tarbutt [Canada]	Safe	See 6 June 1918 - 56 Squadron

SE.5 A4853

T/o Valheureux for operations over Third Army front and damaged beyond worth while repair after a heavy crash during landing. Following in the steps of three prototype SE.5 [A4561-4563] the last of which was used operationally on the Western Front until damaged beyond repair on the 24 of February 1918, when a No 84 Squadron pilot, Lieutenant R E Duke, lost control on take off from Flez [his foot slipped off the rudder bar and the SE.5 swung and crashed], a batch of twenty-four aircraft [A4845-A4868] were ordered from the Royal Aircraft Factory, Farnborough on the 16th of October 1916. Thus, Canadian born Fraser Coventry Tarbutt now had the misfortune to wreck the ninth production aircraft and the earliest surviving example of a SE.5 since the formation of the Royal Air Force on the 1st of April. Issued to the squadron at London Colney as 'C2' by 24 March 1917, it crossed the Channel to St Omer on the 7th of April 1917, moving to Vert Galand on the 20th and remained with '56' until the 10th of August 1917, by which time it had either claimed or shared in the destruction of nine hostile machines. Still in good condition, 'A4853' was flown to Filescamp Farm on the 12th of August for use by No 60 Squadron but nine days later was given up to storage where it remained until taken in hand by No 84 Squadron on the 22nd of October. With '84' Lieutenant J S Ralston claimed an Albatros near Menin on the last day of October but on the 23rd of November, while in the care of Captain K M St C G Leake force-landed and fell into a shell hole. Taken to a repair facility and thence to storage this veteran SE.5 found its way to No 56 Squadron, now at Valheureux on the 3rd of April 1918. Despite its mishaps 'A4853' flew for a total of one hundred and fifty-nine hours and five minutes.

64 Squadron	Lt M L Howard [Canada]	Safe	See 25 July 1918 - 64 Squadron

SE.5a B125 Y

T/o Izel-lès-Hameau for practice flying but lost control in the slipstream of the aircraft in front of him; crashed and damaged beyond repair. Operating on the Western Front since arriving at St Omer from Sedgeford on the 14th of October 1917, and led by Major B E Smythies who had the distinction of being its commanding officer from formation on the 1st of August 1916, until December 1918, this was the squadron's first loss since the formation of the Royal Air Force. Bearing in mind the pace of operations throughout April, this was a remarkable run of good fortune.

65 Squadron	2Lt M A Newnham	Safe	Unemployed list 18 March 1919: Lt DFC

F.1 Camel D1801

T/o Bertangles for an offensive patrol during which Maurice Ashdown Newnham attacked an enemy two-seater but was himself engaged and driven down by a quintet of scouts from *Jasta 5*, one of which is thought to have been flown by *Leutnant* J Mai. A time [German] of 1415, is quoted and the location given as Morcourt. Maurice's award was *gazetted* on 3 December 1918, supplement 31046; *'This officer has taken part in several night-bombing raids and in 102 offensive patrols, many of which he has led with ability and success. On the night of 23rd-24th September Lt Newnham carried out a very successful long distance raid on an enemy aerodrome. Owing to heavy rain and a strong west wind he had difficulty in reaching his objective. Undeterred by this, he succeeded, and effectively bombed the aerodrome, obtaining two direct hits on a large Zeppelin shed. He then attacked other objectives, descending to ground level to do so. He returned to our lines after a two and half hour flight.'* On the 20th of April 1923, Maurice Ashdown Newnham was granted a commission, in the rank of flying officer, in Class A of the Reserve of Air Force Officers, but still so ranked resigned his commission on the 10th of January 1930 [*gazetted* respectively in issues 32816 and 33576]. Then, on Armistice Day 1939, he was appointed to a hostilities only commission, as a pilot officer, in the Administrative and Special Duties Branch [issue 34747 of 5 December 1939]. Like so many of these 'hostilities only' appointments, Maurice Newnham served on with the postwar air force and on the 1st of April 1947, and now holding the rank of group captain, he was conferred by His Majesty The King of Norway with the King Haakon VII Liberty Cross, as promulgated in issue 38577 of that same date. Eventually, he had to relinquish his commission [3 August 1954] under the provisions of the Navy, Army and Air Force Reserves Act of 1954, retaining his rank. While still a serving officer, and now appointed to the Most Excellent Order of the British Empire, he wrote 'Prelude to Glory - The Story of the Creation of Britain's Parachute Army' [Sampson Low, Marston & Co Ltd], 1948, copies of which may still be found on second-hand book sellers sites with, appropriately, the plain cover reflecting the colour of the airborne forces cap.

65 Squadron	2L J McM MacLennan	Safe
F.1 Camel D6448		

T/o Bertangles similarly tasked and crashed, owing to a thick mist, on landing; wrecked.

73 Squadron	Lt A N Baker [Canada]	Injured Arras Flying Services Memorial
F.1 Camel D1776		

T/o 1200 Beauvois for an offensive patrol and was last sighted east of Messines [just inside Belgium] and scene of heavy fighting between the 7th and 14th of June 1917, when divisions of General Sir Herbert Plummer's British Second Army fought a successful battle, securing the Messines Ridge. The action was a prelude to the Third Battle of Ypres [31 July to 10 November 1917] now regarded by historians as one of the most horrific engagements of the Great War. Albert Nathaniel Bake is reported to have been alive when reached by the Germans but died, I suspect, soon after and was probably buried close to where he crashed, since when all trace of his grave has been lost. Built by Proctor and Company Limited, 'D1776' was the first of a batch of two hundred airframes [D1776-D1975] and shipped to France arriving circa 14 March 1918, and to No 73 Squadron on the 1st of April.

74 Squadron	Lt P F C Howe	Safe
SE.5a B8496		

T/o Clairmarais to test firing the aircraft's guns and reported to have crashed on landing. Although salvaged, it is suspected 'B8496' had made its final flight. This was Lieutenant Howe's second crash in less than a week [see summary for 19 April 1918].

84 Squadron	2Lt C F C Wilson	Safe
SE.5a B676		

T/o Bertangles for the dual purposes of practice flying and testing the aircraft's guns. Reported as being wrecked following too fast a landing.

84 Squadron	Captain K A Lister Kaye	Injured
SE.5a D276		

T/o Bertangles for an offensive patrol during which 'D276' was attacked by an enemy aircraft. Hit in its Viper engine [and, I suspect, wounding the pilot] and while attempting a forced landing flew into a telegraph pole and crashed at Blagny-Tronville in the Somme.

95 Squadron	2Lt J J Miller [USA]	+	Shotwick [St Michael] Churchyard
Avro 504J C599			

T/o Shotwick for continuation training but while in the process of turning at a low airspeed lost control and crashed. John Jewett Miller was born at Claremont in New Hampshire.

98 Squadron	Lt C J Gillan	pow
DH.9 C6079	Lt W Duce	pow

T/o 1130 Alquines having being briefed for a raid on Gheluvelt and was lost owing to engine failure, the DH when last sighted was gliding on a westerly heading between the target and Gheluwe. Delivered to the squadron at Old Sarum by 23 February 1918, 'C6079' flew to France on the 1st of April and during an operation on the 21st of April, the same crew attacked an enemy kite balloon. The balloon's observer was seen to jump, but his parachute failed to deploy. This incident took place between 0645 and 0715; the balloon, it is reported, failed to catch fire.

98 Squadron	Captain R W Bell [Canada]	Safe	See 30 April 1918 - 98 Squadron
DH.9 C6083	Lt A A Malcolm	Safe	See 30 April 1918 - 98 Squadron

T/o Alquines and on return to the airfield from a raid crash-landed owing to fog shrouding the landing area. The previous Sunday, Captain Bell and Lieutenant Malcolm shared in the destruction of an Albatros near Armentières, their fellow squadron colleagues in this engagement being Captain D V D Marshall and Second Lieutenant H A Lamb [see Roll of Honour entries for 9 July 1918] flying in 'C6105'.

106 Squadron	Lt H M Whitcut	+	Tidworth Military Cemetery
DH.4 B5489	2Lt G J Downey [Canada]	+	Tidworth Military Cemetery
	2Lt F A Richardson	+	Tidworth Military Cemetery

T/o Andover and merely reported as "crashed". All three casualties are recorded in the cemetery register as serving with various infantry battalions and in descending order of the crew matrix these are reported as; 5th Battalion Staffordshire Regiment, 3rd Battalion King's Own [Royal Lancaster Regiment] and 1st Battalion East Yorkshire Regiment. A further conundrum arises for according to squadron records No 106 Squadron was never a recipient of the DH.4. Formed at Andover on 30 September 1917, as a corps reconnaissance unit it was equipped throughout with RE.8, moving to Fermoy in Ireland on 30 May 1918 and remaining here until disbanding on 8 October 1919. Furthermore, as far as I can ascertain, '106' did not exist as a training squadron.

Note. Andrew Pentland advises the official reported into the accident carries a comment *'could not stand the strain of stunting with three passengers.'*

148 Squadron	Lt G Baker	Safe
FE.2d A6486		

T/o Ford Junction and in the company of the rest of the squadron set a course for Auchel in the Pas-de-Calais from where, it was envisaged, the commencement of night bombing operations would commence. Nearing the French coast, Lieutenant Baker's aircraft developed an engine fault which forced him to alight in the sea off Cap Gris Nez from where he was picked up by the crew of a French trawler. From searches carried out by Oliver Clutton-Brock, it seems this was squadron's first 'casualty' since forming at Andover [Major Ivor Thomas Lloyd,*South Wales Borderers] on 10 February 1918 and transfer to Ford Junction on the 1st of March.

* Major Ivor Thomas Lloyd was the sole commander of No 148 Squadron during the *Great War* and was still in post when the squadron returned to Tangmere on 17 February 1919, still equipped with FEs and disbanded here on the last day of June. In the month prior to his appointment to a permanent commission on 1 August 1919, Major Lloyd took command of No 58 Squadron [Handley Page O/400]. In the years leading up to his retirement [at his own request] on the last day of July 1939, Ivor's service was typical for that of a permanent officer. His retirement, however, was brief [less than a month] for with war now almost a certainty Group Captain Lloyd was recalled and spent the next six years with Coastal Command, finally leaving the service on 29 March 1946, his rank now being air commodore. Born on the 1st of August 1896, Ivor Thomas Lloyd died on 28th October 1966.

Note. Oliver Clutton-Brock, who has researched, and published, the history of No 148 Squadron, has supplied a list of known FE.2b and FE.2d serials; of the former B7795, B7808, B7815, B7816, B7838, B7840 [written off 22 May 1918], B7843, B7847, B7872, C9794, C9824, C9826, D9117, D9187, D9749, D9764, D9776, D9781, D9935, D9936, D9937, D9940, D9993, E7093 and F5851 and of the latter A6406 [subsequently rebuilt as F5866 following a flying accident on 27 May 1918], A6409 [written off 17-18 June 1918], A6411, A6450 [written off 23 May 1918], A6452, A6463, A6464, A6486 [ditched 25 April 1918], A6504, A6517, A6529, A6569, A6579, A6592, A6599, A6600 [rebuilt as H7178] and B1879.

199 Squadron*	2Lt H G Achurch	+	St Neots Cemetery
FE.2b A5616			

T/o Rochford for continuation training at night but lost his bearings and flew into high ground. On impact a Holt flare ignited and the FE was burnt out.

* The inclusion of No 199 Squadron within the parameters set for the period is something of a grey area. According to Air-Britain's *The Squadrons of the Royal Air Force and Commonwealth,* No 199 Squadron formed at Rochford on the 1st of June 1917, from No 99[Depot] Squadron *as a training unit for pilots intended for service with the night bomber squadrons in France.'* Although its task was 'training' it was recognised as a squadron and as such I have decided to report its losses within the scope of this volume, and in those succeeding.

201 Squadron	Captain S W Rosevear DSC*	+	St Hilaire Cemetery extension, Frevent.
F.1 Camel B6231	[Canada]		

T/o Noeux and while making a practice dive on a target failed to pull up and crashed near Noeux-lès-Auxi in the Pas-de-Calais. The citations for his awards appeared in *The London Gazette* supplement 30386 of 17 November 1917 and supplement 30635 of 17 April 1918; in order they read; *'For conspicuous gallantry and devotion to duty. He has destroyed several hostile machines, and has also attacked and scattered parties of enemy infantry from low altitudes, on one occasion from a height of only 100 feet.'*, the First Bar paying attention to a particular episode in his service; *'For the skill and gallantry displayed on the 15th March 1918, when he attacked a formation of eight enemy aircraft, destroying two of the enemy machines. This officer has destroyed numerous enemy machines and is a very skilful and dashing fighter pilot.'* The aerodrome website lists twenty-five combat victories credited to Stanley Wallace Rosevear, the first being on the 14th of August 1917, when he destroyed an Albatros northeast of Ypres while his final success was gained three days before his death with a brace of Pfalz DIIIs over Hangard. The table suggests he had two favoured aircraft; Sopwith Triplane N6299 and F.1 Camel B6428 [see my summary for 22 April 1918].

206 Squadron	Lt W L Coleridge	Safe	Unemployed list 13 February 1919: Lt
DH.9 B7605	2Lt R W Brigstock	Safe	

T/o Alquines and on return from an operational bombing sortie crashed on landing. Lieutenant Coleridge transferred from the Machine Gun Company to the Royal Flying Corps on 9 November 1917 [*gazetted* in issue 30429 published on 14 December 1917].

This day, April 25th, is now perpetuated as ANZAC Day in memory of the sacrifice made by the Imperial Forces of Australia and New Zealand in the *Great War.*

Friday 26 April 1918
The Right Honourable William Weir, 1st Baron Weir, appointed President of the Air Council in succession to Lord Rothermere. Previously heading the aeronautics branch of the Ministry of Munitions his duties as President of the Air Council are reported in depth by Richard Overy in his book *The Birth of the RAF 1918.* Squadron losses on this day appears to have been confined to home based squadrons.

33 Squadron	2Lt L J Van Staden	+	Gainsborough General Cemetery
FE.2b B407	[South Africa]		
	2Lt W R Bilson	Safe	

T/o Braham Moor and flew into the ground after erroneously switching off the petrol feed from the main tank. Laurens Jacobus Van Staden's entry in the cemetery is devoid of age and next of kin details; it is known, however, that he was twenty-four years of age when killed. His name is commemorated on the 'Roll of Honour' table issued by the Air Ministry and repeated in *Flight* May 30, 1918. Second Lieutenant Van Staden was one of many cadets commissioned to the General List [in his case 30 July 1917] promulgated in supplement 30270 of *The London Gazette* 5 September 1917.

Note. At the time of this loss, the only one traced during the period being reported, the squadron, commanded by Major C G Burge, was operating as a Home Defence squadron protecting the North Midlands from enemy night intrusion. As a measure of the difficulties faced by the Home Defence squadrons No 33 Squadron failed to intercept a single airship despite mounting numerous patrols in the hope of success.

36 Squadron	Lt S N Jones	Injured
FE.2b A6582	Lt J M J Le Mee	Injured

T/o Newcastle*for a special patrol on behalf of the Navy and while over the sea, and about a mile from the shore, lost control and fell from one hundred feet into the water.

* Newcastle was the squadron's headquarters, while detached flights were maintained at Seaton Carew, Hylton and Ashington. This would appear to be the only reported loss for the period under investigation.

| 50 Squadron | 2Lt L L Morgan MC | + | Canterbury Cemetery, Kent |
| SE.5a C5342 | | | |

T/o Bekesbourne and while banking steeply at one hundred and fifty feet lost control and dived onto a railway embankment on the northern edge of the airfield. This was a tragic end to a very gallant officer for Swansea born Lewis Laugharne Morgan had been discharged from the Royal Flying Corps after losing his right leg when shot down over France in 1917. Determined to play his part and continue to fly, and now fitted with an artificial limb, he rejoined the service in March. Lewis Laugharne Morgan was commissioned to the Welsh Regiment on 5 August 1916 [*gazetted* 17 August 1916, supplement 29710]. A non-digitised document pertaining to Second Lieutenant Morgan is held at The National Archives in Class WO 374/48777. A website, titled *Mumbles at War,* which I have pleasure in acknowledging, reports that on the 24th of May 1917, he flew over the Allied lines at under a one hundred feet and destroyed an enemy kite balloon, followed by the destruction of an enemy scout, but sustained a fracture to his right leg which had to be amputated. Although shown as being a recipient of the Military Cross, I have yet to find the citation.

Note. At the time of this loss the squadron, commanded by Major A de B Brandon, was finding very little trade in its rôle as a Home Defence squadron covering the southeast coastal region.

| 109 Squadron* | 2Lt F G Edwards | Injured Macclesfield Cemetery |
| DH.4 B5486 | | |

T/o Stonehenge for a practice flight during which the DH was put into a steep dive and when recovering to level flight the airframe was overstressed resulting in the tail unit breaking away. Nineteen year old Frank Graham Edwards was commissioned, following a cadetship, on 30 November 1917 [*gazetted* 4 December 1917, issue 30414] survived the impact but was grievously injured, resulting in his death on 3 May 1918. His entry in the cemetery register is devoid of unit details. According to records that have survived the passage of time No 109 Squadron was earmarked as a day bomber unit and equipped with DH.9 but, I assume, some DH.4 were introduced for training purposes.

* Similar to my observations regarding No 199 Squadron [my summary for FE.2b A5616 on 25 April 1918, refers], No 109 Squadron is believed to have operated in a training capacity despite being earmarked for day bombing duties. James Halley in his Air-Britain publication *The Squadrons of the Royal Air Force and Common-wealth* but *'remained a training nucleus.'*

| 149 Squadron | 2Lt L C Tonkin | Injured |
| FE.2b A6507 | 2Lt F H Thompson | Safe |

T/o Ford but was obliged to make a forced landing in a field and it was while taking off that the FE failed to clear some trees and crashed; damaged beyond repair.

217 Squadron   DH.4 A7829   Reported as having been badly shot about [though it may not have been on this date] and after languishing at No 4 Aircraft Supply Depot at Guines until 26 November 1918, when, as Andrew Pentland reports, it was awaiting shipment to No 2 Salvage Section Richbiro' presumably for scrap. Details of the last crew to fly A7829 have not been recorded.

Saturday 27 April 1918
The Second Battle of Villers-Brettoneux petered out. Nevertheless, as many future summaries will show, aerial support for Allied forces tied down in this area was considerable.

| 1 Squadron | Lt F A Nesbitt | Injured |
| SE.5a C1104 | | |

T/o 1800 Clairmarais for an offensive during which Lieutenant Nesbitt was engaged in combat; wounded, he force-landed at Rexpoëde [Nord] some fifteen km southeast of Dunkirk.

| 2 Squadron | 2Lt S H Warner | Safe |
| FK.8 C3575 | 2Lt J Watson | Safe |

T/o Hesdigneul tasked for an artillery patrol during which a thick mist enveloped the area. Subsequently, the crew force-landed but had the misfortune to collide with telegraph wires near Beuvry in the Pas-de-Calais. On squadron charge since 21 March 1918, 'C3575' had been well used, flying for a total of fifty-seven hours.

| 8 Squadron | 2Lt J Stuart | Safe |
| FK.8 D5015 | Lt H L Cox | Safe |

T/o Auxi-le-Château with orders to carry out a line patrol and while doing so was subjected to machine gun fire from the ground. According to the 'D' serial listings, 'D5015' which arrived with the squadron on 8 April 1918, was salvaged and sent for repair; however, it appears to have languished until the 3rd of September 1918, when it was struck off charge as being not worth repairing with twenty-five hours and thirty-five minutes of flying recorded.

| 21 Squadron | Lt Savage | Safe |
| RE.8 B4104 | | |

T/o Bruay intending to return to Floringhem but *en route* flew into clouds and became uncertain of his position; sighting an airfield, which turned out to be Abbeville, Lieutenant Savage force-landed but damaged his aircraft in the process. Salvaged, and sent for repair, 'B4104' languished until 5 July 1918, when it was deemed not worth the cost of repair and with twenty-two hours and twenty minutes of flying to its credit it was struck off charge.

| 24 Squadron | Lt J A E R Daley | Safe |
| SE.5a B79 | | |

T/o Conteville for an offensive patrol and was shot down near Langeau *[sic]*. This particular SE.5a had an interesting service life in that on its delivery to the squadron by Lieutenant G F Hunter [Unemployed List 12th February 1919] on the 2nd of January 1918, it crashed heavily on arrival at Villers-Brettoneux and it was not until the 3rd of March 1918, that it was reissued. On the 15th of March, at around 1020, Lieutenant Harold Bolton Redler*sent down a Fokker DrI out of control over Premont [Aisne], just over nineteen km southeast of Cambrai [this was one of his three combat successes while attached to the squadron; either prior to or after his time with '40' he gained a further seven], and this was followed on the 26th March with a Scout 'flamed' by Lieutenant J A E R Daley in the vicinity of Croix. In the mid-afternoon of the 7th of April 1918, Second Lieutenant W C Lambert of the United States Air Service snapped up an Albatros near Moreuil [Somme] and he followed this on the 12th with a long combat which ended at 1630 with another Albatros, its fuselage painted yellow, going down out of control at an undisclosed location.

* Born on the 27th of January 1897, Harold Bolton Redler hailed from Boschbeek, Newlands, Cape Town, and at the time of his death on the 21st of June 1918, was attached to No 1 Fighting School at Turnberry, Ayrshire. On the day that he died he had accompanied Captain Ian Henry David Henderson, formerly of the Argyll and Sutherland Highlanders, to test the Lewis gun fitted to DH.9 D1018 and it seems that while in a climbing turn control was lost and the DH crashed with fatal consequences. At the Court of Inquiry held to determine the cause of the crash it was stated that although the crew appear to have changed places during the test, this was not a contributory factor. Harold Redler's funeral was arranged by relatives and he is buried in Somerset at West Monkton [St Augustine] Churchyard, while Captain Henderson rests in Ayrshire at Girvan [Doune] Cemetery. Both officers were twenty-one years of age and both held the Military Cross. It is further noted that Ian Henry David Henderson's father was the much decorated General Sir David Henderson who for the first year of the *Great War* commanded the Royal Flying Corps in the Field and, subsequently, was instrumental in the establishment of the Royal Air Force. However, he did not enjoy the best of health and with the arrival of Trenchard's replacement, Sykes, he tendered his resignation to Rothermere. Postwar, he was appointed as the First Director-General of the League of Red Cross Societies and it while holding this prestigious post that he died in Geneva, Switzerland, on 17th of August 1921. He was fifty-nine years of age.

29 Squadron	2Lt R J MacLachlan		Injured
SE.5a D3515			

T/o St Omer authorised for a practice flight. Owing to engine failure over the Pas-de-Calais near Tatinghem* Second Lieutenant MacLachlan force-landed but while doing so had the misfortune to run up against a raised road which resulted in 'D3515' turning onto its back.

* A former commune in the Pas-de-Calais west-southwest of St Omer, Tatinghem merged on the 1st of January 2016 to form a new commune 'Saint-Martin-lez-Tatinghem'.

106 Squadron	Lt N C Kearney	+	Putney Vale Cemetery
RE.8 C2424			

T/o Andover for continuation training but crashed, owing to engine failure, at Weyhill some two miles west-north-west of the airfield. As with so many deaths from the home based squadrons, no unit detail has been appended against Lieutenant Norman Charles Kearney's entry in the cemetery register. Formed on 30 September 1917, with Corps reconnaissance duties in mind the squadron eventually went to Ireland and was lodged at Fermoy in Co Cork.

129 Squadron	Lt W G Whalley	+	Euston [St Genevieve] Churchyard
DH.9 D2810	F/S G L Evans	+	Bristol [Arnos Vale] Cemetery

T/o Duxford and crashed following structural failure of the tailplane. Although his age has not been recorded, Flight Sergeant Gilbert Lawrence Evans*service number is shown as '712' thereby identifying service with the Royal Flying Corps since 1913.

* Andrew Pentland provides a most interesting observation taken from *A Contemptible Little Flying Corps* by Ian McIness and with contributions from J V Webb [Naval and Military Press, New edition, 2009], in that Gilbert Evans joined as a direct entrant on the 22nd of May 1913, and served in France with No 5 Squadron [various types] from 14th August 1914 [main body of squadron to Maubeuge on 18th August 1914], thus having the honour to be included in the original Royal Flying Corps contingent committed to operations on the Western Front.

Sunday 28 April 1918
During the day came the welcome news that American troops had entered the lines on the Northern battle front and coming under control of the French. Continued heavy fighting in the Ypres Sector where the Belgian army contained vigorous thrusts from the Germans, while south of Villers-Bretonneux at Hangard Wood attacks by the enemy were checked.

59 Squadron	Lt C C E Robinson	+	Doullens Communal Cemetery extension No 2
RE.8 B6520	2Lt P Thornton	+	Doullens Communal Cemetery extension No 2

T/o Vert Galand tasked for a patrol and eyewitnesses report seeing the crew climb away and at around three hundred feet appeared to make a turn to port. At this point the RE.8 went into a spin and dived vertically into the ground. Prior to joining the Royal Flying Corps, twenty-four year old Percy Thornton had seen active service in Egypt and France with the 15th Battalion, West Yorkshire Regiment.

84 Squadron	Lt A F Matthews USAS		Injured
SE.5a D3506			

T/o Bertangles to practice firing in the course of which Lieutenant Matthews stalled and crashed, his injuries being described as 'slight'.

Monday 29 April 1918
Noteworthy in that although a German attack succeeded in capturing the Scherpenberg, a high point northwest of Kemmelberg, the long drawn out campaign collectively known as the *Battle of Lys* drew to a close. Similar to all campaigns along the Western Front, and particularly in 1918, it had been a 'bloody' experience for all partici-pants with casualties running to many thousands.

| 4 Squadron | Lt A Buchanan | Injured |
| RE.8 B6480 | Lt H Sainsbury | Injured |

T/o St Omer for an offensive patrol during which engine failure occurred which in turn necessitated a forced landing at map reference 36aC22c. This particular RE.8, taken on squadron charge on the last day of October 1917, logged [for the time] an impressive two hundred and twenty seven hours and twenty-five minutes.

| 10 Squadron | Lt F W Burdick | Safe |
| FK.8 B3327 | 2Lt A C Chinton | Safe |

T/o Droglandt for a *Flash* reconnaissance and was obliged to force-land at map reference M2a77 after taking a direct hit from a shell. Taken on charge 9 January 1918, 'B3327' flew for a total of one hundred and forty hours and fifty minutes.

35 Squadron	Lt R W Keoffenheim	Injured Crouy British Cemetery, Crouy-sur-Somme
FK.8 B5789	[served as Trubridge]	
	2Lt H Gittins	Safe

T/o Poulainville briefed to conduct a contact patrol in the course of which the FK.8 was attacked by a hostile aircraft, wounding Lieutenant Trubridge who force-landed at map reference 62DO19D00. Nineteen year old Roland William Trubridge of Gosforth in Northumberland died from his wounds on 6 May 1918. From its first flight circa September 1917, and acceptance by the squadron on the 1st of October, 'B5789' flew a total of one hundred and eighty-two hours and five minutes. It appears the engine was salvaged.

| 46 Squadron | 2Lt E J Smith | + | Roclincourt Military Cemetery |
| F.1 Camel C1617* | | | |

T/o 1120 Filescamp for a counter attack patrol and shot down, in flames, at around 1120 just inside the Allied lines at map reference 51BB4, possibly near Rocklincourt in the Pas-de-Calais and east of the Arras to Lens highway and a little over four km north-northeast of Arras. Taken on squadron charge on 8 March 1918, 'C1617' in its relatively short operational life shot down, or shared in the destruction of three hostile machines, all at the hands of Captain S P Smith, and a kite balloon, downed at 1315 on the 3rd of April by Ernest Smith.

* Andrew Pentland has forwarded a copy of Army Form W 3347 where No 46 Squadron is shown as being attached to No 10 Wing and that Second Lieutenant Smith was operating over 1st Army Front. The report also notes that the airframe had accumulated approximately fifty hours and fifty-three minutes and the engine forty-one hours and thirty minutes, approximately.

| 53 Squadron | Lt H W Auerbach | Safe |
| RE.8 A3629 | 2Lt A Todd | Safe |

T/o Clairmarais heading for Kemmel tasked for a counter attack patrol. Force-landed K31 owing to engine failure. Issued to No 12 Squadron on 5 August 1917, 'A3629' lost engine power while flying at four hundred feet on the 23rd of November, forced landing in a field Ruyaulcourt and before coming to a stop dropped into a depression in the ground. The crew, Lieutenant C J S Dearlove and Lieutenant T R Scott were not hurt and 'A3629' was salvaged and sent for repair. Completed, it arrived with No 53 Squadron on 24 February 1918.

| 64 Squadron | 2Lt D Lloyd-Evans | Safe | See 30 August 1918 - 64 Squadron |
| SE.5a B124 | | | |

T/o Izel-lès-Hameau for practice flying and on return to the airfield touched down in a strong crosswind and flipped over. Issued to No 24 Squadron on 16 February 1918, 'B124' accounted for a trio of hostile aircraft between the 26th of February and the 12th of March, all credited to Second Lieutenant H B Richardson. Given up four days later to No 2 Aeroplane Supply Depot, 'B124' arrived at Izel-lès-Hameau forty-eight hours later and before being written off shot down three more enemy aircraft.

| 74 Squadron | Lt G R Savage | Injured |
| SE.5a B8409 | | |

T/o Calirmarais for an evening patrol and reported to have spun to the ground in fading light.

| 74 Squadron | Lt J R Piggott | Safe |
| SE.5a D267 | | |

T/o Clairmarais for an offensive patrol and reported to have lost his way owing to ground mist; attempted to force-land but crashed, ending up in a field that had been put to the plough.

| 84 Squadron | Lt B Stefansson | Safe |
| SE.5a D3914 | | |

T/o Bertangles and while in flight the 'CC' bracket broke loose causing the radiator to become detached from the longeron. Salvaged, 'D3914' with only five hours and ten minutes of flight time to its credit was struck off charge on 3 May 1918.

| 99 Squadron | CaptainR W Bell | Safe |
| DH.9 B7641 | Lt A A Malcolm | Safe |

T/o St Omer ordered for bombing operations and on return to the airfield a gust of wind caused a wing to lift resulting in the opposite wing digging into the ground. Salvaged, but struck off charge on 4 May 1918. 'B7641' had been on squadron establishment for a mere forty-eight hours.

| 99 Squadron | Lt C J Stanfield | Injured |
| DH.9 C6095 | Lt N C McDonald | Injured |

T/o St Omer similarly tasked on completion of which the crew landed at Icques [having lost their way] but ran onto a ridge and nosed over; damaged beyond repair.

| 99 Squadron | Lt C G Tysoe | pow |
| DH.9 D5571 | 2Lt C V Carr | pow |

T/o 0750 St Omer tasked for a raid on Menen in the Belgian province of West-Vlaanderen and was last sighted going down between Geluwe and Wervik. The Air Ministry 'Roll of Honour' report, as repeated in *Flight* May 30th 1918, includes the names of both officers in the 'Missing' category, Second Lieutenant Carr shown as attached from the Duke of Wellington's Rifles.

| 206 Squadron | Lt J V Turner | Safe | |
| DH.9 B7591 | 2Lt E W Tatnall | Safe | Unemployed list 16 February 1919: 2Lt |

T/o Alquines for bombing operations and wrecked after turning over in a ploughed field in which the DH had force-landed at Beutin a little over eight km east-southeast of Etaples in the Pas-de-Calais. Arriving with No 6 Royal Naval Air Squadron on 27 February 1918, 'B7591' with Flight Commander T F Le Mesurier*and Petty Officer J J Ryan was flying in the vicinity of the battle lines during the early afternoon on the 9th of March when half-a-dozen Albatros CVs were sighted and in the ensuing engagement one was shot down and observed to burst into flames near trenches occupied by the French. Of the former Royal Naval Air Squadrons taken into the fold of the newly established Royal Air Force, '206, was the first to lose ten of its aircraft on operational duties.

* Thomas Frank Le Mesurier was awarded a Distinguished Service Cross on 12 May 1917, the citation being published in the fourth supplement to *The London Gazette,* issue 30066, of 11 May 1917; *'For conspicuous work as a pilot of a bombing machine. Has taken part in fourteen raids and numerous fighter patrols.'* A First Bar followed on 29 August 1917; *'For consistent skill and courage in leading his flight on bombing raids, particularly on the 28th of July.'* And within less than a month [14th of September] a Mention in a Despatch, the relevant issues being 30258 and 30285. A second Bar to the Distinguished Service Cross was published on 21 June 1918, supplement 30756; *'For gallantry and consistent good work. He has at all times displayed the utmost gallantry, and by his determination and skill has set a very fine example to the pilots of his squadron. On the 23rd April 1918, in spite of bad weather conditions, he successfully dropped bombs on the Ostend Docks from a height of 800 feet amidst very intense anti-aircraft fire and machine-gun fire. He also made valuable obser-vations. He has taken part in many bomb raids, and has destroyed or driven down out of control several enemy machines.'*

| 210 Squadron | Lt H L Nelson | + | Arras Flying Services Memorial |
| F.1 Camel B3809 | | | |

T/o Lièttres for an offensive patrol; hit by anti-aircraft fire in the early afternoon and crashed to earth. Eighteen years of age and from Bedford Park in London, Harold Ludlow Nelson commenced his brief military life with the Royal Naval Air Service.

Tuesday 30 April 1918

4 Squadron	Lt H W Girdlestone	+	Longuenesse [St Omer] Souvenir Cemetery
RE.8 B734	Lt R Homersham	+	Longuenesse [St Omer] Souvenir Cemetery

T/o St Omer for an operational patrol and destroyed near the airfield in a midair collision with the RE summarised below. Twenty year old Horace Wilfred Girdlestone's headstone is inscribed; *'Pro Fide Et Patria'*he was formerly of the Royal Garrison Artillery, while Ronald Homersham came to the Royal Flying Corps by way of the 4th Battalion, East Yorkshire Regiment. His headstone is inscribed; *'Too Perfect For This World Called To Higher Service Our Beloved Son.'*

* Translates as 'For Faith and Fatherland'; it is also the motto of the originally Muldoon family and has also been incorporated in the mottos of several schools.

4 Squadron	Lt L J Sweeney MC [Canada]	+	Longuenesse [St Omer] Souvenir Cemetery
RE.8 D4833	Lt J C Stack [USA]	+	Longuenesse [St Omer] Souvenir Cemetery

T/o St Omer similarly ordered and destroyed in the manner outlined above. The citation for the award of the Military Cross in regard to Leo John Sweeney of Vancouver, British Columbia, appeared in supplement 30813 of the *Gazette* published on 26 July 1918; *'For conspicuous gallantry and devotion to duty. When leading a bombing raid this officer attacked enemy troops and transport with bombs and machine-gun fire from 500 feet, causing a great many casualties. Although his observer was wounded and his machine badly damaged, he succeeded in landing behind our lines. During two subsequent low flights he caused many casualties, his observer being again wounded and his machine badly damaged.'* James Charles Stack of Chicago, Illinois, but now married to Eva Stack of Dundalk, was formerly of the Labour Corps. It will be recalled that eight days previously, flying with Second Lieutenant Chesney, he had fought off the attentions of five enemy aircraft.

4 Squadron AusFC	Lt A D Pate	Safe
F.1 Camel B2535		

T/o Clairmarais for a practice flight and, it is reported, crashed close to the aerodrome as a result of Lieutenant Pate 'choking' the engine. Accepted by the squadron on 19 January 1918, 'B2535' claimed three, possibly, four hostile aircraft between the 21st of March and the 10th of April, all by Lieutenant A H Cobby. Two [possibly three] were Albatros scouts, the first driven down during the morning over the Pas-de-Calais east of Arras at Brebières and the last, also a morning combat, near Estaires. In between he downed a Pfalz DIII which broke up southeast of Arras.

98 Squadron	Captain R W Bell [Canada]	Safe	17 May 1918 - 98 Squadron
DH.9 B7641	Lt A A Malcolm	Safe	17 May 1918 - 98 Squadron

T/o Alquines and on return to base from bombing duties, and in the process of landing, a strong gust of wind caught the DH at a critical moment which resulted in a wing touching the ground. Damaged beyond repair. Both officers had been involved in a crash on 25 April 1918.

So ended the first month of air operations by the newly formed Royal Air Force, a month that had witnessed much activity over the Western Front where the squadrons had carried out numerous operational tasks in support of the ground forces, as well as independent patrolling, frequently engaging with the enemy's highly skilled scout pilots. Appropriately, in light of the contribution made the Royal Air Force received its first 'Battle Honour', the official wording being as follows; *"For squadrons participating in operations in support of the Allied offensive against German Armed Forces during the Battle of Lys, April 9-29, 1918."* In a well written article by Andrew Thomas featuring No 98 Squadron, published in the April 2018 issue of *Flypast* [which I gratefully acknowledge], he comments; *'... although only 98 and 210 Squadrons chose to carry it on their Standards.'*

Wednesday 1 May 1918

1 Squadron   Lt B H Moody   Safe   Unemployed list 3 February 1920: Lt
SE.5a B632
T/o Clairmarais to practice formation flying and on landing the axle fractured and the aircraft lost a wheel. Salvaged for possible repair, 'B632' with one hundred and twenty-one hours and fifty-five minutes flying time recorded was struck off charge on 4 May 1918.

29 Squadron   Lt A E Reed   Safe   See 6 May 1918 - 29 Squadron
SE.5a D3940
T/o St Omer to patrol the twenty odd km corridor between Hazebrouck and Poperinghe but lost his bearings and while making a precautionary landing was obliged to swerve in order to avoid running into a cart. Moments later the tail-skid came into contact with a tent, after which control was lost and 'D3940' was damaged beyond repair. This was the squadron's first operational loss of a SE.5a, the four previous write offs all occurring during practice flying.

49 Squadron   Lt D S Cramb   Injured Unemployed list 16 April 1919
DH.9 D5554   Sgt F A Bardsley   Injured
T/o Petite Synthe for an exercise in formation flying and on return to the airfield and preparing to land stalled while turning and dived to the ground, the crew escaping with minor injuries. At No 2 Aircraft Acceptance Park Hendon by 26 February 1918, 'D5554' arrived with the squadron on the 2nd of April, having initially been earmarked for the mobilisation at Old Sarum of No 99 Squadron. I strongly suspect the pilot to be Douglas Stuart Cramb who received an hostilities only commission as a pilot officer in the Training Branch on 8 April 1941 [*gazetted* 11 July 1941, issue 35217]. However, for reasons not stated, his commission was terminated on the 15th of May 1943, as promulgated in supplement 36044 of 8 June 1943; he was still ranked pilot officer. Turning to the squadron's website, it is recorded here that Lieutenant Cramb reported to the squadron on the 23rd of April 1918, and was removed from establishment on the 1st of May; undoubtedly owing to his injuries. Sergeant Bardsley, too, was taken off establishment, thereby suggesting their injuries may have been more serious that first envisaged.

218 Squadron   Lt E R Lawson   Safe   Unemployed list 3 February 1919: Lt
DH.4 N6404*   Lt L H Herridge   Safe
T/o Dover and on return overshot the airfield and went round again. On their second approach [and I suspect visibility may have been poor] Lieutenant Lawson flew into a flagstaff which sent the DH crashing into Guston Road between the villages of Guston and Esst Langdon and just inland from St Margaret's at Cliffe. Although uninjured both officers were quite badly shaken by their experiences.

* According to *The DH.4/DH.9 file*, 'N6404' was a well traveled aircraft. Following initial acceptance at Hendon by the week ending 27 October 1917, by November 3rd it was at Grain and thence to Dover where it is recorded as arriving on December 10th. Two days later it was taken over by No 2 Squadron Royal Naval Air Service but by 17 January 1918, it had transferred to No 6 Squadron Royal Naval Air Service followed on March 7th to No 11 Squadron Royal Naval Air Service. At the end of the next seven days it had transferred once again, this time to No 12 Squadron Royal Naval Air Service before being earmarked for issue to No 218 Squadron which formed at Dover on 24 April 1918. A DH.9 squadron from the start, I can only assume a handful of DH.4s were used as it worked up in readiness for its departure to France and Petite Synthe on the 23rd of May.

Thursday 2 May 1918
Following two 'quiet' days aerial activity over the Western Front resumed with a vengeance with hundreds of offensive sorties flown, resulting in a plethora of losses and aircraft damaged to varying degrees of severity.

3 Squadron   2Lt G L D Hall   +   Doullens Communal Cemetery extension No 2
F.1 Camel B5583
T/o Valheureux for a practice flight which concluded with eighteen year old Geoffrey Lawrence Dobney Hall of Muswell Hill, London, diving headlong into the ground. A simple inscription marks his headstone; *'For Whom Thanks Be To God.'*

4 Squadron AusFC   Lt L R Sinclair   Safe   See 14 May 1918 - 4 Squadron AusFC
F.1 Camel B2527
T/o Clairmarais and wrecked following a crash in a field adjacent to the aerodrome, owing to Lieutenant Sinclair 'choking' the engine as he departed for a practice flight.

11 Squadron   Lt R F Mullins   Safe
Bristol F.2b C869   Lt H M Stewart   Safe
T/o Remaisnil for a reconnaissance sortie subsequently encountering a thick mist; force-landed near Beauvais [airfield] but ran into a ditch sustaining damage that was deemed not worth repairing. Lieutenant Mullins was seconded to the Royal Flying Corps on 24 October 1917 [*gazetted* 17 November 1917, supplement 30385].

13 Squadron   Lt C E Everard   Safe   Unemployed list 18 January 1919: Lt
RE.8 A3572 *Johore No 5* 2Lt J Evans   Safe
T/o Izel-lès-Hameau for a puff test during which a forced landing was made some three km to the east of the airfield. Then, taking off the RE flew into telegraph wires, crashed and damaged beyond repair. Initially operated by No 15 Squadron, 'A3572' was damaged during operations on 10 December 1917 [Lieutenant S D Morrison and Second Lieutenant W K Whittle]. Repaired, it arrived with No 13 Squadron on 6 March, and when written off had recorded a useful two hundred and forty-six hours and thirty minutes flying. Lieutenant Everard had served with the Essex Regiment.

15 Squadron   2Lt S A Young   Injured
RE.8 B6508   Lt J A FitzHerbert MC [Australia]Injured
T/o Izel-lès-Hameau for a patrol, on return from which the crew force-landed in a field that had been put to the plough near Villers-Bocage, their RE.8 having suffered complete engine failure. Both officers sustained serious injuries. Lieutenant John Aloysius FitzHerbert first commissioned to the Royal Garrison Artillery with effect from 26 October 1916, was seconded to the Royal Flying Corps on 22 January 1918, as published in supplement 30535 of the paper issued on 21 February 1918. His name appears along with many hundreds *gazetted* with the Military Cross on New Year's Day 1917, as published in The *Edinburg Gazette* issue 13033. Prior to arriving in the United Kingdom, he had attended universities in Australia at Sydney and Adelaide, the latter holding a collection of papers for Lieutenant FitzHerbert under reference MSS 0030. At Sydney in 1913, he attained a Bachelor of Arts degree and postwar, at Adelaide, a Master of Arts degree. Scanning through the plethora of information reported for this officer, it appears he returned to Australia as a passenger aboard the SS *Orvieto* out from London, a date of 3 July 1920, is quoted but I am uncertain if this was the date of sailing, or arrival in Australia.

20 Squadron   Lt P B Holgate   Safe
Bristol F.2b C4826
T/o Boisdinghem for a practice flight and on landing flew into bank which damaged the Bristol beyond repair. Accepted by the squadron on 9 December 1917, 'C4826' had logged one hundred and twenty hours and thirty-five minutes of flying, a creditable total. Owing to ill-health Lieutenant Holgate's commission was relinquished on 12 October 1918.

23 Squadron   Captain L M Mansbridge   Injured
5F.1 Dolphin C4154
T/o St Omer for a practice flight and owing to engine failure crashed near the aerodrome; salvaged, the airframe was struck off charge six days later, thereby becoming the first of its type written off from the squadron which until of late had flown French built Spads. Including its despatch to the Western Front, by air, and acceptance by the squadron from No 87 Squadron on 27 April 1918, 'C4154' had accumulated a miserly two hours and twenty-seven minutes flying. Captain Mansbridge, who at the time of his accident was attached to headquarters, had been seconded as a second lieutenant to the Royal Flying Corps on the 7th of January 1917, from the Dorset Regiment [*gazetted* 23 January 1917, issue 29913]. Postwar, he returned to his regiment, resigning his commission on 15 December 1920, by which time he had reverted to his substantive rank of lieutenant [*gazetted* in supplement 32195 published on 17 January 1921.

29 Squadron   Lt A Bevan   Safe
SE.5a D3925

T/o St Omer tasked to patrol the twenty km corridor between the French market town of Hazebrouck and the key Belgian rail centre of Poperinghe, the gateway for Allied troops moving up to the northern part of the Ypres Salient. To the British soldiers at the time, it was always referred to as 'Pops'. On his return, Lieutenant Bevan stalled on his approach, resulting in 'D3925' being damaged beyond repair.

35 Squadron   2Lt C S Booker   Safe   See 19 May 1918 - 35 Squadron
FK.8 C8562   Mechanic Starkey   Safe

T/o Villers-Bocage*for a practice shoot and on return, and landing, struck the top of FK.8 C8589 [see below].

35 Squadron   FK.8 C8589   Struck by the FK.8 summarised above while parked on the airfield, both machines being damaged beyond repair.

* Although I have indicated Villers-Bocage, this accident my have occurred at Poulainville from where the squadron arrived at its new base at Villers-Bocage during the day.

40 Squadron   Lt H H Wood   Safe   See 12 June 1918 - 40 Squadron
SE.5a D3526

T/o 1340 Brauy for a line patrol and crashed twenty-five minutes later while attempting to land. A former cadet, Henry Harben Wood was commissioned to the General List of the Royal Flying Corp as a second lieutenant, on probation, with effect from 27 February 1917 [gazetted 6 March 1917, supplement 29975]. Trevor Henshaw notes that 'D3526' was in action on the 1st of April 1918, when Canadian born Second Lieutenant W L Harrison shot down a two-seater soon after midday near Izel-lès-Équerchin in the Pas-de-Calais.

43 Squadron   Lt G Hamilton   pow
F.1 Camel B2482

T/o Avesnes-le-Comte for a practice flight during which Lieutenant Hamilton must have strayed over the lines for he was later reported to be in enemy hands. A presentation Camel 'B2482' operated with No 4 Squadron AusFC as *Australia No 1, South Australia No 1, The Sidney Kidman* until it was damaged in a forced landing near Doullens [Lieutenant F S Woodward] on the 13th of January 1918.

46 Squadron   Lt L C Hickey   +   Arras Flying Services Memorial
F.1 Camel C1685

T/o Filescamp for a contact operational patrol and was last sighted over Estaires [Nord] and about to engage with half-a-dozen enemy scouts.

56 Squadron   Major R Balcombe-Brown MC   +   Carnoy Military Cemetery
SE.5a C1796   A mention in a Despatch [New Zealand]

T/o 1040 Valheureux for a special mission and was last sighted at around 1130 in combat over Martinpuich in the Pas-de-Calais, some twenty-six km south of Arras. Rainsford Balcombe-Brown, reports Errol Martyn, was the highest ranking New Zealander to lose his life in the *Great War*. He was a very experienced fighter pilot with eight hundred and eighty flying hours to his credit and since November 1917, had been at the helm of No 56 Squadron. Formerly of the Royal Field Artillery, since attached to the Royal Flying Corps, Rainsford's award appeared in a supplement to *The London Gazette* of 27 July 1916, the citation appearing on page 7431; *'For conspicuous gallantry and skill. He attacked an enemy kite balloon*and brought it down in flames. He was flying in a type of machine unfamiliar to him owing to the absence through wounds of the regular pilot. At dawn he commenced to learn the machine, and the same evening brought down the kite.'*

* Attacking kite balloons was far more hazardous than some may imagine. Put up for observation purposes with an observer equipped with strong binoculars and a parachute of sorts, balloons were usually well defended and any approach by an aircraft with ill-intent invariably resulted in a curtain of defensive fire being directed in its path. Furthermore, in the case of the balloon bursting into flames, the attacking pilot probably had only seconds in which to bank away to avoid being caught up in the flaming mass of canvas as it fell to the ground.

| 64 Squadron | Lt J J Carroll | Safe | See 18 May 1918 - 64 Squadron |

SE.5a B8263

T/o Izel-lès-Hameau for practice flying and as a consequence of landing in the backwash of another aircraft lost control and tipped onto one wing. Salvaged, but was struck off charge four days later.

| 64 Squadron | 2Lt J F T Barrett | Safe | See 6 July 1918 - 64 Squadron |

SE.5a C1100

T/o Izel-lès-Hameau for an offensive patrol over 1st Army front and failed to return. John Francis Tufnell Barrett, commissioned to the General List, was confirmed in his appointment of second lieutenant on 15 September 1917 [*gazetted* 9 October 1917, supplement 30327]. Postwar, he was granted a short service commission in the rank of flying officer on 16 September 1919 [*gazetted* 16 September 1919, issue 31554]. His service between the two wars was outstanding. Posted to Iraq and attached to No 84 Squadron, *The London Gazette* of 6 June 1924, issue 32943, reports his awarded of the Distinguished Flying Cross '*... for distinguished service rendered during operations in Iraq in 1922'.* A Distinguished Service Order followed, with effect from 3 April 1928, also for services in Iraq and promulgated in *The Edinburgh Gazette* of 6 April 1928, issue 14432. His final accolade was A mention in a despatch, *gazetted* on 24 September 1941, supplement 35284. During the Second World War and now promoted group captain, and Station Commander at North Luffenham, he continued to involve himself in hazardous operations, paying the ultimate price during a raid to Berlin on the 2nd-3rd September 1941, when he accompanied Wing Commander George Engebret Valantine, commanding No 61 Squadron, their Manchester L7388 being shot down by *Flak* over the capital. For a fuller report in respect of both officers, please refer to my summaries for 2-3 September 1941, in my second volume dedicated to the losses from Bomber Command.

| 64 Squadron | Lt T Rose | Safe | |

SE.5a C5392

T/o Izel-lès-Hameau tasked for an offensive patrol during a connecting rod snapped, damaging the crankcase. It appears no spare Hispano-Suiza engine was available and a replacement Viper would take too long to install; consequently, the airframe was struck off charge on 8 May 1918. Arriving with the squadron on 13 March 1918, Lieutenant Rose accounted for a two-seater, sent down in flames during the early evening of 23 April, followed on the 29th with a Pfalz D going down out of control.

| 65 Squadron | 2Lt W H D Knight | + | Heath Cemetery, Harbonnieres |

F.1 Camel D6546

T/o 1140 Bertangles for an offensive patrol and when last seen by fellow members of the patrol eighteen year old William Henry Duncan Knight was horribly outnumbered, being attacked by up to a dozen hostile machines operating over the Somme between Le Hamel and Cerisy. His headstone carries the inscription; *Blessed Are The Pure In Heart For They Shall See God.'*

| 66 Squadron | Lt W H Robinson [Canada] | Injured | Montecchio Precalcino Communal Cemetery |

F.1 Camel B3840 F

T/o San Pietro and came to grief near the aerodrome after losing control recovering from a steep dive. William Hartley Robinson died later the same day from his injuries; he was twenty-five years of age and came from Toronto, a fact repeated by his parents on his headstone. His aircraft, 'B3840', had survived for ten months. By 5 July 1917, it was being held at the Aeroplane Acceptance Park at Lympne from where it was issued on the 29th of the month to No 70 Squadron at Estrée Blanche where it was coded C-4, to which its first pilot, Lieutenant E C Gribben added the name *'Pat'.* On the 10th and 13th of August, Lieutenant Gribben, operating over the Ypres Salient, now the scene of renewed heavy fighting, shot down three hostile aircraft and may have added to his score but, and no doubt to his chagrin, a fellow squadron pilot, Second Lieutenant I C F Agnew, had the misfortune to crash 'B3840' while landing on the 16th. Following repair it was taken in hand by No 3 Squadron on the 5th of October but attempting to land at Warloy Baillon*Second Lieutenant G S McGregor misjudged his approach and nosed over. This necessitated further repair on completion of which it went to No 46 Squadron at Filescamp on the 24th of November. Ill-fortune followed for two days after acceptance Lieutenant R K McConnel crashed while landing from a practice flight. Restored to good order, the Camel was prepared for transfer by rail to Italy where it was issued to No 66 Squadron on 27 January 1918. Here it survived a minor landing accident when Second Lieutenant A E Rudge arrived on the airfield rather heavily on the 8th of February.

* At the time No 3 Squadron was based at Lechelle but moved to Warloy Baillon on the 10th of October; thus, it is possible Second Lieutenant McGregor had been authorised to carry out a pre-move inspection of the airfield.

79 Squadron	Captain H P Rushforth MC	Injured See 20 May 1918 - 79 Squadron

5F.1 Dolphin C4030

T/o Beauvais for an offensive patrol during which the Dolphin ran low on fuel. Sighting the airfield at Clairmarais, Captain Rushforth made an approach to land but at five hundred feet his engine 'cut' and he ended up running into a hedge. Taken on charge on the 1st of April 1918, 'C4030' was struck off charge on 18 May 1918, with a total of thirteen hours and thirty minutes flying. As a second lieutenant, Henry Philip Rushforth had been commissioned to the General List on 28 November 1916, promulgated 18 December 1916, supplement 29869. Initially he was attached to No 27 Squadron, subsequently being attached to No 85 Squadron on its formation at Upavon on the 1st of August 1917. It was, however, with No 79 Squadron that he was awarded the Military Cross; *'For conspicuous gallantry and devotion to duty in leading bombing raids, the majority of which have been on distant objectives. Notably on one occasion, he led a most successful raid under extreme adverse weather conditions, in spite of which the objective was reached and bombed from a low altitude, after which the whole formation of eight machines returned in safety, after a total flight of over five hours. The success of the operation was due to his determination and fine leadership.'* [The *Edinburg Gazette* 19 September 1917, supplement 13143]. Postwar, he was granted a short service commission on 19 October 1919 [*gazetted* 24th October 1919, issue 31616].

79 Squadron	2Lt A C R Tate	+	St Pol British Cemetery, St Pol-sur-Ternoise

5F.1 Dolphin C4126

T/o Beauvais similarly tasked and when last sighted was in a steep nose dive, and on fire, over Bernicourt *[sic]*. It will be recalled that Alan Charles Richmond Tate had crashed on the advanced landing ground at Beaumetz on 11 April 1918, and when extracted from beneath his overturned Dolphin was taken to hospital for attention to some painful facial injuries. His father had served with the India Army Medical Service, retiring in the rank of colonel and it was on his recommendation that Alan's gravestone was inscribed; *'He Knew No Fear But The Fear Of The Lord RIP.'*

Friday 3 May 1918

1 Squadron AusFC	Lt J K Curwen-Walker AusFC	+	Ramleh War Cemetery
Bristol F.2b A7198	Corporal N P B Jensen AusFC	+	Ramleh War Cemetery

T/o Ramleh for a practice flight and, as reported by Trevor Henshaw, stalled and completely wrecked in the ensuing crash. Thirty year old Jack Keith Curwen-Walker's grave is marked with the inscription; *'My Beloved First Born.'* Corporal Jensen's entry is devoid of age and details of his next of kin. Andrew Pentland, during his trawl of air documents pertaining to movements, discovered that 'A7198' was flown to Waddington from Filton on 23 July 1917, and taken in hand by No 82 Squadron. Its subsequent despatch to the Middle East has not been recorded.

2 Squadron AusFC	Lt E D Cummings	Safe See 8 June 1918 - 2 Squadron AusFC

SE.5a B188

T/o 1005 Fouquerolles for an offensive patrol and while to the northeast of Méteren*sighted, and shot down, a Fokker DrI only to be himself attacked and driven down. Owing to the proximity of the lines, the SE.5a had to be abandoned to its fate.

* Méteren is in the d*épartement du Nord* but so close to the border, Lieutenant Cummings may well have made his landing in Belgium.

2 Squadron AusFC	Captain R C Phillips MC	Safe

SE.5a D3535

T/o Fouquerolles similarly tasked and reported to have run low on fuel thereby necessitating an emergency landing which, in the event, was attempted at Trangy [sic] but the Very pistol slipped from its socket and jammed the flying controls. Salvaged, 'D3535' was struck off charge three days later as not worth repairing.

2 Squadron AusFC	Lt E D Cameron	Safe
SE.5a D3923		

T/o Fouquerolles similarly ordered but ran short of fuel, forced landing in 'No Mans Land' near Méteren [see my asterisk note for B188 above], this location being shown in *The SE.5 File*. However, AIR 1/855 indicates Lieutenant Cameron came down in the Pas-de-Calais near Auchel, which is forty odd km south-southwest of Méteren.

7 Squadron	Lt F J Sanders	+	Ebblinghem Military Cemetery
RE.8 B6505			

T/o Droglandt authorised for practice flying but it seems Frederic Joseph Sanders was using Clairmarais for take off and landings as the report in AIR 1/855 indicates he spun in from between one hundred and fifty and one hundred feet near No 53 Squadron, which at the time was based here.

15 Squadron	Lt H J Browne	+	Querrieu British Cemetery
RE.8 C2361	2Lt L J Derrick	+	Querrieu British Cemetery

T/o Vert Galand having received orders to carry out a photographic reconnaissance mission during which the RE was shot down through the efforts of three enemy triplanes, falling in flames over the Somme near Buire-sur-l'Ancre roughly thirteen km east-northeast from where both now rest. The headstone of eighteen year old Harold Johnston Browne has been inscribed; *'He Fought The Good Fight On Whose Soul Sweet Jesus Have Mercy'.* Leslie James Derrick's military life began with The Buffs [East Kent Regiment]; his headstone carries the words; *'Not My Will But Thine Be Done Gone On To Some Better Thing.'* They were the squadron's first fatalities since the 1st of April 1918.

19 Squadron	Captain G Chadwick	pow
5F.1 Dolphin C3828		

T/o Savy for an offensive patrol over the Pas-de-Calais in the direction of Neuve-Chappelle where Captain Chadwick was last seen going down out of control. Previously of the Manchester Regiment, Territorial Forces, his name appears in *Flight* May 30, 1918, under the heading 'Missing', while the magazine's issue of August 1st, 1918, confirms his status as a prisoner of war, wounded.

20 Squadron	Lt T W Williamson	Safe	
Bristol F.2b C4856	Mechanic S W Melbourne	Safe	See 16 July 1918 - 49 Squadron

T/o Boisdinghem for an offensive patrol during which the crew lost there way; force-landed near Henneveux in the Pas-de-Calais some thirteen km east of Boulogne. Neither airman suffered injury, but Mechanic Melbourne was rather shaken up by the experience. 'C4856' was struck off charge on 8 May 1918, with thirty hours and six minutes of flying to its credit.

27 Squadron	Lt H P Schoeman	Safe	Unemployed list 9 October 1919: Lt
DH.4 A7740	2Lt W Spencer	Safe	See 10 May 1918 - 27 Squadron

T/o Ruisseauville for bombing operations on return to the airfield Lieutenant Schoeman was late in 'flaring' and 'A7740' was damaged beyond repair. First used by No 49 Squadron, it had been badly shot about by anti-aircraft while raiding Cambrai on 29 November 1917, Second Lieutenant G S Stewart and Lieutenant D D Richardson escaping injury. Second Lieutenant Spencer had been involved in a serious crash on 12 April 1918.

27 Squadron	2Lt G E Ffrench	Safe	See 23 May 1918 - 27 Squadron
DH.4 B2092	Sgt V Cummins	Safe	

T/o 0630 Ruisseauville tasked for a raid but owing to 'B2092' developing a rough running engine the crew fell behind the rest of their formation. Isolated, the DH seemed an easy target for a patrolling enemy scout and in the wake of its attack George Ffrench was obliged to force-land, coming down just to the north of Kemmel [West-Vlaaderen] in an area that had witnessed ferocious fighting almost throughout the war and such was its proximity to German positions salvage of the aircraft was impossible. Although conjecture on my part, I consider it likely it was subsequently destroyed by shall fire. Details of George Ffrench's birthplace, next of kin and commission are reported in the summary for 12 April 1918.

| 35 Squadron | Lt J E R Hyson | Injured |
| FK.8 D5016 | 2Lt F H McNay | Safe |

T/o Villers-Bocage tasked for an operational patrol; on return, crashed while landing. On squadron charge from 3 April 1918, 'D5016' accumulated forty-three hours and fifteen minutes in its one month of active service. Second Lieutenant McNay was confirmed as an observer officers on the 1st of June 1918, as *gazetted* in issue 30572 of the paper published on 18 June 1918.

| 41 Squadron | Lt A Goby [Canada] | Safe |
| SE.5a C5301 | | |

T/o Serny for practice flying, a detail that ended with Lieutenant Goby landing and running against a ridge which damaged his aircraft beyond repair. 'C5301' was the first aircraft in a batch of one hundred and fifty airframes ordered from Vickers Limited at their Crayford facility in Kent and was at Farnborough by 20 November 1917, before passing through the hands of Nos 1 and 2 Air Issues, reaching No 24 Squadron at Matigny on 8 March. During the early afternoon of the 11th, and flown by Lieutenant E W Lindeberg, it shared in the downing of an enemy two-seater east of Bellenglise*in the *département du Aisne*. However, four days later it was lodged with No 2 Aeroplane Supply Depot from where it was issued on the 17th of March to No 41 Squadron. Lieutenant Goby of the Canadian Expeditionary was seconded to the Royal Flying Corps on 19 October 1917, remaining so until relinquishing his commission on 18 March 1919, when he returned for duty with the Saskatchewan Regiment [promulgated in *The London Gazette* on 16 May 1919, issue 31343].

* The entry for Bellenglise on *Wikipedia* [which I acknowledge] has an interesting historical reference, relevant to the *Great War* for it was here, on the 28th of August 1914, a Friday, that the French 10th Regiment of Territorial Infantry, comprising mainly of soldiers from the local *département,* clashed with a strong force of seasoned invading German forces. Nevertheless, the Territorials acquitted themselves well before being forced to yield with many hundreds being captured. Posted on the same site is the famous photograph of men of the British 137th Brigade gathered *en mass* on the canal bank at Riqueval being addressed on the 2nd of October 1918, by Brigadier-General J V Campbell from the nearby bridge following the crossing of the St Quentin Canal.

| 46 Squadron | 2Lt R L G Skinner | + | Arras Flying Services Memorial |
| F.1 Camel B7357 | | | |

T/o Filescamp for an offensive patrol and was last seen by his flight northwest of Don [sic] engaged in combat. Prior to transferring to the Royal Flying Corps, twenty year old Robert Leonard Grahame Skinner had served with the 1st/2nd Battalion Black Watch [Royal Highlanders]. From Callander in Perthshire he was the son of the Reverend Henry Leonard Skinner and Susanna Maria Skinner. 'B7357' arrived in France by sea from Newhaven and first saw service with No 65 Squadron. Following overhaul, during which it was fitted with a Le Rhône 9J, it was allocated to No 46 Squadron on 21 April 1918.

| 48 Squadron | 2Lt A C G Brown | pow | Heath Cemetery, Harbonnieres |
| Bristol F.2b C814 | Cpl A W Sainsbury | pow | |

T/o Bertangles to carry out a reconnaissance of enemy positions around Villers-Bretonneux; failed to return. Alexander Claud Garden Brown, whose home was at Whitwell on the Isle of Wight, died in enemy hands from his wounds on the 6th of May 1918. 'C814' flew for a total of twenty-two hours and thirty minutes; it arrived with the squadron as recently as the 17th of April.

| 53 Squadron | Lt H T Rushton | Injured | Unemployment list 14 August 1919: Lt |
| RE.8 C2311 | 2Lt J B Sanders | Injured | Unemployment list 28 May 1919: Lt |

T/o Clairmarais tasked for photographic reconnaissance; brought down near Abeele by hostile machines. The RE had been in squadron hands for less than a week and had flown for just four hours and forty-five minutes. Herbert Thomas Rushton was commissioned to the General List of the Royal Flying Corps on the 2nd of February 1918 [supplement 30515 of 8 February 1918]. During the Second World War he returned to the service and was commissioned to the Training Branch on 2 April 1941 [issue 35158 of 9 May 1941]. Rising to squadron leader rank, he was appointed to The Most Excellent Order the British Empire [Military Division] in the King's Birthday Honours list of 14 June 1945, as promulgated on that date, supplement 37119. At some time in the postwar years he joined the Training Branch of the Royal Air Force Volunteer Reserve, but relinquished his commission [ranked pilot officer] on 1 July 1947 [*gazetted* 23 January1951, supplement 39129].

| 54 Squadron | Lt A R Stewart | + | Les Baraques Military Cemetery, Sangatte |
| F.1 Camel C1677 *Basuto* | | | |

T/o Caffiers authorised to practice low flying. While doing so it seems Archibald Ross Stewart dived his aircraft but while trying to recover to level flight 'C1677' broke up and crashed near Wadenthun in the Pas-de-Calais, a little under fifteen km southwest of the port of Calais. This particular Camel was presented By the Paramount Chief and Basuto Nation. It was taken on squadron charge on 20 April 1918. Eyewitnesses to the accident estimate its height was around two thousand feet when it was seen to come apart.

| 62 Squadron | Lt H C M Nangle | Injured | Unemployment list 13 June 1919: Lt |
| Bristol F.2b B1245 | 2Lt T C Cooper | Injured | |

T/o Planques tasked for an offensive patrol but before becoming airborne ran into a FE.2b [airframe serial not reported] belonging to No 58 Squadron.

| 62 Squadron | Lt P R Hampton | pow | |
| Bristol F.2b C4744 | Lt L C Lane | pow | |

T/o Planques for an offensive patrol and was last sighted going down behind the enemy lines, both officers were wounded. The Roll of Honour released by the Air Ministry and published in *Flight* May 30, 1918, shows Lieutenant Hampton's name under the 'Missing' heading, while the magazine's issue of July 1918, confirms he was being held prisoner, and believed wounded, this being confirmed by the paper on August 8, 1918. With effect from 14 January 1920, Lieutenant Hampton, reluctantly, had to relinquish his commission owing to ill-health which had been contracted on active service.

| 64 Squadron | Lt W C Daniel | Safe | Unemployed list 28 September 1919: Lt |
| SE.5a B2 | | | |

T/o Izel-lès-Hameau for an offensive patrol in the course of which Lieutenant Daniel 'flamed' a Rumpler two-seat reconnaissance aircraft over Mercatel in the Pas-de-Calais, but was himself shot about and at around 1055 he force-landed amongst old trench workings, the SE.5a being wrecked as a result.

| 64 Squadron | Lt W P Southwell | Safe | |
| SE.5a B697 | | | |

T/o Izel-lès-Hameau similarly tasked and in an attempt to force land at map reference 37DG21D collided with telegraph wires and crashed. Reallocated from an intended training rôle, 'B697' was flown to France and taken in hand by the squadron on 28 January 1918.

| 73 Squadron | 2Lt A F Dawes | pow | |
| F.1 Camel D6480 | | | |

T/o Beauvois for an offensive patrol and when last seen by the flight he was flying in a westerly direction, apparently under control, in the vicinity of Messines, the scene of much heavy ground fighting of late. In its issue of July 18, 1918, *Flight* reports Second Lieutenant Dawes as being confirmed as a prisoner of war. He was repatriated on 18 December 1918.

| 73 Squadron | Lt R R Rowe | pow | Arras Flying Services Memorial |
| F.1 Camel D6536 | | | |

T/o Beauvois similarly tasked and was last sighted over Flanders in the vicinity of Bois de Ploegsteert. Lieutenant Rowe's name appears in *Flight* June 6, 1918, under the heading 'Missing'; sadly, Robert Ronald Rowe, alive when found by his captors, died on the day he was reported 'missing' since when his grave has been lost.

| 98 Squadron | Lt R A Holiday MM | + | Arras Flying Services Memorial |
| DH.9 C6101 | 2Lt C B Whyte [Canada] | + | Arras Flying Services Memorial |

T/o 1200 Alquines after briefing for a raid on Menin during which the crew came under attack from a force of enemy aircraft estimated at eighteen in total. Against such odds the crew stood little chance of escape and when last seen their DH was going down, burning and breaking up in an almost vertical plunge near Gheluvelt* some nine km east-southeast from Ypres. Richard Alan Holiday was *gazetted* to the General List of the Royal Flying Corps on 24 May 1917 [supplement 30141 of 20 June 1917]. Cecil Bertram Whyte was formerly of the Royal Scots, thus suggesting he joined our armed services having crossed the Atlantic from his native Canada and the city of Edmonton in Alberta. In conclusion, 'C6101' was issued to the squadron prior to its deployment from Old Sarum to France on the 1st of April 1918. The deaths of these two officers were the first suffered by the squadron since deploying to France.

* Students of military history, and in particular those whose interest lies in delving into the early engagements of the *Great War* will no doubt be familiar with the now famous actions of late October 1914, when the 2nd Battalion Worcester Regiment fought so bravely to stem the German advance towards Ypres, retaking the village of Gheluvelt and with it the lessening of enemy pressure being put on our defences of the Menin road.

| 98 Squadron | Lt S B Welch | Injured | See 25 August 1918 - 49 Squadron |
| DH.9 C6174 | Lt C T de Guise [Canada] | Injured | |

T/o Alquines tasked for a reconnaissance sortie and on return, and approaching the airfield, stalled at around fifty feet and crashed. Salvaged, the airframe was struck off charge on 8 May 1918, twelve hours and thirty minutes flying recorded. Originally intended for No 104 Squadron 'C6174' was issued to No 98 Squadron on the 22nd of April 1918. Of the Quebec Regiment, Canadian Imperial Forces, ceased his secondment on 31 March 1919, as promulgated in issue 31333 published on 9 May 1919.

| 142 Squadron | Captain W H Williams | + | Ramleh War Cemetery |
| Martinsyde G100 A3495 | | | |

T/o Ramleh for a practice flight armed with bombs and, as historian Trevor Henshaw reports, crashed on the airfield circa 1750, a fire breaking out on impact. The crash was witnessed by Mechanic William Hewitt Fell who immediately ran towards the wreckage to render aid; tragically, as he neared the scene one of the bombs exploded and he was mortally injured. William Humphrey Williams was formerly of the 6th Battalion Lancashire Fusiliers. His headstone reflects his Welsh origins; *'Preswylfa Carnarvon North Wales'*.

| 205 Squadron | Lt R Scott | + | Hangard Communal Cemetery extension |
| DH.4 D9243 | 2Lt T A Humphrey MM | + | Hangard Communal Cemetery extension |

T/o 1610 Bois de Roche and was last sighted over the Somme in a flat spin near the railway station at Chaulnes but I suggest the eventual crash occurred near the village of Fontaine-lès-Cappy, a little under ten km to the north as memorials 4 and 3 respectively exist here for the two officers; a note on the Commonwealth War Graves Commission website indicates that following the armistice burials from the churchyard extension at Fontaine-lès-Cappy have been opened and the remains interred in the extension at Hangard which lies about twenty-four km to the west-southwest. Twenty-four year old Thomas Albert Humphrey undoubtedly won his Military Medal pre-commissioning which was *gazetted* on 28 August 1917 issue 30257, and going on to serve with the 8th Battalion The Queen's [Royal West Surrey Regiment]. At the time of their deaths, the area in which they fell had been the scene of intense fighting during the period of the German spring offensive of March 1918, Hangard being the junction between the Commonwealth forces of the Fifth Army and the French Army and it was not until the 8th of August 1918 that the 1st and 2nd Canadian Mounted Rifles succeeded in flushing out the Germans from Hangard and its environs.

| 206 Squadron | Lt A E Steel | + | Arras Flying Services Memorial |
| DH.9 C2157 | 2Lt A Slinger | + | Arras Flying Services Memorial |

T/o 1741 Alquines for an operational mission and was observed between 1800 and 1900 [I can only think there was a wide variation in the precise time] to be going down in flames between Bailleul and Kemmel, the two locations separate by about ten km lie west-northwest and north-west of Armentières in the *département du Nord* and nestled against the border with Belgium. Nineteen year old Arthur Edward Steel had served formerly with the 21st Battalion, Middlesex Regiment; his Manchester born observer was of the same age. Their DH had been on squadron charge since 21 April 1918.

Saturday 4 May 1918

1 Squadron	Lt D W Hughes	Injured
SE.5a C1107		

T/o Clairmarais tasked for patrol operations and wrecked after crashing near Renescure, a commune in the *département du Nord*, owing to engine failure. On the 16th of April 1918, while on an offensive patrol, 'C1107' was hit by fire from the ground causing the pilot, Captain J S Windsor MC*a painful wound to one of his wrists. 'C1107' had been on squadron charge since 12 April 1918.

* *The London Gazette* supplement 30444 published on Christmas Eve 1917, shows Captain Windsor MC as remaining seconded from the South Wales Border Regiment. A date of 1 July 1917, has been appended against his name which, I suspect, indicates promotion to the rank of captain. His Royal Air Force commission ceased with effect from 9 February 1920 [at the time he was ranked flight lieutenant] on return to his regiment and with which he served until being placed on retired pay on 9 November 1947, having exceeded the age limit for retirement. At the time his rank was that of Major [Lieutenant-Colonel War Substantive] but was granted the honorary rank of Brigadier, *gazetted* 11 November 1947, supplement 38119.

4 Squadron AusFC	Lt B W Wright	+	Outtersteene Communal Cemetery extension,
F.1 Camel B5629			Bailleul

T/o 1735 Clairmarais for an offensive patrol, which was to include bombing, and when last seen by his fellow pilots at around 1805, was on fire near Vieux-Berquin, a commune in the *département du Nord*. Bernard Wilfred Wright hailed from Hemel Hempstead in Hertfordshire. This was the squadron's tenth operational loss since the 1st of April while five other Camels had been wrecked in training accidents, resulting overall in the deaths of three pilots and one reported to have fallen into enemy hands.

7 Squadron	Lt E S Wood	Injured
RE.8 B7727	Lt G A Mountain	Injured Unemployed list 8 April 1919: Lt

T/o Droglandt having been briefed for artillery observation but before becoming airborne swung and crashed into three light tenders, effectively wrecking the RE [and no doubt causing no little damage to the tenders]. This particular RE had already been rebuilt following a landing accident at No 1 Air Issues on 28 March 1918, subsequently arriving with No 7 Squadron on 21 April. Its total flying hours are reported as seventeen hours and twenty-five minutes.

11 Squadron	Lt R K Harrison	Safe
Bristol F.2b B1309	Sgt R D Mason	Safe

T/o Remaisnil for a reconnaissance mission but owing to heavy mist made a precautionary landing near Rouen. When conditions improved, the crew took off but crashed into a tree which damaged their aircraft beyond repair and it was struck off charge on the last day of the month. 'B1309' had been issued to the squadron on 29 March 1918; its flying hours total has not been recorded.

16 Squadron	2Lt Buick	Safe
RE.8 C5058	2Lt Donald	Safe

T/o Camblain l'Abbé having received instructions for artillery observation; ran low on fuel and force-landed near Bully-Grenay in the Pas-de-Calais, some twenty km north-northwest of Arras. Salvaged, a decision was made that repairs would not be worth the cost and the airframe was struck off charge on 8 May 1918, with sixty-nine hours and fifty-five minutes of recorded flying time, most of which would have been since 26 February 1918, when it was accepted by the squadron.

24 Squadron	Lt R A Slipper	pow
SE.5a C1793		

T/o Conteville and failed to return from an offensive patrol. Lieutenant Slipper, who was wounded, was named on the Air Ministry list, repeated in *Flight* May 30, 1918, under the heading 'Missing'. His repatriation was notified on 30 December 1918.

54 Squadron	Lt R E Taylor	Safe
F.1 Camel C6702*		

T/o Caffiers authorised to practice flying at low altitude but crashed almost immediately.

* AIR 1/855 [as Andrew Pentland reports] indicates 'B6702' which leads me to think that the Camel may have carried the letter 'B', though Air-Britain's *Camel File* notes that 'C6702' had been seriously damaged on the 12th of March 1918, while being tested by No 3 Squadron [Warloy Baillon] at the machine gun range when owing to incorrect timing on the CC interrupter gear the propeller was shot through resulting in excessive vibration. Taken for repair, it is suggested [in the File] the airframe may have been incorrectly painted as 'B6702'.

60 Squadron	2Lt R G Lewis	Safe
SE.5a D3913		

T/o Boffles for an offensive patrol but owing to engine failure left the patrol and force-landed on a French airfield near Poix; overturned and damaged beyond repair. 'D3913' had logged forty-two hours and twenty-five minutes.

74 Squadron	Captain W E Young	Safe
SE.5a D271		

T/o Calirmarais South for an offensive patrol and on return landed on soft and uneven ground resulting in the undercarriage collapsing. During the evening of 12 April 1918, Captain Young, while on patrol over Belgium, downed an Albatros south of Poperinghe.

210 Squadron	Lt W L Davidson USAS	Injured
F.1 Camel B5651		

T/o St Omer having received orders for an offensive patrol, which included bombing. On return Lieutenant Davidson allowed his approach speed to decay to a point where he stalled at fifty feet and spun in. Although not seriously injured, he was nevertheless badly shaken. His aircraft was the first in a batch of one hundred airframes produced by Clayton and Shuttleworth Limited of Lincoln.

Sunday 5 May 1918

16 Squadron	Lt J Grimshaw	Injured
RE.8 A3839		

T/o Camblain l'Abbé authorised to practice flying on type but owing to his inexperience Lieutenant Grimshaw made a flat turn at one hundred feet, lost control and crashed, sustaining severe injuries.

52 Squadron	Lt L S Worthing	Safe	Unemployed list 7 June 1919: Lt
RE.8 B2262	2Lt F D Gaiger	Safe	

T/o Mont de Soissons Farm to transit to the squadron's new base at Fismes [having been lodged for forty-eight hours at Serches] but *en route* the RE's engine failed and the crew sideslipped in from five hundred feet. Lieutenant Worthing was transferred from the Cheshire Regiment to the General List of the Royal Flying Corps on the 18th of July 1917, as promulgated in supplement 30270 of 5 September 1917. As a private soldier he had been commissioned to the Cheshire Regiment from The London Regiment, Territorial Forces, with effect from the 30th of January 1916 [*gazetted* in supplement 29494 of 1 March 1916].

107 Squadron	Lt R H Horwood	Injured
DH.6 C1959	2Lt D P Scott	Injured

T/o Lake Down for a training exercise during which the control column became jammed behind the instrument panel. Out of control, 'C1959' came down heavily and was, it is believed, damaged beyond repair.

131 Squadron	Lt J M R Miller	Injured
DH.6 C6657	Mechanic C R Clack	Injured

T/o Shawbury for a training flight and while banking to the right allowed the nose to drop and with insufficient height in which to recover the DH hit the ground. Charles Richard Clack died from his injuries later in the day.

Monday 6 May 1918

1 Squadron	Lt B D Clark	Injured	
SE.5a C1074			

T/o Clairmarais for an offensive patrol during which his petrol tank was shot through. Despite this, Lieutenant Clark struggled back to base, approaching the airfield from the north in storm conditions and it was here that he crashed into some trees.

1 Squadron	Lt K C Mills	Safe	See 8 August 1918 - 1 Squadron
SE.5a C5374			

T/o Clairmarais for an offensive patrol in the course of which Kenneth Charles Mills and his aircraft became the object for intensive anti-aircraft fire. Badly shot about, he landed safely and though 'C5374' was salvaged, the airframe was struck off charge five days later. On squadron charge 6 April 1918, it accounted for three hostile aircraft, one being shared, all at the hands of Lieutenant Mills. His commission to the General List of the Royal Flying Corps, effective 10 May 1917, was published in *The London Gazette* supplement 30100 of the 29th May 1917.

2 Squadron	Lt O E Sharpe	Safe	
FK.8 D5022	Captain Beighley	Safe	

T/o Hesdigneul to show Captain Beighley, an infantry officer, a sight of the lines from the air. On return Lieutenant Sharpe overshot the airfield and finished up in a ditch. Salvaged, 'D5022' languished until 25 June 1918, when it was struck off charge with a total of fifteen hours and fifty minutes flying time annotated.

2 Squadron	Lt J Stuart	Injured	See 8 July 1918 - 2 Squadron
FK.8 D5027			

T/o Hesdigneul for practice flying, a detail that ended with a landing crash. Similar to the FK.8 summarised above, 'D5027' languished until 29 June 1918, when with eight hours and twenty-five minutes flight time recorded, it was struck off charge.

3 Squadron AusFC	Captain H D E Ralfe AusFC	+	Vignacourt British Cemetery
RE.8 A4404	Lt W A J Buckland AusFC	+	Vignacourt British Cemetery

T/o Villers-Bocage for a counter attack patrol and was seen to go down, out of control, and streaming flames after being attacked by a quartet of enemy triplanes. 'A4404' had been on squadron establishment since the 22nd of October 1917, and had logged a total of one hundred and thirty-eight hours and forty-five minutes flying. The son of the late Henry Ralfe, a Sydney Barrister-at-Law, Henry's mother [now the Honourable Mrs Holmes a Court] requested, and had approved, the following inscription for her son's headstone; *'Beloved Son I Thank My God Upon Ever Remembrance Of You.'* That inscribed for his observer reads; *'Until The Day Dawns And Shadows Flee Away.'*

12 Squadron	2Lt G B Leslie	Safe	See 12 October 1918 - 12 Squadron
RE.8 C2249 *Gambia No 4*	2Lt S Soothill	Safe	

T/o Soncamp for a test flight and crashed into telegraph wires after overshooting Ascq, base for No 5 Squadron. George Buchanan Leslie was one of many commissioned to the General List of the Royal Flying Corps on the 27th of September 1917 [*gazetted* 3 October 1917, supplement 30320]. Second Lieutenant Soothill relinquished his commission, owing to wounds, on 14 August 1919.

18 Squadron	2Lt H Leach	Safe	
DH.4 A7816	Lt J Fenwick	Safe	

T/o Serny to practice firing at targets; damaged beyond repair after landing heavily on ground that was hard and rough.

24 Squadron   Lt J A E R Daly   Safe
SE.5a C1846
T/o Conteville for a practice flight and crashed, owing to engine failure, near the aerodrome. The loss of 'C1846' is also reported for the 5th of May 1918. It had been on squadron establishment since the 29th of April 1918.

29 Squadron   Lt A E Reed   Safe   See 11 June 1918 - 29 Squadron
SE.5a C5330
T/o St Omer for a practice flight and on return, and landing, a wheel parted company with the axle resulting in 'C5330' turning over. Taken in hand on the 1st of the month, it had achieved a mere four hours and twenty minutes flying in total. For the pilot it was his second crash in less than a week [see my summary for the 2nd]

29 Squadron   Sgt A S Cardno   +   Arras Flying Services Memorial
SE.5A D5956   A mention in a Despatch
T/o St Omer for a line patrol over the *Forêt de Nieppe* and failed to return thus becoming the first pilot from the squadron to lose his life since conversion to SE.5a scouts. Allen Scott Cardno's*service number '206' identifies him as a direct entrant to the Royal Flying Corps in 1912, though whether or not he trained immediately as a pilot I am not able to say. However, *Flight* January 11, 1917, repeated the long list of those who received A mention in a Despatch as released on 13 November 1916, and reported in a supplement to *The London Gazette* published on 2 January 1917. His entry on the Commonwealth War Graves Commission website is devoid of age and next of kin.

* Andrew Pentland, quoting from *Cross & Cockade Volume 2* pages 102 and 114, show enlistment on 5 June 1912, and crossing to France on 12 August 1914, attached to Royal Flying Corps Headquarters.

40 Squadron   Lt G Watson   Safe   See 20 May 1918
SE.5a D3513
T/o 1100 Brauy for an offensive patrol but on return to the aerodrome forty minutes later George Watson mis-judged his approach and hit the chimney of a nearby house. The impact removed most of the undercarriage unit resulting in 'D3513' being struck off charges 18 June 1918.

53 Squadron   Lt S H Evans   Safe
RE.8 B4101   2Lt L F Thurlow*   Safe   Unemployed list 27 February 1919: 2Lt
T/o Clairmarais for a night patrol in the direction of Kemmel where of late the fighting had been intense with the enemy gaining the upper hand, though suffering many casualties. Force-landed in a field near Abeele airfield owing to engine failure. Arriving with the squadron on 29 April 1918, 'B4101' was written off with a mere seven hours and twenty-five minutes flying to its credit.

* An Acting Pilot Officer Leslie Frank Thurlow was confirmed in his appointment and graded as a Pilot Officer on 8 November 1939, under the heading Auxiliary Air Force and No 903[County of London] Squadron which came under the aegis of Balloon Command. However, by December 1941, he was attached to the Administrative and Special Duties Branch and continued to serve until relinquishing his commission on under the provisions of the Navy, Army and Air Force Reserves Act 1954. His rank is shown as flight lieutenant.

62 Squadron   Lt G Palardy [USA]   Injured Huby St-Leu British Cemetery
Bristol F.2b C4602
T/o Planques for a practice flight which ended with the Bristol stalling and nose diving into the ground on, or near the airfield. On reaching the crash site, rescuers found Guy Parady had been very severely crushed by the impact and, sadly, he died from his injuries on the 7th May. Born at Fitchburg in Worcester County, Massachusetts, his headstone carries the words; *'Tes Parents Fiers De Toi Pleurent Et Esperent Repose En Paix'* which translates as 'Your proud parents of thee cry and hope rest in peace'.

74 Squadron   Captain W J Cairnes   Safe   See 1 June 1918 - 74 Squadron
SE.5a C6385

T/o Clairmarais for an offensive patrol during which the aircraft's Very pistol was accidentally discharged, setting fire to a longeron. William Jameson Cairnes, late of the 1st Battalion Leinster Regiment, landed safely but 'C6385' was struck off charge on 11 May 1918. Captain Cairnes had served almost from the beginning of the war, his commission to the 5th Battalion Leinster Regiment being *gazetted* on 22 September 1914, issue 28910.

| 74 Squadron | Lt H E Dolan MC | Safe | See 12 May 1918 - 74 Squadron |
| SE.5a B173 | | | |

T/o Clairmarais for an offensive patrol and on return, and while taxying, the left side wheel dropped into a deep rut and the resulting shock caused the undercarriage struts to fail. Since the beginning of April, Henry Eric Dolan had sent down an Albatros east of Merville [Nord] early on the 12th, followed during the late morning of the 29th by another Albatros, this time over West-Vlaanderen near Dickebusch. Then, twenty-four hours later his keen aim accounted for a Halberstadt which force-landed in the fighting area where it was destroyed by shell fire.

| 88 Squadron | Lt Foster | Safe |
| Bristol F.2b C4713 | Lt Chilton | Safe |

T/o Capelle to practice gunnery; on return landed on a road and turned over. Struck off charge on 11 May 1918, with thirty-two hours and twenty minutes flying time recorded. During the day the squadron was declared ready to start operations and in the remaining months of the war it gained a reputation as being one of the most aggressive fighter squadron operating on the Western Front.

| 101 Squadron | Lt S A Hustwitt [Canada] | pow |
| FE.2b C9787 | Lt N A Smith | pow |

T/o Famechon for a special road reconnaissance Estrée to Brie; failed to return. Lieutenant Hustwitt of the Canadian Engineers was seconded to the Royal Flying Corps on 5 June 1917, *gazetted* 29 June 1917, supplement 30157. Released from captivity [notification of this was reported in the Boxing Day 1918, issue of *Flight*], he was appointed to the rank of temporary captain [within the Canadian Engineers] on 5 December 1918, promulgated 11 August 1919, supplement 31500. The repatriation of his observer was reported in the same issue where his initials are recorded as 'L A'.

| 103 Squadron | Lt G F Townsend | Injured |
| DH.9 D1690 | | |

T/o Norwich [No 3 Aeroplane Acceptance Park] for delivery to No 103 Squadron at Old Sarum but *en route* flew into low cloud and mist and while attempting to land lost control and spun to the ground. Lieutenant Townsend's injuries were not thought to be serious. Some documents show the accident occurring on the 7th, but this was the day during which the wreckage was surveyed for possible salvage.

204 Squadron   F.1 Camel B3892   Reported to have crashed whilst landing [presumably at Cappelle].

| 211 Squadron | Lt G H Baker | Safe |
| DH.9 B7625 | 2Lt T B Dodwell | Safe |

T/o Petite Synthe for aerial gunnery practice and wrecked in a heavy landing that resulted in a smashed undercarriage.

Tuesday 7 May 1918
1 Squadron   SE.5a B8506   While parked at Clairmarias struck and damaged beyond repair by an unidentified RE.8. Salvaged, 'B8506' was struck off charge on 11 May 1918.

| 8 Squadron | Lt D J M Miller | Injured |
| FK.8 C8434 | Lt H Wisnekowitz MC | Injured |

T/o Auxi-le-Château having received orders for a bombing operations but on lifting into the air flew into trees and crashed. Since its arrival with the squadron on 16 March 1918, 'C8434' had logged seventy hours and fifty-five minutes flying. On 22 June 1918, supplement 30761, of *The London Gazette* carried the citation for Lieutenant Wisnekowitz's award of the Military Cross; *'For conspicuous gallantry and devotion to duty. On one occasion, during a very thick mist, he and his pilot* [Lieutenant Lionel Conrad Hooton] *by flying very low, despite very heavy machine-gun fire, succeeded in locating the enemy's position. Though their machine was hit in all the vital parts, it was flown back to the aerodrome in safety. On a later occasion, while on contact patrol, during failing light they succeeded in locating accurately the position of the enemy. They have shown the utmost gallantry and skill during recent operations, and have carried out their duties with the greatest courage and determination.'* As an observer officer Harry Wisenekowitz was granted a short service commission on 12 September 1919, promulgated that day in issue 31548. Subsequently, transferred to the Reserve of Air Force Officers, he was transferred from Class B to Class C with effect from 20th August 1928. A document pertaining to him, non-digitised, is available from The National Archives under WO 339/115148.

10 Squadron	Lt W Hughes	Safe	See 13 May 1918 - 10 Squadron
FK.8 C8521	2Lt H G Hooker	Injured	Unemployed list 21 May 1919: 2Lt

T/o Droglandt having received instructions for a *Flash* reconnaissance during which the FK came under attack from a hostile aircraft forcing the crew to descend near Peselhoek, a hamlet in West-Vlaanderen which at the time was an important rail hub for supplies being sent to the British Second Army holding Ypres. Although only a hamlet, its location was of prime importance within the Ypres Salient. Second Lieutenant Hooker was slightly wounded.

18 Squadron   DH.4 A8064   Damaged beyond repair after being struck by a Bristol Fighter [see below]. On 21 April 1918, when flown by Second Lieutenant A C Atkey and Lieutenant P W Anderson [both officers are named in various summaries], tasked for a photographic reconnaissance of the Aubers area of the département of Nord and scene of hard fighting in the spring of 1915, came under attack from no less that five Pfalz scouts, one of which was sent down out of control.

19 Squadron	2Lt W G Brown [Canada]	+	Aubigny Communal Cemetery extension
5F.1 Dolphin C3841			

T/o Savy with authorisation to carry out a practice flight during which twenty-one year old William Gordon Brown of Motherwell, Ontario, crashed near the airfield. His headstone is inscribed; *'I See My Pilot Face To Face'.*

27 Squadron	Lt E A Coghlan	Safe	Unemployed list 5 May 1919: Lt
DH.4 B2139	Lt V F S Dunton	Safe	Unemployed list 20 February 1919: Lt

T/o Ruisseauville and on return to base following target practice landed safely and came to a halt; then, as the crew prepared to move off so their aircraft was dealt a crippling blow by DH.4 D9242 flown by a 25 Squadron crew Lieutenant J Loupinksy and Sergeant J R White. Apart from a nasty fright, neither crew were hurt and 'D9242' was sent for a rebuild, emerging with a new airframe serial 'F6136'. Victor Frederick Shapley Dunton returned to the Royal Air Force in 1939, and was commissioned on 14 February 1939 to the Administrative and Special Duties Branch [*gazetted* 21 February 1939, issue 34600]. His service continued until relinquishing his commission, in the rank of squadron leaders, under the provisions of the Navy, Army and Air Force Reserves Act 1954.

84 Squadron	Lt H O MacDonald	Safe	Unemployed list 25 July 1919: Lt
SE.5a B134			

T/o Bertangles for an air test and damaged beyond repair following a forced landing in a ploughed field, owing to engine failure.

Wednesday 8 May 1918

1 Squadron C Flight	Captain C C Clark	pow	Gosport [Ann's Hill] Cemetery
SE.5a B8410			

T/o Clairmarais for an offensive patrol and shot down over territory in the hands of the enemy. Cecil Christian Clark was one of seventy-four graduates from the Royal Military Academy all *gazetted* in the rank of Second Lieutenant on 10 May 1916. Fifty-two, including Second Lieutenant Clark went either to the Royal Horse or the Royal Field Artillery, while the remainder were assigned to units within the Royal Garrison Artillery and it is interesting to note that his association with the Royal Regiment of Artillery remained with him throughout the 1920s and '30s when his service was in the Reserve of Air Force Officers*. I strongly suspect he left the air force after the *Great War* but on 23 August 1920 he was granted a short service commission, in the rank of flight lieutenant [*gazetted* 27 August 1920, issue 32032]. However, less than two years later he put in his resignation papers [effective 1 April 1922 and *gazetted* in issue 32673 published on 18 April 1922], but on 23 July 1929 he was commissioned as a flying officer in class A of the afore mentioned Reserve of Air Force Officers, reverting to class C 23 July 1935 only to return to class A a year later with promotion to squadron leader promulgated on 30 June 1939, the relevant issues for these *Gazette* entries being 33519, 34182, 34366 and 34654. By the early winter of 1939, he was attached to No 2 Anti-Aircraft Co-operation Unit at Gosport and it was when flying Skua L2981 in the late evening of the last day of November that he crashed into shallow water at Fareham Creek; Cecil was forty-two years old. During the *Great War* he was credited with seven combat victories and three shared with fellow pilots.

* Each time that he left the air force his retained rank reflects prior army service; lieutenant and captain being mentioned in respect of the Reserve of Royal Artillery Officers. In preparing the general summary, I acknowledge the Sussex History forum website.

1 Squadron	Lt P J Clayson	Safe	Placed on the retired list on account of ill-
SE.5a C1095			health 16 April 1929: F/L MC DFC

T/o Clairmarias similarly tasked; returned with his aircraft so badly shot about that it was deemed beyond any worthwhile repair; struck off charge 12 May 1918, with forty-nine hours and twenty-nine minutes of flying recorded. Please see my summary for 1 April 1918, concerning Percy Jack Clayson's commission and award citations.

1 Squadron	2Lt J C Wood	pow
SE.5a C6408		

T/o Clairmarais similarly tasked and when last seen by other members of the patrol Second Lieutenant Wood's aircraft was over the lines and to the northeast of Kemmel. With these three losses No 1 Squadron now equalled No 54 Squadron in the number of fighters lost in action or in training accidents, namely twenty-six apiece.

3 Squadron AusFC	Lt A H Penhall	Safe
RE.8 C5079	Lt O G Witcombe	Safe

T/o Villers-Bocage for a contact patrol in the course of which Lieutenant Penhall thought his aircraft had caught fire. Sighting the airfield at Bertangles he attempted to force-land, but lost control and spun in. As no injuries are reported, I suspect the RE was fairly close to the ground when the spin developed.

4 Squadron	Lt D W M Miller	Safe	Unemployed list 16 June 1919: Lt DFC
RE.8 B7734	2Lt A Shrives	Safe	

T/o St Omer briefed for a photographic reconnaissance duty but while travelling at speed collided with a Red Cross tender. Accepted on 15 April 1918, 'B7734' was scrapped with twenty-eight hours and forty minutes flying.

10 Squadron	Lt H L Storrs	Safe	See 1 June 1918 - 10 Squadron
FK.8 B3363	Mechanic Mackey	Safe	

T/o Droglandt for an engine test but during the take off run the undercarriage was damaged. However, the test was continued but on return, and landing, the airframe was damaged beyond repair. Accepted by the squadron on 19 February 1918, 'B3363' had logged a total of ninety-nine flying hours.

23 Squadron	2Lt V R Pauline [Canada]	+	Longuenesse [St Omer] Souvenir Cemetery
5F.1 Dolphin C4149			

T/o St Omer authorised for a practice flight but Victor Reginald Pauline was seen to climb far too steeply and as a consequence of doing so the Dolphin stalled and spun to the ground. Twenty years of age and from Victoria in British Columbia, his headstone bears the inscription; *'He Left All Rose Up And Followed Him'.* This was the squadron's second loss of a Dolphin and the first resulting in loss of life.

29 Squadron	2Lt R H Walker	Injured
SE.5a D3568		

T/o St Omer with instructions to carry out a line patrol; damaged beyond repair following engine failure and an attempted forced landing near Lambres [Pas-de-Calais], sixteen km northwest of Béthune, where 'D3568' flew into telegraph wires. Second Lieutenant Walker had been involved in a crash on 23 April 1918 [see my summary for details].

41 Squadron	Lt W E Shields	Safe	See 16 May 1918 - 41 Squadron
SE.5a B138			

T/o 1315 Serny for an offensive patrol; returned, badly shot about and following examination struck from charge. 'B138' had been on squadron strength since the last day of March 1918.

41 Squadron	Lt F R McCall*[Canada]	Safe	See 9 June 1918 - 41 Squadron
SE.5a B8235			

T/o Serny authorised for practice flying during which Lieutenant McCall indulged in 'stunting' to the extent that he overstressed the airframe. His appointment from the Canadian Expeditionary Force to the Royal Flying Corps on 22 November 1917, was promulgated a month later to the date in supplement 30443. On 16 August 1918, supplement 30845, he was *gazetted* with the Military Cross; *'For conspicuous gallantry and devotion to duty. While observing artillery fire he attacked an enemy scout and destroyed it. He has set a fine example of courage and determination on all occasions, and has rendered most valuable service.'* Oddly, at the time of this reporting of a Military Cross a First Bar had already been promulgated, supplement 30761 of 22 June 1918; *'For conspicuous gallantry and devotion to duty. Whilst engaged on photographic work, he observed a hostile scout, on which he dived and fired a burst from his machine gun. The enemy machine went down in a steep dive out of control. On a later occasion he engaged two hostile two-seater planes, which immediately turned East. Though a steady rate of fire was kept up against him, he continued the attack, during which the observer of one of the hostile machines collapsed in the cockpit, other observers reporting this machine crashed to earth in enemy lines. He has always displayed the greatest gallantry and determination in carrying out his work, and has set a very high example to his squadron.'* In parenthesis it states his Military Cross was *gazetted* in March. Salvaged for inspection the decision was made on the 12th to strike 'B8235' off charge with sixty-one hours and ten minutes flying in total.

* His entry on *Wikipedia* reports him as Frederick Robert Gordon McCall, showing his honours as the Distinguished Service Order, Military Cross and First Bar, and Distinguished Flying Cross. The citations that I show in the summary, according to *Wikipdia,* pertain to his service attached to No 13 Squadron [RE.8] for which I have my doubts, while the Distinguished Service Order and Distinguished Flying Cross were gained while serving with No 41 Squadron. Frederick was born in Vernon, British Columbia on 4 December 1896, and died 22nd January 1949, in Calgary, Alberta.

43 Squadron	2Lt T M O'Neil	+	Arras Flying Services Memorial
F.1 Camel C8298			

T/o 1220 Avesnes-le-Comte for an offensive patrol over the *département du Nord* and when last sighted by his formation Thomas Michael O'Neil, late of the Royal Dublin Fusiliers was tumbling from the sky, seemingly out of control, to the east of Bailleul. On the 3rd of April 1918, Second Lieutenant O'Neil had shared in the destruction of a Fokker DrI over Morlancourt [Somme], some twenty-six km northeast of Amiens.

53 Squadron	Lt G L Dobell	Safe	See 23 June 1918 - 53 Squadron
RE.8 B8097	Lt C E Willows	Safe	Unemployed list 10 April 1919: Lt

T/o Clairmarais tasked for a counter attack patrol in the direction of Kemmel and was obliged to force-land at map reference P25c with its petrol tank shot through. It is possible, though there are no indications as such, that the RE was recovered and repaired. Lieutenant Dobell had been involved in a crash on 13 April 1918 [see my summary for the day in question]. Although already serving as an observer officer, officially Lieutenant Willows's appointment was made on 8 June 1918, it being noted that he was lately of the London Rifles, Territorial Force [*gazetted* 21 June 1918, issue 30759].

56 Squadron	2Lt H L Mulroy	Safe
SE.5a B8274		

T/o Valheureux for a practice flight which ended with Second Lieutenant Mulroy walking away from a crash landing. Accepted by the squadron on 22 April, 'B8274' logged a total of nineteen hours and fifty-five minutes flying.

64 Squadron SE.5a B8492	Lt B A Walderdine	Safe	Unemployed list 11 January 1919: Lt

T/o Izel-lès-Hameau for an offensive patrol during which engine failure occurred, leading to a forced landing among trenches at map reference 51CW9A55. Bernard Albert Walkerdine returned to the service following the outbreak of the Second World War and was commissioned, with effect from 11 July 1940, to the Administrative and Special Duties Branch [issue 34915 of 6 August 1940], and continued to serve until relinquishing his commission on 7 September 1954, under the provisions of the Navy, Army and Air Force Reserves Act of 1954.

64 Squadron SE.5a C6461	Lt W H Farrow	Safe	Unemployed list 21 April 1919: Lt DFC

T/o Izel-lès-Hameau similarly tasked but in the misty weather lost his way and while forced landing had the misfortune to turn over near Tangry in the Pas-de-Calais some forty km northwest of Arras.

64 Squadron SE.5a C9604	Lt A C Hendry	Safe	Unemployed list 4 February 1919: Lt MC

T/o Izel-lès-Hameau for a practice flight but on landing was hit, and damaged beyond repair, by an unidentified RE.8. Arriving with the squadron on 23 January 1918, 'C9604' flew, in total, ninety-three hours and five minutes.

74 Squadron SE.5a B8502	Lt J R Piggott	Safe	Unemployed list 5 March 1919: Lt

T/o Clairmarais for a special reconnaissance which was to be flown at a low altitude. During the sortie 'B8502' came under a hail of ground fire and was totally wrecked in a forced landing at map reference XX16B94.

74 Squadron SE.5a B8373	2Lt R E Bright	+	Arras Flying Services Memorial

T/o Clairmarais for an offensive patrol and was last seen east of Zillebeke. Delivered to the squadron at London Colney on 20 February 1918, 'B8373' arrived at St Omer from Goldhangar [where the squadron had been lodged for the past five days] on 30 March. Including testing and movements, it had achieved a total of fifty-three hours and twenty-five minutes flying.

74 Squadron SE.5a C1078	Lt P J Stuart-Smith [Canada]	+	Arras Flying Services Memorial

T/o Clairmarais similarly ordered and last seen by other pilots in the patrol in the same area as that for Second Lieutenant Bright. Philip James Stuart-Smith had come to the Royal Flying Corps by way of the Canadian Corps, Cavalry Regiment.

74 Squadron SE.5a C6445	Lt C E L Skedden [USA]	+	Ebblinghem Military Cemetery

T/o Clairmarais similarly tasked and was observed by the patrol to break up at around one thousand feet, the main debris bursting into flames on hitting the ground. Please refer to my summaries for 24 April 1918, for details concerning Charles Edwin Lloyd Skedden.

79 Squadron   5F.1 Dolphin C3835   Wrecked at Beauvais after being hit, while parked in a hangar, by a DH which was landing at the time. 'C3835' was received by the squadron on 8 April 1918, and had flown for a total of six-teen hours, including ferrying to the Western Front.

201 Squadron F.1 Camel B6427	Lt B L McCarthy	Safe	Unemployed list 7 August 1919: Lt

T/o Noeux for a practice flight but lost control in the crosswind and ended up balanced on its nose. Although not extensively damaged, 'B6427' languished throughout the summer and into the autumn when it was decided not to carry out repairs and the airframe was struck off charge on the last day of October 1918.

208 Squadron	Captain R McDonald [Canada] +	Arras Flying Services Memorial	
F.1 Camel D1852			

T/o Serny with orders to carry out a special reconnaissance at low level. When last seen, the Camel was to the east of Proven [possibly Proven East airfield]. Arriving in France from No 4 Aeroplane Acceptance Park Lincoln and assigned on 11 April 1918, to No 208 Squadron, 'D1852' was soon in action, a two-seater being shot down by Roderick McDonald southwest of Hénin-Liétard [Pas-de-Calais] in the morning of the 21st, resulting in the deaths of *Lieutnant* Heinrich Grabhorn and *Lieutnant* Otto Baltzer.

210 Squadron	Captain E S Arnold	Safe
F.1 Camel B6276		

T/o St Omer for an offensive patrol and was badly shot about over the frontier town of Armentières. Captain Arnold landed safely, but 'B6276' to use the jargon of the day was deleted on 20 May 1918, as not worth repairing [general fatigue].

Wednesday-Thursday 8-9 May 1918

98 Squadron	Lt L T Hockey	Safe	
DH.9 C6154	Lt H B B Wilson	Safe	See 15 May 1918 - 98 Squadron

T/o Alquines having received instructions for a bombing raid on Menin. On return, and landing, turned sharply in order to avoid colliding with another machine and in doing so one of the DH's wheels sank into a deep rut which caused the undercarriage to collapse. The airframe was struck off charge on 14 May 1918.

Thursday 9 May 1918

2 Squadron	Lt R L Johnston [Canada]	+	Guards Cemetery, Windy Corner, Cuinchy*
FK.8 B5792	Lt A J Melanson [Canada]	+	Arras Flying Services Memorial

T/o 1115 Hesdigneul and was last sighted at around 1150 over Rue de Marais [sic]. Shot down ten minutes later in combat with four hostile aircraft. Robin Louis Johnston of St John in New Brunswick was a Bachelor of Science graduate from McGill University. His observer, Albert Joseph Melanson, also hailed from New Brunswick [South Bathurst] and had commenced his service with the Canadian Forestry Commission. It will be recalled he had survived a serious crash landing on Chocques aerodrome on 17 April [see my summary for that date].

* The cemetery at 'Windy Corner', Cuinchy is in the Pas-de-Calais and about seven km to the east of Béthune. For a detailed description of its origins, please access the Commonwealth War Graves Commission website.

2 Squadron	Lt H I Pole	Injured	Unemployed list 7 April 1919: Lt
FK.8 C3566	Lt E A Jenkinson	Safe	Unemployed list 30 December 1919: Lt

T/o Hesdigneul for a night reconnaissance and wrecked after flying into trees near the airfield. It is not clear if this accident occurred on take off, or on completion of the mission. Lieutenant Jenkinson is reported to have been badly shaken.

3 Squadron	2Lt M C Kinney	Injured
F.1 Camel B5445		

T/o Valheureux for a wireless interception duty but 'choked' the engine, lost control and turned over. Lieutenant Kinney escaped serious injury. 'B5445' was included in the returns of aircraft held at the end of June by No 2 Advanced Salvage Dump, thereby raising the possibility of a rebuild. However, as there are no further entries I have indicated its demise in the statistics for the squadron.

22 Squadron	Lt S F H Thompson	Safe	See 27 September 1918 - 22 Squadron
Bristol F.2b B1164	Sgt L Kendrick	Injured	

T/o Serny for operations over First Army [General Sir Henry Horne] front during which the Bristol was attacked circa 1845 by a Pfalz DIII near Douai [Nord], which was driven down out of control. However, the encounter left 'B1164' badly shot about and with Sergeant Kendrick suffering from a slight arm wound. On return to Serny the fighter was deemed beyond any worthwhile repair. Samuel Frederick Henry Thompson was an outstanding pilot whose service started with his appointment as a temporary second lieutenant on 22 March 1915 [*gazetted* on the 2nd of April 1915, issue 29118]. Attached to the Army Service Corps, Samuel subsequently transferred to the Royal Flying Corps and was *gazetted* with the Military Cross on 16 September 1918; *'For conspicuous gallantry and devotion to duty as a fighting pilot. During recent operations he destroyed five enemy machines. He showed great courage and skill, and by his keenness and dash sets a fine example to all.'* Subsequent to his death, *The Edinburgh Gazette* of 4 November 1918, issue 13346, carried the citation for his award of the Distinguished Flying Cross; *'This officer has carried out numerous offensive patrols, displaying the most marked bravery and determination. His boldness in attack and utter disregard of personal danger affords a most inspiring example to his brother pilots. Since June 1st last he has destroyed eleven enemy aeroplanes.'* His biography reported by *Wikipedia* shows he was born in the London borough of Bow on 30 August 1890, his father, Samuel Whitell Thompson being a medical practitioner. By the time of the 1911 Census the family had moved to Blackheath and Samuel was studying civil engineering. His flying career was not without its problems for in the wake of crashing a No 20 Squadron Bristol F.2b on 27 October 1917, he was posted to No 22 Squadron and it was while attached to '22' that his extraordinary fighting skills came to the fore.

27 Squadron	Lt C E Hutcheson	Safe	See 19 May 1918 - 27 Squadron
DH.4 B2145	Lt H E Gooding	Safe	Unemployed list 26 January 1919: Lt

T/o Ruisseauville for bombing operations over Cambrai but following the bursting of its radiator, which led to almost immediate engine seizure, force-landed near the hamlet and nearby airfield of Treizennes not far from Aire-sur-la-Lys in the Pas-de-Calais. 'B2145' arrived at No 27 Squadron on 23 April 1918 and two days later had a 'meeting' with DH.9 'A7622' sustaining minimal damage. On the eve of the merger between the Royal Naval Air Service and the Royal Flying Corps, Lieutenant Gooding, formerly of the Manchester Regiment, was officially transferred [in the rank of temporary Second Lieutenant] to the General List and with seniority of rank effective from the 5th of March 1918 [*gazetted* 3 May 1918, issue 30670]. I strongly suspect he was on the strength of No 27 Squadron at the time of his 'official' transfer for on 11 March 1918, when flying with Second Lieutenant E J Smith [see my summary for 3rd April 1918], both emerged unhurt when their DH.4 A7625 crashed on landing.

29 Squadron	Lt C J Venter	Safe	See 22 May 1919 - 29 Squadron
SE.5a D301	[South Africa]		

T/o St Omer for operations over Armentières where, in combat, 'D301' was badly shot about. Despatched by sea to France, 'D301' arrived at St Omer and No 29 Squadron on 23 April 1918. Lieutenant Venter's name appears on The South African Military History Society website where, it is noted, he became a flight commander with No 29 Squadron and sometimes joined in combat with No 74 Squadron; subsequently, he rose to the rank of Major General.

29 Squadron	2Lt T Ratcliffe	pow	Unemployed list 15 March 1919: Lt
SE.5a D3566			

T/o 0840 St Omer also tasked for operations over Armentières where Second Lieutenant Ratcliffe was last seen, in combat, at around 0950. Strong belief that he was a prisoner of war published in *Flight* July 11, 1918.

43 Squadron	Lt S Birch	pow	
F.1 Camel D1790			

T/o 1425 Avesnes-le-Comte for an offensive patrol from which Lieutenant Birch failed to return. Confirmation of his prisoner of war status was published in *Flight* August 8, 1918.

43 Squadron	Lt A H Whitford-Hawkey	+	Arras Flying Services Memorial
F.1 Camel D1821			

T/o 1740 Avesnes-le-Comte for an offensive patrol and it is the opinion of pilots in the area that this eighteen year old Cornishman, Anthony Henry Whitford-Hawkey, may well have been the pilot of a Camel observed falling in flames southeast of Albert. Born on the 3rd of April 1899, a young Anthony attended Nash House preparatory school at Burnham in Somerset before entering Sherborne School*[The Green] in 1913. Here he excelled at rugby football and rose to the rank of sergeant with the school's Officer Cadet Corps before leaving on 20 June 1917, in order to enlist in the Royal Flying Corps. Commemorated on Sherborne School's Roll of Honour, it is noted that Anthony arrived in France in March 1918. Before his death, Anthony wrote of his experiences in the Royal Flying Corps, these being published in the November 1917, issue of *The Shirburnian* in which he described his time at Farnborough through to flying training at Netheravon. He ended his missive with the words; *'I hope to be going solo soon, and that's when the fun begins. Hoping that I have not taken up too much precious space.'*.

* I am indebted to Sherborne School's archives for the brief biographical notes regarding Lieutenant Whitford-Hawkey.

| 49 Squadron C Flight | Lt G A Leckie [Canada] | + | Arras Flying Services Memorial |
| DH.9 C6094 | Lt G R Cuttle MC [Australia] | + | Arras Flying Services Memorial |

T/o 0940 Conteville tasked for a raid on rail communications at Péronne and when last seen just after noon was in a glide, apparently under control, east of Bray-sur-Somme. George Robin Cuttle's entry on the Commonwealth War Graves Commission website indicates he was *gazetted* in July 1916, and while attached to the 50th Battery, Royal Field Artillery, gained the Military Cross in November 1916, during an engagement at Butte de Warlencourt on the Somme. Later, he took part in the 1917 *Battle of Arras* during which he was attached to the Royal Scots, 9th Division, where he assisted in working artillery pieces captured from the Germans. A website, devoted to the Robinvale Regional War Memorial [which I acknowledge], indicates that Lieutenant Cuttle's parents arrived in France in 1923, and following a lengthy search identified wreckage from 'C6094' in a field near Caix. In memory of their son, Herbert and Margaret Cuttle, renamed their new settlement on the Murray 'Robinvale' and a further tribute was the naming of the town's square 'Caix Square'. Information posted on the squadron's website indicates George Arthur Leckie was posted in on the 12th of February 1918, while his observer reported as recently as 20 April.

| 54 Squadron | Lt C R Borkland | Safe | Unemployed list 29 January 1919: Lt |
| F.1 Camel D6517 | | | |

T/o Caffiers to practice flying in formation and while in the vicinity of Courtbourne *[sic]*, Lieutenant Borkland fainted, coming to his senses in time to crash-land.

| 57 Squadron | Lt L de V Weiner | Injured | |
| DH.4 D8411 | Lt R W Rumsby MC | Injured | Huby-St Leu British Cemetery |

T/o 1005 Le Quesnoy having been briefed for a photographic reconnaissance mission during which the DH was attacked by enemy fighters and its flying controls badly damaged. Lieutenant Weiner managed to regain Le Quesnoy but while attempting a forced landing 'D8411' stalled and spun in just off the landing area. Richard William Rumsby, formerly of the 9th Battalion Royal Sussex Regiment was *gazetted* with the Military Cross in a supplement to the paper published on 14 August 1917, issue 30234, at which time he had yet to transfer to the air arm. The citation reads; *'For conspicuous gallantry and devotion to duty. When in charge of a mopping-out party, he did valuable work in support of the leading company, afterwards displaying great skill and initiative in making reconnaissances and collecting men who had gone astray. He has done similar excellent work on previous occasions.'*

| 66 Squadron | Lt F C Vincent | Injured |
| F.1 Camel B2356 | | |

T/o San Pietro and believed to have been damaged beyond worthwhile repair before becoming properly airborne. Between 18 September 1917, when it was accepted by No 70 Squadron, and the time of its probable demise, this Camel accounted for five enemy aircraft. During the morning of October 10th, two Albatros scouts were sent down; both during encounters over Belgium with the first falling in flames near Westroosbeke and the second south of the Houthulst Forest. Ten days later, and again over West-Vlaanderen, a two-seater fell with its wings folding up over Rumbeke Aerodrome - all credited to Second Lieutenant F G Quigley*though the latter was shared in part with a squadron colleague, Second Lieutenant C W Primeau. Then, on the 27th Second

Lieutenant M S C Gordon crashed on take off and 'B2356' was struck for repairs. Sent by rail to Italy and San Pietro on the 5th of April, its career came close to being ended on the 15th when a wheel came off during take off but, fortunately, damage was not too serious and 'B2356' was back in the air by the 24th. Then, during activity in the late morning of 3 May, Lieutenant A F Bartlett shot down an Albatros near Treviso followed by another Albatros over Ormelle.

* Later promoted captain, Canadian born Frank Granger Quigley chalked up a remarkable score of thirty-three aerial victories, the majority against fighters, before being wounded in action on 27 March 1918. Admitted to a hospital at Le Touquet he made a good recovery before returning to Canada to convalesce further. Deemed fit to resume active flying, Frank Quigley embarked for Liverpool in October 1918 but within two days of the ship docking at Liverpool he was dead [20th], a victim of the scourge of influenza. His body was returned to Canada for burial in Toronto [Mount Pleasant] Cemetery. His entry in the cemetery register showing that he had been awarded a Distinguished Service Order and a Military Cross and First Bar, a very courageous Canadian.

| 66 Squadron | Lt L A A Bernard | Safe |
| F.1 Camel B7389 T | | |

T/o San Pietro but lost his bearings and in the forced landing near Legnano, some twenty km or thereabouts northwest of Milano, the Camel was damaged beyond worthwhile repair, Lieutenant Bernard escaping unhurt but rather badly shocked by his experience.

| 79 Squadron | Lt J C Brooks | Safe | Unemployed list 10 January 1919: Lt |
| 5F.1 Dolphin C4047 | | | |

T/o Beauvais for an offensive patrol and on return, and preparing to land, stalled while banking and turned over; damaged beyond repair.

| 83 Squadron | Lt J C Hopkins | Injured | Unemployed list 26 April 1919: Lt |
| FE.2b A5734 | 2Lt M B Joseph | Injured | |

T/o Franqueville tasked for bombing operations on Péronne; crashed into a haystack near the flare path, turned over and damaged beyond repair. 'A5734' flew for a total of forty-six hours and nineteen minutes.

| 84 Squadron | Lt S B Echert | Safe |
| SE.5a C5446 | | |

T/o Bertangles and with the rest of the patrol set out for Villers-Bretonneux where a general engagement with hostile aircraft took place, Lieutenant Echert's aircraft being shot through by an Albatros. Although he was able to return, for 'C5446' its flying days were over.

| 100 Squadron | Captain H T O Windsor | Injured |
| FE.2b A5625 | Sgt A Smallman | Injured |

T/o 1630 Ochey*for a sortie that ended with the crew making a precautionary landing in a field near Maulan, a commune in the *département du Meuse* some sixty km west-northwest from Ochey and it was while attempting to take off from here that the FE went out of control and crashed.

* Ochey was a familiar aerodrome for No 100 Squadron having first made its association on the 11th of October 1917. On the 1st of April, the squadron moved to Villesneux but returned to Ochey on the 9th of May [the loss of 'A5625' being likely the first since its return] and remained here until the 10th of August when it transferred to Xaffévillers.

| 108 Squadron | 2Lt A Harman | Injured |
| BE.2e A1359 | | |

T/o Lake Down for a training exercise and on return failed to flare when landing and crashed heavily. This is the only report recorded against this serial and though I cannot be certain, I suspect the BE was damaged beyond repair. At the time the main establishment of the squadron was the DH.9; in July 1918, the squadron arrived on the Western Front for bombing operations, principally against targets in Belgium.

| 149 Squadron | Captain R W Scholes | Injured |
| FE.2b B469 | Mechanic Stelling | Injured |

T/o Ford*for a training flight but before becoming airborne crashed into the hedge bordering the airfield. At this point the nose dug into the soft ground and 'B469' was effectively wrecked.

* Also referred to as Yapton.

| 201 Squadron | Lt F Newton | + | Adanac Military Cemetery, Miraumont |
| F.1 Camel D3375 | | | |

T/o Noeux for an offensive patrol over the Somme and when last seen in the general vicinity of Bapaume and being heavily assaulted by at least eight Pfalz scouts. His headstone is inscribed with the words; *'They Are And They Are With God.'* From Tonbridge in Kent, Fleming Newton was aged nineteen.

| 205 Squadron | Captain C R Lupton DSC | + | Vignacourt British Cemetery |
| DH.4 N6009* | Airman A G Wood | + | Vignacourt British Cemetery |

T/o Bois de Roche tasked for an attack on Chaulnes Railway Station [Somme] and to the horror of crews in the formation, as they were returning to base, Charles Roger Lupton's aircraft broke up in the air giving the crew no chance whatsoever of survival. For an assessment of his service, please refer to my summary of 17 April 1918. Prior to its loss, the DH had been involved in a series of combats - all in March 1918 and on two occasions with Charles Lupton at the controls. The first, on the 16th resulted in the shooting down of two enemy aircraft, a feat shared with Charles Bartlett [the resolute Naylor accompanying him] who was piloting DH.4 A7644. The second time was during the afternoon of the 22nd when over the *département du Aisne* and southwest of Vendhuile where an Albatros was despatched. In between, on the 18th, Flight Sub-Lieutenant G E Siedle and his observer Sergeant W J H Middleton claimed an unidentified enemy aircraft which, subsequently, was disallowed.

* The 'N' series of airframe numbers were used twice; the first time during the *Great War* and the second time during World War Two when amongst the various types so adorned was a batch of Stirling bombers. Thus, 'N6009' was carried by a Stirling I of No 7 Squadron shot down during the night of 20-21 April 1941.

| 206 Squadron | Lt E A Burn | Safe | See 15 May 1918 - 206 Squadron |
| DH.9 B7595 | 2Lt A H Mitchener | Safe | See 15 May 1918 - 206 Squadron |

T/o Alquines and damaged beyond repair having been hit by shrapnel from anti-aircraft fire near Melville *[sic]*. First issued to No 11 Squadron Royal Naval Air Service on 20 March 1918, B7595 transferred to No 6 Squadron Royal Naval Air Service three days later.

| 211 Squadron | Lt F J Islip | Safe | Unemployed list 14 October 1919: Lt |
| DH.9 B7637 | 2Lt E Cooke | Injured | |

T/o Petite Synthe for a bombing raid and it was when flying between Oostende and Nieupoort that the DHs came under attack from enemy fighters, Frederick John Islip's aircraft being so badly shot about that following a technical inspection the airframe was deemed beyond reasonable repair. Frederick's service postwar followed an interesting course; granted a short service commission on 8 February 1921 [*gazetted* 22 February 1921, issue 32235] he [I suspect] spent most of the next three years overseas until posted to the Royal Air Force Depot [Uxbridge] on 13 December 1924, on transfer to Home Establishment and release to the Reserve Class A on 9 February 1925. His eventual release from service was *gazetted* on 16 March 1937, issue 34380, effective 8 February 1937 and retaining his rank of flying officer. However, on the outbreak of the Second World War, Frederick volunteered his services and was commissioned with effect from 31 December 1939 [issue 34784 published on 2 February 1940] to the Administrative and Special Duties Branch and allocated the service number '77154' though at a date unknown he reverted to his original service identity of '09219'. He continued to serve postwar until his commission was relinquished under the provisions of the Navy, Army and Air Force Reserves Act 1954, leaving the air force on 13 July 1954, in the rank of flight lieutenant.

| 213 Squadron | Lt R T Whiteley | Safe |
| F.1 Camel B3896 | | |

T/o Bergues for an offensive patrol, returning to base badly shot about and deemed uneconomical to repair.

Friday 10 May 1918

A days of considerable air activity, and one which is remembered by No 80 Squadron for the loss of five of their Camels, and two others needing repair following an evening patrol over the Somme. Three of the pilots were killed and one taken prisoner of war. No 27 Squadron suffered four losses during bombing operations, six crew paying with their lives.

2 Squadron AusFC	2Lt D'A K J Stutterd	Injured	
SE.5a D3512			

T/o Fouquerolles having received orders to carry out a photographic reconnaissance in the course of which his aircraft suffered engine failure, brought about by ignition failure, and crashed.

27 Squadron	Captain G B S McBain DFC	+	Assevillers New British Cemetery
DH.4 A7514	Lt W Spencer	+	Assevillers New British Cemetery

T/o 0505 Beauvois tasked for a bombing raid and shot down in a general engagement southwest of Péronne, the bombers having come under attack from enemy scouts estimated between twenty and thirty in number. William Spencer was nineteen years of age. Efforts to trace the award made to Captain George Brown Sievwright McBain have, so far, failed; however, the Auction House Morton & Eden, in association with Sotheby's in November 2013, published the results of a recent medals sale in which Lot 308, Captain Brown's Victory Medal, described as 'extremely fine' sold for £110, £70 over the starting bid.

27 Squadron	Lt S W Taylor	Safe	
DH.4 B2078	Lt W H Gibson	Injured	

T/o 0505 Ruisseauville similarly ordered. Lieutenant Gibson was struck by a bullet and very severely wounded but with commendable courage he continued to give protective fire. At the first available opportunity Lieutenant Taylor set his aircraft down near the hamlet of Bertangles*. Five days earlier Lieutenant Taylor and his observer Sergeant V Cummins fought with Albatros scouts and in a running engagement sent one down over the Somme near Péronne.

* Bertangles deserves its place in the history of the *Great War* for it was in the cemetery, some distance from the hamlet, that the Australian Flying Corps arranged the funeral with full military honours for *Rittmeister* Manfred Freiherr von Richthofen ['The Red Baron'] on 22 April 1918. A photograph showing his coffin, laden with flowers, and borne on the shoulders of bare-headed soldiers led by a military Chaplin reading from a prayer book, appears in the photograph section of Richard Overy's excellent account of the forming of the Royal Air Force. The photograph also shows an Australian 'Guard of Honour' from No 3 Squadron Australian Flying Corps, wearing their distinctive hats with the upturned brim, with rifles at the 'present' and with two officers in the background saluting the cortège. It was to be but temporary for after the armistice his body was exhumed and taken to a Germany military cemetery at Fricourt. Again, it was not permanent for Manfred's brother arranged for a burial in Berlin and then, with yet another war over, this world renowned fighter pilot was taken in 1975 to Wiesbaden.

27 Squadron	2Lt L E Dunnett	+	Caix British Cemetery
DH.4 B2081	2Lt D H Prosser	+	Caix British Cemetery

T/o 1705 Beauvois with instructions to bomb a target near Bertangles and in a general engagement with a strong force of enemy scouts, estimated to have been between twenty and thirty strong, shot down in flames southwest of Péronne. Lawrence Edwin Dunnett was nineteen; his headstone carries the words; *I Hail The Glory Dawning In Emmanuel's Land.'*

27 Squadron	Lt A H Hill	+	Caix British Cemetery
DH.4 B2087	Sgt S R Richmond	+	Caix British Cemetery

T/o 1705 Beauvois similarly tasked and lost in the manner described above. Accepted on Christmas Day 1917, 'B2081' flown by Second Lieutenants W J Henney and P S Driver claimed at Albatros in the vicinity of Maria Aeltre [see 23 May 1918] but in turn was badly shot about and repairs kept the DH on the ground until 26th March when it resumed active service. Arthur Haddon Hill was one of a large number of officers commissioned to the General List of the Royal Flying Corps, 21 June 1917, their names appearing in issue 30170 of *The London Gazette* published on 6 July 1917. Stanley Robert Richmond joined the Royal Flying Corps in 1915.

| 32 Squadron | Lt K G P Hendrie | Safe | Unemployed list 27 January 1919: Lt |
| SE.5a C9614 | | | |

T/o Beauvois for an offensive patrol; on return, overshot and on running onto uneven ground turned over and caught fire. On charge from 31 March 1918, 'C9614' accomplished forty hours of flying. Kelvin Gladstone Peter Hendrie was one of hundreds commissioned to the Administrative and Special Duties Branch for the duration of hostilities, his being effective on the day that war was declared [*gazetted* 26 September 1939, issue 34694]. However, 'flying a desk' seems not to appeal and now ranked flying officer a transfer on the 1st of November 1940, to the General Duties Branch was promulgated 3 January 1941, issue 35032, but this entry was duly cancelled in the *Gazette* 28 January 1941, issue 35057. The reason for this short lived change from administration to a possible return to flying is not known and when promotion from flight lieutenant to squadron leader [temporary] on 1st January 1944, was reported, Kelvin Hendrie was still anchored to his desk.

| 48 Squadron | Lt N G Stransom | + | Heath Cemetery, Harbonnieres |
| Bristol F.2b B1299 | Private C V Taylor | + | Heath Cemetery, Harbonnieres |

T/o Bertangles for an offensive patrol, armed with bombs. Last seen spinning down over the Somme and well to the southeast of Amiens near Maricourt following an attack from hostile aircraft. Norman Gardner Stransom was educated at Framlingham College in Suffolk; his headstones is inscribed' *I Thank My God On Every Remembrance Of Thee'*. From Rochford in Essex, Charles Vickers Taylor was nineteen.

| 50 Squadron | 2Lt L H Streten | Injured |
| BE.2e A2973 | Cpl W H Hodgson | Injured |

T/o Bekesbourne but stalled and crashed; damaged beyond reasonable repair.

| 56 Squadron | Lt J E Doyle | Safe | See 6 September 1918 - 56 Squadron |
| SE.5a B8256 | [South Africa] | | |

T/o Valheureux for practice flying; landed badly and damaged 'B8256' beyond repair. Struck four days later with flying hours totalling thirty-nine and thirty minutes.

| 79 Squadron | Lt H A Miller | Safe | Unemployed list 20 May 1919: Lt |
| 5F.1 Dolphin C4180 | | | |

T/o Beauvais for an offensive patrol but, it is believed, the Dolphin's engine failed and Lieutenant Miller landed in a field that had been put to the plough near the airfield. On touch down, the wheels became stuck in the furrows, causing 'C4180' to flip onto its back.

| 80 Squadron | 2Lt A W Rowdon | + | Arras Flying Services Memorial |
| F.1 Camel B2463 | | | |

T/o 1700 La Bellevue for an offensive patrol over the Somme from which Alfred William Rowdon failed to return. Prior to arriving with the squadron, 'B2463' had seen service with Nos 70 and 43 Squadrons, its usage with these units being terminated as a result of crashes - fortunately without serious consequences for the pilots involved.

| 80 Squadron | 2Lt G A Whately [Canada] | + | Arras Flying Services Memorial |
| F.1 Camel D6419 | | | |

T/o 1700 La Bellevue similarly tasked. George Alfred Whately is reported as being, prewar, a student in the Engineering Department at Toronto University. 'D6419' was issued to the squadron on 22 March 1918.

| 80 Squadron | 2Lt A V Jones | pow |
| F.1 Camel D6457 | | |

T/o 1700 La Bellevue similarly tasked; failed to return. Wounded, Second Lieutenant Jones was repatriated on 13 December 1918.

| 80 Squadron | 2Lt H V Barker* | Safe | Unemployed list 9 May 1919: Lt |
| F.1 Camel D6591 V | | | |

T/o 1700 La Bellevue similarly tasked during which Second Lieutenant Barker drove down a Fokker DrI out of control near Morcourt, little more than a hamlet east of Amiens and on the banks of the River Somme. The engagement took place at around 1855, and attracted the attention of three more DrIs which, in a running fight going in west-northwesterly direction, between them, avenged the downing of their colleague by forcing down the Camel which crash-landed a mere fifty metres inside enemy lines, and near their outpost at Bouzencourt on the south bank of the same river roughly six km from Morcourt. Not surprisingly, it is reported that Second Lieutenant Barker who quickly reached 'friendly territory' sustained 'slight shock'.

* Although I cannot be absolutely certain, it is possible that Lieutenant Barker returned to the service, commissoned to the Reserve of Air Force Officers for a Squadron Leader Henry Victor Barker lost his life on the 10th of October 1941, and is buried in Middlesbrough [Acklam] Cemetery. His entry on the Commonwealth War Graves Commission website describes him as a 'pilot' and reports his age as '42', making it feasible that he served in the *Great War*.

| 80 Squadron | Lt C G S Shields | + | Cerisy-Gailly Military Cemetery |
| F.1 Camel D6619 | | | |

T/o 1700 La Bellevue similarly tasked; failed to return. 'D6619' had been with the squadron for just eight days.

| 84 Squadron | Lt C F Falkenburg | Safe | Commission relinquished on ceasing to be |
| SE.5a B8272 | [Canada] | | employed 9 May 1919: Captain DFC |

T/o Bertangles for an offensive patrol in the course of which a connecting rod fractured; in landing back at base, 'B8272' turned over and was damaged beyond repair. Notification of Lieutenant Falkenburg's attachment to the Royal Air Force appeared in *The London Gazette* 30887 of 6 September 1918, and that he was to ranked captain [A] with effect from 9 August 1918 [*Flight* November 22, 1917, however, lists his attachment to the Royal Flying Corps amongst a myriad of names extracted from *The London Gazette*] of an earlier date. He was formerly of the Canadian Expeditionary Force, Quebec Regiment.

| 93 Squadron | Sgt W Gibson | Injured | |
| Avro 504A A3404 | | | |

T/o Tangmere but while banking at one hundred feet Sergeant Gibson lost control, stalled and crashed. Formed at Croydon on 23 September 1917, intended for fighter duties on the Western Front, the squadron did not become operational and disbanded before the armistice.

| 98 Squadron | Lt F A Laughlin | Safe | Unemployed list 18 May 1919: Lt DFC |
| DH.9 B7650 | Airman R J Weston | Safe | |

T/o Alquines tasked with others for a bombing mission during which the DHs came under anti-aircraft fire. Shrapnel from one burst struck the engine of 'B7650' but the crew were able to re-cross the lines and force-land just to the east of trenches held by the British. Frederick Andrew Laughlin received a commission to the General List of the Royal Flying Corps on 17 August 1917 [*gazetted* 30 October 1917, issue 30359]. By the autumn of 1918, he was ranked temporary captain and as such was awarded a Distinguished Flying Cross, the citation published on page 3534 of *The Edinburgh Gazette* [issue 13325] reads; '*While bombing an important railway station the formation, of which this officer was leader, was attacked by about twenty enemy scouts. In the engagement that ensued two enemy aeroplanes were destroyed and a third driven down out of control. These results were largely due to his excellent leadership. He has taken part in forty bomb raids, the objectives of many being far over the enemy lines. His knowledge of navigation and skill as a leader have been invaluable in enabling the formation to reach the objectives.*' A record for Lieutenant Laughlin is held at The National Archives under AIR 79/649/70143.

Saturday 11 May 1918

| 1 Squadron | Lt C A Pelletier [Canada] | + | Arras Flying Services Memorial |
| SE.5a C6444 | | | |

T/o Clairmarais for an offensive patrol and in an engagement over the *département du Nord* Charles Adolphe Pelletier was seen to spin away in the vicinity of Bailleul. From Ottawa, he came to the Royal Flying Corps by way of the Canadian Engineers.

| 1 Squadron | Lt H S Hennessy [Canada] | Safe | See 5 June 1918 - 1 Squadron |
| SE.5a D332 | | | |

T/o Clairmarais similarly tasked but in the bad weather [rain and mist prevailed over the patrol area] Lieutenant Hennessy lost his way and having run out of petrol he force-landed at map reference S19 T25d52. 'D332' had survived a mere five days of operational service.

| 4 Squadron AusFC | Lt A Finnie AusFC | Safe | See 22 May 1918 - 4 Squadron AusFC |
| F.1 Camel B5647 | | | |

T/o Clairmarais for an offensive patrol during which he assisted in driving down an Albatros out of control near Armentières. However, on returning to Clairmarais the weather had closed in and Alexander Finnie for the second time in a month crashed while landing [see my summary for 18 April 1918, when No 4 Squadron Australian Flying Corps was based at Bruay].

| 4 Squadron AusFC | Lt O C Barry [Australia] | + | Arras Flying Services Memorial |
| F.1 Camel B7480 | | | |

T/o Clairmarais similarly tasked and shot down circa 1945, in flames, near Armentières. 'B7480' was the last airframe in a batch of two hundred built by Ruston, Proctor and Company Limited of Lincoln, with deliveries reaching the Aeroplane Acceptance Park at Lincoln by mid-December 1917. In the case of 'B7480', it was shipped to France during February 1918, arriving with the squadron on 8 April. To conclude, Owen Cressy Barry, twenty five years of age, was born at Harwood Island in New South Wales, but had probably moved to Neutral Bay [New South Wales] by the time of his enlistment.

| 4 Squadron AusFC | Lt P K Schafer MM | Safe |
| F.1 Camel D1863 | | |

T/o Clairmarais similarly instructed and, subsequently, owing to fog force-landed near Wormhoudt*in the *département du Nord*. Lieutenant Schafer won his Military Medal as an infantry lance corporal [*gazetted* 21 September 1916, supplement 29758]. Prior to the forced landing, Lieutenant Schafer had shared in the driving down of an Albatros near Armentières.

* Wormhoudt will be for ever remembered as the place in May 1940, where on the 28th close on one hundred Allied prisoners of war were murdered by the *Waffen-SS* the perpetrators being from the 1st SS Division *Leibstandarte SS Adolf Hitler*. Postwar, it was said that specifically the soldiers involved in this war crime were from the 2nd Battalion, commanded by *Haupsturmführer* Wilhelm Mohnke, who emphatically denied ever giving such orders. Although strenuous efforts were made to bring to justice those responsible, it proved impossible to bring a sufficiently strong case for a prosecution to proceed. See my summary for No 80 Squadron and Lieutenant Pell on 12 April 1918, for additional information concerning these war crimes.

| 4 Squadron AusFC | Lt F W Webster | Injured |
| F.1 Camel D1884 | | |

T/o Clairmarais similarly charged and was lost in circumstances similar to those reported above.

| 24 Squadron | Captain I D R McDonald | Safe | See 22 September 1920 - 84 Squadron |
| SE.5a C9613 | [British West Indies] | | |

T/o Conteville for practice flying but either during take off, or on return, 'C9613' was effectively wrecked after running into a hole. Commissioned to the General List of the Royal Flying Corps on 27 February 1917 [*gazetted* 8 March 1917, supplement 29975], Ian Donald Roy McDonald had a distinguished war record. A Military Cross was *gazetted* on 16 September 1918, supplement 30901; *'For conspicuous gallantry and devotion to duty. With seven scouts he attacked eighteen enemy machines, of which three were destroyed and one driven down completely out of control. When driven down to within 200 feet of the ground by two enemy machines owing to a choked engine, he turned on them and drove one down. He has in all destroyed eleven enemy aircraft and carried out valuable work in attacking enemy troops on the ground.'* The Edinburgh Gazette meanwhile of 7th August 1918, supplement 13300, published the citation for his Distinguished Flying Cross; *'A dashing fighter pilot. In the past two months he has destroyed five enemy machines and brought down two others out of control. At all times he shows a fine offensive spirit and complete disregard of danger.'* His entry on *Wikipedia* reports his coming into the world on the 9th of September 1898, in the British West Indies, crossing the Atlantic to serve in the Royal Flying Corps. A table of victories indicates his first three successes [commencing 15 November 1917] were achieved in De Havilland DH.5s followed by seventeen flying the SE.5a, six of these falling to the guns of 'C9613'. Postwar, following a brief spell back in the British West Indies recovering from the stress of war which had left him with eye strain, he was appointed as a permanent officer on the 1st of August 1919. His tragic death on the 22nd of September 1920, will be reported in a third volume.

28 Squadron	Lt E G Forder	pow

F.1 Camel B2455 X

T/o Grossa and last seen at 1005; claimed by *Oberleutnant* Frank Linke-Crawford*of of *Flik 51J*. It is recorded that Lieutenant Border landed his aircraft intact and, subsequently, it was painted in Austrian markings.

* Born on the 8th of August 1893 at Krakau, then a provincial Austro-Hungarian city, Frank Linke-Crawford initially saw service on the Eastern Front where he commanded an infantry unit. However, his health was not good and it is mooted that his medical condition was a factor in his request to transfer to the air service. Regarded by all who served with him as a fine leader of men he was shot down by Italian scouts on the 30th of July 1918. First laid to rest in Slovenia, his grave is now in Salzburg.

29 Squadron	Lt E Osborne	Safe

SE.5a D3933

T/o St Omer for an offensive patrol and on return he made a heavy landing through avoiding collision with a Camel. Salvaged, 'D3933' was struck off charge on 15 May 1918, with its record card annotated with total flying of twenty-seven hours and thirty minutes.

38 Squadron	Lt H L Hopkins [USA]	+	Hornchurch [St Andrew] Churchyard

RE.8 E58

T/o Melton Mowbray and having climbed to four hundred feet stalled; spun in. Harry Lynn Hopkins had been attached from No 185[Night Training] Squadron. His entry in the cemetery register is devoid of age and next of kin detail.

Note. Andrew Pentland reports that although Commonwealth War Graves Commission shows Harry Lynn Hopkins as attached to No 185 Squadron, the casualty report indicates No 189[Night Training] Squadron. Andrew also reports that a next of kin address for Newark New Jersey and a strong indication that he had trained in Canada and America with the Curtiss JN-4 included in the types flown.

40 Squadron	Lt L H Sutton	Injured Unemployed list 3 February 1919: Lt

SE.5a B157

T/o 1625 Bruay for an offensive patrol; possibly obliged to return early having developed engine trouble and at 1710 crash-landed in a field near the aerodrome that had been put to the plough.

41 Squadron	Lt C H Marchant*	Safe

SE.5a C6352

T/o Serny for an offensive patrol on return from which, and landing, 'C6352' ran into ruts and the resultant damage was deemed not to be worth the cost of repair. Arrived from No 2 Air Issues on 4 February 1918, with Lieutenant Marchant at the controls, 'C6352' flew for a total of seventy-eight hours and fifty minutes, including factory testing and ferry to France.

* Although I am unable to be certain, I strongly suspect the Lieutenant Clarence Henry Martin of No 5 Fighting School who died in Egypt on the 3rd of March 1919, is one and the same person. Aged twenty-three, he is

buried in Cairo War Cemetery where his headstone is inscribed with his honour; *'Croix De Guerre Avec Palme'* which had been awarded to him for his services in France.

| 41 Squadron | Lt R H Stacey | Injured | |
| SE.5a D3442 | | | |

T/o Serny similarly tasked and returned with his aircraft so badly shot about in combat, and himself wounded, that it was struck off charge on 14 May 1918. Lieutenant Stacey's commission had to be relinquished on 16 April 1919, owing to the condition of his health.

| 98 Squadron | Lt A A Sevastopulo | Safe | Unemployed list 8 February 1918: Lt |
| DH.9 C6176 | Lt F Smethurst | Safe | Unemployed list 10 March 1919: Lt |

T/o Alquines for a practice flight which ended with the crew flying into a tree while landing. 'C6176' arrived in France from Old Sarum on the 1st of April 1918. It would seem both officers were pilots for on the 8th of May, Lieutenant Smethurst, accompanied by Lieutenant E G T Chubb drove down a hostile aircraft during the evening of 8 May, while on operations in the vicinity of Menin-Wervicq.

| 206 Squadron | Lt G A Pitt | Safe | Unemployed list 4 February 1918: Lt |
| DH.9 B7587 | 2Lt C E Anketell MM | + | Longuenesse [St Oner] Souvenir Cemetery |

T/o 1707 Alquines with others to bomb the railway station at Armentières*north of Lille and close to the border with Belgium and where in October 1914 joint Franco-British forces were engaged in a fierce battle with the advancing German 6th Army. The raid was intercepted by enemy scouts which, I suspect, mortally wounded Charles Edward Anketell*and in turn resulted in a forced landing near Winnezeele a commune straddling the present A25 in the Nord *département*. Second Lieutenant Anketell's entry in the cemetery register indicates he had been awarded a Military Medal but his commissioning details published in *The London Gazette* issue 30206 on 27 July 1917, records him as one of many cadets commissioned on the 27th to the infantry and in Charles's case to the Regiment of Fusiliers. There is no mention of a previous award; he had been involved in a serious crash on the 12th of April 1918, which wrote off the DH in which he was flying. Errol Martyn, however, has added additional information; *'Anketell lived in New Zealand prior to the war, but his place of birth and when he immigrated is unknown. Prior to the Royal Fusiliers he was with the Royal Navy Reserve and thus served with all three of the Services - Navy, Army and Air Force. His MM was won during Army service.'*

| 206 Squadron | Lt C N Hyslop | Safe | See 5 June 1918 - 206 Squadron |
| DH.9 B7602 | 2Lt W T Ganter | Safe | See 19 May 1918 - 206 Squadron |

T/o Alquines [possibly tasked for the same operation reported above] and came down at Wylder, a commune in the Pas-de-Calais. Second Lieutenant Ganter was appointed to the General List as a temporary second Lieutenant on 9 November 1917 [*gazetted* 7 December 1917, issue 30418], probably from the rank of air mechanic for he is recorded as such on his medal card which is held at The National Archives under WO 372/7/198885.

| 206 Squadron | Lt L Child | Injured | |
| DH.9 C2154 | 2Lt F W Chester | Safe | |

T/o Alquines tasked for bombing but on becoming airborne the engine failed and the DH crashed just off the aerodrome. Owing to ill-health, which was detected during his war service, Second Lieutenant Chester relinquished his commission on Christmas Day 1918.

| 210 Squadron | Lt S C Joseph | Safe | |
| F.1 Camel B6228 | | | |

T/o St Omer for an offensive patrol and carrying bombs [and, I suspect, heading for the same area that was being targeted by No 4 Squadron AusFC]. During the operation, the squadron's aircraft experienced most inclement weather and Lieutenant Joseph, in avoiding a tree which loomed up out of the mist, crash-landed about a km east of Esquelbecq [Nord]. Salvaged, 'B6228' was struck off charge on 20 May 1918, as being overtaken by general fatigue.

| 210 Squadron | Lt M F Sutton | Safe | Unemployed list 27 September 1919: Lt |
| F.1 Camel B6256 | | | |

T/o St Omer similarly briefed and, subsequently, force-landed at Wormhoudt [Nord]. [See my summary for the loss here of No 4 Squadron AusFC Camel D1863]. 'B6256' was deleted on the same day, and for the same reason, as annotated against 'B6228'.

210 Squadron   Lt B A P L d'Etchegoyen   Injured Arneke British Cemetery
F.1 Camel D3377
T/o St Omer similarly tasked and, subsequently, force-landed near Rubrouck [Nord]. Described as being a native of Ipsden in the County of Oxfordshire, his father was Count Paul d'Etchegoyen of Château de Montfleaux of St-Denis-de-Gastines [Mayenne], France, Louis Paul Bryant Albert d'Etchegoyen died from his injuries on the 13th of May; his headstone has been inscribed; *'Church of England'*.

224 Squadron   2Lt S J Chamberlain   Safe
DH.4 B2122   Lt J Ellingham   Safe
T/o Alimini tasked for a raid on the seaplane base at Cattaro and on return to base swung on touch down and collided with a hangar, damaging the DH beyond repair.

Saturday-Sunday 11-12 May 1918
214 Squadron   Lt J V Ould   Injured
Handley Page O/100   Lt W H Matthews   Injured
3130   Lt D R Tullis   Injured Unemployed list 26 January 1919: Lt
T/o Coudekerque with the intention of bombing the docks at Oostende and on return, owing to ground fog, crash landed at Montlemaitre [sic]. An entry in *The London Gazette* 14 October 1919, issue 31598, indicates transfer from the Air Branch to the Administrative Branch on 18 September 1919, of Lieutenant Ould in the rank of flying officer.

Sunday 12 May 1918
During the day the DH.9 force operating on the Western Front was boosted by the arrival from Old Sarum by the main body of No 103 Squadron led by their Commanding Officer Major E N Fuller, the odd machine and crew having arrived at Serny three days previously.

22 Squadron   2Lt C E Tylor   pow
Bristol F.2b B1162*   2Lt A V Bollins   pow   Unemployed list 10 September 1919: P/O
T/o Serny for an offensive patrol and was last seen, under control, between Armentières and Merville. Both officers were named in *Flight* June 6, 1918, under the 'Missing' banner, noting that Second Lieutenant Bollins was late of the King's Liverpool Regiment. Second Lieutenant Tylor was confirmed as a prisoner of war in the magazine's issue of July 4, 1918, but was thought to be wounded. A month later [August 8th], *Flight* confirmed that Second Lieutenant Bollins was a prisoner of war. Both were repatriated towards the end of December, the pilot on the 29th followed the next day by his observer.

* It was, Trevor Henshaw reports, while flying 'B1162' on the 2nd of April 1918, Second Lieutenant G E Gurdon [accompanied by Second Lieutenant A J H Thornton] secured the first of his twenty-two combat victories when he drove down a Fokker DrI out of control near Vauvillers.

29 Squadron   Lt C M Wilson [Canada]   Safe   See 14 October 1918 - 29 Squadron
SE.5a D306
T/o St Omer for a line patrol and wrecked while landing owing to strong and gusting wind. Received by the squadron as recently as the 7th May, 'D306' was written off with a mere seven hours and forty-five minutes flying in total.

58 Squadron   2Lt J Handley   pow
FE.2b B497   2Lt J B Birkhead   pow
T/o Fauquembergues with instructions to bomb a target identified as Don; failed to return. Both officers are reported to have been wounded, their names appearing under the 'Missing' banner in *Flight* June 6th, 1918,

where it is noted Second Lieutenant Birkhead had been attached to the Royal Air Force from the West Yorkshire Regiment.

| 74 Squadron | Lt H E Dolan MC | + | La Laiterie Military Cemetery |

SE.5a B7733

T/o Clairmarais for an offensive patrol; failed to return. Fellow pilots returned to report seeing a SE.5a go down in the vicinity of Wulverghem [West-Vlaanderen]; this may have been Henry Eric Dolan's machine. His Military Cross was *gazetted* in the New Year's Honours list 1917 [supplement 29886], where it is indicated he was attached to Headquarters Royal Field Artillery.

| 74 Squadron | Captain C B Glynn | Safe |

SE.5a C6446

T/o Clairmarais authorised to carry out a test of the aircraft's guns. On return Captain Glynn made what is described in the accident report as an *'erratic landing'* which damaged 'C6446' beyond repair. Previously of the Liverpool Regiment, Territorial Forces, he was seconded to the Royal Flying Corps on 10 May 1917, as promulgated in supplement 30104 of 31 May 1917. It seems he returned to the territorials and under the provisions of A.O. 166/21 as amended by A.O. 332/21, relinquished his commission on 30 September 1921 [supplement 32542 of 7 December 1921] at which time he was attached to the 10th Battalion The King's Regiment; he is shown as being a recipient of the Distinguished Flying Cross.

| 74 Squadron | Lt G M Atkinson | Injured |

SE.5a D266

T/o Clairmarais for an offensive patrol and written off in a crash near the airfield owing to pressure failure.

Monday 13 May 1918

| 10 Squadron | Lt W Hughes | Safe | See 29 June 1918 - 10 Squadron |
| FK.8 B3301 | 2Lt F C Peacock | Safe | See 29 June 1918 - 10 Squadron |

T/o Droglandt for artillery observation duties during which the crew force-landed at map reference 27K4c65, both officers being badly shaken. Second Lieutenant Peacock, late of the Royal Field Artillery, subsequently transferred to the Administrative Branch.

Tuesday 14 May 1918

| 4 Squadron AusFC | 2Lt R G Smallwood | Safe |

F.1 Camel B5213

T/o 1750 Clairmarais for a special mission during which Second Lieutenant Smallwood got the better of a Pfalz in the vicinity of Ypres, but his own aircraft sustained substantial damage and, it is believed, was later struck off charge. The next day, and while flying in Camel D6520, he made a poor landing on return from a patrol, but on this occasion his aircraft was repaired [see my summary for 20 April 1918, where Second Lieutenant Smallwood wrote of a Camel].

| 4 Squadron AusFC | Lt L R Sinclair | pow |

F.1 Camel D1818

T/o 1750 Clairmarais similarly tasked and was last sighted over Belgium and south of Zillebeke [West-Vlaanderen]. At the time Zillebeke was a village, but since 1976, has been merged into the environs of Ypres. I suspect that while being held prisoner Lieutenant Sinclair's health took a turn for the worse thereby leading to the relinquishment of his commission on 17 June 1919.

| 18 Squadron | Lt R T Minors* | Safe | See 2 September 1918 - 18 Squadron |
| DH.4 A7839 | Lt W H Lyall | Safe | See 2 September 1918 - 18 Squadron |

T/o Serny tasked for bombing only for the engine to 'choke' and then 'cut'. Damaged beyond repair in the emergency landing that followed. On 26 March 1918, when being flown by Lt R B Smith and Sergeant A O A Pollard, a successful engagement took place near Vaux [sic] with a Fokker DrI being sent down out of control.

* I am reasonably confident that Lieutenant R T Minors is Reginald Towers Minors whose name, along with two fellow privates, appears in a supplement to *The London Gazette* issue 29268 of 17 August 1915, under the heading Territorial Force Reserve - General List where the trio previously with the 28th [County of London] Battalion, The London Regiment [Artists' Rifles] were commissioned as second lieutenants with effect from 20th August 1915. I am also reasonably certain that postwar, and now promoted captain, he died on 27 March 1919, and is buried in Belgrade Cemetery. For Sergeant Pollard, see my summary for DH.4 A7815 on 4th September 1918.

| 18 Squadron | Lt F J Morgan | Injured | Aire Communal Cemetery |
| DH.4 A7998 | 2Lt S T J Helmore | + | Tannay British Cemetery, Thiennes |

T/o Serny ordered for a photographic reconnaissance sortie during which the DH came under sustained anti-aircraft fire and in the early evening came down in the Forêt de Nieppe*, Frederick James Morgan being critically injured and, subsequently, dying from his wounds on the 16th. Both officers had served formerly with the Royal Fusilier, Frederick with the 7th Battalion and his observer with the 23rd Battalion. From their entries in the cemetery registers, it is noted that both lay within the area controlled by the British 5th Division with the first service burials at Tannay taking place in April 1918. Their deaths were the first sustained by the squadron since the 1st of April 1918.

| 23 Squadron | Lt B W Fletcher | Safe |
| 5F.1 Dolphin C3812 | | |

T/o St Omer authorised for a practice flight; damaged beyond repair following a heavy landing. On 27 April 1918 Captain A A N D Pentland delivered 'C3812' to No 87 Squadron recently arrived at St Omer from Hounslow, but on the 27th it was reallocated to No 23 Squadron. Its total flying time was a mere seven hours and thirty-eight minutes.

| 24 Squadron | Lt E G McMurtrie | Injured |
| SE.5a B8500 | | |

T/o Conteville for an offensive patrol and, owing to engine failure, crash-landed at Surcamps, base for the FE.2b equipped No 102 Squadron. Lieutenant McMurtrie features in a crash on 21 April 1918 [see my summary for details].

| 29 Squadron | Lt T S Harrison | Safe |
| SE.5a D5958 | | |

T/o St Omer for an engine test and on return Lieutenant Harrison misjudged his approach and crashed onto a road, wiping off the undercarriage. Accepted by the squadron 0n 19 April 1918, and including delivery 'D5958' had flown for a total of twenty-six hours and fifteen minutes.

| 41 Squadron | Lt R S Milani | Safe | Unemployed list 24 March 1919: Lt |
| SE.5a B69 | | | |

T/o Serny for an air test and damaged beyond any worthwhile repair following a heavy landing which resulted in the undercarriage collapsing. Prior to its issue to No 41 Squadron, 'B69' operated as 'U' with No 40 Squadron and in the hands of Captain Oswald Horsley*forced down four enemy aircraft between the 28th of December 1917 and the 9th of March 1918.

* Captain Oswald Horsley MC and mentioned in a despatch was killed on the 19th of August 1918, along with Captain Hugh Archibald Renwick in a flying accident involving RE.8 A4205. Oswald Horsley is buried in Steep [All Saints] Churchyard, Hampshire [he was the younger son of Sir Victor Horsley], while Hugh Renwick rests in Farnborough [Victoria Road] Cemetery. An extremely detailed report as to the cause of the crash at Arborfield can be read on the Arborfield History website, which I have pleasure in acknowledging. Taken from the Inquest held at Wokingham it appears that failure of part of the port wing structure occurred at roughly two thousand feet after which the RE.8 spiralled to the ground and was completely smashed. The subsequent verdict read; *'Accidental death through falling through the air in an aeroplane, owing to the failure of the wing structure.'*

| 55 Squadron | 2Lt S Sephton [South Africa] | + | Charmes Military Cemetery, Essegney |
| DH.4 A7548 | 2Lt H A Nash | + | Charmes Military Cemetery, Essegney |

T/o Tantonville for a practice flight during which control was lost and the DH dived to the ground. Stanley Sephton was born on 19 February 1899, and hailed from Glengyle, New England in South Africa's Cape Province. At nineteen years of age [Commonwealth War Graves Commission indicates he was eighteen] he could not have been with the squadron for any length of time.

| 60 Squadron | Lt R A Kilpatrick | Safe |
| SE.5a B176 | | |

T/o Boffles for an offensive patrol but owing to a failing engine Lieutenant Kilpatrick peeled away and while landing on an unidentified aerodrome, but possibly Tingry in the Pas-de-Calais, he crashed.

| 70 Squadron | 2Lt K H Wallace | Safe | See 4 September 1918 - 70 Squadron |
| F.1 Camel B7473 | | | |

T/o Ramaisnil for a practice flight; crashed on landing. Kenneth Houston Wallace was one of dozens of cadets commissioned on the 30th of August 1917, to the General List, Royal Flying Corps [gazetted 18th September 1917, supplement 30392]. His Camel was at No 4 Aeroplane Acceptance Park Lincoln by 8 February 1918, and was taken on squadron charge on 5 March 1918. Before being written off it shared in the destruction of a kite balloon and drove down two hostile machines [Second Lieutenant W M Carlaw and Captain F G Quigley].

| 84 Squadron | Lt A F Matthews | Safe |
| SE.5a C5448 | | |

T/o Bertangles to practice his flying skills on type, an exercise that ended in engine failure and a crash-landing on a nearby French airfield where 'C5448' ended up in a bush. Examination of the engine revealed a fractured connecting rod.

| 112 Squadron | Captain A A C Garnons- | + | Horsham [Hills] Cemetery |
| F.1 Camel D6625 | Williams*MC | | |

T/o Throwley authorised to carry out stall turns. It seems control was lost at around two thousand five hundred feet with 'D6625' falling to earth. An inquiry into the circumstances of Alexander Aylmer Curtis Garnons-Williams death put forward the suggestion that he may have fainted. Prior to transferring to the Royal Flying Corps in March 1917, he had served with the South Wales Borderers, having been commissioned as an ex-cadet on 15th August 1914, to the 3rd Battalion [gazetted 11 September 1914, issue 28899]. During his time on the Western Front, he was badly wounded during the Second Battle of Ypres and invalided home; recovered, he returned to France to see action at Loos and on the Somme from July through to November.

* I am reasonably confident, bearing in mind the surname, that there is a connection with Miles Herbert Garnons-Williams, one of fifteen ex-Britannia Royal Naval Cadets that arrived at Cranwell in February 1920 as the first entry of flight cadets. Graduating with a permanent commission he retired in the rank of Group Captain post-Second World War. Another 'Garnons-Williams', Lieutenant-Colonel Henry Fenton Garnons-Williams was killed in France on 10 November 1939, in the crash of a No 13 Squadron Lysander.

Wednesday 15 May 1918

| 11 Squadron | Lt H W Sellars MC | + | Arras Flying Services Memorial |
| Bristol F.2b C845 | Lt C C Robson | pow | |

T/o Remaisnil to carry out a patrol over a corridor of roughly thirty km from southeast of Amiens to southeast of Albert and when last seen was trying to fight off a hostile aircraft over Bouchou [sic]. Herbert Whiteley Sellars was commissioned to the General List, Royal Flying Corps on 3 June 1916 [gazetted 14 June 1916, supplement 29622]. His award appeared in the Gazette on 21 June 1918, supplement 30761; 'For conspicuous gallantry and devotion to duty. Whilst on offensive patrol, he attacked a hostile two-seater machine, which dived vertically and eventually crashed. Having attacked another two-seater machine, which dived down over the enemy's lines, he engaged three hostile scouts, at which the nearest of which his observer fired two bursts at 75 yards range, causing the enemy machine to crash down in flames. His skill and gallantry have been most marked.' Biographical notes for Herbert, as recorded on Wikipedia, indicate he was born on 11 June 1896, and following schooling at The Leas, Hoylake and Loretto School, Musselburgh, he was entered to go up to Cambridge to study at Gonville and Casius College [I suspect, however, war intervened which put paid to his university ambitions]. His entry continues by stating he learnt to fly at Hendon with the Beatty School, and in the month before he enlisted was granted Royal Aero Club Aviator's Certificate No 2852. His first squadron attachment was with No 25 Squadron, flying FE.2b before converting to DH.4 which '25' used for long-range reconnaissance and bombing; he joined No 11 Squadron circa March 1918. Under the heading 'Missing', *Flight* June 13th, 1918, records Lieutenant Charles Crichton Robson's name as appearing in the list of casualties advised by the Air Ministry. Confirmation of his prisoner of war status appeared in the magazine's issue of September 5th, 1918, noting his award of the Military Cross. His biography, as reported by *Wikipedia,* shows he was born in Liverpool on 11 June 1896, and that prior to joining No 11 Squadron he flew FE.2b equipped No 25 Squadron.

11 Squadron	Captain J V Aspinall	+	Arras Flying Services Memorial
Bristol F.2b C4882	Lt P V Dornonville de la Cour [Denmark]	+	Arras Flying Services Memorial

T/o Remaisnil tasked likewise and lost in the same circumstances as those reported above. Thirty-nine year old Paul Victor Dornonville de la Cour had been attached from the South African Infantry and had formerly served, as had his father Colonel Victor Dornonville de la Cour, in the Danish Cavalry. It is further noted that Paul had fought in the South African War and at the time when he was posted 'missing' his parents were residing in the Earls Court district of London.

23 Squadron	Lt K D Macpherson	Safe
5F.1 Dolphin C4146		

T/o St Omer for a practice flight but became lost. Sighting an airfield, which turned out to be Beauvois [then being used by No 32 Squadron], Lieutenant Macpherson landed only to overshoot the landing area and on entering a ditch his aircraft turned over. On squadron charge since 27 April 1918, 'C4146' was a write off with a mere six hours and twelve minutes flying to its credit. This was the squadron's last casualty while based at St Omer; the next day '23' transferred to Bertangles, roughly one hundred km away to the south.

27 Squadron	Lt H Wild	Safe	See 16 June 1918 - 27 Squadron
DH.4 A7544	Airman W Hilton	Safe	See 19 May 1918 - 27 Squadron

T/o Ruisseauville for practice flying and damaged beyond repair after making an emergency landing in a field that had been put to the plough. Harold Wild was one of many ex-cadets granted the temporary rank of second lieutenant on being commissioned to the General List of the Royal Flying Corps on 19 July 1917 [*gazetted* in issue 30221 published on 7 August 1917].

29 Squadron	Captain R C L Holmes MC	Safe
SE.5a D5990		

T/o St Omer for an offensive patrol; on return, and making ready to land, Captain Holmes lost control and from fifty feet sideslipped to the ground. A relatively new arrival on the squadron, 'D5990' was short by fifty-five minutes of ten hours flying.

40 Squadron	2Lt W L Andrew	pow
SE.5a D3956		

T/o 1645 Bruay along with squadron colleagues for an early evening patrol and was last sighted three quarters of an hour later diving in pursuit of an enemy aircraft. The list of war casualties repeated in *Flight* June 6, 1918, records him as 'missing'. In its issue of February 4, 1919, Second Lieutenant Andrew [now promoted Lieutenant] is named in the list for 20 January 1919 of repatriated prisoners of war.

48 Squadron	Captain C G D Napier MC DCM	+	Arras Flying Services Memorial
Bristol F.2b B1337	Sergeant P Murphy	+	Arras Flying Services Memorial

T/o Bertangles tasked for operations to La Motte and was last sighted in the area going down on fire. Charles George Douglas Napier as a lance-sergeant attached to the 47th Divisional Cyclist Company [Territorial Force] was *gazetted* with the Distinguished Conduct Medal on 28 February 1916, promulgated in *The Edinburgh Gazette* issue 12909. The citation, which can be found on *Wikipedia* where his service life is charted in some detail, reads; *'For conspicuous gallantry on the 25th and 26th May 1915, at Givenchy. After the withdrawal of a bombing party, and having become separated from it, he remained in the trenches with a Serjeant and some men of another Battalion, and greatly assisted this small party by the use of his bombs in retaining possession of a captured trench.'* By the early autumn of 1917, he had transferred to the Royal Flying Corps, briefly serving with No 20 Squadron before joining No 48 Squadron early in 1918. Between the 7th of February and his death, he accounted for nine hostile aircraft, the last three victories being achieved during one afternoon patrol on the 9th of May when three Fokker scouts were driven down out of control. The citation for his Military Cross, promulgated after his death, reads; *On one occasion during a low-flying bombing attack he descended to a height of 100 feet and dropped four bombs amongst a body of enemy troops, causing heavy casualties and scattering the enemy in all directions. Later, whilst on an offensive patrol, he observed an enemy two-seater and two scouts. He fired twenty rounds at the two-seater, with the result that it crashed, and then attacked one of the scouts, which turned over completely, and finally went down in a vertical nose dive. In all he has to his credit two enemy machines crashed and four driven down out of control. He has displayed the greatest judgement, determination and daring.'* [*gazetted* 21 June 1918, supplement 30761]. The action referred to in the citation regarding the shooting down of a two-seater and a scout took place at first light on the 16th of March. To conclude, a document relating to Captain Napier is held in The National Archives under WO 339/115888.

| 49 Squadron | Captain W G Chambers | + | Arras Flying Services Memorial |
| DH.9 C6177 | Lt R C Burky USAS | + | Suresnes American Cemetery, Paris |

T/o Conteville having received orders for a photographic reconnaissance sortie from which the crew failed to return. William Geoffrey Chambers had seen service with the 1st/2nd Battalion Lincolnshire Regiment, and along with many others receiving his commission on 3 April 1915 [*gazetted* 2 April 1915, issue 29118]. Captain Chambers had been attached since 8 November 1917. The squadron's website has three photographs featuring William Chambers, all taken during his training. Raymond C Burky came to the squadron as recently as the 14th of April, and, as remarked on the website, may have survived the crash long enough to be taken to a hospital in Paris.

| 54 Squadron | Lt A H Peters | + | Les Baraques Military Cemetery, Sangatte. |
| F.1 Camel D6607 | | | |

T/o Caffiers in the company of others to practice formation flying and it was while so engaged that eighteen year old Albert Henry Peters lost control in a turn and from a height of one hundred feet spun to the ground. His headstone bears the inscription; *'Fondly Remembered And Never To Be Forgotten By His Loving Parents.'* The death of Lieutenant Peters was the tenth while pursuing operational tasks by the squadron since the 1st of April.

| 55 Squadron | 2Lt A C Hill | Safe | |
| DH.4 A7592 | 2Lt J G Quinton | Safe | See 30 August 1918 - 55 Squadron |

T/o Tantonville with others to practice flying as a formation and on landing, crashed and damaged beyond repair.

| 56 Squadron | 2Lt A L Garrett | Safe | Unemployed list 27 March 1919: Lt |
| SE.5a B101 | | | |

T/o Valheureux for a counter attack patrol and wrecked in a forced landing along a line of old trench works. Moments earlier a connecting rod snapped leading to total engine failure.

| 56 Squadron | Lt T Durrant | Safe | See 16 May 1918 - 56 Squadron |
| SE.5a B8367 | | | |

T/o Valheureux for an operational sortie but ran into a hollow, turned over and damaged beyond repair. Originally intended for No 74 Squadron 'B8367' was delivered to No 56 Squadron on 25 March 1918.

| 57 Squadron | Captain F L Mond | + | Doullens Communal Cemetery extension 2 |
| DH.4 A7645 | Lt E M Martyn [Canada] | + | Doullens Communal Cemetery extension 2 |

T/o 0950 Le Quesnoy tasked for a photographic reconnaissance mission during which the DH was intercepted circa 1130 by enemy fighters west of Bouzencourt near Corbie in the Picardy region. Francis Leopold Mond was commissioned, in the rank of Second Lieutenant, to the 6th London Brigade on 29 August 1914 [*gazetted* in issue 28881, published on 28 August 1914]. Subsequently, he is believed to have served with the Royal Field Artillery while his Canadian observer had transferred to flying duties from the 19th Battalion Canadian Infantry. 'A7645' had been involved in a landing accident on what is described as a *'new aerodrome'* on 29 March 1918, its crew being reported as Second Lieutenant D P Trollip and Lieutenant J D Moses, neither of whom were injured [for further details regarding these officers, please refer to my summary for 1 April 1918]. For much additional information pertaining to Captain Mond and Lieutenant Martyn, please refer to the Western Front Association website which I have pleasure in acknowledging. Here, it is reported, the crew had attacked an ammunition dump near Bapaume.

| 57 Squadron | Lt E H Piper | + | Carnoy Military Cemetery |
| DH.4 A7725 | 2Lt H L B Crabbe | + | Carnoy Military Cemetery |

T/o 0950 Le Quesnoy similarly tasked; failed to return. 'A7725' first saw service with No 25 Squadron but was badly damaged when it struck the top of an old trench when carrying out an emergency landing on 30 November 1917, Second Lieutenant H G Milnes and his observer Captain J H Graham being assisted away from the crash quite badly shaken. Following repairs and storage, it arrived with No 57 Squadron on 2 April. An ex-cadet, Edward Hoernlé Piper was commissioned to the General List of the Royal Flying Corps on 7 June 1917 [*gazetted* 6 July 1917, issue 30170]. Although known to be buried at Carnoy, his grave, and that of his observer, cannot be positively identified and, therefore, the two officers have Special Memorials 9 and 10 respectively. Second Lieutenant Hubert Lyon Bingham Crabbe was formerly of the 3rd [King's Own] Hussars having been *gazetted* to the Special Reserve of Officers [Cavalry] from his Officer Cadet Unit on 21 December 1916 and published in a supplement to the paper first published on 5 January 1917, issue 29895. Their deaths took the squadron's total to twelve since the 1st of April.

| 58 Squadron | 2Lt J E Philpott | Injured Unemployed list 16 March 1919: Lt |
| FE.2b A5675 | 2Lt F W Roadhouse | Injured Unemployed list 13 May 1919: 2Lt |

T/o Fauquembergues for an offensive patrol but crashed almost immediately running into a deep hollow and turning over. Taken on charge on 3 April 1918, 'A5675' logged a minute over twenty-three hours flying. I am of the belief that Second Lieutenant Philpott returned to the service on 5 December 1942, when a pilot officer John Edward Philpott was commissioned to the Administrative and Special Duties Branch [supplement 35940 of 16 March 1943], though subsequent entries are yet to be traced.

| 60 Squadron | 2Lt R A Kirkpatrick | Safe |
| SE.5a B567 | | |

T/o Floringhem tasked for an offensive patrol and on return overshot and crashed onto a road; damaged beyond repair. This brought the squadron's operational losses since the 1st of April to ten, two pilots being killed.

| 70 Squadron | 2Lt J Williamson | + | Arras Flying Services Memorial |
| F.1 Camel D6438 | | | |

T/o 0635 Ramaisnil for an offensive patrol over Rossignal Wood and was seen to spin to the ground at map reference 57D L22.

| 74 Squadron | Lt P F C Howe | Safe | See 2 June 1918 - 74 Squadron |
| SE.5a C1112 | | | |

T/o Clairmarais for an offensive patrol on return from which Lieutenant Howe overshot, ran down a slope and crashed against a fence. For Lieutenant Howe this was his third accident since the formation of the Royal Air Force [see my summaries for 19 and 25 April 1918].

| 74 Squadron | Lt L M Nixon | Safe | See 17 May 1918 - 74 Squadron |
| SE.5a C6414 | | | |

T/o Clairmarais similarly tasked and on return, and landing, struck a ridge which damaged 'C6414' beyond repair. Struck off charge on 23 May 1918, having flown for forty-eight hours and fifteen minutes.

| 83 Squadron | Lt Symmons | Safe |
| FE.2b A5712 | Lt Garrett | Injured |

T/o Franqueville tasked for bombing operations and on return collided with an unidentified machine on landing. 'A5712' was struck from charge as not worth repairing with a total flying time of forty hours and thirty-seven minutes.

86 Squadron   2Lt C M Sankey MC   +   Hanwell [City of Westminster] Cemetery
F.1 Camel B7396

T/o Northolt for a training exercise but while making a turn at fifty feet, downwind, stalled and spun in. On impact the Camel burst into flames. Delivered to No 4 Aeroplane Acceptance Park at Lincoln on, or by, 19 January 1918, 'B7396' was on No 70 Squadron establishment at Poperinghe by 17 February, displaying the letter 'G'. However, it was returned to England on the 16th of March and was probably issued to No 86 Squadron soon after. Prior to his transfer to the Royal Flying Corps, Cecil Martin Sankey distinguished himself in action on the Western Front, his bravery being recognised with the Military Cross *gazetted* on 12 March 1917, supplement 29981; *'For conspicuous gallantry and devotion to duty. He led his company in a most successful raid against the enemy's trenches. He himself killed one of the enemy and wounded another, whom he brought back to our lines.'* [The citation has all the 'hall marks' of an intelligence gathering operation which frequently led to casualties on both sides].

87 Squadron   Lt L N Hollinghurst   Safe   Retirement 27 December 1952:
5F.1 Dolphin C4167   Air Chief Marshal GBE KCB DFC Twice mentioned in a despatch

T/o Petite Synthe for an offensive patrol during which the Dolphin's engine failed and in the ensuing forced landing hit a tree near Moeres*thus becoming the squadron's first loss since arriving at St Omer on 23 April 1918. Leslie Norman Hollinghurst having received his flying training in Egypt joined the squadron in April 1918, having spent part of 1917 and into 1918 as a test pilot, latterly with No 2 Air Issues. He was destined to serve with '87' for the remainder of the war, gaining the Distinguished Flying Cross; *'Since 25th April this officer has destroyed four enemy aeroplanes and driven down one out of control. At all times he displays great deter-mination and cool courage, notably on 20th September, when, although his petrol tank had been shot through and his machine badly damaged, he attacked and destroyed a Fokker biplane that was starting to fire on another member of the patrol, thereby saving the life of a brother Officer. On numerous other occasions Lt Hollinghurst by his gallantry has saved from disaster other members of his patrol'* [credit; Air of Authority website]. Postwar, he was appointed to a permanent commission [with effect from 12 December 1919, after which his career followed the pattern associated with permanent officers, this being a mix of flying duties interspersed with staff positions. Knighted, his last appointment before retirement on 27 December 1952, was as Air Member for Personnel. In retirement he continued to give valued service, not least to the Boy Scout movement. In 1971, he attended the annual D-Day commemorations in Normandy and it was while returning home on the 8th of June that he collapsed and died.

* Probably Les Moëres in the *département du Nord.*

98 Squadron   Lt W Lamont   pow
DH.9 C6103   Lt H B B Wilson   pow   Hamburg Cemetery

T/o 1730 Alquines tasked for bombing and was last sighted flying below the main formation with flames coming from the aircraft's centre section. At the time the DHs were over Belgium and west of Kortrijk [West-Vlaanderen]. It would seem Hamish Blacklock Bowes Wilson sustained serious burns for he is reported to have died on the 18th of July 1918.

100 Squadron   2Lt D S Anderson   pow
FE.2b B498   Mechanic H O'Connor   pow

T/o Villeseneux to transit to Ochey which had been occupied by the squadron the day before; failed to arrive. Second Lieutenant Anderson's name appears under the heading 'Missing' in *Flight* June 20, 1918, and it was not until the magazine's issue of November 14, 1918, that he was confirmed as a prisoner of war.

110 Squadron   2Lt R T Finke   Injured
FK.8 B9643

T/o Sedgeford and while trying to make a steeply banked turn lost control and crashed, Second Lieutenant Finks being severely injured.

120 Squadron	Major P J V Lavarack MC*	+	Newcastle-upon-Tyne [St Andrew's and
RE.8 B8902			Jesmond] Cemetery
	2Lt R A H Brittain	+	Newcastle-upon-Tyne [St Andrews's and
			Jesmond] Cemetery

T/o Cramlington only for the engine to fail and for some inexplicable reason the pilot flying the RE [which was fitted with dual controls] attempted a stall turn at a mere eighty feet. One of the earliest entries in *The London Gazette* concerning Philip James Vaughan Lavarack is dated 22 December 1914 [issue 29015] when on that date, under the banner Staff for Royal Engineer Services, he was one of five appointees to the post of temporary Inspector of Works and Honorary Lieutenants. The next entry, where his full name is given, comes on 26 May 1917 [supplement 30095], by which time he has been appointed to the General List of the Royal Flying Corps and the occasion of his award of the Military Cross; *'For conspicuous gallantry and devotion to duty. While on a photographic patrol he shot down and destroyed a hostile machine. He has done consistently good work in artillery observation and photography throughout the operations.'* Promoted temporary captain, the First Bar was promulgated on 7 March 1918 [supplement 30561]; *'For conspicuous gallantry and devotion to duty. When attacked on artillery patrol by eight enemy aircraft he succeeded in driving down one machine, the rest being driven off east. Later, he drove off three scouts badly hit, which could not be followed, owing to the clouds. In the last month he has fought and driven off enemy aircraft on seven occasions, and afterwards completed his work.'*

206 Squadron	Lt E A Burn	Safe	See 9 May 1918 - 206 Squadron
DH.9 C1175	2Lt A H Mitchener	Safe	See 9 May 1918 - 206 Squadron

T/o Alquines having received orders for a photographic reconnaissance detail and wrecked after flying into telegraph wires to the west of Boisdinghem a hamlet in the Pas-de-Calais west of the present E15 highway and some twelve km due west of St Omer. The war took its toll on the health of Second Lieutenant Mitchener to the extent that he was obliged to relinquish his commission on 15 February 1919.

207 Squadron	Captain W J Mair	Injured
RE.8 A4469	Lt W A George	Injured

T/o Andover and having climbed to three thousand feet entered a bank of cloud and it was while turning that control was lost and the RE spun in.

208 Squadron	Lt M C Howell	Injured
F.1 Camel D6516		

T/o Serny for an offensive patrol only to collide with a DH.9 that was in the process of taxying, Lieutenant Howell sustaining a slight concussion. His aircraft, which had been with the squadron for a week was damaged beyond repair.

209 Squadron	2Lt O G Brittorous	+	Arras Flying Services Memorial
F.1 Camel B5666			

T/o Bertangles for an offensive patrol and was probably shot down at around 1115 by an Albatros scout near Beaufort. Oswald George Brittorous, age nineteen and from Manchester, is described as being a 'Civil Servant' prior to enlistment.

209 Squadron	Lt G Wilson	+	Arras Flying Services Memorial
F.1 Camel B6257			

T/o Bertangles similarly tasked and when last sighted was engaged in a fight with a triplane. Geoffrey Wilson was late of the 19th Divisional Train, Army Service Corps. Both Camels had arrived with the squadron on the 10th of May 1918.

Note. AIR 1/855 indicates the patrol witnessed Camels spinning down near 'Igancourt' which, possibly, is a misprint for 'Agincourt' [Azincourt] in the Pas-de-Calais.

| 210 Squadron | Lt M S Kelly [Canada] | + | Ebblinghem Military Cemetery |

F.1 Camel B7160

T/o St Omer for an offensive patrol and collided near the Allied lines with the Camel, summarised below, after being hit by anti-aircraft fire. Magnus Sigunour Kelly had first enlisted with the Manitoba Regiment, Canadian Infantry.

| 210 Squadron | Lt F V Hall | + | Ebblinghem Miltary Cemetery |

F.1 Camel D3385

T/o St Omer similarly tasked and lost in the circumstances described above, the midair collision ripping away the tailplane of 'D3385'. His headstone is inscribed; *For Whom We Return Thanks To God.'*

| 211 Squadron | Lt C K Flower* | + | Dunkirk Town Cemetery |
| DH.9 B7600 | 2Lt I A B MacTavish* | + | Dunkirk Town Cemetery |

T/o Petite Synthe for practice flying but when climbing out the engine failed. At this point Charles Kenneth Flower made the fatal decision in turning back to the airfield instead of landing straight ahead. As the DH banked, control was lost and 'B7600' spun to the ground bursting into flames on impact.

* Lieutenant Flower's and Second Lieutenant MacTavish's entries in the cemetery register show both as belonging to No 218 Squadron which at the time was stationed at Dover but soon to cross the Channel on the 23rd and take up residence at Petite Synthe. Consequently, their Roll of Honour entries show No 211 Squadron.

Thursday 16 May 1918

| 5 Squadron | Lt F Nash | Safe |
| RE.8 B6566 | Lt E Shamper [Canada] | Injured |

T/o Ascq having received orders for an artillery patrol but swung badly and collided with a hut. Accepted by the squadron on 18 March 1918, 'B6566' flew for fifty-five hours and twenty-five minutes. Lieutenant Shamper, whose injuries were slight, had been attached as an observer officer from the Quebec Regiment, Canadian Expeditionary Force.

| 7 Squadron | Lt J Buckley | Safe |
| RE.8 A4425 *Punjab 51 Malwa* | Lt A T Harper | Safe |

T/o Droglandt for artillery observation. On return crashed while landing; deemed not worth the cost of repair. Originally to No 6 Squadron on 17 October 1917, only to be damaged while on operations on 29 October [Lieutenants Egner and King], repaired and issued to No 7 Squadron on Boxing Day. Flew for a total of one hundred and seventy-two hours and twenty minutes. Postwar, Lieutenant Buckley was granted a short service commission.

| 7 Squadron | Lt C Sutherland | Injured |
| RE.8 D4836 | 2Lt R C Mais [BWI] | Injured |

T/o Droglandt for a *Flash* reconnaissance but swung badly and flew into the airfield's wind gauge. Damaged beyond repair, the airframe was struck off charge on 3 June 1918, and though with only seventeen hours and ten minutes recorded it was considered the cost to repair was not worth the money. Roderick Cameron Mais was commissioned in the rank of pilot officer, for the duration of hostilities, in the Administrative and Special Duties Branch on 12 September 1940 [*gazetted* 5 November 1940, issue 34986]. He resigned his commission on the 29th of March 1946, retaining the rank of flight lieutenant.

| 8 Squadron | Captain A V Milton | Injured Unemployed list 11 February 1919: Captain |
| FK.8 B306 | 2Lt A J Ord | Injured Unemployed list 22 March 1919: 2Lt |

T/o Auxi-le-Château tasked for bombing operations but before becoming safely airborne the propeller hit the ground and the crew crash-landed just beyond the airfield.

| 20 Squadron | 2Lt F E Boulton | pow |
| Bristol F.2b B1232 | 2Lt H G Holman [Canada] | pow Unemployed list 21 March 1919: Lt |

T/o Boisdinghem for an offensive patrol and was last seen crossing the lines; failed to return and, subsequently, both officers were reported wounded, their names appearing in *Flight* July 11, 1918, where it was confirmed that Second Lieutenant Holman was, indeed, in a wounded condition. Of the Canadian Engineers, he was promoted temporary captain on Armistice Day 1918, as promulgated in supplement 31311 of 26 April 1919.

23 Squadron	2Lt A H P Pehrson	Injured	Unemployed list 9 March 1919: Lt
5F.1 Dolphin C3869			

T/o St Omer intending to transit to the squadron's new base at Bertangles but on becoming airborne the engine 'cut' and the Dolphin crashed.

23 Squadron	Lt C E Walton	Injured
5F.1 Dolphin C4147		

T/o St Omer with the same intention but *en route* Lieutenant Walton lost his goggles [presumably they came off and were blown away in the slipstream leaving, I suspect, Lieutenant Walton with streaming eyes] and his attempt to land at Tantonville resulted in a crash. I believe he later transferred from the Air Branch to the Administrative Branch as a 'Lieutenant C E Walton [A]' was so moved on 19 March 1919, issue 31293 of 15th April 1919.

41 Squadron	Lt W E Shields	Safe	See 3 June 1918 - 41 Squadron
SE.5a B123			

T/o Serny and crashed at Floringhem in the Pas-de-Calais, some seventeen km southeast of the airfield, its flying controls shot through. Initially to No 40 Squadron on 19 February 1918, but sent to Air Issues on 21st March, 'B123' arrived with No 41 Squadron twenty-four hours before the Royal Air Force came into being. It will be recalled that Lieutenant Shields had been badly shot up, though fortunately without injury, during a patrol on the 8th of May 1918.

55 Squadron	Lt R C Sansom	+	Niederzwehren Cemetery, Kassel
DH.4 A7477 F	Airman G C Smith	+	Niederzwehren Cemetery, Kassel

T/o Tantonville for a bombing raid on Saarbrücken and seen by crews similarly engaged going down, burning, over the target area. Roland Charles Sansom was commissioned to the General List of the Royal Flying Corps on 29 July 1917 [*gazetted* 4 September 1917, issue 30270]. His father, Charles Sansom, had been honoured with the The Most Distinguished Order of St Michael and Saint George.

56 Squadron	Captain T Durrant	+	Dantzig Alley British Cemetery, Mametz
SE.5a B183 A			

T/o 1850 Valheureux for an offensive patrol and was last seen over the Somme doing battle with a triplane northeast of Albert. A skilful Scout pilot, Trevor Durrant personally destroyed or shared in the destruction of seven hostile aircraft between the 6th of April and the 13th of May 1918. His first victim was a two-seater reconnaissance aircraft north of Lamotte and the last another two-seater reconnaissance machine identified as a LVG CVI southwest of Beacourt [*sic*]. Trevor Durrant had crashed twenty-four hours previously while taking off for an operational mission [see my summary for details].

56 Squadron	Lt P H Ritter [USAS]	Safe
SE.5a B4880*		

T/o Valheureux for a practice flight and while firing at a target on the ground Lieutenant Ritter, to his concern, shot away part of the propeller. Forced landing, he finished up in trees at Bois de la Naours**in the *département de la Somme*. This particularly SE.5a was not in prime condition for just four days earlier Second Lieutenant F C Tarbutt had been obliged to return early from a patrol as 'B4880' was unable to keep up with the rest of the formation. Not surprisingly, it was struck off charge on 19 May 1918, with, it is noted, a useful total of one hundred and nineteen hours and forty minutes flying to its credit.

* Concerning 'B4880' *The SE.5a File* shows issue to the squadron on 11 December 1917, after which it accounted for two Albatros scouts; the first on 19th February [shared] and the second on 22nd March, both credited to Captain F Billings. The entry then continues; *'On practice flight part of propellor shot off damaging*

one plane and lateral control, FL, struck tree 1905 16.5.18 [Lt P H Ritter USAS injured]; SOC 2 Advanced Salvage Dump 19.5.18.' But a rider has been appended; *'BUT Combat report has Fokker DrI in flames NE of Albert 20.15 16.5.18 [Lt F C Tarbutt]; Sqdn Daily Report has B4880 for both Tarbutt [in the air 1850-2026] and Ritter [crashing 1905].*

** The area where Lieutenant Ritter force-landed is now regarded as one of the most important sites regarding the *Great War* for in the vast network of underground caves historians have found masses of 'graffiti' surviving from the period. Work on examining these remarkable 'scrawls' continues, while visitors are able to take conducted tours of these impressive galleries.

56 Squadron	Captain A L Cuffe	Safe
SE.5a B8494		

T/o Valheureux for a practice flight but while running at speed damaged the undercarriage. Continuing the duty, he subsequently forced landed at Beauvois, base for No 32 Squadron, but overturned; damaged beyond repair 'B8494' had flown for fifteen hours and forty minutes in total.

60 Squadron	2Lt R G Lewis	Safe
SE.5a C5449		

T/o from an undisclosed location where Second Lewis had force-landed twenty-fours previously, but on reaching Boffles he overshot and ran onto a road where 'C5449' turned over; wrecked. On squadron charge since 6 May 1918, it had logged, in total, a mere three hours and fifty minutes flying.

60 Squadron	2Lt H N J Proctor	+	Red Cross Corner Cemetery, Beugny
SE.5a D3912			

T/o Boffles for an offensive patrol and was seen for the final time, in combat, near Bapaume [Pas-de-Calais] and he probably fell some five km away to the northeast at Beugny. Nineteen years of age, Herbert Nevil Jack would never again look out over the waters of the Bristol Channel from his home in Weston-super-Mare.

62 Squadron	Lt C H Arnison	Injured	
Bristol F.2b C4859	Lt C D Wells MC	+	Corbie Communal Cemetery extension
	A mention in a despatch		

T/o Planques for an offensive patrol and became involved in aerial combat over the Somme. In the *mêlée* Lieutenant Arnison was wounded and his observer killed. Most likely in an attempt to get medical help for his colleague, a forced landing was made near Corbie, some fifteen km east of Amiens, but twenty-one year old Charles Douglas Wells was beyond aid. Commissioned to the 7th Battalion Royal Lancaster Regiment on the 2nd of December 1914 [he could only have been seventeen at the time and must have been among those who answered the 'call to arms' made at the outbreak of war] as published in issue 28995 of the *Gazette* of 4th December 1914, he was *gazetted* with the Military Cross in the New Year's Honours List of 1918 [supplement 30450 1 January 1918]. Charles Henry Arnison made a good recovery, subsequently winning a Military Cross; *'For conspicuous gallantry and devotion to duty. He has destroyed four enemy aircraft and driven down four others completely out of control. He has always shown the greatest skill, keenness and gallantry, and has been largely instrumental in the fine achievements of his squadron.'* [supplement 30901 of 16 September 1918]. It is noted, however, that with effect from 6 October 1920, he was placed on the retired list owing to injuries. At the time he held the rank of flying officer. Returning to the service in the Second World War and commissioned in the Royal Air Force Volunteer Reserve, his commission was relinquished on 11 May 1954, under the provisions of the Navy, Army and Air Force Reserves Act of 1954; at the time he was ranked flight lieutenant. Born on the 13th of January 1893, Henry Arniston died on the 4th of September 1974.

64 Squadron	Lt S B Reece	Safe	Unemployed list 2 March 1919: Lt
SE.5a C1859			

T/o Izel-lès-Hameau for an offensive patrol during which enemy aircraft were engaged. Picking what he thought was a good target, Lieutenant Reece dived steeply and while doing so he heard a distinctive snap, after which he found his aircraft difficult to control. Forced landing near Vert Galand an inspection revealed a broken rear spar. Salvaged, 'C1859' was struck off charge on 21 May 1918.

65 Squadron   Captain J A Grenier   Safe
F.1 Camel D6578   [Canada]

T/o Bertangles for a practice flight but while landing lost control and sideslipped to the ground where, on impact, the Camel turned over. Captain Grenier of the Canadian Expeditionary Force was attached to the Royal Flying Corps on 20 November 1917 [*gazetted* 13 December 1917, supplement 30425].

70 Squadron   2Lt W S Dann   +   Doullens Communal Cemetery extension
F.1 Camel D1886

T/o Ramaisnil with instructions to carry our a patrol at low level; force-landed, with fatal consequences, over one thousand metres to the south of the church at Basseux in the Pas-de-Calais, twelve km southwest of Arras. Wilfrid Steven Dann had served previously with the 3rd Battalion The Buffs [East Kent Regiment]. His head-stone bears a message from his widow; '*In Proud And Everliving Memory Of My Beloved Husband From Eve.*'

79 Squadron   Lt H C Taylor   Injured See 27 June 1918 - 79 Squadron
5F.1 Dolphin C4046

T/o Beauvais to transit to the squadron's new home at Ste Marie Cappel. Landing, Lieutenant Taylor struck a ridge and turned over, thereby have the dubious distinction of writing off the squadron's first Dolphin at their new base. His injuries were not thought to be too serious.

82 Squadron   Lt L S Kiggell   Safe
FK.8 B5764   2Lt M P E Harrisson*   Safe

T/o Agenvilliers having being briefed for bombing operations but while travelling at speed a wheel detached from its axle, though the crew managed to stagger into the air and continue with the sortie. However, before reaching their objective engine trouble forced an early return and on landing the undercarriage collapsed. On charge since the 7th of the month, 'B5764' was struck off charge on the 2nd of June with thirty-six hours and twenty minutes flying credited. Both officers had an army background; Lieutenant Kiggell was attached to the General List of the Royal Flying Corps from the Royal Warwickshire Regiment with effect from 31 August 1918, as prom-ulgated in supplement 30354 of 27 October 1917, while his observer was of the Royal East Kent Regiment who had to relinquish his commission, owing to ill-health, on 31 July 1919.

* The son of Major Arthur Henry Portal Harrisson, Montagu Philip Everson Harrisson, having recovered his well-being returned to army duty, rose in rank to match that of his father, and by the winter of 1944-1945 was in Egypt attached to his old regiment, The Buffs [Royal East Kent Regiment] in whose service he died on the 29th of January 1945. He is buried in Heliopolis War Cemetery where his headstone carries the words; '*Come Unto Me All Ye That Labour, And Are Heavy Laden, And I Will Give You Rest.*'

84 Squadron   Captain H P Smith   Injured
SE.5a C1847

T/o Bertangles for an offensive patrol during which Captain Smith's aircraft was hit in the engine while fighting with an enemy aircraft. Wounded, he force-landed in 'No Man's Land' near Villers-Bretonneux, 'C1847' catching fire. On charge since 11 May 1918, 'C1847' flew for just nine hours and twenty minutes in total.

98 Squadron   Lt A G Baker   Safe
DH.9 C6100   Mechanic D Wentworth   Safe

T/o Alquines tasked for bombing but returned with engine trouble. Landing, the DH bounced and when Lieu-tenant Baker opened the throttle to go round again the engine failed to respond and moments later the crew were walking away from a crash-landing. Salvaged, subsequent inspection deemed the damage was so severe it was struck off charge on 21 May 1918.

98 Squadron   Lt J H Bryer   Injured
DH.9 C6105   Mechanic R J Weston   Injured

T/o Alquines similarly tasked but turned back with engine trouble and while in the landing area lost control, and spun to the ground. Salvaged, 'C6105' was struck off charge on 22 May 1918. As the conflict progressed so the health of Lieutenant Bryer's failed and with effect from 29 January 1919, his commission was relinquished.

| 102 Squadron* | 2Lt S C Mimmack | Injured |
| FE.2b A5611 | Lt A E G Bailey | Injured |

T/o Surcamps for operations during which the air pressure dropped alarmingly and in the ensuing emergency landing the FE flew into trees near Domart en Ponthieu.

* No 102 Squadron arrived in France as a night bomber squadron on 24 September 1917, being first based at St André-aux-Bois before moving to Izel-lès-Hameau from where on the night of 30th September-1st October the squadron despatched five crews to bomb a stores dump at Dechy. Four claim to have hit the target while a fifth failed to return. The write off, here summarised, was the first since the 1st of April, a remarkable run of good fortune.

| 201 Squadron | Lt R H Hemmens | Safe | Unemployed list 1 May 1919: Lt |
| F.1 Camel B6211 | | | |

T/o Noeux for an offensive patrol and on return to Noeux overshot the landing area and finished up in a cornfield damaged beyond worthwhile repair, general fatigue being quoted as one reason. Reginald Hewlett Hemmens began his service as a cadet and was commissioned to the General List of the Royal Flying Corps on the 11th of October 1917 [gazetted 17 October 1917, supplement 30337]. He returned to the service in the Second World War, being granted a hostilities only commission on 28 March 1941, in the Equipment Branch, promulgated 25 April 1941, issue 35145. He continued to be employed postwar until relinquishing his commission on 13 July 1954, under the provisions of the Navy, Army and Air Force Reserves Act 1954. His rank at the time was flight lieutenant.

| 203 Squadron | Captain P R White | pow |
| F.1 Camel D3353 | | |

T/o possibly from Lièttres for an offensive patrol and when seen for the last time was trying to escape the attention of half-a-dozen Pfalz scouts on the north side of La Bassée [see my summary below for No 208 Squadron]. Captain White was repatriated on Christmas Day 1918, a magnificent present for his family and friends.

| 206 Squadron | Lt S Gillott | Safe | |
| DH.9 B7654 | 2Lt F S Ganter | Safe | See 11 May 1918 - 206 Squadron |

T/o Alquines ordered for bombing and reported to have crashed when landing. For notes regarding Second Lieutenant Ganter, please refer to my summary for 10 May 1918.

| 208 Squadron | Lt W E Cowan | pow | Unemployed list 24 March 1919: Lt |
| F.1 Camel D9540 | | | |

T/o 0630 Serny for an early morning patrol and when last seen by his fellow pilots was flying, under control, north of La Bassée in the Nord département and being chased by two hostile scouts. According to Air-Britain's Camel File Lieutenant Cowan was claimed by Lieutnant von Marwitz of Jasta 30 at 0840 [German time] over the Pas-de-Calais at Lorgies which straddles the boundary twixt the two départements and in distance is around three km north-northwest of La Bassée. Flight, in their August 8, 1918, issue confirmed Lieutenant Cowan's status as a prisoner of war; he was repatriated on 30 December 1918.

Friday 17 May 1918

| 2 Squadron AusFC | Captain M Jones | Safe |
| SE.5a B571 | | |

T/o Fouquerolles for an offensive patrol to Bapaume. On return, and landing, the axle broke causing damage that was deemed not worth repairing. While in the care of No 84 Squadron, Second Lieutenant C L Stubbs force-landed in a ploughed field near Chocques airfield on 14 October 1917. Following repairs, 'B571' arrived with the squadron on 15 March.

| 4 Squadron AusFC | Lt R Moore | Safe |
| F.1 Camel B5625 | | |

T/o Clairmarais authorised to make a practice flight; crashed on landing and wrecked.

5 Squadron	Lt S H Vickers	Safe	
RE.8 E7	2Lt C E Gardener	Safe	See 2 September 1918 - 5 Squadron

T/o Le Hameau having received instructions for an artillery patrol but moments after becoming airborne Lieutenant Vickers 'choked' the engine causing 'E7' to sideslip to the ground. On, or by, 20 March 1918, this RE.8 was at the Aeroplane Acceptance Park at Coventry, having previously been earmarked for training, and was in the hands of the squadron on the last day of the month. Including testing and transit, it achieved fifty-three hours and twenty minutes flying.

11 Squadron	Major R F S Morton	Safe
Bristol F.2b C911	Lt H R Kincaid [Canada]	Injured

T/o Remaisnil for a practice flight but on return misjudged his approach and flew into a tree. Rowland Francis Storrs Morton [he had commanded No 11 Squadron since August 1917] was badly shaken and was admitted to No 3 Casualty Clearing Station while Lieutenant Kincaid [whom I suspect went to the same clearing station] escaped with minor injuries. Seconded for duty with the Royal Flying Corps on 8 January 1918, from the Canadian Expeditionary Force [*gazetted* 7 February 1918, supplement 30513], his attachment ceased on 3 July 1919, when he returned to duty with the Eastern Ontario Regiment, as notified on 30th July 1919, supplement 31481. It is noted from his entry that he had been awarded the Military Cross. Returning to Major Morton, the accident ended his tenure of command [Major H P Davey taking his place] and four days after the crash he returned to England aboard the *Carisbrook Castle*. Remaining in the service, he was appointed to a permanent commission on the 1st of August 1919, and when he relinquished the rank of acting air commodore on 24th August 1939,*served until 25 June 1943, at which date he reverted to the retired list as a group captain. Although little is known of his subsequent service, the website devoted to officers attaining air rank notes he was commissioned, temporarily, as Commander [Air] in the Royal Navy with effect from the 1st of November 1943. Born 25th October 1887, he died on 3 April 1953.

* It seems he retired as a wing commander in 1937, but was recalled to take up the appointment of Air Officer Commanding No 31[Barrage Balloon] Group.

24 Squadron	2Lt W C Lambert [USA]	Safe	Unemployed list 6 September 1919: F/L DFC
SE.5a C1082			

T/o Conteville for an offensive mission during which a connecting rod snapped. A forced landing was carried out close to the airfield, but the flying days for 'C1082' were at an end. On squadron establishment since 17 March 1918, its total flying hours are recorded as eighty-two hours and three minutes. William Carpenter Lambert's biography on *Wikipedia* indicates he was born on 18 August 1894, at Ironton in Lawrence County, Ohio, and by the outbreak of the *Great War* was employed as a chemist working in Buffalo, New York. Like many Americans, the declaration of war in Europe opened up the chance for adventure and quitting his job William crossed into Canada and enlisted with the Royal Regiment of Canadian Artillery. However, it seems he soon left the artillery and with his chemist's background joined Canadian Explosives Limited. Then, early in 1917, he sailed for England having being successful in joining the Royal Flying Corps [he had an experience of flying seven years earlier in a Wright biplane]. His training completed, William was attached to No 24 Squadron on the 20th of March 1918, serving with '24' until 20 August 1918, when he was sent to England to recover from stress brought about by an enemy raid on the squadron's aerodrome [probably Bertangles, but possibly Conteville]. In the Second World War he enlisted with the United States Army Air Force, retiring in the rank of lieutenant-colonel in 1954. His death occurred on 19 March 1982. Returning to his time with No 24 Squadron, William attained the rank of temporary captain and was *gazetted* with the Distinguished Flying Cross on 3rd August 1918, supplement 30827; *'He has destroyed six enemy machines and driven down four others out of control, displaying at all times dash and determination. On one occasion, when attacked by two Fokker biplanes, he drove down one, engaged the other at twenty yards range, and crashed it to earth.'*

24 Squadron	Lt E Harrison	+	Arras Flying Services Memorial
SE.5a C1105			

T/o Conteville similarly tasked and was seen 'flamed' by an enemy aircraft over Foucaucourt-en-Santerre in the *département du Somme*; Edward Harrison was formerly of the Royal Engineers.

| 32 Squadron | 2Lt K P G Hendrie | Injured |
| SE.5a B627 | | |

T/o from a forced landing site near St Pol and on reaching Beauvois had the misfortune to come down in standing corn. A technical inspection resulted in the airframe being struck off charge on 18 May 1918, with sixty-one hours in total being appended to its record card.

| 32 Squadron | Lt D J Russell | pow |
| SE.5a B8393 | | |

T/o Beauvois for an offensive patrol over the Pas-de-Calais and along the corridor between Mametz and Vitry-en-Artois, a distance of around sixty km north-northeast of Amiens. Held at Karlsruhe, Lieutenant Russel was repatriated on 30 December 1918.

| 35 Squadron | 2Lt M G W Stewart | Safe | Unemployed list 19 February 1919: Lt DFC |
| FK.8 C8449 | 2Lt A E Harris | Safe | |

T/o Villers Bocage for an operational patrol and owing to engine failure was obliged to force-land at Hédauville [Somme] some five km northwest of Albert.

| 40 Squadron | Lt S P Kerr | Injured |
| SE.5a B189 S | | |

T/o 1945 Bruay for an evening offensive patrol and on return to aerodrome the light was beginning to fade and this resulted in Lieutenant Kerr misjudging his approach and at 2055, he flew into a line of telegraph wires and crashed into a house. Taken on charge on 20 March 1918, 'B189' saw plenty of action and before being wrecked destroyed four hostile machines.

| 40 Squadron | Lt L Seymour | pow |
| SE.5a D3555 | | |

T/o 0700 Bruay for an offensive patrol and was last seen by his colleagues at 0845 when he discharged a red flare and set off in pursuit of a formation of hostile aircraft flying near Bois-de-Biez. Turning to *Flight* their issue of June 27, 1918, in which the Roll of Honour list is repeated shows Lieutenant Seymour classified as 'missing' while the list published on 1 November 1918, and repeated in *Flight* November 7, 1918, confirms his status as a prisoner of war and suffering from wounds.

| 54 Squadron | Lt J H Spence | Safe | See 16 July 1918 - 54 Squadron. |
| F.1 Camel B2529 | | | |

T/o Caffiers with others tasked for formation flying practice and reported to have crashed in the sea off Hardelot-Plage in the Pas-de-Calais while attempting to force-land with engine failure. In the same Camel, James Hamilton Spence had a minor landing accident on the 8th of May; 'B2529' arrived with the squadron on 20 April, prior to which it had been on the strength of No 73 Squadron until it was struck for repairs on 22 March 1918.

| 57 Squadron | 2Lt A Newman MC | Injured |
| DH.4 A7723 | Lt E G Pernet | Injured |

T/o Le Quesnoy having been briefed for bombing and during the sortie, and flying at ten thousand feet, a piston broke, fracturing the crankcase. Force-landed near Treizennes. Although on active service since November 1917, when it was issued to No 25 Squadron, an accident on the 26th of the month resulted in lengthy repairs and it was not until the 16th of May that 'A7723' arrived at Le Quesnoy; thus, it flew for only a mere ten hours.

| 60 Squadron | 2Lt A Beck | Safe |
| SE.5a B8268 | | |

T/o Boffles for an offensive patrol but ran onto a road and damaged beyond repair. On 20 January 1918, while being flown on a gunnery practice detail by Lieutenant Crosbee 'B8268' was poorly handled during landing which resulted in the undercarriage giving way, finishing up on its nose. This ended its time with No 24 Squadron and following salvage and repair was issued to No 60 Squadron on the 5th of April.

60 Squadron | 2Lt C R Henderson | Safe
SE.5a B8415

T/o Boffles similarly tasked but left the formation owing to the engine 'choking'; uncertain of his position, and with the engine failing, Second Lieutenant Henderson force-landed at Capelle*near Hazebrouck [Nord].

* Probably the airfield at Ste Marie Cappel which lies some to two to three km north of Hazebrouck.

65 Squadron | Lt H J Leavitt | pow | Resigned commission 31 May 1919: Lt
F.1 Camel D1791*

T/o 1700 Bertangles for an offensive patrol and when last seen was going down, apparently under control, from one thousand feet over the Somme near Bécordel-Bécourt, two km east of Albert. Lieutenant Leavitt's status as a prisoner of war was confirmed by the Air Ministry in their list of casualties, repeated in *Flight* July 4th, 1918.

* See my summary for 20 May 1918, for notes relating to this aircraft.

70 Squadron | 2Lt V W H Hillyard | pow | Unemployed list 26 February 1919: Lt
F.1 Camel C8242

T/o Remaisnil for an offensive patrol and was last seen in the early afternoon about a km or more to the east of Aveluy Wood and was eventually shot down, so it is reported, near Bray-sur-Somme. *Flight* June 13, 1918, names Second Lieutenant Hillyard [amongst many others] as 'missing' and in their issue of July 4, 1918, confirms his status as a prisoner of war.

74 Squadron | 2Lt L F Barton | + | Ebblinghem Military Cemetery
SE.5a C1854

T/o Clairmarais for an offensive patrol over the *département du Nord* in the course of which the patrol ran into concentrated anti-aircraft fire, one of the bursts 'flaming' 'C1854' which went down at map reference 36AQ26C. Lambert Francis Barton was nineteen years of age.

74 Squadron | Lt W C Stewart | Safe
SE.5a C1867

T/o Clairmarais authorised to make a practice flight during which a misjudged landing damaged 'C1867' beyond repair. At Brooklands Aeroplane Acceptance Park by 29 April 1918, it was flown over to France on the 8th of May and reached '74' on the 14th. In total it had achieved a mere four hours and ten minutes of flying.

74 Squadron | 2Lt L M Nixon | + | Merville Communal Cemetery extension
SE.5a C6404

T/o Clairmarais tasked for operations and when last seen by fellow members of the patrol 'C6404' was falling, on fire, over La Gorgue airfield. It will be recalled eighteen year old Leigh Morphew Nixon had crashed forty-eight hours previously [see my summary for details]. He was the son of Captain R M and Mrs A C Nixon of Clapham Common, London. His rank in the cemetery register is described as 'Flight Lieutenant', while inscribed on his headstone are the words; *'Borne On Wings Of High Enterprise To The Presence Of God Where He Rests.'*

74 Squadron | Lt S L Russell | Safe | Unemployed list 22 August 1919: Lt
SE.5a C6407

T/o Clairmarais similarly charged. On return, and with a failing engine, struck a ridge [another report says a road] and turned over.

84 Squadron | Lt S T Tipper | Safe | See 18 May 1918 - 84 Squadron
SE.5a C5444

T/o Bertangles for a practice flight from which Sidney Thomas Tipper made such a poorly judged landing that 'C5444' was deemed not to be worth the cost of repair.

| 84 Squadron | Lt M L Newhall USAS | Safe |
| SE.5a C5447 | | |

T/o Bertangles for an offensive mission but while climbing away had to sideslip in order to avoid flying into a Camel that crossed his path. Although a collision was avoided, Lieutenant Newhall had insufficient height in which to recover and in the ensuing crash 'C5447' was wrecked.

| 84 Squadron | Lt W J B Neil | Safe |
| SE.5a C6410 | | |

T/o Bertangles for an offensive patrol on return from which 'C6410' was damaged beyond repair following a poor landing.

| 98 Squadron | Lt R E Dubber [Canada] | Safe | See 18 July 1918 - 107 Squadron |
| DH.9 C6142 | Sgt E R McDonald | Safe | |

T/o 0435 Alquines ordered for a raid on Armentières and was shot about so badly that the airframe was deemed beyond worthwhile repair.

| 98 Squadron | Lt F H Reilly | Safe |
| DH.9 D1667 | Lt R McK Hall [Canada] | Safe |

T/o Alquines similarly ordered and badly shot about by anti-aircraft fire while flying east of the lines. Returned safely and the DH was salvaged for inspection and possible repair. However, the damage was such that the airframe was struck off charge on 21 May 1918. Lieutenant Hall of the Quebec Regiment was seconded for duty with the Royal Flying Corps on 17 October 1917, but it was not until 1918, that the administrators caught up with his movements, promulgating his secondment in supplement 30842 of 14 August 1918.

| 98 Squadron | Captain R W Bell [Canada] | + | Arras Flying Services Memorial |
| DH.9 D5630 | Lt A A Malcolm | + | Arras Flying Services Memorial |

T/o 0430 Alquines for a high-level reconnaissance of Hazebrouck in the Nord *département*. Shot down over the Somme when south of Thiepval. Ralph William Bell, born 17 May 1886, had died on his birthday. It will be recalled that he had been involved in serious crashes on 25 and 30 April 1918; prior to transferring to the Royal Flying Corps his service had been with the Western Ontario Regiment. Alan Alexander Malcolm began his service with the 17th Lancers, Duke of Cambridge's Own; he was the regular observer for Captain Bell.

| 100 Squadron | 2Lt R H Sawyer | Injured | Died on active service 3 August 1918: 2Lt |
| FE.2b A864 | 2Lt F H Chainey | Injured | |

T/o Ochey tasked for bombing at night and while returning to base force-landed, owing to engine failure, near Pompey [Meurthe-et-Moselle], both members of crew sustaining slight bruising. 'A864' was written off just nine days before its first anniversary in squadron service, in which time it had logged one hundred and sixty-one hours and six minutes. Robert Henry Sawyer's death occurred in the United Kingdom; he is buried in Ealing Cemetery.

| 100 Squadron | 2Lt J C Williamson | pow |
| FE.2b B492 | Lt N F Penroddocke | pow |

T/o Ochey tasked for a night raid on Thionville in the *département du Moselle* from which the crew failed to return. Both officers are named in *Flight* June 13, 1918, which repeats the Air Ministry list of casualties. It is noted that Lieutenant Penroddocke had been attached from the Army Service Corps. Both were repatriated in December 1918, Second Lieutenant Williamson on Christmas Day and his observer on the 30th. Remaining in the army, supplement 35611 of *The London Gazette* 30 June 1942, promulgates his appointment as attached to the Sudan Defence Force with the rank of local lieutenant-colonel.

| 102 Squadron | Lt A S Kelly | Safe | Unemployed list 14 March 1919: Lt |
| FE.2b B7782 | Lt W J Harvey | Safe | |

T/o Surcamps for a night bombing raid during which 'B7782' was hit by anti-aircraft fire and force-landed near Douchy-les-Ayette in the Pas-de-Calais some thirteen km south-southwest of Arras. The village, like so many in this part of France, has a Commonwealth War Graves Commission cemetery in which close on seven hundred servicemen are either buried or commemorated on a special memorial.

| 103 Squadron | Lt H R Herbert | Injured | |
| DH.9 D5594 | 2Lt H T G Robey | Injured Unemployed list 7 March 1919: 2Lt | |

T/o Serny authorised for a practice flight. On return Lieutenant Herbert failed to notice that he was heading towards telegraph wires which he duly struck, and from a height of twenty feet the DH dived to the ground and was damaged beyond repair. 'D5594' had arrived at Serny on the 9th of May 1918, three days ahead of the rest of the squadron which flew in from Old Sarum on the 12th having worked up in the United Kingdom since forming at Beaulieu on the 1st of September 1917. Thus, Lieutenant Herbert earned the unwanted accolade of writing off the squadron's first DH.9 on the Western Front. Second Lieutenant Robey was formerly of the King's Own Scottish Borderers, his commission to the regiment being resigned on his appointment to the Royal Air Force on 11 May 1918, promulgated in supplement 31146 of 28 January 1919.

| 203 Squadron | 2Lt E R Prideaux | + | Arras Flying Services Memorial |
| F.1 Camel B6408 | [South Africa] | | |

T/o 1030 Filescamp for an offensive patrol and about forty-five minutes into the patrol the Camels were set upon my a mixture of Pfalz scouts and Triplanes, the latter type being estimated at fifteen in number. One of the Pfalz scouts was 'flamed' but on the debit side a Camel was seen falling out of control near Merville in the *département du Nord,* and this might well have been Edwin Ravenhill Prideaux's aircraft. In due course a telegram advising he was 'missing in action' would be sent to his parents at Mowbray in the Cape Province.

Saturday 18 May 1918

| 4 Squadron AusFC | Captain G F Malley MC | Injured |
| F.1 Camel C8261 | [Australia] | |

T/o Clairmarais for an offensive patrol during which 'C8261' came under anti-aircraft fire, wounding Garnet Francis Malley. On return the Camel was sent for repair, but close examination deemed it was not worth the cost and it was struck off charge on 14 June 1918. Born on 2 November 1892, Garnet Malley first saw active service as an infantryman with the Australian Imperial Force before volunteering in 1917, for flying duties. Posted to the Western Front, where he joined No 4 Squadron Australian Flying Corps, he quickly made his mark as a scout pilot and was rewarded with the Military Cross on 22 June 1918, supplement 30761; *'For conspicuous gallantry and devotion to duty. When on offensive and low-flying patrol he attacked one of two hostile scouts, which eventually turned over and fell out of control, being seen to crash by another pilot. Later, a general engagement ensued with four enemy scouts, one of which he attacked, with the result that it fell completely out of control and crashed. Prior to this occasion he had also shot down out of control another hostile machine. His courage and able leadership have resulted in his patrol carrying out excellent work under the most adverse conditions.'* Post-war he was awarded the Air Force Cross, this being *gazetted* 3 June 1919, supplement 31378. Returning to his native Australia, Captain Malley soon tired of civilian life and in 1925, joined the Royal Australian Air Force. His biography on *Wikipedia* records his involvement in 1931, as aviation advisor to China where he worked closely with Madame Chiang Kai-Shek; subsequently, he was able to observe at first hand tactics employed by the Japanese Air Force during the Sino-Japanese War, though his reports on the conflict appear to have been largely ignored by the Australian military. Continuing to serve throughout the Second World War, his duties centred on intelligence work. In retirement he bought a plantation on the Island of Fiji from where his death at the age of sixty-eight was reported from Vanua Balavu on 20 May 1961.

| 4 Squadron AusFC | Major W A McClaughry MC | Safe |
| F.1 Camel D1874 | [Australia] | |

T/o Clairmarais for a special mission which ended, in the dark, with the Camel wrecked in a sunken road near Lillers in the Pas-de-Calais fifteen km northwest of Béthune. Major Wilfred Ashton McClaughry, born in Adelaide on the 26th of November 1894, began his military service with the 9th Light Horse Regiment before transferring in 1916, to the Royal Flying Corps. Postwar, he was granted a permanent commission in the Royal Air Force and apart from the period between September 1924 and February 1928, when he commanded No 8 Squadron [DH.9A] at Hinaidi in Iraq, he was mainly concerned with Staff Duties, a notable appointment being Director of Training at the Air Ministry where on 29 November 1938, he took over from Air Commodore Robert Leckie DSO

DSC DFC. In mid-September 1940, at the height of the *Battle of Britain,* he became Air Officer Commanding No 9 Group which had recently re-formed at Barton Hall, Preston, with responsibilities for the air defence of north-west England, this being followed in the summer of 1942, when he was ordered to the Middle East as Air Officer Commanding Air Headquarters Egypt and it was here that he died in an air crash at Cairo on the 4th of January 1943. His headstone in Helioplis War Cemetery is inscribed; *'A Man Of Valour, Forceful, Skilled, Yet Human, Modest, Kind.'* His impressive list of honours read: CB DSO MC DFC.

| 10 Squadron | Lt C T Aulph | Safe | Unemployed list 14 August 1919: Lt |
| FK.8 C8546 | Lt F W Rushton | Injured | Unemployed list 20 May 1919: Lt MC |

T/o Droglandt with orders to carry out artillery observations but engine failure overtook the crew who force-landed at map reference 27K16a35. 'C8546' arrived with the squadron on 29 April 1918, and including test flying and ferrying from the United Kingdom had logged twenty-six hours and five minutes.

| 10 Squadron | Lt A A Webster | Safe |
| FK.8 D5009 | 2Lt G A Cameron | Safe |

T/o Droglandt similarly charged; force-landed at map reference F26d62 owing to engine failure. On charge since 10 April 1918, 'D5009' logged in total fifty-three hours and fifty minutes flying.

| 15 Squadron | Lt F C U Dymant | Safe | Unemployed list 13 June 1919 |
| RE.8 B2276 | Lt J T Wyre | Injured | Unemployed list 8 August 1919: F/O |

T/o Vert Galand tasked for artillery observation and written off near the aerodrome owing to the engine seizing, Lieutenant Wyre being recorded as 'wounded'. Salvaged, 'B2276' was deemed not worth the cost of repair. As a temporary second lieutenant, Lieutenant Wyre had been attached to the Royal Flying Corps for observer duties from the Dorset Regiment as recently as 8 March.

| 15 Squadron | 2Lt S Fine | + | Contay British Cemetery, Contay* |
| RE.8 C5047 | 2Lt R A Fraser | + | Contay British Cemetery, Contay |

T/o Vert Galand similarly ordered and it was while returning to Vert Galand that the crew encountered very heavy rain which reduced visibility considerably. Flying at seven hundred feet over the Somme [possibly trying to establish their position], control was lost and the RE spun into Vadencourt Wood. Soloman Fine was nineteen years of age; his headstone carries the inscription; *'Precious In The Sight Of The Lord Is The Death Of His Loving Ones.'* His observer was of the same age; his parents requested, and had approved; *'Until The Day Breaks'.*

* Sited close to the village of Contay [Somme], this Commonwealth War Graves Commission cemetery is, surely, one of the most beautiful of all their major burial grounds. Origins of the site date back to August 1916, when the 49th Casualty Clearing Station was established at Contay; today, well in excess of one thousand one hundred servicemen now rest in the most pleasant of countryside surroundings. The photograph posted on their website shows a gentle sloping field with the overlooking bank shielding the rows of headstones with a well established hedge and trees now growing to maturity over which in the *Great War* was a much war defiled landscape.

| 20 Squadron | Lt T W Williamson | Safe |
| Bristol F.2b B1279 | Corporal W H Foster | Injured |

T/o Boisdinghem for an offensive patrol during which the crew came under fire from the ground, this wounding Corporal Foster. Lieutenant Williamson force-landed his damaged aircraft near Vlamertinghe [West-Vlaanderen] which at the time was one of the many villages near Ypres and today is incorporated within the city some five km to the west where a Commonwealth military cemetery has been established. Accepted by the squadron on the 11th of March 1918, 'B1279' had been in constant use and when written off had accumulated one hundred and three hours and twenty-three minutes flying.

| 32 Squadron | Captain E W C G de V Pery | + | Vis-en-Artois British Cemetery, Haucourt |
| SE.5a C9615 | | | |

T/o Beauvois for operations and was reported by members of his patrol to be going down, spinning from ten thousand feet, over Étaing in the Pas-de-Calais. Educated at Eton, Captain Edmond William Claude Gerard de Vere Pery, Viscount Glentworth, was the son of William Henry de Vere Sheaffe Pery, 4th Earl of Limerick, of Dromore Castle, Pallaskenry, Co Limerick. Prior to joining the Royal Flying Corps, Captain Pery served with the Warwickshire Yeomanry. His photograph is among the extensive Imperial War Museum collections of military memorabilia and is identified by catalogue number HU 122602. His death was the first from the squadron since the 1st of April 1918.

| 32 Squadron | Lt G E B Lawson | Safe | Unemployed list 5 June 1919: Lt |
| SE.5a D331 | | | |

T/o Beauvois similarly charged and specifically to patrol over the *département du Nord* between Marquoin and Douai. Engaging with enemy scouts, Lieutenant Lawson dived on a potential opponent but his would be victim got the better of him, climbing and then firing a short burst into the SE's engine which obliged Lieutenant Lawson to force-land some eight km to the west of Arras.

| 41 Squadron | Lt A S Hemming | Safe | See 13 June 1918 - 41 Squadron |
| SE.5a D3939 | | | |

T/o Serny for a practice flight and on landing ran against a ridge which damaged 'D3939' beyond repair. The next day No 41 Squadron moved to Estrée-Blanche. Since the 1st of April, the squadron had lost five of their aircraft on operations and, now, an equal amount in training; thankfully the pilots involved escaping with little more than a shaking.

| 55 Squadron | Lt C E Reynolds | Injured | See 23 October 1918 - 55 Squadron |
| DH.4 A7593 O | 2Lt J E Reynolds | + | Charmes Military Cemetery, Essegney |

T/o Tantonville for a raid on the cathedral city of Köln and on return crashed close to the airfield. John Eric Reynolds entry in the cemetery register has no indication of his age or next of kin.

| 60 Squadron | 2Lt G M Duncan | Safe | |
| SE.5a C5450 | | | |

T/o Boffles for a practice flight; damaged beyond repair after crashing onto a road. On charge on 6 May 1918, 'C5450' was struck off charge the next day with four hours and fifty-five minutes flying in total.

| 64 Squadron | Lt J J Carroll | Safe | See 31 May 1918 - 64 Squadron |
| SE.5a B8516 | | | |

T/o Izel-lèz-Hameau for an offensive patrol but force-landed, and turned over, near Wagonlieu in the Pas-de-Calais after being overtaken with a failing engine. This was Lieutenant Carroll's second serious accident in the month, the first being on the 2nd.

| 64 Squadron | Lt W P Southall | Safe | See 28 May 1918 - 64 Squadron |
| SE.5a C6470 | | | |

T/o Izel-lèz-Hameau similarly tasked, returning from the mission so badly shot about that it was struck off charge four days later.

| 64 Squadron | Lt W C Daniel | Safe | Unemployed list 28 September 1919: Lt |
| D336 '5' | | | |

T/o Izel-lès-Hameau similarly ordered and sighting the enemy ho dived to attack but as his descent steepened so the leading edges of the top planes collapsed. Shaken quite badly he managed to recover to base where 'D335' was written off as not worth repairing on 23 May 1918.

| 65 Squadron | Lt K P Hunt | pow | |
| F.1 Camel B7178 | | | |

T/o 0900 Bertangles for an offensive patrol and was last seen between Albert and Bray-sur-Somme heavily engaged in a fight with a dozen Albatros scouts.

65 Squadron   Lt W F Scott-Kerr   pow
F.1 Camel C8256
T/o 0900 Bertangles and lost in the manner described above. It can be safely stated that both pilots were able to force-land for the option of baling out from Allied aircraft in the *Great War* was non-existent. The names of both officers appeared under the 'Missing' heading with the reproduction in *Flight* June 13, 1918, of the official Air Ministry list of casualties. Lieutenant Scott-Kerr was late of the Lothian and Border Horse. He was among a large group of officers repatriated on Boxing Day 1918.

81 Squadron   Lt G S Tunstall [Canada]   +   Lincoln [Newport] Cemetery
5F.1 Dolphin C8023
T/o Scampton for a training sortie and crashed out of control following a tight turn during which the Dolphin stalled. George Stanley Tunstall was late of the 16th Battalion, Canadian Infantry, Manitoba Regiment.

84 Squadron   Lt B Stefansson [Canada]   Safe
SE.5a B7833
T/o Bertangles for an offensive patrol which ended with Lieutenant Stefansson undershooting his attempt to land at Vert Galand. Formerly of the Manitoba Regiment, Canadian Expeditionary Force, Lieutenant Stefansson was seconded to the Royal Flying Corps on 28 September 1917 [*gazetted* 22 March 1918, supplement 30589].

84 Squadron   Lt S T Tipper   Safe   Unemployed list 15 October 1919: Lt
SE.5a C1882
T/o from No 2 Air Issues and on reaching Bertangles landed badly; with a mere one hour and fifteen minutes flying [including factory testing and delivery to France] 'C1882' would never take to the skies again. This was his second 'write off' in twenty-four hours. In the Second World War, Sidney Tipper returned to the service and when obliged to relinquish his commission on the 1st of October 1954, under the provisions of the Navy, Army and Air Force Reserves Act 1954, he was permitted to retain the rank of wing commander.

88 Squadron   Lt L G S Gadpaille [BWI]   +   Arras Flying Services Memorial
Bristol F.2b C783   2Lt S Griffin   +   Arras Flying Services Memorial
T/o Capelle for operations over the Ypres Salient and it was here that the Bristol was last seen heading earth-wards in a spinning nosedive. Louis Granville Surridge Gadpaille hailed from Jamaica; his observer came from Ennis in Co Clare. This was the squadron's first operational loss since arriving on the Western Front.

98 Squadron   Lt A M Phillips   Safe
DH.9 B7634   Lt N C McDonald   Safe
While manned and parked on the airfield at Alquines was struck, and damaged beyond repair, by the DH summarised below.

98 Squadron   Lt G D Horton [Canada]   Safe   See 19 May 1918 - 98 Squadron
DH.9 C6073   Lt C P Harrison   Safe   See 27 May 1918 - 98 Squadron
T/o Alquines for an operational sortie but the engine 'cut' and in the emergency landing that followed, 'C6073' ran into the DH shown above. Information concerning Gifford D Horton appears in my summary for the 31st of May, while Lieutenant Harrison had been involved in a serious crash on the 18th [see my summary for details].

119 Squadron   Lt R G Spratt   Injured
DH.6 C7248   Private C A Baker   +
T/o Duxford authorised for a training flight; lost control, stalled and crashed.

149 Squadron   2Lt C H P Hughes   Injured
FE.2b C9792   Captain G Robinson MC   Injured Wye [SS Gregory and Martin] Churchyard
T/o Ford for continuation training and crashed, heavily, after sideslipping. Delivered to Norwich with the intention of issue to No 148 Squadron, 'C9792' was taken over by No 149 Squadron on 29 April 1918. Canadian born George Robinson, late of the Canadian Corps Cavalry Regiment died the next day from his injuries. I suspect

he was the first officer to lose his life in an air accident since the formation of the squadron at Ford on the 3rd of March 1918.

| 205 Squadron | 2Lt H C R Conron | + | Arras Flying Services Memorial |
| DH.4 D8401 | 2Lt J Finningan | + | Arras Flying Services Memorial |

T/o Bois de Roche for a raid on the railway station at Chaulnes [Somme] and last seen in the vicinity of Aubercourt.

| 210 Squadron | Lt J Hollick | + | Arras Flying Services Memorial |
| F.1 Camel D3390 | | | |

T/o 0930 St Omer in company with the Camel summarised below, both pilots having being briefed to carry out a special mission, which according to a report in AIR 1/969 was to *'interrupt wireless'*.

| 210 Squadron | 2Lt M F Sutton | pow |
| F.1 Camel D3391 | | |

T/o 0930 St Omer similarly instructed. Evidence presented in Air-Britain's *Camel File* points to both Camels being shot down by *Unteroffizier* Pech of *Jasta* 29 who claimed a Camel at 1145 near Lestrem in the Pas-de-Calais and five minutes later a second over Merville Wood. Second Lieutenant Sutton's name appears in *Flight* June 13, 1918, under the heading 'Missing'. Both aircraft had arrived with the squadron during May, 'D3390' on the 14th followed two days later by 'D3391'. Their flying hours are shown as fifteen hours and fifty minutes and eight hours and five minutes respectively.

Saturday-Sunday 18-19 May 1918

214 Squadron	Captain V E G Sieveking DSC*	+	Zeebrugge Churchyard
Handley Page O/400	Lt H A H Roe	+	Zeebrugge Churchyard
C3487	Mechanic F Spencer	pow	

T/o Coudekerque having received instructions for a bombing raid on the port of Zeebrugge. Valentine Edgar Sieveking [his third Christian name 'Giberne' is omitted from *The London Gazette* entries] was appointed temporary Sub-Lieutenant in the Royal Naval Volunteer Reserve on 7 December 1915 [*gazetted* 10 December 1915, issue 29398]. On 28 June 1917, supplement 30147, he was *gazetted* with The Distinguished Service Cross; *'In recognition of his services on the night 3rd to 4th May 1917, when he dropped bombs on Ostend seaplane station with good results, making two trips.'* The First Bar followed on 17 April 1918, supplement 30635; *'For skill and determination in attacking enemy aerodromes, docks, etc., with bombs. On the night of the 17th-18th February 1918, he carried out two bombing attacks on Bruges Docks, and on the following night he again carried out two attacks, one on St Denis Westrem Aerodrome and one on Bruges Docks. His zeal and determination cannot be too highly praised.'* Mechanic Spencer was taken into captivity in a wounded state. 'C3487' was flown from Farnborough to Coudekerque for No 214 Squadron 20 April 1918, and in total flew for twenty-one hours and thirty minutes.

Sunday 19 May 1918

During the day Major J C Quinnel led No 104 Squadron from Andover for duties on the Western Front and following a sojourn of just twenty-four hours at St Omer flew on to Azelot [Meurthe et Moselle] where it would remain to after the armistice. Also of interest on this day Lieutenant A A Leitch of No 65 Squadron at Bertangles was authorised to test fly the prototype Sopwith TF.2 Salamander E5429 and on return to the airfield he crash-landed after side-slipping at very low altitude to avoid a parked Dolphin and an ambulance. According to the movement card for 'E5429' it was tested in the United Kingdom on 11 May 1918, and after ferrying to France was allotted to No 65 Squadron on the 17th. In the wake of the accident a total of seven hours and forty-five minutes was appended to the movement card but although it was deemed not worth repairing, this has been questioned. Nevertheless, this 'incident' on the 19th of May 1918, certainly predates the information posted on *Wikipedia* that … *two were in France in October 1918.'* According to *British Military Aircraft Serials 1878-1987* compiled by Bruce Robertson and published by Midland Counties Publications, 1987, 'E5429' was the first aircraft in a small batch of six prototypes built by Sopwith with the type being intended for use in the ground attack rôle. A search on the web for details concerning 'E5429' provides two photographs, both taken at Brooklands, one on the 1st of May 1918, and the second on the 9th with Captain H B Robin Rowell in the cockpit preparing to fly the Salamander to France. It is believed 'E5429' took to the air for the first time on 27 April 1918.

1 Squadron	Lt C S T Lavers	Safe

SE.5a C1103

T/o Clarimarais for an offensive patrol. On return bounced heavily on landing and its second arrival on *terra firma* damaged 'C1103' beyond repair. Andrew Pentland has noted that its transit from Farnborough to Marquise on the 18th of April 1918, was the sole cross-Channel air movement of the day owing to inclement weather. On the 20th it was flown to Clairmarais and allotted to No 1 Squadron, and when written off had, in total, flown for sixty-five hours and twenty-five minutes, indicating high usage. An entry in *The London Gazette* of 22 February 1918 [supplement 30537] reports Lieutenant Lavers to be formerly of the West Yorkshire Regiment, Special Reserve. Postwar, he was one of the many officers appointed to a permanent commission on 1 August 1919. However, it seems he returned to the army as *Gazette* of 5 April 1921, supplement 32281, under War Office 'Special Appointment' heading shows Lieutenant C S T Lavers DFC granted the rank of captain while attached to the 4th Battalion West Yorkshire Regiment.

2 Squadron AusFC	Lt E D Cameron	Safe

SE.5a C5443

T/o Fouquerolles and with others tasked for the patrol headed in the direction of Armentières but was obliged to make a forced landing owing to a broken connecting rod. 'C5443', which had been with the squadron since 4th May 1918, was struck off charge on 21 May 1918; in total it amassed a mere ten hours of flight. It was the tenth operational loss for the squadron since the 1st of April, thankfully without any fatalities.

3 Squadron	2Lt F J Brotheridge	+	Arras Flying Services Memorial

F.1 Camel D6433

T/o 0630 Valheureux having been briefed to intercept wireless transmissions during which nineteen year old Frederick John Brotheridge shared with Captain J W Aldred MC [F.1 Camel C1655] in the destruction of a two-seater. Lieutenant Brotheridge was last seen over Mesnil-Martinsart, a commune in the Somme thirty-five km northeast from Amiens.

4 Squadron	Lt F W McChesney	Injured
RE.8 B5062	2Lt P Hughes	Injured

T/o St Omer having received orders for an artillery observation patrol but within seconds of becoming airborne flew into a tree. Despatched to the Western Front by air in September 1917, 'B5062' went to No 5 Squadron on 14 October and remained on establishment until 25 March, when on return from a night reconnaissance Second Lieutenants A E Ellis and A Bechervaise came down in a ploughed field adjacent to La Gorgue. Salvaged, the airframe was though to be damaged beyond repair [at the time it had logged one hundred and ninety flying hours]. However, further examination resulted in repairs being authorised and on the 1st of May, it was issued to No 4 Squadron. Its second 'mishap' proved terminal and now with two hundred and sixty two hours to its credit, it was struck off charge on 23 May 1918.

19 Squadron	Major A D Carter [Canada]	pow

5F.1 Dolphin C4017

T/o Savy for an offensive patrol and when last seen was east of La Bassée in the Nord *département,* site of fierce fighting between the 10th of October and 2nd November 1914, when both sides concentrated their forces in readiness for the *First Battle of Ypres.* Major Albert Desbrisay Carter made a forced landing in enemy held territory; his name appears in *Flight* July 18, 1918, reproducing the Roll of Honour list for notified casualties, under the heading 'Previously missing, now reported Prisoners in German hands'; he was repatriated on the 13th of December 1918. Formerly of the New Brunswick Regiment, Canadian Infantry, Major Carter lost his life on the 22nd of May 1919, while testing a captured German Fokker DVII which broke up in the air over the air-field at Shoreham. At the time he was attached to No 1 Training Group, though it seems the Fokker was being held by No 123 Squadron of the recently formed Canadian Air Force. Albert Desbrisay Carter is buried in Old Shoreham Cemetery where his headstone is inscribed with the words; *'He Did That Which Was His Duty To Do'.* It is noted he held the Distinguished Service Cross and Bar, and *Croix de Guerre* [Belgium].

23 Squadron   Lt J T McKay   Safe   See 22 May 1918 - 23 Squadron
5F.1 Dolphin C3865

T/o Bertangles tasked for *Aerial Sentry**duty; struck a ridge landing; damaged beyond repair. This was the squadron's first operational loss since exchanging their Spads for Dolphins, but in respect of the latter six had been written off in practice flying, resulting in one fatality.

* I am of the opinion these duties were flown close to the frontline in order to mask the sound of heavy material in the form of tanks and artillery being positioned by the Allies in preparations of the buildup of the British and French ground forces preparing for offensive action later in the summer. It may well be that I am wrong in my assumption and, therefore, I welcome correction.

27 Squadron   Lt C E Hutcheson   Safe   See 30 October 1918 - 27 Squadron
DH.4 B2068   Airman W Hilton   Safe

T/o Ruisseauville for an air test; crashed on landing. 'B2068' had been with the squadron for eight days. Both airmen had survived recent crashes; Lieutenant Hutcheson on the 9th and Airman Hilton on the 15th.

27 Squadron   2Lt F J Bull   pow   Unemployed list 1 September 1919: F/O
DH.4 B2129   2Lt C B Law   pow

T/o Ruisseauville having received orders to raid targets at Valenciennes [Nord] during which the crew experienced engine failure, leading to a forced landing behind enemy lines east of Arras. The names of both officers appear under the heading of 'Missing' in *Flight* June 13,1918, Second Lieutenant Law being attached from the Hussars. Confirmation that they were prisoners of war was reported in *Flight* August 8, 1918, both being repatriated on 30 December 1918.

29 Squadron   Captain H G White   Safe
SE.5a D3942

T/o St Omer tasked for operations in the vicinity of Estaires during which Captain White, who twenty-four hours earlier had shot down an enemy scout near Merville, came within an 'inch' of losing his own life when a Pfalz struck the top planes of 'D3942' before peeling away to break up in the air. With his aircraft barely under control he force-landed near Bailleul [Nord].

29 Squadron   Lt H M Hutton   Safe   See 23 May 1918 - 29 Squadron
SE.5a D5965

T/o St Omer similarly tasked. Returned safely, but so badly shot about that 'D5965' was struck off charge on 24th May 1918, as not worth repairing.

35 Squadron   2Lt C S Booker   Safe   See 3 July 1918 - 35 Squadron
FK.8 C8591   2Lt A Gilchrist   Safe   See 20 May 1918 - 35 Squadron

T/o Villers-Bocage for operations during which the crew force-landed at Bresle, a hamlet in the Somme roughly twenty-eight km northwest of Amiens. Salvaged, the FK.8 was struck off charge as not worth the expense of repair on 3 June 1918. Archibald Gilchrist was late of the 1st/4th Battalion Rifle Brigade.

49 Squadron   Captain W Milton   Injured
DH.9 C6160   Lt T F Harvey   Safe   See 7 June 1918 - 49 Squadron

T/o 0505 Conteville with orders to bomb targets at Bray-sur-Somme but having climbed to two hundred feet the engine 'cut' and Captain Milton turned to land at Bois de Roche [No 205 Squadron], but crashed in the attempt.

49 Squadron   Lt F D Nevin   +   Heath Cemetery, Herbonnières
DH.9 D1002   Sgt H Barfoot   +   Heath Cemetery, Harbonnières

T/o 0505 Conteville similarly ordered and was last sighted over the Somme near Harbonnières. Frederick Desmond Nevin was nineteen years of age; his memory is perpetuated with the words; *'His Few But Glorious Years Will Live Immortally.'* In contrast, Herbert Barfoot was thirty-four, his headstone bearing the words; *'Until The Day Break And The Shadows Flee Away.'* He had been with the squadron since 28 December 1917, while Lieutenant Nevin arrived on 25 February 1918.

60 Squadron	Lt A W Saunders	Safe	
SE.5a C9536			

T/o Boffles for an evening offensive patrol and on return, with dusk encroaching, he failed to see the ridge that lay in his path and upon running onto it he damaged 'C9536' beyond repair. From the Aeroplane Acceptance Park at Brooklands, it was flown across the Channel on or by the 3rd of January 1918, and from No 1 Air Issues reached the squadron, then at Ste Marie Cappel, on the 7th; in total it accumulated one hundred and forty hours and twenty minutes flying.

62 Squadron	Lt D A Savage	Safe	Unemployed list 15 June 1919: Lt MC
Bristol F.2b B1336	Lt E W Collis	Safe	Unemployed list 12 April 1919: Lt

T/o Planques as part of a patrol making for the Corbie area of the Somme where hostile aircraft were encountered. Lieutenant Savage immediately engaged two of the machines, diving towards them but was then himself attacked. Shot about, he force-landed near Corbie and close enough to the lines for the undercarriage of his Bristol to be ripped off by barbed wire entanglements. Lieutenant Collis was appointed as an observer officer with effect from 11 April 1918; he was formerly of the Manchester Regiment, Territorial Forces, and is believed to have returned to army duties following the transfer notified above. Accepted by the squadron on 24th March 1918, 'B1336' flew for a total of fifty hours and forty-five minutes.

62 Squadron	2Lt H C Hunter	pow	Unemployed list 10 July 1919:" Lt
Bristol F.2b C796	Sgt J Lake	pow	

T/o Planques similarly ordered and was last seen by the patrol flying in the top formation in the target area.

62 Squadron	2Lt H A Clarke	pow	
Bristol F.2b C4630	Captain H Claye	pow	Unemployed list 10 April 1919: Captain

T/o Planques similarly ordered and appears to have suffered the same fate that eventually befell that for the Bristol summarised above.

62 Squadron	2Lt F Atkinson	pow	Niederzwehren Cemetery, Kassel
Bristol F.2b C4751	Sgt C Brammar	pow	

T/o Planques similarly ordered and probably went down in the same area as the two Bristols featured above. Nineteen year old Frank Atkinson died the 10th of July 1918.

Note. The Air Ministry release of names of casualties, as reproduced in *Flight* June 20, 1918, reports the names of Captain Claye [Sherwood Foresters attached Royal Air Force], Second Lieutenants Clarke and Hunter, all under the heading 'Missing'. For reasons best known only to the authorities at the time, information pertaining to non-commissioned officers are omitted from these lists; however, Andrew Pentland, in his examination of the plethora of documents associated with the Royal Air Force in the *Great War* indicates Sergeant Brammar was wounded, while there seems to be some dispute as to the surname of Sergeant 'Lake' where some papers show 'Lake' and others 'Luke'. Furthermore, one set of records indicates Second Lieutenant C G Capel as being the pilot of 'C4751' and *Flight* in its issue of June 13, 1918, records the name of this officer under the heading 'Wounded' but with no indication that he was made a prisoner of war; there are no further reports of this officer under Air Ministry releases for 1918. Meanwhile, *The London Gazette* issue 31539 of 5th September 1919, reports Flying Officer Capel as reverting to the unemployed list with effect from 9 August 1919.

80 Squadron	2Lt A J Patenaude	pow	Unemployed list 30 April 1919
F.1 Camel B2429			

T/o 1850 La Bellevue for formation practice and was last sighted in the vicinity of Doullens [Somme]. Fitted with a Clerget 9B and reported at No 4 Aeroplane Acceptance Park Lincoln on 8 October 1917, 'B2429' saw extensive operational service ahead of its arrival with No 80 Squadron by which time it had been fitted with a La Rhône 9J. Second Lieutenant Patenaude's name appears on the Roll of Honour list published on the 1st of August 1918, and reported in *Flight* August 8th, 1918, confirmed as a prisoner of war.

82 Squadron	Lt H F Flowers [Canada]	Safe	See 14 October 1918 - 82 Squadron
FK.8 C8559	2Lt S G Dyson	Safe	See 1 June 1918 - 82 Squadron

T/o Agenvilliers for bombing operations over the Somme on targets in the *Forêt de Crécy.* During the operation the crew landed at Bertangles [roughly forty km southeast of Agenvilliers] to top up with water, but ran into a bank which wrecked their aircraft. 'C8559' was at the Aeroplane Acceptance Park at Newcastle by 2 April 1918, from where it flew across the Channel that same day and taken in hand on the 7th by No 82 Squadron. Well used, it flew for a total of fifty-three hours. Humphrey French Flowers was commissioned to the Royal Field Artillery, 5 August 1915, following service as a private soldier with the Inns of Court Officers Training Corps [*gazetted* 19 August 1915, supplement 29268]. His attachment to the Royal Flying Corps, effective from 11th March 1918, was promulgated in supplement 30641 of 20 April 1918.

| 84 Squadron | Lt E M Hammer USAS | + | Meuse-Argonne American Cemetery |
| SE.5a C6449 | | | |

T/o Bertangles for an offensive patrol and was last seen diving towards an enemy aircraft east of Wiencourt-l'Équipée [Somme], twenty-two km east of Amiens. Formerly of the Air Service Signal Corps, Earl M Hammer was a Californian.

| 98 Squadron | Lt G D Horton [Canada] | Safe | See 31 May 1918 - 98 Squadron |
| DH.9 C1174 | Lt H J McConnel [USA] | Safe | See 31 May 1918 - 98 Squadron |

T/o Alquines tasked for bombing operations but having risen to a height of a mere ten feet the engine 'cut' and the DH stalled back to the ground - wrecked. Details for both officers are reported in my summary for the 31st of May. For Lieutenant Horton this was his second crash in twenty-four hours.

| 104 Squadron | Sgt W Gunn | + | Penton Mewsey [Holy Trinity] Churchyard |
| DH.9 D5633 | Mechanic T T House | + | Penton Mewsey [Holy Trinity] Churchyard |

T/o Andover during which a nail worked loose and jammed the rudder bars and while trying to overcome the problem airspeed was lost and the DH stalled into the ground, possibly at Penton Mewsey a mile or so to the north of Andover. Thomas Trewitt House's unit is shown as No 215 Squadron; I have retained this in the Roll of Honour while indicating attachment to No 104 Squadron. This tragedy may have occurred as the crew set forth for St Omer.

| 109 Squadron | 2Lt J C A Barker [Canada] | + | Durrington Cemetery |
| DH.4 B5541 | Airman J Stillman | injured | |

T/o Stonehenge and when on approach to land stalled and dived to the ground.

| 206 Squadron | 2Lt F G Reddie | + | Arras Flying Service Memorial |
| DH.9 B7594 | 2Lt A C Howell-Jones | + | Arras Flying Services Memorial |

T/o Alquines in the company of others who later reported seeing Francis Graham Reddie and Athol Cuthbert Howell-Jones in the early evening over Belgium trying to fight off enemy scouts. From the St John's Wood district of London and Clifton near Bristol respectively, neither officer could have been long with the squadron for both were merely eighteen years of age.

| 206 Squadron | Lt R H Stainbank | Safe | |
| DH.9 C6152 *Shanghai Britons* | 2Lt F C Taylor | Safe | See 22 May 1918 - 206 Squadron |

T/o Alquines tasked for bombing and written on return as a consequence of making a bad landing. Received from No 1 Air Issues on the 1st of April 1918, 'C6152' achieved forty-six hours and twenty-two minutes of flying, including testing and transit to France. Lieutenant Stainbank's appointment to the Royal Flying Corps was promulgated on 10 April 1918, supplement 30621, and was effective from 9 March of that year.

| 206 Squadron | 2Lt B F Dunford | + | Arras Flying Services Memorial |
| DH.9 C6159 | 2Lt F F Collins | + | Arras Flying Services Memorial |

T/o Alquines for an early morning bombing operation and was last seen over Belgium being engaged by hostile aircraft northwest of Roeselare [West Vlaanderen]. Accepted as recently as 16 May, including testing and transit 'C6159' flew for a mere eight hours and thirty-two minutes. Bertram Fred Dunford was nineteen, his observer twenty-five.

206 Squadron	2Lt H Mitchell	pow	
DH.9 C6161	Airman C F Costen	pow	

T/o 1815 Alquines for operations and when last sighted was west of the lines near Menin and leaving the formation following combat. Presumed to have been driven down in territory held by the enemy. Arriving at Alquines on the 17th of May, 'C6161' flew for a total of just three hours and thirty-nine minutes, which included testing and transit to the Western Front. This had been a bad day for the squadron, the four losses taking the total to twenty-one destroyed on operations with nine airmen killed and two in captivity, while two of their DH.9s had been lost in training accidents, all since the 1st of April.

211 Squadron	Lt N A Taylerson	+	Zeebrugge Churchyard
DH.9 D2784	Lt C L Bray	+	Zeebrugge Churchyard

T/o 1100 Petite Synthe for an operational sortie and was last seen by fellow squadron colleagues in the vicinity of Nieuwpoort-Ooostende. Believed to have crashed at Uytkerke an area in West-Vlaanderen just below the port of Blankenberge. Accepted by the squadron on 7 April 1918, 'D2784' raided the Zeebrugge Mole on the 9th of May during which enemy scouts were encountered, one of which, a Fokker DrI was sent down by Lieutenant W Gilman and his observer Second Lieutenant R Lardner.

Monday 20 May 1918

The website Lewisham War Memorials, which I have pleasure in acknowledging, report that on Whit Monday at around 1140 a German Gotha bomber dropped a fifty kg bomb into Sangley Road which damaged forty-four properties and killing a man and injuring a women. Then, shortly after midday more bombs fell in the Leahurst road area causing significant damage to shops and houses and causing the deaths of two soldiers and injuries to two others, plus civilians including a child. At around the same time a bomb a bomb exploded in the Sydenham Road and Fairlawn Park area killing thirteen civilians and five soldiers. Local historian, John Hook, to whom I pay generous tribute, identifies one John Jacob Klingels, a naturalised German, who was in the street when the bomb fell.

2 Squadron	Lt T H Crossman	Safe	See 23 May 1918 - 2 Squadron
FK.8 D5020	Lt L C Spence MC [Canada]	Injured	See 23 May 1918 - 2 Squadron

T/o Hesdigneul tasked for artillery observation but before becoming airborne crashed against a bank and was damaged beyond repair. 'D5020' had survived just over a month of operations after arriving with the squadron on the 15th of April 1918. In total, it flew for seventy-seven hours and fifteen minutes including makers test and ferrying by air to France. Lyell Campbell Spence, formerly of the Canadian Field Artillery won his Military Cross with the artillery, *gazetted* 7 March 1918, supplement 30561; *'For conspicuous gallantry and devotion to duty as forward observation officer during an attack. He established his station in the assembly trench and sent back most valuable information both to the artillery and infantry. When the shelling became so intense that the wire could not be maintained he repeatedly passed through heavy enemy barrages with valuable information. He showed the greatest initiative, courage and determination throughout the operations.'*

3 Squadron AusFC	Captain E J Jones	Injured	
RE.8 B8876	2Lt A L D Taylor AusFC	+	Vignacourt British Cemetery

T/o Villers-Bocage with instructions to carry out artillery observation during which the RE came under sustained assault from half-a-dozen triplanes. The engagement left Captain Jones wounded and his observer dead; his headstone is inscribed; *'Aer Ardua Ad Astra'* where the first word should have been *'Per'* [Through adversity to the stars]. Although Captain Jones managed to recover to Villers-Bocage, 'B8876' was so badly shot about that it was struck off charge on the 2nd of June 1918. Between mid-November 1917, and May 20th, it had flown one hundred and twenty-eight hours and thirty-five minutes, most of this total being logged following issue to the squadron on 5 February.

11 Squadron	Lt A T Walker	Injured	Unemployed list 23 January 1919: Lt
Bristol F.2b C925	Sgt W A Fraser	Injured	

T/o Remaisnil authorised for a practice flight but on return, and landing, ran into the area of butts used by No 70 Squadron; damaged beyond repair.

| 16 Squadron | Lt Milner | Safe |
| RE.8 B7853 | Lt Evans | Injured |

T/o Camblain l'Abbé briefed to bomb a supply dump at Rouvroy*but while flying at three thousand five hundred feet over Méricourt [Pas-de-Calais] the RE lost engine power and the crew force-landed at map reference S19b50.

* There are several locations in France and Belgium named 'Rouvroy', but with the incident here summarised I suspect it was Rouvroy in the Pas-de-Calais and just to the east of Méricourt.

| 22 Squadron | 2Lt C H Dunster | Safe |
| Bristol F.2b C4747 | 2Lt J H Umney | Safe | Unemployed list 17 January 1919: 2Lt |

T/o Serny for an offensive patrol in the course of which the Bristol was hit in its engine by shrapnel from an anti-aircraft shell burst. Returned to Serny, but crashed during landing. On charge since 11 April 1918, 'C4747' achieved sixty hours and ten minutes flying in total. Lieutenant Dunster relinquished his commission, on account of ill-health which developed during the war, on 24 April 1919. Subsequently, his well being restored, Charles Horace Dunster came forward a second time and was commissioned as a pilot officer to the Administrative and Special Duties Branch on 19 September 1939 [*gazetted* 26 September 1939, issue 34694]. Eventually attaining wing commander rank his commission was relinquished under the provisions of the Army, Navy and Air Force Reserves Act 1954.

| 23 Squadron | Lt C A Crysler [Canada] | + | Adelaide Cemetery, Villers-Bretonneux |
| 5F.1 Dolphin C3807 | | | |

T/o Bertangles for an offensive patrol and shot down, in combat, to crash at map reference 62DO28. Returning pilots reported seeing nineteen year old Carleton Aquilla Crysler of Delhin, Ontario, going down in flames after being attacked by at least seven enemy scouts.

| 23 Squadron | Lt A O Bentley | Safe | See 6 June 1918 - 23 Squadron |
| 5F.1 Dolphin C4135 | | | |

T/o Bertangles similarly tasked and on return, and landing, struck a ridge which effectively ended the service life of 'C4135' which until then had accumulated eleven hours and twenty-two minutes flying.

| 23 Squadron | Lt C L A Sherwood | Injured | See 1 July 1918 - 23 Squadron |
| 5F.1 Dolphin C4153 | | | |

T/o Bertangles authorised to make a practice flight. Landed, but lost control while turning [presumably to taxi back to the hangars] and damaged beyond repair. According records, 'C4153' had flown the same number of hours and minutes as 'C4135'.

| 24 Squadron | Lt R T Mark | Safe | Unemployed list 9 April 1919: Lt MC* |
| SE.5a C5367 | | | |

T/o Conteville for an offensive patrol and damaged beyond repair here following a forced landing brought about by the fabric stripping from the airframe during combat. Ronald Turnbull Mark was *gazetted* with the Military Cross on 22 June 1918, supplement 30761; '*For conspicuous gallantry and devotion to duty. He showed great determination and resource during operations in attacking enemy troops and transport with machine gun fire. Observing some enemy transport in a village, he attacked it repeatedly and caused it to stampede. While on an offensive patrol he attacked and destroyed an enemy two-seater machine. He has destroyed one other enemy machine and driven down others out of control.*'Supplement 30901 of 16 September 1918, reports the citation for the First Bar; '*For conspicuous gallantry and devotion to duty. This officer and another pilot were escorting a formation of machines engaged on bombing a village, when seven enemy scouts attacked the bombers. They both attacked these scouts, but at the outset the other pilot's machine was set on fire, and 2nd Lt Mark's right-hand top plane broke. During the fight that ensued each came to the rescue of the other. 2nd Lt Mark first caused the other pilot's pursuer to break off his attack, and then the other pilot shot down the scout attacking 2nd Lt Mark. The action of both these officers, in practically unmanœuvrable machines, in coming to the rescue of each other in turn showed courage and self-sacrifice of a very high order.*' Returning to the service in the Second World War, Lieutenant Mark was commissioned, as an acting pilot officer, to the Administrative and

Special Duties Branch on the 2nd of April 1940, promulgated in issue 34838 of 26 April 1940. In the New Year's Honours List for January 1946, and now an acting wing commander, he was *gazetted* [issue 37407] with the Most Excellent Order [Military Division] of the British Empire. He also received a mention in a despatch.

24 Squadron	Captain C N Lowe	Safe
SE.5a D275		

T/o Conteville and damaged beyond repair having engaged in combat with the enemy. On establishment since the 8th of April 1918, 'D275' flew in total for seventy-three hours and fifteen minutes.

25 Squadron	Lt A H Herring	+	Aulnoye Communal Cemetery
DH.4 D9239	2Lt R S Lasker [Australia]	+	Aulnoye Communal Cemetery

T/o 0800 Ruisseauville for a bombing raid on the rail centre of Aulnoye-Aymeries*in the Nord *département* and practically nestling on the border with Belgium. Flying at 15,000 feet the DH took a direct hit from anti-aircraft fire, caught fire and plunged to the ground. Both officers were commissioned to the General List of the Royal Flying Corps in 1917 [19 July and 12 August to be precise], their names being *gazetted* in issues 30221 and 30279 published on 7 August and 11 September 1917 respectively. For the widowed mother of twenty year old Albert Henry Herring this was the second time that tragedy had struck for on 24 April 1915, Albert's elder brother, Private Reginald Frank Herring serving with the 13th Battalion Canadian Infantry was reported 'missing in action'. His remains were never identified and he is commemorated at Ypres on the panels of the Menin Gate. Robert Sydney Lasker hailed from Newcastle in New South Wales.

* in the early part of the nineteenth century Aulnoye-Aymeries was little more than a hamlet but with the coming of the railway so its importance grew immeasurably for it is here that the main Paris to Brussels line connects with the Calais-Lille-Thionwille line.

35 Squadron	2Lt G J Gunyon	Safe	
FK.8 C3703	2Lt A Gilchrist	Safe	See 3 July 1918 - 35 Squadron

T/o Villers-Bocage to observe artillery shooting; damaged beyond repair following loss of a wheel while landing. Second Lieutenant Gilchrist had been involved in a forced landing the previous day [see my summary for details]. Gerald James Gunyon was commissioned to the General List of the Royal Flying Corps on 16 August 1917, promulgated on 11 September 1917, supplement 30279. A document in respect of Second Lieutenant Gunyon is held by The National Archives under AIR 79/433/46634, while The Imperial War Museum has a photograph showing him in his pilot's uniform standing in front of what could be an FK.8; catalogue number HU 122633.

40 Squadron	Lt G Watson	Injured Arras Flying Services Memorial
SE.5a D3938		

T/o 0855 Brauy for an offensive patrol during which the squadron clashed with enemy Scouts, identified as Pfalz, and at approximately 0940, George Watson went down to crash out of control. It seems he survived the impact but died soon after from his wounds. David Gunby indicates George fell to the guns of *Lieutnant* Ober-länder. Earlier in the month [see my summary for 6 May 1918] he had written off a SE.5a in a landing accident.

41 Squadron	Lt H E Watson	Safe	Unemployed list 18 January 1919: Lt
SE.5a B635			

T/o Estrée Blanche for practice flying but landed heavily, possibly at Marquise, the repair park attached to No 1 Aeroplane Supply Depot. The squadron had moved to Estrée Blanche from Serny twenty-fours previously. On squadron establishment since 15 November 1917, 'B635' had flown a very useful one hundred and sixteen hours and fifteen minutes.

41 Squadron	Captain C N Russell	Safe
SE.5a D5991		

T/o Estrée Blanche for an offensive patrol; wrecked on return after striking a ridge while landing. 'D5991' had been on squadron establishment for just three days and including the usual test and ferry flying had a mere six hours and twenty minutes recorded.

| 57 Squadron | Lt R Willey | + | Huby-St Leu British Cemetery |
| DH.4 A7406 | 2Lt H S G Palmer | Injured | Unemployed list 20 February 1919: 2Lt |

T/o Le Quesnoy taked for bombing operations over Bapaume only to fly into the airfield's wind gauge and dive back to the ground, bursting into flames on impact. Reginald Willey may have been American for his father, Harry Ide Willey is reported as having held the position of Surveyor General for California. Both officers had been involved in a serious crash on the 12th of April 1918 [see my summary for details].

| 65 Squadron | Captain L E Whitehead | + | Arras Flying Services Memorial |
| F.1 Camel D1876 | | | |

T/o Bertangles for an evening patrol over the lines during which the Camels came up against a strong force of enemy scouts. When last seen, Lewis Ewart Whitehead was twisting and turning in combat with a quintet of Fokker Drls southeast of Albert. The combat life of 'D1876' although not extensive [it arrived with the squadron on 15 April 1918] was quite hectic, particularly during operations over the Somme. On the 2nd of May, it sent a two-seater down, smoke trailing, in the early afternoon near Cerisy-Lamotte, followed the next day by another two-seater [this time shared with Second Lieutenant S W Crane flying 'D1791'] which was driven down, intact, near Heilly, its observer dead and pilot wounded, and captured. Then, on the 15th, 'D1876' accounted for an Albatros southeast of Villers-Bretonneux with a second Albatros in the same area on the 17th; all credited to Captain Whitehead.

| 74 Squadron | Lt H E O'Hara | Injured | See 25 May 1918 - 74 Squadron |
| SE.5a C1811 | | | |

T/o Clairmarais for a practice flight but before becoming airborne crashed against a fence.

| 74 Squadron | Lt H G Clements [Canada] | Safe | See 12 June 1918 - 74 Squadron |
| SE.5a D6068 | | | |

T/o Clairmarais for an offensive patrol and wrecked in a forced landing at map reference 28H16, following failure of the engine to respond to opening up after diving. Lieutenant Clements was attached to the Royal Flying Corps from the Alberta Regiment.

| 79 Squadron | Captain H P Rushforth MC | Injured | See 23 May 1918 - 79 Squadron |
| 5F.1 Dolphin C3901 Z | | | |

T/o Ste Marie Cappel for an offensive patrol during which Henry Philip Rushforth became embroiled in combat and was forced down inside the Allied lines near Wippenbach [sic], his petrol tank being shot through. Forced landing in a field of crops, the Dolphin turned over; it had completed sixty-eight hours and sixteen minutes flying. An excellent photograph of this Dolphin can be viewed on the Rise of Flight website, which I have pleasure in acknowledging. For details of Captain Rushforth's commission and award, please return to my summaries for the 2nd of May 1918.

| 80 Squadron | Lt J R Paisley | Injured | Unemployed list 5 February 1919: Lt |
| F.1 Camel D6499 | | | |

T/o La Bellevue for a practice patrol during which Lieutenant Paisley fired the aircraft's Very pistol to indicate to the rest of the pilots that they should return to base. Unfortunately, the round struck one of the Camel's struts and bounced off and into the cockpit, filling it with smoke. Disorientated, he crashed near the aerodrome.

| 84 Squadron | Lt R J Fyfe | Safe | See 18 June 1918 - 84 Squadron |
| SE.5a B7850 | | | |

T/o Bertangles heading with the rest of the patrol to Villers-Bretonneux. On return Lieutenant Fyfe landed with a force that damaged his aircraft beyond repair; it had been with the squadron for just twenty-four hours.

| 87 Squadron | Major J C Callaghan MC | Safe | See 2 July 1918 - 87 Squadron |
| 5F.1 Dolphin C4168 | | | |

T/o Petite Synthe to test the Dolphin's engine and on return crashed while avoiding another aircraft. Major Joseph Cruess Callaghan had taken over command of the squadron from Captain C J W Darwin, who had formed the squadron at Upavon on the 1st of September 1917, at Hounslow in February 1918, and under his leadership worked up on Dolphins in readiness for deployment to the Western Front, this being implement on the 23rd of April, when the squadron arrived at St Omer [see my brief notes for the day in question]. Late of the 7th Battalion Royal Munster Fusiliers, Major Callaghan gained the Military Cross on 14 February 1917 [issue 13051 of *The Edinburgh Gazette*]; *'For conspicuous gallantry in action. He displayed marked courage and skill on several occasions carrying out night bombing operations. On one occasion he extinguished a hostile search-light.'*

210 Squadron	Lt C Marsden	Safe
F.1 Camel D3366		

T/o St Omer for a test flight but as it passed between two hangars so it collided with a parked DH.9. Not surprisingly, Lieutenant Marsden clambered from the wreckage of his Camel somewhat shaken.

Tuesday 21 May 1918

1 Squadron	Lt K J P Laing	Safe	Unemployed list 2 February 1919: Lt
SE.5a C9621			

T/o Clairmarais for a special mission to Merville; came up against hostile aircraft and emerged from the ensuing combat badly shot about. Salvaged, but struck off charge on 27 May 1918. On squadron charge since 27 March 1918, 'C9621', including test and transit flying, logged eighty-one hours and fourteen minutes in the air.

5 Squadron	Lt S H Vickers	Safe	Unemployed list 6 February 1919: Lt
RE.8 B7805	2Lt A C Dutton	Safe	

T/o Ascq for artillery observation duties but Lieutenant Vickers lost control in the cross-wind and crashed. On establishment since 6 February 1918, 'B7805' had logged a useful one hundred and seven hours and thirty minutes flying. Following the Armistice, Second Lieutenant Dutton, now a recipient of the Distinguished Flying Cross, returned for duties with the 4th Battalion Royal West Kent, continuing to serve in various capacities until 28 January 1949, when having exceeded the age limited, entered retirement with the rank of honorary major.

8 Squadron	Lt A Trewheler	Safe
FK.8 B245		

T/o Auxi-le-Château for an air test and wrecked on return after flying into the top of tree while approaching the landing area. Delivered the previous June to No 2 Squadron 'B245' was damaged on the 16th of the month when on return from artillery observation, Second Lieutenant F W Crawford landing safely only to turn into a ditch adjoining Hesdigneul airfield. Repaired, it arrived with No 8 Squadron on 29 December. In total, it flew for one hundred and forty-six hours and ten minutes. Formerly of the 3rd Battalion, King's Own Regiment, Lieutenant Trewheler returned to army duty but relinquished his commission on the 29 December 1920, retaining his rank [*gazetted* 31 January 1921, supplement 32211].

9 Squadron	Lt H E Price	Safe
RE.8 A3930	2Lt Bassett	Safe

T/o Calais for an air test and, presumed, wrecked on landing owing to misjudgement on the part of the pilot. One hundred and sixty-four hours and twenty-five minutes flying time recorded since being despatched from the Air Acceptance Park at Kenley in early October 1917, and arriving with the squadron on the 23rd of that month.

16 Squadron	Lt Duffy	Safe
Bristol F.2b*A7259	Lt North	Safe

T/o Camblain l'Abbé tasked for artillery observation but the Bristol's engine failed and the crew found themselves clambering from the wreckage after hitting a tree at Villers-a- Bois a km or less east-northeast from the airfield..

* No 16 Squadron's equipment at the time was the RE.8 and this non-standard issue appears to have been shared with No 22 Squadron which was based at Serny. Postwar, No 16 Squadron would operate Bristol F.2bs between April 1924 and January 1931.

19 Squadron   Lt J D de Pencier [Canada]   Safe   See 17 May 1920 - 12 Squadron
5F.1 Dolphin C4019
T/o Capelle for operations; force-landed, and damaged beyond repair, near Béthune in the Pas-de-Calais.

21 Squadron   Lt Dobeson   Safe
RE.8 B4075   Mechanic Lamgden   Safe
T/o Floringham to test the aircraft's engine but on return did the airframe no good at all by landing in a bush. Salvaged, it was written off four days later; flying hours eight and fifteen minutes.

25 Squadron   Lt R P Bufton*   Safe
DH.4 A7565   Sgt W C Elliott   Safe
T/o Ruisseauville ordered for bombing operations at Marquise but before becoming airborne crashed into a No 27 Squadron machine [summarised below] which was stationary on the airfield, the fuselage of 'A7565' being severed in half. First used by No 55 Squadron, it had force-landed at Beaumaris on 12 September 1917, with engine trouble during bombing operations, the crew escaping unharmed. Sent for repair it was not until early January that it emerged fit and well and issued to No 25 Squadron. Then, on 9 March a cylinder burst leading to an emergency landing near Bailleul and a second spell in the repair shops before returning to the squadron on the 20th of May.

* Although I am not one hundred percent certain, I strongly suspect Lieutenant R P Bufton to be Reginald Percy Bufton who was granted a commission in the Administrative and Special Duties Branch for the duration of hostilities, effective 18 March 1940, and *gazetted* in issue 34831 published on 16 April 1940. He remained with the postwar air force and eventually relinquished his commission under the provisions of the Navy, Army and Air Force Reserves Act 1954, retaining his rank of flight lieutenant.

25 Squadron   Lt L L K Straw [South Africa] Safe   See 14 October 1918 - 25 Squadron
DH.4 D9251   2Lt H H Watson   Safe   See 9 June 1918 - 25 Squadron
T/o Ruisseauville briefed for reconnaissance during the course of which the DH came under anti-aircraft fire, shrapnel from one burst puncturing the fuel tank. Limping for home the crew managed to cross the lines and with the engine spluttering force-landed amid the shell holes. Lionel Lifford Kay Straw, son of Major William Pennington Straw of Hill Crest in the Natal, had first seen service with the South African Horse in the German East Africa campaign. He was commissioned as a temporary second lieutenant to the General List of the Royal Flying Corps on 30 August 1917 [*gazetted* 18 September 1917, issue 30292].

27 Squadron   Lt D B Robertson   Safe
DH.4 A7710   Sgt S B Percival   Safe
Elizabeth Campbell of Inverell Station
T/o Ruisseauville ordered for bombing operations only for the engine to fail and within seconds of becoming airborne the DH was down in a cornfield and damaged beyond worthwhile repair.

27 Squadron   Lt S W Taylor   Safe
DH.4 B2083   2Lt D Moore   Injured
T/o Ruisseauville also tasked but owing to engine problems was obliged to return some ten minutes later. Then, when stationary on the airfield was struck by a DH.4 from No 25 Squadron [summarised above]. Second Lieutenant Moore was struck on the head, sustaining a fracture to his lower right jaw.

40 Squadron   Lt D S Poler USAS   Safe   See 7 June 1918 - 40 Squadron
SE.5a D3561
T/o 1635 Bruay for an offensive patrol returning just over two hours later. However, Lieutenant Poler held off to high and by doing so he stalled, crashed and turned over. This was the first of what would be five 'adventures' for the young American all from which, thankfully, he emerged unharmed.

40 Squadron   Lt D F Murmann   Safe   Unemployed list 5 January 1919: Lt
SE.5a D5968

T/o Bruay for operations over the coal mining area of Northern France towards Lens where Lieutenant Murmann drove down an Albatros, but was badly shot about in return. Landed back at Bruay, and though his aircraft was salvaged it was struck off charge on 24 May 1918.

| 42 Squadron | Lt W Ledlie | Safe |
| RE.8 A3624 | 2Lt W D Potter | Injured |

T/o Rély for an artillery observation patrol; crashed, owing to engine failure, near Serny. Between 17 November 1917, and 18 March, No 42 Squadron was seconded to No 7 Brigade control for operations on the Italian front.

| 54 Squadron | Lt W K Wilson | Safe | See 6 June 1918 - 54 Squadron |
| F.1 Camel B9307 | | | |

T/o Cathiers for flying practice, an exercise that ended with the Camel on its back following a misjudged landing. At No 3 Aeroplane Acceptance Park Norwich by 28 January 1918, 'B9307' served with two home based squadrons, namely '77' and '44' before going to the Western Front and, following overhaul, flown to Clairmarais on 24 April and issued to No 54 Squadron, leaving five days later for Caffiers where its flying days came to an end, thirty-five hours and eight minutes being recorded as its total.

| 55 Squadron | 2Lt H E Townsend | pow |
| DH.4 A7791 R | Airman J Greenaway | pow |

T/o Tantonville briefed for a raid on the Belgian city of Charleroi in Hainaut province. Last sighted north of the French fortress city of Verdun-sur-Meuse, more commonly referred to as 'Verdun' and the site of some of the most destructive and costly fighting by the defending French armies of the *Great War.* A summary featuring Second Lieutenant Townsend is reported on 20 April 1918; he was repatriated on 18 December 1918. 'A7791' had been on squadron establishment since Christmas Eve 1917.

| 60 Squadron | 2Lt R G Lewis | Safe |
| SE.5a B8419 | | |

T/o Boffles for an offensive patrol and was so badly shot about in aerial combat that on return it was declared *hors de combat* and was struck off charge on the 27th of May 1918, after thirteen hours and twenty minutes flying; it had served the squadron for just five days.

| 64 Squadron | Lt S B Reece | pow | Unemployed list 2 March 1919: Lt |
| SE.5a B7737 | | | |

T/o Izel-lèz-Hameau for an offensive patrol and was east of the lines when last spotted over the River Scarpe. Under the heading 'Missing', *Flight* [repeating the Air Ministry list] June 20, 1918, names Lieutenant Reece.

| 70 Squadron | 2Lt J F Higgins | Safe |
| F.1 Camel D1826 | | |

T/o Boisdinghem for an offensive patrol but was overtaken by engine trouble and in forced landing hit a tree and crashed at map reference 51CT20.

| 73 Squadron | 2Lt J L Brewster | + | Arras Flying Services Memorial |
| F.1 Camel D6604 | | | |

T/o 1730 Beauvois for an evening sortie and last sighted by other pilots in the patrol seemingly under control to the west of Armentières. 'D6604' had been accepted by the squadron from No 2 Air Issues on 18 May 1918.

| 73 Squadron | Lt T G Drew-Brook | pow |
| F.1 Camel D9539 | | |

T/o Beauvois for an evening patrol and was seen at around 1830, under control, near La Bassée [Nord] Reported as 'Missing' by the Air Ministry, and repeated as such in *Flight* June 20, 1918. By August the Air Ministry advised that Lieutenant Drew-Brook had been classified as 'Wounded' [*Flight* August 8, 1918]. It was most likely that the wounds sustained by Lieutenant Drew-Brook were the main factor that on 30 September 1919, led to him to relinquish his commission.

75 Squadron   2Lt T F Scott MM [Canada]   +   East Harling Cemetery
BE.12 B727
T/o Elmswell and having climbed to eighty feet stalled and dived back to the ground, bursting into flames on impact. Prior to undergoing flying training, Tom Farrar Scott had served with the Canadian Medical Corps. He was commissioned to the General List of the Royal Flying Corps on 20 January 1918 [*gazetted* 26 January 1918, supplement 30496]. His entry on the Canadian Virtual War Memorial shows he was born in Montreal on the 16th of April 1894. A non digitised record for Second Lieutenant Scott is held by The National Archives under WO 339/124123. Commanded by Major C S Ross his squadron saw no action whatsoever.

78 Squadron   2Lt C G Joyce [South Africa]   Injured Hornchurch [St Andrew] Churchyard
F.1 Camel D6677
T/o Sutton's Farm and while coming into land Cyril Gordon Joyce 'choked' the engine [a Le Rhône 9J] and probably distracted failed to notice he was heading straight for a tree. Lifted from the wreckage with very severe injuries he died twenty-four hours later. Soon, a telegram of condolence would be speeding on its way to his parents, the Reverend J W and Mrs Joyce of 429 Fox Street, Johannesburg in the Transvaal.

88 Squadron   2Lt C G Scobie [Canada]   +   Arras Flying Services Memorial
Bristol F.2b B1341   2Lt F J D Hudson   +   Arras Flying Services Memorial
T/o Capelle in the company of others for an offensive patrol in the direction of Oostende during which the Bristols were heavily engaged by at least twelve enemy scouts; failed to return. Caldwell Groves Scobie was twenty years of age and hailed from Ottawa. His observer was a year younger and came from the West Hampstead district of London.

88 Squadron   2Lt K O Millar [Canada]   +   Arras Flying Services Memorial
Bristol F.2b C839   2Lt S Davidson   +   Coxyde Military Cemetery
T/o Capelle similarly tasked and lost in the manner described above. Keith Ogilvie Millar was nineteen, and from Winnipeg; Sydney Davidson came from Hull, his headstone being inscribed; *'His The Strife And Reward Ours The Sorrow'.*

98 Squadron   Lt A M Phillips   Safe
DH.9 C6166   Lt N C MacDonald   Safe
T/o Alquines with instructions to bomb the key rail communication centre at Roeselare where supplies to the enemy pressing the defences of Ypres Salient were channelled. During the raid the DH lost an intake pipe and the cowling from the engine, possibly as a result of the anti-aircraft fire that was present over the target area. The crew, however, maintained control, gliding down to crash-land behind the Allied lines at map reference 27NEF24C97. 'C6166' arrived with the squadron on the 18th of May 1918, by way of No 7 Aeroplane Acceptance Park Kenley and No 1 Air Issues; it had achieved a total of nine hours and fifty minutes flying and had the unwanted distinction of being the twentieth DH.9 lost from the squadron in the course of operational duties.

110 Squadron   Captain G J MacLean   Injured
DH.9 C6089   Mechanic E A E Hart   Injured
T/o Sedgeford for a training flight during which the leading edge of the tailplane failed; damaged beyond repair in the ensuing forced landing. Neither the pilot or his observer were seriously hurt.

211 Squadron   2Lt H E Tansley MC   pow   Retired 15 September 1944: G/C MC
DH.9 B7661   2Lt N B Harris   pow
T/o 1015 Petite Synthe for a bombing raid and was last sighted over the aerodrome at Varssenaere [apparently referred to by the Germans as Jabbeke] lagging behind the formation. Herbert Edwin Tansley, formerly of the King's Royal Rifle Corps gained his Military Cross for; *'Conspicuous gallantry and enterprise during a bomb attack by aircraft on an important enemy railway bridge. A subsequent reconnaissance showed that the whole of the centre section of the bridge had collapsed into the river, thereby interrupting important enemy commun- ications'* [*gazetted* 9 January 1917, issue 29898]. It appears that despite the obvious inference that the raid was carried out by aeroplanes, Herbert, then a second lieutenant, was still serving with the King's Royal Rifle Corps

and his seconding to the Royal Naval Air Service only became effective on 7 June 1917, as *gazetted* in issue 30193 published on 20 July 1917. From his many entries in *The London Gazette* it seems he remained attached to the now newly formed Royal Air Force though issue 32795 which appeared on 13 February 1923, reports his transfer, effective the next day, from the King's Royal Rifle Corps to the Cheshire Regiment in the rank of lieutenant and with seniority backdated to 10 April 1917. However, his commission to the Cheshire Regiment ended on 17 December 1924, on his acceptance of a permanent commission to the Stores Branch [later retitled Equipment Branch] of the Royal Air Force. Further investigation into his military service suggests that by the autumn of 1941, he was serving in the Far East and was present, probably in Singapore, when Japan entered the war for held at The National Archives under AIR 20/5593 Malaya Operations 1941-1942 - Equipment which features a lengthy report submitted by Herbert, now holding the rank of group captain, and including an assessment of the supply to the air force of Buffalos, Catalina Flying Boats and Hurricanes along with observations on salvage both in Singapore and, subsequently, Java and Sumatra.

Note. During the raid on Varssenaere [Jabbeke], strong enemy reaction occurred which resulted in the forced landing of DH.9 B7604 crewed by Lieutenant R F C Metcalfe and Second Lieutenant D R Bradley, both of No 211 Squadron. Not only did they have to fight off the attention from five enemy scouts but also had to contend with anti-aircraft fire and were fortunate to emerge unscathed after coming down west of the trench lines. 'B7604' was recovered and by the 25th of June 1918, had been rebuilt and given the serial 'F5847' [see my summary for 1 October 1918 and its new owners, No 108 Squadron].

Tuesday-Wednesday 21-22 May 1918

216 Squadron	Lt H L Le Roy	pow	
Handley Page O/100	2Lt R W Peat	pow	Unemployed list 2 March 1919: Lt
3134	Mechanic W J L Twite	pow	

T/o Ochey tasked for bombing operations; failed to return. The names of both officers are reported under the heading 'Missing' in *Flight's* reproduction of the Air Ministry list in their issue of June 20, 1918. The same magazine confirmed Lieutenant Peat's status as a prisoner of war in their issue of August 8, 1918. This crew were the first to be reported missing from the squadron since the formation of the Royal Air Force.

Wednesday 22 May 1918

By close of play No 85 Squadron, now commanded by the legendary Canadian 'Ace' Major William Avery 'Billy' Bishop, was ensconced at Marquise having flown in from Hounslow. Equipped with the SE.5a the squadron's rôle was fighter patrolling and ground attack duties, tasks which were carried out with vigour.

| 4 Squadron AusFC | Lt E V Culverwell | | Safe |
| F.1 Camel B7382 | | | |

T/o Clairmarais for an offensive patrol and to include bombing; suffered engine failure at ten thousand feet and force-landed just yards inside the Allied lines near Strazeele Station, east of Hazebrouck in the *département du Nord*. Owing to the closeness of the enemy, and in order to prevent the possibility of 'B7382' falling into their hands, Lieutenant Culverwell set light to his aircraft.

| 4 Squadron AusFC | Lt G Nowland AusFC | + | Pont-du-Hem Military Cemetery, La Gorgue |
| F.1 Camel D1909 | | | |

T/o Clairmarais in the company of others for an offensive patrol and it was at around 1130 when George Nowland spotted an enemy kite balloon near Neuf-Berquin [Nord]. Diving to attack he failed to see his squadron friend, Alexander Finnie, and with a sickening crash his Camel smashed into 'D1924', both machines crashing to the ground. Alexander, who came from Botany in New South Wales had walked away from two landing crashes, summarised on the 18th of April and 11th of May 1918. George Nowland came from North Fitzroy in the State of Victoria and his loss was so felt that his mother had his headstone inscribed *'He Lived And Died For Us Mother, Brother And Sisters Our Hero.'*

| 4 Squadron AusFC | Lt A Finnie AusFC | + | Pont-due-Hem Military Cemetery, La Gorgue |
| F.1 Camel D1924 | | | |

T/o Clairmarais and tragically lost in the manner described above. His parents had the following inscribed on his headstone; *'Forever With The Lord'*. First of the Australian Flying Corps squadrons operating on the Western Front to lose ten aircraft, these losses brought to twenty-one Camels struck from their establishment during operations since the 1st of April. Five pilots had been killed and a sixth had died in one of the training accidents that had befallen the squadron.

| 7 Squadron | Lt E W Fletcher | Safe |
| RE.8 B5066 *Johore No 8* 2Lt L Harrison | | Safe |

T/o Droglandt tasked to carry out artillery observation but collided with another machine and damaged beyond repair. Received by the squadron on 14 October 1917, this presentation aircraft from the Government of Johore flew for a total of one hundred and eighty three hours and ten minutes, indicating excellent servicing and reliability. Formerly of the Essex Regiment, Lieutenant Fletcher gained the Distinguished Flying Cross and a postwar entry in *The London Gazette* [supplement 32550 of 15 December 1921] shows his promotion to captain within the 7th Battalion.

| 10 Squadron | Lt S C P Slattery | Safe | See 6 June 1918 - 10 Squadron |
| FK.8 C8605 | 2Lt M T Stanley | Safe | Unemployed list 10 October 1919: Lt |

T/o Droglandt having been briefed for artillery observation. On return, and landing, ran the length of the airfield to finish up in a ditch. The impact must have been severe for 'C8605' was deemed not worth the expense of repair and with just seven hours and five minutes of airborne time to its credit it was struck off charge on the 20th of May 1918. As a second lieutenant serving with the Oxfordshire and Buckinghamshire Regiment, Lieutenant Slattery had been seconded to the Royal Flying Corps on 17 July 1917, promulgated in supplement 30221 of 8 August 1917. Postwar, he returned to his regiment and was a career soldier for the better part of the next three decades before retiring in the rank of major on the 28th of February 1946, as published in supplement 37517 of 2 April 1946. His final entry in *The London Gazette* appeared on 29 June 1948, with the announcement that he had exceeded the age limit for recall to service [supplement 38336].

| 18 Squadron | 2Lt A Green | Safe |
| DH.4 A8026 | Lt F Loly | Safe |

T/o Serny for an operational flight that went on until dusk at which point the crew lost their bearings. Sighting what he considered was a suitable field, Second Lieutenant Green made his approach but in the gloom he failed to see a ridge running across his path. On landing the wheels caught the ridge and the DH's momentum flipped it onto its back.

| 23 Squadron | Lt J T McKay | Safe | See 9 June 1918 - 23 Squadron |
| 5F.1 Dolphin C4152 | | | |

T/o Bertangles for an offensive patrol but on becoming airborne the engine 'cut' and the Dolphin came down in a field near the airfield. Moments late, Lieutenant McKay was scrambling out from beneath his inverted machine.

| 29 Squadron | 2Lt E G Latham | Injured |
| SE.5a D3929 | | |

T/o St Omer tasked for an offensive patrol during which engine failure occurred and in the attempt to force-land Second Lieutenant Latham stalled while avoiding flying into a tree and crashed at map reference 36aG6. Accepted by the squadron on the 12th of April 1918, 'D3929' was involved in a landing accident five days later in which Lieutenant J Bursey was injured. Damage to the SE.5a was relatively minor and repairs were carried out on site.

| 29 Squadron | Lt C J Venter | Safe | Unemployed list 7 November 1919: Lt DFC |
| SE.5a D3937 | [South Africa] | | |

T/o St Omer similarly tasked and crashed at map reference 27V15C88 in circumstances not too dissimilar to those reported above, though in Lieutenant Venter's case he hit the tree. For notes regarding this officer, please refer to my summary for 9 May 1918.

29 Squadron   Lt L E Bickel   Safe   See 7 June 1918 - 29 Squadron
SE.5a D5957

T/o St Omer tasked for a line patrol. On return failed to flatten out sufficiently and crash-landed, damaging his aircraft beyond repair.

29 Squadron   Lt R H Humphries   Safe
SE.5a D5983

T/o St Omer for an offensive patrol and on return wrecked in the manner described above.

35 Squadron   2Lt C R Strudwick*   Safe
FK.8 C3535   2Lt A E Sherwood   Safe   See 27 May 1918 - 35 Squadron

T/o Villers Bocage authorised to make a practice flight. On return to the airfield Second Lieutenant Strudwick banked too steeply, lost control and crashed.

* See my asterisked note for No 10 Squadron on the 1st of April 1918.

35 Squadron   Captain L S Kiggell   Safe   Unemployed list 16 April 1919: Captain
FK.8 C8628   2Lt J A Weller   Safe   See 9 June 1918 - 35 Squadron

T/o Villers-Bocage having received orders to patrol the Albert area. Hit by anti-aircraft fire, the crew brought their FK.8 down to a forced landing near Baizieux [Somme]. Including testing, transit and squadron usage, 'C8628' flew for the meagre total of five hours and fifty-five minutes. Formerly of the Royal Warwickshire Regiment, Captain Kiggell was transferred to the General List of the Royal Flying Corps on 31 August 1917; at the time he was ranked second lieutenant [*gazetted* 27 October 1917, supplement 30354].

37 Squadron   2Lt W M Burfoot   +   Chevening [St Botolph] Churchyard
SE.5a B658

T/o Woodham Mortimer*and destroyed following engine failure and loss of control as the pilot made the fatal error of turning downwind.

* No 37 Squadron had a number of detached bases; Goldhangar, Stow Maries and Rochford, and the crash that took the life of William Martin Burfoot, late of the 3rd Battalion, Dorset Regiment, may have occurred at one of these airfields.

40 Squadron   Lt H W Clarke   Safe   See 1 July 1918 - 40 Squadron
SE.5a D3922

T/o 1805 Bruay authorised for his first practice flight on type; lost control and crashed when landing half-an-hour later. It is believed the loss of 'D3922' was the first SE.5a written off by No 40 Squadron from a non-operational flight since the formation of the Royal Air Force on the 1st of April 1918. Hubert William Clarke was one of five replacement pilots drafted to the squadron between the 14th and 23rd of May 1918, and so may well have been on his first venture into the air since his arrival.

41 Squadron   Lt E F H Davis   Safe   See 5 July 1918 - 41 Squadron
SE.5a B76

T/o Estrée Blanche for operations over Béthune; wrecked following connecting rod failure which led to a fracture of the crankcase and an ensuing forced landing.

41 Squadron   Lt W J Gillespie   Safe
SE.5a B8259

T/o Estrée Blanche similarly tasked and on return it was discovered that an exhaust valve had fractured, as had one of the piston heads. Subsequently, it was decided repairs were not worth while and with ninety-four hours and five minutes credited flying 'B8259' was struck off charge on 29 May 1918.

56 Squadron   2Lt J H Acton   Injured
SE.5a C5435

T/o Valheureux for a cpunter attack patrol during which Second Lieutenant Acton got into difficulties while flying at one thousand five feet and with the engine full on he sideslipped and hit the ground at map reference 57BH19 where, it is reported, 'C5435' caught fire. Accepted by the squadron on the last day of March 1918, it had flown for a total of forty-five hours and thirty minutes. Owing to ill-health, which developed during the war, Lieutenant Acton relinquished his commission on 12 April 1919.

64 Squadron	Lt G A Rainer	pow
SE.5a B132 V		

T/o 0930 Izel-lès-Hameau for an offensive patrol and when last sighted was well inside enemy held territory. Lieutenant George Adrian Rainer drove down an Albatros over Brebières in the Pas-de-Calais during the morning of 16th May 1918. He is named in the War Office list for prisoners published on the 1st of August 1918, and repeated in the August 8, 1918, issue of *Flight*.

64 Squadron	Lt G Wood	Safe
SE.5a C6471		

T/o Izel-lès-Hameau for an offensive patrol but owing to engine failure Lieutenant Wood was obliged to seek a forced landing and while doing so his aircraft turned over. On squadron charge since 19 May 1918, 'C6471' had logged just six hours and thirty-five minutes flying in total.

73 Squadron	Lt R Mortimer USAS	+	Suresnes American Cemetery*
F.1 Camel D1907			

T/o Beauvais in the company of Second Lieutenant H C Hayes who was flying 'D1800', both being authorised to practice aerial combat. During the exercise the two Camels collided and although a slightly injured Hayes managed to force-land, Richard Mortimer lost control and spun in near Humières in the Pas-de-Calais.

* Located just outside of Paris, the cemetery covers seven point five acres and is the resting place for United States servicemen from both wars, the majority from the *Great War* numbering one thousand nine hundred and forty-one.

74 Squadron	Lt T G Sifton	Safe
SE.5a C1869		

T/o from No 1 Air Issues having been ordered to collect and ferry 'C1869' to the squadron's base at Clairmarais where, on landing, he ran against a ridge which tipped the aircraft onto a wingtip and at the same time, to quote from the accident report, *'swept away the undercarriage'*. Including its transit by air from the United Kingdom, 'C1869' flew for just one hour and fifty minutes. An entry in *The London Gazette* 31 January 1919, supplement 31154, indicates Lieutenant Sifton of the 1st Battalion Monmouthshire Regiment was to remain seconded to the Royal Air Force.

83 Squadron	Lt N S Jones	Safe
FE.2b B495	2Lt T H Singleton	Safe

T/o Franqueville for bombing operations but was obliged to force-land after enemy ground fire shot away the petrol pipe. Salvaged, the airframe was struck off charge on 7 June 1918.

84 Squadron	Lt E E Biccard	Injured Unemployed list 20 April 1919: Lt
SE.5a C6442		

T/o Bertangles for an offensive patrol but before becoming airborne collided with another aircraft. Lieutenant Biccard's injuries, fortunately, were not too serious.

87 Squadron	Lt R A Hewat	Safe See 14 August 1918 - 87 Squadron
5F.1 Dolphin C4024		

T/o Petite Synthe with the intention of ferrying the Dolphin to Estrée-lès-Crécy where the squadron was due to move to on the 27th. Before reaching his destination Richard Alexander Hewat realised he was running low on fuel and force-landed at Fécamp, damaging 'C4024' beyond repair.

| 98 Squadron | Lt G D Horton | Safe | See 31 May 1918 - 98 Squadron |
| DH.9 C6223 | Lt H J McConnel [USA] | Safe | See 31 May 1918 - 98 Squadron |

With its engine running, and preparing to take off from St Omer [where the crew had force-landed on 19 May] to return to Alquines, the DH was struck and severely damaged by a Camel that was in the process of getting airborne. Initially, it was thought the damage to 'C6223' could be repaired, but after languishing for nearly two months the airframe was struck off charge on 5 July 1918.

| 148 Squadron | Lt C C Grant-Baker | Safe | Unemployed list 13 April 1919: Lt |
| FE.2b B7840 | 2Lt A M Pearson | Safe | |

T/o Sains-lès-Pernes tasked for bombing but at that vital moment of becoming airborne the engine 'cut' and the crew force-landed just beyond the airfield. Languished until 14 August 1918, at which time it was decided the airframe was not worth the cost of repair and it was struck off charge after twenty-eight hours of flying. This was the squadron's first serious accident since arriving in France and moving to its operational base on the 3rd of May 1918. As far as I can ascertain, No 148 Squadron was the sole Royal Air Force user of Sains-lès-Pernes which is in the Pas-de-Calais some forty-three km northwest of Arras.

| 206 Squadron | Captain G L E Stevens | Safe | Unemployed list 29 September 1919: Captain |
| DH.9 C6163 | Lt L A Christian | Safe | Unemployed list 23 August 1919: F/O DFC |

T/o 1205 Alquines tasked for a bombing raid in the course of which the DH was badly damaged by shrapnel from anti-aircraft fire. Force-landed at base and, subsequently, deemed damaged beyond repair. 'C6163' arrived with the squadron on 20 May 1918.

| 206 Squadron | 2Lt E P Morgan | Injured | Longuenesse [St Omer] Souvenir Cemetery |
| DH.9 D1695 | 2Lt F C Taylor | + | Longuenesse [St Omer] Souvenir Cemetery |

T/o Alquines for an operational sortie but while climbing away Edward Percival Morgan lost control, spun back to the ground whereupon the DH burst into flames. Gravely injured, he died later in the day. His headstone carries the inscription 'Animae Magnae Prodigus'*while the words on the headstone for his nineteen year old observer are; 'Safe By Night And Day Until We Meet Again'.

* Seeking a translation, the website 'The One True Blog' reporting from James Miller's book Examined Lives and the ending of the author's essay on Socrates quotes [the German philosopher] Nietzsche; I know of no better aim of life than that of perishing animae magnae prodigus, in pursuit of the great and the impossible.'

| 209 Squadron | Lt C T Evans*USAS | Injured | |
| F.1 Camel C58 | | | |

T/o Vignacourt with the intention of returning to Bertangles but on becoming airborne sideslipped and nose-dived to the ground. 'C58' was the fifty-eighth airframe in a batch of two hundred Camels built by the Nieuport and General Aircraft Company Limited at Cricklewood, much of the early production being delivered to various training establishments.

* See my asterisk note in the second volume for 19 July 1918.

| 210 Squadron | Lt A S Highstone | Safe | |
| F.1 Camel D3365 | | | |

T/o St Omer for practice flying in the course of which Lieutenant Highstone 'choked' the engine which led to a forced landing near the airfield. On squadron charge 14 May 1918, Lieutenant A L Jones, assisted by Lieutenant H A Patey [F.1 Camel D3391 [see 18 May 1918]] drove down a Rumpler over the Nord département northeast of Bailleul during the morning of the 17th.

| 250 Squadron | Not named | | |
| DH.9 C1301 | Not named | | |

T/o Padstow and wrecked when landing.

Thursday 23 May 1918

2 Squadron	Lt G H Allison	Safe	Commission relinquished 11 May 1954: F/L
FK.8 B3367	2Lt H Pritchett	Safe	

T/o Hesdigneul tasked for artillery observation on return from which 'B3367' was caught by a sudden gust of wind at the crucial moment of landing and before Lieutenant Allison could regain control his aircraft swung and crashed against a hut used for messing. Salvaged, it was struck off charge on 29 May 1918, eight-four hours and twenty minutes flying being recorded. For Lieutenant Allison, this was his third serious crash since the formation of the Royal Air Force, the two previous having occurred on the 15th and 19th of April [for details, please refer to my summaries].

2 Squadron	Lt T H Crossman	Safe	
FK.8 C8526	Lt L C Spence MC [Canada]	Injured	Pernes British Cemetery

T/o Hesdigneul similarly tasked during which the crew came under sustained attack from five hostile aircraft over the village of Le Touret [Pas-de-Calais], five km northeast of Béthune, their fire mortally wounding Lyell Campbell Spence who died while undergoing treatment on 25 May 1918. For details of his previous crash, and that of Lieutenant Crossman also, please refer back to my summary for 20th May 1918, in which the citation for Lieutenant Spence's Military Cross is appended. Following a technical inspection 'C8526' was struck off charge on 27 May 1918.

4 Squadron	Lt M Stuart-Menteth	Safe	
RE.8 A4640	2Lt W Brennan	Safe	

Colony of Mauritius No 5
T/o St Omer tasked for artillery observation and on return, and while in the process of landing, caught by a sudden and severe gust of wind which turned the RE on to its back. 'A4640' initially served with No 21 Squadron but on 23 March 1918, a wheel came off on landing at La Lovie which necessitated a spell spent undergoing repair; Second Lieutenants Norman and Findlay, fortunately, required no attention whatsoever. Restored to good order, it was received by No 4 Squadron a mere three days before it was wrecked.

9 Squadron	Lt L M Hill	Safe	
RE.8 A3657	Lt Houlton	Safe	

T/o Calais to practice contact patrol procedures but crashed on the aerodrome; wrecked. Accepted by the squadron on 21 October 1917, 'A3657' logged a most creditable one hundred and forty hours and forty minutes flying, this including testing [it is noted that test pilot E H Lawford test flew 'A3657' ten days prior to its delivery to Proven where No 9 Squadron was then based].

15 Squadron	Lt A C Hardy	Safe	
RE.8 B821	2Lt P H Dixon	Safe	

T/o Vert Galand for a patrol during which the RE.8 entered cloud. Soon after doing so the engine began to fail as a consequence of moisture getting into the carburettor and Lieutenant Hardy had little option but to seek a forced landing. This he accomplished near Varennes [Somme] roughly midway between Amiens to the south-west and Arras to the northeast, ending with 'B821' running into a trench system. Salvaged, it was struck off charge on 11 June 1918.

27 Squadron	Captain A E Palfreyman	+	Ruddervoorde*Communal Cemetery
DH.4 A7840	[Australia]		
	2Lt W I Crawford	pow	Unemployed list 18 December 1919: 2Lt

T/o 0610 Ruisseauville to bomb Thourout [sic] and last seen by other crews in the formation under attack from enemy fighters west of Maria Aaltre probably in the vicinity of Ruddervoorde in the Belgian province of West-Vlaanderen and roughly a dozen km south of Brugge. 'A7840' began its Western Front service on 5 December 1917, with No 49 Squadron in whose hands it was badly damaged five days later in a forced landing, owing to the radiator losing its water, Second Lieutenant W H Valentine and Second Lieutenant F C Aulagnier emerging unharmed. Following repairs it was accepted by No 27 Squadron on 6 May 1918 and over the next fortnight it accounted for two enemy aircraft, the first [unidentified] during the evening of the 10th, by Lieutenant G E Ffrench and Second Lieutenant F A Gledhill near Bray [probably Bray-sur-Somme] and the second, a Pfalz DIV, in the mid-morning of the 20th, Captain Audubon Eric Palfreyman and Lieutenant W G Hurrell - their victim reported as having the front part of its fuselage painted red with the rest camouflaged. Second Lieutenant Crawford's removal to the unemployed list was as the result of wounds.

* There are four burials here from the *Great War,* three being the final resting places of DH.4 officers who died after the formation of the independent air force. The fourth, and first burial, is that for Corporal R Reilly of the Army Service Corps, attached to the 7th Cavalry Brigade, Field Artillery, and whom I suspect died when being held captive.

27 Squadron	Lt G E Ffrench	+	Pernes British Cemetery
DH.9 D5616	Sgt F Y McLaughlan	+	Pernes British Cemetery

T/o 0610 Ruisseauville tasked for operations to Maria-Aalter in the Belgian province of Oost-Vlaanderen and was lost in most unusual circumstances in that the engine fell out of its frame. Completely unbalanced the DH went down out of control to crash at Sains-lès-Pernes, a commune in the Pas-de-Calais, west of the cemetery where the crew are buried and roughly twenty odd km east of Ruisseauville. I cannot be certain if the crew were outbound at the time, or on the home leg. George Edward Ffrench was eighteen years of age and was not long out of training. It is noted his father was the Reverend Le B Edward Ffrench of Kilconnell Rectory, Ballinasloe, Co Galway. George had served with the Officer Training Corps at Trent College, Derbyshire. His headstone bears the inscription; *'Of Kilconnell, Co Galway Underneath Are The Everlasting Arms.'* His observer, two years his senior, is remembered by the words; *'God Knew The Measure Of His Service Father, Mother.'*

29 Squadron	Lt H M Hutton	Safe	Unemployed list 22 April 1919: Lt
SE.5a D5989			

T/o St Omer tasked for a line patrol on return from which 'D5989' was caught by a sudden gust of wind which caused it to turn over as it touched down. For information concerning Lieutenant Hutton's previous crash, please refer to my summary for 19 May 1918.

35 Squadron	Lt A Macgregor	Safe
FK.8 C8446	2Lt G F Sharp	Safe

T/o Villers Bocage for operational patrol duties during which the crew came under attack from enemy aircraft. Although their adversaries were successfully eluded, on return to base it was discovered longerons and the main spar had been shot through and, thus, 'C8446' was struck off charge on 4 June 1918, as not being worth the cost of repair. Despatched, crated, by sea it was assembled and issued to the squadron on 25 March 1918, and in total had flown for eighty-nine hours and fifty signalling high usage.

70 Squadron	2Lt A L Stockenstrom	+	Arras Flying Services Memorial
F.1 Camel D1902	[South Africa]		

T/o for an offensive patrol during which other pilots in the flight saw Andries Lars Stockenstrom dive past other Camels and it is believed 'D1902' broke up in the vicinity of Courcelette [Somme], a hamlet some forty-eight km northeast of Amiens. Andries Stockenstrom was the son of Sir Andries Stockenstrom, 3rd Baronet, of Pretoria, South Africa.

79 Squadron	Captain H P Rushforth MC	Safe	Retirement 20 May 1920: F/L MC
5F.1 Dolphin C4179			A mention in a despatch

T/o Ste Marie Cappel for an offensive patrol. On return, and landing the Dolphin struck an obstruction which smashed the undercarriage and caused the aircraft to turn over. For summaries featuring Captain Rushforth, please return to the 2nd and 20th of May 1918.

101 Squadron	2Lt J D Anderson	Safe	
FE.2b A6578	2Lt T H D Silvers	Safe	Unemployed list 17 January 1919: Lt

T/o Famechon tasked for a bombing raid on Bois de Tailles *[sic]* and while so engaged had to force-land following fracture of the camshaft. Soon after coming down, 'A6578' caught fire. On charge since 22 March 1918, 'A6578' flew, including testing and transit, forty-five hours and forty minutes.

| 102 Squadron | 2Lt A B Whiteside*[Canada] | Safe |
| FE.2b A5649 | Lt E F Howard | Safe | Commission relinquished 19 April 1919: Lt MC |

T/o Surcamps for a night bombing raid but when about to cross the lines engine failure occurred [Norman Franks writing on page 21 of his excellent *Fallen Eagles* states 'A5649' was fired upon by anti-aircraft guns and it was shrapnel from a near miss that hit the engine, causing it to fail] and a forced landing was made at Ficheux in the Pas-de-Calais ten km south of Arras. Postwar, and while awaiting release from the service, Arthur Barlow Whiteside was attached to No 2 School of Navigation and Bomb Dropping at Andover [some documents refer to this Andover based unit as 'Weyhill']. Among the various types held was, for the time, the impressive Handley Page O/400 twin-engined heavy bomber and it was in the early hours of 22 April 1919, that he was selected by Major Thomas Archibald Bachelor to accompany him for a test flight in 'F3758'. With Major Bachelor [a much decorated officer who had recently flown operations with the type attached to No 214 Squadron] at the controls, the crew of six and a naval passenger, Captain W R Adkins, took off at 0230, but the climb out was sluggish and within seconds of becoming airborne 'F3758' hit the roof of an airfield building, crashed to the ground and burst into flames. Amazingly, Lieutenant E A Westall was thrown clear, though was injured, while Flight Sergeant H H Heales and Corporal E G Ward were also ejected from the aircraft and though shocked were otherwise unhurt. The rest were not so fortunate and perished in the blaze, both pilots being laid to rest with full military honours in Penton Mewsey [Holy Trinity] Churchyard, where Arthur's headstone carries the inscription; *'He Ws Faithful To The End.'* During his time on the Western Front he gained the Military Cross and First Bar, the first of which was awarded on 24 August 1918 and the second less than a month later on 16 September, supplements 30682 and 30901 respectively. In order, the citations read; *'For conspicuous gallantry and devotion to duty. He carried out several night bombing raids with great success, attacking enemy aerodromes and billets, often from a low altitude. On one occasion he attacked a train with his machine gun from a height of 100 feet. He showed splendid skill and initiative.' 'For conspicuous gallantry and devotion to duty. This officer has taken part in over fifty night bombing raids, many of which, carried out at heights considerably under 1,000 feet, and in adverse weather conditions, were only successful through the skill and energy displayed by him by discovering and attacking his objective. On one night in particular , after having successfully bombed a large ammunition dump, which was set on fire and blown up, he proceeded to drop bombs on a town which held large numbers of the enemy, also firing from a low altitude with his machine gun on the roads leading to it. Returning to his squadron he obtained more bombs and ammunition, and with the same observer proceeded to drop bombs on a train behind enemy lines. On several occasions his machine was badly knocked about by enemy fire from the ground. The devotion to duty and disregard of danger displayed by this officer have been admirable examples to all members of his squadron.'* Lieutenant Howard was formerly of the Royal Field Artillery

* Son of the Reverend Arthur Whiteside of Victoria in British Columbia, Arthur Barlow Whiteside was born to his parents at Fort Quappelle, Saskatchewan, and is known to have attended McGill University.

| 148 Squadron | F/S J Helingoe | Safe |
| FE.2b A6450 | Lt Kendrick | Safe |

T/o Sains-lès-Pernes for the dual purpose of conducting an engine test and to familiarise the crew with the local area. During the flight 'A6450' lost engine power and a forced landing was carried out near the station at Frévent in the Pas-de-Calais and roughly twenty-six km south-southwest from the airfield. Salvaged, it languished until 20 June 1918, when it was struck off charge; its total flying hours are noted as eighteen hours and ten minutes.

| 209 Squadron | 2Lt A W Aird [Canada] | + | Arras Flying Services Memorial |
| F.1 Camel B7250 | | | |

T/o Bertangles for what has been described as wireless interception; observed to dive towards a hostile two-seater but, it seems, Arthur William Aird lost control of his aircraft which crashed, on fire, at Lamotte-Warfusée [Somme], some five hundred metres south of le Hamel. 'B7250' arrived in France by way of the Aeroplane Acceptance Park at Lincoln, Fairlop and Dover early in 1918, and before its loss shared in the destruction of at least four enemy aircraft, all credited to Captain O W Redgate. Thus far, since the 1st of April, the squadron had lost five of their aircraft on operations resulting in the deaths of the pilots.

Friday 24 May 1918

2 Squadron	Lt S H Warner	Safe	Unemployed list 8 May 1919: Lt
FK.8 B6901	2Lt H S Lindfield	Safe	Unemployed list 1 April 1920: Lt

T/o Hesdigneul for artillery observation duties and on return, and landing, came down rather heavily causing the axle and wheels to buckle. Salvaged, it was struck off charge on 29 May 1918, with a most creditable one hundred and forty-one hours and fifteen minutes flying recorded. It is described as a FK.8 experimental.

45 Squadron	Lt H J Watts	Injured
F.1 Camel B6282 O		

T/o Grossa and reported to have crashed in the River Brenta after colliding with a line of telegraph poles. An extremely well-used Came 'B6282' was packed at Ascot and thence via Newhaven arrived in France and issued to No 70 Squadron at Poperinghe on 17 September 1917, but twelve days later Second Lieutenant I S Micheal crashed while landing and the Camel was struck for repairs. When taken over by No 45 Squadron on the 1st of November, at Ste Marie Cappel the squadron was soon to transfer from operations on the Western Front to duties in Italy, arriving at Padova on 16 December and thence to Grossa forty-eight hours later. However, during its last few days over the Ypres Salient in drove down a couple of Albatros scouts while in Italy it succeeded in crashing three more Albatros types, all at the hands of Second Lieutenant T F Williams [who, I suspect, was responsible for the two victories aforementioned]. Then, with Lieutenant J H Dewhirst at the controls, two more hostile machines were accounted for before Lieutenant Watts had his unfortunate accident.

74 Squadron	Lt A C Kiddie	Safe	Unemployed list 20 February 1919: Lt
SE.5a C6450			

T/o Clairmarais for a special mission during which 'C6450' was roughly treated by hostile fire over the Ypres Salient southeast of Meteren and on its return was deemed as damaged beyond repair. Arriving with the squadron on 21 April 1918, it immediately became the favoured aircraft for Lieutenant Kiddie who in the early evening of the 19th of May 'flamed' an enemy kite balloon west of Armentières followed by a Pfalz scout which he drove down out of control northeast of Merville [Nord] in the early morning of the 21st.

76 Squadron	2Lt B A Ross	Injured
BE.2e 6301		

T/o Ripon*for a night patrol but became lost and while attempting a forced landing came down in a wood.

* No 76 Squadron, commanded by Major A C Wilson, maintained detachments at Copmanthorpe, Helperby and Catterick, thus the incident here summarised may have occurred during a sortie from one of these stations. The history of this squadron has been published under the title *To See The Dawn Breaking* in which I cover its activities in both wars and postwar when it was equipped with Canberra bombers and which between March 1956 and November 1959, were detached to Australia. During this period the squadron maintained detachments on Christmas Island in connection with Operation *Grapple* [nuclear weapons testing]. It is interesting to reflect that at this time airmen who served with the squadron during the *Great War* might well have read some of the limited reports published about their post-Second World War colleagues engaged in what was quite hazardous flying as they took air samples from the aftermath of the atomic bomb explosions.

226 Squadron	Lt P B S Wood	+	Taranto Town Cemetery extension
DH.4	Airman F Johnson	+	Taranto Town Cemetery extension

T/o Pissone and reported to have crashed; the aircraft's serial and duty are, as yet, not known. Nineteen year old Patrick Bryan Sandford Wood was a Fellow of Gonville and Caius College, Cambridge; his observer was twenty-one years of age. No 226 Squadron came under the aegis of No 67 Wing.

250 Squadron	*Not named*	Safe
DH.9 B7665	*Not named*	Safe

T/o Padstow probably for an anti-submarine sortie during which the DH ditched. Its crew were rescued and the hulk towed ashore by a trawler.

Saturday 25 May 1918

41 Squadron   F.1 Camel D3569   While parked, and ready for operations, at Estrée Blanche was struck and damaged beyond repair by a No 46 Squadron [based at Lièttres] F.1 Camel B2353 which was landing. This incident has not been recorded against its movements record and I believe there is a strong case to question the accuracy of the identity of the No 46 Squadron aircraft.

44 Squadron   Lt H J L Taylor   Injured
F.1/3 'Comic' type Camel B9287
T/o Hainault Farm and wrecked following a stall, while turning, at two hundred feet. The resultant crash left Lieutenant Taylor very severely injured. One of a clutch of Home Defence squadrons and under their leadership of Major G W Murliss-Green achieved some success in combating the threat posed by the Gotha night raiders.

74 Squadron   Lt H E O'Hara   +   Ebblinghem Military Cemetery
SE.5a C6483
T/o Clairmarais for a practice flight but while turning downwind Henry Eyre O'Hara stalled and crashed, his aircraft going up in flames. This was his second crash while practice flying, the first being on 20 May 1918 [see my summary for details]. His headstone is inscribed with the simple inscription; *'Thy Will Be Done RIP'.*

79 Squadron   2Lt P D P Hamilton   Injured
5F.1 Dolphin C4128
T/o Ste Marie Cappel for offensive patrolling over the Ypres Salient where Second Lieutenant Hamilton was driven down, wounded, to crash within the Allied lines. With his health failing, Lieutenant Hamilton was compelled to relinquish his commission on 16 April 1919.

104 Squadron   Lt W Bruce*[Canada]   +   Commercy French National Cemetery
DH.9 C6266   Sgt D G Smith   +   Chambieres French National Cemetery, Metz
T/o from an unidentified airfield in England [possibly Andover where the squadron had been based before departing to France on 19 May 1918] with the intention of making for Azelot but landed with engine problems at Sézanne in the *département du Marne.* With the faults rectified, the crew took off to continue their transit but would seem to have become lost and, subsequently, came down behind enemy lines at around 1130 near Pont-à-Mousson in the Meurthe-et-Moselle *département.* I strongly suspect that David Gordon Smith, described as a 'Chief Motor Mechanic', survived the crash for the distance between his place of burial and that for Canadian born William Bruce [formerly of the Saskatchewan Regiment] is in the region of between sixty and seventy km.

* His parents address in the cemetery register indicates they were domicile in Scotland at Inverness; interestingley, there are only two Commonwealth burials at Commercy where around two thousand French servicemen lie, one being William Bruce and one whose identity could not be established. Also worthy of further research is that Pont-à-Mousson is at least forty km northeast of Commercy which raises questions as to why was William's body taken that distance for burial, though I am aware that this probably took place post-armistice.

119 Squadron   2Lt E O Scarborough   +   Cambridge City Cemetery
BE.2e C7022
T/o Duxford and lost control while making a flat turn at low altitude; crashed and caught fire. Twenty-one years of age and from Minthorpe in Westmoreland his headstone is inscribed; *'Eternal Rest Give Unto Him O Lord.'*

131 Squadron   2Lt G Roper [USA]   +   Shawbury [St Mary the Virgin] Churchyard
DH.9 D5613
T/o Shawbury and burnt out after stalling in a turn. George Roper hailed from Steubenville in Jefferson County, Ohio.

Sunday 26 May 1918
According to most records No 10 Squadron, based at Droglandt, commenced receiving Bristol F.2b fighters to operate alongside their FK.8s in June 1918; however, Bristol F.2b A7300, a presentation aircraft from *Maharajah Bahadur Sir Ramaeswar Singh of Darbhanga* [his fourth], which arrived with No 22 Squadron at Estrée Blanche

on 21 October 1917, came to No 10 Squadron as early as 22 April [it had been brought back on charge following an accident on 12 March when Second Lieutenant J E Gurdon of No 22 Squadron misjudged his landing following a practice flight], and was badly damaged on the 26th of May when Lieutenant S C P Slattery [see my summary for 22nd May], accompanied by Second Lieutenant J C Anderson, made a heavy landing on return from observing artillery action. Although struck off charge, further examination of the airframe deemed it suitable for repair and on completion of the rebuild it was given a new airframe serial 'F5819'. As such it was issued to a unit referred to as 'L Flight' on the 4th of August 1918. Its future service was brief; on the 21st of the month it landed from artillery observation and photography operations on rough ground and was damaged beyond any further repair; it had, in total, achieved forty-one flying hours.

| 4 Squadron AusFC | 2Lt G F Pierce | Injured |
| F.1 Camel D1896 | | |

T/o Clairmarais tasked for an offensive patrol, and to include bombing. On return, and preparing to land, stalled while banking and spun in damaging the Camel to the extent that repairs were deemed not worth the cost.

| 18 Squadron | 2Lt L J Balderson | Safe |
| DH.4 A7682 | Airman G Bridge | Safe |

T/o Serny for an engine test and when landing across the wind the DH tipped onto its left wing followed almost immediately with the undercarriage giving way. Accepted by No 49 Squadron*at Dover on 8 November 1917, 'A7682' went with the squadron to France on the 12th and before being given up to No 18 Squadron on 8 May 1918, shot down three enemy fighters; 13 January, in the morning, a Fokker DrI near Cambrai, the same type, and again near Cambrai, in the afternoon of 2 February and an Albatros DV on 26 February, the victorious crews being reported as Second Lieutenant H L Rough and Second Lieutenant V Dreschfeld [see my summary for 25 August 1918], Second Lieutenant D S Stewart and Lieutenant D D Richardson and Lieutenant R Mitton and Second Lieutenant B S B Bayliss. This state of affairs continued with No 18 Squadron with Second Lieutenant L J Balderson [see my summary for this officer on 11 April 1918] with Lieutenant G Bullen sending down an Albatros and a Fokker DrI in quick succession the day before the accident which wrote off 'A7682'.

* Additional information pertaining to some of the squadron crews mentioned above can be found on the excellent No 49 Squadron Association website.

| 32 Squadron | Lt M E De Zee | Safe |
| SE.5a C9537 | | |

T/o Beauvois for a practice formation flight and on return to the airfield made a heavy landing which damaged the undercarriage and left the SE.5a balanced on its nose. This was the second, and final, crash involving 'C9537' for on 18 December 1917, Second Lieutenant J B Corcoran took off from Brooklands with the intention of delivering 'C9537' to France but having climbed to around fifty feet lost control and sideslipped to the ground, injuring himself in the process. Repaired, it eventually reached No 32 Squadron on 8 March; its total flying hours are recorded as eighty hours and five minutes. Lieutenant M E De Zee, commissioned to the General List of the Royal Flying Corps, was confirmed in his rank [second lieutenant] on Christmas Eve 1917 [*gazetted* 19 April 1918, supplement 30639].

| 77 Squadron | 2Lt F Sansome | Injured |
| BE.2 4146 | | |

T/o Penston and crashed following an inflight fire. To the best of my knowledge this was the first serious crash involving the squadron since the 1st of April 1918, Formed as a home defence squadron on 1 October 1916, with its headquarters at Edinburgh detached flights were established at Whiteburn, New Haggerston and Penston. On 13 April 1917, the squadron's headquarters transferred to Turnhouse after which Penston appears to have been the sole detached flight. At the time of Second Lieutenant Sansome's crash the squadron was commanded by Major A Somervail.

| 98 Squadron | Lt W S Eason | Safe | Commission relinquished 13 July 1918: Lt |
| DH.9 C2151 | | | |

T/o Coudekerque with other crews from the squadron to practice flying as a formation and on landing ran into a ditch and damaged beyond repair. Built by F W Berwick and Company, London, 'C2151' was the first off from a production line of eighty aircraft and was delivered to Kenley and No 7 Aircraft Acceptance Park on 23 March 1918. Earmarked for the Expeditionary Force, the DH was in the process of being ferried by Lieutenant H Shaw to Penhurst in Sussex on 26 April when an inflight fire necessitated an emergency landing. Fortunately, the damage was not too severe and following repairs 'C2151' arrived with No 98 Squadron on 17 May. In the early afternoon of the 14th, Captain E A Fawcus and Lieutenant G D Dardis drove down an enemy scout west of Comines in the *département du Nord*. This was the squadron's first non-operational crash since the 1st of April.

| 102 Squadron | 2Lt F W Butt | + | Doullens Communal Cemetery extension No 2 |
| FE.2b B458 | Lt F N Phillips | Injured | Unemployed list 10 October 1919: Lt |

T/o Surcamps tasked for night bombing during which engine failure overtook the crew and while attempting to force-land nineteen year old Frank Wilfred Butt crashed out of control at Hénu in the Pas-de-Calais. Educated at Brighton College, Frank joined the Officer Training Corps attached to the Inns of Court. His father, who was deceased, had graduated from Balliol College, Oxford with a Master of Arts degree and, subsequently, was Rector of Rodmartin in Gloucestershire. Second Lieutenant Butt's headstone is inscribed; *'Their Names Shall Be Held In Everlasting Remembrance.'*

| 103 Squadron | Lt D McK Darroch | Safe | Unemployed list 12 July 1919: Lt |
| DH.9 D5605 | Mechanic W J Westcott | Safe | |

T/o Serny for a bombing sortie on return from which Lieutenant Darroch approached the landing area flying in a cross-wind. All might have been well but when just about to land another aircraft passed in front of him; pulling up to avoid a collision he semi-stalled and crash-landed, damaging the DH beyond repair. This was the squadron's first operational loss since arriving in France on 12 May 1918.

| 206 Squadron | Lt T H Wood | Safe |
| DH.9 D5606 | | |

T/o Alquines authorised to make a local practice flight; crashed on landing. Salvaged, the DH languished until the 5th of July 1918, when it was struck off charge as not worth repairing.

211 Squadron	Captain T F Le Mesurier DSC**	Injured	Dunkirk Town Cemetery
DH.9 D1693	A mention in a despatch		
	2Lt R Lardner	+	Dunkirk Town Cemetery

T/o 1010 Petite Synthe for a test flight [the DH having been received on the squadron ten days previously] with additional drift wires fitted. Passing over some trenches near Pervijze in the Belgian province of West-Vlaanderen a few km northwest from Diksmuide, and flying at only twenty feet, eyewitnesses report the port wing as folding up. Frederick Thomas Le Mesurier, twenty-one years of age, died later in the day from his injuries. His headstone at Dunkirk reads; *'He Is Not Here, He Has Risen On The Wings Of Resurrection.'* For information regarding the honours bestowed on this gallant officer, please refer to my asterisk note appended to my summary for 'B7591' on 29 April 1918.

Monday 27 May 1918
Opening day of the *Third Battle of the Aisne* which, in reality, was a resumption of the *Kaiserschlacht* offensive launched by the German army in March. Similar to the initial success of the spring attack, the battle went well and the Chemin des Dames Ridge was recaptured as drive and determination by the attackers pressed the French and British divisions back to within fifty-six km of the French capital. But, although the allies had suffered heavy losses*the cost to the attackers was higher and the fighting petered out during the first week of June.

* The 2nd Battalion Devonshire Regiment recorded a total of five hundred and fifty-two casualties on this first day of fighting with only between forty and fifty men of the battalion managing to cross the Aisne and join up with elements of the British forces engaged in a fighting withdrawal. In recognition of the outstanding bravery of the Devons a unique battle honour was conferred upon them, namely the Bois des Buttes. At Guyencourt the 1st Battalion Wiltshire Regiment was caught up in the fighting and an extract from their War Diary reads; *'1 a.m. enemy starts a heavy gas bombardment which last until 5 a.m. when he commenced to attack the forward Battn*

line held by the 8th Div.' For the remainder of the day the Wiltshires were hard pressed trying to hold the line and during a fighting withdrawal in the evening their commanding officer Lieutenant-Colonel Furze DSO MC was killed.

3 Squadron	Captain D J Bell MC*	+	Arras Flying Services Memorial
F.1 Camel C6730	[South Africa]		

T/o Valheureux for wireless interception operations and when last seen was engaging an enemy two-seater, then falling away and breaking up in area map reference 57DR32. Of Johannesburg in the Transvaal, Douglas John Bell saw action in German South West Africa, at the time attached to the Transvaal Light Horse. His *Wikipedia* entry indicates he took his flying instruction following enlistment with the Royal Flying Corps on the 1st of June 1916, and was awarded his Aviator's Certificate on the 22nd of September of that year. His first attachment was to No 27 Squadron for bombing duties, subsequently followed by service with No 78 Squadron on home defence duties, during which he clashed with a Gotha bomber on the 25th of September 1917, eventually driving it down to crash in the North Sea. Returning to the France, he was attached No 3 Squadron for flight commander duties with effect from 13th February. The citation for his first award of the Military Cross appeared in *The London Gazette* 18 June 1917, supplement 30135, and reflects on his service with No 27 Squadron; *'For conspicuous gallantry and devotion to duty when in command of a long distance bomb raid. Owing to good leader-ship and skill a large ammunition dump was destroyed. Later, he single-handed carried out a difficult mission and succeeded in reaching his objective under extremely adverse weather conditions.'* Supplement 30681 of 13th May 1918, reports the citation for the First Bar, gained with No 3 Squadron; *'For conspicuous gallantry and devotion to duty. He has led his formation with great skill and has destroyed three enemy aeroplanes and driven down two others, one of which was seen to be completely out of control. The high state of efficiency which his flight has attained is due to his splendid example and fearless leadership.'*

4 Squadron	Lt A H Maltby	Safe	See 4 June 1918 - 4 Squadron
RE.8 B4100	2Lt J B P Simms	Safe	See 4 June 1918 - 4 Squadron

T/o St Omer with orders to observe artillery in the Vieux-Berquin region southeast of Hazebrouck [Nord]. While so engaged, the crew were attacked by a quintet of hostile aircraft resulting in 'B4100' being so badly shot about that it was struck off charge on 8 June 1918.

4 Squadron	Lt F C Daniel	Safe
RE.8 E88	2Lt J A A Malhiot [Canada]	Injured

T/o St Omer similarly tasked but owing to engine failure the crew crash-landed at map reference 36aD5. Second Lieutenant Malhiot was not too seriously injured. From the Aeroplane Acceptance Park at Coventry 'E88' was flown across the Channel and following a week or so at No 1 Air Issues was delivered to the squadron on 24 May 1918; in total, it flew for twelve hours and twenty-five minutes. Second Lieutenant Malhiot was granted a temporary commission, in the rank shown above, with effect from 26 May 1918, as an observer officer. His former service had been with the Canadian Railway Service, Canadian Expeditionary Force [issue 30803 of 19 July 1918]. His secondment ceased on 16 December 1918 [promulgated in supplement 31137, of 22nd January 1919].

15 Squadron	Lt G A Griffin	Safe
RE.8 B2277	2Lt A E Sherwood*	Safe

T/o Vert Galand tasked for an artillery patrol in the course of which the crew came under ground fire and were obliged to force-land after the petrol [feed] pipe was shot away. Gliding down, Lieutenant Griffin arrived near Englebelmer [Somme] and had the misfortune to run into a shell hole. Supplement 31790 of 23 February 1920, under the heading 'Royal Flying Corps' *[sic]* records; *'Temp. 2nd Lt G A Griffin, attd R Dub Fus, and to be transfd RFC Gen List 10th Mar 1918.'*

* There were two A E Sherwood's, both second lieutenant observers, flying on the Western Front at this time, one as shown above and the other with No 35 Squadron.

20 Squadron	Sgt A Stansfield	Safe
Bristol F.2b B1193	2Lt J Tulloch	Injured

T/o Boisdinghem and force-landed at Clairmarais South shot about by enemy fire while carrying out an offensive patrol, Second Lieutenant Tulloch requiring medical treatment for wounds which were not thought to be serious. First allocated on the 5th of January 1918, to No 48 Squadron at Flez, 'B1193' was damaged on the 21st of February when Lieutenant W A McMichael and Second Lieutenant W Hart crash-landed on return from an artillery observation patrol, neither officer suffering injury. Salvaged, and repaired, the Bristol arrived with No 20 Squadron on 23 April. Overall, it had logged sixty-four hours and twenty-six minutes flying.

| 29 Squadron | Lt H G White | Safe | |
| SE.5a D5962 | | | |

T/o St Omer for a practice flight that was over before becoming airborne when Lieutenant White lost control, swung and crashed. Salvaged, the airframe was struck off charge on 2 June 1918.

| 29 Squadron | Lt C E Bickel | Injured | Unemployed list 5 February 1919: Lt |
| SE.5a D5966 | | | |

T/o St Omer tasked to carry out a line patrol during which Lt Bickel was attacked by enemy aircraft. With his controls badly damaged, he force-landed at Ostreville a km or so to the northeast of St Pol-sur-Ternoise in the Pas-de-Calais. His injuries, happily, proved to be only slight.

| 35 Squadron | Lt W E Joseph | Safe | |
| FK.8 C8525 | 2Lt A E Sherwood | Safe | See 4 October 1918 - 35 Squadron |

T/o Villers-Bocage tasked for operations in the vicinity of Albert. Force-landed, owing to engine failure, and ran into the trench systems; damaged beyond repair. Second Lieutenant Sherwood had walked away from a serious crash five days previously - see my summary for Second Lieutenant C R Strudwick for details.

| 35 Squadron | 2Lt A B Hughes | Injured | |
| FK.8 C8588 | 2Lt G F Sharp | Injured | |

T/o Villers Bocage tasked to observe an artillery shoot during which the crew came under intense machine-gun fire from the ground which damaged both the engine and the flying controls. Force-landed near Buire [Aisne].

| 52 Squadron | 2Lt C C A Beaumont | + | Berry-au-Bac Military Cemetery |
| RE.8 B5147 | 2Lt F Whitehouse | + | Berry-au-Bac Military Cemetery |

T/o 0505 Fismes*for an armed patrol over the lines; believed shot down by an enemy scout - possibly in the vicinity of Craonne [Aisne]. Christopher Charles Audley Beaumont is reported to have received his commission on 25 October 1917. His observer was nineteen years of age.

52 Squadron   RE.8 B5891 and D4970 both abandoned at Fismes having been damaged by enemy shell fire.

* During the day No 52 Squadron took up temporary residence at Cramaille before moving in quick succession to Anthenay and Trecon arriving at the latter on the 29th and remaining here for a month before moving, once again, this time to Auxi-le-Château on the last day of June 1918. As a corps reconnaissance squadron No 52 Squadron was active on the Western Front from 18 November 1916 to 17 February 1919 when it returned to Netheravon in Wiltshire. Apart from the three RE.8s identified here, It is possible the squadron lost a fourth machine for named on the Arras Flying Services Memorial are Lieutenant Charles Reay Coffey and Corporal George Anderson Chichton, Lieutenant Coffey having been awarded a *Croix de Guerre avec Palme.* However, both may have perished during the shell fire that fell on the airfield.

| 57 Squadron | Lt A Newman MC | Safe | See 8 December 1918 - 57 Squadron |
| DH.4 'A7142' | Sgt P S Tidy | Safe | See 7 June 1918 - 57 Squadron |

T/o Le Quesnoy and on landing ran into a partly filled shell hole and damaged beyond repair. The airframe serial for this DH is erroneous and was probably mis-painted on the fuselage and tail either ahead of delivery or during servicing. It will be recalled that Lieutenant Newman had been slightly injured on 16 May 1918.

| 65 Squadron | 2Lt A R Bolay | + | Vignacourt British Cemetery |
| F.1 Camel D1787 *Peking Britons No 3* | | | |

T/o Bertangles to practice flying on type but got into a flat spin from which Albert Richard Bolay was unable to recover. There are no next of kin details appended against his entry in the register, neither is his age given.

79 Squadron   Lt F I Lord   Safe
5F.1 Dolphin D3645
T/o Ste Marie Cappel for a test flight, the Dolphin having arrived with the squadron five days previously but while flying at two hundred feet the engine lost power and in the ensuing forced landing Lieutenant Lord touched down on uneven ground and before he could arrest his progress ran into a trench which damaged 'D3645' beyond repair. Including a test and ferry from Brooklands, it had flown for just three hours and thirty-five minutes.

91 Squadron   2Lt A T Wyman [USA]   Injured Chichester Cemetery
Sopwith Pup B5360
T/o Tangmere and crashed out of control; it is believed Alfred Theodore Wyman fainted; he died a few hours after the crash. A graduate of Massachusetts Institute of Technology [class of 1916], his home was at Fitchburg in Worcester County, Massachusetts.

98 Squadron   Lt R L Tilly   Safe   Unemployed list 22 February 1919: Lt
DH.9 C6108   Lt C P Harrison   Safe   See 28 May 1918 - 98 Squadron
T/o Coudekerque tasked for bombing but soon after becoming airborne a wing dropped resulting in a crash-landing. Languished, 'C6108' was struck off charge on 5 July 1918. This DH.9 arrived with the squadron while at Old Sarum and flew to France with the main body on the day of formation of the Royal Air Force. It was much favoured by the observer, Lieutenant Harrison who on the 21st of April and on the 8th of May, drove down enemy scouts out of control, that on the 8th having wounded his pilot Lieutenant C C MacDonald.

99 Squadron   Lt D A McDonald   pow
DH.9 C6137   2Lt F H Blaxhill   pow
T/o 0955 Tantonville in a formation tasked for bombing and heading for Bénestroff*in the *département du Moselle* and when last sighted was in combat with hostile machines north of Dieuze and south of the target area, and being chased down in a controlled spin from two thousand feet. I am unable to say if the crew had attacked their objective or were preparing to do so. Second Lieutenant Blaxhill's name appears under the 'Missing' banner as published in *Flight* June 20, 1918.

* Bensdorf as it was known to the Germans, and as it appears in records contemporary to operations on the Western Front.

100 Squadron   Lt D L Kirk   Evaded
FE.2b A5779   Lt W Richards   Evaded
T/o Ochey for a night bombing attack on targets at Creutzwald*in the *département du Moselle*. Subsequently, the crew crossed, by foot, into Allied lines. Accepted by the squadron on 7 April 1918, 'A5779' flew for thirty-one hours and twenty-five minutes, including testing and transit.

* Known in 1918, as Creutzwald-la-Croix, its name since 1961 has been shortened to 'Creutzwald'. With its locality on the Franco-German border, the nearby Warndt forest is managed by both countries.

203 Squadron   Captain R A Little*DSO* DSC*   +   Wavans British Cemetery
F.1 Camel D3416   *Croix de Guerre avec Palme* [Australia]
T/o Filescamp at night to intercept a reported enemy bomber. Subsequently, the wreckage of the Camel was found at Nœux-lès-Auxi just inside the border between the Pas-de-Calais and the Somme *départements*. Melbourne born Robert Alexander Little was still alive when found but died from his wounds soon after. Formerly of the Royal Naval Air Service, he was one of the most decorated airmen of the *Great* War [uniquely, all were awarded during his Royal Naval Air Service]. As a flight sub-lieutenant his first Distinguished Service Cross citation appeared in *The London Gazette* [issue 29947] on 16th February 1917; *'For conspicuous bravery in successfully attacking and bringing down hostile machines on several occasions. On 11th November 1916, he*

attacked and brought down a hostile machine in flames. On 12th December 1916, he attacked a German machine at a range of 50 yards; this machine was brought down in a nose-dive. On 20th December 1916, he dived at a hostile machine, and opened fire at 25 yards range; the observer was seen to fall down inside the machine, which went down in a spinning nose-dive. On first January 1917, he attacked an enemy scout, which turned over on its back and came down completely out of control.' This was followed on 29 June 1917, supplement 30147, by the First Bar; *'For exceptional daring and skill in aerial fighting on many occasions, of which the following are examples:- 'On the 28th April 1917, he destroyed an Aviatik; on the 29th April he shot down a hostile scout, which crashed. On the 30th April, with three other machines he went up after hostile machines and saw a big fight going on between fighter escorts and hostile aircraft. Flt-Lieut Little attacked one at fifty yards range, and brought it down out of control. A few minutes later he attacked a red scout with a larger machine than the rest. This machine was handled with great skill, but by clever manœuvring Flt-Lieut Little got into a good position and shot it down out of control.'* Supplement 30227 of 11 August 1917, carried the citation for the first of his award of the Distinguished Service Order; *'For gallantry in action and for exceptional skill and daring in aerial combats. Since the 9th of May 1917, besides having driven off numerous artillery aeroplane and damaged six hostile machines, he has destroyed six others. On the 26th June 1917, an Aviatik being seen from the aerodrome he went up to attack it. He engaged it and fired a burst at close range, and the enemy machine stalled and went down in flames.'* The First Bar to the Distinguished Service Order was promulgated on 14th September 1917, supplement 30285; *'For exceptional gallantry and skill in aerial fighting. On 16th July 1917, he observed two Aviatiks flying low over the lines. He dived on the nearest one, firing a long burst at very close range. The enemy machine dived straight away, and Flt-Lieut Little followed him closely down to 500ft, the enemy machine falling out of control.'* His headstone is inscribed thus; *'Croix De Guerre With Star"His Ever Loving Wife And Little Son Blymp Also His Living Father.'*

* Biographical notes reported on *Wikipedia* show that he was born on 19 July 1895, and on arriving in England in 1915, undertook flying instruction at his own expense. Arriving on the Western Front in 1916, he flew Sopwith Pups, Triplanes and Camels and in twelve months of operations accounted for thirty-eight enemy aircraft, all with No Squadron Royal Naval Air Service. Rested in July 1917, he returned to the Front in March 1918, joining No 3 Squadron Royal Naval Air Squadron [subsequently becoming No 203 Squadron following the merger] and shot down three more hostiles before his death, as described in the above summary. He was age twenty-two and is believed to have been the most outstanding Australian 'Ace' of the *Great War*.

209 Squadron   Captain C N Jones   Safe
F.1 Camel B3897
T/o Bertangles for practice flying and on return to the airfield, and committed to landing, collided with a vehicle described as a *'French wagon'*.

Note. As will have been observed, this day witnessed the deaths of two decorated flight commanders.

Monday-Tuesday 27-28 May 1918
98 Squadron   Lt A C Tilly   Safe
DH.9 C1180   Lt C P Harrison   Safe
T/o Coudekerque for bombing operations only to crash, heavily, into a field of standing corn that adjoined the airfield and colliding with a cart in the process; wrecked. This was the third crash in the month of May featuring Lieutenant Harrison.

Tuesday 28 May 1918
2 Squadron   Lt C E Preece   Safe
FK.8 C8582   Lt H S Woodman   Safe
T/o Hesdigneul for photographic reconnaissance and while over Auchy*was hit by shrapnel from anti-aircraft fire which caused such extensive damage to the airframe that it was struck off charge on 25 June 1918. The death on 18 February 1919, of Charles Evered Preece will be summarised in Volume 2.

* Probably Auchy-les-Mines in the Pas-de-Calais.

| 2 Squadron | Lt L Daly | | Safe | See 17 June 1918 - 2 Squadron |
| FK.8 C8600 | 2Lt F S E McRae | | Safe | |

T/o Hesdigneul tasked to observe artillery but returned early with a failing engine and on landing 'C8600' ran into a ditch and damaged to the extent that repairs were not sanctioned. Its service life, which began at the Aeroplane Acceptance Park at Newcastle was relatively brief, arriving with the squadron from No 1 Air Issues on the 7th of May 1918, in total 'C8600' flew for twenty-seven hours and ten minutes.

| 2 Squadron AusFC | Lt L J Primrose AusFC | | Safe | See 4 June 1918 - 2 Squadron AusFC |
| SE.5a B194 | | | | |

T/o Fouquerolles tasked for operations in the vicinity of Albert only to crash-land with air pressure failure; salvaged, but written off two days later as not worth the cost of repair. Leslie John Primrose had been obliged to make an emergency landing near Amiens on the 4th of April 1918, when the oil tank on his SE.5a was shot through [see my summary for that date].

| 8 Squadron | Lt R Grice | | Safe | |
| FK.8 C8586 | 2Lt S H Smith | | Safe | |

T/o Auxi-le-Château carrying bombs and was so badly shot about over Fricourt [Somme] by enemy aircraft that it was struck off charge on 13 June 1918.

| 12 Squadron | 2Lt R W Locheed | + | Bac-du-Sud British Cemetery, Bailleulval |
| RE.8 B832 | [Canada] | | |

T/o Soncamp authorised to practice landings but while flying at a thousand feet appeared to lose control and entering a slow spiral he failed to recover before hitting the ground roughly two km from the airfield. According to the aircraft's movements record 'B832' had already undergone a rebuilt and was tested on 29 January 1918 by E H Lawford. Ferried to France, it was taken on charge by the squadron on 22 March 1918. Its flying hours are recorded as one hundred and thirty-one and forty minutes which suggests this includes its rebuild flying.

| 15 Squadron | Lt F C U Dymant | | Safe | Unemployed list 13 June 1919: Lt |
| RE.8 B7713 | Sgt R Morgan | | Safe | |

T/o Vert Galand for a test flight during which the crew came down, in a forced landing, near Orville following an engine fire. It would appear that their aircraft continued to burn for it was written off that same day without any attempts to salvage; seventy-three flying hours in total, including testing and ferrying from Coventry and usage by the squadron since 27 March 1918. It was the tenth aircraft lost from the squadron since the 1st of April, and the first while in the process of non-operational duties.

| 20 Squadron | Lt R G Bennett | + | Arras Flying Services Memorial |
| Bristol F.2b C4763 | Lt G C T Salter MC | + | Arras Flying Services Memorial |

T/o Boisdinghem for an offensive patrol and was last seen near Neuf-Berquin [Nord]. Formerly of the East Yorkshire Regiment and Machine-gun Corps, Geoffrey George Taylor Salter's Military Cross was *gazetted* 20th June 1917, in the Edinburgh edition, issue 13105; *'For conspicuous gallantry and devotion to duty. He handled his Tank with the greatest skill and gallantry, and although under heavy fire, he cleared a trench of the enemy, which he handed over to the infantry.'*

| 23 Squadron | Lt H M Sinclair | | Safe | See 18 June 1918 - 23 Squadron |
| 5F.1 Dolphin C3914 | | | | |

T/o Bertangles for a practice flight and landing ran into Dolphin C3873. Salvaged, 'C3914' was declared not worth repairing on 9 June 1918.

23 Squadron   5F.1 Dolphin C3873   Struck by the Dolphin summarised above and damaged beyond repair. Struck off charge 30 May 1918, with thirty-nine hours and forty-three minutes of flying recorded. First adopted by No 87 Squadron, 'C3873' arrived with the squadron on 27 April 1918.

| 41 Squadron | Lt R S Milani | | pow | |
| SE.5a B8394 | | | | |

T/o Estrée Blanche for an offensive patrol and when last sighted by others in the patrol Lieutenant Milani was fighting with two enemy aircraft over Fresnes-lès-Montauban in the Pas-de-Calais. Wounded, Lieutenant Milani was repatriated on the 14th of December 1918. Untraced via *The London Gazette,* his name and initials are confirmed in *Flight* August 15, 1918, where his status as a prisoner of war is confirmed.

54 Squadron	Lt R C Crowden	Safe	See 18 June 1918 - 54 Squadron
F.1 Camel B7293			

T/o Caffiers with other squadron pilots to practice the art of flying as a formation but damaged beyond repair after running onto uneven ground.

64 Squadron	2Lt W P Southall	+	Arras Flying Services Memorial
SE.5a C6455			

T/o Izel-lès-Hameau for an offensive patrol and was last seen by other pilots in the patrol going down, on fire, near Locon in the Pas-de-Calais some eight km north of Béthune.

65 Squadron	Lt J A Sykes	Safe	See 16 June 1918 - 65 Squadron
F.1 Camel C8278			

T/o Bertangles and headed for Fienvillers to view a French machine but on arrival crashed and was damaged beyond repair. Delivered to No 4 Aeroplane Acceptance Park Lincoln by 4 March 1918, and accepted by the squadron on the 24th, 'C8278' had an extremely busy two months of operational service during which it shot down, or shared in the destruction of fourteen hostile machines, many being two-seater reconnaissance types. Thirteen of the fourteen are credited to Captain P J Gilmour, holder of the Military Cross and First Bar. With such active flying it is not surprising that it logged a total of one hundred and four hours and fifty minutes flying.

65 Squadron	2Lt W B Craib	+	Arras Flying Services Memorial
F.1 Camel C8280			

T/o Bertangles for an offensive patrol and when last sighted at around 0930 was in a steep dive over the Somme west of Lamotte.*The "movements records" for 'C8280' are similar to that for 'C8278' summarised above, arriving at Bertangles on the 27th of March. Favoured by Lieutenant A A Leitch [see 19 May 1918]. It accounted for two hostile machines; a Pfalz DIII on the 9th of May and a Fokker DrI on the 15th. In total 'C8280' flew for ninety-one hours and forty-five minutes.

* Some documents quote 'La Motte' and others 'Lamotte'; if the latter is correct, then it might well be what is known since 1974 as Lamotte-Warfusée some twenty-six km east of Amiens.

84 Squadron	Captain A F W Beaumont	Safe
SE.5a C1772	Proctor [South Africa]	

T/o Bertangles heading for operations over Villers-Bretonneux and it was whilst so engaged that anti-aircraft fire shot away the propeller of his aircraft. A successful forced landing was accomplished near Allonville [Somme]. For detailed notes concerning Captain Beaumont Proctor, please refer to my asterisk note appended to the summary for 'B597' of No 1 Squadron. 'C1772' had an eventful eight weeks or so of active service; on squadron strength since the last day of March it accounted for, or shared in the destruction, of no less than thirteen enemy aircraft, ten of which were credited, or in part, to Captain Beaumont Proctor.

85 Squadron	Lt E C Brown	Safe
SE.5a C1896		

T/o No 1 Air Issues and on arrival at Petite Synthe crash-landed and was damaged beyond repair. Including a test at Brooklands and ferry to France, 'C1896' flew for just one hour and thirty-five minutes.

85 Squadron	Captain C B A Baker	Safe
SE.5a C6500		

T/o Petite Synthe for practice firing; crashed on return to the airfield. Initially intended for No 92 Squadron at Tangmere, 'C6500' arrived at Petite Synthe on 15 May 1918. In total, it flew for seven hours and ten minutes.

87 Squadron   Lt C H Cahill   Injured Unemployed list 9 March 1920: Lt
5F.1 Dolphin C4165

T/o Estrée-lès-Crecy heading, with other pilots, for Hesdin for inspection by a general. *En route* the engine failed and Lieutenant Cahill was slightly injured when forced landing near Le Quesnoy airfield. I am confident that Charles Howard Cahill, initially commissioned to the General List of the Royal Flying Corps [*gazetted* 5th September 1917, supplement 30270], returned to Royal Air Force within the same year as his discharge and was granted a short service commission on 15 October in the rank of flying officer [*gazetted* 26 October 1920, 32098] and though his early service is yet to be traced, he was attached to No 1 Squadron [Snipe] at Hinaidi with effect from 5 December 1923, and a year later joining No 70 Squadron [Vernon], also based at Hinaidi and still ranked flying officer. Returning to the United Kingdom, and now promoted flight lieutenant, he joined the Marine Aircraft Experimental Establishment at Felixstowe on 4 January 1927 [a year previously, he was appointed to a permanent commission on New Year's Day, promulgated 9 February 1926, issue 33131]. It would seem Flight Lieutenant Cahill spent several years at Felixstowe, possibly until 21 June 1934, when he was attached to No XV Squadron [Hart] at Abingdon. Meanwhile, he had been awarded the Air Force Cross [*gazetted* 2 January 1933, supplement 33898], this being followed seven years later by the Distinguished Flying Cross, published in issue 34831 of the 16th of April 1940. It is known that postwar he received a commission in the Royal Air Force Volunteer Reserve, Training Branch.

87 Squadron   Lt N Sales   Safe   See 30 June 1918 - 87 Squadron
5F.1 Dolphin C4174

T/o Estrée-lès-Crecy and on landing a wheel dropped into a hole, turning the Dolphin on to its back; damaged beyond repair.

87 Squadron   Lt D J Allan   Safe   See 15 June 1918 - 87 Squadron
5F.1 Dolphin C4177

T/o Estrée-les-Crecy and on landing ran in to long grass and turned over; damaged beyond repair. The accident to 'C4177' and 'C4174' occurred at Hesdin.

98 Squadron   Lt F H Reilly [Canada]   Injured Stalhille Churchyard
DH.9 B7674   Lt R McK Hall [Canada]   +   Stalhille Churchyard

T/o 0400 Coudekerque for a raid on targets near Bruges; came under attack from two enemy scouts and sent down near the village of Stalhille [West-Vlaanderen] which lies just to the east of Oostende and west of the target area. Frederick Holmes Reilly who died soon after the crash from his wounds and Russell McKay Hall of the Canadian Infantry [Regimental Depot Quebec] attached to No 98 Squadron are the sole *Great War* burials in the churchyard.

100 Squadron   2Lt V R Brown   pow
FE.2b B448   Private A Johnson   pow

T/o Ochey having received instructions for a bombing raid on targets at Metz. From Farnborough to France by air, 'B448' was received from No 2 Air Issues on 9 January 1918. Including makers testing, ferry and squadron usage, 'B448' logged seventy-six hours and twenty minutes flying.

208 Squadron   Lt W E Holland   Safe   Unemployed list 15 October 1919: Lt
F.1 Camel B5621

T/o Serny for flying practice but having flown away from the vicinity of the airfield Lieutenant Holland realised he was 'lost' and in making a forced landing at Estrée*turned over. This ended the flying days for 'B5621' which had had a relatively long existence since first being issued to No 65 Squadron on 22 January 1918 [originally, 'B5621' had been earmarked for No 80 Squadron]. On the 30th of that month, with Major G P Howe [he was not the squadron's commander but may have been attached as a supernumerary] at the controls, the Camel was driven down over the Ypres Salient between Poelkapelle and Westrozebeke in what was now a wasteland northeast of Ypres. Damage, if any, must have been slight for it was flying again by 12th February and four days later Lieutenant E C Eaton [see my summary for 26 June 1918] sent down an Albatros over the Salient between Moorslede and Dadeizele, villages east-northeast of Ypres. Shortly after this success, it was sent for an overhaul during which it underwent an engine change and following testing was issued to No 208 Squadron on the 16th of May. In total, 'B5621' flew for seventy hours and twenty-five minutes.

* Possibly 'Estrée-Blanche' in the Pas-de-Calais, though as observant readers will be aware there were airfields at Estrée-en-Chaussée and Estrées-lès-Crecy, both in the Somme *département* with the latter often being recorded as 'Estrée-lès-Crecy'.

| 210 Squadron | Lt D M McGregor* | Safe |
| F.1 Camel B3940 | | |

T/o St Omer for a practice flight but as the Camel lifted into the air so the port wheel came off. Returning to the airfield Lieutenant McGregor tried to keep his aircraft balanced as he touched down but was unable to prevent it from turning over; damaged beyond repair.

* By July 1918, Lieutenant Donald Mallock McGregor had returned to the United Kingdom and was serving with No 45 Training Depot Station at North Cerney in Gloucestershire where he lost his life on 16 July 1918; he is buried Edinburgh [Grange] Cemetery.

| 217 Squadron | Lt Col P F M Fellowes DSO | pow |
| DH.4 A8065 | Sgt F H Pritchard | pow |

T/o 0235 Bergues for a raid on the lock gate at Zeebrugge during which the DH was driven down into the North Sea from where the crew were picked up by a destroyer, Lieutenant-Colonel Fellowes requiring treatment for his wounds. Earlier in the month 'A8065' had attacked enemy shipping on two occasions, each time when crewed by Lieutenant G B Coward and Private S F Briggs. Peregrine Forbes Morant Fellowes, meanwhile, was born two days before Christmas 1883 in St Kilda in the State of Victoria, Australia of English parents [his father had been sent to Australia in connection with organisation of the Australian army]. In his youth Peregrine became a naval cadet at the Britannia Naval College Dartmouth and from where he graduated. However, he resigned his commission on 26 October 1910, and after returning to military service in 1914, he applied for flying training and, subsequently, achieved his Aviators' Certificate No 1696 from The Royal Aero Club of the United Kingdom on the 5th of September 1915, after qualifying at Royal Naval Air Station Chingford on Maurice Farman Biplanes. A year to the day before the formation of the Royal Air Force, he took over command on No 2 Squadron Royal Naval Air Service but it was in the spring of 1918, that he came to prominence following the now historic raid by the Royal Navy on the Mole at Zeebrugge on 23 April 1918. For this, and further operations at Oostende, he is mentioned in the official despatch published in the Second Supplement to *The London Gazette* issue 31189 published on 18 February 1919. Postwar, he was granted a permanent commission in the rank of lieutenant-colonel on 1 August 1919 [*gazetted* in issue 31189 of that date] after which his service was mainly devoted to Staff Duties. His final appointment was Air Officer Commanding No 23 Group during which he was responsible for organising the 1933 Everest Air Expedition. In retirement he lived at Pietermauritzberg in South Africa from where his death was announced on 12 June 1955.

Note. In preparing this summary I acknowledge material published in various issues of *Flight* and the most informative RAF Commands - A History of RAF Organisation website.

Wednesday 29 May 1918

| 1 Squadron | Lt K Laing | Safe |
| SE.5a C1853 | | |

T/o Clairmarais South for an offensive patrol during which Lieutenant Laing force-landed at map reference 27W1a55 following total engine failure in the aftermath a connecting rod breakage. Accepted by the squadron on 9 May 1918, 'C1853' flew for twenty-six hours and forty-nine minutes in total.

| 2 Squadron AusFC | Lt Hammond | Safe |
| SE.5a D3514 | | |

T/o Fouquerolles for a practice flight during which Lieutenant Hammond was obliged to force-land, on the aerodrome, owing to a malfunctioning carburettor.

6 Squadron	Lt Holt	Safe
RE.8 B8874	Lt Hemery	Safe

T/o Lt Crotoy having been briefed to carry out photographic reconnaissance but within seconds of becoming airborne engine failure occurred and the crew flew into telegraph wires and crashed. Taken to No 2 Advanced Salvage Dump 'B8874' was struck off charge on 112 June 1918. Although the manner in which this aircraft was written off was not particularly remarkable, its loss deserves a special mention in that as far as I can tell this was the squadron's first since the formation of the Royal Air Force two months previously. As a Corps reconnaissance squadron it arrived on the Western Front as early as 7 October 1914, and though undoubtedly suffering losses since then, a trouble free run of eight weeks against the background of recent operations is worthy of comment.

8 Squadron	Lt H N Young*	Safe	See 8 July 1918 - 8 Squadron
FK.8 B3382	2Lt L W Norman	Safe	Unemployed list 11 April 1919: 2Lt

T/o Auxi-le-Château tasked for bombing, returning to base with the front longeron shot through by anti-aircraft fire. Although salvaged, it is thought the flying days were over for 'B3382' which up to this point amounted to one hundred and eight hours and twenty-five minutes.

* Although I cannot be absolutely certain, I strongly suspect that Lieutenant Young remained in the postwar air force and was granted a short service commission on 19 October 1919 [*gazetted* 24 October 1919, issue 31616]. It is noted from the entry that he held the Distinguished Flying Cross. Further searches identity a Flying Officer H N Young as losing his life on 13 July 1921, in the service of No 12 Squadron, and with a First Bar to his award, plus a mention in a despatch. He is buried in Shropshire at Prees [St Chad] Churchyard. My suspicions are, however, supported by a post submitted on 22 February 2008, by 'Dolphin''Major General' in response to a question in respect of Flying Officer Young put to members of the Great War Forum website by Sergeant-Major Kevin Mears. I hope to elaborate further in the second volume.

8 Squadron	Lt T G Jefferies	Safe
FK.8 C8584	Corporal Bolton	Safe

T/o Auxi-le-Château and flew to Conteville where a machine [unidentified] had force-landed. Taking off to return to base Lieutenant Jefferies ran into a hole and as a consequence the undercarriage collapsed. Salvaged, the airframe was struck off charge on 16 June 1918. Lieutenant Jefferies was formerly of the Royal Field Artillery and postwar he returned to army duties; however, his commission was relinquished on the 1st of April 1920, retaining his rank of lieutenant. It is noted that he had been awarded the Distinguished Flying Cross.

19 Squadron	Lt R E White	Safe
5F.1 Dolphin C3820		

T/o Savy where on return from a practice flight the Dolphin ran into deep ruts which effectively damaged the airframe beyond repair. On squadron establishment since 29 December 1917, 'C3820' flew for a total of ninety-nine hours and four minutes.

20 Squadron	Lt T C Trail	Injured	
Bristol F.2b C856	2Lt P G Jones	Safe	See 2 July 1918 - 20 Squadron

T/o Boisdinghem for operations during which a longeron was shot through and the tail adjustment mechanism shot away. On return to Boisdinghem Lieutenant Trail was unable to control his landing and crashed near the airfield. His injuries were not too serious.

29 Squadron	Lt C G Ross	Safe
SE.5a D5981		

T/o St Omer for operations. On return landed with drift and crashed out of control. On squadron strength since the 15th of the month, 'D5981' flew a total of twenty-nine hours and twenty-five minutes, including testing and transit to France.

42 Squadron	2Lt F V Sheard	Injured	Unemployed list 29 June 1919: Lt
RE.8 B876	Lt M C Sexton	Injured	Unemployed list 11 April 1919: Lt

T/o Rély with instructions to proceed to the Merville area and here to carry out photographic reconnaissance. While doing so the crew attracted the attention of hostile aircraft and, subsequently, they force-landed [both being wounded] at Treizennes airfield. Both officers are named in *Flight* June 20 1918, under the heading 'Wounded', Lieutenant Sexton being reported as formerly of the King's Liverpool Regiment.

55 Squadron	2Lt A C Hill	Safe
DH.4 A7560	Sgt A Boocock	Safe See 26 June 1918 - 55 Squadron

T/o Tantonville ordered for bombing operations and crashed out of control. Flown to France from Hendon and issued to the squadron on 13 August 1917, 'A7650' had undergone a series of repairs or overhauls for un-specified reasons and following this latest mishap languished until 14 July when it was declared not worth repairing. In just on a year of service it had flown for a total of one hundred and seventeen hours and twenty-five minutes.

79 Squadron	Lt F W Gillet [USA]	Safe Unemployed list 7 March 1919: Lt DFC
5F.1 Dolphin C3830		

T/o Ste Marie Cappel with orders to carry out a line patrol. On return Lieutenant Gillett's*approach was rather slow and as a consequence he lost control at twenty feet, sideslipping to the ground.

* Biographical notes on *Wikipedia* state that American born Francis Warrington Gillet was the highest scoring Sopwith Dolphin pilot in the *Great War* with twenty aerial victories to his credit. It is also stated that on promotion to captain on 14 October 1918, he briefly held command of No 79 Squadron, but this is not supported by John Rawlings excellent *Fighter Squadrons of the RAF and their Aircraft.* Born 28 November 1895 in Baltimore, Mary-land, Francis Gillet [he is referred to as 'Gillett' in Royal Air Force documents] died at the age of 74 in Baltimore on the 21st of December 1969. To his many friends he was known as 'Razors'.

100 Squadron	2Lt F R Johnson	Safe
FE.2b A8950		

T/o Ochey for a practice flight and on return, and landing, a strong gust of wind tipped 'A8950' onto its starboard wing. Salvaged, it languished for a month before being struck off charge on 1 July 1918. The "movements record" for 'A8950' indicates allotment at Farnborough on 23 April 1917, and to No 25 Squadron at Auchel two days later. By 10 July it appears to be undergoing major overhaul before being issued to No 100 Squadron on the 7th of March, on which date the term 'pom pom' has been added to the "record". Its total hours of flying are shown as one hundred and seventy eight and one minute.

123 Squadron	2Lt J E Machin	+ Biddulph [St Lawrence] Churchyard
DH.9 D2807		

T/o Duxford for continuation training but following loss of engine power, stalled, crashed and burst into flames. One of the many ancestry websites features John Egbert Machin with photographs showing him standing along-side a BE.2e and with his fellow trainee pilots. His headstone carries the words; *'He Gave His Life For England, But His Soul To God. Gone But Not Forgotten.'*

211 Squadron	2Lt E T M Routledge	Safe See 16 June 1918 - 211 Squadron
DH.9 D5624	Corporal H Lindsay	Safe

T/o Petite Synthe for bombing operations and on return Lieutenant Routledge noticed two aircraft stationary on the landing area. Electing to land cross-wind 'D5624' swung and ended up on its nose and partially balanced by the starboard wing. Salvaged, it languished until 5 July 1918, when it was struck off charge.

Thursday 30 May 1918

3 Squadron	Lt C P Macklin [USA]	+ Arras Flying Services Memorial
F.1 Camel D6483		

T/o Valheureux with other pilots briefed to escort RE.8s from No 59 Squadron up from Vert Galand. Sighted by enemy scouts, the formation came under attack from at least six hostile aircraft and nineteen year old Charles Purcell Macklin went down, streaming flames, to crash east of Achiet-le-Petit, a commune in the Pas-de-Calais. His parents address is recorded as The Edgewater Beach Hotel in Chicago.

4 Squadron AusFC   Lt E C Crosse   Safe
F.1 Camel D1846
T/o Clairmarais for an offensive patrol carrying bombs. Force-landed, owing to engine failure, and ran into a trench as map reference 27U1A55.

8 Squadron   2Lt C F Putwaine   Safe
FK.8 B5771   2Lt W L Norman   Safe
T/o Auxi-le-Château tasked for bombing damaging the undercarriage; the crew continued with their mission but on return 'B5771' crash-landed and was damaged beyond repair. The engine, however, was salvaged but the rest of the airframe was struck off charge on 14 June 1918, with thirty-one hours and fifteen minutes recorded flying time. Initially issued to No 82 Squadron on 31 March 1918, it was damaged while landing from a line patrol on the 4th of April [Second Lieutenant N S MacGregor and Second Lieutenant C E E Boult] at which point it had logged fifteen hours and forty-five minutes. Repaired, it arrived at Auxi-le-Château on 16 May.

9 Squadron   Lt L M Hill   Injured
RE.8 B5100   2Lt T M Haslett   Injured
T/o Calais authorised for a practice flight and wrecked, owing to an error of judgement, while landing. On charge from 1 Air Issues on 15 November 1917, 'B5100' flew for a very creditable one hundred and sixteen hours and thirty-five minutes. Formerly of the Royal Field Artillery, Second Lieutenant Haslett returned to army duties post-war and served until 1 April 1920, when he relinquished his commission, retaining the rank of lieutenant [supplement 32013 of the *Gazette* published on 10 August 1920].

10 Squadron   Lt L H Short   Injured Unemployed list 1 September 1919: F/O MC
FK.8 C8522   2Lt A C Clinton   Injured Unemployed list 7 November 1919: Lt
T/o Droglandt briefed for artillery observation duties in the course of which their aircraft came under anti-aircraft fire, a burst from one shell completely shredding the lower starboard wing and wounding both officers. Exerting ever ounce of his piloting skill Lieutenant Short managed to force-land at map reference 28G6c88. Salvaged, the airframe was struck off charge on 3 June 1918, with fifty-six hours and twenty minutes flying time recorded. Regarding Second Lieutenant Clinton, I believe he returned to the service in the rank of flying officer on being granted a short service commission on 15 August 1920, as promulgated in issue 32032 of 27 August 1920. If my assumption is correct, then he remained in the Reserve of Air Force Officers until 10 February 1954, when his commission was relinquished under the provisions of the Navy, Army and Air Force Reserves Act 1954.

18 Squadron   2Lt J W Mellish   Safe
DH.4 A7498   Lt B J Blackett   Safe   Unemployed list 4 April 1919: Lt
T/o Serny tasked for bombing and on return Second Lieutenant Mellish landed with a force so heavy that he effectively ended the flying days of 'A7498' which was struck off charge on 3 June 1918. Interestingly, this seems to be the only entry in *The DH.4/DH.9 File* for this officer.

29 Squadron   Lt D Watt   Injured
SE.5a B8275
T/o St Omer for a practice flight but soon after leaving the airfield the engine failed and in the ensuing crash-landing 'B8275' was damaged beyond repair. Although received No 1 Aeroplane Acceptance Park Coventry by the 7th December 1917, it seems this aircraft was held in storage until flown to France on 27 May and issued two days later to No 29 Squadron.

32 Squadron   Lt E McD Jarvis   Safe   See 6 June 1918 - 32 Squadron
SE.5a B166
T/o Beauvois for an offensive patrol and crashed in a forced landing at Estrée Blanche occasioned by petrol feed problems.

40 Squadron   2Lt G D V Russell   Safe
SE.5a B178

T/o 1430 Buary for a practice flight [Second Lieutenant Russell had only recently arrived with the squadron] but clipped the top of a chimney, crashed and went up in flames, a badly shocked but otherwise uninjured pilot escaped. Under the heading 'Flying Branch' [*The London Gazette* 21 May 1918, issue 30694], Second Lieutenant Russell is recorded as being promoted to his rank on the 2nd of April 1918, his status, along with fellow officers, switching from administration to pilots qualified on aeroplanes and seaplanes. Postwar, I believe he joined the East Lancashire Regiment and continued to serve with the regiment until an entry in *The London Gazette* of 8 February 1949, supplement 38533, reports; *'Major G D V Russell having exceeded the age limit for retirement is placed on ret. pay, 7th Feb, 1949, and is granted the hon. rank of Lt-Col.'*

| 43 Squadron | Lt P T Bruce | + | Arras Flying Services Memorial |
| F.1 Camel D1793 | | | |

T/o 1340 Avesnes-le-Comte for an offensive patrol and was last seen, in combat, in the vicinity of Flers *[sic]*. Nineteen years of age, Philip Thomson Bruce began his military service in the Territorial Forces and was commissioned to the 10th Battalion The King's Liverpool Regiment on 27 June 1917 [*gazetted* 11 July 1917, supplement 30178] and, as recorded in his entry on the Commonwealth War Graves Commission website, had served previously with No 87 Squadron.

| 46 Squadron | Lt F H Cave | Safe | Unemployed list 20 June 1919: Lt |
| F.1 Camel C6729 | | | |

T/o Lièttres for an offensive patrol carrying bombs. Over the battle lines the Camel's engine failed and Lieutenant Cave turned for home and may well have landed safely but it seems he misjudged his approach and crash-landed. Salvaged, 'C6729' was struck off charge on 3 June 1918.

| 46 Squadron | Lt G R Priestley | Injured | Unemployed list 24 May 1919: Lt |
| F.1 Camel D6601 | | | |

T/o Lièttres for an offensive patrol but before becoming airborne ran at high speed into standing corn and grass, turning over as a result and leaving Lieutenant Priestley seriously injured.

| 48 Squadron | 2Lt W B Yuille [Canada] | + | Longueau British Cemetery |
| Bristol F.2b C871 | 2Lt W D Davidson | + | Longueau British Cemetery |

T/o Bertangles for an offensive patrol to St Moreuil and was seen to go down, burning. William Beresford Yuille's headstone carries the words; *'God Shall Wipe Away All Tears From Our Eyes'*. William's observer was nineteen years of age.

| 49 Squadron | Lt R H B Stevens | + | St Riquier British Cemetery |
| DH.9 D462 | Private L C Norman | + | St Riquier British Cemetery |

T/o Conteville for a bombing raid on Roziers *[sic]*, which the crew accomplished, and it was on the return leg and flying at twelve thousand feet that the DH suffered structural failure, probably as a result of anti-aircraft fire. Intended for No 218 Squadron, 'D462' was diverted to the squadron on 26 May 1918. Richard Henry Barkwood Stevens was posted to the squadron earlier in the month on the 7th, Leonard Charles Norman was attached on the 25th of April 1918.

| 51 Squadron | 2Lt J R W Farfan | Injured | |
| FE.2b A5764 | Mechanic L Cohen | Injured | |

T/o Marham and crashed while in the process of making a slow turn. Commanded by Major H Wyllie the squadron saw little in the way of activity as a Home Defence squadron.

| 52 Squadron | Lt H P Illsley [Canada] | Safe | |
| RE.8 A3447 | 2Lt J W Benton | Injured | Terlincthun British Cemetery, Wimille |

T/o Trecon tasked for a situation patrol over the lines in the course of which John Walter Benton was badly wounded. Realising the serious situation in which his observer was in, Lieutenant Illsley [seconded from the Quebec Regiment] force-landed close to the field dressing station at Chambrecy and in doing so had the misfortune to damage the RE.8 which, subsequently, had to be abandoned. Sadly, it was all to no avail for John Benton succumbed to his wounds the next day. 'A3447' had until this point led an extensive operational life commencing on 5 Jun 1917, when it was issued to No 21 Squadron at La Lovie; however, eight days later it was given up to No 4 Squadron at Abeele and served with the squadron until 20 March 1918, on which date a casualty report filed in AIR 1/853 states *'time expired only fuselage and tailplane remain.'* It had flown for an impressive total of three hundred and fifteen hours and fifty minutes. For reasons known only to the authorities, 'A3447' was sent to No 1 Advanced Salvage Dump where work was put in hand to return the RE.8 to flying standards and this being achieved it was issued to No 52 Squadron, then operating from Cramaille, on 27 May. Including test flying, transiting between airfields and its final operational sortie its final total came to three hundred and twenty-two hours and five minutes. To conclude this summary, Lieutenant Illsley's secondment ceased on the 13th of March 1919.

60 Squadron	Lt J Headlam	+	St Hilaire Cemetery extension, Frevent
SE.5a C5381			

T/o Boffles to practice firing at targets laid out on the ground. It would seem nineteen year old John Headlam overstressed his aircraft for eyewitnesses report seeing the wings fold up, sending it hurtling to the ground. The inscription on his headstone reads; *'Blessed Are The Pure In Heart For They Shall See God.'*

60 Squadron	Lt K P Campbell [Canada]	Safe	See 1 June 1918 - 60 Squadron
SE.5a D328			

T/o Boffles for an offensive patrol during which the air pressure mechanism failed and the propeller ceased to turn. Crashed while attempting to land at Vert Galand airfield.

70 Squadron	Lt W A Scott [Canada]	pow
F.1 Camel D6640		

T/o 1110 Ramaisnil for an offensive patrol and was last sighted by other pilots in the patrol east of Albert. Arriving in France from No 3 Aeroplane Acceptance Park Norwich, 'D6640' was issued to the squadron as recently as 14th May. Confirmation of his status as a prisoner of war, Lieutenant Scott's name is reported in *Flight* June 27, 1918, where it is noted he was late of the Canadian Forestry Corps. On the same page reporting the Roll of Honour, *Flight* includes the following interesting snippet: *'The first detachment of American airmen last week left Rome for the Italian front, where they at once went into action. These airmen - all volunteers - received their instruction in flying in Italian aviation schools. They were accompanied by Mr La Guardia, of the United States Congress, and on their departure were greeted by Signor Chiesa the Commissioner for Aviation.'*

82 Squadron	Lt H F Flowers [Canada]	Injured	See 14 October 1918 - 82 Squadron
FK.8 C8554	Lt S G Dyson	Injured	Vignacourt British Cemetery

T/o Agenvilliers and headed for targets at Bonnay [possibly the commune of Bonnay in the *département du Saône-et-Loire*] but when eight Fokker Triplanes swooped down the formation split up and with both officers wounded a forced landing was made. Stanley Gilbert Dyson died on the 1st of June 1918; his widowed mother requesting, and being granted, the following poignant inscription for his headstone; *'My son, My Son.'*

85 Squadron	Captain E L Benbow MC	+	Duhallow ADS*Cemetery
SE.5a C1862			

T/o 1855 Petite Synthe to search for a reported enemy aircraft; failed to return. Under the heading 'Special Reserve of Officers', Edwin Louis Benbow was commissioned as a second lieutenant to the Royal Field Artillery on 7 October 1914 [*gazetted* 6 October 1914, issue 28926]. The award of the Military Cross was promulgated on 13 February 1917 [by which time he had transferred to the Royal Flying Corps] supplement 29940; *'For conspicuous gallantry in action. He has on several occasions displayed great courage and skill, and has destroyed four enemy machines under difficult conditions.'* Born at Abbotsbury in Dorset, his parents subsequently moved to Italy. Edwin's headstone bears the inscription; *'A Chevalier Sans Reproche'* [A Knight beyond reproach]. His death was first since the squadron arrived in France and the first since operating Camels in lieu of the Dolphins which had been used at Hounslow while working up for deployment during which, and since the 1st of April 1918, had resulted in one fatality as my summary for 8 April reports.

85 Squadron	Lt H E Thomson	Safe
SE.5a C6485		

T/o Petite Synthe for an offensive patrol during which 'C6485' lost engine power and in the forced landing five km from the airfield came down on uneven ground and was damaged beyond repair. On charge from 15 May 1918, including test and ferrying 'C6485' flew for just ten hours and fifty minutes.

98 Squadron	Lt L W Strugnell MM	Safe	See 16 June 1918 - 98 Squadron
DH.9 C1205	Sgt C Lomax	Safe	See 16 June 1918 - 98 Squadron

T/o Coudekerque for a bombing operation and on return to the airfield, and landing, was obliged to swerve violently in order to a avoid a collision with a parked Handley Page aircraft. In doing so the DH turned over and was damaged beyond repair. Twenty-five year old Leonard William Strugnell from Clapham Junction began his service life in the ranks of the London Regiment and as a corporal was awarded the Military Medal [*gazetted* in the supplement to *The London Gazette* of 16 February 1917, issue 29953]. Commissioned as a temporary second lieutenant he was attached to the Middlesex Regiment on 26 September 1917 [issue 30330 of 9th October 1917] and, subsequently, transferred to the Royal Air Force by 22 April 1918 [*gazetted* 24 May 1918, issue 30702].

98 Squadron	Lt W S Eason	Safe	Commission relinquished 13 July 1918, on
DH.9 C6238			ceasing to be employed: Lt

T/o Coudekerque for a practice flight and on return, and landing, one of the wheels became jammed in a rut which caused such damage that the airframe was struck off charge on 5 July 1918. Although I cannot be certain, I believe Lieutenant Eason may well have transferred from the army and the above entry may reflect his return to army duties.

100 Squadron	2Lt G H Box	Safe
FE.2b A5580	Lt R K Inches	Safe

T/o Ochey tasked for a night raid but while still in the process of taxying their aircraft ran into a rut and lost its undercarriage. The resultant damage to the rest of the airframe was such that it was consigned for scrap having logged one hundred and fourteen hours and thirty-three minutes flying.

120 Squadron	2Lt V C Lashford	+	Cardiff [Cathays] Cemetery
RE.8 C2393			

T/o Cramlington for his first solo on type but got into a nosedive from which he failed to recover.

Friday 31 May 1918
During the day No 38 Squadron FE.2b arrived at Capelle as a night bomber squadron having previously operated as a Home Defence squadron countering Zeppelin raids over the Midlands.

2 Squadron	Lt F J Collison	Safe	
FK.8 C3583	2Lt W S Melvin	Safe	See 23 August 1918 - 2 Squadron

Punjab No 22 Simla Hills

T/o Hesdigneul to practice procedures for a contact patrol during which the top petrol tank ran dry near Bouvigny*and the FK.8 was damaged beyond repair in the forced landing at map reference 44bQ22b. On squadron charge since 19 February 1918, 'C3583' had achieved, in total, one hundred and sixty-three hours and twenty-five minutes flying.

* Probably Bouvigny-Boyeffles in the Pas-de-Calais. Once a mining village, it is now surrounded by woods and farmland.

4 Squadron AusFC	Lt A D Pate	Injured
F.1 Camel D1959		

T/o Clairmarais for an offensive patrol but swung out of control and crashed into trees bordering the airfield. Lieutenant Pate was no stranger to 'D1959' for in his hands he shot down two enemy aircraft, the first on the 20th of May and the second on the 22nd, both during the course of early morning patrols. His name is mentioned in F M Cutlack's book *The Australian Flying Corps in the Western and Eastern Theatres of war 1914-1918*.

| 18 Squadron | Lt G Leitch | Safe |
| DH.4 A7810 | Captain D Gale | Safe |

T/o Serny tasked for photography but was obliged to force-land in a cornfield southwest of Doullens [Somme] but when attempting to take off and return to base, failed to clear a hedge and wrecked in the ensuing crash.

| 18 Squadron | 2Lt J Waugh | Safe | See 20 April 1918 - 18 Squadron |
| DH.4 A7990 | 2Lt E Walker | Safe | |

T/o Serny tasked for a raid on Erquinhem-Lys [Nord]. At around midday the bombers were set upon by a formation of enemy fighters, estimated to be fourteen in number, but by coolly directing his fire Second Lieutenant Walker quickly sent one down out of control, and a second was also despatched though this may have been through the action of Second Lieutenant Waugh. On return, however, a misjudged landing damaged their aircraft beyond repair. Taken in hand on 17 March 1918, 'A7990' had its fair share of action when on the 12th of April, Lieutenant F J Morgan and Sergeant M V Kilroy shared in the destruction of an enemy aircraft near Estaries.

| 29 Squadron | Lt F R Brand | Safe | See 27 June 1918 - 29 Squadron |
| SE.5a D6159 | | | |

T/o St Omer and wrecked here on return from an offensive patrol during which enemy machine-gun fire damaged the undercarriage. Accepted just four days previously, 'D6159' logged a total of nine hours and fifteen minutes flying.

| 32 Squadron | Lt G F C Caswell | Safe | Unemployed list 11 February 1919: Lt |
| SE.5a C1890 | | | |

T/o Beauvois for operations northwest of Cambrai and along the twenty-one km corridor between Douai to the north and Marquion to the south. On return, and landing, 'C1890' struck a ridge which caused the undercarriage to collapse. Accepted as recently as 19 May, it had flown in total twenty hours and thirty minutes.

| 42 Squadron | Lt J Weight [South Africa] | Safe | See 4 July 1918 - 42 Squadron |
| RE.8 B5045 | | | |

T/o Rély for a practice flight which ended in a very heavy landing. A survivor of the squadron's detachment to Italy, 'B5045' flew for a very creditable two hundred and five hours and fifty minutes.

55 Squadron	Lt J L K Anderson	+	Niederzwehren Cemetery, Kassel
DH.4 A7825	[South Africa]		
	Sgt H Nelle	+	Niederzwehren Cemetery, Kassel

T/o Tantonville for bombing operations and was last seen going down in flames, following an attack from a fighter, over Karlsruhe. From Cramilt, East Griqualand [south of the Colony of Natal] received his commission on 3 May 1917 [gazetted 15 May 1917, issue 30074]. His observer's service number '101947' identifies him as either enlisting from civilian life, or a transfer from another arm of the services.

| 60 Squadron | 2Lt R G Lewis | Safe |
| SE.5a D2966 | | |

T/o Boffles for an offensive patrol and wrecked, owing to the engine overheating, in a forced landing near the air-field at Noeux occupied at the time by No 201 Squadron.

| 64 Squadron | Lt J J Carroll | Safe | Resigned his commission 15 January 1919: Lt |
| SE.5a C6448 | | | |

T/o Izel-lès-Hameau for an offensive patrol; wrecked while forced landing, owing to engine failure, near Grand Servins in the Pas-de-Calais. For the third time in the month [see my summaries for the 2nd and 18th] Lieutenant Carroll emerged relatively unscathed.

| 70 Squadron | 2Lt W E Taylor [USA] | + | Beacon Cemetery, Sailly-Laurette |
| F.1 Camel C8217 | | | |

T/o Ramaisnil for an offensive patrol and was shot down southwest of Albert and probably in the general vicinity of Sailly-Laurette some nine km distant from Albert. At the age of thirty William Edward Taylor from Pasadena in Los Angeles County, California, was above the age associated with scout pilots. Accepted by the squadron on 11th March 1918, 'C8217' destroyed, or shared, six hostile scouts and a kite balloon, four, including the kite balloon at the hands of Captain F E Hobson and two by Second Lieutenant H N C Robinson.

| 74 Squadron | Lt S Carlin*MC DCM | Safe | See 25 June 1918 - 74 Squadron |
| SE.5a C6460 | | | |

T/o Clairmarais for an offensive patrol but owing to his engine boiling over Lieutenant Carlin was obliged to force-land near Saint-Silvestre-Cappel [Nord] and within sight of the airfield at Ste Marie Cappel.

* By all accounts Sydney Carlin was a remarkable man for his biography, reported on *Wikipedia,* indicates he enlisted with the 18th Royal Hussars in 1908, but, it seems, army life did not suit him and for the then costly sum of eighteen pounds he bought himself out in 1909, and worked as a farm labourer. However, with the advent of the *Great War* he re-enlisted, again with the 18th Royal Hussars [the army refunding him nine pounds] and in 1915, distinguished himself in action winning the Distinguished Conduct Medal. Commissioned, it would appear he transferred to the Royal Engineers, this being indicated by the citation for his award of the Military Cross [*gazetted* in issue 13001 of *The Edinburgh Gazette*]; *'For conspicuous gallantry during operations. Under continuous shell fire he laid out a fire trench, brought up his section, dug the trench, and with his men held it against a counter-attack. He was seriously wounded.'* The action referred to in the citation took place on the Somme during the *Battle of Delville Wood* [15 July to 3 September 1916], during which the wounds to one of his legs led to it being amputated. Amazingly, his application to transfer to the Royal Flying Corps and flying duties was accepted and by May 1918, he was attached to No 74 Squadron where he was affectionately nicknamed 'Timbertoes'. Such was his aggressive approach to flying, he was awarded the Distinguished Flying Cross [issue 13346 of *The Edinburgh Gazette* of 4 November 1918 [at which time he was a prisoner of war]]; *'A gallant and determined pilot, who sets a fine example to his squadron. Although handicapped by the loss of a leg, he is bold and skilful in attack, and has destroyed four balloons and shot down two enemy machines.'* With the outbreak of the Second World War, Sydney came forward and was accepted for flying duties as a commissioned air gunner flying in the *Battle of Britain* with No 264 Squadron [Defiants, and after the battle with No 151 Squadron and, it is said, unofficially with No 311[Czech] Squadron [Wellingtons]. Tragically, during the night of 7-8 May 1941, the *Luftwaffe* bombed Wittering airfield and Pilot Officer Sydney Carlin was seriously wounded. Admitted to Peterborough Hospital this gallant airman died on the 9th of May 1941, and was cremated at Hull Crematorium where he is commemorated on Screen Wall, Panel 1.

| 80 Squadron | 2Lt E J Lainchbury | Safe | Unemployed list 16 April 1919: Lt |
| F.1 Camel C1661 | | | |

T/o La Bellevue for practice flying and crashed near the aerodrome following engine failure; damaged beyond worthwhile repair. Issued to No 46 Squadron on 23 March 1918, 'C1661' while being flown by Second Lieutenant Gerald Arthur Lamburn*on 10 April 1918, was badly shot about in the course of a low-level sortie over the British Third Army front. Repaired, 'C1551' arrived with No 80 Squadron on 25 May 1918.

* See No 46 Squadron summary for 19 July 1918, reported in my second volume.

| 98 Squadron | Captain G D Horton [Canada] | + | Bedford House Cemetery |
| DH.9 B7657 | Lt H J McConnell [USA] | + | Larch Wood [Railway Cutting] Cemetery |

T/o 1215 Coudekerque with others for a raid on the docks at Bruges; last seen spiralling earthwards victim of anti-aircraft fire. Concerning Gifford Horton, it seems his substantive rank was second lieutenant and his appointment to temporary captain was made only five days prior to his death, these details appearing on page 6590 of *The London Gazette* issue 30727 published on 4 June 1918. His American born observer, Harold Jeffrey McConnell hailed from Spokane in the northwestern state of Washington, though his entry in the cemetery register hints at a family connection with County Down in Ireland [at the time of Harold's death the partition of Ireland had yet to take place]. Both had survived a serious take off crash from the squadron's previous base, Alquines on the the 19th of May, while the previous day Captain Horton with Lieutenant Harrison as his observer had a similar mishap.

98 Squadron	Lt I A Peers [USA]	Safe
DH.9 D1013	Airman D Wentworth	Safe

T/o 1215 Coudekerque similarly tasked and was so badly shot about by anti-aircraft fire that on return it was deemed not worth repairing and was struck off charge on 5 July 1918.

100 Squadron	Lt J Henry	Safe
FE.2b A5564	2Lt P Wilkins	Safe

T/o Ochey having been briefed for a night attack on Metz but while travelling at speed struck a rut and lost its undercarriage. One hundred and seventeen hours and seven minutes flying recorded since its first flight in August 1917.

246 Squadron	Lt E S Dean	Injured
Kangaroo B9971	Signalman W C Hazelwood	Injured

T/o Seaton Carew and ditched, owing to fuel problems, in Robin Hood's Bay.

Saturday 1 June 1918

This busy day ended with twenty-four squadron aircraft written off and was marred additionally by an unusual accident which cost the life of the pilot, though his aircraft was salvaged and [it is believed] following repair returned to service. Second Lieutenant Thomas Edmund Simpson of No 65 Squadron took off from Bertangles in F.1 Camel C8277 but owing to engine trouble he force-landed near a French aerodrome at Breteuil [sic]. Running onto soft ground 'C8277' turned onto its back, a shaken, but otherwise unharmed, pilot extracting himself from the cockpit. It seems that he went to the front of his aircraft and was in the process of examining the damage when without warning the twin Vickers machine-guns mounted ahead of the cockpit fired killing Second Lieutenant Simpson; he is buried in Vigancourt British Cemetery where his headstone carries the words; *'He Served His King Until The King Of Kings Called Him RIP.'* Salvaged, 'C8277', as indicated, underwent repairs and returned to service, being issued to No 151 Squadron, a night fighter squadron which by September 1918, was based at Vignacourt. My summary for 20-21 September records its demise, though some documentation states that it was deemed not worth repairing on 11 June 1918. During the day No 41 Squadron moved to Conteville and linked up with No 24 Squadron, while No 54 Squadron took their Camels to St Omer.

2 Squadron AusFC	Lt A R Rackett AusFC	pow
SE.5a B525		

T/o 1800 Fouquerolles for an offensive patrol and when last seen was over the Somme and well to the east of Villers-Brettoneux. Named on the War Office list, and repeated in *Flight* June 28th, 1918, as 'Missing', his status as a prisoner of war appeared in the magazine's issue of August 1, 1918.

3 Squadron	Lt G F Young	Injured See 2 September 1918 - 3 Squadron
F.1 Camel D6477 Y		

T/o Valheureux for an air test and on return to the airfield clipped the tops of trees and, out of control, plunged through the roof of RE7 hangar belonging to the resident No 56 Squadron. Lieutenant Young's injuries, happily, proved not to be serious.

4 Squadron AusFC	2Lt A Rintoul AusFC	pow
F.1 Camel C8231		

T/o 1410 Clairmarais for an offensive patrol and to include bombing. Last seen flying, under control, at fourteen thousand feet over Bac St Maur [sic]. On establishment since 15 April 1918, 'C8231' accounted for Albatros scouts on the 2nd and 3rd of May, both by Lieutenant E R Jeffree. Confirmation that he was a prisoner of war was published in *Flight* July 11, 1918.

10 Squadron	Lt H L Storrs	Safe	See 20 June 1918 - 10 Squadron
FK.8 C8561	Lt J H Hirst	Safe	Unemployed list 1 April 1920: Lt

T/o Droglandt for a *Flash* reconnaissance during which the crew force-landed at map reference 28B19a59 owing to engine failure. See my summary for 8 May 1918, for an 'incident' involving Henry Lionel Storrs.

24 Squadron | Lt J N Clarke | Safe
SE.5a C1845

To Conteville authorised for practice flying; damaged beyond repair following a heavy landing. Crated, and shipped via Newhaven, 'C1845' was taken on charge on 26 April 1918, and in total accomplished fifty-nine hours of flight.

40 Squadron | Major R S Dallas DSO DSC* | + | Pernes British Cemetery
SE.5a D3530 | Twice mentioned in despatches *Croix de Guerre* [France] [Australia]

T/o Bruay for a lone offensive patrol during which his aircraft was attacked by a trio of enemy scouts and shot down out of control. For an appreciation of this officer, who had been wounded as recently as the 14th of April 1918 [see my summary for this date], I recommend you obtain David Gunby's *Sweeping the Skies* where Roderic Stanley Dallas receives full coverage of his time as the squadron's commanding officer, plus photographs on pages 48 and 56. As is obvious from his decorations, Roderic came to the squadron via the Royal Naval Air Service with a reputation of resolution and above average skill as a fighter pilot. To give added substance to David's writing, I now present the citations for his Distinguished Service Cross and First Bar, published respectively in supplements to the *Gazettes* of 5 September 1916 and 22 June 1917 [issues 29736 and 3017]; *'Flight Sub-Lieut Dallas, in addition to performing consistently good work in reconnaissance and fighting patrols since December 1915, has been brought to notice by the Vice-Admiral, Dover Patrol, for the specially gallant manner in which he has carried out his duties. Amongst other exploits is the following: On the 21st May 1916, he sighted at least 12 hostile machines, which had been bombing Dunkerque. He attacked one at 7,000 feet, and then attacked a second machine close to him. After reloading, he climbed to 10,000 feet, and attacked a large two-seater hostile machine off Westende. The machine took fire and nose-dived seawards. Another enemy machine appeared, which he engaged and chased to the shore, but had to abandon owing to having used up all his ammunition'.* Now promoted Flight Commander he gained a First Bar; *'In recognition of his services on the 23rd April 1917, when with two other machines he engaged a formation of nine hostile scouts and two-seater machines. Two two-seater machines were shot down, one of them by Flt-Cdr Dallas unassisted.'* His Distinguished Service Order was *gazetted,* without a citation appended, in a supplement to the paper of 23 April 1918, issue 30654. In conclusion, David shows Roderic's squadron as No 1 Royal Naval Air Service and on his arrival with No 40 Squadron on 15 March 1918, his victory tally stood at twenty-three. A biography [David advises] of this outstanding airman by Adrian Hellwig was published by Grub Street in 2006 under the title *Australian Hawk over the Western Front.* And, in conclusion, David has discovered in the April 1959, edition of the *'Royal Air Force Flying Review'*, page 49, an eyewitness account of Major Dallas's death written by Harold Rayner, formerly of the Royal Engineers.

40 Squadron | Lt N D Willis | Safe | See 9 June 1918 - 40 Squadron
SE.5a D6117

T/o 1630 Bruay for an offensive patrol and bombing but was obliged to force-land near Lillers in the Pas-de-Calais for when over Merville his engine failed to function.

41 Squadron | Lt J A Gordon | Injured
SE.5a C5436

T/o Estreé Blanche for Conteville via Lièttres and on arrival landed heavily and was damaged beyond repair. Lieutenant Gordon's injuries were not serious.

41 Squadron | Lt W H Jordan | Safe | See 13 June 1918 - 41 Squadron
SE.5a C6396

T/o Estreé Blanche for Conteville via Lièttres and reported to have overshot the aerodrome and crashed into a field of standing corn at Le Crecy.

45 Squadron | Lt E McN Hand | pow
F.1 Camel B6423 T

T/o Grossa for an offensive patrol and shot down in combat, Lieutenant Hand going into captivity in a wounded state. On squadron charge while still operating over the Ypres Salient 'B6423' drove down a brace of enemy aircraft ahead of transferring to Italy where it continued to score at the hands of Captain J C B Firth. The Second

Lieutenant G H Bush weighed in by driving down two more hostiles before Captain Firth sent down a couple before Lieutenant Hands was captured.

| 45 Squadron | Lt F J Jones | + | Montecchio Precalcino Communal Cemetery |
| F.1 Camel B7307 R | | | extension |

T/o Grossa similarly charged and was last seen falling out of control, inverted, and before hitting the ground nineteen year old Francis Joseph Jones was seen to fall out of the cockpit.

52 Squadron	Lt G A B Ross *Croix de Guerre* +	Terlincthun British Cemetery, Wimille
RE.8 B7738	[France] [South Africa]	
	2Lt A Nugent *Croix de Guerre* +	Terlincthun British Cemetery, Wimille

T/o Trecon with orders to carry out an artillery observation patrol over the lines. During their mission their air-craft was shot down by an enemy scout, falling into a wood behind the allied lines. From Durban in South Africa and a cadet graduate from the Inns of Court Officer Training Corps, *gazetted* second lieutenant on probation with effect from 24 June 1916 in supplement 29643 published on 27 June 1916, George Augustus Bellair Ross was attached to the 6th Battalion King's Liverpool Regiment. His eighteen year old observer, Anthony Nugent, was commissioned as a temporary second lieutenant to the General List on the last day of November 1917 [*gazetted* 4 December 1917]. By the spring of 1918, the names of both officers had been brought to the attention of the French Government, their decorations being promulgated in a supplement of *The London Gazette* issue 30913 published on 20 September 1918.

| 52 Squadron | Lt T E Sharp | Safe |
| RE.8 B8888 | 2Lt W H Bentley | Safe |

T/o Trecon similarly charged and driven down over the Somme by three enemy scouts east of Damery eight km northwest of Roye. Taken on charge on the last day of March 1918, 'B8888' flew, including transit and tests, for eighty hours.

| 52 Squadron | Lt T E Sharp | Safe |
| FK.8 E177 | 2Lt W H Bentley | Safe |

T/o Trecon tasked for artillery observation but failed to leave the ground, nosing over and damaged beyond repair. Sent to France in a crate, it arrived with the squadron twenty-four hours previously and, therefore, I suspect that much of the three hours and five minutes flying recorded took place in England. Although I cannot be certain, I am of the opinion that the crew transferred to 'B8888'; see the summary above.

| 54 Squadron | Lt W A Hunter | Safe |
| F.1 Camel B7172 | | |

T/o Caffiers to transit with the squadron to their new base at St Omer where, on arrival, Lieutenant Hunter banked steeply, stalled and crashed.

| 55 Squadron | Lt L De G Godet [Bermuda] | + | Chambieres French National Cemetery, Metz |
| DH.4 A7482 B | 2Lt A Haley | + | Chambieres French National Cemetery, Metz |

T/o Tantonville and set a course for Metz where other crews in the formation returned to report seeing 'A7482' breaking up in the air as it dived toward the target. From Bermuda's capital, Hamilton, Lennock De Graaff Godet was commissioned to the General List of the Royal Flying Corps on 5 April 1917 [*gazetted* 22 May 1917, issue 30087]. His observer, Arthur Haley, came to the Royal Flying Corps by way of the Essex Regiment. A photo-graph of their aircraft, when in service with No 25 Squadron, appears on page 27 of *The DH.4/DH.9 File*.

| 56 Squadron | Lt E R Ortner | Safe | Unemployed list 30 May 1919: Lt |
| SE.5a B624 | | | |

T/o Valheureux for operations over Third Army front. On return landed heavily and damaged beyond worthwhile repair. First operated by No 41 Squadron, 'B624' arrived with the squadron on 17 May 1918, and in total flew for one hundred and one hours and thirty minutes.

60 Squadron   Lt K P Campbell [Canada]   Safe   See 27 June 1918 - 60 Squadron
SE.5a D6152

T/o Boffles for an offensive patrol on return from which Lieutenant Campbell landed heavily and collapsed the undercarriage. Salvaged, 'D6152' which had flown to France from Brooklands in late May had lasted for less than a week. Its total flying came to just thirteen hours. This was his third serious crash; my summaries for 2nd April and 30 May 1918, describe his previous mishaps.

74 Squadron   Captain W J Cairnes   +   Arras Flying Services Memorial
SE.5a C6443

T/o Clairmarais for an offensive patrol and when last seen was in combat northeast of Estaries. William Jameson Cairnes had come to the Royal Flying Corps by way of the 1st Battalion Leinster Regiment.

80 Squadron   Lt E G Hayes   Safe   Unemployed list 31 May 1919: Lt
F.1 Camel C8232

T/o La Bellevue for a practice flight which ended with Lieutenant Hayes flying into telegraph wires near the air-field as he prepared to land.

82 Squadron   Lt W G Mackenzie   Safe
FK.8 C8527   Lt J H M Yeomans   Safe

T/o Agenvilliers tasked for bombing. Hit by anti-aircraft fire but returned and landed safely; however, while taxying a wheel fell into a deep rut resulting in the airframe being damaged beyond repair. Struck off charge with a total of ninety-four hours and ten minutes flying on 14 June 1918.

83 Squadron   Lt B W Knuckey   Safe
FE.2b A5665   2Lt A Macinnes   Safe

T/o Franqueville tasked for bombing but on becoming airborne stalled and crashed. Shipped, crated, to France 'A5665' was issued to the squadron on 24 March 1918, and when struck off charge on 13 June 1918, had a total of forty-one hours and twenty minutes flying.

84 Squadron   Lt M L Newhall USAS   Safe
SE.5a C6409

T/o Bertangles and headed for Villers Bretonneux and an offensive patrol. On return landed with a force that damaged the airframe beyond repair.

107 Squadron   Lt O J Marchbank   Injured Durrington Cemetery
DH.9 D5657   Lt K Kennedy   Injured

T/o Lake Down for continuation training and on return to the airfield the crew experienced some form of engine trouble, and, as a consequence, the DH stalled and dived into the ground injuring both officers. Ogilvie James Marchbank, originally of Glasgow but now attached from the Canadian Engineers died the next day from his injuries.

107 Squadron   2Lt R R Bourner   +   Tunbridge Wells Cemetery
DH.9 D5682   Boy J Durrant   +   Northampton [Kingsthorpe] Cemetery

T/o Lake Down similarly charged and reported to have dived to the ground after stalling at a low altitude.

Note. Three days after these two awful accidents No 107 Squadron, now declared ready for operations, departed Lake Down for Le Quesnoy in the département *du Nord*.

211 Squadron   2Lt H H Palmer   Safe   Unemployed list 12 March 1919: 2Lt
DH.9 C2180   2Lt J S Muir   Safe

T/o Petite Synthe tasked for bombing and on return landed heavily, damaging the airframe beyond repair. Reported at No 2 Aeroplane Acceptance Park Hendon by 8 May 1918, 'C2180' arrived with the squadron on the 22nd from No 1 Air Issues.

Sunday 2 June 1918

1 Squadron   Captain K S Henderson   +   Arras Flying Services Memorial
SE.5a C1113   [Australia]
T/o Clairmarais South for an offensive patrol and when last sighted Kenneth Selby Henderson was over Bailleul.

1 Squadron   Lt D Knight   Safe
SE.5a C6479
T/o Clairmarais South similarly tasked during which Lieutenant Knight was driven down by three enemy scouts, crash-landing just two hundred metres or so inside the Allied lines west of Steenwerck a commune inside the *département du Nord* from the neighbouring Pas-de-Calais and within a couple of km of the Franco-Belgium border.

2 Squadron AusFC   Lt Cox   Safe
SE.5a B8400
T/o Fouquerolles for an offensive patrol during which the engine seized. Salvaged, repairs were not put in hand and 'B8400' was struck off charge on 11 June 1918.

4 Squadron AusFC   Lt G S Jones-Evans   Safe
F.1 Camel B7394
T/o Clairmarais for a practice flight and on return to the airfield Lieutenant Jones-Evans misjudged his approach and stalled in from twenty feet.

7 Squadron   Lt L H Brown   Safe
FK.8 D4837
T/o Droglandt and wrecked after completely misjudging his approach to land at Clairmarais. Received by way of Kenley and No 1 Air Issues, 'D4837' flew for a total of seventy-one hours and fifty minutes, mostly since the 4th of May 1918.

8 Squadron   2Lt N Young   Safe
FK.8 D5074   2Lt H B Davis   Safe
T/o Auxi-le-Château for a bombing mission during which the crew came under accurate anti-aircraft fire which obliged them to force-land near Bresle [Somme], twenty-six northwest of Amiens with their rudder controls shot away.

23 Squadron   Captain A B Fairclough   Safe
F5.1 Dolphin C4151
T/o Bertangles for an air test and damaged beyond repair when on landing the Dolphin struck a ridge, turning 'C4151' onto it back.

25 Squadron   Lt J R Zieman [Canada]   pow
DH.4 A7882   2Lt H Tannenbaum   pow   Unemployed list 2 March 1919: 2Lt
T/o 0400 Ruisseauville for a dawn raid on Cambrai during which the DH lost engine power and force-landed. The plight of the crew were spotted with the pilot setting light to their aircraft in order to prevent it from falling into enemy hands. Both officers are named under the 'Missing' banner in *Flight* June 20, 1918, where it is noted Lieutenant Zieman was formerly of the Ontario Regiment, Canadian Infantry. His status as a prisoner of war was confirmed by the magazine in its issue of July 11, 1918, while Second Lieutenant Tannenbaum was reported as a prisoner of war in the August 15, 1918, issue.

29 Squadron   Lt T S Harris   Safe
SE.5a D6157
T/o St Omer and wrecked here when on return from a line patrol the engine failed as Lieutenant Harris prepared to land.

| 35 Squadron | Lt N C Bennison | Safe |
| FK.8 D5018 | Lt P Pickering | Safe |

T/o Hetomesnil to visit aerodromes but while travelling at speed had to swerve in order to avoid a collision. Out of control 'D5018' crashed against the side of a road, leaving Lieutenant Pickering badly shaken, but otherwise unharmed.

| 49 Squadron | Lt H Ford | Injured See 30 October 1918 - 49 Squadron |
| DH.9 C6183 | Mechanic S E Carr | Injured |

T/o Conteville*to attack targets in the Somme near Rosières-en-Santerre but was obliged to force-land, coming down in a wheat field near Longpré-les-Corps-Saints well to the northwest of Amiens.

* That same day No 49 Squadron departed Conteville for Fourneuil.

| 54 Squadron | Captain W R Fish MC* | + | Ebblinghem Military Cemetery |
| F.1 Camel E1589 | | | |

T/o St Omer tasked for a line patrol and destroyed in a midair collision with Camel C1667 [summarised below]. The citations for the awards of the Military Cross and First Bar were reported on pages 7410 and 7398 respectively of supplement 30761 of the paper issued on 22 June 1918. In order they read; *'For conspicuous gallantry and devotion to duty. While on reconnaissance, observing a number of enemy troops and transport on a road, he engaged these, diving on them from a height of 500 feet. Throughout he was subjected to the most violent machine-gun and rifle fire from the ground, but he succeeded in scattering the enemy in all directions and inflicting heavy casualties on them. He has also destroyed several enemy machines, and his personal example and determination have been on the greatest value to his squadron.'* The citation for the First Bar; *'For conspicuous gallantry and devotion to duty. While leading a patrol in very bad weather he saw the enemy's infantry advancing in an attack on our trenches, which he knew were not strongly held. There were nine enemy scouts patrolling above their lines, but he led his patrol down immediately beneath them and under heavy machine-gun fire from the ground, and concentrated his fire on the advancing enemy infantry. Largely owing to his determined and courageous action, the enemy's attack was repulsed.'* A memorial plaque commemorated Captain William Raymond Fish may be seen in All Saints Church in Broomhill Road, Ilford in Greater London.

| 54 Squadron | Lt C F R Price-Hughes | Safe |
| F.1 Camel C1667 | | |

T/o St Omer similarly tasked and lost in the circumstances outlined above. Lieutenant Price-Hughes, I suspect, made a controlled crash-landing for *The Camel File* carries the annotation 'shock'. These were the first operational losses from the squadron since taking up residence at St Omer and follow a run of training mishaps.

| 56 Squadron | Lt R H Ritter | Safe |
| SE.5a B8238 | | |

T/o Valheureux in the company of other pilots to practice flying in formation. All went well until the cowling came off Lieutenant Ritter's aircraft and sighting the airfield at Noeux he made a forced landing but, unfortunately, before coming to a stop he ran into the station's bomb dump, damaging 'B8238' beyond repair. First issued to No 41 Squadron on 25 March 1918, it had been with the squadron since the 17th of May.

| 56 Squadron | 2Lt C B Stenning | Safe See 13 June 1918 - 56 Squadron |
| SE.5a C5432 | | |

T/o Valheureux for a counter attack patrol and on return overshot the airfield and turned over; damaged beyond repair. On charge since 29 March 1918, including transit and tests it had flown a total of seventy-five hours and five minutes.

| 59 Squadron | Lt R J F Wells | Injured |
| RE.8 C2234 | Lt B Instone | Injured |

T/o Vert Galand for a patrol but having climbed to between one hundred and fifty and two hundred feet, Lieutenant Wells put on left rudder but failed to bank at the same time; consequently, 'C2234' entered a flat spin and with the engine on full power sank back to the ground.

64 Squadron	Lt W J Cockburn	Injured	
SE.5a C6476			

T/o Izel-lès-Hameau for a practice flight during which a connecting rod snapped; in the ensuing emergency landing 'C6476' crashed and was consumed by fire. Accepted by the squadron twenty-four hours earlier, it had, including testing and transit, flown for just six hours and twenty minutes.

65 Squadron	2Lt A Devitt	+	Arras Flying Services Memorial
F.1 Camel D6562			

T/o 1730 Bertangles for an offensive patrol over the Somme and it is believed to have been 'flamed' by *Leutnant* J Mai of *Jasta 5* south of Hangard. On establishment 7 April 1918, 'D6562' sent down two enemy aircraft while being flown by Lieutenant J L M White, the first an Albatros on the 9th of May and ten days later a two-seater reconnaissance aircraft which he attacked southeast of Villers-Bretonneux.

74 Squadron	Lt P F C Howe	Safe	See 15 June 1918 - 74 Squadron
SE.5a C6472			

T/o Clairmarais tasked for an offensive patrol to Staple in the *département du Nord* during which Lieutenant Howe was overtaken by engine failure. Forced landing, he came down in a wheat field where his aircraft finished up, wrecked, in a ditch. Please consult my summaries for the three previous 'adventures' concerning Lieutenant Howe; 19 and 25 April, and 15 May 1918.

74 Squadron   SE.5a D278   Damaged beyond repair after being hit by a Camel [not identified] which was landing at Clairmarais.

79 Squadron	Lt C A Howse	Safe	
5F.1 Dolphin C4029			

T/o Ste Marie Cappel and headed for Bailleul where he came under attack from at least seven enemy scouts. Although Lieutenant Howse eventually shook off his assailants, his aircraft was so badly shot about that it was struck off charge on 7 June 1918, as not worth repairing.

82 Squadron	Lt A V P Davey	+	St Riquier British Cemetery
FK.8 C3525	Lt L G Heigham-Plumptre	Injured	St Riquier British Cemetery

T/o Agenvillers but swung sharply to starboard and before the RE.8 could be brought under control it smashed into a lorry travelling along the road bordering the airfield. On impact it burst into flames. Formerly of the Royal Field Artillery, Albert Victor Patrick Davey's parents submitted the following inscription to be carved on his headstone; *'Of Wyoming Bexley Heath, Kent Jesus Mercy RIP'*. Leslie Graham Heigham-Plumptre died from his injuries on the 4th of June; his inscription comes from the 4th line of Psalm twenty-one; *'Thou Gavest Him A Long Life Even For Ever And Ever.'* Before becoming an observer with the Royal Flying Corps, Leslie Heigham-Plumptre had served with the Bedfordshire Regiment.

88 Squadron	Lt Des Lauriers	Safe	
Bristol F.2b C879	2Lt West	Safe	

T/o Capelle for an offensive patrol in the direction of Oostende and wrecked while making a forced landing on the airfield at Petite Synthe.

208 Squadron	Lt P M Dennett	+	Arras Flying Services Memorial
F.1 Camel D1854			

T/o Serny for an offensive patrol and shot down between Merville and Estaries in the *département du Nord*. Pruett Mullens Dennett was nineteen.

211 Squadron	Lt G T Scott	Safe	Unemployed list 29 June 1919: Lt
DH.9 B7629 K	2Lt P R Thornton	Safe	

T/o Petite Synthe tasked for bombing operations only to fly into a railway signal post and crash out of control.

Monday 3 June 1918

5 Squadron	Lt F Nash	Safe
RE.8 C2330	Sgt F Crossley	Safe

T/o from an unidentified forced landing site intending to return to Le Hameau but 'chocked' the engine, clipped a bank and came down at map reference J27.

15 Squadron	Lt A E Fitness	Injured
RE.8 C4596	Lt H A Chippindale	Injured

T/o Vert Galand tasked for artillery observation duties but flew into a telegraph pole and crashed out of control. Sent to France by sea, 'C4596' arrived with the squadron on 4 May 1918, since when the better part of its sixty-two hours and twenty-five minutes flying had been from Vert Galand.

28 Squadron	Lt R C Muir	Safe
F.1 Camel B2364		

T/o 0900 Grossa for an operational patrol and was last seen, in a glide, and being bracketed by anti-aircraft fire as he made for the allied lines near San Pietro in Gu in the province of Padua some fifty km northwest of Venice. Page 16 of *The Camel File* notes that 'B2364' was the first to be delivered to No 3 Squadron at Lechelle on the 25th September 1917. On the 1st of December, Lieutenant W R Haggas crashed while landing and 'B2364' was struck for repairs, eventually arriving in Italy and taken over by No 28 Squadron on the 4th of May. Lieutenant Muir returned to his unit on the 13th of June.

32 Squadron	Lt P Macfarlane	Injured See 21 June 1918 - 32 Squadron
SE.5a C1066		

T/o Beauvois in the company of other pilots from the squadron heading for Fouquerolles where Lieutenant Macfarlane stalled and crashed, thereby writing off the squadron's first aircraft at their new home.

41 Squadron	Lt W E Shields	Safe Unemployed list 1 March 1919: Captain DFC
SE.5a D329		

T/o Conteville for operations over the Albert area; lingered too long and out of petrol crashed near Marieux, a commune in the Somme and bordering the Pas-de-Calais. Lieutenant Shields was by now well to the northwest of Albert [see summaries featuring this officer on 8 and 16 May 1918].

42 Squadron	Lt G J Cooper	Safe
RE.8 B5895		

T/o Rély authorised for flying practice, an exercise that ended with Lieutenant Cooper stalling into the ground. Issued way back on the last day of October 1917, when the squadron was based at La Gorgue 'B5895' had come through the squadron's detachment to Italy unscathed and when damaged beyond repair had flown for a total of two hundred and twenty-eight hours and thirty minutes.

54 Squadron	Lt T H Bevan	Safe
F.1 Camel B9285		

T/o St Omer authorised for flying practice but as 'B9285' climbed away so Lieutenant Bevan 'chocked' the engine and moments later he was emerging from the wreck of his aircraft which had come to rest up against a fence.

55 Squadron	2Lt J R Bell	Safe
DH.4 D9268	Sgt E V Clare	Safe

T/o Tantonville but lost contact with the formation when in the process of changing tanks. Force-landed near the commune of Martigny-les-Bains [Vosges], then a quite small village but since well extended.

73 Squadron	Lt C W H Douglas USAS	Safe
F.1 Camel D6476		

T/o Beauvois to transit to the squadron's new base at Fouquerolles where he landed downwind and fell into a sunken road, the Camel turning over. Arriving with the squadron on the last day of March, its flying days had come to an end.

74 Squadron	Captain G B Glynn	Safe
SE.5a D6879		

T/o Clairmarais for an offensive patrol shedding during which an oil pipe fractured; wrecked in a forced landing at Ste Marie Cappel.

82 Squadron	Lt E E Showler	Safe
FK.8 D5013	2Lt M P E Harrison	Safe

T/o Agenvilliers for bombing operations and on becoming airborne a wheel fell away. The crew continued with their task but 'D5013' was damaged beyond repair while landing back at base.

84 Squadron	Lt D B Jones DCM	Safe	See 3 July 1918 - 84 Squadron
SE.5a B8396			

T/o Bertangles for flying practice and damaged beyond repair following a heavy landing. Accepted as recently as 10 May, 'B8396' logged thirty hours and fifteen minutes flying.

85 Squadron	Lt E W Springs	Safe
SE.5a C1885		

T/o Petite Synthe for a line patrol; wrecked on return during landing. Between testing at Brooklands in mid-May and its demise, 'C1885' had flown for eighteen hours and thirty-five minutes.

Tuesday 4 June 1918

2 Squadron	Captain J H Mitchell	Safe
FK.8 B3320	Major Brooks*	Safe

T/o Hesdigneul tasked for a special mission only for the engine to fail. Seconds later 'B3320' came to a stop in a trench bordering the airfield, damaged beyond repair. At the Aeroplane Acceptance Park Newcastle by 17th November 1917, it was flown to France in January 1918, and stored until issued to the squadron on 5 March. In total, it flew a creditable one hundred and twenty-one hours and thirty-five minutes.

* I suspect 'Major Brooks' may have been an army officer for at the time No 2 Squadron was commanded by Major W R Snow [16 August 1917 to 28 August 1918].

2 Squadron	Lt C M Johnson	Safe	See 6 June 1918 - 2 Squadron
FK.8 C8573	Lt C G Johnson	Safe	

T/o Hesdigneul tasked for artillery observation duties on return from which Lieutenant Johnson overshot and ran into a trench bordering the airfield.

2 Squadron AusFC	2Lt H E Hamilton	Safe
SE.5a B70		

T/o Fouquerolles for a practice flight only for the engine to 'cut' which resulted in a crash landing, damaging the fighter beyond repair.

2 Squadron AusFC	Lt L J Primrose AusFC	+	Catenoy French National Cemetery
SE.5a C5441			

T/o Fouquerolles having been given instruction to practice making a patrol in the direction of Clermont [IOise]. However, it is believed Leslie John Primrose was indulging in *contour chasing* when his engine failed causing him to crash out of control. There are only two airmen from the *Great War* buried at Catenoy; Lieutenant Primrose is one and Lieutenant Leonard Charles Welford of No 80 Squadron, killed three days later, is the other.

3 Squadron	Lt J R Montgomery	Safe	See 16 September 1918 - 3 Squadron
F.1 Camel B7386			

T/o Valheureux having received orders for wireless interception and it was on return that Lieutenant Montgomery crashed while attempting to land. Arriving in France by sea from Newhaven, 'B7386' was accepted by No 43 Squadron on 7 March 1918, and before being struck to No 1 Air Issues on the 20th of the month, Second Lieutenant M F Peiler crashed a brace of Albatros scouts east of La Bassée in the early afternoon of the 13th.

From No 1 Air Issues, 'B7386' arrived at Valheureux on 15 April, and while flown on a patrol by Lieutenant Tipton of the United States Air Service on 10 May, shared in the destruction of a Rumpler two-seater.

4 Squadron	Lt A H Maltby	+	Arras Flying Services Memorial
RE.8 E38	2Lt J B P Simms	+	Arras Flying Services Memorial

T/o St Omer for artillery observation duties and while over map reference 36AK9d33 was 'flamed' by enemy aircraft. Records for this relatively new RE.8 indicate it was flown to France from Coventry early in April and issued to the squadron on the 19th, since when it had been in constant use logging one hundred and twenty-seven hours, including delivery. Alfred Henry Maltby was eighteen, his observer, who was formerly of the 3rd Battalion Northumberland Fusiliers, nineteen.

35 Squadron	2Lt G N Hardwick	Safe	See 7 July 1918 - 35 Squadron
FK.8 B3390	2Lt J T Thursfield	Safe	

T/o Villers-Bocage for an offensive patrol and on return Second Lieutenant Hardwick landed heavily, damaging 'B3390' beyond worthwhile repair. The airframe was struck off charge on 12 June 1918, with flying totals reported as being five minutes short of one hundred and six hours.

48 Squadron	Lt E A Foord	Safe	See 7 June 1918 - 48 Squadron
Bristol F.2b C793	2Lt J J Mackenzie	Safe	

T/o from an unidentified forced landing site and on reaching Bertangles made a poor approach and crashed.

54 Squadron	2Lt C H Atkinson	Safe	See 7 June 1918 - 54 Squadron
F.1 Camel D6587			

T/o St Omer for a transit flight to a new aerodrome identified in *The Camel File* as 'Blangy' where, on landing, the Camel ran into long grass and was damaged beyond repair. Struck of charge six days later. Although I cannot be certain, the 'Blangy' referred too may have been Blangy-sur-Bresle which is over a hundred km south-southwest of St Omer and about fifty km west-northwest of Amiens. This was the first of three Camels written off by Charles Henry Atkinson who very tragically would be killed in the fourth.

79 Squadron	Lt E A Coapman	Safe
5F.1 Dolphin C3821		

T/o Ste Marie Cappel for an offensive patrol but having just left the ground the Dolphin's air pressure system failed and Lieutenant Coapman force-landed roughly a km or so from the airfield coming down in a field of crops and turning over.

80 Squadron	Lt L C Welford	Safe	See 7 June 1918 - 80 Squadron
F.1 Camel D6414			

T/o Fouquerolles with the intention of carrying out a practice in patrolling; damaged beyond repair following engine failure and a forced landing in a wheat field near Breuil *[sic]*. The loss of 'D6414' was the first from the squadron since arriving at Fouquerolles from La Bellevue twenty-four hours previously. For Lieutenant Welford this was his second visit to a wheat field in less than a week for it was while making a practice flight in Camel B9237 on 31 May that his flight ended, inverted, in such a field. On that occasion damage was slight and the Camel was repaired and given a new airframe serial 'F6148' [see my summary for 25 July 1918]. Sadly, Leonard Charles Welford would lose his life three days later.

84 Squadron	Lt W E Lunnon	Injured
SE.5a B8403		

T/o Bertangles and headed for the familiar patrol area over Villers-Bretonneux. Reported to have stalled and crashed on the aerodrome, but it is not clear if this was prior to reaching the patrol's objective or on completion of the sortie. What is clear 'B8403' had given useful service and, including the usual tests and ferrying, had achieved one hundred and thirty-five hours and five minutes flying.

84 Squadron	Lt W J B Nell	Safe
SE.5a C1097		

T/o Bertangles similarly tasked; following engine failure force-landed in a field cropped with wheat and damaged beyond repair. Including factory testing and transit by air to France [early March 1918], 'C1097' flew for a total of eighty-six hours and thirty minutes.

85 Squadron	Lt E C Brown	Safe	See 18 October 1918 - 85 Squadron
SE.5a D6873			

T/o Petite Synthe for a line patrol and on return crashed during landing. Tested and flown to France from Coventry and acceptance by the squadron on 29 May 1918, 'D6873' managed just twelve hours and twenty minutes flying.

103 Squadron	Captain H Turner	Safe	See 6 June 1918 - 103 Squadron
DH.9 C6151	Lt R E Dodds	Safe	

T/o Serny to carry out a reconnaissance but within seconds of becoming airborne the engine 'cut' and moments later 'C6151 was somersaulting to destruction having collided with a farm barrow. From the wreckage emerged two very shaken airmen. Issued to the squadron at Old Sarum during its working up for service on the Western Front, the DH is reported to have flown to Serny on the 9th of May 1918, three days ahead of the main body. In total, it had flown for forty-four hours and fifteen minutes.

202 Squadron	Lt L H Pearson	Safe	Unemployed list 13 February 1919: Lt
DH.4 A7930	Sgt S E Allatson	Safe	

T/o Bergues for an operational sortie during which its rudder was shot away in an attack from fighters. With commendable skill, Lieutenant Pearson landed the DH on a beach near Fort-Mardyk [Nord] facing the English Channel at Dunkirk. Samuel Eli Allatson received the *Medaille Militaire* conferred on him by the Government of the French Republic and *gazetted* in issue 31170 of 7 February 1919. To the best of my knowledge the loss of this aircraft was the first sustained by the squadron on operational duties since re-numbering on the 1st of April from No 2 Squadron Royal Naval Air Service, though a training flight on the 21st resulted in the squadron's first fatality.

Wednesday 5 June 1918
During the day No 107 Squadron [commanded by Major J R Howett] and their DH.9s arrived at Le Quesnoy from Lake Down in Wiltshire.

1 Squadron	2Lt A F Scroggs	Injured	Retirement 16 October 1946: G/C
SE.5a C6416			

T/o 1105 Clairmarais for a line patrol during which Second Lieutenant Scroggs was wounded; force-landed to the north of Hazebrouck [Nord]. Mention of 'C6416' appears in my summary for D277 on the 16th of April 1918. Meanwhile, *Motor Sport* in their September 1965 issue carries the following announcement, which I am pleased to acknowledge; *'Readers will be sorry to learn of the death at the end of July of Group Captain A F Scroggs, whose successes with vintage two-stroke, chain driven Trojan cars have so often been featured in MOTOR SPORT. "Scroggie", as he was known to all of us in the Trojan Owners' Club, was our Chairman from the outset; he just had to be...'* The appreciation, penned by Don Williams, Trojan Owners Club Historian, continues by drawing attention to the group captain's service in the two world wars; flying fighters in the *Great War* and on technical testing of Spitfires in the second conflict. An exponent of motor trialing [The famed Land's End was his favourite] he was a familiar competitor known to many as he tackled the rutted and stone-strewn gradients where in the oft cold days of such events his *'exceedingly mature leather flying coat'* was a reminder of his days in the open cockpits of Scouts of more than forty decades past. As with so many of his era, Group Captain Scroggs was ever willing to pass on his knowledge to the less experienced members of the Trojan Owners' Club.

1 Squadron	2Lt H S Hennessy	+	Arras Flying Services Memorial
SE.5a D337	[Canada]		

T/o Clairmarais similarly ordered and was last seen above the clouds in combat with a number of enemy scouts. *Flight* June 20, 1918, reports his name under the heading 'Missing' and the same paper [August 22, 1918] carries this rather poignant item; *'Any information relating to Sec Lieut H S Hennessey RAF reported missing*

June 5th, would be gratefully received by N/S O C Whitby, No 2 Canadian General Hospital, BEF France.' The reporting of Harold Stephen Hennessy's surname may have led to some confusion for it was variously reported as 'Hennessey' and 'Hennesy'. Sadly, for Nurse Whitby there would be no happy outcome.

8 Squadron	Lt F V Fennell	Safe	See 30 June 1918 - 8 Squadron
FK.8 D5029	2Lt G G Ashton	Safe	See 23 July 1918 - 8 Squadron

T/o Auxi-le-Château for a bombing sortie. On return, and with the airfield coming into view, the petrol ran out and 'D5029' came down in a wood and was totally wrecked.

9 Squadron	2Lt R N Essel	Safe
RE.8 A4394		

T/o Calais for solo practice flying and on return to the airfield flared too high, stalled and crashed; wrecked. Taken on charge on the last day of August 1917, 'A4394' appears to have enjoyed trouble free service up to this point, accumulating two hundred and six flying hours.

10 Squadron	Lt T McM Shields	Safe
FK.8 B3398		

T/o Droglandt with newly arrived Lieutenant Shields authorised to practice circuits and landings. All did not go according to plan for he crashed on landing, damaging 'B3398' beyond repair. Arriving in France by sea, it collided with Sopwith 5F.1 Dolphin C3796 on landing at No 1 Aeroplane Supply Depot on 15 February 1918, Lieutenant E W Walls escaping injury. Reconstructed, it was issued to the squadron on 25 March. Including testing, 'B3398' logged one hundred and twenty-two hours and thirty-five minutes flying.

12 Squadron	Lt B H Garrett	Injured
RE.8 C2261	Lt C E Binns	Injured

T/o Soncamp for artillery observation duties and on return, and landing, collided with RE.8 C2375 which was parked on the airfield and unoccupied. Damage to 'C2261' was such that it was struck off charge on 13 June 1918, as not worth the cost of repair.

12 Squadron   RE.8 C2375   Wrecked at Soncamp in the circumstances described above.

20 Squadron	Lt J E W Sugden	pow
Bristol F.2b B1114	2Lt R J Gregory	pow

T/o Boisdinghem for an offensive patrol and was last seen near Armentières. John Eric Warley Sugden received a commission on the General List of the Royal Flying Corps on 16 August 1917, as promulgated in the *Gazette* of 11 September 1917, supplement 30279. He was repatriated from captivity, along with Second Lieutenant Gregory, on 13 December 1918. On the 1st of September 1939, John Sugden was commissioned to the Administrative and Special Duties Branch [*gazetted* 20 October 1939, issue 34713]. His commission while ranked squadron leader was relinquished under the provisions of the Navy, Army and Air Force Reserves Act of 1954. A document relating to his *Great War* service is held by The National Archives under WO 339/112166.

20 Squadron	Lt E A Magee	pow
Bristol F.2b C817	Sgt W O'Neill	pow

T/o Boisdinghem similarly charged and lost in the circumstances recorded above. Lieutenant Magee's name [and that of Lieutenant Sugden above] appear in *Flight* August 29, 1918, under the heading 'In the hands of the Enemy' which repeats the official list circulated by the German authorities for claims of aircraft that fell into their hands on the Western Front during June 1918. It would seem aircraft recognition was not their strong point as both officers are listed under the DH.4 table.

Note. Andrew Pentland, who has delved into the myriad of Royal Air Force documents for the period, advises that the crew combinations for the two Bristols differ, depending which report is read. What is clear, however, all four airmen ended the day as prisoners of war.

| 22 Squadron | Lt J E Gurdon | Safe |
| Bristol F.2b A7243 | Sgt J H Hall | Injured |

T/o Serny for operations over First Army Front during which longerons and spars were shot through by enemy aircraft, thus effectively ending the flying days for the Bristol. Sergeant Hall's injuries were not too serious.

| 22 Squadron | 2Lt C H Dunster | pow | |
| Bristol F.2b B1253 | Sgt L A F Young | + | Merville Communal Cemetery extension |

T/o Serny similarly charged and when last seen was going down, under control, near Lestrem. Second Lieutenant Dunster was repatriated on 18 December 1918. His observer's grave is marked with the simple inscription 'Sleep On Beloved.'

| 29 Squadron | Lt H W Clarke | Safe |
| SE.5a B93 | | |

T/o St Omer for an offensive patrol and force-landed with a seized engine at Floringhem in the Pas-de-Calais some forty-five km south-southeast of St Omer.

| 40 Squadron | Lt H W Clarke | Safe | See 1 July 1918 - 40 Squadron |
| SE.5a B93 | | | |

T/o Bryas for an offensive patrol and while returning to base the engine seized, Lieutenant Clarke forced landing on Floringhem airfield. Struck off charge 10 June 1918, with only nine hours and thirty minutes flying in total. It was the squadron's first casualty since arriving at Bryas from Bruay the previous day.

| 46 Squadron | 2Lt J H Smith | Safe |
| F.1 Camel B5409 | | |

T/o Lièttres for a counter attack patrol and on return drifted and lost a wheel on touch down; damaged beyond repair.

| 49 Squadron | Lt C A B Beattie | Safe | |
| DH.9 D7221 | Sgt A I Boyack | + | Marissel French National Cemetery |

T/o Fourneuil ordered for bombing. Badly shot about and on return crashed into trees two km from Clermont [sic] though some sources suggest the DH ran up against a tree on landing at base. It is not clear if eighteen year old Alexander Ian Boyack was killed in combat, or in the subsequent crash.

| 53 Squadron | Lt T C Welch | Safe |
| RE.8 B4093 | | |

T/o Clairmarais and flew to Alquines to practice night circuits and landings and it was here that Lieutenant Welch misjudged an approach and crashed. Salvaged, 'B4093' with seventy-four hours and fifteen minutes total flying was struck off charge on 10 June 1918.

| 54 Squadron | Lt R E Taylor | Safe |
| F.1 Camel C6709 | | |

T/o St Omer for an offensive patrol during which, and possibly unknown to Lieutenant Taylor, a wheel fell off; thus, on return to St Omer the Camel crashed and was damaged beyond repair. Initially used by No 80 Squadron, 'C6709' had been damaged in a crash-landing near Ypres on 28 February 1918, and while undergoing repair the Clerget 9B engine was replaced with a Le Rhône 9J. Issue to No 54 Squadron took place on the 16th of April. Total flying hours fifty-two and forty-five minutes.

| 54 Squadron | Lt I P Graeb | Safe |
| F.1 Camel D6416 | | |

T/o St Omer intending to carry out a line patrol but 'choked' the engine and crashed.

| 73 Squadron | Lt G W Gorman | Safe |
| F.1 Camel C8284 | | |

T/o Fouquerolles for an air test. On return landed in long grass with the tail up and overturned; damaged beyond repair.

73 Squadron   Lt C W H Douglass   Safe
F.1 Camel D1814
T/o Fouquerolles for an offensive patrol and on return turned onto its back while landing. This time 'D1814' was damaged beyond repair, a fate that nearly befell the Camel on the 17th of April 1918, when it crashed on landing at Avesnes-le-Comte from a formation practice flight flown by Lieutenant C Mitchell of No 43 Squadron. Taken for repair it arrived with No 73 Squadron forty-eight hours before it was written off.

74 Squadron   SE.5a D334   Written off at Clairmarais in unusual circumstances; as Lieutenant R A Birch taxied for take off there came a crunching sound and moments later the entire fuselage structure collapsed around him. Such was the extent of the damage that 'D334' was reduced to produce.

79 Squadron   Captain L S Ladd   Safe
5F.1 Dolphin C3964
T/o Ste Marie Cappel shedding a tyre as it lifted off. Captain Ladd continued with the patrol but on return, and landing, the damaged undercarriage resulted in the Dolphin turning onto its back.

84 Squadron   Lt A F Mathews USAS   Safe
SE.5a B535
T/o Bertangles heading for the skies above Villers-Bretonneux and on return to the airfield, crashed. This particular SE.5a had been on squadron charge for a mere twenty-four hours having previously seen service with No 60 Squadron between 19 September and the 30th of November 1917, during which time it had been damaged by enemy gunfire on the 20th of September [Captain J K Law] and an operational crash on 29th November [Lieutenant J D McCall] after which it was struck for repairs on the 30th. Following storage, it was issued to No 68 Squadron on 9 January 1918, '68' becoming No 2 Squadron AusFC five days later and continued in use until again sent for repairs on 5 March 1918.

85 Squadron   Captain C R B MacDonald   Safe
SE.5a D6863
T/o Petite Synthe heading for Neuve Chappelle*and a line patrol during which the engine failed and in the forced landing that followed Captain MacDonald crashed.

* Sight of one of the many key battles of the *Great War* initiated by the Allies and recorded as taking place between 10th and 13th of March 1915, where the ground forces greatly aided by the aerial photographs taken by the Royal Flying Corps that enabled the attack front to mapped in detail to a depth of one thousand five hundred yards.

89 Squadron   2Lt F H N Sessions   +   Mount Jerome Cemetery
SE.5a D264
T/o Thetford for a training flight during which nineteen year old Frederick Harold Norman Sessions attempted to make a slow turn and while doing so he stalled and crashed; on impact the 'D264'; went up in flames. From Rathmines, Dublin, he was returned across the Irish Sea for burial near his home. He was late of the Royal Dublin Fusiliers.

96 Squadron   2Lt E S Hart [USA]   +   Amityville Cemetery
F.1 Camel C8304
T/o Shotwick for continuation training during which the Camel stalled at two thousand feet, diving to the ground. From Bayshore on Long Island, New York, Eric Stanley Hart was taken back across the Atlantic for burial in his home State. Fitted with a Clerget 9B, 'C8304' was received by the squadron on 20 May 1918.

100 Squadron   2Lt H J Crofts   Safe
FE.2b A5606   2Lt O Sherwood   Safe

T/o Ochey tasked for night bombing but ran on to a ridge at speed and smashed the undercarriage.

103 Squadron	Lt E A Windridge	Safe	See 9 June 1918 - 103 Squadron
DH.9 C6251	2Lt V W Allen MC MM	Safe	See 9 June 1918 - 103 Squadron
	[South Africa]		

T/o Serny with orders to proceed to Fourneuil but at flying five hundred feet the engine seized and the DH was wrecked in the ensuing forced landing near Fontaine-les-Herman in the Pas-de-Calais.

203 Squadron	Lt A N Webster	+	Brown's Road Military Cemetery, Festubert
F.1 Camel B7220			

T/o Filescamp for an offensive patrol during which nineteen year old Arthur Nugent Webster was attacked by an enemy scout which dived from the clouds and poured a lethal burst of machine-gun fire into the Camel over Richebourg St Vaast*in the Pas-de-Calais some nine km northeast of Béthune. His headstone bears the inscription; *'Fell In Aerial Battle, "They Shall Mount Up With Wings As Eagles"'.*

* I commend readers to visit the Imperial War Museum website where an amazing three minute black and white film can be viewed showing scenes of devastation to buildings and the church at Richebourg St Vaast; the early part of the film shows British troops filing through the ruins of the churchyard. It is believed the film was shot as early as 1915, and is indicative of the damage caused by enemy shell fire on the village [one of the shells that hit the church blew a circular hole clean through one of the walls of the tower].

206 Squadron	Lt C M Hyslop	Safe	See 11 May 1918 - 206 Squadron
DH.9 B7658	Sgt J W Pacey	Safe	See 29 July 1918 - 206 Squadron

T/o Boisdinghem and with the rest of the squadron set out for Alquines*where the DH crashed on landing.

* This was the second time since the 1st of April 1918 that No 206 Squadron had departed Boisdinghem for Alquines, the previous occasion being 15 April; then on May 29th the squadron returned to Boisdinghem and remained here for just over a week.

Thursday 6 June 1918
During the day the Independent Force, Royal Air Force, came into being under the command of Major-General Sir Hugh Trenchard, an event which receives excellent coverage in Richard Overy's *The Birth of the RAF 1918.*

Also, on this day what was to become known as the 'bombing campaign'*got under way, the honour of being first to operate falling to No 55 Squadron and its sister squadron No 99 Squadron both lodged at Azelot. The city of Koblenz was chosen as the focal point for No 55 Squadron and crews were briefed to attack factories, the railway station and barracks; a dozen DH.4s were mustered from which ten crews claim success. No 99 Squadron sent eleven of their DH.9s to bomb rail facilities at Thionville in the Moselle, five crews returning to say they had identified the target.

On the ground the *Third Battle of the Aisne* came to a halt with the enemy's supply lines over extended and their infantry exhausted from eleven days of fierce fighting; the French and British had lost considerable ground but their front now held firm.

* Although termed as the 'bombing campaign' raiding by both sides had been taking place almost since day one of the war for on 22 September 1914 airship sheds at Düsseldorf and Köln were attacked by four Royal Naval Air Service aircraft, each armed with twenty pound Hales bombs. Only the shed at Düsseldorf was identified by a single aircraft and though bombs were dropped it seems one missed and the other failed to explode. A portent of events that would mark many of the early missions of the Second World War.

2 Squadron	Lt C M Johnson	+	Barlin Communal Cemetery extension
FK.8 C8570	2Lt J H Hay	Injured	

T/o Hesdigneul for artillery observations duties and on return, and preparing to land, stalled at one hundred and fifty feet and crashed to the ground. Cecil Marland Johnson, nineteen years of age, had walked away from a landing accident two days previously [see my summary for details]. His headstone is marked quite simply; *'Ever Remembered'.* Considering the height from which 'C8570' stalled, it was a miracle that Second Lieutenant Hay was not killed, though I very much suspect his engagement with air operations was over; on 12 April 1919, he relinquished his commission, the relevant entry in *The London Gazette* recording it was on account of ill-health.

| 10 Squadron | Lt S C P Slattery | Safe |
| FK.8 C8599 | 2Lt W W Hewitt | Safe |

T/o Droglandt for artillery observation work and wrecked following a forced landing at map reference 28A25b29. Lieutenant Slattery had survived a crash on 22 May 1918 [see my summary for the day in question].

| 19 Squadron | Lt J Hewson | Safe |
| F5.1 Dolphin C3940 | | |

T/o Savy for an offensive patrol during which the engine failed and in the forced landing near Pernes in the Pas-de-Calais the Dolphin turned onto it back. Including factory testing, transit and usage since being issued to the squadron on 8 March 1918, 'C3940' had flown for eighty-one hours and forty-six minutes.

| 23 Squadron | Lt A O Bentley | Safe |
| 5F.1 Dolphin C4184 | | |

T/o Bertangles to patrol the Allied inner defensive line, remaining over the area until dusk. On regaining the airfield the light was fast fading and this was a contributory factor in the crash that followed. Lieutenant Bentley had crashed on landing on 20 May 1918 [see my summary for details].

| 27 Squadron | Major G D Hill | Safe |
| DH.4 B2071 R | 2Lt C H F Nesbitt | Injured |

T/o Fourneuil to bomb Flaby [sic] and on the return flight came under attack from fighters whose fire wounded Second Lieutenant Nesbitt. A force-landed was carried out near the city of Beauvais, capital of the Oise *département*. Following two false starts with No 27 Squadron [down to its poor quality of build and pre-delivery servicing], 'B2071' arrived for a third time on 27 March 1918. While being flown by Captain S Anderson and Lieutenant W J Crawford it was involved in at least two combats, the first during the morning of 18 May with a claim for a red nosed Albatros and the second two days later for a Pfalz DIII despatched near Valenciennes-Anzin. The first claim was disallowed but the second granted.

| 27 Squadron | Lt M F Cunningham [Canada] | + | Arras Flying Services Memorial |
| DH.4 B2080 | 2Lt W J Stockins | + | Arras Flying Services Memorial |

T/o 0820 Fourneuil and reported to have left the formation when east of the trench lines [presumably while over enemy held territory or over the wilderness formed by 'No Mans' land]. Further information indicates the DH was under control when over Chaulnes [Somme] a village through which the present E19 runs in a north-south direction. Six months previously, and on 28 December 1917, Second Lieutenant C H Gannaway and Second Lieutenant F R D Wickhand had the misfortune to crash when in the process of taking off in 'B2080' and it was not until the 15th of May that the DH was returned to the squadron. Twenty year old Michael Francis Cunningham from Ottawa was commissioned on 21 March 1917 [*gazetted* 15 June 1917, issue 30132], while his twenty-two year old observer was commissioned to the 22nd Battalion London Regiment on 26 April 1917 having passed through an officer cadet unit [issue 30073 published on 15 May 1917].

| 29 Squadron | Lt H White | Safe | See 9 June 1918 - 29 Squadron |
| SE.5a D3931 | | | |

T/o St Omer for an offensive patrol and on return, and preparing to land, stalled at around twenty feet and crashed on the aerodrome.

| 32 Squadron | Lt E McD Jarvis | + | Marissel French National Cemetery |
| SE.5a B131 | | | |

T/o Fouquerolles for an offensive patrol but for reasons that are yet to be determined turned back and on arrival over base stalled and dived to the ground. On the 7th of April 1918, with Captain Douglas Munroe Faure* [Unemployed List 6 September 1919] at the controls, B131 sent down a Fokker DrI over the Somme near Démuin. Eric McDonald Jarvis had been obliged to force-land seven days previously after experiencing petrol feed difficulties [see my summary for 30 May 1918 for further information].

* Douglas Munro Faure was commissioned as a pilot officer to the Administrative and Special Duties Branch on the 23rd of August 1939 [*gazetted* 8 September 1939, supplement 34674] and continued to serve until the 9th of July 1954, when he relinquished his commission, retaining the rank of wing commander, under the provisions of the Navy, Army and Air Force Reserves Act, 1954.

| 32 Squadron | Lt R E L MacBean | Safe |
| SE.5 C1791 | | |

T/o Fouquerolles to patrol a twenty-two km corridor running south-southeast from Montdidier to Lassigny taking in the *départements* of the Somme and Oise. Returned to base badly shot about from an encounter with a hostile aircraft.

| 40 Squadron | Lt P V Burwell USAS | Safe | See 11 June 1918 - 40 Squadron |
| SE.5a D3540 K | | | |

T/o 1100 Bryas for an offensive patrol and bombing; on return crash-landed to the southwest of the airfield, collapsing the port undercarriage and damaging the SE.5a beyond repair.

| 54 Squadron | Lt W K Wilson | Injured See 21 June 1918 - 54 Squadron |
| F.1 Camel D6609 | | |

T/o St Omer ordered for a line patrol but when the engine 'cut' while climbing away the Camel crashed out of control near the aerodrome. For Lieutenant Wilson, help was quickly to hand; fortunately his injuries were not too serious and within days he was back in the air.

| 57 Squadron | Lt W E Green | Safe |
| DH.4 A7904 | 2Lt R H Shepherd | Safe |

T/o Le Quesnoy having received instructions for bombing operations over Bapaume. On return, and when trying to land crashed into hangars; damaged beyond economical repair. Accepted by No 57 Squadron on 4 January 1918, 'A7904' had seen its fair share of action with three aerial victories to its credit, two coming in its first month of active service when at midday on the 6th it downed an Albatros near Lichtervelde in the Belgian province of West-Vlaaderen; then on the 25th, again over West-Vlaaderen it sent another Albatros down, this time near Torhout. Finally, in late morning on the last day of March a Pfalz was sent tumbling out of the sky near Bapaume. Lieutenant Green was the victor for the first and third victories, his observers being Second Lieutenant E H Wilson and Second Lieutenant H S Gros respectively, while Second Lieutenant J M Allen and Second Lieutenant F R S Wakeford claimed the second.

| 57 Squadron | Lt W H Kilbourne | Safe | See 30 June 1918 - 57 Squadron |
| DH.4 E4628 | Corporal J Simmons | Safe | |

T/o Le Quesnoy for an air test but Lieutenant Kilbourne eased the control column a shade too far forward resulting in the propeller clipping the ground; damaged beyond repair. This accident, I believe, was first from the squadron of a non-operational nature.

| 59 Squadron | Lt H M Golding | Safe |
| RE.8 D4812 | 2Lt A J Bridge | Safe |

T/o Vert Galand for operations during which enemy ground fire shot away what are described as 'extensions' as the crew dived to machine-gun troops. Force-landed at map reference 57DNEF20D central.

| 60 Squadron | Lt F Williams | Safe |
| Bristol F.2b C965 | 2Lt W Hodgkinson | Safe |

T/o from an unidentified forced landing site and reaching Planques, and landing, swung and crashed against a hangar; damaged beyond repair.

| 65 Squadron | 2Lt L A Durrant | + | Vignacourt British Cemetery |
| F.1 Camel B9298 | | | |

T/o Bertangles to practice firing at ground targets in the course of which Lombe Atthill Durrant overstressed his aircraft while pulling up from a dive, both sets of wings folding up and sending 'B9298' hurtling into the ground.

| 66 Squadron | Lt F N Marchant | + | Montecchio Precalcino Communal Cemetery |
| F.1 Camel B2338 | | | extension |

T/o San Pietro but owing to engine trouble made an emergency landing on an Italian airfield. Following attention, nineteen year old Frederick Newland Marchant took off but when banking steeply to starboard lost control ands pun in at Castello di Godega in Treviso province. Prior to being railed down to Italy, 'B2338' had been used on the Western Front, first by No 45 Squadron and then by No 3 Squadron. With the former it crashed on landing on 18 September 1917 and with the latter it overturned in a forced landing on the 2nd of December. Second Lieutenant B R Davies*was at the controls in the landing mishap while it was a somewhat shaken Second Lieutenant H M Beck*that crawled out from his inverted machine in December.

* Neither survived the war; flying F.1 Camel B6205 Lieutenant Basil Raymond Davies failed to return from an offensive patrol two days after his landing accident. He is buried in Belgium at Dadizeele New British Cemetery while Second Lieutenant Herbert Musgrove Beck was attached to No 6 Squadron [Bertangles] to give the squadron's RE.8 crews' experience in warding off fighter attacks. During one such training exercise on the 22nd of January 1918, he got into a spin at the perilously low height of five hundred feet and was unable to recover the situation before his Camel B9141 hit the ground; he rests in St Pierre Cemetery, Amiens.

| 84 Squadron | Lt J E Reid | Safe | See 15 June 1918 - 84 Squadron |
| SE.5a C6495 | | | |

T/o Bertangles for operations over Villers-Bretonneux; force-landed owing to engine failure near the front line at Laviéville [Somme] twenty-six km northeast from Amiens.

| 87 Squadron | Lt H A R Biziou | Safe | See 28 June 1918 - 87 Squadron |
| 5F.1 Dolphin C4166 | | | |

T/o Estreé-les-Crecy for an air test; on return, overshot and ended up on its back in a field of corn. This Dolphin was one of the squadron's initial establishments at Hounslow and arrived at St Omer with the main body on the 23rd of April 1918. Henry Arthur Richard Biziou lost his life on the 14th of July 1919, while attached to the Royal Aircraft Establishment [Experimental Squadron] at Farnborough, when his SE.5a D7014 collided in the air above Farnborough with Avro 504K E3621, the latter piloted by Lieutenant Leonard Arthur Herbert who was accompanied by a civilian mechanic Mr C Highly, both of whom were killed. Weather conditions were misty and this may have been a contributory factor. Lieutenant Biziou was *gazetted* [Edinburgh] with the Distinguished Flying Cross on 5 December 1918, issue 13363; *'A most successful leader of marked gallantry. During recent operations he has destroyed four enemy aeroplanes and driven down one out of control, two of these accounted for in one engagement on September 15th with a number of Fokker biplanes. In addition he has driven down a hostile balloon.'*

101 Squadron   FE.2b A6478   Struck, and damaged beyond repair by the FE.2b summarised below, while parked on the aerodrome. Total flying time forty-five hours and forty-five minutes.

| 101 Squadron | Lt T Aldous | Safe |
| FE.2b A6494 | 2Lt P K Chapman | Safe |

T/o Famechon tasked for bombing and on return, and landing, collided with the FE.2b shown above. Accepted by the squadron on 2 April 1918, 'A6494' was struck off charge on 15 June 1918. In total, it flew for sixty eight hours and fifty minutes.

| 103 Squadron | Captain H Turner | + | Vignemont French National Cemetery |
| DH.9 C6203 | 2Lt G Webb | + | Vignemont French National Cemetery |

T/o Serny for bombing operations over the Somme on targets near Roye and when last seen was in a glide, making for the lines and being hounded by four enemy aircraft over woods near Warsy-Lignières some ten km west of the target area. The deaths of Henry Taylor, subsequently honoured by the French with the *Croix de Guerre,* and George Webb, formerly of the 1st/2nd Battalion South Staffordshire Regiment, were the first since the squadron arrived in France from Old Sarum on the 12th of May 1918. Captain Turner had survived a take off crash forty-eight hours earlier. Their deaths were the first from the squadron since its arrival of on the Western Front.

203 Squadron   Lt C F Brown   Safe   See 27 July 1918 - 203 Squadron
F.1 Camel D3403
T/o Filescamp for an offensive patrol along the corridor between Merville and Estaries. On return landed on rough ground sustaining damage that was deemed uneconomical to repair.

206 Squadron   Lt F Daltrey   Injured
DH.9 C2187   2Lt M G Penny   Safe
T/o Alquines for a long distance reconnaissance to Samur [sic] during which the DH's oil tank burst followed soon after by engine failure. In the forced landing that followed, Lieutenant Daltrey sustained minor injuries.

206 Squadron   Captain J W Mathews   Safe
DH.9 C6180   Lt C Knight   Safe
T/o Alquines tasked for bombing and reported to have crash-landed at Clairmarais owing to engine failure. Struck off charge as not worth the cost of repair on 5 July 1918. The two DHs here summarised were the first to be lost from the squadron since arriving at Alquines the previous day from Boisdinghem.

Friday 7 June 1918
5 Squadron   Lt E A Locke-Waters   Safe
RE.8 B5113   Lt M J Wyatt   Safe
T/o Le Hameua intending to carry out a patrol, as ordered, but engine trouble intervened and the crew crash-landed on the aerodrome. Flown to France from Coventry in January 1918, 'B5113' arrived with the squadron from No 1 Air Issues on 20 February and overall managed a useful ninety-seven hours and eight minutes flying.

8 Squadron   2Lt F A Whittall   Safe   See 18 June 1918 - 8 Squadron
FK.8 B3394   2Lt A J Ord   Safe   See 18 June 1918 - 8 Squadron
T/o Auxi-le-Château for a bombing operation during which the crew experienced engine trouble. Landing at the airfield used by No 2 Advanced Salvaged Dump the undercarriage was 'swept away'. This ended the flying days for 'B3394' which in total logged one hundred and forty-nine hours and thirty minutes.

12 Squadron   Lt A L Allan   Safe
RE.8 D4824   Captain Butcher   Safe
T/o Soncamp for an air test but while over Bavincourt [Pas-de-Calais] engine failure occurred and 'D4824' came to grief on landing. Including testing and ferrying, and its use by the squadron since 27 April 1918, it had flown for fifteen minutes short of seventy-seven hours.

15 Squadron   Lt G A Griffin   Injured
RE.8 C2443   2Lt W R S Fox   Injured See 22 August 1918 - 15 Squadron
T/o Vert Galand for a patrol and on return Lieutenant Griffin was unable to throttle back owing to the mechanism being jammed. As a consequence a high speed landing resulted in 'C2443' overshooting and finishing up damaged beyond repair in barbed wire. Neither officer was badly hurt.

24 Squadron   Lt J J Dawe   +   Rosieres Communal Cemetery extension
SE.5a B611
T/o Conteville tasked for an offensive patrol over the Somme to Rosieres where, it would seem, nineteen year old James Jeffery Dawe fell to earth. His headstone carries the words; *'A Faithful Soldier & Servant Unto His Life's End'*. His aircraft had survived for close on nine months. Flown to France from Brooklands in October 1917, it went first to No 41 Squadron at Lealvillers on 27 October but on the 22nd of December when piloted by Second Lieutenant E F H Davis it was badly damaged after side slipping following the pilot 'choking' the engine. At this point it had achieved in the region of thirty-seven flying hours. Repaired, it arrived with No 24 Squadron on 7 April, and from then on until its demise was in constant use. In total, 'B611' logged one hundred and sixty-eight hours and forty minutes.

25 Squadron   Lt J Loupinsky   Safe   See 10 July 1918 - 25 Squadron
DH.4 A8075   Sgt J R Wright   Safe   See 10 July 1918 - 25 Squadron

T/o Ruisseauville having received orders for bombing operations and damaged beyond repair following a heavy landing.

25 Squadron	Lt L A Hacklett	pow	Killed on active service 26 February 1919:
DH.4 D9266	Sgt W C Elliott	pow	

T/o 0830 Ruisseauville and seen by crews in the formation to be going down, under control, southwest of Valenciennes [Nord] after being hit by anti-aircraft fire. Leslie Arnold Hacklett was commissioned on 26 May 1916 to the Northumberland Fusiliers [*gazetted* 2 June 1916, issue 29607]. Although I have no firm evidence that Leslie was present on the Western Front for the opening day of the Somme Offensive on 1 July 1916, elements of the Northumberland Fusiliers appear on the Order of Battle as attached to the 34th Division, 102nd [Tyneside Scottish] Brigade and 103rd [Tyneside Irish] Brigade. Following his release from captivity and return to flying duties, Leslie was killed on Wednesday 26 February 1919 when after taking off from Hendon in DH.4 'F5743' for a passenger carrying flight to Paris he lost his bearings and in the continuation of the accident report *'was endeavouring to land, stalled while turning near the ground, resulting in a nose-dive into an* [English] *orchard.'* His passenger, Lieutenant S Graham Royal Naval Volunteer Reserve attached to the Ministry of Shipping was gravely injured. It would seem that Lieutenant Hacklett, who rests in Heston [St Leonard] Churchyard, had been detached for this duty as 'F5743' was a relatively new aircraft and had been delivered to Hendon and No 2 Aircraft Acceptance Park from where it was drawn for the flight to Paris.

29 Squadron	Lt L E Bickel	Safe	Unemployed List 5 February 1919: Lt
SE.5a B8240			

T/o St Omer for an offensive patrol and for the second time in his service Lieutenant Bickel landed with a force sufficient to damage his aircraft beyond repair; his previous accident occurring on the 22nd of May 1918.

29 Squadron	Lt L S Court	Injured See 1 July 1918 - 29 Squadron
SE.5a C9544		

T/o St Omer similarly tasked; ran out of petrol and crashed while attempting to land. Lieutenant Court was not too seriously injured [I suspect this crash was after his accident in 'D5967']..

29 Squadron	2Lt L S Court	Safe
SE.5a D5967		

T/o St Omer similarly tasked and crashed on return when the propeller stopped as Lieutenant Court prepared to land. Arriving in France by air from Brooklands, 'D5967' was accepted by the squadron on 23 April 1918. Overall it achieved sixty-nine hours and forty minutes flying.

40 Squadron	Lt D S Poler USAS	Safe See 8 June 1918 - 40 Squadron
SE.5a D3941		

T/o 0635 Bryas for an offensive patrol and returned badly shot about after exchanging fire with a two-seater. Lieutenant Poler was unscathed but the SE.5a was considered damaged beyond repair as was struck off charge on 12 June 1918. This was the American's second 'adventure', the first being summarised on 21 May 1918, and, as indicated above he would be the subject of a third mishap twenty-four hours later.

41 Squadron	Major G H Bowman DSO MC*	Safe
SE.5a C9533		

T/o Serny to make the transit to the squadron's base at Conteville where on arrival, and landing, the undercarriage collapsed. Intended for No 56 Squadron, this proved to be a 'paper issue' and 'C9533' was taken on squadron charge on 9 February 1918, and when struck off charge at No 2 Advanced Salvage Dump had flown for a total of seventy-seven hours and five minutes. Geoffrey Hilton Bowman had succeeded Major F J Powell as commanding officer of the squadron in January 1918, remaining 'at the helm' until February 1919. The award of the Military Cross was *gazetted* in supplement 30287 of the paper issued on 17 September 1917; *'For conspicuous gallantry and devotion to duty. He has taken part in many offensive patrols, which he led on twenty occasions, in the course of which four enemy aircraft were destroyed and twelve others driven down out of control. Although outnumbered by five to one on one occasion he handled his patrol of four machines with such skill and gallantry that after a very severe fight he was able to withdraw them without loss, having destroyed at least two enemy machines and driven down one out of control. His fearlessness and fine offensive spirit have been a splendid example to others.'* Shortly after taking command of the squadron, he was *gazetted* with the Distinguished Service Order [sixth supplement to the paper published on 26 March 1918], while the Edinburgh edition of the paper published on 21 March 1918 [issue 13226] the citation for the First Bar to Major Bowman's Military Cross; *'For conspicuous gallantry and devotion to duty in leading twenty-five offensive patrols in two months, shooting down five enemy aircraft and showing marked skill as a leader.'* Postwar, the Distinguished Flying Cross was added to his list of gallantry awards [supplement 31378 of 3 June 1919], while on the 1st of August of that year, and now reverted to his substantive rank of captain, he was appointed to a permanent commission. By this time one further honour had been bestowed upon him, namely the *Croix de Guerre* [Belgium]. His biography, reported on *Wikipedia,* shows he was born in Manchester on 2 May 1891, his military service commencing with the 3rd Battalion Royal Warwickshire Regiment . Seconded to the Royal Flying Corps in 1916, he flew operationally with Nos 29 and 56 Squadrons. His inter-war service was extensive and when retiring, at his request, on 20 January 1937, he held the rank of group captain. Recalled to the air force two days before the outbreak of the Second World War, Group Captain Bowman retired for a second time on 15 December 1941. His death at the age of seventy-eight was announced on 25 March 1970.

| 49 Squadron | Lt G S Ramsay | Safe | See 8 August 1918 - 49 Squadron |
| DH.9 C1176 | Airman H Knowles | Safe | |

T/o Fourneuil for a practice flight during which the engine failed which, in turn, led to a crash-landing; damaged beyond repair. Arriving at Conteville on the 6th of May, 'C1176' was soon inaction for shortly after midday on the 9th a Fokker DrI was sent down, out of control, east of Bray-sur-Somme by Lieutenant F W Lowen and Second Lieutenant J Sharp. Then, flying over the Somme and in the vicinity of Harbonnières, during the early evening of the 19th, Lieutenant Lowen, this time accompanied by Lieutenant F B Dennison, came upon an enemy scout which was duly despatched in an earthwards direction, apparently out of control.

| 49 Squadron | Lt A H Curtis | Safe | |
| DH.9 C6114 M | Sgt A Davis | Safe | |

T/o Fourneuil with orders to bomb targets at Fresnoy-lès-Roye [Somme] during which the DH was hit by anti-aircraft fire and force-landed at Remy [sic].

| 49 Squadron | Lt G C McEwan | + | Noyon New British Cemetery |
| DH.9 C6184 | Lt T F Harvey | + | Arras Flying Services Memorial |

T/o Fourneuil dual tasked for bombing and photographic reconnaissance; last seen going down out of control following combat with an enemy aircraft in the vicinity of Appily [sic].

| 54 Squadron | 2Lt C H Atkinson | Safe | See 26 June 1918 - 54 Squadron |
| F.1 Camel C1690 | | | |

T/o St Omer for a line patrol during which the Camel's engine failed and in attempting to stretch his glide to reach the airfield at Droglandt Charles Henry Atkinson crashed, ending up in a ditch, writing off his second aircraft in the space of three days.

| 56 Squadron | 2Lt C Parry | Safe | |
| SE.5a B144 D | | | |

T/o Valheureux for an offensive patrol during which Second Lieutenant Parry 'flamed' a two-seat aircraft southeast of Achiet-le-Petit in the Pas-de-Calais, twenty-one km south of Arras and 'crashed' a second to the northeast of Grévillers, about seven km east-southeast from where his first victim went down. However, the fight had not been all one sided for on return to Valheureux his SE.5a was found to be so badly shot about that it was struck from charge.

| 57 Squadron | Captain H Liver | Safe | Unemployed list 1 February 1919: Lt |
| DH.4 A7771 | Sgt P S Tidy | Safe | See 27 May 1918 - 57 Squadron |

T/o Le Quesnoy for an operational sortie and when in the vicinity of Bapaume the DH was struck by shrapnel from bursting anti-aircraft fire, thereby necessitating an emergency landing. Damaged beyond repair.

62 Squadron | Lt R G Taggart | Safe
Bristol F.2b C779 | 2Lt I P A Aitken | Safe

T/o Planques for an offensive patrol only to collided with Bristol F.2b C953. Damage to 'C953' must have been minimal for nothing of the incident appears in its documents; however, 'C779' was declared not worth repair and was probably struck off charge on 21 June 1918, with sixty-eight hours and five minutes flying time recorded.

74 Squadron | Lt F L C Link | + | Ebblinghem Military Cemetery
SE.5a C6491

T/o Clairmarais for a line patrol but nineteen year old Frederick Leslie Cuff Link climbed too steeply, stalled and dived into a field adjacent to the airfield. His death was the occasion of the squadron's thirtieth operational loss since the 1st of April 1918, Lieutenant Link being the eleventh fatality associated with operations during this period.

79 Squadron | Major M W Noel* | Safe
5F.1 Dolphin C4224

T/o Ste Marie Cappel leading an offensive patrol which for Major Noel ended with a forced landing near Eecke a commune in the *département du Nord* [dominated by a tall water tower], seven km northeast of Hazebrouck following engine failure at ten thousand feet. 'C4224' was a new aircraft and had been on squadron for just eight days; overall it flew for just ten hours and twenty minutes.

* Major Noel commanded No 79 Squadron from its formation at Gosport on 8 August 1917, until June 1918, when he was succeeded by Major A R Arnold.

79 Squadron | Lt H E Taylor | Safe
5F.1 Dolphin D3668

T/o Ste Marie Cappel to practice firing on ground targets near Clairmarais. During the detail, a petrol pipe fractured and Lieutenant Taylor force-landed, running into a hedge, at map reference 27N70B41. On charge since 27 May 1918, 'D3668' flew for fifteen hours and thirty minutes in total.

80 Squadron | Lt L C Welford | + | Catenoy French National Cemetery
F.1 Camel B7294

T/o Fouquerolles for an offensive patrol and it was while returning to base that the engine failed. Unable to control his descent, Leonard Charles Welford crashed. In his brief operational life he had crashed twice, the first time on 31 May [his Camel on that occasion was salvaged and repaired, and is summarised on 25 July 1918] and the second on the 4th of June. He is one of only two airmen from the *Great War* buried at Catenoy, the other being Lieutenant Leslie John Primrose of No 2 Squadron AusFC whose passing is recorded on the 4th of June 1918.

103 Squadron | Lt D M Darroch | Safe
DH.9 C6194 | Mechanic W J Westcott | Safe

T/o Serny for a bombing sortie and on return overshot the airfield. Salvaged, but struck off charge 9 July 1918.

213 Squadron | 2Lt J E Greene [Canada] | Safe | See 14 October 1918 - 213 Squadron
F.1 Camel B6330

T/o Bergues order to carry out a fleet patrol at low-level. Wrecked, owing to engine failure, which necessitated forced landing on the beach some three to four km south of Bray Dunes. On touch down the wheels dug in and the Camel overturned. Initially accepted on 3 April 1918, 'B6330' was struck for inspection on the 22nd and only returned to the squadron three days before the accident, here summarised. Canadian born John Edmund Greene was an experienced pilot and as his association with no less than nine different Camels show, he was a fighter pilot *par excellence*. He is mentioned in my summary for Second Lieutenant Edmund Charles Toy who was killed when flying with No 210 Squadron on 25 August 1918.

217 Squadron | Lt J H Hardman | Safe | Unemployed list 7 March 1919: Lt
DH.4 A7762 | Sgt F W Shufflebotham Safe | See | 28 September 1918 - 217 Squadron

T/o Bergues ordered for bombing operations and written off in a landing accident.

Saturday 8 June 1918
From Azelot [Meurthe et Moselle] No 104 Squadron flew its first operational sorties of the war, twelve DH.9s being sent to attack the railway station at Metz-Sablon. Nine crews claim to have attacked the target while three others turned back, presumably with technical problems.

1 Squadron	Lt B H Moody	Safe	Unemployed List 3 February 1920: Lt
SE.5a B130			

T/o Clairmarais with other pilots ordered for a line patrol and on return landed safely but so badly shot about that 'B130' was struck from charge.

2 Squadron	Lt H K Baron	Safe
FK.8 D5030	Lt F A Baker	Safe

T/o Hesdigneul and headed for Rély where Lieutenant Baron intended to demonstrate dual circuits and landing with Lieutenant Baker, a pilot newly arrived on the squadron. To his embarrassment he swung while taking off and 'D5030' turned onto its nose and was damaged beyond repair. Flown to France from Newcastle early in April 1918, 'D5030' had been well used since issue to the squadron on the 1st of May, clocking up a grand total of one hundred and sixty-three hours and fifty minutes. The next day, No 2 Squadron moved the short distance west to Floringhem having been based at Hesdigneul for the past three years.

2 Squadron AusFC	Lt E D Cummings	Safe	See 16 June 1918 - 2 Squadron AusFC
SE.5a B195			

T/o Fouquerolles for operations over the Roye area but crash-landed soon after with engine failure. This was Lieutenant Cummings's third crash, summaries for the two previous accidents being reported on 22 April and 3rd May 1918.

2 Squadron AusFC	Captain E L Simonson	Safe
SE.5a D6187		

T/o Fouquerolles for operations over the Somme in the direction of Péronne during which a connecting rod broke resulting in a forced landing near Compregnie [sic].

2 Squadron AusFC	Lt R W Sexton	Safe
SE.5a D6191		

T/o Fouquerolles heading for operations over Noyen; force-landed on the side of a hill near St Laurent following loss of oil pressure. See my summary for 5 April 1918, concerning Lieutenant Sexton.

9 Squadron	Lt W H Sangway	Safe
RE.8 A3825	Lt E A Easterbrook	Safe

T/o Estrée-en-Chaussée for camera gun practice but owing to an error of judgement came to grief in an unspecified manner. On squadron establishment since 21 September 1917, 'A3825' logged two hundred and sixty-six hours and fifty minutes flying.

10 Squadron	Lt S Jukes	Safe
FK.8 C8556	2Lt W H Stanley	Safe

T/o Droglandt for a counter attack patrol but force-landed almost immediately, just beyond the airfield, owing to major engine failure. Delivered to France from Newcastle, 'C8556' was accepted by the squadron on 15 April 1918, and when written off had flown for a total of one hundred and one hours and fifty five minutes. An asterisk note regarding Lieutenant Jukes accompanies my summary for 7 April 1918.

10 Squadron	Lt H McL Ferguson*	Safe	Commission relinquished 1 April 1920: Lt
FK.8 D5032	Lt D I Melhado*	Safe	Commission relinquished 1 April 1920: Lt

T/o Droglandt authorised to carry out a practice reconnaissance; force-landed near the aerodrome owing to engine failure. On the 16th of April 1918, this FK.8 crewed by Lieutenant L H Short and Second Lieutenant

Edward Keith Harker departed Droglandt at 1300 for a sortie over the Zillebeke to Dranoutre area and during the operation came under heavy anti-aircraft fire and machine-gun fire from the ground. Then, having drawn clear a trio of hostile aircraft swooped on 'D5032' but were unable to inflict any lasting damage and the crew landed at base circa 1420. Here it was discovered that Edward Harker had been badly wounded, either as a consequence of the ground fire or from the aerial encounter. Taken to one of the nearby casualty clearing stations he died from his wounds on 18 April. Formerly of the Royal Garrison Artillery, twenty year old Second Lieutenant Harker rests in Belgium at Haringhe [Bandaghem] Military Cemetery. When written off 'D5032' had accumulated a total of one hundred and twenty-eight hours and twenty-five minutes flying.

* Both officers were formerly of the Royal Field Artillery and had returned to army duty prior to relinquishing their commissions.

| 22 Squadron | Lt C W M Thompson | Safe |
| Bristol F.2b C4894 | Mechanic Rich | Safe |

T/o Serny to test the aircraft's wireless equipment; on return landed heavily causing major damage. Salvaged, the airframe languished until 8 August 1918, when it was deemed to be not worth repairing. In total 'C4894' logged one hundred hours and twenty-five minutes flying.

| 28 Squadron | Lt G D McLeod [Canada] | pow | Montreal [Mount Royal] Cemetery |
| F.1 Camel B2316 H | | | |

T/o Grossa for an offensive patrol; last sighted at around 0950 diving from 12,000 feet towards an enemy aircraft in the vicinity of Pordenone in the province of the same name in northeast Italy. Subsequently, reported down in territory held by the Austrians. Lieutenant McLeod was badly wounded and following the armistice and his return to Canada he died as a result of his injuries on 22 January 1919. His squadron details are omitted from his entry in the cemetery register. Reported at the Air Acceptance Park at Lincoln by 4 August 1917, 'B2316' was initially taken on by No 70 Squadron on the 17th, but the following month on the 15th crashed when taking off from Poperinghe, Second Lieutenant H Ibbotson escaping unhurt. Repaired, the Camel next went to Filescamp where it was accepted by No 46 Squadron but within a fortnight it was again in need of repair following a combat on the 23rd of November [Second Lieutenant H N C Robinson]. This time repairs and storage lasted until the last day of April 1918 when it arrived, by rail, with '28' for operations on the Italian front.

| 32 Squadron | Lt S W Graham | Safe | See 9 June 1918 - 32 Squadron |
| SE.5a B8514 | | | |

T/o Fouquerolles and headed for operations in the Fresnoy-lès-Roye area of the Somme. On return Lieutenant Graham overshot his approach and 'B8514' was damaged beyond repair after becoming entangled in wire fencing.

| 40 Squadron | Lt D S Poler USAS | Safe | See 23 June 1918 - 40 Squadron |
| SE.5a D3505 | | | |

T/o 1055 Bryas detailed for escort duties and on making his return to Bryas at 1155, Lieutenant Poler touched down on one wheel and nosed over; the third SE.5a to be wrecked in his hands.

| 41 Squadron | Lt W G Claxton | Safe |
| SE.5a C8877 | | |

T/o Conteville for operations over Montdidier; force-landed with a seized engine and damaged beyond repair.

| 56 Squadron | 2 Lt L N Franklin | Safe | See 4 July 1918 - 56 Squadron |
| SE.5a B8413 | | | |

T/o Valheureux authorised to carry out a practice flight which ended with 'B8413' on its back, in long grass, following a misjudged landing.

| 85 Squadron | Captain A C Randall | Safe | See 7 July 1918 - 85 Squadron |
| SE.5a C1901 | | | |

T/o Petite Synthe for an air test and damaged beyond repair following a heavy landing. Postwar, Captain Randall was appointed to a permanent commission.

85 Squadron	Lt M C McGregor	Safe
SE.5a C6492		

T/o Petite Synthe for an offensive patrol and on return landed heavily; damaged beyond repair.

103 Squadron	Lt V Mercer-Smith	Safe	See 15 June 1918 - 103 Squadron
DH.9 C2177	2Lt A E Durling	Safe	

T/o Serny for bombing during which the crew force-landed at Longueil*after the aircraft's water circulation failed to function.

* Possibly Longueil-Annel or Longueil-Saint-Marie, both communes being in the *département du Oise.*

205 Squadron	Lt J C Wilson	Safe
DH.4 A7739	Sgt S M MacKay	Safe

T/o Bois de Roche and wrecked in a landing accident on return from bombing operations over Rosieres. The favoured aircraft for Lieutenant [later captain] Euan Dickson*'A7739' may accurately be described as being in the thick of it where air fighting was concerned. During the morning of 16 March an Albatros DV was sent down over the aerodrome at Busigny, southwest of Le Cateau while the day after becoming No 205 Squadron [1st of April] it came under attack from six enemy aircraft in the vicinity of Péronne. Despite the heat of air fighting, the crew reported that the Pfalz DIII sent down had green and yellow markings. On the 6th, near Abancourt [Oise], in mid-afternoon a trio of triplanes and a black Pfalz with crosses on a white background decided to engage the DH, but Second Lieutenant W H Scott [Captain Dickson's observer] was up to the matter in hand and the Pfalz was duly despatched. Then, during the late afternoon of the 22nd, this time with Gunlayer C V Robinson occupying the rear cockpit, a Fokker DrI was sent earthwards over Chaulnes [Somme]. The following day, with Gunlayer C V Middleton as his observer, an evening battle which lasted for ten minutes finally ended with another Fokker DrI falling near the railway station at Chaulnes. Sergeant McKay features in summaries reported on the 1st and 24th of April 1918.

* Born in Sheffield on the last day of March 1892, Euan Dickson emigrated circa 1912 to New Zealand but returned to his homeland in 1916, and was commissioned in the July as a Flight Sub-Lieutenant and it was while ranked as such that he was awarded a Distinguished Service Cross, published without a citation in *The Edinburgh Gazette* issue 13182 of 21 December 1917. To this was added a First Bar [issue 30654 of *The London Gazette* published on 23 April 1918, the citation reading; *'For conspicuous gallantry in attacking enemy aircraft and in carrying out bombing raids. On the 16th March, 1918, he went to the assistance of a machine of his formation which was being attacked at close quarters by twelve enemy scouts. Despite the fact that all the guns on his machine were useless owing to lack of ammunition, he turned and charged the hostile formation, splitting it up and diverting their attention from the other machine, thus undoubtedly saving it. On other occasions he has brought down enemy machines and taken part in many daylight bombing raids, at all times showing utter fearlessness and great determinations.'* Following the merger of the two air arms, a Distinguished Flying Cross was awarded and the citation in *The Edinburgh Gazette* issue 13325 published on 23 September 1918 reads; *'Since 17th April, 1918, this officer has led eighty-four successful bombing raids. His leadership has been conspicuous for remarkable bravery, skill, and determination. On one raid directed against a town in occupation by the enemy he obtained seven direct hits on the railway station and four on a dump outside. Thrice on a prior date he led his flight to attack enemy billets and horse lines, descending to low altitudes and engaging enemy troops on the ground.'* Leaving the air force in 1919, with a *Croix de Guerre* added to his decorations, he returned to New Zealand where he died in Auckland on 10 March 1980. There are several websites devoted to this officer and I recommend a reading of the notes and observations published on *Wikipedia.*

Sunday 9 June 1918

2 Squadron AusFC	Lt W Q Adams	Safe
SE.5a D3429		

T/o Fouquerolles for an offensive patrol during which 'D3429' was hit by hostile fire and on return to base, and landing, the undercarriage gave way causing damage that was deemed uneconomical to put right. The second production aircraft off the line from a contract awarded to Vickers at Weybridge, 'D3429' was issued to the squadron on 30 March 1918, and was in continuous action up until the events here outlined. During this time it shared in the destruction of three enemy aircraft, while on the 1st and 2nd of June Lieutenant Adams bagged a brace of Pfalz scouts.

19 Squadron	Lt W A Hunter	Injured	
5F.1 Dolphin C4134			

T/o Savy for a line patrol and shot down over the Pas-de-Calais near Béthune. Lieutenant Hunter was wounded in the engagement.

23 Squadron	Lt J T McKay	Safe	See 3 July 1918 - 23 Squadron
5F.1 Dolphin C4133			

T/o Bertangles for an offensive patrol of the inner perimeter; lost engine power and wrecked in a forced landing at Allonville [Somme], five km north of Amiens. It will recalled that John Thomas McKay had survived serious crashes on the 19th and 22nd May 1918 [see my summaries for details].

25 Squadron	Lt R G Dobeson	Safe	Unemployed list 5 August 1919: F/O
DH.4 A7602	Airman F E Warren	Safe	

T/o Ruisseauville for a test flight and damaged beyond repair following a heavy landing. This, I believe, was the squadron's first non-operational loss since the 1st of April.

25 Squadron	Lt A E Hulme	Safe	See 20 July 1918 - 25 Squadron
DH.4 A7775	Airman W Gray	Safe	

T/o Ruisseauville tasked for bombing operations and damaged beyond repair following a crash-landing in a ploughed field near Gironcourt [possibly Gironcourt-sur-Vraine in the Vosges].

25 Squadron	Lt L F V Atkinson	Injured	
DH.4 D9272	2Lt H H Watson	Safe	See 2 July 1918 - 25 Squadron

T/o Ruisseauville tasked for bombing operations over Valenciennes and was rendered very second-hand after crashing into a tree when landing. For Second Lieutenant this was his second 'incident', the first being on 21st May 1918, when he was crewing with South African, Lieutenant L L K Straw [see my summary for details].

29 Squadron	Lt H White	Safe	
SE.5a D6192			

T/o St Omer for an offensive patrol and wrecked here when Lieutenant White landed with a force sufficient to damage his aircraft beyond repair. My summary on 6 June 1918, regarding this officer records a similar mishap.

32 Squadron	Captain W A Tyrrell	+	Beauvais Communal Cemetery
SE.5a B8391			

T/o Fouquerolles for operations along the corridor between Montdidier and Lassigny and it was while strafing enemy troops that his aircraft was bracketed by anti-aircraft fire. Wounded, Walter Alexander Tyrrell managed to climb to around a thousand feet when he appears to have fainted, crashing to earth near Maignelay*where 'B8391' went up in flames. Before the month was out, his elder brother Captain John Marcus Tyrrell, late of the 3rd Reserve Battalion Royal Irish Fusiliers, attached as a staff pilot with No 1 Aeroplane Supply Depot St Omer died; he is buried in Boulogne Eastern Cemetery. In due course, Walter Tyrrell was awarded the Military Cross [gazetted 16 September 1918, supplement 30901]; 'For conspicuous gallantry and devotion to duty. On one day this officer attacked two enemy triplanes, destroying one and driving down the other out of control. After this he was attacked by two other machines, one of which he forced to land, taking the occupants prisoner. On various other occasions he has destroyed or driven down out of control enemy machines'. The inscription. On his head-stone is very much in the language and thinking of the time; 'Stout Fellow.'

* Probably Maignelay-Montigny in the département due Oise.

32 Squadron	Lt S W Graham	Safe
SE.5a D6867		

T/o Fouquerolles charged for operations as outlined above in the course of which he was wounded and, subsequently, force-landed close to No 43 Squadron lines.

34 Squadron	Captain T C Lowe MC	Injured
Bristol F.2b C913	2Lt A S Withers	Injured

T/o Villaveria for a reconnaissance sortie and on return crash-landed on the aerodrome; damaged beyond repair. Trevor Henshaw, in his records for losses from the Italian front, shows 'C913' belonging to Z Flight. As an observer officer Second Lieutenant Withers was confirmed in his appointment on 17 May 1918, promulgated in *The London Gazette* 23 July 1918, issue 30808. He returned to the service in the Second World War and was commissioned to the Administrative and Special Duties Branch on 28 June 1940 [*gazetted* 16 July 1940, issue 34898] and served until relinquishing his commission under the provisions of the Navy, Army and Air Force Reserves Act 1954, retaining his rank of squadron leader.

35 Squadron	Lt J M Brown [Canada]	Safe	See 3 October 1918 - 35 Squadron
FK.8 D5050	2Lt J A Weller	Safe	

T/o Villers Bocage and set forth for the Albert area. During the patrol the crew experienced major engine failure when a cylinder head cracked; force-landed near Béhencourt [Somme] some ten km east-southeast of the air-field. On squadron charge 28 May 1918, 'D5050' was struck off charge on 12 June 1918, having achieved a total of thirty-two hours and fifteen minutes flying. On 14 December 1918, owing to wounds, Second Lieutenant Weller had to relinquish his commission.

40 Squadron	Lt N D Willis	Safe	See 27 September 1918 - 40 Squadron
SE.5a D3971			

T/o 1055 Bryas tasked for escort duties but at 1235 had to make a forced landing at Avesne-le-Comte in the Pas-de-Calais some twenty-one km west-southwest from Arras.

41 Squadron	Lt F R McCall [Canada]	Safe
SE.5a D5959		

T/o Conteville for operations in the direction of Moreuil [Somme] and following an engagement with a hostile machine force-landed near Berny [*sic*]. For biographical notes concerning Frederick Robert McCall, please consult my summary for 8 May 1918.

43 Squadron	Lt J H Johnson	+	Thiescourt French National Cemetery
F.1 Camel D1844			

T/o 0855 Fouquerolles for a special mission from which Lieutenant Johnson failed to return; prior to his loss, and while at the controls of 'D1844' he drove down an Albatros scout out of control on 30 May 1918. It is almost a certainty that he came down just to the west of Noyon in the *département du Oise* at, or close to the commune of Thiescourt where John Hercules Johnson is the sole British serviceman from the *Great War* buried here.

49 Squadron	Lt G Ezard	Injured	
DH.9 D5596	Lt C A B Beattie	Safe	See 16 July 1918 - 49 Squadron

T/o Fourneuil for what is described as a 'travelling flight' and it would appear the crew became uncertain of their position for a landing was made at Le Quesnoy, home of No 57 Squadron, to request onward directions. Subsequently, the crew took off but while climbing away the engine failed and 'D5596' went down into a wood and was completely wrecked. Interestingly, the squadron's website indicates Lieutenant George Ezard as being attached to the squadron on 25 March 1918, and posted out, believed injured, ten days prior to the accident here summarised. Cameron Alexander Bell Beattie had been posted in on 10 May 1918, and his subsequent fate is described in my summary for 16 July 1918.

60 Squadron	Lt G M Duncan	Injured
SE.5a B8398		

T/o Boffles and while in flight the generator wheel broke, fragments puncturing the radiator and injuring Lieutenant Duncan who, in some discomfort, crash-landed in a cornfield near Pas [sic]. Including the usual factory tests and ferrying to France, 'B8398' flew for twenty-three hours and thirty-five minutes.

| 73 Squadron | 2Lt R A Baring | + | Arras Flying Services Memorial |

SE.5a B5244

T/o 1930 Fouquerolles tasked for low level strafing attacks and when last seen was flying southwest of Tricot in the *département du Oise*. Nineteen years of age, and from Chandlers Ford in Hampshire, his widowed mother would bear the pain of losing this her fourth son; two appear to have emigrated to Australia where on the outbreak of war they joined the Australian Imperial Force. Twenty-three year old Private Charles Alexander Baring serving with the 52nd Battalion Australian Infantry was first to die fighting on the Somme on the 4th of September 1916; he is commemorated on the Villers-Bretonneux Memorial. Less that a year later, on 2 April 1917, Lance Corporal Ernest Baring, at twenty-seven the eldest, fell fighting with the 56th Battalion Australian Infantry; he is buried in the Pas-de-Calais at Vaulx Hill Cemetery. Nearly a year would pass before Second Lieutenant Cecil Christopher Baring, age twenty, and who was born in at Simla in India, died on the opening day of the German Spring Offensive. At the time Cecil was attached to the 8th Battalion Queen's Own [Royal West Kent Regiment] of the 72nd Brigade, 24th Division; he rests in Roye New British Cemetery in the Somme. Now, the youngest of her sons was gone. It is noted that the entry for Cecil Baring shows his father was the late Reverend Francis Henry Baring.

| 73 Squadron | Lt H Jenkinson | Safe | See 11 June 1918 - 73 Squadron |

F.1 Camel D6592

T/o 1930 Fouquerolles similarly charged and was shot up by anti-aircraft fire which carried away the rear spar from the bottom port plane; gliding over the lines to force-land at Godenvillers [Oise] some seven to eight km south-southwest of Montdidier. Bravely, despite intense shelling of the area, Lieutenant Jenkinson managed to torch 'D6592' in order to prevent it from falling into enemy hands.

| 82 Squadron | Lt Kitchingman* | Safe |
| FK.8 C3701 | Lt Bardsly | Safe |

T/o Quevenvillers for a patrol during which a close burst of anti aircraft fire tilted the FK.8 so violently that acid from the aircraft's accumulator spilt. This caused such corrosive damage that it was struck off charge on 26th June 1918.

* Probably Lieutenant C G Kitchingman confirmed in the rank of second lieutenant on 12 February 1918 [*gazetted* in supplement 30584 of 19 March 1918], subsequently placed on the unemployed list 19 April 1919.

| 84 Squadron | Captain J V Sorsoleil MC | Safe |
| SE.5a B8233 | [Canada] |

T/o Bertangles leading a patrol to Villers-Bretonneux where a German scout pilot*had the audacity to shoot off John Victor Sorsolleil's propeller. Maintaining control, Captain Sorsoleil force-landed near Les Alençons. From Coventry 'B8233' on arrival in France went first to No 56 Squadron but was badly damaged while landing at Lavieville on the 6th of January 1918, from a forced landing near Albert, the pilot being named as Lieutenant Hastings-Trew. Repaired, 'B8233' was issued to No 84 Squadron on 12 March; in total it flew one hundred and sixty-three hours and thirty-five minutes. Born in Peterborough, Ontario on 2 June 1898, John Sorsoleil gained his Military Cross on 22 April 1918, supplement 30643; '*For conspicuous gallantry and devotion to duty. While on patrol with three other scouts he engaged a hostile formation of ten scouts, driving one of these down. While climbing to rejoin his patrol he was attacked by an enemy scout, upon which he opened fire at close range, bringing it down spinning, with the result that it crashed to earth. He has also driven down one enemy machine in flames, and sent another crashing to earth, where it was destroyed. His gallantry and skill have been most conspicuous.*' His tour of duty on the Western Front ended towards the end of June, after which he posted for instructional duties at an aerodrome in England. Captain Sorsoleil died at the comparatively early age of fifty-eight on 4 September 1956.

* Some sources suggest the propeller was shot away by anti-aircraft fire.

| 103 Squadron | Lt J G H Crispin | Safe |
| DH.9 C6155 | Lt E A Wadsworth | Safe |

T/o 1825 Serny for a bombing raid coming under anti-aircraft fire which shot through airframe to the extent that it was struck off charge on 13 July 1918. This particular DH.9 had been intended for issue to No 99 Squadron, but while being ferried to France on the 4th of May 1918, by Lieutenant N S Harper [see my summary for 25 June 1918] and Corporal Harding overshot the aerodrome [presumably Tantonville] and running into a trench did the undercarriage no little good. Repaired, it was issued to No 103 Squadron later in the month.

103 Squadron	Lt E A Windridge	+	Bouchoir New British Cemetery
DH.9 D1007	2Lt V W Allen MC MM	+	Bouchoir New British Cemetery
	[South Africa]		

T/o 1945 Serny and was reported by returning crews to have been last sighted with the formation still behind enemy lines. Four days previously these two officers had walked away from a forced landing which effectively wrote off their DH. Since arriving with the squadron as recently as 25 May, 'D1007' had seen plenty of action. Second Lieutenant I W Leiper and Private J Buffery engaging with enemy scouts on the 6th and 9th of June, crashing one just over an hour before Lieutenant Windridge took off for his final sortie. Victor William Allen had served with the South African Infantry, attached to the 4th Regiment.

| 203 Squadron | 2Lt C Marsden | pow |
| F.1 Camel B7163 | | |

T/o Filescamp for an offensive patrol joining up, it would seem, with Camels from No 210 Squadron out from Ste Marie Cappel and at around 0830 driven down, along with the Camel summarised below, following a sharp fight over Bois de Ploegsteert in West-Vlaanderen. Second Lieutenant Marsden was repatriated on 13 December 1918; his Camel had flown in total forty-four hours and three minutes.

| 210 Squadron | 2Lt W Breckenridge | pow |
| F.1 Camel D3348 | | |

T/o Ste Marie Cappel and went down in the manner described above; his name, along with Second Lieutenant Marsden's, appeared under the heading 'Missing' in *Flight* July 4, 1918.

| 224 Squadron | Lt W F Salton | + | Otranto Town Cemetery |
| DH.4 D1773 | Airman S W James | Injured | Otranto Town Cemetery |

T/o Alimini and crashed soon after. Both casualties are shown on the Commonwealth War Graves Commission website as attached to No 66 Wing which at the time of their deaths was officially referred to as No 66 [Naval] Wing, this title being bestowed on the former No 6 Wing Royal Naval Air Service on the day that the Royal Naval Air Service and the Royal Flying Corps merged to become the independent Royal Air Force. Three squadrons operated under its aegis; Nos 223, 224 and 225 Squadrons. Situated on Italy's Salento peninsular and looking out towards the Strait of Ortranto which connects the Adriatic Sea with the Ionian Sea the cemetery has ten service burials from the *Great War* five Royal Naval Air Service and five Royal Air Force. Untraced in *The London Gazette* William Fletcher Salton's name appears on the list released from the Admiralty in October 1917, and recorded in *Flight* October 25, 1917. Sidney Whitehouse James's service number '208399' shows enlistment to the Royal Naval Air Service in 1915 and his subsequent transfer to the air force in April 1918.

Monday 10 June 1918

| 27 Squadron | 2Lt T Noad | + | Verberie French National Cemetery |
| DH.4 A7677 G | Sgt G Sterling | + | Verberie French National Cemetery |

T/o Fourneuil with orders to carry out, with others, a low strafing attack. Seen to break up over Gournay.*George Sterling's service number '187954' indicates he was probably transferred from another arm of the forces circa March 1918. He was nineteen years of age.

* There are six locations in France with 'Gournay' as the lead name; here I suspect it was Gournay-sur-Aronde in the Oise *département* which is roughly thirty km north-northwest from Verberie.

32 Squadron   Lt A A Callender [USA]   Safe   See 30 October 1918 - 32 Squadron
SE.5a C1884

T/o Fouquerolles heading for the area Montdidier-Cuvilly-Roye to seek out targets for ground strafing. Force-landed southeast of Compaigne [sic] following combat with a hostile aircraft.

32 Squadron   Lt P Hooper [USAS]   +
SE.5a C9626

T/o Fouquerolles for an offensive patrol and reported to have spiralled down to crash near the Château de Sorel at Orville-Sorel in the *département de la Somme.*

43 Squadron   Lt W K Macfarlane   Safe
F.1 Camel C8299

T/o 0545 Fouquerolles for a special mission to Gournay-sur-Aronde and Hémévillers [Oise]; crashed after flying into a balloon cable, visibility being described as 'misty'.

43 Squadron   Lt C C Banks MC   Safe
F.1 Camel D1809

T/o 1835 Fouquerolles for an offensive patrol during which Lieutenant Banks sent down an Albatros at around 1915 north of Monchy-le-Preux in the Pas-de-Calais; however, in the exchange of fire his petrol tank was holed and roughly fifteen minutes later he crash-landed near Bois de Ressons where he set fire to the Camel as he was aware of enemy troops advancing in the area. A photograph of Second Lieutenant Charles Chaplin Banks of the 4th Battalion Royal Welsh Fusiliers is in the extensive collection of military photographs at the Imperial War Museum [HU113280]. It is a formal image showing him with his service cap, 'Sam Browne' and Flying Badge clearly showing 'RFC'. The citation for his Military Cross was published on 9 February 1918, in supplement 30517 of that date and it is clear he gained his award while serving with a Home Defence squadron; *'For conspicuous gallantry displayed when they*engaged a Gotha raiding London. During the engagement, which lasted a considerable time, they were continually under fire from the enemy machine.'* From the Oxford University Contingent, Senior Division, Officers Training Corps, Charles Banks was initially commissioned to the 5th[Flintshire] Battalion, The Royal Welsh Fusiliers on 10 December 1914 [supplement 29001 of 9th December 1914]. Postwar, he was *gazetted* with the Distinguished Flying Cross on 8th February 1919, issue 31170; *'A brilliant and skilful airman who has been conspicuous for his success in aerial combats. On 30 October he, single-handed, engaged five enemy aeroplanes and drove one down out of control. In the fight his aileron controls were shot away, but by skilful handling and a cool presence of mind he brought his machine back and made a successful landing. In addition to the above Capt Banks has accounted for nine other enemy machines.'* His biography, reported on *Wikipedia,* shows he was born in the Hampstead district of London on 17 December 1893, and died at the age of seventy-eight at Lewes in Sussex on 21 December 1971.

* Temporary Captain George Henry Hackwill was the other pilot so honoured, both serving with No 44 Squadron and flying F.1 Camels identified in *The Camel File* as 'B2402' [Captain Hackwill] and 'B3827' [Second Lieutenant Banks], their victim being a Gotha DV 938/16 which crashed at Wickford in Essex circa 2210 on the 25th of January 1918. At the time No 44 Squadron was operating from Hainault Farm.

49 Squadron   Lt L R Charron [Canada]   Safe
DH.9 D5585   Lt F B Dennison USAS   Injured

T/o Fourneuil to bomb targets at Montdidier during which the bombers were attacked by enemy scouts, fire from a Pfalz wounding Lieutenant Frederick Browne Dennison whose weapon had jammed, thereby ending his service with the squadron which had lasted for less than a month. His skipper, however, served between the 10th of March and the 10th of August 1918. On return to base, and examined, 'D5585' was struck off charge on 9 July 1918.

73 Squadron   Lt B W de B Leyson USAS   pow
F.1 Camel D1963

T/o 0600 Fouquerolles having received instructions for low level strafing; last seen trying to attach himself to a formation of SE.5s.

73 Squadron	Lt J Balfour	Safe
F.1 Camel D8117		

T/o 0640 Fouquerolles similarly briefed. Twenty-five minutes after leaving and flying over the Somme southwest of Rollot, Lieutenant Balfour drove down an Albatros out of control, but in the fight his petrol tank was shot through and he force-landed near Cernoy [sic]. With Rollot on the border between the *départements* of Somme and Oise, it is likely that both aircraft came down in Oise.

103 Squadron	Lt F H Sillem	Safe	See 12 June 1918 - 103 Squadron
DH.9 C6157	Sgt H W Cornell	Safe	See 12 June 1918 - 103 Squadron

T/o Serny for bombing operations and reported crashed near Château de Laversine in the *département du Oise* home of the polo playing Robert de Rothschild, son of Baron Gustave de Rothschild who acquired the land on which it stands in 1874. This particular DH.9 arrived in France on 9 May 1918, three days ahead of the main body.

206 Squadron	Lt E H P Bailey	Safe	See 11 August 1918 - 206 Squadron
DH.9 D459	2Lt W D McKinnon	Safe	

T/o Alquines for a line patrol on return from which Lieutenant Bailey crashed during landing. His previous mishap is summarised on 12 April 1918.

210 Squadron	Captain J G Manuel DSC	+	Y Farm Military Cemetery, Bois-Grenier
F.1 Camel B7249	[Canada]		

T/o Ste Marie Cappel for an offensive patrol during which John Gerald Manuel dived towards an enemy aircraft and while doing so collided with the Camel featured below, both aircraft breaking up with debris falling between Laventie to the north and Neuve Chappelle on the south, a corridor of about five km south-southeast of Estaries these communes in the winding border country of the *départements* of Nord and Pas-de-Calais. Captain Manuel gained his Distinguished Service Cross for actions taken in the late summer of 1917, as *gazetted* 19 December 1917 in supplement 30437; *'For conspicuous gallantry and devotion to duty in air fights and bombing raids, particularly on the 26th September 1917, when he attacked alone the Abeele Aerodrome, dropping his bombs from about 1,500 feet with good results. A machine-gun then opened fire on him, but he dived down low and silenced it by firing fifty rounds from his machine gun.'*

210 Squadron	2Lt F C Dodd	+	Y Farm Military Cemetery, Bois-Grenier
F.1 Camel D9590			

T/o Ste Marie Cappel similarly tasked and lost in the manner described above.

218 Squadron	2Lt R W Robinson [Canada]	+	Bergen-op-Zoom War Cemetery
DH.9 B7667	Private H A Claydon	+	Les Baraques Military Cemetery, Sangatte

T/o Petite Synthe tasked for bombing but inclement weather prevented the squadron from making any attacks and the formation turned for home, 'B7667' being last sighted flying between 12,000 and 14,000 feet, above the clouds, off Nieuwpoort after which it is assumed the DH went down in the sea resulting in the deaths of the crew by drowning. Eventually the sea gave up both bodies. Their details on the Commonwealth War Graves Commission website, I suggest, indicate the dates that they found for Ralph Walter Robinson is shown as dying on the 11th of June and Harold Alfred Claydon on the 25th of July 1918. Both, however, will be commemorated on the 10th of June 1918. They were the first from the squadron to lose their lives since forming at Dover on the 28th of April 1918.

Tuesday 11 June 1918

Twenty-four hours after losing the DH reported in my summary above, No 218 Squadron opened its account for the *Great War* with eleven of their aircraft bombing a variety of targets at Oostende, including docks, the harbour basin, the railway station and nearby sidings. Operations over the *départements* of Somme and Oise were intense; at Fouquerolles No 73 Squadron had their Camels in the air throughout the day, mainly engaged on low level strafing of troops south of Montdidier and paying a high price with at least seven aircraft driven down, crashed or damaged beyond repair owing to enemy opposition.

1 Squadron   Lt H A Kullberg [USA]   Safe   Unemployed list 12 July 1919: Lt DFC
SE.5a C6441
T/o Clairmarais South for a practice in formation flying and on return to the airfield, and landing, ran into a grass cutter machine and wrecked. Howard Albert Kullberg was born on 10 September 1896, in Somerville, Middlesex County, Massachusetts and desirous to join in the fight against Germany he crossed into Canada in August 1917, and enlisted with the Royal Flying Corps. In France he proved a skilful fighter pilot and Norman Franks [whom I acknowledge] states he was *gazetted* with the Distinguished Flying Cross on 2 November 1918. Norman reports, in his book *Fallen Eagles,* that Howard Kullberg, now a civilian but remaining much connected with aviation, died on Tuesday 5 August 1924, while instructing a Mr Henry Dunbar, their aircraft going out of control and crashing from two thousand feet near Hudson, Ohio.

29 Squadron   Lt A E Reed   Safe   See 12 June 1918 - 29 Squadron
SE.5a E1260
T/o St Omer and with other pilots from the squadron headed for their new home at Vignacourt roughly one hundred km away to the south and some seventeen km north-northwest from Amiens. On landing, Lieutenant Reed had to swerve, violently, in order to avoid colliding with a Camel and in doing so the undercarriage was, in the parlance of the day, *'swiped away.'*

32 Squadron   Lt H L W Flynn   Safe
SE.5a C1899
T/o Fouquerolles heading for operations along the Montdidier to Roye corridor. During the sortie Lieutenant Flynn force-landed on Épineuse aerodrome with an overheating engine and all might have been well had he not run into an old shell hole that had not been filled, thus ended the flying days for 'C1899'.

39 Squadron   2Lt E C Slaght   Injured Unemployed list 29 October 1919: Lt
Bristol F.2b C971   2Lt F J West   Injured
T/o North Weald and on landing crashed and turned over. Commanded by Major W T Holland, the squadron was charged with Home Defence and with its proximity to the East Coast was one of the most successful, particularly during the late summer of 1916, when on the 3rd of September Lieutenant William Leefe Robinson intercepted the airship SL.11 and following a long running fight drove it down to destruction near the village of Cuffley in Hertfordshire, an action that was to win him the Victoria Cross. His biography is reported in full by Chaz Bowyer in his book *For Valour - The Air VCs.*

40 Squadron   Lt W A Morris*   Safe   See 1 July 1918 - 40 Squadron
SE.5a C5320
T/o 1925 Bryas for an offensive patrol and on becoming airborne the port wheel came off. Lieutenant Morris continued with his mission but on return to the airfield at 2100, he was unable to prevent a heavy landing which damaged the SE.5a beyond worthwhile repair.

* Although I cannot be certain, a Lieutenant W A Morris was killed on the 2nd of October 1918, while flying with No 41 Squadron, an SE.5a equipped Scout squadron based at Droglandt.

40 Squadron   Lt P V Burwell USAS   Safe   See 9 August 1918 - 40 Squadron
SE.5a C8876
T/o 1925 Bryas similarly charged but turned back with engine trouble and crashed while attempting to land at 1955. It will be recalled that Lieutenant Burwell had crashed while landing on the 6th of June 1918, for details please see my summary for that data.

40 Squadron   Lt N S Cameron   Safe   See 26 June 1918 - 40 Squadron
SE.5a D6188
T/o Bryas for a line patrol and on return crashed while landing. Flown to France from Brooklands, 'D6188' was accepted by the squadron four days previously.

41 Squadron	Lt M E Gadd	Safe	See 16 June 1918 - 41 Squadron
SE.5a B7787			

T/o Conteville for an offensive patrol and on return, and landing on some rough ground, the V-strut snapped damaging 'B7787' beyond repair.

49 Squadron	Lt R C Stokes	Safe	See 18 June 1918 - 49 Squadron
DH.9 C2185	2Lt C E Pullen	Safe	

T/o Fourneuil for bombing duties during which the airframe sustained major damage from enemy fire; force-landed at Fouquerolles and though salvaged 'C2185' was struck off charge as not worth the cost of repair on 17th July 1918.

49 Squadron	Lt C Bowman	Safe
DH.9 D7201	Lt V Gordon	Injured

T/o Fourneuil for bombing operations during which the crew sent an Albatros down out of control over Cuvilly [Oise], the time being around 1500. Thirty minutes later an attack from a hostile aircraft near Mointierz resulted in the controls being shot away and leaving Lieutenant Gordon in a wounded state. Clifford Bowman was to gain a Distinguished Flying Cross, the citation appearing in *The Edinburgh Gazette* 4th November 1918, issue 13346; *'A fine leader, conspicuous for his courage and cool judgement, who has taken part in over fifty bombing raids, in the majority as leader. On one occasion the formation he was leading was attacked by fifteen Fokkers. In despite of determined efforts on the part of these hostile machines the objective was successfully bombed, direct hits being obtained. By skilful manœuvring the formation returned safely, having destroyed four enemy aeroplanes during the flight. On the evening of the same day when again leading an attack on the same objective the formation was attacked by twenty hostile machines; having destroyed four of them he brought the formation safely back over our lines.'* This particular DH.9 was the first off the line of one hundred aircraft built at Yeovil by the Westland Aircraft Works. Flown to Filton by 20 May 1918, it reached the squadron the day before it was lost from operations.

57 Squadron	Lt T G Rhodes	+	Huby-St Leu British Cemetery
DH.4 D9261	Lt E D Spencer [Canada]	+	Huby-St Leu British Cemetery

T/o Le Quesnoy for bombing operations only for the engine to 'cut' and crash out of control. His cadetship successfully completed Thomas George Rhodes was commissioned on 30 May 1917 to the West Riding Regiment and was attached to the 3rd Battalion Duke of Wellington's [*gazetted* 12 June 1917, issue 30129]. From Vancouver, Evan David Spencer was still on the strength of the 5th Battalion, Canadian Railway Troops though detached for service with the Royal Air Force.

73 Squadron	Lt J I Carpenter USAS	Injured
F.1 Camel B2351		

T/o 1300 Fouquerolles with squadron colleagues to strafe enemy infantry and was last seen over the départment of Oise near Cuvilly. It is believed, however, that his Camel went down to the north of Rollot which is roughly six km or so north-northwest from where he was last sighted. Very badly wounded he died from his injuries on the 19th. Similar to so many of the autumn 1917 issues, 'B2351' had had an eventful life; on the 28th of December it crashed when landing from a patrol flown by by Second Lieutenant M H Orcutt*attached to No 43 Squadron. Repaired locally, it was damaged on the 16th of January when Lieutenant H E Thomson ran into a ditch. This time the damage was of a more serious nature requiring the attention of a repair park where its Clerget 9B was replaced with a Rhône 9J. On 23 March it was taken over by No 46 Squadron but on the historic 1st of April Second Lieutenant E R Watt made rather a hash of his landing; once again 'B2351' was removed for repairs. Issued to No 73 Squadron on the 1st of June, it seems its Rhône had been exchanged for a 160 h p Clerget.

* Maurice Hitchcock Orcutt died on the 1st of March 1918, when he stalled F.1 Camel B5628 and spun in; he is buried in Merville Communal Cemetery where his entry is incorrectly shown as 'No 3 Squadron'.

73 Squadron	Lt O M Baldwin	Safe
F.1 Camel D1832		

T/o 1345 Fouquerolles for low level strafing around Rollot; returned to base so badly shot about that it was struck off charge on 4 July 1918.

73 Squadron   Captain W H Hubbard   Safe
F.1 Camel D1841   [Canada]
T/o 1500 Fouquerolles for an offensive patrol and an hour later Captain Hubbard added to his tally of hostile machines destroyed, or driven down, by crashing a Fokker DVII three km northeast of Rollot. However, his opponent did not go down without putting up fierce resistance and such was the damage inflicted on 'D1841' it was struck off charge on 4 July 1918. It was well favoured by William Henry Hubbard who crashed at least five enemy aircraft, all scouts, while at the controls of 'D1841' and almost certainly assisted in his eventual award of the Distinguished Flying Cross, followed by a First Bar; *'During recent operations he has repeatedly descended to low altitudes to release his bombs and to open machine-gun fire on troops and transport. He has shown the greatest gallantry, judgement and presence of mind. On several occasions he has attacked and driven down out of control enemy aeroplanes.'* [supplement 30827 of 3 August 1918]; *'This officer has shown great bravery and devotion to duty both in destroying enemy aircraft - ten of which he has accounted for - and in silencing anti-Tank guns. On 27th September, flying at altitudes between 200 and 1,500 feet, he engaged and silenced many anti-Tank guns, thereby rendering valuable service. He at the same time completed a detailed and accurate reconnaissance of the area, locating the position of our troops.'* [issue 13363 of *The Edinburgh Gazette* 5th December 1918]. Born 19 May 1896, William Hubbard died on 19 June 1960.

73 Squadron   Lt C W H Douglas USAS   +
F.1 Camel D1962
T/o 1345 Fouquerolles for low level strafing and was seen thirty minutes later diving across the lines to attack targets near Cuvilly [Oise] and about two km southeast of Rollot in the Somme.

73 Squadron   Lt W G Peters   Safe
F.1 Camel D6456
T/o Fouquerolles for an offensive patrol and damaged beyond repair on return in the wake of a heavy landing. It is recorded in *The Camel File* that 'D6456' was the *'Wing Commander's communications a/c'*.

73 Squadron   Lt H Jenkinson   Safe
F.1 Camel D6636 *Johannesburg No 2*
T/o Fouquerolles for an offensive patrol; hit by anti-aircraft fire and left barely controllable and though Lieutenant Jenkinson [see my summary for 9 June 1918] succeeded in returning to base 'D6636' was struck off charge four days later.

73 Squadron   Lt J H Ackerman USAS   Injured
F.1 Camel D9382
T/o 1315 Fouquerolles for low level strafing and it was less than an hour later over the Somme near Rollot that Lieutenant Ackerman sent a Fokker DVII tumbling out of control, though himself received a painful arm wound. Forced landing, the fuselage of 'D9382' broke in two pieces, though according to *The Camel File* parts were salvaged under conditions of heavy shell fire. Without a doubt this had been the worst operational day for the pilots of the squadron since the 1st of April.

103 Squadron   2Lt W R McGee [South Africa] +   Arras Flying Services Memorial
DH.9 C6172   2Lt H Thompson   +   Arras Flying Services Memorial
T/o 1430 Serny to bomb targets in the Montdidier area and it was near Montdidier that the wreckage of their aircraft and their bodies*were found the next day. Wilfred Raworth McGee came from St Pietermaritzburg in Natal province. He was thirty-one years of age, his observer was nineteen.

* I can only surmise that they were buried close to where they fell, since when their graves have been lost.

205 Squadron   Lt W E MacPherson   Safe
DH.4 D9260   Lt C F Ambler   Safe

T/o Bois de Roche and on return to the airfield smashed into DH.4 'N6004' [summarised below]. During the course of a raid in the early morning of 20 May 1918, Lieutenant R Chalmers and Second Lieutenant S H Hamblin shot down a Pfalz DIII.

205 Squadron	Captain J Gamon DSC	Safe	Unemployed list 11 June 1919 - Capt DSC
DH.4 N6004	Sgt P L Richards	Safe	

T/o Bois de Roche and written off in the manner outlined above. Accepted as long ago as 24 July 1917 when No 205 Squadron existed as No 5 Squadron Royal Naval Air Service, 'N6004' had at least four enemy aircraft destroyed to its credit, all with Captain John Gamon at the controls; the first, during the morning of 30 March with Sub-Lieutenant F H Stringer was reported as a Fokker DrI, followed in the evening of 23 April and with Lieutenant R Scott occupying the rear cockpit another Fokker DrI 'flamed' and a Pfalz out of control, were claimed over the Somme and in the general vicinity of Chaulnes railway station. The Pas-de-Calais was the scene for his fourth success in 'N6004' [and his seventh in total] when with Sergeant J Jones a Pfalz DIII was sent crashing near Méricourt. John Gamon is remembered on a number of websites, one of which records that he was the middle of three sons, his elder brother Sydney Percival Gamon having been commissioned to the Cheshire Regiment and serving with the 5th Battalion transferred to the Royal Flying Corps only to be killed in a flying accident in South Essex on 23 March 1918. At his inquest a verdict of "Accidental Death" was returned [*Flight* April 4th, 1918]. Ranked captain, he is buried in Neston Cemetery. Tragedy, it is reported, struck the family again when Geoffrey Alexander Percival Gamon died on 24 October 1934 in Cairo while in the service of Imperial Airways. John Gamon's passing occurred on 5 December 1976, since when a cloister window in Cheshire Cathedral now commemorates all three brothers and their father. As can be seen from the crew matrix, John, born on 25 July 1898, was awarded the Distinguished Service Cross, the citation for which, as repeated on *Wikipedia* reads; '*For conspicuous gallantry and devotion to duty. On 30 March 1918, whilst returning from a bombing raid, he was attacked by three enemy triplanes, one of which he brought down and drove off the other two. He has carried out very many bombing raids on enemy lines of communication, aerodromes, and dumps. His work has always been of the greatest merit, and he has set a splendid example to those around him.*' With the Second World War showing no signs of imminent ending the Royal Air Force was in need of hundreds of experience men to handle the plethora of administrative tasks it was to the Administrative and Special Duties Branch that John Gamon returned on 27 September 1940 [*gazetted* 29 October 1940, issue 34982], continuing to serve long after the cessation of hostilities.

208 Squadron	Lt R L Johns	+	Aire Communal Cemetery
F.1 Camel D6698			

T/o Serny for a test flight which tragically ended when Reginald Leach Johns lost control while banking left and spun in at Treizennes airfield. His headstone is inscribed thus; '*His Loved Ones Honour Him He Was The Life & Soul Of The Sqdn*"*His C O*'.

210 Squadron	Lt N Mason	+	Ebblinghem Military Cemetery
F.1 Camel B7155			

T/o Ste Marie Cappel for a practice flight during which nineteen year old Nelson Mason dived steeply and in pulling out overstressed the airframe resulting in the wings folding.

Wednesday 12 June 1918

1 Squadron	Lt E E Owen	Safe	See 16 June 1918 - 1 Squadron
SE.5a B8512			

T/o Clairmarais South authorised for practice flying during which Lieutenant Owen overstressed the airframe while pulling up sharply from a dive and force-landed at map reference 36ab20b22 where it was found three of the aircraft's main spars were fractured. Struck off charge 19 June 1918.

2 Squadron AusFC	Lt T J Hammond AusFC	+	Arras Flying Services Memorial
SE.5a D3960			

T/o Fouquerolles for an offensive patrol and was lost sight of after the patrol left Noyon [Oise]. Themetre James Hammond was the first pilot from the squadron to be killed on operations since the 1st of April 1918.

4 Squadron AusFC   2Lt W S Martin AusFC   +   Ebblinghem Military Cemetery
F.1 Camel B5646

T/o 1040 Clairmarais for what, sadly, was to be William Stanley Martin's last offensive patrol, a patrol during which he acquitted himself valiantly. Flying in the company of Captain E J K McCloughry, a noted Australian flying 'Ace', William shared with his flight commander in the total destruction of one kite balloon and left a second one smoking, these encounters taking place between 1140 and 1150. Then, with midday approaching, he made a solo attack on an enemy scout which he drove down near Meteren just inside the border with Belgium and on the northwest side of Bailleul [Nord]. Soon after he was attacked by another scout and fell away out of control. In his all too short life he accounted for two enemy aircraft.

40 Squadron   Lt H H Wood   Safe   See 12 August 1918 - 40 Squadron
SE.5a D6002

T/o 2010 Bryas for an offensive patrol but on return at 2055 stalled and crashed heavily. It will be recalled that Henry Harben Wood had had a similar accident on the 2nd of May 1918; for details of this, and information regarding his commission, please refer to my summary for that date.

43 Squadron   Lt J G Beck   Safe
F.1 Camel D1885

T/o 1025 Fouquerolles for an offensive patrol; drove down a Fokker DrI over Ribécourt-Dreslincourt [Oise] but was himself shot about resulting in 'D1885' being struck off charge on 4 July 1918.

43 Squadron   Lt P W R Arundel   Safe   See 8 August 1918 - 43 Squadron
F.1 Camel D1917

T/o Fouquerolles for an offensive patrol during which the Camel's petrol tank was shot through. A forced landing was carried out circa 1230 in a cornfield whereupon 'D1917' flipped onto its back. Accepted as a temporary second lieutenant, on probation, Philip Walter Rivers Arundel was confirmed in his rank on 26 February 1918 [gazetted 26 March 1918, issue 30600].

55 Squadron   Lt M G Jones MC   +   Charmes Military Cemetery, Essegney
DH.4 A7650 C   2Lt T E Brewer   +   Charmes Military Cemetery, Essegney

T/o Azelot to conduct a height test and having climbed to a point above Chenevrières [Meurthe-et-Moselle] came under attack from an enemy aircraft and sent down out of control west of the trench lines. Max Greville Jones, formerly of the Northumberland Fusiliers won his Military Cross as a temporary second lieutenant serving with the 1st Battalion, the citation reading; *'For conspicuous coolness and ability in getting his men through wire under heavy fire during an attack. He did excellent work until he was wounded, clearing trenches and consolidated the position won.'* [gazetted in both The London Gazette and The Edinburgh Gazette issues 29584 and 12939, published on 16th and 18th May 1916 respectively]. With No 55 Squadron on the 13th September 1917, 'A7650' accounted for two Albatros DIIIs during a raid over Germany on 24 March 1918, when being flown by Second Lieutenant W Legge and Sergeant A S Allan. Their first success came shortly after midday in the vicinity of Mannheim and the second half-an-hour or so later at Germingen [sic].

74 Squadron   Lt G F Thompson   pow
SE.5a C6497

T/o 1905 Clairmarais for an offensive patrol and is reported as last being sighted at fifteen thousand feet going down in a spin northwest of Armentières. Lieutenant Thompson must have retained control as there was no luxury of a parachute to aid his survival. Along with many of his fellow prisoners of war he was repatriated on the 13th of December 1918.

74 Squadron   Lt H G Clements [Canada]   Safe
SE.5a C9584

T/o Clairmarais similarly charged; on return landed on that part of the airfield where the ground was uneven. Struck off charge 16 June 1918; in total 'C9584' had flown for one hundred and six hours and fifteen minutes. Lieutenant Clements took his retirement from the Royal Air Force in the United Kingdom.

85 Squadron   Lt J D Canning   Safe
SE.5a D6566

T/o Petite Synthe having collected 'D6566' which had been left behind on the squadron's move the previous day and on arrival at St Omer Lieutenant Canning crashed on landing.

95 Squadron   Lt H N Hastie [Canada]   Injured   Shotwick [St Michael] Churchyard
Sopwith Pup C278

T/o Shotwick for a training flight in the course of which Harry Nelson Hastie flew his aircraft into the ground, turning onto its back as a consequence. He succumbed to his injuries later in the day. His headstone has been inscribed with the words; *'Safe In The Arms Of Jesus'.*

98 Squadron   Lt F C Wilton   Safe
DH.9 C1208   Sgt J H Reed   Safe

T/o 1000 Ruisseauville for a bombing operation. Last sighted going down east of the trench lines and south of Bois de Biez possibly as a consequence of enemy action. Annotated 'Safe', Both airmen made there way through the lines. Frank Beamish Wilson was *gazetted* with the Distinguished Flying Cross on 2 November 1918, supplement 30989; *'On 9th August Captain Wilson observed that the enemy were bringing up reinforcements in lorries to meet a French attack. Descending to a low altitude, he dropped bombs, and, causing considerable damage, he stopped their advance. He then attacked with machine gun fire the troops descending from the lorries. By this prompt action Captain Wilson rendered very valuable service.'*

Note. Supplement 30989 of *The London Gazette* published on 1 November 1918, provides a goldmine of citations regarding awards made to personnel of the Royal Air Force.

98 Squadron   DH.9 C6118   Hit by bomb fragments during an enemy raid on the aerodrome during the night of 5-6 June 1918, and deemed not worth repairing.

103 Squadron   Lt F H Sillem   Safe
DH.9 C6185   Sgt H W Cornell   Safe

T/o Serny for bombing operations but crashed within seconds of becoming airborne when a bomb fell off upsetting the aircraft's trim. For the crew this was their second crash in forty-eight hours.

121 Squadron   2Lt T M Tyson   +   Narborough [All Saints] Churchard
FK.3 B8827

T/o Narborough for an unauthorised flight; stalled at a low altitude and on hitting the ground burst into flames. Described in the cemetery register as a second lieutenant, other documents show Thomas Mashiter Tyson as a flight cadet. Also, the register shows his unit as No 2 School of Aeronautics.

150 Squadron   Captain H J Scales MC   +   Sarigol Military Cemetery, Kriston
F.1 Camel C1597

T/o Kirec and crashed in unknown circumstances. Four days previously Herbert James Scales drove down a Aviatik DD. He was commissioned to the General List on 24 May 1916, from the rank of lance corporal serving with the City of London Yeomanry [Territorial Forces], promulgated 4 July 1916, issue 29651 of *The London Gazette.* The announcement of his award appeared in the New Year's Honours list 1918, as repeated in *The Edinburgh Gazette* issue 13186. His headstone is inscribed with words most appropriate; *'This Life Cut Off 'Neath Foreign Skies Still Lives In Hearts At Home'.*

206 Squadron   Sgt R Jackson   Safe
DH.9 C6158   Private W S Blyth   Safe

T/o Alquines tasked for bombing on return from which Sergeant Jackson overshot the landing area and crashed against a trailer. For the time an all non-commissioned crew was unusual.

206 Squadron   Lt H Steir USAS   Safe
DH.9 D5696   2Lt W G Duncan   Safe   See 24 June 1918 - 206 Squadron

T/o Alquines having received orders for a bombing raid on St Inglevert. Reported to have crash-landed on the aerodrome and overshot into a sunken road, engine overheating being a contributory cause. From No 2 Aeroplane Acceptance Park Hendon 'D5696' having been re-allotted from No 108 Squadron at Lake Down, the DH eventually arrived at Alquines on 7 June 1918.

211 Squadron	Lt L F Drake	Safe	See 13 June 1918 - 211 Squadron
DH.9 B7638	2Lt N G Breeze	Safe	See 13 June 1918 - 211 Squadron

T/o Petite Synthe tasked for bombing and written off, damaged beyond repair, following a forced landing in a field that had been put to the plough. A report concerning this states that the observers belt dropped through the hole in the fuselage floor [to facilitate photography] and was carried by the slipstream into a longeron which then fractured.

217 Squadron	Lt H S Matthews	Injured
DH.4 A7878	Private E Farley	Injured

T/o Bergues and damaged beyond worthwhile repair after landing from bombing operations and running into a lorry.

Wednesday-Thursday 12-13 June 1918 - Cambrai-Le Cateau-St Quentin-Peronne

83 Squadron	Captain J Weaver	pow
FE.2b D9762	2Lt J L Brown	pow

T/o Franqueville having been briefed to carry out a long night reconnaissance of the locations shown above; it would seem the crew were in wireless contact with base on a frequency that an enemy interception team managed to monitor for it is reported that the last message transmitted from 'D9762' was jammed by Bruges. It is believed both members of crew were repatriated on, or around, 18 December 1918.

Thursday 13 June 1918

1 Squadron	Lt E T S Kelly [Canada]	pow	Cabaret-Rouge British Cemetery, Souchez
SE.5a B8508			

T/o Clairmarais South and was last seen by other pilots engaged on the patrol in combat over the Pas-de-Calais south of Laventie, a commune some sixteen km northeast of Béthune. From Picton in Ontario, nineteen year old Ernest Tilton Sumpter Kelly died from his wounds on the 15th of June 1918. His death, the sixth from the squadron on operations, occurred on the occasion of the squadron losing its thirtieth fighter so charged since the 1st of April. In addition, nine of their establishment had been lost in other circumstances.

29 Squadron	Lt H A Whittaker	Safe	See 21 June 1918 - 29 Squadron
SE.5a D5970			

T/o Vignacourt for an evening offensive patrol on return from which the light was fast fading and this was a contributory factor in Lieutenant Whittaker coming down in a cornfield off the aerodrome. Salvaged, 'D5970' was struck off charge the next day. Taken on squadron charge 8 May 1918, it was flown by various pilots who between them accounted for four enemy aircraft, some being shared with others from the squadron.

29 Squadron	2Lt F T Arnold	Safe
SE.5a D6017		

T/o Vignacourt similarly tasked and damaged beyond repair in the manner described above. It had been on squadron strength since 27 May 1918.

37 Squadron	Captain S H Starey	Injured	Unemployed list 15 January 1919: Captain
F.1 Camel D9574			

T/o Stow Maries for a practice flight; crashed following engine failure in a turn, severely injuring the pilot. It is noted that 'D9574' while being tested at No 3 Aeroplane Acceptance Park Norwich on the 4th of June 1918, displayed symptoms of excessive engine [Lt Rhône 9J] vibrations. The Camel was delivered to the squadron on the 11th.

39 Squadron	Lt J L Boles [Canada]	+	North Weald Bassett [St Andrew] Churchyard
Bristol F.2b C4815	Cadet J W MacKay	+	Edinburgh [Grange] Cemetery

T/o North Weald and crashed, owing to engine failure; burnt.

41 Squadron   Lt A S Hemming   Safe
SE.5a C1071
T/o Conteville for an offensive patrol; wrecked on return and while landing. For Lieutenant Hemming this was his second landing accident, the first being at Serny on 18 May 1918, during practice flying.

41 Squadron   Lt W H Jordan   Safe   See 16 June 1918 - 41 Squadron
SE.5a D6020
T/o Conteville to patrol over Albert and the surrounding area; written off on return in a heavy landing. Lieutenant Jordan's previous accident had taken place on the 1st of June 1918, when his SE.5a ended up in a cornfield.

49 Squadron   1Lt H H Giles USAS   pow
DH.9 D1723   2Lt E M Nicholas   pow
T/o 1055 Fourneuil for an attack on targets at Ricquesbourg and was last seen going down, but under control, near Orvilliers. First Lieutenant Giles had been attached to the squadron on the last day of May 1918; his observer had arrived just twenty-four hours ago!

53 Squadron   Lt W H Williams   Injured
RE.8 C2291   2Lt T D Raby   Injured
T/o Clarmarais having received instructions for a *Flash* reconnaissance towards Kemmel. During the sortie the crew experienced problems with the engine and while forced landing at map reference 27U16a had the misfortune to fly into a line of telegraph wires which damaged their aircraft beyond repair.

55 Squadron   Lt W Legge   +   Cologne Southern Cemetery
DH.4 A7466 P   2Lt A McKenzie   +   Cologne Southern Cemetery
T/o Azelot with order to bomb Treves*and was last sighted going down in flames following sustained attacks from enemy fighters. Both officers hailed from Scotland.

* Formerly referred to by this name in English, it is now commonly known at Trier, a beautiful city on the Moselle in the wine growing region of the western Rhineland-Palatinate.

55 Squadron   Sgt A W Mepsted   Safe
DH.4 A7535   Sgt Brass   Safe
T/o Azelot in the company of others to practice flying in formation which was of paramount importance when engaged on bombing operations. Damaged beyond worthwhile repair after turning over when landing.

56 Squadron   2Lt C B Stenning   Safe
SE.5a C9566
T/o Valheureux for an offensive patrol; badly shot about and force-landed at map reference 57D07 central. Please refer to my summary for 2 June 1918, for details of Second Lieutenant Stenning's crash at Valheureux.

60 Squadron   2Lt R G Lewis   pow
SE.5a C9498
T/o Boffles for an offensive patrol and seen by his fellow pilots to go down over the Somme *département* with a failing engine to force-land between the communes of Ablaincourt and Chaulnes. Second Lieutenant Lewis was among those repatriated on 13 December 1918.

60 Squadron   Captain J D Belgrave MC*   +   Grove Town Cemetery, Meaulte
SE.5a D5988
T/o Boffles for a first light offensive patrol and at around 0445 shared*in the destruction of an enemy two-seater east of Albert, but return fire from the enemy aircraft sent James Dacres Belgrave down out of control. A Gentleman Cadet from the Royal Military College Sandhurst, James Belgrave was commissioned to The Oxfordshire and Buckinghamshire Light Infantry on 15 December 1914 [*gazetted* 15 December 1914, issue 29007]. Trans-

ferring to the Royal Flying Corps he was *gazetted* with the Military Cross on 18 July 1917, supplement 30188; *'For conspicuous gallantry and devotion to duty. On at least five occasions he successfully engaged and shot down hostile aeroplanes, and has consistently shown great courage and determination to get to the closest range; an invaluable example in a fighting squadron.'* The First Bar was awarded posthumous on 16 September 1918, supplement 30901; *'For conspicuous gallantry and devotion to duty while leading offensive patrols. In four days he destroyed two enemy machines and drove down four others. The odds were heavy against him, and he did magnificent work.'*

* Lieutenant H A Gordon flying SE.5a E1261.

| 64 Squadron | Captain P S Burge MC MM | Safe | 24 July 1918 - 64 Squadron |
| SE.5a B58 | | | |

T/o Izel-lès-Hameau for an offensive patrol and on return to the airfield, and while taxying, the undercarriage collapsed. The damage was such that repairs were deemed inappropriate. As with many of the early SE.5a production, 'B58' first saw service as 'J' with No 56 Squadron until an accident on 4 December 1917, condemned it to a repair facility. Arriving with No 64 Squadron on the 24th of March 1918, it was much favoured by Lieutenant A A Duffus and Captain Philip Scott Burge who between them claimed four hostile aircraft. In regard to Captain Burge, he is reported in *The London Gazette* for 8 March 1917, supplement 29975, as being commissioned to the General List of the Royal Flying Corps along with a host of fellow cadets with effect from the 27th of February 1917.

| 85 Squadron | Lt C R Hall | pow | |
| SE.5a B7830 | | | |

T/o 1855 St Omer for an offensive patrol and when last seen was between Ypres and Bailleul flying under control at eight thousand feet. It is reported that Lieutenant Hall was brought down by anti-aircraft fire. Lieutenant Hall was repatriated on 13 December 1918.

| 98 Squadron | 2Lt W V Thomas | Safe | |
| DH.9 C2184 | | | |

T/o Ruisseauville for a test flight [the DH had arrived with the squadron five days previously] and on landing ran into a hollow. This spun the aircraft round and damaged the airframe beyond worthwhile repair.

| 98 Squadron | Lt I V Lawrence | Safe | |
| DH.9 D467 | Lt J R Jackman | Safe | |

T/o Ruisseauville similarly charged, their DH having arrived the previous day, and while preparing to land and having descended to two hundred feet flew into turbulent air and crash landed. Salvaged, the airframe was struck off charge on 19 June 1918.

| 104 Squadron | 2Lt W J Rivett-Carnac | Injured | |
| DH.9 C6277 | Sgt W E Flexman | Injured | Charmes Military Cemetery, Essegny |

T/o Azelot tasked for a bombing raid on Hagendingen*and during the sortie the DH came under attack from enemy aircraft and driven down near Toul [Meurthe-et-Moselle], both members of crew sustaining wounds from which Walter Edward Flexman died later in the day. Their DH had arrived in France with the main body of the squadron from Andover on 19 May 1918, landing at St Omer. The crew were the squadron's first casualties since commencing bombing operations.

* Hagendingen was the German interpretation for Hagondange in the Moselle *département* and is located around twenty km north of Metz.

| 211 Squadron | Lt L F Drake | Safe | See 12 June 1918 - 211 Squadron |
| DH.9 B7621 | 2Lt N G Breeze | Safe | See 12 June 1918 - 211 Squadron |

T/o Petite Synthe and wrecked in a landing accident on its return from bombing operations.

| 224 Squadron | Lt E L Bragg | Safe | See 21 July 1918 - 224 Squadron |
| DH.4 B9500 | Lt P E Linder | Safe | |

T/o Almini and reported as being damaged by a seaplane; no further information available. Twenty-four hours later No 224 Squadron transferred to Andrano in the province of Lecce in southeast Italy.

Thursday-Friday 13-14 June 1918 - Oostende docks
Attacked by ten FE.2b bombers from No 38 Squadron based at Capelle and mounting their first offensive sorties since arriving on the Western Front from the United Kingdom on the last day of May 1918.

Friday 14 June 1918
| 17 Squadron | Lt S W Sparks [South Africa] | Injured | Lahana Military Cemetery |
| FK.8 | | | |

T/o Mikra Bay and crashed while practice flying. In *The Sky Their Battlefield* Trevor Henshaw indicates Seba Walter Sparks of Komgha in the Cape Province as dying from his injuries forty-eight hours later, but his death, as shown on the Commonwealth War Graves Commission website suggests he died on the day of the accident.

| 19 Squadron | Lt G W Northridge | Safe |
| 5F.1 Dolphin B7849 | | |

T/o Savy for an offensive patrol in the course of which the engine's oil pressure fell to such an extent that Lieutenant Northridge had little option but to seek a forced landing. This was eventually accomplished in the area of the Forêt de Nieppe. Considered for salvage, the airframe was deemed beyond repair and was struck off charge with just thirteen hours and eight minutes of flying in total on 19 June 1918.

| 35 Squadron | Lt M C Sonnenberg | Safe |
| FK.8 C8545 | 2Lt J T Thursfield | Injured |

T/o Villers-Bocage for a dusk patrol towards Aucheux*during which the crew were attacked by a hostile aircraft that left Second Lieutenant Thursfield in a wounded state. Anxious to get his observer medical help, Lieutenant Sonnenberg force-landed on a road but was unable to prevent his aircraft from running into a ditch which damaged the airframe beyond repair.

* Probably Aucheux-en-Amiénois in the Somme and roughly ten km northwest of Albert.

| 48 Squadron | 2Lt B M Battey | Safe |
| Bristol F.2b C932 | Sgt H F Watson | Safe |

T/o Bertangles heading for reconnaissance operations in the vicinity of Villers-Bretonneux and it was while carrying out the detail that the Bristol's propeller was shot away. Force-landed and overturned in a wheat field near Querrieu [Somme] on the banks of the Hallue river some eleven km northeast of Amiens.

| 54 Squadron | Captain R A Jones | Safe |
| F.1 Camel B9137 | | |

T/o Vignacourt for a weather test and in uncertain light crash-landed on return, running into long grass. This did little good to 'B9137' which with only eight hours and five minutes airborne time to its credit was struck off charge there and then.

| 63 Squadron | Lt J L Warwick | + | Baghdad [North Gate] War Cemetery |
| RE.8 A4661 | Captain T J Keating | + | Baghdad [North Gate] War Cemetery |

T/o Baghdad and crashed in circumstances yet to be explained. Thomas Joseph Keating of Ballinamult of Co Waterford was formerly of the Royal Field Artillery.

| 73 Squadron | 2Lt D B Sinclair | Safe |
| F.1 Camel D1833 | | |

T/o Fouquerolles to practice flying and on return completely misjudged his approach and crashed. Similar to that of the Camel summarised above, 'D1833' looked in a sorry state but in this case it languished until 4 July 1918.

| 79 Squadron | Lt E Taylor [USA] | Safe | See 25 August 1918 - 79 Squadron |
| 5F.1 Dolphin C8071 | | | |

T/o Ste Marie Cappel for an offensive patrol and on return crashed; damaged beyond repair. Taken on charge as recently as 8 June 1918, 'C8071' flew, in total, for twelve hours and fifteen minutes.

| 80 Squadron | 2Lt G Wignall | Safe | Unemployed list 26 February 1919: 2Lt |
| F.1 Camel C1590 | | | |

T/o Fouquerolles for a practice flight but became lost and on landing at a French airfield [Tille] running into long grass badly damaged. Salvaged, the Camel was sent for repair but was struck off charge on 7th July 1918, as not worth repairing. This was its second crash, the first while in the hands of No 73 Squadron when on 26 March 1918, Second Lieutenant Pilditch crashed at Cachy where until two days earlier the squadron, now lodged at Remaisnil, had been based.

| 80 Squadron | 2Lt A R Melbourne | + | Arras Flying Services Memorial |
| F.1 Camel D6420 | | | |

T/o 1820 Fouquerolles for an offensive patrol over the Oise in the direction of Ribécourt-Dreslincourt; lost without trace.

| 80 Squadron | 2Lt P R Beare | Injured | |
| F.1 Camel D6597 | | | |

T/o 1820 Fouquerolles similarly tasked and was driven down to crash on the Allied side of the lines near Ribécourt-Dreslincourt [Oise] from where a wounded Second Lieutenant Beare was taken for treatment at a French hospital.

| 80 Squadron | Lt W R Archibald [Canada] | Safe | See 27 June 1918 - 80 Squadron |
| F.1 Camel D6611 | | | |

T/o Fouquerolles for a practice flight but mishandled the throttle and 'chocked' the engine; crashed.

| 100 Squadron | 2Lt V C Kirtley | Safe | |
| FE.2b A5787 | | | |

T/o Ochey for a practice flight but before becoming airborne ran onto ground so rutted that the aircraft was damaged beyond repair. On squadron establishment since 28 February 1918, it had, in total, flown for fifty-seven hours and thirty-five minutes.

| 204 Squadron | Lt S C J Askin | Safe | Unemployed list 29 September 1919: Lt |
| F.1 Camel B3869 *Basutoland No 5 Lerotholi* | | | |

T/o Téteghem and reported to have been damaged beyond repair in a forced landing. Interestingly, against its airframe serial this incident has not been recorded, but there is no doubt it was beyond repair as the final entry reads; *'SOC 4ASD general fatigue and age FH191.85' [sic].*

Saturday 15 June 1918

| 3 Squadron AusFC | 2Lt S Jones AusFC | + | Vignacourt British Cemetery |
| RE.8 A3817 | Lt S A Loram AusFC | + | Vignacourt British Cemetery |

T/o Villers-Bocage tasked for an artillery observation patrol. When over Flesscelles [Somme] Second Lieutenant Jones banked the aircraft but lost control and spun to the ground; on impact the RE went up in flames. Allotted to the squadron [when it was known as No 69 Squadron] on 11 September 1917, 'A3817' had been well used and when lost had flown for a total of three hundred and seventeen hours and twenty-five minutes. It seems probable that twenty-five year old Stanley Arthur Loram had emigrated to Australia for his parents lived at Alphington in the south-southwest suburbs of Exeter, the county town of Devon. His headstone carries the words; *'Let Those Who Come After See To It That His Name Be Not Forgotten.'*

| 8 Squadron | Lt F M F West | Safe | |
| FK.8 C8631 | Lt T M Doley | Safe | |

T/o Auxi-le-Château ordered for bombing but owing to engine failure force-landed on Vert Galand airfield. Struck off charge 24 June 1918, with an overall total of twenty-four hours and thirty-five minutes flying.

| 21 Squadron | Lt Chisholme | Injured |
| RE.8 B4086 | Lt Allenby | Safe |

T/o Floringhem tasked for a counter attack patrol but on return, and just about to land, a strong gust of wind sent the RE.8 crashing out of control.

| 28 Squadron | Lt J G Russell [Canada] | Injured | Montecchio Precalcino Communal Cemetery |
| F.1 Camel B7351 | | | extension |

T/o Grossa but within moments of leaving the ground James Gordon Russell lost control, spun and crashed. During its service with squadron 'B7351' accounted for four hostile aircraft and a kite balloon. Lieutenant Russell's headstone bears an inscription taken from the fourth verse of Rudyard Kipling patriotic 1914 poem 'For All We Have And Are'; *'There's But One Task For All For Each One Life To Give'*.

| 29 Squadron | Lt W L Douglas | Safe |
| SE.5a D6153 | | |

T/o Vignacourt for an offensive patrol and wrecked in an attempted landing at Izel-lès-Hameau airfield.

| 45 Squadron | Lt A J Haines | Safe | See 10 August 1918 - 45 Squadron |
| F.1 Camel B2443 K | | | |

T/o Grossa and reported to have force-landed. Salvaged, it is though this was the end of its active life.

| 74 Squadron | Lt P F C Howe | Safe | Unemployed list 29 July 1919: Lt |
| SE.5a D6854 | | | |

T/o Clairmarais for an offensive patrol during which an oil pipe fractured and on landing Lieutenant Howe ran into a ditch, damaging 'D6854' beyond repair. His score for aircraft written off in his charge now totalled five; see summaries for 19 and 25 April, 15 May and 2 June 1918.

| 84 Squadron | Lt J E Reid | Safe |
| SE.5a C9519 | | |

T/o Bertangles for operations over Villers-Bretonneux and on return damaged beyond repair following a heavy landing. It will be recalled that Lieutenant Reid had crash landed [away from the airfield] during operations to the same area on 6 June 1918. 'C9519' arrived with the squadron on 3 April 1918, and including testing and transit flew for a respectable one hundred and twenty-two hours and twenty-five minutes.

| 87 Squadron | Lt D J Allan | Injured |
| 5F.1 Dolphin C4161 | | |

T/o Estrée-les-Crecy for an offensive patrol and it was on the return leg that Lieutenant Allan experienced problems with the Dolphin's engine. Sighting the airfield at Bertangles he decided to land, but approached from downwind and as a consequence landed fast and struck a ridge. It will be recalled he had been involved in a landing accident on 28 May 1918.

| 103 Squadron | 2Lt V Mercer-Smith | pow |
| DH.9 C2200 | Sgt J Hamilton | pow |

T/o 1000 Serny for bombing operations on targets at Roye and when last seen was flying between the target area and the Allied lines. Both airmen were taken into captivity in a wounded state. See my summary for 8 June 1918, in which Second Lieutenant Mercer-Smith is featured. Repatriation for the two airmen came on 13th December 1918.

| 218 Squadron | Lt C F Smith | Safe |
| DH.9 C1210 | Sgt R S Joysey | Safe |

T/o Petite Synthe for bombing operations and on return to the airfield crashed; struck to one of the many salvage sections it is thought 'C1210' never flew again, though there are indications that it was returned to the United Kingdom and by October was at No 2 Salvage Section Richboro.

Sunday 16 June 1918
A day of intense air activity with squadrons operating from first light until dusk.

1 Squadron	Lt E E Owen	Safe
SE.5a C1898		

T/o Clairmarais South for an offensive patrol on return from which Lieutenant Owen misjudged his approach and on touch down ran into a mess hut that was under construction. Summaries for 21 April and 12 June 1918, detail his previous 'escapades'.

1 Squadron	Lt H B Parkinson	Safe
SE.5a C8842		

T/o Clairmarais South for an offensive patrol during which the thermometer shattered; force-landed in standing crops and damaged beyond repair. Arriving with the squadron ten days previously 'C8842' in total flew for twenty-one hours and fifty-seven minutes.

2 Squadron AusFC	Lt E D Cummings	Safe
SE.5a C5442		

T/o Fourquerolles heading for operations over the Compèigne [Oise] area but owing to engine failure force-landed, and damaged beyond repair, at Verrines [sic]. Lieutenant Cummings had been involved in three previous crashes; see my summaries for 22 April, 3 May and 8 June 1918.

4 Squadron	Lt P A Bertrand	+	Outtersteene Communal Cemetery extn
RE.8 B823	2Lt C Levick	+	Arras Flying Services Memorial

T/o St Omer for a reconnaissance sortie and while flying at four thousand feet over Merris [Nord] took a direct hit from anti-aircraft fire, the force of the strike completely shattering the RE.8 into pieces. The son of Captain Felix Bertrand of Manchester Square, London, eighteen year old Philippe Angus Bertrand's headstone is inscribed; 'Sans Peur Et Sans Reproche' [without fear without reproach]. Although on squadron charge since 23rd March 1918, 'B823' had spent much of its time undergoing repair; a forced landing during artillery observation duties by Lieutenants R P Ziegler and A W Miller on 24 March came close to ending its service and it was not until 5 June that it was deemed fit to resume operations. Consequently, its total flying only amounted to twenty-five hours and fifty-five minutes.

4 Squadron	Captain F W Burdick MC	+	Aval Wood Military Cemetery, Vieux-Berquin
RE.8 B6656	Lt S C Shillingford	+	Meteren Military Cemetery

T/o St Omer for a photographic reconnaissance sortie; subsequently it was reported that an RE.8 had been seen to take a direct hit from anti-aircraft fire and crash at map reference 27X25b98. Formerly of the Inns of Court Officers Training Corps and the 20th Battalion London Regiment, Frederick William Burdick was *gazetted* with the Military Cross on 16 September 1918, supplement 30901; *'For conspicuous gallantry and devotion to duty. This officer has carried out several contact patrols and brought in accurate information, and has bombed and machine-gunned enemy troops from a low altitude, under bad weather conditions. He has also carried out many successful flights, and on one occasion landed his machine after a direct hit from a shell.'* Stanley Charles Shillingford was late of the 2nd Battalion Royal Fusiliers.

Note. The citation makes reference to Captain Burdick landing his aircraft after taking a direct hit from a shell and with his burial location different from that of his observer it seems feasible that he may have survived long enough to be taken to a field hospital. This, though, is conjecture on my part.

10 Squadron	Captain E H Comber-Taylor	+	Esquelbecq Military Cemetery
Bristol F.2b C967	2Lt G A Cameron	Injured	

T/o Droglandt having received instructions for artillery observation but shortly after becoming airborne stalled and crashed, Second Lieutenant Cameron being pulled from the wreckage with very serious injuries. On charge since 27 May 1918, 'C967' was one of several Bristol F.2b types attached to the squadron, this particular example logging a total of forty-one hours and five minutes flying.

10 Squadron	Lt G A E Norgarb	Safe	
FK.8 C8574	2Lt J C Anderson	Safe	See 18 June 1918 - 10 Squadron

T/o Droglant for a counter attack patrol in the course of which the engine failed, leading to a forced landing at map reference G23b54

27 Squadron	2Lt C H Gannaway	+	Hangard Communal Cemetery extension
DH.4 A7597	Sgt W E A Brooks	+	Hangard Communal Cemetery extension

T/o 0855 Fourneuil for a raid and was last sighted on fire over the Somme engaged in combat with two enemy machines three km, or thereabouts, west of Roye. Both were nineteen years of age. Charles Henry Gannaway was commissioned to the Royal Flying Corps, General List, on 5 July 1917 [*gazetted* in issue 30203, 24th July 1917]. His observer was formerly of the Royal Fusiliers and although recorded in the cemetery register as 'Royal Air Force' his squadron details are omitted. 'A7597' had first been issued to No 18 Squadron and before being badly damaged in a landing accident on 26 November 1917 [Lieutenant W N Bussell and Lieutenant E M Farncombe], had, three days earlier, downed an Albatros [Second Lieutenant C Evans and Mechanic K A Gellan].

27 Squadron	Captain S Anderson	Injured	
DH.4 B2113	Lt J H Holland	Injured	Marissel French National Cemetery

T/o Fourneuil for operations during which the DH ran into a swarm of enemy fighters, one of which the crew sent down, spinning, near Roye. However, continuous firing passes from the scouts inflicted terrible damage on both 'B2110' and its crew and barely able to control his aircraft Captain Anderson force-landed [possibly near the Cathedral town of Beauvais]. It is reported that Lieutenant Holland maintained return fire throughout, despite being mortally wounded; rushed to a hospital - possibly at Marissel where the French had various casualty facilities - he died the same day. Formerly of the 22nd Battalion Royal Fusilier his squadron details are omitted from the cemetery register. It will be recalled he had been involved in a forced landing on the day that the Royal Air Force emerged as an independent force. Some reports say that Captain Anderson died from his wounds, but this was not the case.

27 Squadron	Lt H Wild	+	Bouchoir New British Cemetery
DH.9 C6107 P	Sgt E Scott	+	Bouchoir New British Cemetery

T/o 0855 Fourneuil heading for operations in the direction of Roye and when last seen was being attacked from behind by an enemy scout west of the target area.

27 Squadron	2Lt W H Vick	pow	
DH.9 C6346	Lt F R G Spurgin	+	Roye New British Cemetery

T/o 0855 Fourneuil similarly tasked and was last seen in the target area falling earthwards streaming flames. It would appear, however, that Second Lieutenant Vick managed to crash land, though in a wounded state, and I am reasonably confident that the 'Second Lieutenant H Vick' reported in *Flight* October 3, 1918, as a prisoner of war was the pilot of the DH here summarised. First of the DH.9 squadrons operating since the formation of the Royal Air Force to sustain twenty airmen killed on operations.

32 Squadron	Lt C Wilderspin	Safe
SE.5a C1833		

T/o Fouquerolles for a practice flight but made such a hash of his landing, smashing the undercarriage, that 'C1833' was struck off charge on the 4th of July 1918.

41 Squadron	Lt M E Gadd	Safe
SE.5a D239		

T/o Conteville for an offensive patrol over Montdidier; came down in a cornfield and turned over near Chepoix in the *département du Oise* following engine failure. Summaries for 12 April and 11 June 1918, feature this officer.

| 41 Squadron | Lt W H Jordan | Safe | See 9 October 1918 - 41 Squadron |
| SE.5a E1280 | | | |

T/o Conteville for an offensive patrol towards Albert. Written off in a crash near the airfield owing to failure of the flying controls. It is not clear if the crash occurred on take off or when Lieutenant Jordan [see summaries for the 1st and 13th of June] was returning to base. 'E1280' had been on charge for a mere twenty-four hours and with test and ferry times included its days ended after just six hours and twenty-five minutes.

| 45 Squadron | Lt H B Hudson* | Safe |
| F.1 Camel B3887 P | | |

T/o Grossa and reported to have crashed to the north of Castelfranco Véneto in the province of Treviso.

* Annex M Officers and aircrew of No 45 Squadron 1916-1976 as researched, and subsequently published, by Wing Commander 'Jeff' Jefford in his definitive history of the squadron under the title *The Flying Camels* shows Lieutenant H B Hudson as being on squadron strength between 30 May and 29 July 1918.

| 53 Squadron | 2Lt J N Gatecliff | Safe | See 29 June 1918 - 53 Squadron |
| RE.8 C2405 | | | |

T/o Clairmarais to practice flying on type; landed heavily, damaging the airframe beyond repair.

| 56 Squadron | Lt F C Tarbutt [Canada] | + | Arras Flying Services Memorial |
| SE.5a D6088 | | | |

T/o 0445 Valheureux for a first light offensive mission and was seen by other pilots to break up in the air north of Boyelles in the Pas-de-Calais. Twenty-one years of age Fraser Coventry Tarbutt had been educated at Huntingdon Academy.

| 57 Squadron | Lt C W Peckham | Safe | |
| DH.4 D9248 | 2Lt E I Riley | Safe | See 27 June 1918 - 57 Squadron |

T/o Le Quesnoy for bombing operations over Bapaume and damaged beyond worthwhile repair after smashing its undercarriage in a heavy landing. During the evening of the 6th [June] when raiding enemy positions in the same area, Lieutenant C W Peckham and Sergeant J Grant had 'flamed' a Fokker DrI and sent another down out of control between Ervillers and Vimy but themselves picked up some damage from the return fire and were obliged to make an emergency landing - neither member of crew being hurt in the process.

| 62 Squadron | Lt J M Goller [South Africa] | + | Roye New British Cemetery |
| Bristol F.2b C788 | 2Lt M Ross-Jenkins | + | Roye New British Cemetery |

T/o Planques for an offensive patrol and when last seen was fighting hard over Montdidier. John Morrissey Goller came from Johannesburg.

| 65 Squadron | Lt J A Sykes | + | Heath Cemetery, Harbonnieres |
| F.1 Camel B7347 | | | |

T/o 1855 Bertangles for an evening bombing patrol and was last sighted on an easterly course and heading towards*Foucaucourt. Shipped to France in January 1918, 'B7347' was first used by No 4 Squadron AusFC in whose care it shot down two hostile machines, both by Lieutenant A W Adams. It appears that Lieutenant Adams on securing his second victory, a scout at around 1000 on the 16th of March near Annocullin [Nord], force-landed on La Motte airfield but overturned after clipping the edge of a shell hole and was taken to hospital for treatment for wounds. The squadron, meanwhile, on 27 March, despatched a lorry to recover the Camel only to find that the airfield had been overrun and was now in German hands. However, occupation by the enemy appears to have been temporary for *The Camel File* reports 'B7347' at No 1 Advanced Salvage Dump on the 28th, and struck off charge the same day as not worth repairing. This decision was subsequently overturned and by 18 April the Camel had been brought back on charge and was issued on the 19th of May to No 65 Squadron. Prior to its eventual demise, Lieutenant T M Williams sent down a Pfalz out of control over Bois de Tailleux during the morning of 28th May.

* Probably <u>Foucaucourt</u>-en-Santerre in the Somme and site of an airfield which was in Allied hands by the end of the *Great War.*

| 80 Squadron | 2Lt G H Glasspoole | pow | Unemployed List 17 February 1919: 2Lt |
| F.1 Camel B2524 | | | |

T/o 0730 Fouquerolles for an offensive patrol; shot down at Noyon*[Oise]. Recorded as 'Missing', as published in *Flight* July 11, 1918, confirmation that he was a prisoner of war appeared in the magazine's issue of August 15th, 1918. 'B2524' arrived with the squadron on the 1st of April 1918, transferred from No 73 Squadron.

* Between the 26th and 28th of August 1914, Noyon, roughly one hundred km north-northeast of the French Capital was the very temporary home of General Headquarters of the British Expeditionary Force, falling to the advancing German army on September 1st. French forces re-entered the town on the 18th of March 1917, only for it to be retaken by the Germans in their spring offensive of March 1918, remaining occupied until the French advanced into Noyon on the 29th of August, finally driving out the last of German troops the following day. Nearby is the site of the Commonwealth War Graves Commission Noyon New British Cemetery.

| 80 Squadron | 2Lt G W Hales | Safe | Unemployed List 2 April 1919: Lt |
| F.1 Camel D1797 | | | |

T/o Fouquerolles for an offensive patrol and where, on landing, the Camel turned over; damaged beyond repair. While on the strength of No 54 Squadron, and flown by Second Lieutenant R T Cuffe [see my summaries for 2nd April and the 21st July 1918] on the 3rd of April, was obliged to force-land near St Pol-sur-Tenoise in the Pas-de-Calais after being shot about by a hostile aircraft. Repaired, 'D1797' arrived with the squadron on the 9th of June.

| 83 Squadron | Sgt S C Bracey | + | Vis-en-Artois British Cemetery, Haucourt |
| FE.2b A5780 | 2Lt P Kemp | pow | |

T/o Franqueville with orders for an attack on Cambrai; failed to return. Spencer Charles Bracey with his life fast ebbing managed to crash-land, thereby saving the life of his observer who, subsequently, was repatriated on 13th December 1918.

| 84 Squadron | Lt D B Jones DCM | Safe | See 3 July 1918 - 84 Squadron |
| SE.5a C1871 | | | |

T/o Bertangles authorised for a practice flight which ended with Lieutenant Jones landing with a force sufficient to damage his aircraft beyond repair.

| 85 Squadron | 2Lt H E Thompson* | pow | |
| SE.5a D6876 | | | |

T/o St Omer for an offensive patrol and seen to dive towards the Menin road in the face of intense machine-gun fire from the ground; crash landed and turned over near Kruiseecke [West-Vlaanderen] west of Kortrijk. Second Lieutenant Thompson was among the happy band of ex-prisoners of war repatriated on 13 December 1918.

* In life's many coincidences a Sergeant H E Thompson, a bomb aimer flying with No 78 Squadron, was taken prisoner of war during operations to Plzen on 16-17 April 1943, his details being reported in my fourth volume of Bomber Command's Losses in the Second World War.

| 98 Squadron | Lt L W Strugnell MM | + | Huby-St Leu British Cemetery |
| DH.9 D1010 | Sgt C Lomax* | + | Huby-St Leu British Cemetery |

T/o 0710 Ruisseauville in company with others from the squadron for a raid during which the formation flew into adverse weather conditions and the signal was given for everyone to turn back for home. Leonard William Strugnell's aircraft was observed gliding towards the cloud below and, it is assumed, at some point he lost control and spun in, probably close to where he is and Cecil Lomax are buried in the Pas-de-Calais. Lieutenant Strugnell's headstone is inscribed; *'They Rest In Peace And Await The Eternal Dawn.'* An appreciation of his service is reported in my summary for 30 May 1918, when he, and Cecil, were involved in a serious landing accident. Nineteen year old Cecil served formerly with the 3rd Battalion South Lancashire Regiment and his entry in the cemetery register incorrectly shows him as belonging to No 99 Squadron. His headstone carries the words; *'Though Lost To Sight To Memory Dear.'*

* Purely of academic interest, it is noted that Sergeant Charles Lomax lived with his parents at No 35 London Terrace, Darwen, Lancashire. This address is still extant and, I suggest, the terraced houses along the street have in many cases undergone extensive renovation for prices reported on the Zoopla property website [2017] show variations of between thirty-five thousand pounds and eight-nine thousand pounds!

| 101 Squadron | Captain R O Purry | pow | |
| FE.2b A6424 | 2Lt W H A Rickett | pow | |

T/o Famechon to reconnoitre the Péronne area; failed to return. Both officers are named in *Flight* July 11, 1918, under the heading 'Missing'. Both were repatriated in December 1918, Captain Purry on the 23rd and Second Lieutenant Rickett on the 13th.

| 103 Squadron | 2Lt S Hirst | + | Arras Flying Services Memorial |
| DH.9 C6192 | Lt J M Hughes | + | Arras Flying Services Memorial |

T/o 1000 Serny for bombing operations over Roye during which the DH took a direct hit from anti-aircraft fire, crashing near Crapeaumesnil [Oise]. John Meirion Hughes was commissioned from the Inns of Court Officers Training Corps on 22 January 1916 [*gazetted* 26 January 1916, supplement 29451], joining the 4th Battalion South Lancashire Regiment.

| 131 Squadron | 2Lt A G McGillivray | + | Siddington [All Saints] Churchyard |
| RE.8 D4985 | 2Lt C E Watchorn [Canada] | Injured | Siddington [All Saints] Churchyard |

T/o Shawbury for a training flight during which the RE collided with a flag pole and crashed; Claude Edmund Watchorn of Calgary, Alberta died from his injuries the next day. Together as a crew in the air they now rest side by side in hallowed ground.

| 148 Squadron | 2Lt C E Wharton | pow | |
| FE.2b B7808 | Lt J W Pryor | pow | |

T/o Sains-les-Pernes heading for bombing operations at Douai and when last seen by the formation was making in the direction of the Allied lines. Second Lieutenant Wharton's name appears under the heading 'Missing' as reported by *Flight* July 11, 1918; the same issue names the observer noting he was formerly of the South Lancashire Regiment. Both were repatriated on 13 December 1918.

| 205 Squadron | Lt H G Kirkland | Safe | Unemployed list 3 March 1919: Lt |
| DH.4 A7915 | 2Lt J E Walker | Safe | |

T/o Bois de Roche heading for bombing operations over Rosieres and damaged beyond repair following a landing accident.

| 206 Squadron | Lt A J Garside | Safe | |
| DH.9 C6275 | 2Lt M G Perry | Safe | |

T/o Alquines tasked for bombing and on return wrecked in a heavy landing. Sent out from Hendon during the second week of May 1918, and in squadron hands on the 23rd, 'C6275' flew, in total, for thirty hours and eleven minutes.

| 211 Squadron | 2Lt E T M Routledge | Safe | |
| DH.9 C6167 | 2Lt J F J Peters | Safe | |

T/o Petite Synthe tasked for bombing operations and on return failed to flatten out while landing crosswind; damaged beyond repair. For a summary concerning Second Lieutenant Routledge, please refer to his entry on 29 May 1918. On the 3rd of June 1918, with Lieutenant G H Baker and Second Lieutenant T B Dodwell as the crew 'C6167' force-landed on a beach after being damaged by anti-aircraft fire.

| 250 Squadron | 2Lt A E N Ashford | Injured | Unemployed list 24 July 1919: Lt |
| DH.9 D1714 | 2Lt J D Davidson | Injured | |

T/o Padstow and wrecked here while landing.

Monday 17 June 1918
The intensity of aerial activity of the past twenty-four hours continued throughout the day.

2 Squadron	Lt L Daly	Safe
FK.8 C8512	2lt A J Inkster	Injured Unemployed List 27 January 1920

T/o Floringhem for artillery observation duties and on return following a misjudged approach ended up, damaged beyond repair, in a cornfield. Lieutenant Daly, it will be recalled, had crash-landed at Hesdigneul on 28th May 1918. Second Lieutenant Inkster's injuries are reported as *'slight'*. On 21 April 1918, crewed by Second Lieutenant J W D Farrell*and Lieutenant F Ambler, had a very close encounter over the Pas-de-Calais when it was shot about by seven enemy aircraft, none of which were able to land a telling blow, and, sub-sequently, 'C8512' was recovered from near La Couture and sent for repair. Restored to good order it returned to the squadron via No 1 Air Issues on 25 May 1918.

* On the last day of November 1918, and now ranked lieutenant, Farrell was attached to the Administrative Branch and given the acting rank of captain, as promulgated in issue 31112 of the *Gazette* published on the 7th of January 1919. On 3 July 1919, he reverted to his substantive rank on transfer to the Unemployed List.

3 Squadron	Lt A Hamilton	Safe See 8 August 1918 - 3 Squadron
F.1 Camel D6525		

T/o Valheureux having been briefed for a wireless interception duty only to crash-land, heavily, owing to the engine 'choking' near the railway at Beaumetz [Somme]. Arriving at Valheureux on the last day of March 1918, 'D6525' appears to have been much favoured by Lieutenant E R Maddox MC for he is credited with driving down two Albatros scouts and a Rumpler reconnaissance aircraft, all when flying 'D6625'. His first victory came at midday on the 4th of April while patrolling over the Somme, sending his victim down at Morlancourt some six to seven km south of Albert. Next, and during the early morning of June 3rd, he claimed his second Albatros which he put into a wood near Adinfer in the Pas-de-Calais. His last victim, the Rumpler, fell forty-eight hours later.

11 Squadron	Lt L C H Rutter	Injured
Bristol F.2b C958	Sgt R Allen	Safe

T/o Remaisnil having received orders for a reconnaissance sortie but on becoming airborne the crew were over-taken by engine failure and moments later the Bristol collided with telegraph wires. Sergeant Allen is reported to have been badly shaken.

19 Squadron	2Lt W F Leach	Injured
5F.1 Dolphin C4228		

T/o Savy tasked for an offensive patrol; shot down near Loos [Nord] and taken to hospital where his wounds were treated.

19 Squadron	Lt D P Laird	Safe
5F.1 Dolphin C4062		

T/o Savy similarly tasked and after being shot about force-landed near Ricquinghem a sizeable commune in the Pas-de-Calais.

20 Squadron	Lt G H Zellers	Safe
Bristol F.2b C979	Sgt J D Cormack	Safe See 31 July 1918 - 20 Squadron

T/o Boisdinghem for an offensive patrol and on return, and landing, the Bristol's tail skid sank into a hole. It would appear the damage to the airframe was serious and after languishing until 8 August 1918, it was struck off charge. Flown to France in May 1918, and issued to the squadron on the 28th, it flew in total for forty-six hours and thirty-five minutes.

23 Squadron   Lt C E Walton   Safe
5F.1 Dolphin C4185

T/o Bertangles for an inner offensive patrol during which Lieutenant Walton became embroiled in aerial combat and was driven down to force-land at map reference 62dN28. Although I cannot be absolutely certain, I believe this encounter with hostile aircraft ended the flying service of 'C4185'.

24 Squadron   2Lt J H Southey   Safe
SE.5a D279

T/o Conteville for an offensive patrol and on return the undercarriage collapsed on touch down; damaged beyond repair. Since factory testing and ferry to France and issue to the squadron on 16 March 1918, 'D279' had accumulated one hundred and fifty-nine hours and thirty minutes flying.

41 Squadron   Lt J S Turnbull   +   Arras Flying Services Memorial
SE.5a D3955

T/o Conteville for an offensive patrol to Albert; last sighted diving towards a kite balloon flying near Chuignes in the *département du Somme* and on the south side of the river south-southwest of Cappy. John Seymour Turnbull was late of the Worcestershire Regiment. His death ended a run of extremely good fortune for the squadron for since the 1st of April, despite losing seventeen aircraft on operational duties and nine in other circumstances, this eighteenth loss was the first to result in the death of the pilot.

49 Squadron   Lt E J P Eslin [Canada]   Safe
DH.9 D461   Lt R H van R Schrek [Canada]   Safe

T/o Fourneuil ordered for a bombing raid on Roye-sur-Metz; shot through with shrapnel from anti-aircraft fire. From information reported on the squadron's website, which I gratefully acknowledge, Reginald Hersey van Rennsaeler was attached between 13 May and 25 August 1918.

54 Squadron   Captain R A James   Safe   See 16 July 1918 - 54 Squadron
F.1 Camel B7413

T/o Boisdinghem for an offensive patrol during which Reginald Arthur James became uncertain of his position. Landing at Alquines his aircraft was hit by a DH.9 from the resident No 206 Squadron [see the summary for 'C1181'] and damaged beyond repair. No 54 Squadron had moved into Boisdinghem from Vignacourt the previous day.

56 Squadron   Captain G C Maxwell   Safe
SE.5a B8402

T/o Valheureux for a practice flight during which Captain Maxwell landed at Conteville. Taking off, presumably to return to Valheureux, an undercarriage strut collapsed and 'B8402' was damaged beyond repair.

62 Squadron   Lt G K Runciman   Safe
Bristol F.2b B1343   2Lt A J Todd   Safe

T/o Planques for an offensive sortie and on return crashed in long grass, both officers being badly shaken by the experience. Accepted by the squadron on 29 March 1918, 'B1343' had in total flown for a useful one hundred and four hours and thirty-five minutes.

64 Squadron   Lt G W Schermerhorn   Safe
SE.5a C6402 *Baroda No 11*

T/o Izel-lès-Hameau for a practice flight; on landing turned over and damaged beyond repair. On establishment since 9 May 1918, 'C6402' flown by Lieutenant W H Farrow accounted for three enemy scouts.

73 Squadron   2Lt J A L Champneys   +   Marissel French National Cemetery
F.1 Camel C8289

T/o Fouquerolles for a practice flight; lost control at low altitude and spun to the ground. Prior to its arrival with the squadron 'C8289' had been on the strength of No 70 Squadron and had been damaged on 11 April 1918, when it was hit from above by a No 65 Squadron Camel[see my summaries for the day], its pilot, Lieutenant J Williamson who by coincidence was also engaged in practice flying was unharmed.

79 Squadron	Major M W Noel	Safe
5F.1 Dolphin D3707		

T/o Ste Marie Cappel for an air test and having climbed to eight hundred feet entered a vertical bank from which control was lost and the Dolphin sideslipped and crashed into a wheat field near the aerodrome. Major Noel appears to have escaped serious injury; he had commanded the squadron since its formation at Gosport on the 1st of August 1917, and following his accident command was passed to Major A R Arnold who was destined to lead '79' for the remainder of the war.

86 Squadron	Lt V T Kelly	Injured Commission relinquished 29 January 1920
F.1 Camel F2093		

T/o Northolt and crashed, heavily, after spinning into telegraph wires. Lieutenant Kelly's injuries are described as severe, and I very much doubt if he ever flew again, his commission being relinquished on 290 January 1920, with ill-health, contracted on active service being given as the reason.

98 Squadron	Lt W T J Atkins	pow
DH.9 B9332	Sgt J H Reed	pow

T/o 0715 Ruisseauville tasked, with others, for an attack on the railway station at Cambrai. Here the formation attracted the attention of at least twenty enemy scouts and in the combats that followed 'B9332' was seen going down, east of the lines, but still under control. Its active squadron life had lasted for just nine days. Lieutenant Atkins is named under the heading 'Missing' in *Flight* July 11, 1918.

98 Squadron	Lt D A Macartney	+	Achiet-le-Grand Communal Cemetery extn
DH.9 D1694	Lt J R Jackman	+	Achiet-le-Grand Communal Cemetery extn

T/o 0715 Ruisseauville similarly tasked and shot down, possibly in the vicinity of Achiet-le-Grand in the Pas-de-Calais nineteen km south of Arras. John Robinson Jackman had served with the 6th Battalion Duke of Wellingtons [West Riding Regiment].

98 Squadron	Lt I V Lawrence	Safe
DH.9 D5723	Sgt P J Sprange	Safe

T/o 0715 Ruisseauville similarly ordered but turned back with a failing engine and while attempting to land lost control and came down in a field adjoining the airfield that had been put to the plough. The loss of these three aircraft brought the squadron's losses since arriving in France to thirty on operations, five in non-operational crashes and three written off in unusual circumstances. Fifteen aircrew had died [one in captivity] and six taken prisoner of war.

101 Squadron	Lt W K Mercer	Safe
FE.2b B438	Lt E C Delamain	Safe

T/o Famechon having been briefed for reconnaissance and bombing but on becoming airborne the engine failed and the crew force-landed southeast of the airfield. On squadron strength since 27 October 1917, 'B438' had logged a total [including test and delivery] of one hundred and sixty-six hours and five minutes flying.

206 Squadron	Lt F A Brock	Safe	See 7 August 1918 - 206 Squadron
DH.9 C1181	Corporal L H Hartford USAS	Safe	

T/o Alquines for local flying and reported wrecked after striking Camel B7413 [see my summary for No 54 Squadron]. Taken on squadron charge on the 21st of May, 'C1181', Lieutenant L A Christian and Second Lieutenant E W Tatnall [see 29 June 1918] along with 'C6240', Captain G L E Steven and Lieutenant C Eaton [see 29 June 1918] spotted a Fokker DrI near Bac Saint-Maur [Pas-de-Calais] and in a fierce exchange of fire left the enemy fighter streaming flames as it crashed to the ground.

210 Squadron	2Lt K T Campbell [Canada]	+	Pernes British Cemetery
F.1 Camel D3381			

T/o Ste Marie Cappel for an offensive patrol during which nineteen year old Kenneth Turner Campbell of Winnipeg was shot down circa 0800. His father held the rank of lieutenant-colonel.

210 Squadron   Lt C H Strickland   Injured
F.1 Camel D3424
T/o Ste Marie Cappel similarly charged during which Lieutenant Strickland was wounded in the same aerial combat that claimed the life of his friend summarised above. Force-landed at map reference 36bS9c29.

217 Squadron   2Lt G B Coward   Interned
DH.4 A7935   LtJ F Read   Interned Unemployed list 8 March 1919: Lt
T/o Bergues armed for a raid on the harbour at Zeebrugge. Chased by a quartet of Pfalz fighters and in trying to escape their attention strayed over the border with Holland whereupon the crew came under fire from Dutch batteries. A forced landing was carried out on Soesterburg*airfield, turning onto its back in the process. With Gunlayer G F Briggs, who was wounded, Second Lieutenant Coward had been attacked by some Pfalz DIIIs over Zeebrugge on the last day of May, but on this occasion the DH not only got away but left one of their attackers spiralling down out of control.

* Established as an airfield in 1911 and taken under military control two years later, Soesterburg remained active until December 2008 when flying officially ceased.

Monday-Tuesday 17-18 June 1918
148 Squadron   Lt H B Evans   pow
FE.2b A6409   Lt H S Collett   pow   Unemployed list 15 February 1919: Lt
T/o Sains-les-Pernes for a raid on Estaires in the Nord département during which the FE was caught in searchlights and brought down by ground fire. Both were repatriated on 13 December 1918.

Tuesday 18 June 1918
3 Squadron   Lt O H Nicholson   +   Arras Flying Services Memorial
F.1 Camel C1631   [South Africa]
T/o 1500 Valheureux for an offensive patrol and was last seen an hour later over Neuville-Saint-Vaast in the Pas-de-Calais. A British anti-aircraft battery reported seeing an aircraft hit by enemy fire and falling at map reference A1345AB. For further information concerning Owen Harrow Nicholson, please refer to my summary on 20 April 1918.

3 Squadron   Lt R L Leigh   +   Arras Flying Services Memorial
F.1 Camel D6665
T/o 1500 Valheureux similarly tasked and lost in the manner outlined above. For additional notes regarding Reginald Lea Leigh, please return to my summary for 30 May 1918.

4 Squadron   Lt G T Legge   Safe
RE.8 E43   Lt J S W Moll   Safe
T/o St Omer having received instructions for artillery observation duties but on becoming airborne hit an air pocket and crashed out of control.

4 Squadron AusFC   2Lt A H Lockley AusFC   Safe   See 5 September 1918 - 4 Squadron AusFC
F.1 Camel D1904
T/o Clairmarais with instructions to carry out an offensive patrol but the control lever became caught up in the gun control Bowden wires and before Alexander Hamilton Lockley could free the lever the Camel went out of control and crashed.

8 Squadron   2Lt F A Whittall   Safe
FK.8 B5768   2Lt A J Ord   Safe
T/o Auxi-le-Château tasked for bombing; shot up by enemy aircraft in the vicinity of Méricourt and damaged to the extent that the airframe was struck off charge on 24 June 1918. Arriving in France in January 1918, 'B5768'

was first used by No 10 Squadron until struck for repair following a crash-landing in fog on 23 March. Its service in the hands of No 8 Squadron commenced 3 June and when finally struck had a total of fifty hours and ten minutes flying.

10 Squadron	Lt R I Chapman	Safe
FK.8 C8575	2Lt J C Anderson	Safe

T/o Droglandt for artillery observations duties and wrecked on return after overshooting the landing area. For Second Lieutenant Anderson this was his fourth narrow shave, his previous crashes having occurred on 12 and 17 April, and 16 June 1918.

23 Squadron	Lt H M Sinclair	Safe	See 28 June 1918 - 23 Squadron
5F.1 Dolphin C3874			

T/o Bertangles for an inner offensive patrol during which pressure failure occurred leading to a forced landing near the aerodrome. It is believed this ended the flying days for this Dolphin. Lieutenant Sinclair had survived a practice crash on 28 May 1918 [see my summary for details].

29 Squadron	Lt R G Pierce [South Africa]	Safe	See 2 July 1918 - 29 Squadron
SE.5a C8870			

T/o Vignacourt for an offensive patrol and driven down by scouts to force-land circa 0830 at map reference 36AE28a. No attempt to salvage could be made owing to the proximity of the lines and the risk of coming under enemy fire.

29 Squadron	Lt R G Pierce [South Africa]	Safe	See 2 July 1918 - 29 Squadron
SE.5a C8878			

T/o Vignacourt for an offensive patrol and for the second time in the day Lieutenant Pierce found himself the centre of attraction, this time from anti-aircraft fire which shot through the longeron of his aircraft. Returning to base an examination of his aircraft deemed the damage was such that the airframe, with a mere five hours and fifteen minutes flying to its credit, was not worth the expense of repair.

49 Squadron	Lt R C Stokes	Safe
DH.9 D463	Lt F C Aulagnier	Safe

T/o Fourneuil to continue bombing on targets at Roye-sur-Metz and damaged beyond repair after coming to grief on landing. Languished until struck off charge on 11 July 1918. Rochefort Clive Stokes, according to the squadron's website, experienced a number of crashes during his service which began on 25 April 1918, and ended on 29 October 1918, one such incident occurred on 11 June 1918 [see my summary for details].

54 Squadron	Lt S M Connolly	pow
F.1 Camel D6487		

T/o 0800 Boisdinghem for an offensive patrol and when last sighted at seventeen thousand feet was in a dive, seemingly under control, to the north of Armentières. Under the banner 'In The Hands Of The Enemy' repeating by *Flight* August 29, 1918, the list published by the German authorities for Allied aircraft that came into their hands during the month of June, Lieutenant Connolly is identified not only as a prisoner of war but the airframe serial of his Camel is correctly quoted, thus suggesting he landed with 'D6487' more or less intact. According to the list, sixteen Sopwith Camels fell into their hands during the month.

54 Squadron	Lt J C MacLennan	Safe
F.1 Camel D6669		

T/o Boisdinghem similarly charged but experienced magneto problems and while forced landing collided with telegraph wires near Eecke [Nord], seven km northeast of Hazebrouck.

54 Squadron	Lt R C Crowden	Safe Unemployed List 6 March 1919: Lt MC
F.1 Camel D9403		

T/o Boisdinghem but over the Pas-de-Calais magneto trouble began to make the Le Rhône 9J misfire to such an extent that Roy Charles Crowden had little option but to make an emergency landing. Selecting a suitable field he put the Camel down, but unfortunately the ground sloped away and before he could bring his aircraft to a stop it turned over. Unharmed, he discovered he was down at Esquerdes, a mere ten km southeast of the airfield from which moments ago he had departed. Three days later he was *gazetted* with the Military Cross [supplement 30761]; *'For conspicuous gallantry and devotion to duty during operations. Observing a column of enemy troops marching along a road, he descended to a very low altitude, bombed them, and threw the column into complete confusion. Later on the same day, he attacked and caused heavy casualties to enemy infantry who were advancing across country. On another occasion he attacked one of six enemy scouts and destroyed it. He showed great determination and a splendid offensive spirit.'* Through no fault of his own, Lieutenant Crowden wrote off four Camels, my summaries for the previous three being recorded on the 2nd and 4th of April and the 28th of May 1918. On the 6th of October 1939, he was commissioned to the Administrative and Special Duties Branch [*gazetted* 27 October 1939, supplement 34718] and served until the 6th of January 1943, when as a squadron leader he resigned his commission.

| 56 Squadron | Lt H J Mulroy | + | Arras Flying Services Memorial |
| SE.5a D6098 | | | |

T/o 0745 Valheureux briefed for an attack on the aerodrome at Suzanne*[Somme] during which Herbert James Mulroy was engaged in aerial combat before being hit by anti-aircraft fire and sent crashing into Avéluy Wood. It will be recalled he had written off an SE.5a at Valheureux while practice flying on the 20th of April 1918 [see my summary for the day].

* The French website *Anciens Aerodromes* indicates Suzanne Aerodrome was situated nine km southeast of Albert and between late August 1916 and at least until July 1918, was occupied by units of the German Air Force, including *Jasta 4, Jasta 12* and *Jasta 76*. On 7 September 1918, No 35 Squadron and their FK.8s moved in only to leave on the 13th for Moislains. Three days later, Bristol F.2bs of No 20 Squadron flew in but departed for Proyart on the 24th. It would appear this was the end of Suzanne as an active airfield.

| 74 Squadron | Lt J I T Jones | Safe | |
| SE.5a C1117 | | | |

T/o Clairmarais and damaged beyond repair after running against a ridge on landing. For notes pertaining to Lieutenant Jones, please refer to my summary for 12 April 1918.

| 84 Squadron | Lt P Nielsen [New Zealand] | + | Heath Cemetery, Harbonnières |
| SE.5a C1923 | | | |

T/o 0945 Bertangles for an offensive patrol and when last seen by his colleagues Peter Nielsen was fighting with two enemy aircraft southeast of what Errol Martyn believes was Aubercourt in the Somme département. Prior to his transfer for flying duties, Peter served with the Wellington Mounted Rifles, New Zealand Expeditionary Force.

| 84 Squadron | Lt R J Fyfe | + | Villers-Bretonneux Military Cemetery |
| SE.5a D259 | | | |

T/o Bertangles similarly tasked and was last seen southeast of Abancourt [Oise] in combat with enemy scouts. Robert Joss Fyfe was nineteen years of age and features in my summary for the squadron on 20 May 1918.

| 85 Squadron | Lt J McG Grider USAS | + | |
| SE.5a C1883 | | | |

T/o St Omer for an offensive patrol and when last seen by fellow pilots John McGavock Grider was over enemy lines near Menin. A comprehensive account of his life can be read on the website *The Encyclopedia of Arkansas History & Culture* where it is said he carried with him each time he took off for a patrol a doll presented to him by the British actress Billie Carlton. The account goes on to say that his body was never recovered, but his death was confirmed when a German pilot dropped a weighted note describing Lieutenant Grider's burial. He is now commemorated on the Tablets of the Missing at Flanders Field American Cemetery at Waregem, Belgium. The account features a rather bitter note; it seems John Grider joined No 85 Squadron with two fellow American pilots, Lawrence Callahan and Elliott Springs, the latter having expressed a desire to become a writer and in 1926, Springs published *War Birds: Diary of an Unknown Aviator* which featured in serial form in the magazine

Liberty. Springs, however, failed to mention that his book was based on a diary given to him by John Grider, and though a second edition of *War Birds* acknowledged the source he was sued by John Grider's sister who subsequently received a settlement of $12,500. In 1988, Texas A & M University Press published a revised edition of *War Birds* naming John Grider as the author.

87 Squadron	Lt C A Bryant	Safe
5F.1 Dolphin C3819		

T/o Estrée-les-Crecy tasked for a special patrol between Albert and Arras, a corridor of about thirty-three km. On return, and landing, the Dolphin's axle snapped damaging the airframe beyond repair.

87 Squadron	Captain A A N D Pentland	Safe
5F.1 Dolphin C3827		

T/o Estrée-les-Crecy for a special patrol during which Captain Pentland's Dolphin was shot about by hostile aircraft and damaged beyond worthwhile repair; struck on 24 June 1918, with thirty-eight hours and fifty-four minutes flying in total.

96 Squadron	Lt G C R Hamilton [Canada]	+	Montreal [Mount Royal] Cemetery
F.1 Camel C8305			

T/o Shotwick for a training flight; stalled while banking at two hundred feet and spun in. George Cyril Rae Hamilton's father served in the military, rising in rank to lieutenant-colonel. As will be noted, his parents arranged for their son's body to be brought back to Canada for burial.

103 Squadron	Captain K T Dowding	Safe
DH.9 D7226	Lt C E Eddy	Safe

T/o 1315 Serny for bombing operations; returned at 1600 showing evidence of being heavily engaged in aerial combat. Languished until 13 July 1918, when it was struck off charge.

210 Squadron	Lt C J Shackell [South Africa]	+	Ebbinghem Military Cemetery
F.1 Camel B7148			

T/o Ste-Marie Cappel for a practice flight during which South African born Cecil John Shackell is thought to have fainted. Out of control, his Camel spun in near St-Sylvestre-Cappel, a little under five km south-southeast of the airfield. Arriving on the squadron on May 25th, 'B7148' in its one month of service shared in the destruction of a two seater reconnaissance aircraft and an Albatros scout, on each occasion with Lieutenant Clement Wattson Payton [see my summary for 2 October 1918] at the controls. Lieutenant Shackell is mentioned in my summary for Second Lieutenant Edmund Charles Toy of No 213 Squadron who was killed on 25 August 1918.

Wednesday 19 June 1918

1 Squadron	Lt E M Newman	Safe
SE.5a C1101		

T/o Clairmarais South heading for patrol operations over the lines where 'C1101' was damaged by anti-aircraft fire. Forced landing, Lieutenant Newman ended up in a hedge at map reference 27L1a39. Flown to France in April 1918, it had been on squadron charge since the 21st of that month.

3 Squadron	2Lt W Bonner	+	Bagneux British Cemetery, Gezaincourt
F.1 Camel C6731			

T/o Valheureux to practice dropping incendiary bombs on a target spread out on the airfield but while diving got into a spin and out of control crashed in flames. His headstone has the inscription *'Absent In Body But Present In Spirit'*. Although only twenty-one years of age his entry in the cemetery register indicates he was of the King's Own [Royal Lancaster Regiment] and late of the 5th Battalion Cameron Highlanders.

3 Squadron AusFC	Lt R C Armstrong	Safe
RE.8 B2275	Lt F J Mart	Safe

T/o Villers Bocage for artillery patrol duties but turned back owing to rain which was the main contributory cause for their crash on return to base.

32 Squadron   Lt H Wilson [Canada]   Injured See 1 November 1918 - 32 Squadron
SE.5a C8894
T/o Fouquerolles authorised to carry out a practice flight. On regaining the airfield landed heavily, collapsing the undercarriage and turning over in the process. Fortunately, Lieutenant Wilson's injuries were not serious.

40 Squadron   2Lt G J Strange   Safe   See 24 September 1918 - 40 Squadron
SE.5a D395
T/o 1855 Bryas for an offensive patrol and when over the Pas-de-Calais saw Captain McElroy make a forced landing near the hamlet of Magnicourt-en-Compte. Anxious to assist, Gilbert John Strange landed close by but ran into standing corn and turned over. Formerly a cadet at the Royal Military College, Gilbert was commissioned to the Dorsetshire Regiment on the 4th of July 1917 [*gazetted* 4 July 1917, supplement 30164].

40 Squadron   Captain G E H McElroy*   Safe   See 20 July 1918 - 40 Squadron
SE.5a D5982   MC** DFC*
T/o 1855 Bryas for an offensive patrol but obliged to land following engine failure at Magnicourt-le-Compte in the Pas-de-Calais. In his history of No 40 Squadron, David Gunby charts the service of George Edward Henry McElroy from the time he arrived on the squadron as a novice second lieutenant in August 1917 to join A Flight as a replacement for Lieutenant H A Kennedy who was shot down and killed on the 22nd of August 1917, until his death on the last day of July 1918 [see my summary for details]. Although his name is now largely forgotten in the annals of air force history, George McElroy was an outstanding 'Ace' and was the top scoring scout pilot on No 40 Squadron with thirty-one confirmed victories, practically double that achieved by the legendary Edward Mannock VC during his time the squadron, and who acted as a mentor for George. A fuller appraisal of Captain McElroy's achievements can be read in my summary for 31 July 1918.

* George Edward Henry McElroy's profile, as recorded by *Wikipedia,* is well worth reading, particularly as it reports his strong patriotic Irish background and touches on his time spent with No 24 Squadron.

49 Squadron   Lt J Aitken   Safe   See 16 July 1918 - 49 Squadron
DH.9 D5656 *Royal Marines Plymouth*
T/o Hesdin and set out for Fourneuil where on arrival James Aitken crashed attempting to land. Salvaged, the airframe was struck off charge on 13 July 1918, having failed to last a single day in squadron service.

98 Squadron   2Lt A L Perry-Keene   Safe
DH.9 D1665   Sgt R T Wallace   Safe
T/o Ruisseauville tasked for a bombing sortie during which Second Lieutenant Perry-Keene was taken ill. Shutting down his engine he glided down to crash-land in a roughish field near Wieffe-Effroy in the Pas-de-Calais.

203 Squadron   Lt F G Black   Safe
F.1 Camel D3414
T/o Filescamp for an offensive patrol and damaged beyond repair following a landing where, I suspect, Lieutenant Black attempted to go round again for the accident report states that the engine failed to pick up and 'D3414' finished up in a cornfield. On squadron charge since 19 May 1918, 'D3414' had had a busy life and since 10 June had either shot down or shared in the destruction of around half-a-dozen hostile aircraft, most of these being accomplished by the squadron's Canadian born commanding officer Major Raymond Collishaw. His entry in *Wikipedia,* which is extensive, describes him as the highest scoring Royal Naval Air Service pilot and the second highest scoring Canadian pilot in the *Great War.*

236 Squadron   Lt F St P Harran   Injured Plymouth [Ford Park] Cemetery
DH.9 B7662   Aircraftman F Fairbrother   +   Atherton Cemetery, Lancashire
T/o Mullion and on return from patrol crashed and caught fire near Gaspell *[sic]*, Lieutenant Harran dying the next day from his injuries.

Thursday 20 June 1918
A day of inclement weather with unseasonal strong winds accompanied by heavy squally rain.

8 Squadron	Lt A Hollingworth	Safe	See 25 June 1918 - 8 Squadron
FK.8 C8623	Lt A Carter	Safe	See 25 June 1918 - 8 Squadron

T/o Auxi-le-Château tasked for bombing and on return the crew were faced with heavy rain and a strong gusting wind and the combination of the two elements proved their undoing when it came to landing. Flown out from Newcastle on 9 May 1918, 'C8623' was taken on charge on the 26th and in total flew forty-nine hours and forty-eight minutes.

8 Squadron	Lt F V Fennell	Safe	See 30 June 1918 - 8 Squadron
FK.8 D5059	Lt H D Hewitt	Safe	

T/o Auxi-le-Château similarly instructed and written off on return when Lieutenant Fennell had to take evasive action to avoid colliding with another aircraft, stalling his own machine in the process. Despatched by air from Newcastle early in May 1918, 'D5069' had been on squadron strength since the 6th and in total had logged eight-five hours and thirty-five minutes flying in total.

29 Squadron	Lt W E Durant [Canada]	Safe	See 2 July 1918 - 29 Squadron
SE.5a D6089			

T/o Vignacourt for a line patrol and on return undershot his approach, came down on a road, bounced and before Lieutenant Durant could recover the situation he stalled and crashed.

29 Squadron	Lt H C Rath	Safe	See 26 October 1918 - 29 Squadron
SE.5a E1258			

T/o Vignacourt similarly ordered in the course of which engine failure occurred. Sighting the airfield at Clairmarais South, Lieutenant Rath made his approach but while over a line of sheds stalled and crash-landed. 'E1258' had lasted in service for less than a month and including its factory test and ferry from Brooklands its flying hours came to just twelve.

29 Squadron	Lt H A Whittaker	Safe
SE.5a E1287		

T/o Vignacourt similarly instructed and during the sortie the aircraft's water pump failed. Maintaining control, Lieutenant Whittaker force-landed at map reference 27Q34C53 in a field that had been heavily shelled. His aircraft had logged, in total, a mere four hours and twenty-five minutes.

60 Squadron	2Lt G M Duncan	Safe	Unemployed List 2 June 1919: Lt DFC*
SE.5a D3439			

T/o Boffles for an offensive patrol over the lines. Ran low on fuel and switched to the emergency tank but before he could regain Boffles, Second Lieutenant Duncan became uncertain of his position and was obliged to make an unscheduled landing at Froyelles [Somme] some twenty km west-southwest short of the airfield. 'D3439' was received by the squadron from No 2 Air Issues on 7 April 1918.

* The citation for his Distinguished Flying Cross was published in *Flight* December 12, 1918; *'A courageous fighter and skilful leader who has accounted for seven enemy aeroplanes. On September 5th, while on escort duty, he attacked a formation of five Fokker triplanes; one of these he engaged at close range and it was seen to break up in the air; he then drove down a second out of control.'*

82 Squadron	Captain R T Fagan	Safe
FK.8 C8636	Lt M H Ely	Safe

T/o Quevenvillers tasked for bombing operations during which their aircraft was shot about while over Morlancourt [Somme] by anti-aircraft fire.

101 Squadron	2Lt C B Dove	Safe
FE.2b B7837	Lt R B Lane	Injured

T/o Famechon having received instructions for a reconnaissance mission but failed to become airborne and travelling at high speed the bomber entered a crop field and turned over. Although Lieutenant Lane's injuries were not too serious the experience left his pilot very badly shaken.

209 Squadron	2Lt H Mason	pow
F.1 Camel D3405		

T/o 1725 Bertangles in the company of five other aircraft all heading for operations over Proyart [Somme], thirty-two km east of Amiens.

210 Squadron	2Lt R G Carr	pow
F.1 Camel B7227 C		

T/o 1240 Ste Marie Cappel tasked for what has been described as a 'high patrol' and as reported in *The Camel File* came under attack from a quartet of Fokker DVIIs, one of which flown by Josef Jacobs drove the Camel down in the vicinity of Bousbecque, a largish village on the Franco-Belgium border then in enemy hands. Taken into captivity Second Lieutenant Carr escaped on the 1st of July and made his way to safety. 'B7227' began its service on or by 19 January 1918, when it arrived at No 4 Aeroplane Acceptance Park Lincoln from where by way of Hendon and Dover it made its way to France and to the care of No 8 Squadron Royal Naval Air Service who soon disposed of 'B7227' to No 3 Squadron Royal Naval Air Service. By the end of April it was on charge with No 210 Squadron accounting for three hostile aircraft and four kite balloons [mostly over the Ypres Salient], many of these victories shared with fellow pilots, to add to the two scouts shot down by No 3 Squadron.

Friday 21 June 1918

6 Squadron	Lt Bedworth	Safe
RE.8 C5078	Lt Hay	Safe

T/o Le Crotoy for an instructional flight and on return crash-landed with a force sufficient to damage the RE beyond repair. The official report concluded that the pilot made an error of judgement; Lieutenant Hay is described as a calvary officer.

32 Squadron	Major J C Russell	Safe
SE.5a C1881		

T/o Fouquerolles leading his squadron, which he had commanded since September 1917, to their new base at Ruisseauville where on landing he ran into a sunken road, the impact turning 'C1881' onto its back. Struck off charge 27 June 1918. John Cannan Russell, born on 6 March 1895, initially saw war service with the Royal Engineers before transferring in November 1915, to the Royal Flying Corps. His first operational tour was as a flight commander attached to No 54 Squadron followed by command of No 32 Squadron. Postwar he was appointed to a permanent commission spending much of his time on staff duties, though between April 1924 and May 1926, he commanded No 3 Squadron at Upavon where the squadron flew Gloster Woodcock fighters. Prior to retirement on 6 January 1943, he served as Air Officer Commanding No 1[Indian] Group. Air Commodore John Russell died on the 15th of August 1956.

32 Squadron	Lt P Macfarlane	Safe	See 27 June 1918 - 32 Squadron
SE.5a C1930			

T/o Fouquerolles similarly charged but swung out of control and damaged beyond repair. Peter Macfarlane features in my summary for 3 June 1918, when he had the misfortune to crash at Fouquerolles on arrival from Beauvois.

54 Squadron	Lt W K Wilson	pow	Unemployed list 1 March 1919: Lt
F.1 Camel B6326			

T/o 1620 Boisdinghem for operations over the Ypres sector where he was last seen flying on an easterly heading. Summaries for this officer are reported on 21 May and 6 June 1918. He was repatriated on Boxing Day 1918.

84 Squadron	Lt R Manzer	Safe
SE.5a C1897		

T/o Bertangles to practice diving on a target laid out on the airfield. During one of his dives his aircraft suffered total engine failure and in the ensuing forced landing, just beyond the aerodrome, 'C1897' was damaged beyond repair.

212 Squadron   Lt R C Packe   +   Hollybrook Memorial, Southampton
2F.1 Camel N6608
T/o Yarmouth for a patrol but was obliged to alight in the sea owing to engine failure. Robert Christopher Packe sighted a lightship and brought his Camel down close to it, but, sadly, he was unable to get clear of the cockpit and drowned. Nineteen years of age, he was born and raised on the Falkland Islands.

213 Squadron   Lt K W J Hall   pow
F.1 Camel B7245
T/o Bergues for an offensive patrol along the Belgian coast and was last caught sight of circa 1445 flying at nineteen thousand feet and heading in a north easterly direction between Nieuwpoort and Oostende. This Camel is noteworthy in that on 21 April 1918, while on the strength of No 209 Squadron and flown by Lieutenant W J Mackenzie, it became embroiled in combat where Manfred von Richthofen was present, Mackenzie being slightly wounded and 'B7245' shot about, believed by *Vizefeldwebel* Edgar Scholtz.

Saturday 22 June 1918
2 Squadron AusFC   Captain Simonson   Safe
SE.5a E1265
T/o Bertangles with the intension of transiting to Estree Blanche but *en route* a gear problem arose and Captain Simonson force-landed at Drionville. Seemingly a situation that could be rectified, the damage proved extensive and 'E1265' was struck off charge on 27 June 1918.

10 Squadron   Lt R O Williams   Safe
FK.8 D5166   2Lt W E Grainger   Safe
T/o Droglandt for a counter attack patrol during which an exhaust valve fractured; force-landed, and damaged beyond repair, at map reference 27K12d55. Please consult my summary for 12 April 1918, for details regarding Lieutenant Williams.

29 Squadron   2Lt F T Arnold   Injured
SE.5a D3563
T/o Vignacourt for a line patrol and on return the patrol found the local wind conditions to be extremely strong and in attempting to land Second Lieutenant Arnold made a flat turn, into wind, at thirty feet and promptly spun to the ground.

79 Squadron   Lt H E Snyder   Safe
5F.1 Dolphin C3795
T/o Ste Marie Cappel for an offensive patrol but within seconds of leaving the ground and having climbed to around fifty feet a petrol feed pipe fractured and with his engine failing Lieutenant Snyder crash-landed on to a trench and then skidded onto a drain taking surface water. Issued to the squadron on 26 March 1918, 'C3795' was struck off charge six days later with ninety-two hours and fifty minutes total flying recorded.

Sunday 23 June 1918
Following four days of limited operations owing to weather, flying conditions were markedly improved.

2 Squadron   Lt Rawsthorne   Safe
FK.8 C8598   Lt C G Johnson   Safe
T/o Mazingarbe tasked for artillery observation work but in the poor light crashed against a hangar containing a Bristol F.2b D8025. This was the squadron's first serious crash since arriving at Mazingarbe from Floringhem on the 20th June.

Note. Although the FK.8 was the squadron's principal type, a handful of Bristol F.2b fighters were allocated, one being 'D8025' which on this occasion escaped serious damage. Later issued to 'L' Flight it was written off on the last day of July 1918, when landing from an artillery observation sortie, Lieutenants H O Thornton and A G Fletcher being slightly injured.

7 Squadron	Lt M W C Ridgway	Injured	
RE.8 C2401	2Lt J Forsyth	Injured	

T/o Droglandt tasked for an operational sortie which was over for the crew within moments of becoming airborne when their aircraft flew into telegraph wires. Neither were seriously hurt. Flown to France from Coventry and issued to the squadron on 25 April 1918, 'C2401' was well used logging in total one hundred and thirty-one hours and twenty-five minutes.

20 Squadron	Lt H C McCreary	Safe	See July 1918 - 20 Squadron
Bristol F.2b B1122 *Dominica*	Sgt J D C Summers	Safe	

T/o Boisdinghem for an offensive patrol and force-landed near Tilques in the Hauts-de-France region a little over five km northwest of St Omer. It is believed the Bristol's fuel tank was shot through. Harry Charles McCreary, was one of many commissioned to the General List of the Royal Flying Corps on 6 December 1917, as published in supplement 30425 of the paper issued on 13 December 1917.

40 Squadron	Lt D S Poler USAS	Safe	See 7 August 1918
SE.5a D3969			

T/o 0600 Bryas for an early morning offensive patrol, returning to the aerodrome two hours later. At the time the wind was quite brisk and as Lieutenant Poler was about to touch down a gust caught his aircraft, lifting a wind to the degree that he was unable to control the landing and 'D3969' was damaged beyond repair.

42 Squadron	2Lt H McDonald	Injured	Aire Communal Cemetery
RE.8 C2348	2Lt C A Marsh	Injured	Aire Communal Cemetery

T/o Rély briefed for artillery observation duties but while climbing away lost flying speed in a turn and spun in; on impact the aircraft went up in flames. Rescuers were quickly at the scene and managed to pull both crew to safety but their injuries were so grievous they died the following day. Cuthbert Alban Marsh was formerly of the South Lancashire Regiment.

53 Squadron	Lt G L Dobell	Safe	See 11 August 1918 - 53 Squadron
RE.8 A3619 *Johore No 10*	2Lt J A Lewis	Safe	

T/o Clairmarais for a night investigation around Kemmel and on return Lieutenant Dobell misjudged his approach and failed to flare before hitting the ground with a force sufficient to damage 'A3619' beyond repair. Taken on charge 13 July 1917, 'A3619' had a trouble free life until the incident here summarised, thereby logging a very useful three hundred and sixty-six hours and fifteen minutes flying. Lieutenant Dobell had force-landed during operations on the 8th of May 1918; see my summary for details.

57 Squadron	2Lt C W Peckham	pow	Unemployed list 23 June 1919: Lt
DH.4 A7742	2Lt A J Cobbin	pow	Le Quesnoy Communal Cemetery

T/o 0340 Le Quesnoy for a bombing raid and according to *The DH.4/DH.9 File* was seen under attack from a Fokker DrI west of Montauban-de-Picardie [Somme] and last sighted going down south of Bapaume in the Pas-de-Calais. Both officers are shown as becoming prisoners of war, nineteen year old Arthur John Cobbin dying* from wounds on 14 July 1918. As he is buried in the cemetery close to the airfield from which he departed, this leads me to believe he may have been repatriated. His commission to the General List of the Royal Flying Corps was effective from 19 July 1917 [*gazetted* 7 August 1917, issue 30221]. Common to so many DH.4s of the time, 'A7742' had an eventful service; first employed by No 5 Squadron Royal Naval Air Service, Flight-Sub Lieutenant G B S McBain and Gunlayer W Jones destroyed an Albatros DV near Promour [*sic*] in the late morning of 18th March 1918 and nine days later the same crew came off second best during combat and on landing their machine shed one of its wings, both being pulled from their cockpits suffering from injuries. On 7th June 1918, fully restored for active duty it arrived with No 57 Squadron. Second Lieutenant Peckham was repatriated on 29 November 1918.

* Andrew Pentland has forwarded a note taken from a Red Cross German file indicating Second Lieutenant Cobbin was shot in the upper arm and died in a Field Hospital at Le Quesnoy. Consulting *Flight*, this magazine repeating the Air Ministry Roll of Honour in their issue of July 11, 1918, names both officers under the 'Missing' heading, and in their issue of December 19, 1918, confirms the repatriation of Second Lieutenant Peckham. Meanwhile, in respect of Second Lieutenant Cobbin *Flight* September 19, 1918, records him as wounded and held in captivity.

57 Squadron	2Lt A D R Jones	pow
DH.4 D9276	Sgt J T Ward	pow

T/o 0340 Le Quesnoy similarly tasked and was lost in circumstances similar to those reported above. Taken on charge on 17 June 1918, 'D9276' while being flown by Lieutenant C W Peckham [see my previous summary] and Second Lieutenant E I Riley [destined to join his colleagues from the two crews summarised here following operations on 20 July 1918] on the 19th, accounted for a Fokker DVII between Bapaume and St Léger after which the crew landed on the French airfield at Montagne *[sic]* returning to Le Quesnoy the following day.

87 Squadron	Lt A J Golding	Safe
5F.1 Dolphin C3912		

T/o Estrée-les-Crecy to test fire the guns and while doing so the synchronise mechanism failed and to his concern Lieutenant Golding realised his aircraft was *sans* propeller; maintaining control he came down in a field just off the aerodrome where the Dolphin turned turtle in the long grass and was damaged beyond repair.

100 Squadron	2Lt F S Reed	Safe
FE.2b D9766	Mechanic H C Wickham	Safe

T/o Ochey for a night raid on targets at Metz and while in the vicinity of the lines was hit by anti-aircraft fire and forced down near Landremont in the *département du Meurthe-et-Moselle*. All might have been well but before coming to a stop 'D9766' ran into a deep depression and turned over.

149 Squadron	Lt J W Thompson	pow
FE.2b D9777	2Lt J W Ingram	pow

T/o Alquines tasked for a raid on targets at Armentières; failed to return. Both officers were repatriated on the 13th of December 1918. The loss of this aircraft from operations was the squadron's first since arriving in France from Ford.

206 Squadron	Lt T Roberts	Safe
DH.9 D1699	2Lt R W Brigstock	Safe

T/o Alquines having received orders for photographic reconnaissance sortie in the course of which engine trouble obliged the crew to force-land, which they duly accomplished on Droglandt airfield. Struck off charge on the 27th of June 1918.

217 Squadron	Lt A M Phillips	Safe
DH.4 A7945	Airman H J Tourlaman	Safe

T/o Bergues for an anti-submarine patrol and on return landed heavily, bounced and finished up tipped on its nose. Henry James Tourlaman transferred from the Royal Naval Air Service on the day that the merger with the Royal Flying Corps took place and from which the Royal Air Force was formed. His service number '313935' places him in the block '313001 - 316000'. Postwar he remained in the air force and rose to the rank of sergeant. Thirty-seven years of age, Henry died on 8 January 1921, his entry in the Tottenham Cemetery register showing his unit as 'No 217 Squadron', even though '217' had been a victim of the savage reduction of air force squadrons in the aftermath of the *Great War*.

Monday 24 June 1918

3 Squadron AusFC	Lt F M Lock	Safe
RE.8 A3665	2Lt A G Barrett	Safe

T/o Villers-Bocage tasked for artillery observation over Cerisy. Returned so badly shot about that 'A3665' was deemed uneconomical to repair and with two hundred and eighty-seven hours and ten minutes flying 'in the bank', it was struck off charge on the 5th of July 1918.

| 28 Squadron | Lt C P Uhrich [Canada] | + | Montecchio Precalcino Communal Cemetery |
| F.1 Camel B9306 | | | extension |

T/o Grossa for a practice flight but while flying at two thousand feet near Isola di Cattura spun out of control with fatal consequences for Charles Philip Uhrich from Winkler in Manitoba.

| 35 Squadron | 2Lt C F Brown | Safe |
| FK.8 C8558 | 2Lt H H Creighton | Injured |

T/o Villers Bocage for artillery observation and patrol duties in the course of which their aircraft was hit by shrapnel from a close burst of anti-aircraft fire which damaged the radiator. Forced landing at Rainneville [Somme], some eleven km north of Amiens, repairs were carried out but on taking off the crew had the misfortune to collide with a tree. Second Lieutenant Creighton's injuries are reported as slight.

| 41 Squadron | Lt E J Stephens | Safe |
| SE.5a C8874 | | |

T/o Conteville for an offensive patrol towards Suzanne [sic] and returned to base with the longerons shot through. Struck off charge two days later having, in total, flown for sixteen hours and twenty minutes.

| 58 Squadron | Major J H S Tyssoll* | Injured |
| FE.2 A6495 | Mechanic P A Young | Safe |

T/o Fauquembergues for an air test and on return, and landing, a wingtip caught the ground throwing the aircraft round and snapping the tail boom.

* An unusual surname and as yet untraced via The London Gazette.

| 62 Squadron | Lt T H Broadley | Safe | See 15 September 1918 - 62 Squadron |
| Bristol F.2b B1273 | Sgt F R Bower | Injured | |

T/o Planques for operations in the Lille area during which Sergeant Bower was wounded. Seeking to make an emergency landing in order for his observer to receive immediate treatment, Lieutenant Broadley came down on a dummy airfield at Senlecques, presumably near the commune of the same name in the Pas-de-Calais. On touch down the Bristol was badly damaged and, it is believed, its flying days were over. Sergeant Bower is believed to have made a good recovery.

| 62 Squadron | Lt F Williams | + | Cabaret-Rouge British Cemetery, Souchez |
| Bristol F.2b D8028 | 2lt E Dumville | + | Cabaret-Rouge British Cemetery, Souchez |

T/o Planques for an offensive sortie and when last seen by other pilots engaged on the patrol was being heavily engaged with four to five enemy scouts over Lille.

| 74 Squadron | Lt T G Sifton | Safe |
| SE.5a D6893 | | |

T/o Clairmarais for an offensive patrol during which Lieutenant Sifton force-landed, owing to engine failure, three to four km from Cassel in the département du Nord.

| 98 Squadron | 2Lt E T M Routledge | Safe |
| DH.9 C6287 | 2Lt J F J Peters | Safe |

T/o Drionville tasked for a raid which for the crew ended in a forced landing on a beach near Gravelines*[Nord]. Deemed beyond economical repair, the DH was struck off charge on 27 June 1918.

* Gravelines was a familiar turning point in 1941 for Fighter Command squadrons sweeping the Channel coast in an inducement to draw the Luftwaffe into action.

| 206 Squadron | Lt W C Cutmore | + | Bouchoir New British Cemetery |
| DH.9 D1012 | 2Lt W G Duncan | + | Bouchoir New British Cemetery |

T/o 0330 Alquines briefed for a long reconnaissance and went down east of the lines. William Gardiner Duncan, age thirty-three and married, held a Master of Arts degree. He had been involved in a crash on 12 June 1918 [see my summary for details]. His pilot was only eighteen and his entry in the register indicates he was first laid to rest by the Germans in their cemetery at La Boissiere but whose grave has since been lost. I suspect, therefore, that at Bouchoir he is one of several commemorated by a special memorial.

| 210 Squadron | Lt G A Learn [Canada] | + | Arras Flying Services Memorial |
| F.1 Camel D3367 | | | |

T/o 0900 Ste Marie Cappel with others for an offensive patrol and while over the Ypres sector engaged in combat with a trio of enemy scouts which for Toronto born Gerald Alfred Learn ended with his Camel falling away some three to four km northeast of Zillebeke Lake with its wings folding up.

| 218 Squadron | Lt H V M Hoskins | Injured | Unemployed list 22 April 1919: Lt |
| DH.9 B7656 | | | |

T/o PetiteSynthe for local flying practice during which the DH crashed, severely injuring Lieutenant Hoskins. 'B7656' had already featured in two landing accidents, the first on the 29th of May while being flown by Lieutenant W F Purvis and as recently as the 8th of June with Captain M G Baskerville and Sergeant S H Newton.

Tuesday 25 June 1918

A busy day of operations with the DH.9s of the Independent Force striking at rail communications and at targets inside Germany.

| 1 Squadron | Lt H B Bradley [USA] | + | Arras Flying Services Memorial |
| SE.5a C1102 | | | |

T/o 1725 Clairmarais South and was not seen after passing over Bac-St-Maur in the Pas-de-Calais. Harold Bartlett Bradley was formerly of Montclair in Essex County, New Jersey.

| 2 Squadron AusFC | Lt R L Manuel MC | Safe | |
| SE.5a C1837 | | | |

T/o Lièttres for an offensive patrol during which the engine's oil pressure fell to an alarmingly low level; force-landed, and wrecked, near Eggewaertscapelle [West-Vlaanderen], two to three km southeast of Veurne.

| 8 Squadron | Lt A Hollingworth | Injured | |
| FK.8 D5007 | 2Lt A Carter | + | St Riquer British Cemetery |

T/o Auxi-le-Château ordered for bombing operations and on return crashed out of control near the airfield. Both officers had been involved in a crash-landing on the 20th of June 1918; please refer to my summary for details. Alan Carter's headstone carries the poignant inscription; *'My Son, My Son So Loved So Missed So Mourned.'*

| 24 Squadron | Lt E B Wilson | Injured | |
| SE.5a C1800 | | | |

T/o Conteville for an offensive patrol during which the formation engaged with hostile aircraft over Bouzincourt [Somme]. With his petrol tank on fire Lieutenant Wilson somehow managed to retain control and crash-landed, his aircraft continuing to burn and himself very badly burnt. Despite the severity of his injuries he appears to have made a form of recovery.

| 24 Squadron | Captain C N Lowe | Safe | |
| SE.5a C6452 | | | |

T/o Conteville similarly tasked and force-landed at map reference 57DN10 after fire from the ground shot away the propeller.

| 29 Squadron | Lt F R Brand | Safe | See 27 June 1918 - 29 Squadron |
| SE.5a D8441 | | | |

T/o Vignacourt for an offensive patrol and on return written off in a heavy landing.

| 32 Squadron | Lt C Wilderspin | Safe |
| SE.5a B170 | | |

T/o Ruisseauville with instructions to patrol the thirty odd km corridor between Armentières at the northern end at Carvin away to the south-southeast. Damaged beyond repair after forced landing with a broken centre wire. Subsequently, Lieutenant Wilderspin was transferred to the Administrative Branch and reverted from his status as Lieutenant[A] to plain Lieutenant with effect from 18 January 1919 [*gazetted* 18 April 1919, issue 31302]. As such he ceased to be employed on 20 May 1919, as promulgated in issue 31656 of 25 November 1919.

| 41 Squadron | Lt F W H Martin [Canada] | Safe | See 9 August 1918 - 41 Squadron |
| SE.5a C8873 | | | |

T/o Conteville authorised to make a practice flight but within seconds of leaving the ground the engine failed and in the ensuing crash 'C8873' was wrecked. Little used in its nine days of squadron service, plus ferrying, it had logged a mere two hours and twenty-two minutes flying.

| 43 Squadron | Lt N Wilson | Safe |
| F.1 Camel D6570 | | |

T/o Lièttres for practice flying but misjudged his approach to land and crash-landed in a cornfield; damaged beyond repair. This was the squadron's first serious accident since arriving at Lièttres from Fouquerolles on the 21st of June 1918.

| 48 Squadron | 2Lt F Cabburn | + | Fouquescourt British Cemetery |
| Bristol F.2b C789 | Sgt W Lawder | + | Fouquescourt British Cemetery |

T/o Bertangles for offensive operations with bombs and last seen with its bomb load intact under attack from hostile aircraft near Foucaucourt-en-Santerre [Somme].

| 48 Squadron | Lt N H Muirden | pow | Premont British Cemetery |
| Bristol F.2b C4719 | 2Lt E Roberts | pow | |

T/o Bertangles similarly tasked and when last was going down with its bombs near Foucaucourt-en-Santerre [Somme]. Severely wounded nineteen year old Norman Hadley Muirden managed to force-land; sadly, his wounds proved terminal and he died on the 8th of August 1918. His headstone bears the inscription; *'He Serves Today And Sees God's Face Mid Haven's Hosts'*. Norman's parents are shown in the cemetery register as being of Aberdeen but with a connection to Argentina. It is further noted that his brother fell though his Christian names are omitted. However, I can only find one other serviceman with the surname 'Muirden' becoming a casualty in the *Great War* namely Private Ray Silian Muirden of the 2nd Battalion King's Own Scottish Borders who fell during the *Third Battle of Ypres* on the 4th of October 1917. With no known grave he is commemorated on the Tyne Cot Memorial. His entry is devoid of next of kin. Second Lieutenant Roberts was repatriated on the 13th of December 1918.

| 53 Squadron | 2Lt K D Handel* | Injured | Aire Communal Cemetery |
| RE.8 D4966 | 2Lt H Dyson | Injured | |

T/o Clairmarais for a night patrol and crashed in a forced landing at B6I19b3545. Kenneth Douglas Handel is described in the cemetery register as belonging to No 53 Squadron but attached to No 4 Squadron; however, the airframe serial quoted for this summary indicates he had returned to duty with No 53 Squadron.

* Shown in the register for Aire Communal Cemetery as coming from Ilminster in Somerset, I very much suspect he was a member of the Handel family that ran one of the town's butchery businesses which during the author's time as a pupil at Ilminster Grammar School in the early 1950s is recalled as thriving establishment.

| 54 Squadron | Lt W H Stubbs | + | Aeroplane Cemetery |
| F.1 Camel B7164 | | | |

T/o 1815 Boisdinghem for an offensive patrol and was last sighted forty-five minutes later, under control, to the west of Bailleul; probably came down northeast of Ypres.

54 Squadron	Lt O J F Jones-Lloyd	pow	
F.1 Camel C8238			

T/o Boisdinghem for offensive operations and when last seen was flying at twelve thousand feet, under control, in the vicinity of Forêt de Nieppe. Lieutenant Jones-Lloyd was another of the 13 December 1918, repatriations.

55 Squadron	Lt G A Sweet [Canada]	+	Terlincthun British Cemetery, Wimille
DH.4 B7866	2Lt C F R Goodyear	+	Terlincthun British Cemetery, Wimille

T/o Azelot ordered for a raid on Karlsruhe during which crews in the same formation as 'B7866' witnessed it falling to a fighter attack over Saarbrücken the capital city of the state of Saarland. Since the end of hostilities their remains have been recovered to France. Lieutenant Sweet from Hamilton, Ontario was eighteen; his observer was nineteen and his commissioned was granted on 18 May 1918 [*gazetted* 4 June 1918, issue 30727]. Neither could have had very much operational experience.

60 Squadron	Lt G L Du Cross	Safe	
SE.5a D6182			

T/o Boffles for flying practice and on return to the airfield flattened out far too high and as result stalled and crashed, damaging 'D6182' beyond repair.

74 Squadron	Lt S Carlin MC DCM	Safe	See 1 July 1918 - 74 Squadron
SE.5a C6469			

T/o Clairmarais for an operational sortie and on return landed in a cross-wind and swung, tipping onto its nose. Struck off charge on the last day of June. For an appreciation of Sydney Carlin's service, please refer to my summary for 31 May 1918.

98 Squadron	Lt G Richmond	Safe	
DH.9 C6170	Sgt F Sefton	Safe	

T/o 1610 Drionwill heading for a raid on rail communications at Kortrijk. Intercepted by a formation of hostile scouts the bombers came under sustained attacks and though Lieutenant Richmond made a safe return his aircraft was so badly damaged that it was struck off charge on 29 June 1918.

98 Squadron	Lt H E A Reynolds	Injured	
DH.9 D7228	Lt H A Lamb	Safe	See 9 July 1918 - 98 Squadron

T/o Drionville for bombing operations but within minutes the DH was down, damaged beyond repair, following engine failure and an unsuccessful attempt by Lieutenant Reynolds to return to the airfield. His injuries, thankfully, were not serious.

99 Squadron	Lt N S Harper [Canada]	+	Niederzwehren Cemetery, Kassel
DH.9 D5570	Lt D G Benson [Canada]	+	Niederzwehren Cemetery, Kassel

T/o 0445 Azelot for bombing operations on Offenburg [Baden-Württemberg] and when last sighted was going down between the target area and nearby Strasbourg.

104 Squadron	Lt S C M Pontin	pow	
DH.9 C2170	2Lt J Arnold	pow	

T/o 0935 Azelot for bombing operations over Karlsruhe and it was while homebound that the bombers came under attack from a formation of enemy scouts, one of which drove down Lieutenant Pontin to the east of Vosges and close to the border with France. Both officers appear under the heading 'Missing' in *Flight* July 18th, 1918, with same magazine in their issue of September 19, 1918, confirming they were prisoners of war; Second Lieutenant Arnold prior to joining the Royal Flying Corps served with the King's [Liverpool] Regiment.

149 Squadron	Lt P M Haldiman	Injured	
FE.2b A6497	2Lt S Jones	Safe	

T/o Alquines heading for bombing operations over Armentières; force-landed, and damaged beyond repair, near Ebblinghem [Nord] as a consequence of a water pipe bursting.

201 Squadron   Lt E Nightingale   +   Heath Cemetery, Harbonnieres
F.1 Camel B7278
T/o Noeux for offensive action in the direction of Villers-Bretonneux where the patrol became involved in a fierce fight. On return, Lieutenant Gates said he was positive that the Camel he saw going down under attack from seven of the enemy scouts east of the patrol area was that of Eric Nightingale. Little hope could be expected of his survival as flames were much in evidence streaming from the aircraft. Formerly of the The Buffs [East Kent Regiment] his headstone bears the words; *'Sans Peur Et Sans Reproche The Day Thou Gavest Lord Is Ended.'*

211 Squadron   2Lt F Daltrey   pow
DH.9 C2176   Private R Shephard   +   Arras Flying Services Memorial
T/o 0935 Petite Synthe 'borrowed' from No 206 Squadron [Alquines] and was last seen surrounded by a barrage of anti-aircraft fire a few km east of Oostende. Second Lieutenant Daltry went into captivity in a wounded state; it was not until October 3, 1918, that *Flight* was able to report his name under the Air Ministry's release of September 25th, that he was in German hands, wounded.

211 Squadron   2Lt H H Palmer   Safe
D1021 K   Private W J Atkinson   Safe   See 13 July 1918 - 211 Squadron
T/o Petite Synthe for bombing; sideslipped and crashed on landing. Struck off charge 29 June 1918.

Wednesday 26 June 1918
11 Squadron   Major H B Davey   Injured
Bristol F.2b B1283   Captain J S Chick   Injured
T/o Remaisnil intent on carrying out target firing practice but just as the Bristol was about to lift off its propeller caught the lip of an old shell hole. Climbing, and with the engine vibrating badly, Major Davey lost control at around two hundred feet and sideslipped to a heavy crash landing, Captain Chick receiving severe injuries though he later recovered. Major Davey had assumed command of the squadron from Major R F S Morton during May 1918, handing over to Major R W Heath in the July.

21 Squadron   Lt Peasland   Safe
RE.8 C2351   Lt Taylor   Safe
T/o Floringhem for a dawn reconnaissance but before becoming airborne ran, at speed, into a field of crops and turned over. Despatched to France from Coventry and via Lympne 'C2351' came to the squadron on 28 April 1918, and overall accomplished one hundred and ten hours and forty minutes flying.

22 Squadron   Lt S F H Thompson   Safe   See 27 September 1918 - 22 Squadron
Bristol F.2b C961   Sgt Fletcher   Safe
T/o Serny for an offensive patrol but while traveling at speed the propeller came into contact with a rut and the resultant damage was such that the Bristol was struck off charge on 29 June 1918. Although despatched from the makers early in May and on squadron strength since the 22nd of the month 'C961' had been little used and when struck had a mere five hours and twenty minutes flying recorded. It appears that Samuel Frederick Henry Thompson began his military service commissioned, with effect from 22 March 1915, with the Army Service Corps, his transfer to the Royal Flying Corps as yet not known.

24 Squadron   2Lt W J Miller   Safe   See 17 September 1918 - 24 Squadron
SE.5a C1921
T/o Conteville for a practice flight and on return to the airfield landed across the wind which put an end to the flying days of his aircraft which was struck off charge two days later.

40 Squadron   Lt N S Cameron   Safe   See 28 June 1918 - 40 Squadron
SE.5a D3958
T/o 2000 Bryas for a last light offensive patrol which ended less than an hour later with engine failure. Skilfully, Lieutenant Cameron put the SE.5a down in a cornfield near Le Houpie *[sic]* which ended its days as a flying machine.

41 Squadron   Lt F J Davey   Safe
SE.5a D6189
T/o Contevill for evening operations over Villers-Bretonneux and on regaining base the light was fast dimming and as a consequence Lieutenant Davey misjudged his approach and crashed.

43 Squadron   Lt C W Harman   Injured
F.1 Camel B5433
T/o Lièttres for operations during which Lieutenant Harman was obliged to make an emergency landing owing to engine failure. Arriving in a field, cropped with wheat, near Haverskerque [Nord] he was unable to prevent his aircraft running into a ditch, the impact damaging the airframe beyond repair.

48 Squadron   2Lt J E Doe   pow
Bristol F.2b C818   2Lt A J Elvin   pow
T/o Bertangles and failed to return from a reconnaissance sortie over Villers-Bretonneux. *Flight* in their issue for 29 August 1918, repeated the list issued by the German authorities for Royal Air Force aircraft and personnel [of the latter many are not identified] brought down over their territory during June 1918. Both Second Lieutenants Doe and Elvin are named as being prisoners of war, though their aircraft is described as a *'Sopwith two-seater No 818.'* Their release from captivity was reported on 13 December 1918.

54 Squadron   2Lt C H Atkinson   Safe   See 4 July 1918 - 54 Squadron
F.1 Camel B9251
T/o Boisdinghem for an offensive patrol but tried to become airborne with insufficient airspeed and as a consequence of his actions Charles Henry Atkinson crashed heavily, damaging 'B9251' beyond worthwhile repair. Earlier in the month, on the 4th, he had written off a Camel during a transit flight from St Omer followed three days later by a second Camel [see my summaries for details].

55 Squadron   2Lt F F H Bryan   pow   Unemployed list 20 April 1919: Lt
DH.4 A8073 A   Sgt A Boocock   pow   See 28 May 1918 - 55 Squadron
T/o Azelot tasked for a raid on Karlsruhe during which the DH was intercepted by enemy fighters and shot down near Haguenau [Bas-Rhin] close to the border with Germany. Second Lieutenant Bryan was repatriated on the 14th of December, his observer following on the 23rd.

56 Squadron   Captain A P Thompson   Safe
SE.5a D6022
T/o Valheureux for flying practice and on landing ran onto a ridge, bounced back into the air and his next arrival on *terra firma* collapsed the undercarriage; wrecked.

65 Squadron   Lt E C Eaton [Canada]   +   Bouzincourt Ridge Cemetery, Albert
F.1 Camel D6630   *Croix de Guerre* [France]
T/o 1930 Bertangles and an hour later was seen by other pilots in the patrol to be fighting a quintet of Pfalz scouts northeast of Albert. From Montreal, and late of the Saskatchewan Regimental Depot attached to the Royal Air Force, twenty year old Edward Carter Eaton had shared in the destruction of two enemy scouts, both on the 20th of May 1918; one in the morning and the second late in the evening. His headstone carries the words; *'Unto Thee O Lord Do I Lift Up My Soul.'*

80 Squadron   2Lt B Critchley   Injured Pernes British Cemetery
F.1 Camel D1777
T/o 0630 Lièttres for an early light offensive patrol; shot down by anti-aircraft fire near Annequin in the Pas-de-Calais, a little over six km east-southeast of Béthune. Nineteen year old Burton Critchley from St Annes-on-Sea in Lancashire died the same day from his wounds. Arriving in France by sea, 'D1777' went to No 43 Squadron on 25 March 1918, but was damaged in combat [Captain C F King MC*] on the 3rd of April. It arrived with No 80 Squadron on the last day of May 1918, having undergone repairs at No 2 Advanced Salvage Dump.

* Cecil Frederick King came through the *Great War* unscathed and research by the aviation historian Norman Franks indicates he eventually destroyed, or shared, in the destruction of twenty-two enemy machines, two of these successes being achieved in 'D1777', the first being during the morning of 28 March 1918, when he drove down an Albatros DV east of the road between Albert and Bray. Postwar, and now back in the United Kingdom, he was assigned to flying instructor duties with No 3 Flying School at Sedgeford and it was here on the 24th of January 1919, that he was killed when his Camel C8318 collied in the air with Camel H2724 piloted by a fellow instructor South African born Lieutenant Hector Daniel, also a holder of the Military Cross and who had served alongside Cecil in France. Hector survived the collision, badly shaken, and [I suspect] was present when his friend was laid to rest in Docking [St Mary] Churchyard on 4 February 1919. It is noted that Captain King's entry in the cemetery register incorrectly shows him as belonging to No 33 Squadron. In addition to the Military Cross, he had been *gazetted* with the Distinguished Flying Cross and Norman Franks in his book *Fallen Eagles* states the French government bestowed upon Captain King the *Croix de Guerre avec Palme* in recognition of his good work during the *Second Battle of the Marne* [15 July to 6 August 1918].

| 84 Squadron | Lt E J Reid | Safe |
| SE.5a C1906 | | |

T/o Bertangles and wrecked on landing from a patrol over Villers-Bretonneux. On charge since the 7th of the month 'C1906', including the usual tests and ferrying flew a total of twenty-six hours and fifty-five minutes.

| 84 Squadron | Lt W Pooley | Safe |
| SE.5a D6882 | | |

T/o Bertangles and wrecked here following a heavy landing at the conclusion of a practice flight.

| 86 Squadron | Lt W E I Marshall | + | Liverpool [Anfield] Cemetery |
| F.1 Camel E9977 | | | |

T/o Northolt for a practice flight; lost control and spun in from two thousand feet. Initially with the Army Service Corps [Transport] as a private soldier, William Edward Isley Marshall received a commission and, subsequently, served with the Royal Flying Corps in Italy.

| 104 Squadron | 2Lt C G Jenyns | pow | |
| DH.9 C6256 | 2Lt H C Davis | + | Plaine French National Cemetery |

T/o Azelot tasked for targets at Karlsruhe. Observed to go down east of the lines, probably in the region of Plaine in the *département du Bas-Rhin* just above Colroy-la-Roche. 'C6256' had been issued to the squadron prior to its move to France. Wounded, Second Lieutenant Jenyns is named under one of the 'Missing' headings reported in *Flight* July 25, 1918. It is highly likely that his observer was mortally wounded in the air. His gallant skipper was repatriated on 13 December 1918.

| 206 Squadron | Lt C Eaton | Safe |
| DH.9 D2783 | Lt E W Tatnall | Safe |

T/o 1808 Alquines for bombing operations; hit by anti-aircraft fire and force-landed Elstrée Blanche. Following a technical inspection the DH was struck off charge on 2 July 1918.

| 210 Squadron | 2Lt C D Boothman | + | Pont-du-Hem Military Cemetery, La Gorgue |
| F.1 Camel D9614 | | | |

T/o Ste Marie Cappel for an offensive patrol and driven down near Armentières. 'D9614' had lasted for nine days on squadron charge.

Thursday 27 June 1918
Another day of air activity over the Western Front and one that ended with serious losses in aircraft; at least forty-one Royal Air Force squadron aircraft had been written off either during operations or in training mishaps.

| 2 Squadron | Lt E K Blenkinsop | Safe |
| FK.8 D5028 | | |

T/o Mazingarbe authorised to carry out night landings during which Lieutenant Blenkinsop collided with FK.8 C3581 which was parked on the airfield. Damage to 'C3581' was slight but its reprieve was short lived as my summary for the 9th of July will show.

3 Squadron AusFC	Lt P H Kerr	Injured	
RE.8 A3661	Lt A O'C Brook AusFC	+	Vignacourt British Cemetery

T/o 0640 Villers-Bocage and headed for Corbie tasked for artillery observation duties. A signal from the crew was received circa 0850 and it was probably soon after making this transmission that the crew were set upon by two Pfalz scouts whose fire killed Arthur O'Connor Brook and wounded Lieutenant Kerr who crash-landed near Pont Noyelles. On squadron charge since 11 September 1917, 'A3661' accomplished two hundred and fifty-eight hours and five minutes flying. Arthur's headstone is inscribed; *'Have Mercy Upon Him O Lord And Let Perpetual Light Shine Upon Him.'*

4 Squadron AusFC	Lt J S McD Browne [Canada]	+	Arras Flying Services Memorial
F.1 Camel D9510			

T/o 0840 Clairmarais for an offensive patrol and believed to have been shot down near Bailleul [Nord] by *Vizefeldwebel* Rausch of *Jasta 40*. Nineteen year old John Sandfield McDonald Browne came from Toronto.

5 Squadron	Captain R S Durno	Safe
RE.8 B6680	Lt F W P Clark	Safe

T/o Le Hameau for transit to Izel-lès-Hameau but engine failure intervened and in attempting to land at the airfield at Ostreville came down in a cornfield and turned over. On establishment since 30 March 1918, 'B6680' in total flew one hundred and six hours and thirty minutes.

21 Squadron	Lt Pollard	Injured
RE.8 D4818	Lt Snow	Injured

T/o Floringhem for a dusk artillery patrol and on return lost engine power coming down close to the airfield in a crop field where 'D4818' overturned; neither officer was seriously hurt.

23 Squadron	Lt G W R Pidsley	Safe
5F.1 Dolphin C3910		

T/o Bertangles for an offensive patrol and damaged beyond repair following a forced landing [owing to engine failure] on Hill 155 northeast of Tillot-les-Conty *[sic]*.

23 Squadron	Lt S K C Welinkar [India]	Injured	Hangard Communal Cemeterty extension
5F.1 Dolphin D3691			

T/o 0945 Bertangles for an offensive patrol and when last seen was engaged in a fight with a 'two-seater' near Péronne [Somme], both aircraft on an easterly course and flying between three hundred and four hundred feet. Shri Krishna Chanda Welinkar died from his wounds on 30 June 1918. From Bombay, his headstone has been inscribed with the words; *'To The Honoured Memory Of One Of The Empire's Bravest Sons Who Made The Great Sacrifice.'*

24 Squadron	Lt H F Balmer	Safe
SE.5a B7882		

T/o Conteville and wrecked here when on return from an operational sortie Lieutenant Balmer landed and ran into a deep depression.

25 Squadron	Lt J Webster	pow
DH.4 A7670	2Lt C M Gray	pow

T/o 1715 Ruisseauville with orders for a photographic reconnaissance of Landrecies*[Nord] Second Lieutenant Gray was the first to repatriated followed by his pilot, their respective dates being the 19th and 26th of December 1918.

* Before the first month of the *Great War* was over, the British Expeditionary Force had experienced fierce fighting and a retreat from positions along the Mons Canal was under way with General von Kluck's First Army pressing on towards the town of Landrecies and expecting little in the way of resistance. But, as an advanced force of motor transport entered the town they were met with determined opposition from units of the 4th [Guards] Brigade and in particular the 3rd Battalion of the Coldstreams and in a night [August 25th] action the Guards succeeded in holding up the enemy advance before withdrawing in good order as dawn broke. An excellent account of the battle can be read on the British Battles website, which I acknowledge, and where a highly dramatic interpretation of the 3rd Battalion Coldstreams running towards the German infantry appears in the form of a painting by William Barnes Wollen [born 1857 Leipzig and died 1936 in London].

| 29 Squadron | Lt F R Brand | + | Le Grand Beaumart British Cemetery, |
| SE.5a C9573 | | | Steenwerck |

T/o 0800 Vignacourt for an offensive patrol and was last seen forty-five minutes later in a slow spin near Bailleul [Nord]. Francis Robert Brand had become separated from his flight while fighting with enemy scouts.

| 32 Squadron | Lt P Macfarlane | Safe | See 10 August 1918 - 32 Squadron |
| SE.5a C1907 | | | |

T/o Ruisseauville and set forth for operations over the Lille area. On return, and landing, ran into a hollow whereupon the undercarriage collapsed. For Lieutenant Macfarlane this was his third crash of the month, see my summaries for the 3rd and 21st.

| 46 Squadron | Lt A J Cyr [Canada] | Safe |
| F.1 Camel C1675 | | |

T/o Serny for practice flying and wrecked when on return Lieutenant Cyr landed across the wind.

| 48 Squadron | 1st Lt J M Goad USAS | + | |
| Bristol F2.b C877 | Sgt C Norton | + | Arras Flying Services Memorial |

T/o 0430 Bertangles for an offensive patrol at first light and was shot down circa 0605 over the Somme near Villers-Bretonneux. John Goad's observer, Cyril Norton, was eighteen years of age.

| 48 Squadron | Lt E A Foord [Canada] | + | Villers-Bretonneux Military Cemetery |
| Bristol F.2b C935 | Sgt L James | + | Arras Flying Services Memorial |

T/o 0430 Bertangles similarly tasked and lost in circumstances that mirror those above, crashing in the same vicinity as that for 'C877'. Edward Alec Foord, late of the 78th Battalion, Canadian Infantry, was the only son of the late Arthur Willoughby Foord, Director, Indian Telegraphs, of Faulkner in Manitoba. It is noted that Edward was born in the United Kingdom in the county of Hampshire.

| 49 Squadron | Lt J C Robinson | pow | |
| DH.9 B9334 | 2Lt L G Cocking | pow | Unemployed list 18 February 1919: 2 Lt |

T/o Beauvois and during the sortie hit by anti-aircraft fire circa 1050 and came down to a controlled crash near Seclin in the *départment du Nord*. Neither officer had served for any length of time with the squadron; John Charles Robinson reported a little over a month ago on May 20th, while Leslie Garton Cocking arrived as recently as the 12th. Both were repatriated in December, Second Lieutenant Cocking on the 13th followed the next day by Lieutenant Robinson.

| 57 Squadron | Lt J B Cunningham* | Safe | |
| DH.4 D9257 | 2Lt E I Riley | Safe | See 16 June and 20 July 1918 - 57 Squadron |

T/o Le Quesnoy for a practice flight and on return Lieutenant Cunningham completely misjudged his approach and stalled in from thirty feet, the impact damaging his aircraft beyond repair.

* When checking the name 'J B Cunningham' against Commonwealth War Graves Commission records, a James Brightwell Cunningham of Canadian origin is flagged up for a casualty occurring on 22 August 1918, but with his squadron shown as 'No 205 Squadron'.

60 Squadron   Lt K P Campbell [Canada] Safe
SE.5a C8858

T/o Boffles for an offensive patrol and on return, and while preparing to land one of Lieutenant Campbell's feet became caught up in the rudder bars and unable to control his approach he crashed, wrecking his aircraft. Taken to No 2 Advanced Salvage Dump the airframe was struck off charge on 29 June 1918, with just four hours of flying recorded. This was the pilot's fourth crash, the most recent having occurred on the 1st of June.

64 Squadron   Lt J A van Tilburg   Safe See 30 June 1918 - 64 Squadron
SE.5a B7765

T/o Izel-lès-Hameau for a practice flight and wrecked on the airfield following a heavy landing,

70 Squadron   Lt C McW McMillan   + Arras Flying Services Memorial
F.1 Camel D1905

T/o 0400 Ramaisnil for an offensive patrol at first light and reported as being shot down circa 0535 near Courcelles. Nineteen years of age, Charles McWhirter McMillan had been a student at Leeds University.

70 Squadron   Lt C S Sheldon   + Arras Flying Services Memorial
F.1 Camel D6532

T/o 0705 Ramaisnil for an offensive patrol and when last glimpsed was near Albert.

70 Squadron   2Lt J Fulton   pow
F.1 Camel D9396

T/o 0705 Ramaisnil similarly tasked; last sighted in the same area as reported for Charles Stanley Sheldon. Second Lieutenant Fulton was among the many prisoners of war repatriated on 13 December 1918.

73 Squadron   Lt F S Ganter   + Cabaret-Rouge British Cemetery, Souchez
F.1 Camel C8249

T/o 0845 Ruisseauville for an offensive patrol and believed shot down at around 1015 near Hantay, a commune in the département *du Nord* and close to the border with Belgium.

79 Squadron   Lt H C Taylor   Safe
5F.1 Dolphin B7851

T/o Ste Marie Cappel for an offensive patrol but having climbed to around two hundred feet lost air pressure and came down, heavily, near the airfield. It will be recalled that Lieutenant Taylor had been injured in a crash on 16th May 1918; see my summary for information.

79 Squadron   Captain W A Forsyth   Injured Motor Car Corner Cemetery
5F.1 Dolphin C3806 A mention in a despatch

T/o 0745 Ste Marie Cappel and may well have been brought down in Belgium just to the north of Armentières. The cemetery gains its unique name from the instruction that military cars moving towards the frontlines would not be permitted beyond the point now marked by the cemetery. Begun in June 1917, the cemetery fell into German hands and was held by them between the 10th of April and 29th of September 1918. William Alan Forsyth was rescued alive but died later in the day from his wounds.

79 Squadron   Lt L R Lang   Safe
5F.1 Dolphin C3816

T/o Ste Marie Cappel and was so badly shot about in aerial combat that on return to base the airframe was deemed to be beyond repair. On squadron strength since 9 January 1918, 'C3816' had flown for a grand total of one hundred and sixty-two hours and five minutes, including transit flying from Lympne.

80 Squadron   Lt V S Bennett   Safe
F.1 Camel B9323

T/o Lièttres for operations over Béthune and on return landed in long grass bordering the airfield and turned over.

80 Squadron   Lt W R Archibald [Canada]   +   Arras Flying Services Memorial
F.1 Camel D1789

T/o 0930 Lièttres for an offensive patrol and was last seen in the coal mining area of Lens to La Bassée roughly ten km away to the north. On 11 April 1918, when on the establishment of No 43 Squadron, and while being flown by Lieutenant W H Shell on a practice flight from Asvenes-le-Comte crash-landed on Soncamp airfield, then the base for No 12 Squadron. Repaired, 'D1789' was issued to No 80 Squadron on the 6th of June.

83 Squadron   Lt B M Leete   Safe
FE.2b A5627   Lt H S Winkworth   Safe

T/o Franqueville for a night reconnaissance but owing to a connecting rod breaking the crew force-landed near No 5 lighthouse.

83 Squadron   Lt G E Race   Safe
FE.2b A5713   Lt F V Preston   Safe

T/o Franqueville similarly instructed during which engine failure occurred and in conditions of thick mist the crew force-landed on Ramaisnil airfield where their aircraft crashed into the station's firing butts. The impact left both officers badly shaken and nursing some painful bruises.

84 Squadron   2Lt C R Thompson   Safe
SE.5a B8408

T/o Bertangles for an offensive patrol. Returned to base with significant combat damage; believed struck from charge after removal to No 2 Advanced Salvage Dump. Taken on charge by the squadron on 28 March 1918, 'B8408' found great favour with Captain R A Grosvenor*with nine combat victories in the April followed by two more in May. It is noted that he opened his account with a double during the morning of the 3rd April and ended with another double, again during the morning, on 18th May.

* Robert Arthur Grosvenor's profile, as reported on *Wikipedia,* shows he was born in Chester of the 25th of May 1895, the son of Helen Sheffield and Lieutenant-Colonel Lord Arthur Hugh Grosvenor whose father was the 1st Duke of Westminster. Formerly of the Royal Dragoon Guards 'Robin' [as he was known to his many friends] flew with four squadrons during his flying service, gaining the Military Cross and a First Bar. He died at the relatively early age of fifty-eight on the 12th of June 1953 at Chaddleworth in Berkshire but was taken back to Cheshire for burial in the churchyard at Eccleston Church near Easton Hall. His overall total of success against the enemy was sixteen, two of this total being shared with a fellow pilot.

84 Squadron   Lt D B Jones DCM   Injured Crouy British Cemetery, Crouy-sur-Somme
SE.5a C6453 *Liverpool No 2 Newfoundland*

T/o Bertangles similarly tasked and returned badly shot about and David Bracegirdle Jones so seriously wounded that he died on the 3rd of July 1918. Born in Wales at Rhostryfan in Carnarvonshire, David was in Canada when war was declared. Enlisting with the 6th Battalion of the 1st Canadian Contingent he won the Distinguished Conduct Medal, *gazetted* 14 March 1916, in *The Edinburgh Gazette* issue 12914; '*Lance-Corporal B Jones, Signal Troop, Canadian Calvary Brigade [formerly 6th Battalion, Fort Garry Horse', for conspicuous gallantry and consistent good work when repairing telephone wires under fire, and for general good work.*' His headstone is inscribed thus; '*Asleep In Jesus Blessed Sleep From Which None Ever Wakes To Weep.*'

84 Squadron   Captain J S Ralston MC DFC Safe
SE.5a D333

T/o 0815 Bertangles for an offensive patrol and roughly forty-five minutes later, and now over the Somme and northeast of Villers-Bretonneux, engaged a Pfalz which was sent down out of control. Not long after, however, and still fighting his engine was hit and set on fire. At the time Captain Ralston*was down to two thousand feet and was fortunate to force-land without injury to himself, but his SE.5a went up[in smoke. John Steele Ralston's award of the Distinguished Flying Cross was *gazetted* in supplement 30913 of 21 September 1918; '*An intrepid patrol leader who in recent operations has accounted for three enemy machines and three kite balloons. Recently while on patrol he advanced to attack a kite balloon; on his approach the balloon party began to haul it* *down, but forcing home his attack, he shot the balloon down in flames. In this engagement the officer was seriously wounded. Suffering great pain, he flew back to our lines, but fainted and crashed.'* The fact that he was wounded dates the above action as prior to the 15th of August 1918, for on this date the authorities released the latest list identifying those who were recent casualties and Captain Ralston's name appears under the banner 'Wounded', *Flight* August 22, 1918.

* See my summary for 25 April 1918, for mention of his name when he was attached to No 56 Squadron. Formerly, he was of the Scottish Rifles and had not long recovered from wounds [see *Flight* March 7, 1918]. His *Wikipedia* entry shows him as being born in Bothwell, Lanarkshire on the 27th of April 1897, receiving his education at Glasgow Academy. The entry goes on to say that he served with the 8th Battalion, Scottish Rifles and was commissioned second lieutenant in April 1915. Eighteen months later he won the Military Cross for bravely carrying a wounded soldier to safety under enemy fire; in March 1917 he was seconded to the Royal Flying Corps. It seems he accounted for nine aircraft and a trio of kite balloons; however, the statement that he died on the 25th of July 1918, I suspect may be erroneous. A search for a casualty bearing his name on the Commonwealth War Graves Commission website draws a 'blank' and neither is there a 'Ralston' listed in *Airmen Died in the Great War*.

84 Squadron	Lt R Manzer [Canadian]	Safe	
SE.5a D6902			

T/o 0815 Bertangles similarly tasked and subsequently written off as damaged beyond repair with battle damage, this being confirmed following despatch to No 2 Advanced Salvage Dump.

85 Squadron	Lt A W Springs	Injured	
SE.5a D6851			

T/o St Omer for an offensive patrol and totally wrecked in a crash at Steenbecque in the *département du Nord*. Salvaged, the airframe was struck off charge as not worth repairing on the 1st of July 1918.

98 Squadron	Major E T Newton-Clare	Injured	
DH.9 D5722	Sgt Major H Grainger	Injured	

T/o Drionville for an air test only for the engine to 'cut' and crash back to earth. Major Newton-Clare took over command of the squadron from Major H MacD O'Malley earlier in the month on the 5th; in turn he handed commanded to Major P C Sherren MC on 26 August 1918. Postwar both officers were appointed to permanent commissions.

99 Squadron	Lt E A Chapin [USA]	+	Chambieres French National Cemetery, Metz
DH.9 D1669	2Lt T H Wiggins	+	Chambieres French National Cemetery, Metz

T/o 1415 Azelot for an attack on the station and workshops at Thionville. Flying at thirteen thousand feet the formation came under sustained attack from a dozen enemy aircraft while east of their objective. On fire, the DH was seen to break up in the air. From his research into *Great War* losses, Trevor Henshaw notes that *Leutnant* H Müller of *Jasta 18* submitted a claim for a 'DH.4' at 1625 at Diedenhofen.*Elliot Adams Chapin came from Newton Centre, Massachusetts. His headstone has been inscribed with the words; *'If I Do Not Come Back I Am Not Afraid To Die'.* Thomas Henry Wiggins was late of the 17th Battalion, Lancashire Fusiliers.

* In the *département du Moselle,* 'Diedenhofen was the German interpretation for Thionville.

102 Squadron	Lt L Murphy	Safe	
FE.2b A5725	Lt J P Colin	Injured	

T/o Surcamps tasked for night bombing during which engine failure obliged the crew to force-land near Vauchelles in the *département du Oise*. Briefly on the strength of No 83 Squadron 'A5725' arrived at Surcamps on 25 May 1918, and in total logged sixty-eight hours and forty-three minutes.

102 Squadron	Lt G E Reynolds [Canada]	+	Pont-Remy British Cemetery
FE.2b D9084	Lt E T Clarke	Safe	

T/o Surcamps tasked for a night bombing sortie but soon after becoming airborne engine failure occurred and the bomber crashed while forced landing near the airfield. Gerard Ellis Reynolds had served with Princess Patricia's Canadian Light Infantry [Eastern Ontario Regiment] and had been wounded in September 1916.

103 Squadron	Lt A E T Tyrell	Safe	
DH.9 D464	2Lt I B Corey	Safe	See 29 June 1918 - 103 Squadron

T/o Serny and wrecked here following a misjudged landing on return from formation flying practice.

151 Squadron*	Captain A B Yuille	Safe	Unemployed list 11 March 1919: Captain DFC
F.1 Camel D6405 *Twinkle*			

T/o Famechon for a night patrol but became uncertain of his position. Force-landed, coming down in a cornfield and damaged beyond repair thus becoming the squadron's first 'casualty' since arriving on the Western Front.

* No 151 Squadron formed as a night fighter squadron at Hainault Farm in Essex on the 12th of June 1918, under the command of Major M Green DSO MC, from flights supplied by Nos 44, 78 and 112 Squadrons. Four days later a flight was despatched to France where the squadron's rôle would be to counter German night activity over the Allied airfields. Initially lodged at Marquise the squadron moved to Fontaine-sur-Maye on the 21st and to Famechon on the 25th, its pilots being operational from the start. Captain Yuille had been a flight commander on No 112 Squadron and 'D6405' was his favourite aircraft which he named *Twinkle*.

211 Squadron	Captain J A Gray	Interned	
DH.9 B7620	2Lt J J Comerford	Interned	

T/o Petite Synthe tasked to raid targets at Bruges after which it seems the crew flew in north-northeasterly direction and when nearing the border with neutral Holland [and possibly by now over the province of Seeland] came under sustained anti-aircraft fire in the vicinity of Cadzand before forced landing with slight damage at Nummer Een near the harbour town of Breskens some sixteen km on from Cadzand. 'B7620' subsequently became H433, the purchase cost being offset against the internment charges for Captain Gray and his observer Second Lieutenant Comerford. As H433, the DH was based at Soesterberg where it was used as a training aircraft for pilots of the Dutch East Indies Army.

Thursday-Friday 27-28 June 1918

101 Squadron	Captain R Affleck	Safe	
FE.2b A5745	Major A B Mason	Safe	

T/o Famechon for a special low patrol [and noting the seniority of the crew I suspect the patrol was of significant importance] during which a forced landing was made near Villers Bretonneux brought about by engine failure. Arriving in France by air from Lympne in March 1918, 'A5745' was issued to the squadron on 15 April, and in total flew seventy-three hours and twenty-five minutes.

Friday 28 June 1918

2 Squadron	Lt M W Richardson	Safe	
FK.8 D5061	2Lt J C Gleave	Safe	

T/o Mazingarbe for an artillery patrol during which their aircraft came under heavy anti-aircraft fire in the vicinity of Richebourg in the Pas-de-Calais and practically on the border with the Nord *département*.

2 Squadron	Lt G A Harrison	Safe	
FK.8 D5062	2lt H Rapier	Safe	

T/o Mazingarbe briefed for artillery observation duties and reported to have come down in a cornfield near the airfield when Lieutenant Harrison fainted. With neither officer sustaining injuries, it seems likely the crew were fairly close to the ground at the time. It is not clear if the accident happened ahead of completing their task, or on return.

4 Squadron	Lt R S Burch	+	Borre British Cemetery
RE.8 C4593	2Lt T Garlick	+	Borre British Cemetery

T/o St Omer briefed for artillery observation duties and shot down in flames at map reference 36aE4d54 [possibly in the vicinity of Borre which lies some three km to the east of Hazebrouck].

7 Squadron	Lt J N Rookledge	Safe
RE.8 E108	Mechanic Davies	Safe

T/o Droglandt in the company of other crews to practice formation flying but on becoming airborne Lieutenant Rookledge appears to have swung off line, colliding with the roof of a nearby workshop. On squadron charge since 21 June 1918, 'E108', including tests and ferrying, flew for twelve hours and thirty-five minutes.

12 Squadron	Lt Thomas	Safe
RE.8 C2245	Lt Chadwick	Safe

T/o Soncamp intending to carry out an artillery patrol, as briefed, but swung out of control and collided with a stout post near one of the airfield's gun pits. Salvaged, 'C2245' was struck off charge on 9 July 1918, with one hundred and fifty-six hours and thirty-five minutes flying accumulated from its delivery from Coventry and issue to the squadron on 28 March 1918.

19 Squadron	2Lt W G Lance [Canada]	Safe See 13 August 1918 - 19 Squadron
5F.1 Dolphin C3872		

T/o Savy for a special mission over the Pas-de-Calais during which William George Lance ran into fog and crashed, seemingly without hurt, near Houdain.

19 Squadron	Lt C V Gardiner	Safe
5F.1 Dolphin C4057		

T/o Savy for an offensive patrol and written off, owing to engine failure, in a forced landing near Ablain-Saint-Nazaire in the Pas-de-Calais, twelve km north from Arras.

23 Squadron	Lt H M Sinclair	Safe See 30 June 1918 - 23 Squadron
5F.1 Dolphin C3872		

T/o Bertangles for an offensive patrol and it was while returning to base that the Dolphin's engine overheated to an alarming degree; crash-landed on the airfield and damaged beyond repair, thus becoming the third Dolphin to be written off at the hands of Lieutenant Sinclair [see my summaries for 28 May and 18 June 1918].

25 Squadron	Lt J Webster	pow
DH.4 A7670	2Lt G M Gray	pow

T/o Ruisseauville with order to carry out a photo reconnaissance of Landrecies [Nord] and failed to return. Some reports show this loss as occurring the day previous.

27 Squadron   DH.9 D5704   Damaged beyond repair while parked on the compass course at Ruisseauville having been struck by an SE.5a from No 32 Squadron summarised below.

32 Squadron	Lt H Wilson [Canada]	Safe See 1 November 1918 - 32 Squadron
SE.5a D6858		

T/o Ruisseauville for a practice flight and on return Montreal born Harold Wilson misjudged his approach to land and collided with the DH.9 summarised above.

32 Squadron	Lt S E Farson	Safe
SE.5a C6498		

T/o Ruisseauville for an offensive patrol and on return Lieutenant Farson landed on rough ground which damaged 'C6498' beyond repair; struck off charge on 10 July 1918.

35 Squadron	Lt J Gitsham	Safe See 29 June 1918 - 35 Squadron
FK.8 D5031	2Lt L Wadsworth	Safe See 29 June 1918 - 35 Squadron

T/o Villers Bocage for a dawn patrol during which the crew force-landed colliding as they did so with a wireless mast near Ergnies in the Somme.

| 40 Squadron | Lt N S Cameron | Safe | See 8 July 1918 - 40 Squadron |

40 Squadron
SE.5a C8872
Lt N S Cameron   Safe   See 8 July 1918 - 40 Squadron

T/o 0700 Bryas for an early morning offensive patrol and in circumstances similar to what overtook him during the evening of the 26th June, engine trouble terminated his patrol under less than an hour. This time he was able to crash-land on the airfield at Savy, then being used by No 19 Squadron. An inspection of the SE.5a revealed damage that was not worthwhile repairing.

41 Squadron
SE.5a E1297
Lt F J Davey   Safe

T/o Conteville tasked for operations over Bray-sur-Somme in the course of which the engine failed and the forced landing at Saint-Ouen [Somme] twenty km northwest of Amiens left Lieutenant Davey severely shocked by his experience.

56 Squadron
SE.5a B8421
Lt A L Garrett   pow

T/o Valheureux for an offensive patrol the formation flying at heights between fourteen thousand and sixteen thousand feet. In the vicinity of Miraumont the fighters came under sustained anti-aircraft fire after which Lieutenant Garrett's aircraft could not be seen. His name appears in *Flight* July 25, 1918, under the banner 'Missing' and the same magazine in its issue of September19, 1918, confirmed he was being held as a prisoner of war. His repatriation, along with many others, came on 13 December 1918.

56 Squadron
SE.5a D263
Lt T D Hazen [Canada]   Safe   See 19 August 1918 - 56 Squadron

T/o Valheureux for dawn operations to the southeast of Bray-sur-Somme; with his engine shot through Thomas Douglas Hazen force-landed near Harponville [Somme] some ten to eleven km west-northwest of Albert.

56 Squadron
SE.5a D6086
Lt H Austin   pow

T/o Valheureux similarly tasked and when last seen was fighting hard with an enemy scout at eleven thousand feet between Fricourt to the north and Bray-sur-Somme to the south, a seven km corridor lying east and south-southeast of Albert. Wounded, Lieutenant Austin managed to force-land and was taken prisoner, a fact confirmed in *Flight* September 26, 1918. Repatriation came on 13 December 1918.

87 Squadron
5F.1 Dolphin D3685
Lt H A R Biziou   Safe

T/o Estrée-lès-Crecy for a special patrol but when the engine 'cut' Lieutenant Biziou [see my summary for the 6th of June 1918] was obliged to crash-land, turning over in long grass just beyond the airfield. The following day the squadron packed their bags and headed east-northeast to their new home at Rougefay, some fifteen to eighteen km distant.

88 Squadron   Lt J P West [USA]   +   Larch Wood [Railway Cutting] Cemetery
Bristol F.2b C4880   Private A J Loton   +   Larch Wood [Railway Cutting] Cemetery
T/o Capelle for an offensive patrol during which the formation came under attack over the Houthulst Forest in the Ypres Sector north of Poelcapelle during which 'C4880' was seen to fall away on fire. Subsequently, a Belgian report was received indicating a Bristol had crashed near Clerkem [sic]. John Prout West came from Rutland in Rutland County, Vermont.

125 Squadron   2Lt H A Heritage   +   Hampstead Cemetery
DH.4 A7952
T/o Fowlmere*and when banking allowed the airspeed to drop and was unable to recover from the dive that followed. Herbert Alec Heritage was commissioned on 18 December 1917 [*gazetted* 8 January 1918, issue 30470].

* No 125 Squadron had formed at Old Sarum on 1 February 1918, receiving a mixture of DH.4 and DH.9. Intended for a light bomber rôle, No 125 Squadron disbanded on 1 August 1918, without becoming operational. There is no evidence that the squadron operated from Fowlmere.

151 Squadron	Lt A A Mitchell	Safe
F.1 Camel B5411		

T/o Famechon and wrecked here on landing from a night patrol. Initially issued to No 44 Squadron at Hainault Farm by 29 January 1918, 'B5411' was given up for the formation of No 151 Squadron on 12 June.

217 Squadron	Lt A E Bingham	pow
DH.4 A8023	Lt L J Smith	pow

T/o Bergues and last seen, in the sea, off Oostende following an engagement with an enemy aircraft.' A8023' arrived with No 217 Squadron on 13 June 1918. Lieutenant Bingham was among those repatriated on 13th December while his observer was among those reported for Boxing Day.

Saturday 29 June 1918

In the official communique released from General Headquarters and repeated in *Flight* July 18, 1918, enemy activity over the front was limited, but reports indicate nine of their aircraft were destroyed and eight driven down out of control against a total of five of our aircraft reported 'missing'. Good work was carried out by the reconnaissance squadrons with many photographs being taken. Meanwhile, day bombing was carried out on rail centres at Lille, Kortrijk, Comines and Estaires, these attacks continuing after dusk when railway communications around Tournai came in for close attention.

4 Squadron AusFC	Lt J W Baxter	Safe
F.1 Camel B2520		

T/o Clairmarais for an offensive patrol and damaged beyond repair here following a misjudged landing. Despatched to France in a crate, 'B2520' was issued to No 3 Squadron at Warloy Baillon on 23 November 1917, and in whose hands Captain E Y Hughes accounted for two enemy aircraft before being sent for maintenance on 12 January 1918. Accepted by No 4 Squadron Australian Flying Corps on 20 May, their British Commanding officer, Major F I Tanner*shot down an Albatros during the early evening of the 18th of June in the general vicinity of Merville-Estaires.

* Available for purchase from the Australian War Memorial collection of photographs is a group photograph taken at Clairmarais on 16 June 1918, of the officers, including Major Tanner, of No 4 Squadron Australian Flying Corps. The Accession Number is E02453.

7 Squadron	Lt C A Harvey [Canada]	+	Oosttaverne Wood Cemetery
RE.8 C2474	2Lt G W Osborne	+	Longuenesse [St Omer] Souvenir Cemetery

T/o Droglandt having received orders for a *Flash* reconnaissance and while flying low in much reduced visibility owing to ground fog failed to see a line of trees into which their aircraft smashed, bursting into flames at map reference 27E2c56. As Geoffrey William Osborne is buried in France I consider it possible that he survived the crash, if only for a few hours.

10 Squadron	Lt W Hughes	Safe	See 8 July 1918 - 10 Squadron
FK.8 B3315	2Lt F C Peacock	Safe	See 8 July 1918 - 10 Squadron

T/o Droglandt with orders to carry out a dusk reconnaissance; crashed, and written off, on return to base. For Lieutenant Hughes this was his third major crash [see my summaries for 7th and 13th May 1918] and for his observer his second - see my summary for 13th May 1918.

18 Squadron	Captain H R Gould MC	Safe	See 14 August 1918 - 18 Squadron
DH.4 A8018	Sgt L G Vredenburg	Safe	See 22 July 1918 - 18 Squadron

T/o Serney briefed for a dawn reconnaissance mission and when in flight and passing over ground shielded by a thick mist, a petrol pipe broke and in the ensuing forced landing 'A8018' was damaged beyond repair. During the late evening of 30 May 1918 and when over the Nord *département*, Captain A G Waller and Lieutenant B J

Blackett sent an enemy scout down in flames near Bac sur Maur. For my first summary concerning Captain Gould, please turn back to 8 April 1918.

20 Squadron   Bristol F.2b C889   Burnt out on the ground at Boisdinghem. The Court of Inquiry, having heard the evidence from those concerned, concluded that the most likely cause was a spanner falling onto a lighting set accumulator causing a spark that within seconds had started an uncontrollable blaze.

23 Squadron   Lt H N Compton   Safe
5F.1 Dolphin C4150
T/o Bertangles for an offensive patrol but thought to have turned back having lost pressure and crash-landed near the airfield coming down in long grass and overturning.

25 Squadron   Lt B L Lindley MC   +   Larch Wood [Railway Cutting] Cemetery
DH.4 A7913   [South Africa]
                       2Lt D Boe   pow
T/o 1640 Ruisseauville for a photographic reconnaissance of the Belgian city of Bruges from which it failed to return. Bryant Lutellos Lindley of Claremont in Cape Province was commissioned to the General List of the Royal Flying Corps in the rank of temporary second lieutenant on probation on 2 August 1917 [*gazetted* in issue 30249 published on 24 August 1917]. The citation for his Military Cross appeared in *The London Gazette* issue 30901 of 13 September 1918 and reads; *'For conspicuous gallantry and devotion to duty during recent operations. He carried out several very successful long-distance reconnaissances and bomb raids under adverse weather conditions, and during low-bombing and machine-gun action he did most brilliant work. Throughout he showed great gallantry and skill.'* Bryant Lindley was nineteen years of age. 'A7913' had two aerial victories to its credit; a couple of Pfalz DIIIs shot down on the 10th of March 1918 with Lieutenant J E Pugh and Second Lieutenant W L Dixon in command. It is noted that Lieutenant Pugh held a Military Cross.

32 Squadron   Lt H Wilson [Canada]   Safe   See 1 November 1918 - 32 Squadron
SE.5a C9612 1
T/o Ruisseauville for an offensive patrol but crashed out of control; damaged beyond repair. Delivered to the squadron on the last day of March, 'C9612' sustained slight damage while parked at Beauvois on 22 April when it was struck by SE.5a D273 as it landed - see my summary for details.

35 Squadron   Lt J Gitsham   +   Vignacourt British Cemetery
FK.8 D5051   2Lt L Wadsworth   +   Vignacourt British Cemetery
T/o Villers Bocage tasked for an armed patrol but stalled while executing a climbing turn and nosedived to the ground where the bombs exploded setting fire to the aircraft. James Gitsham and Leonard Wadsworth had lived for just twenty-fours from their accident the previous day.

42 Squadron   Lt W Ledlie   Safe
RE.8 C2478   2Lt J G B Macmillan   Safe
T/o Rély for an artillery patrol but was forced down owing to fog and wrecked while forced landing at Crécy in the Somme.

53 Squadron   2Lt J N Gatecliff   +   Cinq Rues British Cemetery, Hazebrouck
RE.8 D4834   2Lt J Harrison   +   Cinq Rues British Cemetery, Hazebrouck
T/o Clairmarais to observe a bombardment shoot and from reports by other crews so charged was seen to go down in flames. James Noel Gatecliff's headstone has been inscribed with the well known phrase; *'Till The Day Break And The Shadows Fly Away'* while his observer's grave is marked simply *'Rest In Peace'*.

65 Squadron   2Lt R P Whyte   pow
F.1 Camel B7829
T/o 1930 Bertangles for an evening patrol and when seen last by the patrol was over the Somme in the vicinity of Guillaucourt. Second Lieutenant Whyte is named as 'Missing' in *Flight* July 25, 1918; he was repatriated on 13 December 1918. His Camel was a relatively new arrival having reached the squadron on the 17th of June.

80 Squadron   Lt L L McFaul [Canada]   Injured See 10 July 1918 - 80 Squadron
F.1 Camel D6633 N

T/o Lièttres to join with others in formation practice. All went well until the pilots returned to base where Lieutenant McFaul, intent on watching his inside Camel, landed on the edge of the airfield where the grass was long and within seconds 'D6633' was upside down; his injuries, fortunately, were not serious.

87 Squadron   Lt N S Sales   Safe
5F.1 Dolphin D3672

T/o Estrée-lès-Crecy for transit east-northeast to the squadron's new base at Rougefay where on arrival Lieutenant Sales stalled and dived nose first into the ground, seemingly without injury to himself but doing no good to his aircraft which with twenty hours flying in total was struck off charge on the 1st of July 1918.

103 Squadron   Captain A H Curtis   Safe
DH.9 D2857   Lt I B Corey   Safe

T/o Serny tasked for a bombing raid and at some point during the operation collided with a telegraph pole, unseen in the misty conditions. Lieutenant Corey had walked from a crash forty-eight hours previously.

107 Squadron   Lt B E Gammel   Safe
DH.9 B9331   2Lt W Middleton   Safe

T/o Drionville to practice, with other crews, flying in formation and damaged beyond repair in a crash, the location of which not being reported. It seems, however, that when No 107 Squadron left Lake Down in Wiltshire for France on 5 June 1918, 'B9331' was included in the DH formation.

151 Squadron   Lt A C McVie   Safe
F.1 Camel B7322

T/o Famechon for a night patrol but 'choked' the engine; force-landed near Domart [sic]. This particular Camel was first used by No 73 Squadron in whose hands it shot down two enemy aircraft before being damaged by an Albatros while engaged on ground strafing. Repaired, it went to No 80 Squadron notching up another victory before being damaged for a second time. Overhauled, 'B7322' was converted for night flying and was brought to No 151 Squadron twenty-four hours before the incident here reported.

206 Squadron   Lt C Eaton   pow   See 17 June 1918 [summary] - 206 Squadron
DH.9 C1177   2Lt E W Tatnall   pow   See 17 June 1918 [summary] - 206 Squadron

T/o Alquines tasked for a long reconnaissance mission during which the DH descended to low-level and within range of enemy machine gunners whose fire forced the crew to crash-land. Both are named in *Flight* July 25th, 1918, under the 'Missing' heading and both are recorded as prisoners of war in the magazine's issue of September 19, 1918. First issued to No 98 Squadron on 30 April 1918, 'C1177' was flying to the southeast of Ypres on the 2nd of May when Captain R W Bell and his observer Lieutenant A A Malcolm successfully engaged a Pfalz DIII which was last seen spiralling down out of control. However, soon after the DH's engine 'cut' and in the ensuing forced landing was quite badly damaged. Salvaged and sent for repairs, it was issued to No 206 Squadron twenty-four hours before it was reported 'missing'.

211 Squadron   2Lt C O Carson   Safe
DH.9 C6282   Corporal H Lindsay   Safe

T/o Petite Synthe ordered for bombing operations and damaged beyond repair after sideslipping while preparing to land. On 18 June 1918, over Bruges docks, enemy fire wounded the pilot Second Lieutenant J S Forgie but left his observer Second Lieutenant R Simpson unscathed.

213 Squadron   Lt F P Pemble   +   Adinkerke Military Cemetery
F.1 Camel D3333

T/o Bergues for operations and in the vicinity of les Möeres [east-southeast of Dunkerque and virtually on the border with Belgium some ten km northwest from the airfield] collided with Camel D3383, both aircraft crashing to earth. The time of the tragedy occurred circa 1445, and a height of fifteen thousand feet is quoted.

213 Squadron   Lt F L Cattle   +   Adinkerke Military Cemetery
F.1 Camel D3383
T/o Bergues similarly tasked and lost in the manner described above. Both pilots were eighteen years of age; Frank Leonard Cattle had been injured earlier in the year when he crashed while landing at Bergues on 20 April 1918, see my summary for details.

218 Squadron   Lt W F Purvis   Interned
DH.9 C1211 VI   Airman L H Locke   Interned
T/o Petite Synthe to attack the mole at Zeebrugge during which the DH was hit by anti-aircraft fire from coastal batteries. With their engine out of action, the crew commenced gliding down in the direction of neutral Holland and when over the Coastal town of Breskens on Westerschelde commenced firing off red and white flares. Soon after this the crew force-landed, still carrying its bomb load, near Breskens breaking the undercarriage and damaging the lower wings. Salvaged by the Dutch, 'C1211' was transported to Soesterberg where it was painted as *deH434*. On 20 March 1920, the airframe was returned to the Royal Air Force but its days of flying were over. Lieutenant Purvis was confirmed as a second lieutenant, on probation, on the General List on 16th September 1917 [*gazetted* 5 February 1918, issue 30513].

Sunday 30 June 1918
A day which witnessed much aerial fighting with General Headquarters stating that twenty-five hostile aircraft were destroyed and ten others driven down out of control, all for the loss of a single scout. Day and night reconnaissance sorties were flown and the day was also marked by our artillery engaging hostile batteries with some success. At night rail targets were attacked, Tournai again been raided with over seven tons of bombs dropped to good effect. An Air Ministry communique added that at dawn on this day bombers returned safely from a 'visit' to Mannheim where a chemical facility was singled out for attention, while as dusk fell bombers headed for a variety of targets both in the occupied areas and in Germany, rail communications at Zweibrücken and Saarbrücken being mentioned.

4 Squadron AusFC   Lt J W Milner   Safe
F.1 Camel D9549
T/o Clairmarasi to transit to the squadron's new base at Recklinghem. Landed heavily and damaged beyond repair. Issued to the squadron on the first day of the month it flew for a total of fifty-hours and thirty-five minutes, including the mandatory testing and ferrying to France.

8 Squadron   Lt F V Fennell   +   St Riquier British Cemetery
FK.8 B3379
T/o Auxi-le-Château having been authorised to ferry the aircraft to Conteville but while climbing away stalled and spun to the ground. Frederick Vibond Fennell was nineteen years of age.

20 Squadron   Lt T C Traill   Safe
Bristol F.2b C938   2Lt P G Jones   Safe   See 2 July 1918 - 20 Squadron
T/o Boisdinghem and while engaged on their patrol came under fire which holed the rear petrol tank; force-landed near Saint-Momelin [Nord]. Salvaged, 'C938' with an overall total of fifty-three hours and forty-six minutes flying from struck off charge on 5 July 1918.

23 Squadron   Lt H M Sinclair   Safe
5F.1 Dolphin C8003
T/o Bertangles for an offensive patrol and on return finished up in a wood after overshooting the landing area; see my comments re this officer in my summary of 28 June 1918.

27 Squadron   Lt W J Dalziel   Safe
DH.9 D1678   Lt R H Shepherd   Injured
T/o Ruisseauville for bombing operations over Lille and on return, and making ready to land, had to take evasive action in order to avoid a midair collision, but in doing so Lieutenant Dalziel lost control of his aircraft and side-slipped to the ground. Lieutenant Shepherd's injuries were not life threatening.

41 Squadron　　　　　　Lt W E Huxtable　　　　　　Safe
SE.5a D394
T/o Conteville for a practice flight but swung sharply and crashed. At the Court of Inquiry it found that Lieutenant Huxtable was not used to the torque from a 1170 gear engine.

41 Squadron　　　　　　Lt E J Stephens　　　　　　Safe
SE.5a D5961
T/o Conteville for operations over Bray-sur-Somme during which a clash with a hostile scout resulted in 'D5961' being shot about so badly that it was struck off charge three days later. On squadron charge since 27 May 1918, overall its flying came to forty-one hours and fifty-five minutes.

49 Squadron　　　　　　Lt M D Allen　　　　Safe　　See 1 August 1918 - 49 Squadron
DH.9 C2188　　　　　　2Lt J Ross　　　　　Safe　　See 8 August 1918 - 49 Squadron
T/o Beauvois for a practice flight which ended in a crash-landing at Serny airfield. Salvaged, and considered for repair, 'C2188' languished until struck off charge at No 2 Advanced Salvage Dump on 28 July 1918.

54 Squadron　　F.1 Camel B5214　　　　Either at Boisdinghem or Lièttres but most likely at the former, this Camel was badly burnt in embarrassing circumstances. Hangared, a mechanic, named as J N Holmes spilt some petrol which gathered beneath the tailplane of 'B5214'; later, the same airman, now trying to find a tool in the gloom, lit a match which quickly burnt down to scorch the said mechanic's fingers. Flipping the still burning stub aside, it promptly fell into the petrol and that was the end of 'B5214' for although the fire was quickly dowsed the damage to the airframe was such that it was decided not to sanction repairs. I can only imagine the discomfort felt by the mechanic when he was hauled before his superiors to explain his actions. On the 19th of April 1918, 'B5214' had been shot about during an offensive patrol flown by Lieutenant R F W Moore and had only been returned to the squadron twenty-fours hours before its demise. I mention Lièttres for No 54 Squadron moved to this airfield on the 30th.

57 Squadron　　　　　　Lt W H Kilbourne　　　　Safe　　See 1 July 1918 -57 Squadron
DH.4 A7821　　　　　　Sgt A C Lovesey　　　　　Safe　　See 1 July 1918 - 57 Squadron
T/o Le Quesnoy tasked for bombing targets at Vaulx*in the Pas-de-Calais and on return, in a misjudged landing, came down heavily on one wheel; wrecked.

* There are two locations in the Pas-de-Calais; 'Vaulx' and 'Vaulx-Vraucourt', the former is north of the River Somme and roughly a km or so north of Auxi-le-Château while the latter lies to the northeast of Bapaume and thus is likely to have been the objective.

58 Squadron　　　　　　Lt R K Fletcher　　　　　Safe
FE.2b A6462　　　　　　Captain C C Cole　　　　　Safe
T/o Fauquembergues for an air test and at five hundred feet the engine failed. Force-landed on the airfield but the impact was sufficient to damage 'A6462' beyond repair [at least one tyre blew out] and it was struck off charge on 5 July 1918.

64 Squadron　　　　　　Lt M L Howard [Canada]　　　Safe　　See 25 July 1918 - 64 Squadron
SE.5a C6418
T/o Izel-lès-Hameau for an offensive patrol and reported to have turned over in a field near the aerodrome following a connecting rod breaking in the engine. Lieutenant Howard had walked away from a crash on the 25th of April 1918 - see my summary for details.

64 Squadron　　　　　　Lt J A van Tilburg　　　　　Safe
SE.5a D6901
T/o Izel-lès-Hameau for an offensive patrol during which the engine overheated to a degree that an emergency landing could not be avoided. This was duly carried out near Contreville [sic] and while attempting to avoid running into a sunken road Lieutenant van Tilburg [see my summary for 27 June 1918] turned his aircraft over. On establishment for just two days, including test and ferrying, it had logged eight hours and thirty-five minutes.

70 Squadron   Lt D Miller [USA]   +   Wavans British Cemetery
F.1 Camel B3931
T/o Ramaisnil for practice attacks over the aerial range during which Donald Miller pulled up too steeply and as a consequence structural failure occurred with one of the Camel's left wings parting company. Twenty year old Lieutenant Miller was a Member of the Masonic Order and hailed from the West Bronx district of New York.

70 Squadron   2Lt J W Gibson   Safe
F.1 Camel C8212
T/o 1900 Ramaisnil for an evening patrol during which Second Lieutenant Gibson was wounded. In considerable pain he managed to crash-land at map reference 57DP17c71. His aircraft was salvaged and struck off charge on the 25th of July 1918.

70 Squadron   Lt J E Sydie   pow
F.1 Camel D6564
T/o 1900 Ramaisnil similarly tasked and was driven down in combat east of Bray-sur-Somme. Named as 'Missing' in *Flight* July 25, 1918, confirmation that he was a prisoner of war was published in the magazine's issue of September 19, 2018.

82 Squadron   Lt F A Mildred   Safe
FK.8 D5052   2Lt T W Rowlands   Safe
T/o Quevenvillers tasked to carry out artillery observation duties and while in flight, and no doubt to a degree of concern, the crew noticed that a wheel had fallen off. However, a decision was made to carry on with their mission but on return to base Lieutenant Mildred was unable to prevent 'D5052' from crashing.

87 Squadron   2Lt N Sales*   Safe
5F.1 Dolphin C4227
T/o from No 2 Air Issues and headed for Rougefay where on arrival Second Lieutenant Sales stalled as he turned in to land and crashed. Including its ferry by air 'C4227' was now a very sorry sight after just two hours of flying.

* It will be recalled that a Lieutenant N S Sales of No 87 Squadron wrote off a Dolphin the previous day; the possibility that they were brothers and not one and the same person cannot, I suggest, be dismissed.

98 Squadron   Lt H G Goddard   Injured
DH.9 D7230   Sgt C W Moulden   Injured
T/o Drionville ordered for bombing operations but while climbing out Lieutenant Goddard lost control and spun in crashing atop a trailer belonging to No 107 Squadron.

104 Squadron   1Lt W L Deetjen [America]   +
DH.9 D5720   2Lt M H Cole [South Africa]   +   Plaine French National Cemetery
T/o 0500 Azelot for a formation raid on the railway station at Landau in der Pfalz*[Rhineland-Palatinate]. Alerted, the German scouts rose up in force and the bombers had to fight their way in and out, and it was during the home leg that William Ludwig Deetjen and his South African observer, Montague Henry Cole of the 3rd Regiment South African Infantry, but now attached to the Royal Air Force, was seen to drop away streaming flames. It is likely that their DH came down in the vicinity of Plaine in the *département du Bas-Rhin*.

* Described on *Wikipedia* as being surrounded by the *Südliche Weinstraße* [Southern Wine Route].

107 Squadron   Lt R A Arnott   Safe   See 8 July 1918 - 107 Squadron
DH.9 C6269   2Lt H R Whitehead   Safe   See 8 July 1918 - 107 Squadron
T/o Drionville only to run into the DH.9 summarised below. At No 2 Aeroplane Acceptance Park Hendon by the 1st of June 1918, 'C6269' reached the squadron's United Kingdom base at Lake Down on the 4th and departed the next day for France.

107 Squadron	2Lt J K Gaukroger	Safe	See 8 August 1918 - 107 Squadron
DH.9 D5669	2Lt D McN Livingstone	Injured	See 8 July 1918 - 107 Squadron

Wrecked in the circumstances described above. Its service history mirrored that for 'C6269'.

149 Squadron	Captain Russell	Safe
FE.2b D9778	Sgt Clay	Safe

T/o Alquines for a weather check but while running at speed the nose tipped forward and 'D9778' was damaged beyond repair when its propeller was ripped off on striking the stony ground. This was the squadron's first serious crash since arriving in France from Ford on the 2nd of June 1918.

206 Squadron	Lt E A Burn	Injured
DH.9 D5609	2Lt C O Shelswell	Safe

T/o 1414 Alquines with others tasked for a long reconnaissance in the course of which the formation came under sustained attack from hostile scouts and Lieutenant Burns was driven down to force-land in 'No Man's Land' where it fell into a shell hole. Owing to the proximity of the enemy trenches no attempt to salvage the bomber could be made and it was abandoned to its fate.

208 Squadron	Lt J J Mollison	Safe	See 27 August 1918 - 208 Squadron
F.1 Camel D1781			

T/o Serny for an offensive patrol but in the prevailing mist lost his way and force-landed near an engine repair shop. Having satisfied himself on the correct course to take Lieutenant Mollison took off but lost control and crashed.

217 Squadron	Lt C J Moir [Canada]	+	Arras Flying Services Memorial
DH.4 A8013	Sgt E E Hunnisett	+	Arras Flying Services Memorial

T/o 1700 Bergues and set a course for Zeebrugge. Either outbound or on return the crew were intercepted when north of Oostende by enemy machines and attacked so severely that as their aircraft began to go down it broke apart. From Killarney in southwestern Manitoba, Clifford James Moir was one of many ex-cadets commissioned to the General List of the Royal Flying Corps on 17 November 1917 [gazetted 20 November 1917, issue 30395]. Edwin Edward Hunnisett enlisted with the Royal Naval Air Service in 1916. Twenty-four hours before its loss, 'A8013' [Lieutenant R M Berthe] in company with 'A7773' [Lieutenant G R Judge] dropped four 230-lb bombs on a U-boat sighted off the East Dyke.

Acknowledgements

All that has been imparted in over two hundred and seventy pages of summaries has come about through the groundwork, generously shared, by a handful of dedicated aviation historians thereby allowing me the relatively simple task of bringing the myriad strands of their labours into a format that I trust has been informative. It is, therefore, with immense pleasure that I single out two persons; Andrew Pentland whose dedication in searching through the plethora of files held at The National Archives related to the activities of the Royal Air Force in the *Great War* has been nothing short of an outstanding labour of love. And in equal measure historian and author Trevor Henshaw has also delved into records pertaining to the *Great War* period, his investigations taking in air operations across all theatres of war as well as linking, wherever possible, combat claims submitted by the main participants; again, a painstaking process which can only be admired for his thoroughness.

 Both report 'incidents' where the aircraft in question was either repaired, retaining its original identity, or underwent a complete rebuild emerging with a new airframe serial. Such was the nature of air operations at the time, maintaining serviceability imposed a considerable strain on those charged with keeping squadrons up to strength.

My unbridled thanks go to four admired historians whose published work will be familiar to many and who have kindly permitted me to draw on their findings; David Gunby and Errol Martyn of New Zealand and closer to home, Jeff Jefford and Oliver Clutton-Brock. Their willingness to share with me facts reported in their writings have in so many ways enriched the content of my summaries.

Much additional information has come my way through the medium of websites which I have been pleased to acknowledge in the general text. However, it would be remiss of me not to mention Malcom Barrass whose sterling work in compiling Air of Authority - A History of RAF Organisation provides outstanding information, particularly in regard to biographies of officers attaining air rank.

In similar vein the website maintained by No 49 Squadron Association is of the highest quality, its content being continually referred to in the context of summaries regarding the squadron's losses.

By no means least, I extend my warmest gratitude to Dave Gilbert who at the 'eleventh hour' has examined the Roll of Honour content, correcting my errors and providing information that has a bearing on the Roll, as it is now presented.

Finally, heartfelt thanks to my publisher, Simon Hepworth, for his encouragement and who from the outset has had faith in the concept of that I have set out to achieve.

Sources

OFFICIAL

Air Historical Branch [RAF]
Australian War Memorial
Commonwealth War Graves Commission
The Edinburgh Gazette
The London Gazette
The National Archives, Kew

PUBLISHED SOURCES

AIR-BRITAIN [HISTORIANS] LIMITED
Always Prepared : The Story of 207 Squadron Royal Air Force   John Hamlin, 1999
Royal Air Force Flying Training and Support Units   Ray Sturtivant, John Hamlin and
                                                                                   James J Halley MBE, 1997

The Camel File   Ray Sturtivant and Gordon Page, 1993
The DH.4/DH.9 File   Ray Sturtivant and Gordon Page, 1999
The SE.5 File   Ray Sturtivant and Gordon Page, 1996
The Squadrons of the Royal Air Force & Commonwealth 1918-1988   James J Halley MBE, 1988

ALLEN LANE
The Birth of the RAF 1918   Richard Overy, 2018

FETUBI BOOKS
The Sky their Battlefield II - Air Fighting and Air Casualties of the   Trevor Henshaw, 2014
    Great War - British, Commonwealth and United States Air Services
    1912 to 1919

HAYWARD
Airmen Died in the Great War 1914-1918   Chris Hobson and J B Hayward & Son,
    The Roll of Honour of the British and Commonwealth Air Services   1995
    Of the First World War

HUTCHINSON
Douglas Haig The Educated Soldier   John Terraine, 1963

MACDONALD : LONDON
Bomber Squadrons of the RAF and their Aircraft   Philip J R Moyes, 1964
Fighter Squadrons of the RAF and their Aircraft   John D R Rawlings, 1969

MENTION THE WAR PUBLICATIONS
Trusty to the End - The History of 148 [Special Duties] Squadron   Oliver Clutton-Brock, 2017
    1918 - 1945

MIDLAND COUNTIES PUBLICATIONS
British Military Aircraft Serials 1878-1987   Bruce Robertson, 1987

PEN & SWORD AVIATION
Fallen Eagles - Airmen who survived the Great War only to die in   Norman Franks, 2017
  Peacetime
Lost Wings of World War 1 - Downed Airmen on the Western Front   Martin W Bowman, 2014
  1914 - 1918

PENTLAND PRESS
Sweeping the Skies : A History of No 40 Squadron RFC and RAF   David Gunby, 1995
  1915-56

PUTNAM
De Havilland Aircraft since 1915   A J Jackson, 1962

VOLPLANE PRESS
For Your Tomorrow : Volume One : Fates 1915 - 1942   Errol W Martyn, 1998

WILLIAM KIMBER
For Valour : The Air VCs   Chaz Bowyer, 1978

PRIVATE PUBLICATIONS
The Flying Camels - The History of No 45 Sqn RAF   C G Jefford, Wg Cdr MBE BA RAF
                                                       [Retd], 1995
To See The Dawn Breaking : 76 Squadron Operations   W R Chorley, 1981

UNPUBLISHED SOURCES
List of Graduates : The Royal Air Force College Cranwell :
  February 5th, 1920 - December 18th, 1962

Glossary of Terms

AFM	Air Force Medal
AusFC	Australian Flying Corps
BWI	British West Indies
CB	Companion of the Order of the Bath
DCM	Distinguished Conduct Medal
DFC	Distinguished Flying Cross
DSC	Distinguished Service Cross
DSO	Distinguished Service Order
F/L	Flight Lieutenant
F/O	Flying Officer
GBE	Grand Cross of the British Empire
KCB	Knight Commander of the Bath
Km	Kilometre
Lt	Lieutenant
MC	Military Cross
MM	Military Medal
Pow	Prisoner of War
Sgt	Sergeant
T/o	Take off
USA	United States of America
USAS	United States Air Service
WO	War Office
1Lt	First Lieutenant
2Lt	Second Lieutenant
*	When associated with a gallantry award indicates a First and any additional Bar to the honour

Appendix A - Squadron losses table 1st April 1918 - 30th June 1918

Owing to incomplete records it is highly unlikely that the statistics reported are an accurate tally on the number of aircraft and personnel lost during this period. Squadrons that appear not to have lost aircraft between the beginning of April and the end of June are omitted from the table but will feature in the appendix showing the locations of squadrons. Data in the nine columns show:-

1. Operational losses
2. Operational deaths
3. Non-operational losses
4. Non-operational deaths
5. Prisoners-of-war
6. Interned
7. Miscellaneous
8. Totals
9. Area of operations

Section 1 - Royal Air Force

	1	2	3	4	5	6	7	8	9
1 Squadron	34	6	9		7		1	57	Western Front
2 Squadron	28	5	6					39	Western Front
3 Squadron	12	7	5	2	2			28	Western Front
4 Squadron	24	22	3	1	1			51	Western Front
5 Squadron	9	3	2					14	Western Front
6 Squadron	1		1					2	Western Front
7 Squadron	10	4	5	3	2		1	25	Western Front
8 Squadron	20	2	3	1				26	Western Front
9 Squadron	1		5					6	Western Front
10 Squadron	25	5	8					38	Western Front
11 Squadron	9	7	3		1		1	21	Western Front
12 Squadron	4		6	3			1	14	Western Front
13 Squadron	2	2	2					6	Western Front
15 Squadron	11	4	1					16	Western Front
16 Squadron	8	2	1					11	Western Front
17 Squadron	1	2	1	1				5	Balkans
18 Squadron	12	2	7				1	22	Western Front
19 Squadron	12		2	1	2			17	Western Front
20 Squadron	20	4	4		8		1	37	Western Front
21 Squadron	6	2	5	2			1	16	Western Front
22 Squadron	10	7	2		3			22	Western Front
23 Squadron	19	5	11	2	2		1	40	Western Front
24 Squadron	21	3	7		1			32	Western Front
25 Squadron	15	4	1		11		1	32	Western Front
27 Squadron	23	20	4		4		2	53	Western Front
28 Squadron	4	1	3	2	2			12	Italian Front
29 Squadron	38	2	9		1			50	Western Front
32 Squadron	23	4	9		1			37	Western Front
33 Squadron			1	1				2	United Kingdom
34 Squadron	1							1	Italian Front
35 Squadron	27	6	3		1			37	Western Front

Squadron							Total	Theatre
36 Squadron	1						1	United Kingdom
37 Squadron			3	2			5	United Kingdom
38 Squadron	1		3	3			7	United Kingdom
39 Squadron			2	2			4	United Kingdom
40 Squadron	35	3	2		3		43	Western Front
41 Squadron	22	1	11		1	2	37	Western Front
42 Squadron	12	3	3				18	Western Front
43 Squadron	19	7	4	2	6		38	Western Front
44 Squadron			1				1	United Kingdom
45 Squadron	2	1	3		1		7	Italian Front
46 Squadron	8	4	1				13	Western Front
48 Squadron	21	15	3		8		47	Western Front
49 Squadron	19	12	5		5		41	Western Front
50 Squadron			2	1			3	United Kingdom
51 Squadron			1				1	United Kingdom
52 Squadron	12	12	1			3	28	Western Front
53 Squadron	14	6	4				24	Western Front
54 Squadron	35	10	14	3	3	1	66	Western Front
55 Squadron	11	11	5	4	6		37	Western Front
56 Squadron	20	5	10		4		39	Western Front
57 Squadron	19	15	2		4		40	Western Front
58 Squadron	3		2		2		7	Western Front
59 Squadron	4	2	3	1		1	11	Western Front
60 Squadron	22	4	6	1	1		34	Western Front
61 Squadron			1	1			2	United Kingdom
62 Squadron	13	6	1	1	8		29	Western Front
63 Squadron			1	2			3	Middle East
64 Squadron	19	1	7		2		29	Western Front
65 Squadron	24	12	9	4	7		56	Western Front
66 Squadron			6	4			10	Italian Front
70 Squadron	13	7	3	1	4		28	Western Front
73 Squadron	23	7	8	2	6		46	Western Front
74 Squadron	35	11	6	1	1	2	56	Western Front
75 Squadron			1	1			2	United Kingdom
76 Squadron	1						1	United Kingdom
77 Squadron			1				1	United Kingdom
78 Squadron			1	1			2	United Kingdom
79 Squadron	20	2	5	1	1	1	30	Western Front
80 Squadron	20	9	9		4		42	Western Front
81 Squadron			5	5			10	United Kingdom
82 Squadron	15	6	2				23	Western Front
83 Squadron	9	1	1	2	3		16	Western Front
84 Squadron	33	5	14		1		53	Western Front
85 Squadron	10	2	6	1	2		21	Western Front
86 Squadron			4	3			7	United Kingdom
87 Squadron	5		9				14	Western Front
88 Squadron	5	8	1				14	Western Front
89 Squadron			2	2			4	United Kingdom
90 Squadron			1				1	United Kingdom
91 Squadron			1	1			2	United Kingdom
92 Squadron			3	3			6	United Kingdom
93 Squadron			1				1	United Kingdom
94 Squadron								United Kingdom
95 Squadron			2	2			4	United Kingdom

Squadron								Total	Region
96 Squadron			2	2				4	United Kingdom
97 Squadron									United Kingdom
98 Squadron	35	15	6		6		3	69	Western Front
99 Squadron	6	4	1	2	4			17	Western Front
100 Squadron	11		3	2	6	2	1	25	Western Front
101 Squadron	12	3			4		1	20	Western Front
102 Squadron	6	2						8	Western Front
103 Squadron	15	8	3		2			28	Western Front
104 Squadron	4	4	2	4	3			17	Western Front
106 Squadron			2	4				6	United Kingdom
107 Squadron			6	3				9	Western Front
108 Squadron			1					1	United Kingdom
109 Squadron			2	2				4	United Kingdom
110 Squadron			3					3	United Kingdom
111 Squadron	1	1						2	Balkans
112 Squadron			1	1				2	United Kingdom
119 Squadron			2	2				4	United Kingdom
120 Squadron			2	3				5	United Kingdom
121 Squadron			1	1				2	United Kingdom
123 Squadron			2	2				4	United Kingdom
125 Squadron			1	1				2	United Kingdom
129 Squadron			1	2				3	United Kingdom
131 Squadron			4	5				9	United Kingdom
142 Squadron	1	1	1	1				4	Middle East
148 Squadron	3		2		4			9	Western Front
149 Squadron	2		4	1	2			9	Western Front
150 Squadron			1	1				2	Balkans
151 Squadron	3							3	Western Front
199 Squadron			1	1				2	United Kingdom
201 Squadron	6	4	2	1				13	Western Front
202 Squadron	1		1	1				3	Western Front
203 Squadron	10	6	1	1	2			20	Western Front
204 Squadron			1				2	3	Western Front
205 Squadron	14	8	2				1	25	Western Front
206 Squadron	34	13	5		4			56	Western Front
207 Squadron	1	1	1					3	Western Front
208 Squadron	7	3	2	1	2		16	31	Western Front
209 Squadron	6	5	2		1			14	Western Front
210 Squadron	22	10	5	2	4			43	Western Front
211 Squadron	13	3	4	4	3	2		29	Western Front
212 Squadron	1	1						2	United Kingdom
213 Squadron	5	2	1		1			9	Western Front
214 Squadron	4	2		1		3		10	Western Front
216 Squadron	1			3				4	Western Front
217 Squadron	8	2			6	2	1	19	Western Front
218 Squadron	3	2	2			2		9	Western Front
224 Squadron	1		2	2				5	Italian Front
226 Squadron			1	2				3	Italian Front
236 Squadron	1	2						3	United Kingdom
246 Squadron			1					1	United Kingdom
250 Squadron	1		2					3	United Kingdom
Totals	1142	416	399	119	187	9	46	2318	

Note. No 26 Squadron was in the process of returning to the United Kingdom from South Africa without aircraft. Formed at Netheravon in Wiltshire on the 8th of October 1915, from personnel of the South African Flying Unit that had been involved in operations against German South West Africa, the squadron left Netheravon on the 23rd of December for East Africa disembarking at Mombassa on the last day of January 1916, and moving on to Mbuyini the next day, its rôle was to support Imperial troops engaged in opposing the threat from German forces in her East African territories. For the next two years the squadron, equipped in the main with BEs and Henry Farman F.27, numerous reconnaissance sorties were flown. During this period accidents occurred and the historian and author Trevor Henshaw has traced, and report in *The Sky Their Battlefield,* at least fourteen deaths, though not all are associated with flying.

Section 2 - Australian Flying Corps

1 Squadron			1	1				2	Middle East
2 Squadron	20	1	8	1	1		1	32	Western Front
3 Squadron	12	8						20	Western Front
4 Squadron	29	7	8	1	3			48	Western Front
Totals	61	16	17	3	4		1	102	
Combined	1203	432	416	122	191	9	47	2420	

Note. The number of deaths shown in these two sections will be at odds with the Roll of Honour which records both flying and non-flying fatalities. Regarding the area of operations, this reflects the squadron's location as at the 30th of June 1918.

Appendix B - Losses by aircraft type 1st April 1918 - 30th June 1918

Data presented in the columns match to the greater part that which is recorded in Appendix A, except for the ninth column which indicates the squadron's principal rôle, though as the summaries show squadrons often undertook a multitude of tasks with, for example, scout [fighter] squadrons undertaking low-level bombing. Also, squadrons forming in the United Kingdom during 1918, for subsequent service on the Western Front often were issued with aircraft different to those earmarked for their operational task, and example being No 120 Squadron which received Royal Aircraft Factory RE.8s though scheduled to deploy with Airco DH.9As. Statistics for aircraft lost from the Australian Flying Corps are included within the type's overall totals.

Aircraft Manufacturing Company Limited: DH.4

Squadron								Total	Rôle
18 Squadron	12	2	7				1	22	Bombing
25 Squadron	15	4	1		11		1	32	Bombing
27 Squadron	23	20	4		4		2	53	Bombing
55 Squadron	11	11	5	4	6			37	Bombing
57 Squadron	19	15	2		4			40	Bombing
106 Squadron			1	3				4	Reconnaissance
109 Squadron			2	2				4	Training
125 Squadron			1	1				2	Bombing
202 Squadron	1		1	1				3	Bombing
205 Squadron	14	8	2				1	25	Bombing
211 Squadron			1					1	Bombing
217 Squadron	8	2			6	2	1	19	Bombing
218 Squadron			1					1	Bombing
224 Squadron	1		2	2				5	Bombing
226 Squadron			1	2				3	Bombing
Totals	104	62	31	15	31	2	6	251	

Aircraft Manufacturing Company Limited: DH.6

Squadron				Total	Rôle
107 Squadron	1			1	Bombing
119 Squadron	1	1		2	Bombing
123 Squadron	1	1		2	Bombing
131 Squadron	2	2		2	Bombing
Totals	5	4		9	

Aircraft Manufacturing Company Limited: DH.9

Squadron								Total	Rôle
49 Squadron	19	12	5		5			41	Bombing
98 Squadron	35	15	6		6		3	69	Bombing
99 Squadron	6	4	1	2	4			17	Bombing
104 Squadron	4	4	2	4	3			17	Bombing
107 Squadron			5	3				8	Bombing
110 Squadron			2					2	Bombing
123 Squadron			1	1				2	Bombing
129 Squadron			1	2				3	Bombing
131 Squadron			1	1				2	Bombing
206 Squadron	34	13	5		4			56	Bombing

Squadron								Total	Role
211 Squadron	13	3	3	4	3	2		28	Bombing
218 Squadron	3	2	1			2		8	Bombing
236 Squadron	1	2						3	Anti-submarine
250 Squadron	1		2					3	Anti-submarine
Totals	116	55	35	17	25	4	3	255	

Armstrong Whitworth: FK.3

Squadron				Total	Role
121 Squadron		1	1	2	Bombing
Totals		1	1	2	

Armstrong Whitworth: FK.8

Squadron					Total	Role
2 Squadron	28	5	6		39	Reconnaissance
8 Squadron						
10 Squadron						
17 Squadron	1	2			3	Reconnaissance
35 Squadron	27	6	3	1	37	Reconnaissance
82 Squadron	15	6	2		23	Reconnaissance
110 Squadron			1		1	Bombing
Totals	71	19	12	1	103	

Avro Aircraft Company: Avro 504A

Squadron		Total	Role
93 Squadron	1	1	Fighter
Total	1	1	

Avro Aircraft Company: Avro 504J

Squadron			Total	Role
92 Squadron	2	2	4	Fighter
95 Squadron	1	1	2	Training
Totals	3	3	6	

Blackburn Aeroplane and Motor Company: Kangaroo

Squadron		Total	Role
246 Squadron	1	1	Anti-submarine
Total	1	1	

Bristol Aeroplane Company: Bristol F.2b

Squadron							Total	Role
11 Squadron	9	7	3		1	1	21	Fighter
16 Squadron	1						1	Reconnaissance
20 Squadron	20	4	4	8		1	37	Fighter
22 Squadron	10	7	2	3			22	Fighter
34 Squadron	1						1	Fighter
48 Squadron	21	15	3	8			47	Fighter
60 Squadron			1				1	Fighter
62 Squadron	13	6	1	1	8		29	Fighter

Squadron							Total	Role
88 Squadron	5	8	1				14	Fighter

Australian Flying Corps

Squadron							Total	Role
1 Squadron			1	1			2	
Overall totals	78	47	16	2	28	2	175	

Handley Page Limited: HP O/100

Squadron							Total	Role
207 Squadron	1	1					2	Bombing [borrowed by No 215 Squadron]
214 Squadron	3						3	Bombing
216 Squadron	1				3		4	Bombing
Totals	5	1			3		9	

Handley Page Limited: HP O/400

Squadron							Total	Role
214 Squadron	1	2		1			4	Bombing
Totals	1	2		1			4	

Martinsyde Company

Martinsyde G.100

Squadron							Total	Role
142 Squadron			1				1	Bombing
Total			1				1	

Nieuport Company: Nieuport 17

Squadron							Total	Role
29 Squadron	1						1	Fighter
111 Squadron	1	1					2	Fighter
Totals	2	1					3	

Royal Aircraft Factory: BE.2e

Squadron							Total	Role
50 Squadron			1				1	Fighter Home Defence
76 Squadron	1						1	Fighter Home Defence
77 Squadron			1				1	Fighter Home Defence
108 Squadron			1				1	Bombing
119 Squadron			1	1			2	Bombing
Totals	1		4	1			6	

Royal Aircraft Factory: BE.12

Squadron							Total	Role
75 Squadron			1	1			2	Fighter Home Defence
Totals			1	1			2	

Royal Aircraft Factory: FE.2b

Squadron								Total	Role
51 Squadron			1					1	Fighter Home Defence
83 Squadron	9	1	1	2	3			16	Bombing & Reconnaissance
100 Squadron	11		3	2	6	2	1	25	Bombing
101 Squadron	12	3			4		1	20	Bombing
102 Squadron	6	2						8	Bombing
103 Squadron	15	8	3		2			28	Bombing
149 Squadron	2		4	1	2			9	Bombing
199 Squadron			1	1				2	Training
Totals	55	14	13	6	17	2	2	109	

Royal Aircraft Factory: FE.2d

Squadron						Total	Role
33 Squadron			1	1		2	Fighter Home Defence
58 Squadron	3		2		2	7	Bombing
148 Squadron	3		2		4	9	Bombing
Totals	6		5	1	6	18	

Royal Aircraft Factory: RE.8

Squadron								Total	Role
4 Squadron	24	22	3	1	1			51	Reconnaissance
5 Squadron	9	3	2					14	Reconnaissance
6 Squadron	1		1					2	Reconnaissance
7 Squadron	10	4	5	3	2	1		25	Reconnaissance
9 Squadron	1		5					6	Reconnaissance
12 Squadron	4		6	3			1	14	Reconnaissance
13 Squadron	2	2	2					6	Reconnaissance
15 Squadron	11	4	1					16	Reconnaissance
16 Squadron	7	2	1					10	Reconnaissance
21 Squadron	6	2	5	2			1	16	Reconnaissance
42 Squadron	12	3	3					18	Reconnaissance
52 Squadron	12	12	1				3	28	Reconnaissance
53 Squadron	14	6	4					24	Reconnaissance
59 Squadron	4	2	3	1			1	11	Reconnaissance
63 Squadron			1	2				3	Reconnaissance
106 Squadron			1	1				2	Reconnaissance
120 Squadron			2	3				5	Bombing
131 Squadron			1	2				3	Bombing
142 Squadron	1	1						2	Reconnaissance
207 Squadron			1					1	Bombing

Australian Flying Corps

Squadron								Total	Role
3 Squadron	12	8						20	Reconnaissance
Overall totals	130	71	48	12	3	1	6	276	

Royal Aircraft Factory: SE.5

24 Squadron	1						1	Fighter
56 Squadron	1						1	Fighter
Totals	2						2	

Royal Aircraft Factory: SE.5a

1 Squadron	34	6	9		7	1	57	Fighter
24 Squadron	20	3	7		1		31	Fighter
29 Squadron	37	2	9		1		49	Fighter
32 Squadron	23	4	9		1		37	Fighter
40 Squadron	35	3	2		3		43	Fighter
41 Squadron	22	1	11		1	2	37	Fighter
50 Squadron			1	1			2	Fighter Home Defence
56 Squadron	19	5	10		4		38	Fighter
60 Squadron	22	4	5	1	1		33	Fighter
61 Squadron			1	1			2	Fighter Home Defence
64 Squadron	19	1	7		2		29	Fighter
74 Squadron	35	11	6	1	1	2	56	Fighter
84 Squadron	33	5	14		1		53	Fighter
85 Squadron	10	2	4		2		18	Fighter
89 Squadron			1	1			2	Training

Australian Flying Corps

2 Squadron	20	1	8	1	1	1	32	Fighter
Overall totals	329	48	104	6	26	6	519	

Société Pour l'aviation et ses dérivés: SPAD S.7

23 Squadron	1						1	Fighter
Total	1						1	

Société Pour l'aviation et ses dérivés: SPAD S.13

23 Squadron	5	3	2	1	2		13	Fighter
Totals	5	3	2	1	2		13	

Sopwith Aviation Company: F.1 Camel

3 Squadron	12	7	5	2	2		28	Fighter
28 Squadron	4	1	3	2	2		12	Fighter
43 Squadron	19	7	4	2	6		38	Fighter
44 Squadron			1				1	Fighter Home Defence
45 Squadron	2	1	3		1		7	Fighter
46 Squadron	8	4	1				13	Fighter
54 Squadron	35	10	14	3	3	1	66	Fighter
65 Squadron	24	12	9	4	7		56	Fighter
66 Squadron			6	4			10	Fighter

Squadron								Role
70 Squadron	13	7	3	1	4		28	Fighter
73 Squadron	23	7	8	2	6		46	Fighter
78 Squadron			1	1			2	Fighter Home Defence
80 Squadron	20	9	9		4		42	Fighter
81 Squadron		3	3				6	Training
86 Squadron			4	3			7	Training
96 Squadron			2	2			4	Training
112 Squadron			1	1			2	Fighter Home Defence
150 Squadron			1	1			2	Fighter
151 Squadron	3						3	Fighter
201 Squadron	6	4	2	1			13	Fighter
203 Squadron	10	6	1	1	2		20	Fighter
204 Squadron			1			2	3	Fighter
208 Squadron	7	3	2	1	2	16	31	Fighter
209 Squadron	6	5	2		1		14	Fighter
210 Squadron	22	10	5	2	4		43	Fighter
213 Squadron	5	2	1		1		9	Fighter

Australian Flying Corps

4 Squadron	29	7	8	1	3		48	Fighter
Overall totals	248	105	100	33	48	19	544	

Sopwith Aviation Company: 2F.1 Camel

212 Squadron	1	1					2	Anti-submarine
Totals	1	1					2	

Sopwith Aviation Company: 5F.1 Dolphin

19 Squadron	12		2	1	2		17	Fighter & Ground Attack
23 Squadron	13	2	9	1		1	26	Fighter & Ground attack
79 Squadron	20	2	5	1	1	1	30	Fighter & Ground Attack
81 Squadron			2	2			4	Training
85 Squadron			2	1			3	Training
87 Squadron	5		9				14	Fighter & Ground Attack
90 Squadron			1				1	Fighter
Totals	50	4	30	6	3	2	95	

Sopwith Aviation Company: Pup

89 Squadron			1	1			2	Training
91 Squadron			1	1			2	Training
92 Squadron			1	1			2	Fighter
95 Squadron			1	1			2	Training
Totals			4	4			8	

Appendix C - Squadron locations 1st April 1918 - 30th June 1918

The locations reported have been extracted from James J Halley's *The Squadrons of the Royal Air Force & Commonwealth 1918-1988*. Where squadrons in the United Kingdom are recorded, I have, in the majority of cases, restricted the location to the squadron's headquarters. Concerning No 26 Squadron, please refer to my remarks in Appendix A. Concerning the Middle East based squadrons, many had flights detached to various parts of the region.

1 Squadron	Ste Marie Cappel	In situ	Western Front
	Clairmarais	13 April 1918	Western Front
2 Squadron	Hesdigneul	In situ	Western Front
	Floringhem	9 June 1918	Western Front
	Mazingarbe	20 June 1918	Western Front
3 Squadron	Valheureux	In situ	Western Front
4 Squadron	Chocques	In situ	Western Front
	Treizennes	8 April 1918	Western Front
	St Omer	16 April 1918	Western Front
5 Squadron	Ascq	In situ	Western Front
	Le Hameau	25 May 1918	Western Front
6 Squadron	Le Crotoy	In situ	Western Front
7 Squadron	Proven East	In situ	Western Front
	Droglandt	13 April 1918	Western Front
8 Squadron	Vert Galand	In situ	Western Front
	Auxi-le-Château	6 April 1918	Western Front
9 Squadron	Proven	In situ	Western Front
	Calais	11 April 1918	Western Front
	Agenvillers	6 June 1918	Western Front
10 Squadron	Abeele	In situ	Western Front
	Droglandt	12 April 1918	Western Front
11 Squadron	Fienvillers	In situ	Western Front
	Remaisnil	16 April 1918	Western Front
12 Squadron	Soncamp	In situ	Western Front
13 Squadron	Izel-lès-Hameau	In situ	Western Front
14 Squadron	Junction Station	In situ	Palestine
15 Squadron	Fienvillers	In situ	Western Front
	Vert Galand	10 April 1918	Western Front
16 Squadron	Camblain l'Abbe	In situ	Western Front
17 Squadron	Mikra Bay	In situ	Greece
18 Squadron	Treizennes	In situ	Western Front
	Serny	9 April 1918	Western Front
19 Squadron	Savy	In situ	Western Front
20 Squadron	Ste Marie Cappel	In situ	Western Front
	Boisdinghem	13 April 1918	Western Front
21 Squadron	La Lovie	In situ	Western Front
	St Inglevert	13 April 1918	Western Front
	Floringhem	22 April 1918	Western Front
22 Squadron	Vert Galand	In situ	Western Front
	Serny	10 April 1918	Western Front
23 Squadron	Bertangles	In situ	Western Front
	St Omer	29 April 1918	Western Front
	Bertangles	16 May 1918	Western Front

24 Squadron	Conteville	In situ	Western Front
25 Squadron	Ruisseauville	In situ	Western Front
26 Squadron	Cape Town	In situ	South Africa
27 Squadron	Ruisseauville	In situ	Western Front
	Fourneuil	3 June 1918	Western Front
	Ruisseauville	21 June 1918	Western Front
28 Squadron	Grossa	In situ	Italian Front
29 Squadron	La Lovie	In situ	Western Front
	Teteghem	11 April 1918	Western Front
	St Omer	22 April 1918	Western Front
	Vignacourt	11 June 1918	Western Front
30 Squadron	Baquba	In situ	Mesopotamia
31 Squadron	Risalpur	In situ	India
32 Squadron	Beauvois	In situ	Western Front
	Fouquerolles	3 June 1918	Western Front
	Ruisseauville	21 June 1918	Western Front
33 Squadron	Gainsborough	In situ	United Kingdom
	Kirton Lindsey	12 June 1918	United Kingdom
34 Squadron	Villaverla	In situ	Italian Front
35 Squadron	Abbeville	In situ	Western Front
	Poulainville	5 April 1918	Western Front
	Villers-Bocage	2 May 1918	Western Front
36 Squadron	Newcastle	In situ	United Kingdom
37 Squadron	Woodham Mortimer	In situ	United Kingdom
38 Squadron	Melton Mowbray	In situ	United Kingdom
	Capelle	31 May 1918	Western Front
39 Squadron	North Weald	In situ	United Kingdom
40 Squadron	Bruay	In situ	Western Front
	Bryas	4 June 1918	Western Front
41 Squadron	Alquines	In situ	Western Front
	Savy	9 April 1918	Western Front
	Serny	11 April 1918	Western Front
	Estrée Blanche	19 May 1918	Western Front
	Conteville	1 June 1918	Western Front
42 Squadron	Chocques	In situ	Western Front
	Treizennes	9 April 1918	Western Front
	Rély	25 April 1918	Western Front
43 Squadron	Avesnes-le-Comte	In situ	Western Front
	Fouquerolles	3 June 1918	Western Front
	Lièttres	21 June 1918	Western Front
44 Squadron	Hainault Farm	In situ	United Kingdom
45 Squadron	Grossa	In situ	Italian Front
46 Squadron	Filescamp	In situ	Western Front
	Lièttres	16 May 1918	Western Front
	Serny	17 June 1918	Western Front
47 Squadron	Janes	In situ	Greece
48 Squadron	Conteville	In situ	Western Front
	Bertangles	3 April 1918	Western Front
49 Squadron	Petite Synthe	In situ	Western Front
	Conteville	3 May 1918	Western Front
	Fourneuil	2 June 1918	Western Front
	Beauvois	21 June 1918	Western Front
50 Squadron	Bekesbourne	In situ	United Kingdom
51 Squadron	Marham	In situ	United Kingdom

52 Squadron	Abbeville	In situ	Western Front
	Serches	3 May 1918	Western Front
52 Squadron continued	Fismes	5 May 1918	Western Front
	Cramaille	27 May 1918	Western Front
	Anthenay	28 May 1918	Western Front
	Trecon	29 May 1918	Western Front
	Auxi-le-Château	30 June 1918	Western Front
53 Squadron	Boisdinghem	In situ	Western Front
	Abeele	7 April 1918	Western Front
	Clairmarais	13 April 1918	Western Front
54 Squadron	Conteville	In situ	Western Front
	Clairmarais	7 April 1918	Western Front
	Caffiers	29 April 1918	Western Front
	St Omer	1 June 1918	Western Front
	Vignacourt	11 June 1918	Western Front
	Boisdinghem	16 June 1918	Western Front
	Lièttres	30 June 1918	Western Front
55 Squadron	Tantonville	In situ	Western Front
	Azelot	5 June 1918	Western Front
56 Squadron	Valheureux	In situ	Western Front
57 Squadron	Le Quesnoy	In situ	Western Front
58 Squadron	Auchel	In situ	Western Front
	Fauquemberges	23 April 1918	Western Front
59 Squadron	Lealvilliers	In situe	Wester Front
	Vert Galand	12 April 1918	Western Front
60 Squadron	Fienvillers	In situ	Western Front
	Boffles	12 April 1918	Western Front
61 Squadron	Rochford	In situ	United Kingdom
62 Squadron	Planques	In situ	Western Front
63 Squadron	Basra	In situ	Mesopotamia
64 Squadron	Izel-lès-Hameau	In situ	Western Front
65 Squadron	Conteville	In situ	Western Front
	Bertangles	6 April 1918	Western Front
66 Squadron	San Pietro	In situ	Italian Front
70 Squadron	Fienvillers	In situ	Western Front
	Ramaisnil	16 April 1918	Western Front
72 Squadron	Basra	In situ	Mesopotamia
73 Squadron	Beauvois	In situ	Western Front
	Fouquerolles	3 June 1918	Western Front
	Ruisseauville	21 June 1918	Western Front
74 Squadron	Teteghem	In situ	Western Front
	La Lovie	9 April 1918	Western Front
	Clairmarais	11 April 1918	Western Front
75 Squadron	Elmswell	In situ	United Kingdom
	North Weald	22 May 1918	United Kingdom
76 Squadron	Ripon	In situ	United Kingdom
77 Squadron	Penston	In situ	United Kingdom
78 Squadron	Sutton's Farm	In situ	United Kingdom
79 Squadron	Beauvais	In situ	Western Front
	Ste Marie Cappel	16 May 1918	Western Front
80 Squadron	Belleville Farm	In situ	Western Front
	La Bellevue	4 April 1918	Western Front
	Fouquerolles	3 June 1918	Western Front
	Lièttres	21 June 1918	Western Front

81 Squadron	Scampton	In situ	United Kingdom
82 Squadron	Agenvilliers	In situ	Western Front
	Quevenvillers	7 June 1918	Western Front
83 Squadron	Auchel	In situ	Western Front
	Franqueville	2 May 1918	Western Front
84 Squadron	Conteville	In situ	Western Front
	Bertangles	4 April 1918	Western Front
85 Squadron	Marquise	In situ	Western Front
	Petite Synthe	25 May 1918	Western Front
	St Omer	11 June 1918	Western Front
86 Squadron	Northolt	In situ	United Kingdom
87 Squadron	Hounslow	In situ	United Kingdom
	St Omer	23 April 1918	Western Front
	Petite Synthe	27 April 1918	Western Front
	Estrée-les-Crecy	27 May 1918	Western Front
	Rougefay	29 June 1918	Western Front
88 Squadron	Harling Road	In situ	United Kingdom
	Kenley	2 April 1918	United Kingdom
	Capelle	20 April 1918	Western Front
89 Squadron	Harling Road	In situ	United Kingdom
90 Squadron	Shotwick	In situ	United Kingdom
91 Squadron	Tangmere	In situ	United Kingdom
92 Squadron	Tangmere	In situ	United Kingdom
93 Squadron	Tangmere	In situ	United Kingdom
94 Squadron	Harling Road	In situ	United Kingdom
95 Squadron	Shotwick	In situ	United Kingdom
96 Squadron	Shotwick	In situ	United Kingdom
97 Squadron	Netheravon	In situ	United Kingdom
98 Squadron	Coudekerque	In situ	Western Front
	Alquines	13 April 1918	Western Front
	Coudekerque	25 May 1918	Western Front
	Ruisseauville	6 June 1918	Western Front
	Drionville	21 June 1918	Western Front
99 Squadron	Old Sarum	In situ	United Kingdom
	St Omer	25 April 1918	Western Front
	Tantonville	3 May 1918	Western Front
	Azelot	5 June 1918	Western Front
100 Squadron	Villesneux	In situ	Western Front
	Ochey	9 May 1918	Western Front
101 Squadron	Haute Visée	In situ	Western Front
	Famechon	7 April 1918	Western Front
102 Squadron	Izel-lès-Hameau	In site	Western Front
	Surcamps	10 April 1918	Western Front
103 Squadron	Old Sarum	In situ	United Kingdom
	Serny	12 May 1918	Western Front
104 Squadron	Andover	In situ	United Kingdom
	St Omer	19 May 1918	Western Front
	Azelot	20 May 1918	Western Front
105 Squadron	Andover	In situ	United Kingdom
	Omagh	19 May 1918	United Kingdom
106 Squadron	Andover	In situ	United Kingdom
	Fermoy	30 May 1918	United Kingdom

107 Squadron	Lake Down	In situ	United Kingdom
	Le Quesnoy	5 June 1918	Western Front
	Drionville	25 June 1918	Western Front
108 Squadron	Lake Down	In situ	United Kingdom
	Kenley	14 June 1918	United Kingdom
109 Squadron	Stonehenge	In situ	United Kingdom
110 Squadron	Sedgeford	In situ	United Kingdom
	Kenley	15 June 1918	United Kingdom
111 Squadron	Ramleh	In situ	Palestine
112 Squadron	Throwley	In situ	United Kingdom
113 Squadron	Sarona	In situ	Palestine
114 Squadron	Lahore	In situ	India
115 Squadron	Catterick	In situ	United Kingdom
	Netheravon	15 April 1918	United Kingdom
116 Squadron	Netheravon	In situ	United Kingdom
117 Squadron	Waddington	In situ	United Kingdom
	Hucknall	3 April 1918	United Kingdom
118 Squadron	Catterick	In situ	United Kingdom
	Netheravon	15 April 1918	United Kingdom
119 Squadron	Duxford	In situ	United Kingdom
120 Squadron	Cramlington	In situ	United Kingdom
121 Squadron	Narborough	In situ	United Kingdom
122 Squadron	Sedgeford	In situ	United Kingdom
123 Squadron	Duxford	In situ	United Kingdom
124 Squadron	Fowlmere	In situ	United Kingdom
125 Squadron	Old Sarum	In situ	United Kingdom
126 Squadron	Fowlmere	In situ	United Kingdom
127 Squadron	Catterick	In situ	United Kingdom
128 Squadron	Thetford	In situ	United Kingdom
129 Squadron	Duxford	In situ	United Kingdom
130 Squadron	Hucknall	In situ	United Kingdom
131 Squadron	Shawbury	In situ	United Kingdom
132 Squadron	Tern Hill	In situ	United Kingdom
133 Squadron	Tern Hill	In situ	United Kingdom
134 Squadron	Tern Hill	In situ	United Kingdom
135 Squadron*	Hucknall	In situ	United Kingdom
136 Squadron*	Lake Down	In situ	United Kingdom
137 Squadron*	Shawbury	In situ	United Kingdom
140 Squadron	Biggin Hill	1 May 1918	United Kingdom formed
141 Squadron	Biggin Hill	In situ	United Kingdom
142 Squadron	Julis	In situ	Palestine
	Ramleh	18 April 1918	Palestine
143 Squadron	Detling	In situ	United Kingdom
144 Squadron	Port Said	In situ	Egypt
145 Squadron	Aboukir	In situ	Egypt
	Abu Sueir	2 June 1918	Egypt
147 Squadron		1 May 1918	Egypt formed
148 Squadron	Ford	In situ	United Kingdom
	Auchel	25 April 1918	Western Front
	Sains-les-Pernes	3 May 1918	Western Front
149 Squadron	Ford	In situ	United Kingdom
	Marquise	2 June 1918	Western Front
	Quilen	4 June 1918	Western Front
	Alquines	16 June 1918	Western Front

150 Squadron*	Kirec	In situ	Greece
151 Squadron	Hainault Farm	12 June 1918	United Kingdom formed
	Marquise	16 June 1918	Western Front
	Fontaine-sur-Maye	21 June 1918	Western Front
	Famechon	25 June 1918	Western Front
163 Squadron	Waddington	1 June 1918	United Kingdom formed
166 Squadron	Bircham Newton	13 June 1918	United Kingdom formed
186 Squadron*	East Retford	In situ	United Kingdom
187 Squadron*	East Retford	In situ	United Kingdom
188 Squadron	Throwley	In situ	United Kingdom
189 Squadron	Sutton's Farm	In situ	United Kingdom
190 Squadron	Newmarket	In situ	United Kingdom
191 Squadron	Marham	In situ	United Kingdom
192 Squadron	Newmarket	In situ	United Kingdom
198 Squadron	Rochford	In situ	United Kingdom
199 Squadron	Rochford	In situ	United Kingdom
	Harpswell	26 June 1918	United Kingdom
200 Squadron	East Retford	In situ	United Kingdom

* Indicates formation on the 1st of April 1918.

Squadrons between '201' and '211' and '213' and '217' were numbered as such on the 1st of April 1918, following the merging of the Royal Naval Air Service and the Royal Flying Corps, having previously operated as No 1 Squadron Royal Naval Air Service et al.

201 Squadron	Fienvillers	In situ	Western Front
	Noeux	12 April 1918	Western Front
202 Squadron	Bergues	In situ	Western Front
203 Squadron	Treizennes	In situ	Western Front
	Lièttres	9 April 1918	Western Front
	Filescamp	16 May 1918	Western Front
204 Squadron	Bray Dunes	In situ	Western Front
	Teteghem	13 April 1918	Western Front
	Cappelle	30 April 1918	Western Front
	Teteghem	9 May 1918	Western Front
205 Squadron	Bois de Roche	In situ	Western Front
206 Squadron	Ste Marie Cappel	In situ	Western Front
	Boisdinghem	11 April 1918	Western Front
	Alquines	15 April 1918	Western Front
	Boisdinghem	29 May 1918	Western Front
	Alquines	5 June 1918	Western Front
207 Squadron	Coudekerque	In situ	Western Front
	Netheravon	22 April 1918	United Kingdom
	Andover	12 May 1918	United Kingdom
	Ligescourt	7 June 1918	Western Front
208 Squadron	Teteghem	In situ	Western Front
	La Gorgue	2 April 1918	Western Front
	Serny	9 April 1918	Western Front
209 Squadron	Clairmarais	In situ	Western Front
	Bertangles	7 April 1918	Western Front
210 Squadron	Treizennes	In situ	Western Front
	Lièttres	9 April 1918	Western Front
	St Omer	27 April 1918	Western Front
	Ste Marie Cappel	30 May 1918	Western Front

211 Squadron	Petite Synthe	In situ	Western Front
213 Squadron	Bergues	In situ	Western Front
214 Squadron	Coudekerque	In situ	Western Front
	St Inglevert	29 June 1918	Western Front
215 Squadron	Coudekerque	In situ	Western Front
	Netheravon	23 April 1918	United Kingdom
	Andover	15 May 1918	United Kingdom
216 Squadron	Villesneux	In situ	Western Front
	Cramaille	20 April 1918	Western Front
216 Squadron contd	Ochey	9 May 1918	Western Front
217 Squadron	Bergues	In situ	Western Front

Resumption of squadrons formed under the Royal Air Force banner.

218 Squadron	Dover	24 April 1918	United Kingdom formed
	Petite Synthe	23 May 1918	Western Front

Squadrons formed from former Royal Naval Air Service lettered squadrons and Flights.

221 Squadron	Stavros	1 April 1918	Aegean

Formed from D Squadron for anti-submarine duties.

222 Squadron	Thasos	1 April 1918	Aegean

Formed from A and Z Squadrons for anti-submarine duties.

223 Squadron	Mitylene	1 April 1918	Greece

Formed from B Squadron.

224 Squadron	Alimini	1 April 1918	Italy

Formed from 497 and 498 Flights.

225 Squadron	Alimini	1 April 1918	Italy

Formed from 481, 482 and 483 Flights.

226 Squadron	Pizonne	1 April 1918	Italey

Formed from 472, 473 and 474 Flights.

227 Squadron	Pizonne	1 April 1918	Italy

Formed from 499, 550 and 551 Flights.

250 Squadron	Padstow	10 May 1918	United Kingdom

Formed from 494, 500, 501, 502 and 503 Flights.

252 Squadron	Tynemouth	.... May 1918	United Kingdom

Formed from 495, 507, 508 and 509 Flights.

253 Squadron	Bembridge	7 June 1918	United Kingdom

Formed from 412 and 413 Flights.

254 Squadron	Prawle Point	.... May 1918	United Kingdom

Formed from 492, 517 and 518 Flights.

256 Squadron	Sea Houses	.... June 1918	United Kingdom

Formed from 525, 526, 527 and 528 Flights.

Note. The following squadrons are reported to have formed between the 1st of April 1918 and the 30th of June 1918, but at locations yet to be traced and with aircraft unidentified: 160, 161, and 162 Squadrons.

The Roll of Honour
1 April 1918 to 30 June 1918

At the going down of the sun and in the morning
We will remember them

[Laurence Binyon]

The Roll of Honour has been prepared from information held by the Commonwealth War Graves Commission and supported by Chris Hobson's compilation *Airmen Died in the Great War 1914 - 1918*, plus additional notes from material unearthed, relevant to the Roll, by Dave Gilbert and Cathie Hewitt to whom I am exceedingly grateful.

The Roll is being presented in alphabetical sequence of surname and in chronological order of date while the various grades of rank pertaining to airmen, mechanics and privates appear with the singular blanket title of 'Airman', 'Mechanic' and 'Private'.

ROYAL AIR FORCE

Rank	Surname	Name	Date	Squadron
Lieutenant	ADAM Canada	Orval Patrick	1 April 1918	203 Squadron
Captain	BANBURY DSC Canada	Fred Everest	1 April 1918	209 Squadron
Mechanic	CARTER	Leslie George William	1 April 1918	101 Squadron
2nd Lieutenant	GREASLEY	John Richard	1 April 1918	65 Squadron
Lieutenant	HART	William Cecil Frederick Nicol	1 April 1918	57 Squadron
Lieutenant	JOYCE Australia	Norman Roy	1 April 1918	23 Squadron
Mechanic	LANG	Andrew	1 April 1918	116 Squadron
Corporal	LOVELOCK	Edward Charles	1 April 1918	57 Squadron
Lieutenant	MOSES Canada	James David	1 April 1918	57 Squadron
Lieutenant	STONEHOUSE	Ronald	1 April 1918	101 Squadron
2nd Lieutenant	TROLLIP South Africa	Douglas Price	1 April 1918	57 Squadron
2nd Lieutenant	WHITFIELD	Edgar	1 April 1918	57 Squadron
Lieutenant	WINKLEY	Stanley Hugh	1 April 1918	84 Squadron
Lieutenant	CANN	Percy Reginald	2 April 1918	65 Squadron
2nd Lieutenant	CHRISTIE Canada	Edgar Watchorn	2 April 1918	60 Squadron
2nd Lieutenant	CRITCHLEY	Roland	2 April 1918	22 Squadron
Lieutenant	JONES	Evan Davies	2 April 1918 Attached	2 Squadron 10 Squadron
2nd Lieutenant	KNOWLES British West Indies	Arthur Ralph	2 April 1918	11 Squadron
Lieutenant	McLEAN Canada	Donald Gordon	2 April 1918	45 Squadron
Lieutenant	MOORE	Jack Greville	2 April 1918	81 Squadron
Lieutenant	NUNN	Frederick Arthur William	2 April 1918	65 Squadron
2nd Lieutenant	SMITH	Wansey	2 April 1918	10 Squadron
Lieutenant	WILLIAMS	Fred	2 April 1918	22 Squadron

Lieutenant	JONES	Ernest David	3 April 1918	52 Squadron
Lieutenant	MITCHELL	John	3 April 1918	25 Squadron
2nd Lieutenant	MORTIMER	Ernest George Smith	3 April 1918	23 Squadron
		Canada		
2nd Lieutenant	NEWTON	Robert Francis	3 April 1918	52 Squadron
2nd Lieutenant	SALMON-BACKHOUSE	StJohn	3 April 1918	17 Squadron
Lieutenant	STILL	George	3 April 1918	17 Squadron
Lieutenant	CHANT	Earle Marian	4 April 1918	16 Squadron
		Canada		
Private	DRAY	Herbert Walter	4 April 1918	6 Squadron
2nd Lieutenant	HOLMAN	Henry Biorn	4 April 1918	66 Squadron
		South Africa		
Lieutenant	KENNEDY	James Gilbert	4 April 1918	65 Squadron
Sergeant	MITCHELL	Samuel James	4 April 1918	2 Squadron
	AFM			
2nd Lieutenant	ROEBUCK	Leonard	4 April 1918	38 Squadron
2nd Lieutenant	SWAIN	Clifford Maxwell	4 April 1918	52 Squadron
Lieutenant	SWAINE	Sydney William	4 April 1918	52 Squadron
Mechanic	WILTSHIRE	Thomas Bernard	4 April 1918	35 Squadron
2nd Lieutenant	COLLINS	Leslie Ernest	5 April 1918	100 Squadron
2nd Lieutenant	FORD	Norman	5 April 1918	100 Squadron
		Australia		
2nd Lieutenant	BARTLETT	Guy George	6 April 1918	48 Squadron
2nd Lieutenant	BELL	Benedict Godfrey Allen	6 April 1918	48 Squadron
Lieutenant	CARTMEL	George Musgrove	6 April 1918	205 Squadron
2nd Lieutenant	GILLESPIE	Douglas Victor	6 April 1918	70 Squadron
	A mention in a despatch			
2nd Lieutenant	HILTON	Robert	6 April 1918	13 Squadron
Lieutenant	JEWELL	John Belmont	6 April 1918	86 Squadron
Airman	LANE	Alexander James	6 April 1918	205 Squadron
2nd Lieutenant	LEWIS	Henry Stuart	6 April 1918	43 Squadron
	A mention in a despatch Canada			
Lieutenant	MATHER	Edward	6 April 1918	43 Squadron
Lieutenant	PAYNE	Sydney Thomas	6 April 1918	13 Squadron
Captain	SMITH	Sydney Philip	6 April 1918	46 Squadron
Lieutenant	SNEATH	Wilfred Harry	6 April 1918	208 Squadron
2nd Lieutenant	CRAIGIE	Victor Raleigh	7 April 1918	92 Squadron
	USA			
Captain	ENGLAND	Norman Herbert	7 April 1918	92 Squadron
Captain	EYDEN	Herbert	7 April 1918	21 Squadron
	MC			
2nd Lieutenant	HACKMAN	Clifford	7 April 1918	92 Squadron
Sergeant	INGHAM	Frederick	7 April 1918	102 Squadron
Lieutenant	KNIGHT	George Bertram	7 April 1918	53 Squadron
Mechanic	LAWRENCE	George Charles	7 April 1918	19 Squadron
Sergeant	MEAKIN	John	7 April 1918	23 Squadron
Captain	MOORE	Guy Batnwick	7 April 1918	1 Squadron
	MC			
2nd Lieutenant	NAPIER	James	7 April 1918	52 Squadron
Lieutenant	NOLAN	Philip John Noel	7 April 1918	24 Squadron
2nd Lieutenant	WALTERS	Herbert Aidan	7 April 1918	21 Squadron
		South Africa		

Captain	CUTHBERTSON George Chapman MC		8 April 1918	54 Squadron
Corporal	HOLT	John Dronsfield	8 April 1918	8 Squadron
Lieutenant	BION	Rupert Euston	9 April 1918	40 Squadron
2nd Lieutenant	BANNISTER Quinton Wolstenholme Canada		10 April 1918	99 Squadron
2nd Lieutenant	DUERDEN	George	10 April 1918	65 Squadron
Mechanic	HAINES	Charles Seymour	10 April 1918	4 Squadron
2nd Lieutenant	HOLTHOUSE Arthur Reginald Australia		10 April 1918	42 Squadron
2nd Lieutenant	KIDD	Edward John	10 April 1918	99 Squadron
Lieutenant	McKERRELL William Archibald Struthers		10 April 1918	4 Squadron
2nd Lieutenant	SMITH	Donald Graham	10 April 1918	42 Squadron
2nd Lieutenant	STEELE	Thomas Lancaster MC New Zealand	10 April 1918	111 Squadron
2nd Lieutenant	STODDART George Benjamin Johnstone		10 April 1918	65 Squadron
Corporal	WINALL	Arthur Henry	10 April 1918	42 Squadron
Lieutenant	BUTLER	John Ormonde	11 April 1918	3 Squadron
Lieutenant	CRAIG	James	11 April 1918	53 Squadron
Captain	CRAWFORD Kelvin		11 April 1918	60 Squadron
Lieutenant	HUGHES	Harold	11 April 1918	7 Squadron
Captain	JONES	Thomas Bright	11 April 1918	16 Squadron
Lieutenant	KING	Vernon	11 April 1918	16 Squadron
Lieutenant	KING	William Hugh	11 April 1918	7 Squadron
Captain	MacRAE	John Nigel	11 April 1918	83 Squadron
Lieutenant	SMITH	Sidney	11 April 1918	203 Squadron
Flight Sergeant	WESTWOOD Arthur		11 April 1918	83 Squadron
Captain	ALLAN	John Roy DSC Canada	12 April 1918	215 Squadron
Lieutenant	ARNOT	Arthur Alison MacDonald MC	12 April 1918	3 Squadron
Lieutenant	BOYD	Robert Hutton	12 April 1918	5 Squadron
Lieutenant	KORSLUND Mils Franklin USA		12 April 1918	73 Squadron
Captain	MacNAIR	Ian	12 April 1918	54 Squadron
Captain	MACLEAN	Alexander Murchison	12 April 1918	10 Squadron
Lieutenant	MOGRIDGE Lewis		12 April 1918	5 Squadron
2nd Lieutenant	MURRAY	Gordon Lautre South Africa	12 April 1918	80 Squadron
2nd Lieutenant	OWEN-HOLDSWORTH MC	James Philip	12 April 1918	101 Squadron
Lieutenant	PELL	William Augustus Canada	12 April 1918	80 Squadron
Lieutenant	RAMSDEN	Samuel	12 April 1918	4 Squadron
Lieutenant	ROBINSON	Ralph	12 April 1918	206 Squadron
2nd Lieutenant	WESTHOFEN Philip Charles South Africa		12 April 1918	4 Squadron
Lieutenant	WRIGHT	Francis Beattie	12 April 1918	10 Squadron
Captain	AGAR	Egan Zinkan Canada	13 April 1918	54 Squadron
2nd Lieutenant	DENISON	John	13 April 1918	203 Squadron
Lieutenant	GREENWOOD Leonard Aspinall		13 April 1918	43 Squadron
2nd Lieutenant	LEFEBVRE	Rene Hector Canada	13 April 1918	66 Squadron

2nd Lieutenant	MEREDITH Canada	Edward Mercer	13 April 1918	21 Squadron
2nd Lieutenant	PASHBY	Frank Edwin	13 April 1918	53 Squadron
Mechanic	SNOOK	Sydney James	13 April 1918	79 Squadron
2nd Lieutenant	ANDREWS	John Alfred Raymond	14 April 1918	4 Squadron
Lieutenant	DOUGHTY MM	Albert Edward	14 April 1918	4 Squadron
2nd Lieutenant	HEYES	Austin Edward	14 April 1918	21 Squadron
Mechanic	MOORE	George John	14 April 1918	74 Squadron
Mechanic	NICOLS	Frederick Joseph	14 April 1918	2 Squadron
2nd Lieutenant	WALKER	Frank Frederick	14 April 1918	48 Squadron
Lieutenant	BALFOUR	Bernard	15 April 1918	65 Squadron
Sergeant	BELDING	Sydney	15 April 1918	22 Squadron
Mechanic	BROWN	Robert McCulloch	15 April 1918	5 Squadron
Lieutenant	ELLIOTT	Duncan	15 April 1918	4 Squadron
2nd Lieutenant	NAYLOR	Wilson	15 April 1918	4 Squadron
Lieutenant	LEWIS	Henry Stewart	16 April 1918	43 Squadron
		A mention in a despatch *Croix de Guerre* France Canada		
2nd Lieutenant	ST JOHN MILDMAY	Bouverie Walter	16 April 1918	70 Squadron
2nd Lieutenant	COOMBE	Alfred Stanley Naylor	17 April 1918	7 Squadron
2nd Lieutenant	HARGRAVE	William George	17 April 1918	28 Squadron
2nd Lieutenant	HOWE MC	Thomas Sydney Curzon	17 April 1918	54 Squadron
2nd Lieutenant	LIDDELL	Mathew Henry Goldie	17 April 1918	54 Squadron
Lieutenant	LLOYD South Africa	Colin Corden	17 April 1918	54 Squadron
Lieutenant	SWORDER	Norman	17 April 1918	5 Squadron
Lieutenant	WRIGHT	Stephen Sydney	17 April 1918	7 Squadron
Lieutenant	BROOMHALL	Oscar Arthur	18 April 1918	4 Squadron
Lieutenant	LEITH	Sydney Angus	19 April 1918	38 Squadron
Mechanic	TRESTRAIL	John Michael	19 April 1918	52 Squadron
Lieutenant	BRABROOK	Edward John	20 April 1918	8 Squadron
2nd Lieutenant	COLQUHOUN	Archibald Stewart	20 April 1918	79 Squadron
Lieutenant	GOWSALL	Leonard	20 April 1918	4 Squadron
Major	RAYMOND-BARKER MC	Richard 'Dick'	20 April 1918	3 Squadron
Captain	REECE	Frederick Bennett	20 April 1918	4 Squadron
Major	ROWDEN MC	Cuthbert Roger	20 April 1918	78 Squadron
2nd Lieutenant	ROYDS	Thomas Alington	20 April 1918	59 Squadron
Captain	TATTON	Eric	20 April 1918	84 Squadron
		A mention in a despatch		
Sergeant	WILLS	Thomas	20 April 1918	49 Squadron
2nd Lieutenant	BAWLF Canada	David Leland	21 April 1918	203 Squadron
2nd Lieutenant	DINGWALL	John David	21 April 1918	25 Squadron
Lieutenant	MASON	Cecil John	21 April 1918	54 Squadron
Lieutenant	STROUD	Eric Hubert Noel	21 April 1918	53 Squadron
Captain	WHITE MC	Cecil Godfrey	21 April 1918	53 Squadron
Lieutenant	WHITMILL	George Harris	21 April 1918	202 Squadron
Lieutenant	WINTON	Harold Barkley	21 April 1918	1 Squadron
2nd Lieutenant	ALLAN	Ramsey	22 April 1918	2 Squadron

Lieutenant	BEGBIE	Sydney Claude Hamilton	22 April 1918	74 Squadron
2nd Lieutenant	BLYTH	Wilfred Ernest Hill	22 April 1918	88 Squadron
	South Africa			
Sergeant	BURTON	Alfred	22 April 1918	22 Squadron
2nd Lieutenant	CRAIG	Robert Stewart	22 April 1918	12 Squadron
2nd Lieutenant	DEACON	Ernest Cecil Watson	22 April 1918	27 Squadron
2nd Lieutenant	EASTY	Walter Harry	22 April 1918	201 Squadron
Captain	MAGOR	Gerald Atkinson	22 April 1918	201 Squadron
	Canada			
2nd Lieutenant	MUCKLOW	Edward Gerald	22 April 1918	37 Squadron
2nd Lieutenant	PRESCOTT	Lewis William	22 April 1918	23 Squadron
Captain	SAUNDERSON	Samuel Treherne	22 April 1918	131 Squadron
2nd Lieutenant	SHEIL	Charles	22 April 1918	2 Squadron
2nd Lieutenant	WARD	Frank Marshall	22 April 1918	22 Squadron
2nd Lieutenant	SALMONS	William John	23 April 1918	65 Squadron
	MM			
2nd Lieutenant	SOUCHOTTE	Charles Campbell	23 April 1918	57 Squadron
Lieutenant	TOWNSEND	William Henry	23 April 1918	57 Squadron
	USA			
2nd Lieutenant	ACHURCH	Henry Graham	24 April 1918	199 Squadron
Lieutenant	BARRETT	Leland Kelly Willson	24 April 1918	82 Squadron
	USA			
Lieutenant	BROWN	Charles Alexander	24 April 1918	61 Squadron
Lieutenant	HERRON	Kenneth Chester	24 April 1918	82 Squadron
2nd Lieutenant	HODGE	Wilfred	24 April 1918	200 Squadron
2nd Lieutenant	LAMB	Edward Woollard Penistone	24 April 1918	11 Squadron
Sergeant	MAISY	Bertie Joseph	24 April 1918	11 Squadron
2nd Lieutenant	PROCTER	Charles Austin	24 April 1918	82 Squadron
Lieutenant	STOVIN	Frederick Cecil	24 April 1918	209 Squadron
Lieutenant	BAKER	Albert Nathaniel	25 April 1918	73 Squadron
	Canada			
2nd Lieutenant	BOWDEN	Norman	25 April 1918	35 Squadron
Lieutenant	EDDLESTON	Albert	25 April 1918	43 Squadron
Lieutenant	HUNT	Charles Basil	25 April 1918	4 Squadron
Lieutenant	LANKIN	Cyril G	25 April 1918	20 Squadron
Lieutenant	McHATTIE	James William	25 April 1918	20 Squadron
2nd Lieutenant	McINTYRE	David Percival	25 April 1918	10 Squadron
2nd Lieutenant	MILLER	John Jewett	25 April 1918	95 Squadron
	USA			
Lieutenant	REPTON	Charles Tyrwhitt	25 April 1918	142 Squadron
	Croix de Guerre France			
Captain	ROSEVEAR	Stanley Wallace	25 April 1918	201 Squadron
	DSC* Canada			
2nd Lieutenant	WHITWELL	Patrick Henry	25 April 1918	4 Squadron
2nd Lieutenant	WILLIAMS	Alfred Edmund Gerrard	25 April 1918	35 Squadron
Mechanic	ANTHONY	Hubert Frank	26 April 1918	35 Squadron
Lieutenant	MORGAN	Lewis Laugharne	26 April 1918	50 Squadron
	MC			
2nd Lieutenant	VAN STADEN	Laurens Jacobus	26 April 1918	33 Squadron
	South Africa			
Mechanic	WELCH	William	26 April 1918	7 Squadron
Mechanic	CANHAM	Joseph Roy	27 April 1918	72 Squadron
Flight Sergeant	EVANS	Gilbert Lawrence	27 April 1918	129 Squadron
Lieutenant	HUDSON	Frederic 'Derek'	27 April 1918	43 Squadron

Lieutenant	KEARNEY	Norman Charles	27 April 1918	106 Squadron
Lieutenant	WHALLEY	Walter Gilbert	27 April 1918	129 Squadron
Lieutenant	ROBINSON	Cyril Charles Edward	28 April 1918	59 Squadron
2nd Lieutenant	SMITH	Ernest	28 April 1918	46 Squadron
Sergeant	SMITH	Frederick Fieldhouse	28 April 1918	59 Squadron
2nd Lieutenant	THORNTON	Percy	28 April 1918	59 Squadron
2nd Lieutenant	FLEMING	Alfred	29 April 1918	4 Squadron
Lieutenant	NELSON	Harold Ludlow	29 April 1918	210 Squadron
Lieutenant	GIRDLESTON	Horace Wilfred	30 April 1918	4 Squadron
	South Africa			
2nd Lieutenant	HOMERSHAM	Ronald	30 April 1918	4 Squadron
Lieutenant	STACK	James Charles	30 April 1918	4 Squadron

No squadron casualties reported for the 1st of May 1918.

Major	BALCOMBE-	Rainsford	2 May 1918	56 Squadron
	BROWN MC	A mention in a despatch New Zealand		
Lieutenant	HALL	Geoffrey Lawrence Dobney	2 May 1918	3 Squadron
Lieutenant	HICKEY	Leonard Charles	2 May 1918	46 Squadron
2nd Lieutenant	KNIGHT	William Henry Duncan	2 May 1918	65 Squadron
Lieutenant	ROBINSON	William Hartley	2 May 1918	66 Squadron
	Canada			
Lieutenant	TATE	Alan Charles Richmond	2 May 1918	79 Squadron
Mechanic	ALLISON	William Henry	3 May 1918	59 Squadron
Mechanic	BLISS	Thomas Richard	3 May 1918	148 Squadron
Lieutenant	BROWNE	Harold Johnston	3 May 1918	15 Squadron
2nd Lieutenant	DERRICK	Leslie James	3 May 1918	15 Squadron
2nd Lieutenant	EDWARDS	Frank Graham	3 May 1918	109 Squadron
Lieutenant	HOLIDAY	Richard Alan	3 May 1918	98 Squadron
	MM			
2nd Lieutenant	HUMPHREY	Thomas Albert	3 May 1918	205 Squadron
	MM			
Mechanic	PARK	Thomas Richard	3 May 1918	148 Squadron
Lieutenant	PARRY	Samuel	3 May 1918	62 Squadron
Lieutenant	ROWE	Robert Ronald	3 May 1918	73 Squadron
Lieutenant	SANDERS	Frederic Joseph	3 May 1918	7 Squadron
Lieutenant	SCOTT	Raymond	3 May 1918	205 Squadron
	MM			
2nd Lieutenant	SKINNER	Robert Leonard Grahame	3 May 1918	46 Squadron
2nd Lieutenant	SLINGER	Albert	3 May 1918	206 Squadron
Mechanic	SMART	Thomas Alfred Victor	3 May 1918	133 Squadron
Lieutenant	STEEL	Arthur Edward	3 May 1918	206 Squadron
Lieutenant	STEWART	Archibald Ross	3 May 1918	54 Squadron
Private	VINES	Philip James	3 May 1918	148 Squadron
2nd Lieutenant	WHYTE	Cecil Bertram	3 May 1918	98 Squadron
	Canada			
Mechanic	HOWLETT	Percy Charles	4 May 1918	15 Squadron
Lieutenant	STENNETT	William Reginald	4 May 1918	202 Squadron
Lieutenant	WRIGHT	Bernard Wilfred	4 May 1918	4 Squadron
2nd Lieutenant	BARWICK	Richard Laurence Cotter	5 May 1918	93 Squadron
Lieutenant	CARLING	John Burleigh	5 May 1918	109 Squadron
	Canada			
Mechanic	CLACK	Charles Richard	5 May 1918	131 Squadron
2nd Lieutenant	DAVIES	Ralph Llewelyn John	5 May 1918	89 Squadron

2nd Lieutenant	BROWN	Alexander Claud Garden	6 May 1918	48 Squadron
Sergeant	CARDNO	Allen Scott	6 May 1918	29 Squadron
	A mention in a despatch			
Lieutenant	KEOFFENHEM	Roland William	6 May 1918	35 Squadron
	Served as TRUBRIDGE			
Captain	WELLS	William Lewis	6 May 1918	48 Squadron
	MC*			
Lieutenant	BROWN	William Gordon	7 May 1918	19 Squadron
	Canada			
Lieutenant	PALARDY	Guy	7 May 1918	62 Squadron
	USA			
2nd Lieutenant	SCOTT	Reginald Jacob	7 May 1918	111 Squadron
Lieutenant	BRIGHT	Ronald Ernest	8 May 1918	74 Squadron
Captain	McDONALD Roderick		8 May 1918	208 Squadron
	Canada			
2nd Lieutenant	O'NEIL	Thomas Michael	8 May 1918	43 Squadron
2nd Lieutenant	PAULINE	Victor Reginald	8 May 1918	23 Squadron
	Canada			
Lieutenant	STUART-SMITH	Philip James	8 May 1918	74 Squadron
	Canada			
Lieutenant	CUTTLE	George Robin	9 May 1918	49 Squadron
	MC			
Private	HUNT	Asa	9 May 1918	122 Squadron
Lieutenant	JOHNSTON Robert Louis		9 May 1918	2 Squadron
	Canada			
Lieutenant	LECKIE	George Arthur	9 May 1918	49 Squadron
Captain	LUPTON	Charles Roger	9 May 1918	205 Squadron
	DSC			
2nd Lieutenant	NEWTON	Fleming	9 May 1918	201 Squadron
Lieutenant	RUMSBY	Richard William	9 May 1918	57 Squadron
	MC			
Lieutenant	WHITFORD-HAWKEY	Anthony Henry	9 May 1918	43 Squadron
Mechanic	WOOD	Albert George	9 May 1918	205 Squadron
2nd Lieutenant	DUNNETT	Lawrence Edwin	10 May 1918	27 Squadron
Lieutenant	GUTHRIE	John Blair	10 May 1918	34 Squadron
	Canada			
Lieutenant	HILL	Arthur Haddon	10 May 1918	27 Squadron
Captain	McBAIN	George Brown Sievwright	10 May 1918	27 Squadron
	DFC			
2nd Lieutenant	PROSSER	David Harry	10 May 1918	27 Squadron
Sergeant	RICHMOND Stanley Robert		10 May 1918	27 Squadron
Lieutenant	ROWDEN	Alfred William	10 May 1918	80 Squadron
2nd Lieutenant	SHIELDS	Colin Graham Sutherland	10 May 1918	80 Squadron
Lieutenant	SPENCER	William	10 May 1918	27 Squadron
Lieutenant	STRANSOM Norman Garner		10 May 1918	48 Squadron
Private	TAYLOR	Charles Vickers	10 May 1918	48 Squadron
Lieutenant	THORNTON Harold Victor		10 May 1918	34 Squadron
2nd Lieutenant	WHATELY	George Alfred	10 May 1918	80 Squadron
	Canada			
2nd Lieutenant	ANKETELL	Charles Edward	11 May 1918	206 Squadron
	MM			
Mechanic	DOHERTY	P	11 May 1918	6 Squadron

Lieutenant	HOPKINS	Harry Lynn	11 May 1918 Attached	185 Squadron 38 Squadron
Lieutenant	PELLETIER Charles Adolphe Canada		11 May 1918	1 Squadron
Major	VAN POELLNITZ Herman Walter		11 May 1918	72 Squadron
Captain	ARCHIBALD Max Stanfield Eaton MC A mention in a despatch		12 May 1918	18 Squadron
Lieutenant	DOLAN MC	Henry Eric	12 May 1918	74 Squadron
Lieutenant	REID South Africa	John C M	12 May 1918	213 Squadron
Lieutenant	d'ETCHEGOYEN Louis Paul Bryant Adalbert France		13 May 1918	201 Squadron
Lieutenant	BELL	Edward Vaughan	14 May 1918	209 Squadron
Lieutenant	CHISHOLM	Roderick John	14 May 1918	218 Squadron
Captain	EDWARDS	Arthur Strother	14 May 1918	30 Squadron
Captain	GARNONS- Alexander Aylmer Curtis WILLIAMS MC		14 May 1918	112 Squadron
2nd Lieutenant	HELMORE	Stanley Thomas John	14 May 1918	18 Squadron
Corporal	HUDD	Alec James	14 May 1918	4 Squadron
Mechanic	KIMBER	Charles Edmund	14 May 1918	54 Squadron
2nd Lieutenant	NASH	Henry Alfred	14 May 1918	55 Squadron
2nd Lieutenant	SEPHTON South Africa	Stanley	14 May 1918	55 Squadron
Lieutenant	TITCHENER Frank		14 May 1918	202 Squadron
2nd Lieutenant	WALKER	Stephen	14 May 1918	119 Squadron
Captain	ASPINALL	John Vincent	15 May 1918	11 Squadron
Lieutenant	ATHERTON MC	Francis Wright	15 May 1918	30 Squadron
2nd Lieutenant	BRITTAIN	Richard Arthur Henry	15 May 1918	120 Squadron
2nd Lieutenant	BRITTOROUS Oswald George		15 May 1918	209 Squadron
Captain	CHAMBERS William Geoffrey		15 May 1918	49 Squadron
2nd Lieutenant	CRABBE	Hubert Lyon Bingham	15 May 1918	57 Squadron
2nd Lieutenant	FITTON	James Clifford	15 May 1918	48 Squadron
Lieutenant	FLOWER	Charles Kenneth	15 May 1918	211 Squadron
Lieutenant	GLOVER	Clifford Lee	15 May 1918	48 Squadron
Lieutenant	HALL	Frederick Vincent	15 May 1918	210 Squadron
Lieutenant	LANE	Ambrose Godfrey Horneck	15 May 1918	218 Squadron
Major	LAVARACK MC*	Philip James Vaughan	15 May 1918	120 Squadron
Captain	McTAVISH	Ian Arthur Black	15 May 1918	211 Squadron
Captain	MOND	Francis Leopold	15 May 1918	57 Squadron
Sergeant	MURPHY	Patrick	15 May 1918	48 Squadron
Captain	NAPIER MC DCM	Charles George Douglas	15 May 1918	48 Squadron
Lieutenant	PETERS	Albert Henry	15 May 1918	54 Squadron
Lieutenant	PIPER	Edward Hoernle	15 May 1918	57 Squadron
2nd Lieutenant	SANKEY MC	Cecil Martin	15 May 1918	86 Squadron
Lieutenant	SELLARS MC	Herbert Whiteley	15 May 1918	11 Squadron
Mechanic	SUTHURST Frederick		15 May 1918	30 Squadron
Lieutenant	WILLIAMSON James		15 May 1918	70 Squadron
Lieutenant	WILSON	Geoffrey	15 May 1918	209 Squadron

Lieutenant	DANN	Wilfrid Stephen	16 May 1918	70 Squadron
Captain	DURRANT	Trevor	16 May 1918	56 Squadron
Major	HARRISON	James Ingleby	16 May 1918	214 Squadron
Lieutenant	KING	Wilfrid John	16 May 1918	214 Squadron
Lieutenant	MORETON	Norman Houghton	16 May 1918	84 Squadron
Lieutenant	MORGAN	Frederick James	16 May 1918	18 Squadron
Lieutenant	PROCTOR	Herbert Neville Jack	16 May 1918	60 Squadron
Captain	RUSHTON	Cecil George	16 May 1918	214 Squadron
Lieutenant	SANSOM	Roland Charles	16 May 1918	25 Squadron
Mechanic	SMITH	George Charles	16 May 1918	55 Squadron
Lieutenant	WELLS	Charles Douglas	16 May 1918	62 Squadron
	MC A mention in a despatch			
Lieutenant	BARTON	Lambert Francis	17 May 1918	74 Squadron
Captain	BELL	Ralph William	17 May 1918	98 Squadron
	Canada			
Lieutenant	HARRISON	Edward	17 May 1918	24 Squadron
Lieutenant	HEARD	Edward Terence	17 May 1918	8 Squadron
Mechanic	JENNS	Joseph William	17 May 1918	83 Squadron
Lieutenant	MALCOLM	Alan Alexander	17 May 1918	98 Squadron
2nd Lieutenant	NIXON	Leigh Morphew	17 May 1918	74 Squadron
Lieutenant	PRIDEAUX	Edwin Ravenhill	17 May 1918	203 Squadron
	South Africa			
Mechanic	BUTT	Percy	18 May 1918	210 Squadron
Lieutenant	CONRON	Hatton Charles Ronayne	18 May 1918	205 Squadron
Lieutenant	FINE	Soloman	18 May 1918	15 Squadron
2nd Lieutenant	FINNIGAN	Joseph	18 May 1918	205 Squadron
2nd Lieutenant	FRASER	Robert Alexander	18 May 1918	15 Squadron
Lieutenant	GADPAILLE Louis Granville Surridge		18 May 1918	88 Squadron
	British West Indies			
2nd Lieutenant	GRIFFIN	Stephen	18 May 1918	88 Squadron
Lieutenant	HOLLICK	John	18 May 1918	210 Squadron
Captain	PERCY	Edmond William Claud Gerard de Vere	18 May 1918	32 Squadron
	Viscount Glentworth			
2nd Lieutenant	REYNOLDS John Eric		18 May 1918	55 Squadron
Captain	SIEVEKING Valentine Edgar Giberne		18 May 1918	214 Squadron
	DSC*			
Lieutenant	TUNSTALL	George Stanley	18 May 1918	81 Squadron
	Canada			
2nd Lieutenant	BAKER	Joseph Claude Anthony	19 May 1918	109 Squadron
	Canada			
Sergeant	BARFOOT	Herbert	19 May 1918	49 Squadron
Lieutenant	BRAY	Charles Leslie	19 May 1918	211 Squadron
2nd Lieutenant	BROTHERIDGE Frederick John		19 May 1918	3 Squadron
2nd Lieutenant	COLLINS	Frederick Ferdinand	19 May 1918	206 Squadron
Lieutenant	DUNFORD	Bertram Fred	19 May 1918	206 Squadron
Sergeant	GUNN	William	19 May 1918	104 Squadron
Lieutenant	HINDLEY	Aaron	19 May 1918	45 Squadron
Mechanic	HOUSE	Thomas Trewitt	19 May 1918	215 Squadron
			Attached	104 Squadron
2nd Lieutenant	HOWELL-	Athol Cuthbert	19 May 1918	206 Squadron
	JONES			
2nd Lieutenant	NEVIN	Frederick Desmond	19 May 1918	49 Squadron
2nd Lieutenant	REDDIE	Francis Graham	19 May 1918	206 Squadron

Captain	ROBINSON George MC Canada		19 May 1918	149 Squadron
Lieutenant	ROE	Henry Alfred Havilland	19 May 1918	214 Squadron
Lieutenant	TAYLERSON Norman Albert		19 May 1918	211 Squadron
Lieutenant	CRYSLER Canada	Carleton Aquilla	20 May 1918	23 Squadron
Mechanic	ENTWISTLE Thomas		20 May 1918	110 Squadron
Lieutenant	HERRING	Albert Henry	20 May 1918	25 Squadron
2nd Lieutenant	LASKER Australia	Robert Sydney	20 May 1918	25 Squadron
Lieutenant	WATSON	George	20 May 1918	40 Squadron
Captain	WHITEHEAD Lewis Ewart		20 May 1918	65 Squadron
Lieutenant	WILLEY	Reginald	20 May 1918	57 Squadron
2nd Lieutenant	BREWSTER Joseph Lamonby		21 May 1918	73 Squadron
2nd Lieutenant	DAVIDSON	Sydney	21 May 1918	88 Squadron
Mechanic	HAMILTON	George Birl	21 May 1918	105 Squadron
2nd Lieutenant	HUDSON	Frederick James David	21 May 1918	88 Squadron
Lieutenant	MILLAR Canada	Keith Ogilvie	21 May 1918	88 Squadron
Lieutenant	SCOBIE Canada	Caldwell Groves	21 May 1918	88 Squadron
2nd Lieutenant	SCOTT MM Canada	Tom Farrar	21 May 1918	75 Squadron
Sergeant Major	TRAYLOR A mention in a despatch	Finlay Frederick	21 May 1918	26 Squadron
2nd Lieutenant	BURFOOT	William Martin	22 May 1918	37 Squadron
Lieutenant	CLITHEROE James Norman		22 May 1918	53 Squadron
2nd Lieutenant	JOYCE South Africa	Cyril Gordon	22 May 1918	78 Squadron
Lieutenant	MORGAN	Edward Percival	22 May 1918	206 Squadron
Lieutenant	MOYNIHAN Percy Charles		22 May 1918	54 Squadron
2nd Lieutenant	TAYLOR	Frederick Charles	22 May 1918	206 Squadron
2nd Lieutenant	AIRD	Arthur William	23 May 1918	209 Squadron
Mechanic	COLINSKY	Jacob	23 May 1918	15 Squadron
2nd Lieutenant	FFRENCH	George Edward	23 May 1918	27 Squadron
Mechanic	McLAUGHLAN Francis Yates		23 May 1918	27 Squadron
Captain	PALFREYMAN Audubon Eric Australia		23 May 1918	27 Squadron
Lieutenant	STOCKENSTROM Andries Lars South Africa		23 May 1918	70 Squadron
Captain	COLVILL- JONES Argentina	Thomas	24 May 1918	48 Squadron
Airman	JOHNSTON Frederick		24 May 1918	226 Squadron
Lieutenant	WOOD	Patrick Bryan Sandford	24 May 1918	226 Squadron
Lieutenant	BRUCE Canada	William	25 May 1918	104 Squadron
Lieutenant	O'HARA	Henry Eyre	25 May 1918	74 Squadron
2nd Lieutenant	ROPER USA	George	25 May 1918	131 Squadron
2nd Lieutenant	SCARBOROUGH Edward Owen		25 May 1918	119 Squadron
Mechanic	SMITH	David Gordon	25 May 1918	104 Squadron
Lieutenant	SPENCE MC Canada	Lyell Campbell	25 May 1918	2 Squadron
Lieutenant	BUTT	Frank Wilfred	26 May 1918	102 Squadron

2nd Lieutenant	LARDNER	Roland	26 May 1918	211 Squadron
Captain	LE MESURIER DSC**	Thomas Frederick	26 May 1918	211 Squadron
Mechanic	NICKOLLS	Richard George	26 May 1918	30 Squadron
Lieutenant	PEIRCE Canada	George	26 May 1918	4 Squadron
Lieutenant	BARBE	Adrien Espinasson	27 May 1918	111 Squadron
2nd Lieutenant	BEAUMONT	Christopher Charles Audley	27 May 1918	52 Squadron
Captain	BELL MC* South Africa	Douglas John	27 May 1918	3 Squadron
2nd Lieutenant	BOLAY	Albert Richard	27 May 1918	65 Squadron
Lieutenant	COFFEY	Charles Reay	27 May 1918	52 Squadron
Corporal	CHRICHTON	George Anderson	27 May 1918	52 Squadron
Lieutenant	HUTCHESON	Gordon James	27 May 1918	55 Squadron
2nd Lieutenant	WHITEHOUSE	Frank	27 May 1918	52 Squadron
Lieutenant	WYMAN USA	Alfred Theodore	27 May 1918	91 Squadron
Lieutenant	BENNETT	Rex George	28 May 1918	20 Squadron
2nd Lieutenant	CRAIB	William Brice	28 May 1918	65 Squadron
2nd Lieutenant	LOCHEED Canada	Ralph William	28 May 1918	12 Squadron
Lieutenant	REILLY Canada	Frederick Holmes	28 May 1918	98 Squadron
Lieutenant	SALTER MC	Geoffrey Charles Taylor	28 May 1918	20 Squadron
Lieutenant	SOUTHALL	William Percival	28 May 1918	64 Squadron
Mechanic	CROFT	Frank Richard	29 May 1918	12 Squadron
2nd Lieutenant	MACHIN	John Egbert	29 May 1918	123 Squadron
Captain	BENBOW MC	Edwin Louis	30 May 1918	85 Squadron
Mechanic	BRAITHWAITE	Milton	30 May 1918	52 Squadron
Lieutenant	BRUCE	Philip Thomson	30 May 1918	43 Squadron
Mechanic	CUSENS South Africa	Frederic Douglas	30 May 1918 Attached	21 Squadron 3 Squadron AusFC
2nd Lieutenant	DAVIDSON	William Dunlop	30 May 1918	48 Squadron
Lieutenant	HEADLAM	John	30 May 1918	60 Squadron
2nd Lieutenant	LASHFORD	Vincent Clarke	30 May 1918	120 Squadron
Lieutenant	MACKLIN USA	Charles Purcell	30 May 1918	3 Squadron
Private	NORMAN	Leonard Charles	30 May 1918	49 Squadron
Captain	SMITH GRANT	John Gordon Smith Cheetham	30 May 1918	70 Squadron
Lieutenant	STEVENS	Richard Henry Borkwood	30 May 1918	49 Squadron
2nd Lieutenant	YUILLE Canada	William Beresford	30 May 1918	48 Squadron
Lieutenant	ANDERSON South Africa	John Lawrence King	31 May 1918	55 Squadron
2nd Lieutenant	BENTON	John Walter	31 May 1918	52 Squadron
Captain	HORTON Canada	Gifford Davidge	31 May 1918	98 Squadron
Lieutenant	McCONNELL USA	Harold Jettrey	31 May 1918	98 Squadron
Lieutenant	TAYLOR USA	William Edward	31 May 1918	70 Squadron
2nd Lieutenant	BOURNER	Reginald Robert	1 June 1918	107 Squadron

Rank	Surname	Forenames	Date	Squadron
Captain	CAIRNES	William Jameson	1 June 1918	74 Squadron
Major	DALLAS	Roderic Stanley	1 June 1918	40 Squadron
		DSO DSC* Twice mentioned in a despatch *Croix de Guerre* France Australia		
Boy	DURRAN	Jack	1 June 1918	107 Squadron
Lieutenant	DYSON	Stanley Gilbert	1 June 1918	82 Squadron
Lieutenant	GODET	Lennock De Graaff	1 June 1918	55 Squadron
	Bermuda			
2nd Lieutenant	HALEY	Arthur	1 June 1918	55 Squadron
Lieutenant	JONES	Francis Joseph	1 June 1918	45 Squadron
2nd Lieutenant	KEMP	George Hubert	1 June 1918	20 Squadron
2nd Lieutenant	NUGENT	Anthony	1 June 1918	52 Squadron
	Croix de Guerre France			
Lieutenant	ROSS	George Augustus Bellair	1 June 1918	52 Squadron
	Croix de Guerre France South Africa			
2nd Lieutenant	SIMPSON	Thomas Edmund	1 June 1918	65 Squadron
Lieutenant	DAVEY	Albert Victor Patrick	2 June 1918	82 Squadron
Lieutenant	DENNETT	Pruett Mullens	2 June 1918	208 Squadron
2nd Lieutenant	DEVITT	Alan	2 June 1918	65 Squadron
Captain	FISH	William Raymond	2 June 1918	54 Squadron
	MC			
Captain	HENDERSON	Kenneth Selby	2 June 1918	1 Squadron
	Australia			
Lieutenant	MARCHBANK	Ogilvie James	2 June 1918	107 Squadron

No squadron casualties reported for the 3rd of June 1918.

Rank	Surname	Forenames	Date	Squadron
Mechanic	FULLER	Percy Harold	4 June 1918	214 Squadron
2nd Lieutenant	HEIGHAM-PLUMPTRE	Leslie Grantham	4 June 1918	82 Squadron
Mechanic	KEEPAX	W	4 June 1918	214 Squadron
Lieutenant	MALTBY	Alfred Henry	4 June 1918	4 Squadron
Mechanic	REEPAX	William	4 June 1918	14 Squadron
2nd Lieutenant	SIMMS	John Basil Palling	4 June 1918	4 Squadron
Private	WRIGHT	William Arthur	4 June 1918	214 Squadron
Private	ATKINSON	Lawrence Alfred	5 June 1918	103 Squadron
Mechanic	BAIGENT	Edgar	5 June 1918	214 Squadron
Sergeant	BOYACK	Alexander Ian	5 June 1918	49 Squadron
2nd Lieutenant	HART	Eric Stanley	5 June 1918	96 Squadron
	USA			
Lieutenant	HENNESSY	Harold Stephen	5 June 1918	1 Squadron
	Canada			
Mechanic	HORTON	William	5 June 1918	103 Squadron
Mechanic	RANKIN	William Smith	5 June 1918	103 Squadron
2nd Lieutenant	SESSIONS	Frederick Harold Norman	5 June 1918	89 Squadron
Captain	TURNER	Henry	5 June 1918	103 Squadron
	Croix de Guerre France			
2nd Lieutenant	WEBB	George	5 June 1918	103 Squadron
Lieutenant	WEBSTER	Arthur Nugent	5 June 1918	203 Squadron
Sergeant	YOUNG	Lionel Arthur Frederick	5 June 1918	22 Squadron
Lieutenant	CUNNINGHAM	Michael Francis	6 June 1918	27 Squadron
	Canada			
2nd Lieutenant	DURRANT	Lombe Atthill	6 June 1918	65 Squadron
Mechanic	EDWARDS	T	6 June 1918	98 Squadron
Mechanic	GRAY	Percy John	6 June 1918	214 Squadron

Rank	Surname	First names	Date	Squadron
Lieutenant	JARVIS	Eric McDonald	6 June 1918	32 Squadron
2nd Lieutenant	JOHNSON	Cecil Marland	6 June 1918	2 Squadron
Mechanic	JONES	Clarence William	6 June 1918	214 Squadron
Lieutenant	MARCHANT	Frederick Newland	6 June 1918	66 Squadron
Captain	PAYNTER DSC	John de Campbourne	6 June 1918	215 Squadron
2nd Lieutenant	STOCKINS	William James	6 June 1918	27 Squadron
Lieutenant	DAWE	James Jeffery	7 June 1918	24 Squadron
Lieutenant	HARVEY	Thomas Francis	7 June 1918	49 Squadron
2nd Lieutenant	HEATER USA	Roy Esworth	7 June 1918	44 Squadron
Lieutenant	LINK	Frederick Leslie Cuff	7 June 1918	74 Squadron
Lieutenant	McEWAN	George Clapperton	7 June 1918	49 Squadron
Lieutenant	WELFORD	Leonard Charles	7 June 1918	80 Squadron

No squadron casualties reported for the 8th of June 1918.

Rank	Surname	First names	Date	Squadron
2nd Lieutenant	ALLEN MC MM South Africa	Victor William	9 June 1918	103 Squadron
2nd Lieutenant	BARING	Reginald Arthur	9 June 1918	73 Squadron
Lieutenant	GRESWELL Eric Walter		9 June 1918	111 Squadron
Airman	JAMES	Sidney Whitehouse	9 June 1918	224 Squadron
Lieutenant	JOHNSON	John Hercules	9 June 1918	43 Squadron
Mechanic	NOVIS	Arthur John	9 June 1918	7 Squadron
Lieutenant	SALTON	William Fletcher	9 June 1918	224 Squadron
Captain	TYRRELL MC	Walter Alexander	9 June 1918	32 Squadron
Lieutenant	WINDRIDGE Edwin Arthur		9 June 1918	103 Squadron
Private	CLAYDON	Harold Alfred	10 June 1918	218 Squadron
2nd Lieutenant	DODD	Francis Coupe	10 June 1918	210 Squadron
Captain	MANUEL DSC Canada	John Gerald	10 June 1918	210 Squadron
Lieutenant	NOAD	Thomas	10 June 1918	27 Squadron
Sergeant	STERLING	George	10 June 1918	27 Squadron
Flight Sergeant	BYATT	Arthur	11 June 1918	104 Squadron
Mechanic	HARVIE	Alex	11 June 1918	59 Squadron
Lieutenant	JOHNS	Reginald Leach	11 June 1918	208 Squadron
Lieutenant	MASON	Nelson	11 June 1918	210 Squadron
Lieutenant	McGEE South Africa	Wilfred Raworth	11 June 1918	103 Squadron
Lieutenant	RHODES	Thomas George	11 June 1918	57 Squadron
2nd Lieutenant	ROBINSON Canada	Ralph Walker	11 June 1918	218 Squadron
Lieutenant	SPENCER Canada	Evan David	11 June 1918	57 Squadron
2nd Lieutenant	THOMPSON Henry		11 June 1918	103 Squadron
2nd Lieutenant	BREWER	Thomas Elison	12 June 1918	55 Squadron
Lieutenant	HASTIE Canada	Harry Nelson	12 June 1918	95 Squadron
Lieutenant	JONES MC	Max Greville	12 June 1918	55 Squadron
Captain	SCALES MC	Herbert James	12 June 1918	150 Squadron

2nd Lieutenant	TYSON	Thomas Mashiter	12 June 1918	121 Squadron
Flight Cadet	BAKER Canada	William Frank	13 June 1918	191 Squadron
Captain	BELGRAVE James Dacres MC*		13 June 1918	60 Squadron
Lieutenant	BOLES Canada	Jack Lionel	13 June 1918	39 Squadron
Sergeant	FLEXMAN	Waler Edward	13 June 1918	104 Squadron
Lieutenant	LEGGE	William	13 June 1918	55 Squadron
Flight Cadet	MacKAY	John Wood	13 June 1918	39 Squadron
2nd Lieutenant	McKENZIE	Alexander	13 June 1918	55 Squadron
Captain	KEATING	Thomas Joseph	14 June 1918	63 Squadron
2nd Lieutenant	MELBOURNE Arthur Robert		14 June 1918	80 Squadron
Lieutenant	NELSON	James Noel	14 June 1918	213 Squadron
Lieutenant	SPARKS South Africa	Seba Walter	14 June 1918	17 Squadron
Lieutenant	WARWICK	John Lacy	14 June 1918	63 Squadron
Lieutenant	KELLY Canada	Ernest Tilton Sumpter	15 June 1918	1 Squadron
Lieutenant	RUSSELL Canada	James Gordon	15 June 1918	28 Squadron
Lieutenant	BERTRAND Philippe Angus		16 June 1918	4 Squadron
Sergeant	BRACEY	Spencer Charles	16 June 1918	83 Squadron
Sergeant	BROOKS	W E A	16 June 1918	27 Squadron
Captain	BURDOCK MC	Frederick William	16 June 1918	4 Squadron
Captain	COMBER-TAYLOR	Eric Horace	16 June 1918	10 Squadron
Lieutenant	ELLISON	Sydney Wright	16 June 1918	28 Squadron
2nd Lieutenant	GANNAWAY Charles Henry		16 June 1918	27 Squadron
Lieutenant	GOLLER South Africa	John Morrissey	16 June 1918	62 Squadron
2nd Lieutenant	HIRST	Sidney	16 June 1918	103 Squadron
Lieutenant	HOLLAND	Jack Harold	16 June 1918	27 Squadron
Lieutenant	HUGHES	Jack Meirion	16 June 1918	103 Squadron
Sergeant	LEVICK	Cyril	16 June 1918	4 Squadron
Sergeant	LOMAX	Cecil	16 June 1918	98 Squadron
2nd Lieutenant	McGILLIVRAY Alexander George		16 June 1918	131 Squadron
2nd Lieutenant	ROSS-JENKINS	Maurice	16 June 1918	62 Squadron
Sergeant	SCOTT	Ernest	16 June 1918	103 Squadron
Lieutenant	SHILLINGFORD Stanley Charles		16 June 1918	4 Squadron
Lieutenant	SPURGIN	Frederick Robert Godfrey	16 June 1918	27 Squadron
2nd Lieutenant	STEWART South Africa	Harold Malcolm	16 June 1918	27 Squadron
Lieutenant	STRUGNELL Leonard William MM		16 June 1918	98 Squadron
Lieutenant	SYKES	John Acton	16 June 1918	65 Squadron
Lieutenant	TARBUTT Canada	Fraser Coventry	16 June 1918	56 Squadron
2nd Lieutenant	WATCHORN Claude Edmund Canada		16 June 1918	131 Squadron
Lieutenant	WILD	Harold	16 June 1918	27 Squadron

2nd Lieutenant CAMPBELL	Kenneth Turner		17 June 1918	210 Squadron
	Canada			
2nd Lieutenant CHAMPNEYS	John Amyan Ludford		17 June 1918	73 Squadron
Lieutenant	JACKMAN	John Robinson	17 June 1918	98 Squadron
Lieutenant	MACARTNEY	David Allan	17 June 1918	98 Squadron
Lieutenant	TURNBULL	John Seymour	17 June 1918	41 Squadron
2nd Lieutenant BARLOW	Leslie Charles Jackson		18 June 1918	82 Squadron
Lieutenant	FYFE	Robert Joss	18 June 1918	84 Squadron
Lieutenant	HAMILTON	George Cyril Rae	18 June 1918	96 Squadron
	Canada			
Lieutenant	LEIGH	Reginald Lea	18 June 1918	3 Squadron
Lieutenant	MULROY	Herbert James	18 June 1918	56 Squadron
Lieutenant	NICHOLSON	Owen Harrow	18 June 1918	3 Squadron
	South Africa			
Lieutenant	NIELSEN	Peter	18 June 1918	84 Squadron
	New Zealand			
Lieutenant	SHACKELL	Cecil John	18 June 1918	210 Squadron
	South Africa			
Mechanic	WILLIAMSON	Richard	18 June 1918	52 Squadron
2nd Lieutenant BONNER	William		19 June 1918	3 Squadron
Lieutenant	DAVIS	Harold Eborall	19 June 1918	198 Squadron
	MC			
Airman	FAIRBROTHER	Fred	19 June 1918	236 Squadron
Lieutenant	HARRAN	Frank St Patrick	20 June 1918	236 Squadron
Lieutenant	STORRS	Henry Lionel	20 June 1918	10 Squadron
Lieutenant	BANNISTER	Herbert Stanley	21 June 1918	151 Squadron
Lieutenant	PACKE	Robert Christopher	21 June 1918	212 Squadron

No squadron casualties reported for the 22nd of June 1918.

2nd Lieutenant DIXON	William		23 June 1918	25 Squadron
Mechanic	LODGE	William	23 June 1918	34 Squadron
Lieutenant	CUTMORE	William Cecil	24 June 1918	206 Squadron
2nd Lieutenant DUMVILLE	Ernest		24 June 1918	62 Squadron
2nd Lieutenant DUNCAN	William Gardiner		24 June 1918	206 Squadron
Lieutenant	GRAHAM	David Liddell	24 June 1918	47 Squadron
Lieutenant	LEARN	Gerald Alfred	24 June 1918	210 Squadron
	Canada			
2nd Lieutenant LOMAX	Leslie John		24 June 1918	113 Squadron
2nd Lieutenant MARSH	Cuthbert Alban		24 June 1918	42 Squadron
2nd Lieutenant McDONALD	Hugh		24 June 1918	42 Squadron
Mechanic	PROSSER	William Frederick James	24 June 1918	13 Squadron
Lieutenant	UHRICH	Charles Philip	24 June 1918	28 Squadron
	Canada			
Lieutenant	WILLIAMS	Frederick	24 June 1918	62 Squadron
2nd Lieutenant BENSON	Donald Good		25 June 1918	99 Squadron
	Canada			
Lieutenant	BRADLEY	Harold Bartlett	25 June 1918	1 Squadron
	USA			
Lieutenant	CABBURN	Frank	25 June 1918	48 Squadron
2nd Lieutenant CARTER	Alan		25 June 1918	8 Squadron
2nd Lieutenant GOODYEAR	Charles Frederick Richards		25 June 1918	55 Squadron
2nd Lieutenant HANDEL	Kenneth Douglas		25 June 1918	53 Squadron
			Attached	4 Squadron

Lieutenant	HARPER Canada	Norman Stuart	25 June 1918	99 Squadron
2nd Lieutenant	JACKSON Canada	Hugh Arthur Bruce	25 June 1918	104 Squadron
2nd Lieutenant	JENKIN	William Walter Lloyd	25 June 1918	99 Squadron
Sergeant	LAWDER	William Edward	25 June 1918	48 Squadron
Lieutenant	NIGHTINGALE Eric		25 June 1918	201 Squadron
Private	SHEPHARD Richard		25 June 1918	211 Squadron
Lieutenant	STUBBS	William Henry	25 June 1918	54 Squadron
Lieutenant	SWEET Canada	George Arscott	25 June 1918	55 Squadron
2nd Lieutenant	BOOTHMAN Clarence Duckworth		26 June 1918	210 Squadron
Lieutenant	COAPE-ARNOLD	Raymond de Newburgh	26 June 1918	200 Squadron
2nd Lieutenant	CRITCHLEY Burton		26 June 1918	80 Squadron
Private	CROSSLEY Frederick William Canada		26 June 1918	94 Squadron
2nd Lieutenant	DAVIS	Harold Charles	26 June 1918	104 Squadron
2nd Lieutenant	DUNHAM	Marbel Lester	26 June 1918	91 Squadron
Lieutenant	MARSHALL William Edward Isley		26 June 1918	86 Squadron
Lieutenant	ARCHIBALD Walter Roy Canada		27 June 1918	80 Squadron
Lieutenant	BRAND	Francis Robert	27 June 1918	29 Squadron
Lieutenant	BRIGGS	Cyril	27 June 1918	218 Squadron
Lieutenant	CHAPIN USA	Elliot Adams	27 June 1918	99 Squadron
Mechanic	DAWE	Arthur	27 June 1918	17 Squadron
Lieutenant	EVANS	Walter George	27 June 1918	213 Squadron
Lieutenant	FOORD Canada	Edward Alec	27 June 1918	48 Squadron
Captain	FORSYTH A mention in a despatch	William Allan	27 June 1918	79 Squadron
Lieutenant	GANTER	Frederick Spottiswood	27 June 1918	73 Squadron
Sergeant	JAMES	Leonard	27 June 1918	48 Squadron
Lieutenant	McMILLAN	Charles McWhirter	27 June 1918	70 Squadron
Sergeant	NORTON	Cyril	27 June 1918	48 Squadron
Lieutenant	SHELDON	Charles Stanley	27 June 1918	70 Squadron
2nd Lieutenant	WARNER	William Henry	27 June 1918	218 Squadron
2nd Lieutenant	WIGGINS	Thomas Henry	27 June 1918	99 Squadron
Lieutenant	BURCH	Raymond Sanderson	28 June 1918	4 Squadron
2nd Lieutenant	GARLICK	Tom	28 June 1918	4 Squadron
2nd Lieutenant	HERITAGE	Herbert Alec	28 June 1918	125 Squadron
Sergeant	HOSKIN	Stanley William	28 June 1918	38 Squadron
Private	McQUADE	Henry	28 June 1918	40 Squadron
2nd Lieutenant	STEPHENS	Henry Hill	28 June 1918	42 Squadron
Lieutenant	WEST USA	John Prout	28 June 1918	88 Squadron
Lieutenant	WILLIAMS	Frank Stanley	28 June 1918	34 Squadron
Lieutenant	BRADLEY	Walter Robinson	29 June 1918	150 Squadron
Lieutenant	CATTLE	Frank Leonard	29 June 1918	213 Squadron
Lieutenant	GATECLIFF James Noel		29 June 1918	53 Squadron
Lieutenant	GITSHAM	James	29 June 1918	35 Squadron
2nd Lieutenant	HARRISON James		29 June 1918	53 Squadron

Lieutenant	HARTSON	Sidney	29 June 1918	204 Squadron
2nd Lieutenant	HARVEY	Charles Almond	29 June 1918	7 Squadron
		Canada		
Lieutenant	LINDLEY	Bryant Lutellus	29 June 1918	25 Squadron
	MC South Africa			
2nd Lieutenant	OSBORNE	Geoffrey William	29 June 1918	7 Squadron
Lieutenant	PEMBLE	Frederick Philip	29 June 1918	213 Squadron
Mechanic	POULTON	George	29 June 1918	22 Squadron
Mechanic	SAGE	Arthur Patrick	29 June 1918	11 Squadron
2nd Lieutenant	WADSWORTH	Leonard	29 June 1918	25 Squadron
2nd Lieutenant	COLE	Montague Henry	30 June 1918	104 Squadron
	South Africa			
Lieutenant	FENNELL	Frederick Vibond	30 June 1918	8 Squadron
Sergeant	HUNNISETT	Edwin Edward	30 June 1918	217 Squadron
Lieutenant	MILLER	Donald	30 June 1918	70 Squadron
	USA			
Lieutenant	MOIR	Clifford James	30 June 1918	217 Squadron
	Canada			
Lieutenant	SALES	Norman	30 June 1918	87 Squadron
Lieutenant	WELINKAR	Shri Krishna Chanda	30 June 1918	23 Squadron
	India			
Lieutenant	WILSON	Jack Morris	30 June 1918	204 Squadron

AUSTRALIAN FLYING CORPS

Lieutenant	COURTNEY John Classon		7 April 1918	4 Squadron AusFC
	New Zealand			
Lieutenant	WOOLHOUSE Frederick Smith		10 April 1918	4 Squadron AusFC
Lieutenant	BEST	George William	12 April 1918	3 Squadron AusFC
Lieutenant	LEWIS	Owen Gower	12 April 1918	3 Squadron AusFC
Lieutenant	STORCH	Lewis Albert	22 April 1918	4 Squadron AusFC
Lieutenant	BUCKLAND William Alexander John		3 May 1918	3 Squadron AusFC
Lieutenant	CURWEN-	Jack Keith	3 May 1918	1 Squadron AusFC
	WALKER			
Corporal	JENSEN	Neils Peder Berg	3 May 1918	1 Squadron AusFC
Mechanic	FELL	William Hewitt	4 May 1918	1 Squadron AusFC
Captain	RALFE	Henry Douglas Eyre	6 May 1918	3 Squadron AusFC
Lieutenant	BARRY	Owen Cressy	11 May 1918	4 Squadron AusFC
Lieutenant	TAYLOR	Albert Lawrence Deane	20 May 1918	3 Squadron AusFC
Lieutenant	FINNIE	Alexander	22 May 1918	4 Squadron AusFC
Lieutenant	NOWLAND	George	22 May 1918	4 Squadron AusFC
Mechanic	NEWTON	Henry John	30 May 1918	3 Squadron AusFC
Lieutenant	PRIMROSE	Leslie John	4 June 1918	2 Squadron AusFC
Lieutenant	HAMMOND Themetre James		12 June 1918	2 Squadron AusFC
2nd Lieutenant	MARTIN	William Stanley	12 June 1918	2 Squadron AusFC
2nd Lieutenant	JONES	Sydney	15 June 1918	3 Squadron AusFC
2nd Lieutenant	LORAM	Stanley Arthur	15 June 1918	3 Squadron AusFC
Lieutenant	FARQUHAR Wallace Kemmis		26 June 1918	1 Squadron AusFC
Lieutenant	BROOK	Arthur O'Connor	27 June 1918	3 Squadron AusFC
Lieutenant	BROWNE	John Sandfield McDonald	27 June 1918	4 Squadron AusFC
	Canada			
Lieutenant	OXENHAM	Gordon Vincent	27 June 1918	1 Squadron AusFC

CANADIAN INFANTRY

| Lieutenant | TURNER | George James | 10 April 1918 | 142 Squadron |
| Lieutenant | HALL | Russell McKay | 28 May 1918 | 98 Squadron |

SOUTH AFRICAN INFANTRY

| Lieutenant | DORNONVILLE Paul Victor de la Cour | | 15 May 1918 | 11 Squadron |

UNITED STATES AIR SERVICE

1st Lieutenant	HUGHENIN	Stanley	3 April 19018	81 Squadron
Lieutenant	KISSEL	Gustav Herman	12 April 1918	43 Squadron
Lieutenant	SANDFORD Joseph Ralph		12 April 1918	54 Squadron
Lieutenant	WILLIAMS	Charles S	20 April 1918	81 Squadron
Lieutenant	BURKY	Raymond C	15 May 1918	22 Aero Squadron
			Attached	49 Squadron
1st Lieutenant	HAMMER	Earl M	19 May 1918	84 Squadron
Lieutenant	MORTIMER Richard		22 May 1918	73 Squadron
Lieutenant	HOOPER	Parr	10 June 1918	32 Squadron
Lieutenant	CARPENTER Jay Ira		11 June 1918	73 Squadron
Lieutenant	DOUGLAS	Charles W H	11 June 1918	73 Squadron
1st Lieutenant	GRIDER	John McGavock	18 June 1918	85 Squadron
Private	ADAMS	Ernest	26 June 1918	147 Aero Squadron
			Attached	48 Squadron
1st Lieutenant	GOAD	John M	27 June 1918	48 Squadron
1st Lieutenant	DEETJEN	William Ludwig	30 June 1918	104 Squadron

ARMY

2nd Lieutenant	DOWNEY	George Jamieson	25 April 1918	106 Squadron
2nd Lieutenant	RICHARDSON F A		25 April 1918	106 Squadron
Lieutenant	WHITCUT	H M	25 April 1918	106 Squadron

Aircraft Types Used by the
Royal Air Force and Australian Air Corps,
1st April – 30th June 1918

Aircraft Manufacturing Company (Airco) DH4 (Wiki)

Airco DH6 (Wiki)

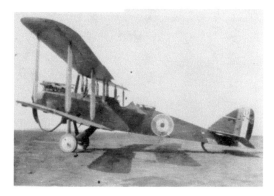

Airco DH9 (White family via Steve Smith)

Armstrong Whitworth FK8 of 35 Sqn RAF (White family via Steve Smith)

Armstrong Whitworth FK3, Thessaloniki, 1918 (Wiki)

Avro 504K (White family via Steve Smith)

Blackburn Kangaroo (Crown Copyright)

Bristol F2b of 35 Sqn RAF (Peter Tresarden via Steve Smith)

Handley Page O/100 (Wiki)

Handley Page O/400 (Wiki)

Nieuport 17 (Wiki)

Nieuport 23 (Wiki)

Royal Aircraft Factory BE12 (Wiki)

Royal Aircraft Factory BE2E of 100 Sqn (Greg Harrison, 100 Sqn historian, via Steve Smith)

Royal Aircraft Factory FE2B of 149 Sqn (Alan Fraser / 149 Sqn Association via Steve Smith)

Royal Aircraft Factory RE8 (White family via Steve Smith)

Royal Aircraft Factory SE5A (White family via Steve Smith)

Sopwith Camel (White family via Steve Smith)

Sopwith Pup (Wiki)

Sopwith Dolphin (Wiki)

Spad S XIII (Wiki)

BV - #0049 - 251024 - C5 - 297/210/19 - PB - 9781911255260 - Gloss Lamination